THE WESTMINSTER CONFESSION OF FAITH AND CATECHISMS

THE

WESTMINSTER CONFESSION OF FAITH AND CATECHISMS

as adopted by
The Presbyterian Church in America

WITH PROOF TEXTS

These Westminster Standards are made available by the Christian Education and Publications Committee of the Presbyterian Church in America.

1-800-283-1357 or www.cepbookstore.com

ISBN 978-0-9793770-0-6

Contents

Preface

In 1643, during a period of civil war, the English "Long Parliament" (under the control of Presbyterian Puritans) convened an Assembly of Divines (mostly Puritan ministers, including a few influential Scottish commissioners) at Westminster Abbey in London. Their task was to advise Parliament on how to bring the Church of England into greater conformity with the Church of Scotland and the Continental Reformed churches. The Westminster Assembly produced documents on doctrine, church government, and worship that have largely defined Presbyterianism down to this day. These documents included a Confession of Faith (1646), a Larger Catechism (1647), and a Shorter Catechism (1647), often collectively called "the Westminster standards." Parliamentary efforts to reconstitute the established Church of England along Presbyterian lines were soon thwarted by the rise to power of Cromwell (who favored Independency) and the expulsion of Presbyterians from Parliament in 1648, and then the restoration of the monarchy in 1660, which quickly led to the reinstitution of Episcopacy and the suppression of Puritanism.

But things were different in Scotland. The General Assembly of the Church of Scotland adopted the Confession of Faith in 1647 and the Catechisms in 1648. The Scottish Parliament ratified them in 1649 and again (after a time of political and religious strife) in 1690. The Presbyterian character of the Church of Scotland was safeguarded when Scotland and England were united under one crown in 1707. Numerous Presbyterian bodies have been formed since then, both in the United Kingdom and around the world, and they have always been constituted on the basis of the Westminster standards (although declension from them has sometimes followed).

When the Presbyterian Church in the United States of America was formed in 1788, it adopted the Westminster standards, as containing the system of doctrine taught in the Holy Scriptures. However, it revised chapters 20.4, 23.3, and 31.2 of the Confession, basically removing the civil magistrate (i.e., the state) from involvement in ecclesiastical matters. It also removed the phrase "tolerating a false religion" from the list of sins forbidden in Answer 109 of the Larger Catechism, and replaced "depopulations" in Answer 142 with "depredation." The Confession was amended again in 1887, when the final sentence of chapter 24.4, which forbade the marrying of the close kindred of one's deceased spouse, was removed.

The Presbyterian Church in the U.S.A. adopted more sweeping revisions of its Confession in 1903. Chapter 16.7, on the works of unregenerate men, was rewritten. The last sentence of chapter 22.3, which forbade the refusing of a proper oath when imposed by lawful authority, was removed. Chapter 25.6, on the head of the church, was rewritten, and the identification of the Roman Catholic pope as the Antichrist was removed. Chapter 34 ("Of the Holy Spirit") was added. Chapter 35 ("Of the Love of God and Missions") was also added. A "Declaratory Statement" explaining chapters 3 and 10.3 (on election and salvation) was appended. The general effect of these additions was to soften the Calvinism of the Confession.

In June 1936, the First General Assembly of the Orthodox Presbyterian Church (called the Presbyterian Church of America until 1939) met to constitute a new denomination as the spiritual heir of the old Presbyterian Church in the U.S.A, which had fallen under modernist control. It elected a Committee on the Constitution and charged it to "present for adoption to the General Assembly meeting in the autumn of 1936 the Westminster Confession of Faith and Catechisms as the confession of the faith of this church." The Committee was instructed to "take as the basis of its consideration the particular form of the Westminster Confession of Faith and Catechisms which appears in the Constitution of the Presbyterian Church in the U.S.A., 1934 edition." The Committee was empowered to recommend the elimination (or retention) of changes to the Confession made in 1903, but to recommend no other changes to "that form of these Standards."

Accordingly, the Committee on the Constitution (consisting of Ned B. Stonehouse [chairman], J. Gresham Machen [*ex officio*], and Murray Forst Thompson) recommended to the Second General Assembly, meeting in November 1936, that the Confession of Faith and

Catechisms be adopted "in the form which they possessed" before the revisions of 1903 (including the Declaratory Statement) were introduced, with two exceptions. The Committee recommended that the change in chapter 22.3 and the removal of the reference to the pope as the Antichrist (but not the other changes) in chapter 25.6 be retained. The Assembly adopted these recommendations. It also rejected a proposal to append a declaratory statement to the Confession that would have declared premillennialism to be consistent with the church standards.

As a preliminary step toward the printing of the doctrinal standards of the Orthodox Presbyterian Church, the Seventh General Assembly (1940) established a Committee on Texts and Proof Texts (consisting of John Murray [chairman], E. J. Young, and Ned B. Stonehouse, who was replaced in 1941 by John H. Skilton) to study the texts and proof texts of those documents.

That Committee submitted to the Eighteenth General Assembly (1951) "the text of the Confession of Faith, together with the proof texts as revised by the Committee." The text, except for the revisions that had been adopted by the Second General Assembly in 1936, was "derived from the original manuscript written by Cornelius Burges in 1646, edited by S. W. Carruthers [in 1937] and published by the Presbyterian Church of England in 1946." That text of the Confession, with a few corrections, was adopted by the Twenty-second General Assembly (1955), approved by nearly all the presbyteries, and adopted again by the Twenty-third General Assembly (1956). The proof texts prepared by the Committee were accepted for publication. The Confession was then published with these proof texts (as citations, not full texts) by the Committee on Christian Education and reprinted by Great Commission Publications.

The Thirty-fourth General Assembly (1967) elected a Committee on Proof Texts for the Catechisms (consisting of E. J. Young [chairman], who died in 1968 and was replaced by John Murray [who died in 1975] and Norman Shepherd, John H. Skilton [the new chairman], George W. Marston, and Richard B. Gaffin, Jr. [beginning in 1971]) to prepare a revised list of proof texts for the Larger and Shorter Catechisms. The Committee presented a list of proof texts for the Shorter Catechism to the Forty-fourth General Assembly

(1977), and the Forty-fifth General Assembly (1978) approved them for publication in an edition of the Shorter Catechism. Great Commission Publications then printed the Shorter Catechism with these proof texts (as citations, not full texts).

The Sixty-sixth General Assembly (1999) elected a Committee on Proof Texts for the Larger Catechism (consisting of Stephen A. Pribble [chairman], George W. Knight III, Steven F. Miller, and Peter J. Wallace). It presented a list of proof texts to the Sixty-seventh General Assembly (2000), and the Sixty-eighth General Assembly (2001) approved the proof texts (with corrections) for publication. One additional change was made by the Seventy-first General Assembly (2004).

The Assembly in 2001 also authorized the Committee on Christian Education to publish the doctrinal standards of the Orthodox Presbyterian Church, with the proof texts prepared by the various Committees over the years. Accordingly, this volume presents to the church the text of the Confession of Faith, as settled upon in 1956, and the text of the Larger and Shorter Catechisms, as received in 1936. It also includes a Scripture index to the proof texts. It is a companion volume to *The Book of Church Order*, which contains the other constitutional documents of the Orthodox Presbyterian Church, namely, the Form of Government, the Book of Discipline, and the Directory for the Public Worship of God.

The Scripture proof texts were originally prepared by the Westminster divines, revised over the years by a succession of committees, and approved for publication by various general assemblies of the OPC, but are not a part of the constitution itself. At the direction of the Sixty-eighth General Assembly, these proof texts are presented largely in full. The King James Version has been used, without prejudice to other translations, since this is the English text that was in use at the time of the Westminster Assembly, the language of which is at times reflected in the Confession and Catechisms.

The Committee on Christian Education has endeavored to publish the texts and proof texts of the Confession and Catechisms as accurately as possible, that is, in accordance with the intention of the general assemblies which adopted them. In ascertaining the approved texts and proof texts, it has been assumed that the general assemblies desired errors, either in the manuscripts with which they were presented, or in the documents as printed, to be corrected. Spelling and capitalization has been regularized and modernized, but the original punctuation and verb forms have been retained. Chapters and sections of the Confession are now enumerated with Arabic numerals, not Roman numerals.

The footnotes to the Confession and Catechisms, containing the proof texts, are enumerated in the traditional manner, that is, by letters of the alphabet (omitting *j* and *v*, as alternative forms for *i* and *u* in the Latin alphabet). In the Confession, the footnotes for each chapter begin with *a;* if *z* is reached, another series of letters begins with *a*. For each of the Catechisms, one series of letters follows another without interruption. The footnote references in the text of the Confession follow the pattern of the original Westminster Confession (except where the text has been amended), but the references in the Catechisms are placed somewhat differently than they were in the past. Where individual answers (or sections of answers) in the Larger Catechism require more than one series of letters (i.e., LC 105, 109, 113, 135, 142, 145, and 151.3), the letters in the second series are distinguished by the prime symbol. Thus, for example, in LC 145, the references begin with *n*, and, after *m* is reached, they continue with *n'*. This will make the Scripture index easier to use.

As a rule, the entire text of the cited proof text is presented, but in a few cases part of an indicated verse has been elided because it is not relevant. Lengthy proof texts (sometimes amounting to one or more full chapters) have been shortened, but enough Scripture is quoted in these instances to establish the doctrine in view. In such cases, the omitted material is marked by an ellipsis. An ellipsis also separates verses when the proof text is not a continuous text.

Sometimes a verse does not form a complete sentence. (Our chapter and verse divisions were not part of the original text of Scripture, but were added, sometimes in unhelpful places, by later editors.) To alert the reader to the fact that a quoted verse begins in the middle of a sentence, an ellipsis has been placed at the beginning of it. And when a verse ends without forming a sentence, an ellipsis has been placed at the end of it. (If the verse forms a grammatical sentence, no ellipsis is added, even though it does not form a complete sentence in the biblical text.)

In the King James Version, each verse begins a new paragraph, and the first word of each verse is capitalized, regardless of its place in the sentence. Also, the first word of each chapter is set entirely in capital letters. In our proof texts, however, these conventions have not been followed. Rather, the biblical text of each proof text runs continuously and is capitalized according to the rules of ordinary prose. However, the KJV's practice of capitalizing the first word of quotations (in lieu of quotation marks) has been retained.

THE
CONFESSION OF FAITH

Chapter 1
Of the Holy Scripture

1. Although the light of nature, and the works of creation and providence do so far manifest the goodness, wisdom, and power of God, as to leave men unexcusable;[a] yet are they not sufficient to give that knowledge of God, and of his will, which is necessary unto salvation.[b] Therefore it pleased the Lord, at sundry times, and in divers manners, to reveal himself, and to declare that his will unto his

a. **Rom. 2:14–15.** For when the Gentiles, which have not the law, do by nature the things contained in the law, these, having not the law, are a law unto themselves: which shew the work of the law written in their hearts, their conscience also bearing witness, and their thoughts the mean while accusing or else excusing one another. **Rom. 1:19–20.** Because that which may be known of God is manifest in them; for God hath shewed it unto them. For the invisible things of him from the creation of the world are clearly seen, being understood by the things that are made, even his eternal power and Godhead; so that they are without excuse. **Ps. 19:1–4.** The heavens declare the glory of God; and the firmament sheweth his handywork. Day unto day uttereth speech, and night unto night sheweth knowledge. There is no speech nor language, where their voice is not heard. Their line is gone out through all the earth, and their words to the end of the world. In them hath he set a tabernacle for the sun. **See Rom. 1:32–2:1.**

b. **John 17:3.** And this is life eternal, that they might know thee the only true God, and Jesus Christ, whom thou hast sent. **1 Cor. 1:21.** For after that in the wisdom of God the world by wisdom knew not God, it pleased God by the foolishness of preaching to save them that believe. **1 Cor. 2:13–14.** … which things also we speak, not in the words which man's wisdom teacheth, but which the Holy Ghost teacheth; comparing spiritual things with spiritual. But the natural man receiveth not the things of the Spirit of God: for they are foolishness unto him: neither can he know them, because they are spiritually discerned.

church;[c] and afterwards, for the better preserving and propagating of the truth, and for the more sure establishment and comfort of the church against the corruption of the flesh, and the malice of Satan and of the world, to commit the same wholly unto writing:[d] which maketh the Holy Scripture to be most necessary;[e] those former ways of God's revealing his will unto his people being now ceased.[f]

2. Under the name of Holy Scripture, or the Word of God written, are now contained all the books of the Old and New Testament, which are these:

c. **Heb. 1:1–2.** God, who at sundry times and in divers manners spake in time past unto the fathers by the prophets, hath in these last days spoken unto us by his Son, whom he hath appointed heir of all things, by whom also he made the worlds.

d. **Luke 1:3–4.** It seemed good to me also, having had perfect understanding of all things from the very first, to write unto thee in order, most excellent Theophilus, that thou mightest know the certainty of those things, wherein thou hast been instructed. **Rom. 15:4.** For whatsoever things were written aforetime were written for our learning, that we through patience and comfort of the scriptures might have hope. **Matt. 4:4, 7, 10.** But he answered and said, It is written, Man shall not live by bread alone, but by every word that proceedeth out of the mouth of God.… Jesus said unto him, It is written again, Thou shalt not tempt the Lord thy God.… Then saith Jesus unto him, Get thee hence, Satan: for it is written, Thou shalt worship the Lord thy God, and him only shalt thou serve. **Isa. 8:20.** To the law and to the testimony: if they speak not according to this word, it is because there is no light in them.

e. **2 Tim. 3:15.** … and that from a child thou hast known the holy scriptures, which are able to make thee wise unto salvation through faith which is in Christ Jesus. **2 Pet. 1:19.** We have also a more sure word of prophecy; whereunto ye do well that ye take heed, as unto a light that shineth in a dark place, until the day dawn, and the day star arise in your hearts.

f. **John 20:31.** But these are written, that ye might believe that Jesus is the Christ, the Son of God; and that believing ye might have life through his name. **1 Cor. 14:37.** If any man think himself to be a prophet, or spiritual, let him acknowledge that the things that I write unto you are the commandments of the Lord. **1 John 5:13.** These things have I written unto you that believe on the name of the Son of God; that ye may know that ye have eternal life, and that ye may believe on the name of the Son of God. **1 Cor. 10:11.** Now all these things happened unto them for ensamples: and they are written for our admonition, upon whom the ends of the world are come. **Heb. 1:1–2.** God, who at sundry times and in divers manners spake in time past unto the fathers by the prophets, hath in these last days spoken unto us by his Son, whom he hath appointed heir of all things, by whom also he made the worlds. **Heb. 2:2–4.** For if the word spoken by angels was stedfast, and every transgression and disobedience received a just recompence of reward; how shall we escape, if we neglect so great salvation; which at the first began to be spoken by the Lord, and was confirmed unto us by them that heard him; God also bearing them witness, both with signs and wonders, and with divers miracles, and gifts of the Holy Ghost, according to his own will?

Of the Old Testament:

Genesis	II Chronicles	Daniel
Exodus	Ezra	Hosea
Leviticus	Nehemiah	Joel
Numbers	Esther	Amos
Deuteronomy	Job	Obadiah
Joshua	Psalms	Jonah
Judges	Proverbs	Micah
Ruth	Ecclesiastes	Nahum
I Samuel	The Song of Songs	Habakkuk
II Samuel	Isaiah	Zephaniah
I Kings	Jeremiah	Haggai
II Kings	Lamentations	Zechariah
I Chronicles	Ezekiel	Malachi

Of the New Testament:

The Gospels	Galatians	The Epistle
according to	Ephesians	of James
Matthew	Philippians	The first and
Mark	Colossians	second Epistles
Luke	Thessalonians I	of Peter
John	Thessalonians II	The first, second,
The Acts of the	to Timothy I	and third Epistles
Apostles	to Timothy II	of John
Paul's Epistles	to Titus	The Epistle
to the Romans	to Philemon	of Jude
Corinthians I	The Epistle to	The Revelation
Corinthians II	the Hebrews	of John

All which are given by inspiration of God to be the rule of faith and life.[g]

g. **Luke 16:29, 31.** Abraham saith unto him, They have Moses and the prophets; let them hear them.... And he said unto him, If they hear not Moses and the prophets, neither will they be persuaded, though one rose from the dead. **Luke 24:27, 44.** And beginning at Moses and all the prophets, he expounded unto them in all the scriptures the things concerning himself.... And he said unto them, These are the words which I spake unto you, while I was yet with you, that all things must be fulfilled, which were written in the law of Moses, and in the prophets, and in the psalms, concerning me. **2 Tim. 3:15–16.** ... and that from a child thou hast known the holy scriptures, which are able to make thee wise unto salvation through faith which is in Christ Jesus. All scripture is given by inspiration of God, and is profitable for doctrine,

3. The books commonly called Apocrypha, not being of divine inspiration, are no part of the canon of the Scripture, and therefore are of no authority in the church of God, nor to be any otherwise approved, or made use of, than other human writings.[h]

4. The authority of the Holy Scripture, for which it ought to be believed, and obeyed, dependeth not upon the testimony of any man, or church; but wholly upon God (who is truth itself) the author thereof: and therefore it is to be received, because it is the Word of God.[i]

5. We may be moved and induced by the testimony of the church to an high and reverent esteem of the Holy Scripture.[k] And the heavenliness of the matter, the efficacy of the doctrine, the majesty of the style, the consent of all the parts, the scope of the whole (which is, to give all glory to God), the full discovery it makes of the only way of man's salvation, the many other incomparable excellencies, and the entire perfection thereof, are arguments whereby it doth abundantly

for reproof, for correction, for instruction in righteousness. **John 5:46–47.** For had ye believed Moses, ye would have believed me: for he wrote of me. But if ye believe not his writings, how shall ye believe my words?

h. **Rev. 22:18–19.** For I testify unto every man that heareth the words of the prophecy of this book, If any man shall add unto these things, God shall add unto him the plagues that are written in this book: and if any man shall take away from the words of the book of this prophecy, God shall take away his part out of the book of life, and out of the holy city, and from the things which are written in this book. **Rom. 3:2.** Much every way: chiefly, because that unto them were committed the oracles of God. **2 Pet. 1:21.** For the prophecy came not in old time by the will of man: but holy men of God spake as they were moved by the Holy Ghost.

i. **2 Pet. 1:19–20.** We have also a more sure word of prophecy; whereunto ye do well that ye take heed, as unto a light that shineth in a dark place, until the day dawn, and the day star arise in your hearts: knowing this first, that no prophecy of the scripture is of any private interpretation. **2 Tim. 3:16.** All scripture is given by inspiration of God, and is profitable for doctrine, for reproof, for correction, for instruction in righteousness. **1 John 5:9.** If we receive the witness of men, the witness of God is greater: for this is the witness of God which he hath testified of his Son. **1 Thess. 2:13.** For this cause also thank we God without ceasing, because, when ye received the word of God which ye heard of us, ye received it not as the word of men, but as it is in truth, the word of God, which effectually worketh also in you that believe. **Rev. 1:1–2.** The Revelation of Jesus Christ, which God gave unto him, to shew unto his servants things which must shortly come to pass; and he sent and signified it by his angel unto his servant John: who bare record of the word of God, and of the testimony of Jesus Christ, and of all things that he saw.

k. **1 Tim. 3:15.** … but if I tarry long, that thou mayest know how thou oughtest to behave thyself in the house of God, which is the church of the living God, the pillar and ground of the truth.

evidence itself to be the Word of God: yet notwithstanding, our full persuasion and assurance of the infallible truth and divine authority thereof, is from the inward work of the Holy Spirit bearing witness by and with the Word in our hearts.[l]

6. The whole counsel of God concerning all things necessary for his own glory, man's salvation, faith and life, is either expressly set down in Scripture, or by good and necessary consequence may be deduced from Scripture: unto which nothing at any time is to be added, whether by new revelations of the Spirit, or traditions of men.[m] Nevertheless, we acknowledge the inward illumination of the Spirit

l. **1 Cor. 2:9–10.** But as it is written, Eye hath not seen, nor ear heard, neither have entered into the heart of man, the things which God hath prepared for them that love him. But God hath revealed them unto us by his Spirit: for the Spirit searcheth all things, yea, the deep things of God. **Heb. 4:12.** For the word of God is quick, and powerful, and sharper than any twoedged sword, piercing even to the dividing asunder of soul and spirit, and of the joints and marrow, and is a discerner of the thoughts and intents of the heart. **John 10:35.** If he called them gods, unto whom the word of God came, and the scripture cannot be broken … **Isa. 55:11.** So shall my word be that goeth forth out of my mouth: it shall not return unto me void, but it shall accomplish that which I please, and it shall prosper in the thing whereto I sent it. **See Rom. 11:36. Ps. 19:7–11.** The law of the Lord is perfect, converting the soul: the testimony of the Lord is sure, making wise the simple. The statutes of the Lord are right, rejoicing the heart: the commandment of the Lord is pure, enlightening the eyes. The fear of the Lord is clean, enduring for ever: the judgments of the Lord are true and righteous altogether. More to be desired are they than gold, yea, than much fine gold: sweeter also than honey and the honeycomb. Moreover by them is thy servant warned: and in keeping of them there is great reward. **See 2 Tim. 3:15. 1 Cor. 2:4–5.** And my speech and my preaching was not with enticing words of man's wisdom, but in demonstration of the Spirit and of power: that your faith should not stand in the wisdom of men, but in the power of God. **1 Thess. 1:5.** For our gospel came not unto you in word only, but also in power, and in the Holy Ghost, and in much assurance; as ye know what manner of men we were among you for your sake. **1 John 2:20, 27.** But ye have an unction from the Holy One, and ye know all things.… But the anointing which ye have received of him abideth in you, and ye need not that any man teach you: but as the same anointing teacheth you of all things, and is truth, and is no lie, and even as it hath taught you, ye shall abide in him. **See Isa. 59:21.**

m. **2 Tim. 3:16–17.** All scripture is given by inspiration of God, and is profitable for doctrine, for reproof, for correction, for instruction in righteousness: that the man of God may be perfect, throughly furnished unto all good works. **Gal. 1:8–9.** But though we, or an angel from heaven, preach any other gospel unto you than that which we have preached unto you, let him be accursed. As we said before, so say I now again, If any man preach any other gospel unto you than that ye have received, let him be accursed. **2 Thess. 2:2.** … that ye be not soon shaken in mind, or be troubled, neither by spirit, nor by word, nor by letter as from us, as that the day of Christ is at hand.

of God to be necessary for the saving understanding of such things as are revealed in the Word:[n] and that there are some circumstances concerning the worship of God, and government of the church, common to human actions and societies, which are to be ordered by the light of nature, and Christian prudence, according to the general rules of the Word, which are always to be observed.[o]

7. All things in Scripture are not alike plain in themselves, nor alike clear unto all:[p] yet those things which are necessary to be known, believed, and observed for salvation, are so clearly propounded, and opened in some place of Scripture or other, that not only the learned, but the unlearned, in a due use of the ordinary means, may attain unto a sufficient understanding of them.[q]

n. **John 6:45.** It is written in the prophets, And they shall be all taught of God. Every man therefore that hath heard, and hath learned of the Father, cometh unto me. **1 Cor. 2:12, 14–15.** Now we have received, not the spirit of the world, but the spirit which is of God; that we might know the things that are freely given to us of God.… But the natural man receiveth not the things of the Spirit of God: for they are foolishness unto him: neither can he know them, because they are spiritually discerned. But he that is spiritual judgeth all things, yet he himself is judged of no man. **Eph. 1:18.** … the eyes of your understanding being enlightened; that ye may know what is the hope of his calling, and what the riches of the glory of his inheritance in the saints. **See 2 Cor. 4:6.**

o. **1 Cor. 11:13–14.** Judge in yourselves: is it comely that a woman pray unto God uncovered? Doth not even nature itself teach you, that, if a man have long hair, it is a shame unto him? **1 Cor. 14:26, 40.** How is it then, brethren? when ye come together, every one of you hath a psalm, hath a doctrine, hath a tongue, hath a revelation, hath an interpretation. Let all things be done unto edifying.… Let all things be done decently and in order.

p. **2 Pet. 3:16.** … as also in all his epistles, speaking in them of these things; in which are some things hard to be understood, which they that are unlearned and unstable wrest, as they do also the other scriptures, unto their own destruction.

q. **Ps. 119:105, 130.** Thy word is a lamp unto my feet, and a light unto my path.… The entrance of thy words giveth light; it giveth understanding unto the simple. **Deut. 29:29.** The secret things belong unto the LORD our God: but those things which are revealed belong unto us and to our children for ever, that we may do all the words of this law. **Deut. 30:10–14.** If thou shalt hearken unto the voice of the LORD thy God, to keep his commandments and his statutes which are written in this book of the law, and if thou turn unto the LORD thy God with all thine heart, and with all thy soul. For this commandment which I command thee this day, it is not hidden from thee, neither is it far off. It is not in heaven, that thou shouldest say, Who shall go up for us to heaven, and bring it unto us, that we may hear it, and do it? Neither is it beyond the sea, that thou shouldest say, Who shall go over the sea for us, and bring it unto us, that we may hear it, and do it? But the word is very nigh unto thee, in thy mouth, and in thy heart, that thou mayest do it. **Acts 17:11.** These were more noble than those

8. The Old Testament in Hebrew (which was the native language of the people of God of old), and the New Testament in Greek (which, at the time of the writing of it, was most generally known to the nations), being immediately inspired by God, and, by his singular care and providence, kept pure in all ages, are therefore authentical;[r] so as, in all controversies of religion, the church is finally to appeal unto them.[s] But, because these original tongues are not known to all the people of God, who have right unto, and interest in the Scriptures, and are commanded, in the fear of God, to read and search them,[t] therefore they are to be translated into the vulgar language of every nation unto which they come,[u] that, the Word of God dwelling plentifully in all, they may worship him in an acceptable manner;[w] and, through patience and comfort of the Scriptures, may have hope.[x]

9. The infallible rule of interpretation of Scripture is the Scripture itself: and therefore, when there is a question about the true and full sense of any Scripture (which is not manifold, but one), it must be

in Thessalonica, in that they received the word with all readiness of mind, and searched the scriptures daily, whether those things were so.

r. **Matt. 5:18.** For verily I say unto you, Till heaven and earth pass, one jot or one tittle shall in no wise pass from the law, till all be fulfilled. **Ps. 119:89.** For ever, O LORD, thy word is settled in heaven.

s. **Isa. 8:20.** To the law and to the testimony: if they speak not according to this word, it is because there is no light in them. **Matt. 15:3, 6.** But he answered and said unto them, Why do ye also transgress the commandment of God by your tradition?… and honour not his father or his mother, he shall be free. Thus have ye made the commandment of God of none effect by your tradition. **Acts 15:15.** And to this agree the words of the prophets; as it is written … **See Luke 16:31.**

t. **John 5:39.** Search the scriptures; for in them ye think ye have eternal life: and they are they which testify of me. **Acts 17:11.** These were more noble than those in Thessalonica, in that they received the word with all readiness of mind, and searched the scriptures daily, whether those things were so. **Rev. 1:3.** Blessed is he that readeth, and they that hear the words of this prophecy, and keep those things which are written therein: for the time is at hand. **See 2 Tim. 3:14–15.**

u. **Matt. 28:19–20.** Go ye therefore, and teach all nations, baptizing them in the name of the Father, and of the Son, and of the Holy Ghost: teaching them to observe all things whatsoever I have commanded you: and, lo, I am with you alway, even unto the end of the world. Amen. **See 1 Cor. 14:6; Mark 15:34.**

w. **Col. 3:16.** Let the word of Christ dwell in you richly in all wisdom; teaching and admonishing one another in psalms and hymns and spiritual songs, singing with grace in your hearts to the Lord. **See Ex. 20:4–6; Matt. 15:7–9.**

x. **Rom. 15:4.** For whatsoever things were written aforetime were written for our learning, that we through patience and comfort of the scriptures might have hope.

searched and known by other places that speak more clearly.[y]

10. The supreme judge by which all controversies of religion are to be determined, and all decrees of councils, opinions of ancient writers, doctrines of men, and private spirits, are to be examined, and in whose sentence we are to rest, can be no other but the Holy Spirit speaking in the Scripture.[z]

Chapter 2
Of God, and of the Holy Trinity

1. There is but one only,[a] living, and true God,[b] who is infinite in being and perfection,[c] a most pure spirit,[d] invisible,[e] without body,

y. **Acts 15:15.** And to this agree the words of the prophets; as it is written ... **John 5:46.** For had ye believed Moses, ye would have believed me: for he wrote of me. **See 2 Pet. 1:20–21.**

z. **Matt. 22:29, 31.** Jesus answered and said unto them, Ye do err, not knowing the scriptures, nor the power of God.... But as touching the resurrection of the dead, have ye not read that which was spoken unto you by God, saying ... **Acts 28:25.** And when they agreed not among themselves, they departed, after that Paul had spoken one word, Well spake the Holy Ghost by Esaias the prophet unto our fathers ... **See 1 John 4:1–6.**

a. **Deut. 6:4.** Hear, O Israel: The LORD our God is one LORD. **1 Cor. 8:4, 6.** As concerning therefore the eating of those things that are offered in sacrifice unto idols, we know that an idol is nothing in the world, and that there is none other God but one.... But to us there is but one God, the Father, of whom are all things, and we in him; and one Lord Jesus Christ, by whom are all things, and we by him. **See Gal. 3:20.**

b. **1 Thess. 1:9.** For they themselves shew of us what manner of entering in we had unto you, and how ye turned to God from idols to serve the living and true God. **Jer. 10:10.** But the LORD is the true God, he is the living God, and an everlasting king: at his wrath the earth shall tremble, and the nations shall not be able to abide his indignation.

c. **Job 11:7–9.** Canst thou by searching find out God? canst thou find out the Almighty unto perfection? It is as high as heaven; what canst thou do? deeper than hell; what canst thou know? The measure thereof is longer than the earth, and broader than the sea. **Job 26:14.** Lo, these are parts of his ways: but how little a portion is heard of him? but the thunder of his power who can understand? **See Ps. 139:6.**

d. **John 4:24.** God is a Spirit: and they that worship him must worship him in spirit and in truth.

e. **1 Tim. 1:17.** Now unto the King eternal, immortal, invisible, the only wise God, be honour and glory for ever and ever. Amen. **See John 1:18.**

parts,[f] or passions;[g] immutable,[h] immense,[i] eternal,[k] incomprehensible,[l] almighty,[m] most wise,[n] most holy,[o] most free,[p] most absolute;[q] working all things according to the counsel of his own immutable and most righteous will,[r] for his own glory;[s] most

f. **Deut. 4:15–16.** Take ye therefore good heed unto yourselves; for ye saw no manner of similitude on the day that the LORD spake unto you in Horeb out of the midst of the fire: lest ye corrupt yourselves, and make you a graven image, the similitude of any figure, the likeness of male or female. **Cf. John 4:24 with Luke 24:39.**

g. **Acts 14:11, 15.** And when the people saw what Paul had done, they lifted up their voices, saying in the speech of Lycaonia, The gods are come down to us in the likeness of men.… and saying, Sirs, why do ye these things? We also are men of like passions with you, and preach unto you that ye should turn from these vanities unto the living God, which made heaven, and earth, and the sea, and all things that are therein.

h. **James 1:17.** Every good gift and every perfect gift is from above, and cometh down from the Father of lights, with whom is no variableness, neither shadow of turning. **Mal. 3:6.** For I am the LORD, I change not; therefore ye sons of Jacob are not consumed.

i. **1 Kings 8:27.** But will God indeed dwell on the earth? behold, the heaven and heaven of heavens cannot contain thee; how much less this house that I have builded? **Jer. 23:23–24.** Am I a God at hand, saith the LORD, and not a God afar off? Can any hide himself in secret places that I shall not see him? saith the LORD. Do not I fill heaven and earth? saith the LORD.

k. **Ps. 90:2.** Before the mountains were brought forth, or ever thou hadst formed the earth and the world, even from everlasting to everlasting, thou art God. **See 1 Tim. 1:17.**

l. **Ps. 145:3.** Great is the LORD, and greatly to be praised; and his greatness is unsearchable. **See Rom. 11:34.**

m. **Gen. 17:1.** And when Abram was ninety years old and nine, the LORD appeared to Abram, and said unto him, I am the Almighty God; walk before me, and be thou perfect. **Rev. 4:8.** And the four beasts had each of them six wings about him; and they were full of eyes within: and they rest not day and night, saying, Holy, holy, holy, Lord God Almighty, which was, and is, and is to come.

n. **Rom. 16:27.** To God only wise, be glory through Jesus Christ for ever. Amen.

o. **Isa. 6:3.** And one cried unto another, and said, Holy, holy, holy, is the LORD of hosts: the whole earth is full of his glory. **See Rev. 4:8.**

p. **Ps. 115:3.** But our God is in the heavens: he hath done whatsoever he hath pleased. **See Isa. 14:24.**

q. **Isa. 45:5–6.** I am the LORD, and there is none else, there is no God beside me: I girded thee, though thou hast not known me: that they may know from the rising of the sun, and from the west, that there is none beside me. I am the LORD, and there is none else. **See Ex. 3:14.**

r. **Eph. 1:11.** … in whom also we have obtained an inheritance, being predestinated according to the purpose of him who worketh all things after the counsel of his own will.

s. **Prov. 16:4.** The LORD hath made all things for himself: yea, even the wicked

loving,[t] gracious, merciful, long-suffering, abundant in goodness and truth, forgiving iniquity, transgression, and sin;[u] the rewarder of them that diligently seek him;[w] and withal, most just, and terrible in his judgments,[x] hating all sin,[y] and who will by no means clear the guilty.[z]

2. God hath all life,[a] glory,[b] goodness,[c] blessedness,[d] in and of himself; and is alone in and unto himself all-sufficient, not standing in need of any creatures which he hath made,[e] nor deriving any glory

for the day of evil. **Rom. 11:36.** For of him, and through him, and to him, are all things: to whom be glory for ever. Amen. **See Rev. 4:11.**

t. **1 John 4:8.** He that loveth not knoweth not God; for God is love. **See 1 John 4:16; John 3:16.**

u. **Ex. 34:6–7.** And the LORD passed by before him, and proclaimed, The LORD, The LORD God, merciful and gracious, longsuffering, and abundant in goodness and truth, keeping mercy for thousands, forgiving iniquity and transgression and sin, and that will by no means clear the guilty; visiting the iniquity of the fathers upon the children, and upon the children's children, unto the third and to the fourth generation.

w. **Heb. 11:6.** But without faith it is impossible to please him: for he that cometh to God must believe that he is, and that he is a rewarder of them that diligently seek him.

x. **Neh. 9:32–33.** Now therefore, our God, the great, the mighty, and the terrible God, who keepest covenant and mercy, let not all the trouble seem little before thee, that hath come upon us, on our kings, on our princes, and on our priests, and on our prophets, and on our fathers, and on all thy people, since the time of the kings of Assyria unto this day. Howbeit thou art just in all that is brought upon us; for thou hast done right, but we have done wickedly. **See Heb. 10:28–31.**

y. **Rom. 1:18.** For the wrath of God is revealed from heaven against all ungodliness and unrighteousness of men, who hold the truth in unrighteousness. **Ps. 5:5–6.** The foolish shall not stand in thy sight: thou hatest all workers of iniquity. Thou shalt destroy them that speak leasing: the LORD will abhor the bloody and deceitful man. **See Ps. 11:5.**

z. **Ex. 34:7a.** … keeping mercy for thousands, forgiving iniquity and transgression and sin, and that will by no means clear the guilty. **See Nah. 1:2–3, 6.**

a. **Jer. 10:10.** But the LORD is the true God, he is the living God, and an everlasting king: at his wrath the earth shall tremble, and the nations shall not be able to abide his indignation. **See John 5:26.**

b. **Acts 7:2.** And he said, Men, brethren, and fathers, hearken; The God of glory appeared unto our father Abraham, when he was in Mesopotamia, before he dwelt in Charran.

c. **Ps. 119:68.** Thou art good, and doest good; teach me thy statutes.

d. **1 Tim. 6:15.** … which in his times he shall shew, who is the blessed and only Potentate, the King of kings, and Lord of lords. **See Rom. 9:5.**

e. **Acts 17:24–25.** God that made the world and all things therein, seeing that he is Lord of heaven and earth, dwelleth not in temples made with hands; neither is worshipped with men's hands, as though he needed any thing, seeing he giveth to all

from them,[f] but only manifesting his own glory in, by, unto, and upon them. He is the alone fountain of all being, of whom, through whom, and to whom are all things;[g] and hath most sovereign dominion over them, to do by them, for them, or upon them whatsoever himself pleaseth.[h] In his sight all things are open and manifest,[i] his knowledge is infinite, infallible, and independent upon the creature,[k] so as nothing is to him contingent, or uncertain.[l] He is most holy in all his counsels, in all his works, and in all his commands.[m] To him is due from angels and men, and every other creature, whatsoever worship, service, or obedience he is pleased to require of them.[n]

life, and breath, and all things.

f. **Luke 17:10.** So likewise ye, when ye shall have done all those things which are commanded you, say, We are unprofitable servants: we have done that which was our duty to do.

g. **Rom. 11:36.** For of him, and through him, and to him, are all things: to whom be glory for ever. Amen.

h. **Rev. 4:11.** Thou art worthy, O Lord, to receive glory and honour and power: for thou hast created all things, and for thy pleasure they are and were created. **Dan. 4:25, 35.** That they shall drive thee from men, and thy dwelling shall be with the beasts of the field, and they shall make thee to eat grass as oxen, and they shall wet thee with the dew of heaven, and seven times shall pass over thee, till thou know that the most High ruleth in the kingdom of men, and giveth it to whomsoever he will.… and all the inhabitants of the earth are reputed as nothing: and he doeth according to his will in the army of heaven, and among the inhabitants of the earth: and none can stay his hand, or say unto him, What doest thou? **See 1 Tim. 6:15.**

i. **Heb. 4:13.** Neither is there any creature that is not manifest in his sight: but all things are naked and opened unto the eyes of him with whom we have to do.

k. **Rom. 11:33–34.** O the depth of the riches both of the wisdom and knowledge of God! how unsearchable are his judgments, and his ways past finding out! For who hath known the mind of the Lord? or who hath been his counsellor? **Ps. 147:5.** Great is our Lord, and of great power: his understanding is infinite.

l. **Acts 15:18.** Known unto God are all his works from the beginning of the world. **Ezek. 11:5.** And the Spirit of the LORD fell upon me, and said unto me, Speak; Thus saith the LORD; Thus have ye said, O house of Israel: for I know the things that come into your mind, every one of them.

m. **Ps. 145:17.** The LORD is righteous in all his ways, and holy in all his works. **Rom. 7:12.** Wherefore the law is holy, and the commandment holy, and just, and good.

n. **Rev. 5:12–14.** Saying with a loud voice, Worthy is the Lamb that was slain to receive power, and riches, and wisdom, and strength, and honour, and glory, and blessing. And every creature which is in heaven, and on the earth, and under the earth, and such as are in the sea, and all that are in them, heard I saying, Blessing, and honour, and glory, and power, be unto him that sitteth upon the throne, and unto the Lamb for ever and ever. And the four beasts said, Amen. And the four and twenty elders fell down and worshipped him that liveth for ever and ever.

3. In the unity of the Godhead there be three persons, of one substance, power, and eternity: God the Father, God the Son, and God the Holy Ghost:[o] the Father is of none, neither begotten, nor proceeding; the Son is eternally begotten of the Father;[p] the Holy Ghost eternally proceeding from the Father and the Son.[q]

Chapter 3
Of God's Eternal Decree

1. God, from all eternity, did, by the most wise and holy counsel of his own will, freely, and unchangeably ordain whatsoever comes to pass:[a] yet so, as thereby neither is God the author of sin,[b] nor is violence offered to the will of the creatures; nor is the liberty or contingency of second causes taken away, but rather established.[c]

o. **Matt. 3:16–17.** And Jesus, when he was baptized, went up straightway out of the water: and, lo, the heavens were opened unto him, and he saw the Spirit of God descending like a dove, and lighting upon him: and lo a voice from heaven, saying, This is my beloved Son, in whom I am well pleased. **Matt. 28:19.** Go ye therefore, and teach all nations, baptizing them in the name of the Father, and of the Son, and of the Holy Ghost. **2 Cor. 13:14.** The grace of the Lord Jesus Christ, and the love of God, and the communion of the Holy Ghost, be with you all. Amen. **See Eph. 2:18.**

p. **John 1:14, 18.** And the Word was made flesh, and dwelt among us, (and we beheld his glory, the glory as of the only begotten of the Father,) full of grace and truth.… No man hath seen God at any time; the only begotten Son, which is in the bosom of the Father, he hath declared him. **See Heb. 1:2–3; Col. 1:15.**

q. **John 15:26.** But when the Comforter is come, whom I will send unto you from the Father, even the Spirit of truth, which proceedeth from the Father, he shall testify of me. **Gal. 4:6.** And because ye are sons, God hath sent forth the Spirit of his Son into your hearts, crying, Abba, Father.

a. **Ps. 33:11.** The counsel of the Lord standeth for ever, the thoughts of his heart to all generations. **Eph. 1:11.** … in whom also we have obtained an inheritance, being predestinated according to the purpose of him who worketh all things after the counsel of his own will. **Heb. 6:17.** Wherein God, willing more abundantly to shew unto the heirs of promise the immutability of his counsel, confirmed it by an oath.

b. **Ps. 5:4.** For thou art not a God that hath pleasure in wickedness: neither shall evil dwell with thee. **James 1:13–14.** Let no man say when he is tempted, I am tempted of God: for God cannot be tempted with evil, neither tempteth he any man: but every man is tempted, when he is drawn away of his own lust, and enticed. **1 John 1:5.** This then is the message which we have heard of him, and declare unto you, that God is light, and in him is no darkness at all. **See Hab. 1:13.**

c. **Acts 2:23.** Him, being delivered by the determinate counsel and foreknowl-

2. Although God knows whatsoever may or can come to pass upon all supposed conditions,[d] yet hath he not decreed anything because he foresaw it as future, or as that which would come to pass upon such conditions.[e]

3. By the decree of God, for the manifestation of his glory, some men and angels[f] are predestinated unto everlasting life; and others foreordained to everlasting death.[g]

edge of God, ye have taken, and by wicked hands have crucified and slain. **Matt. 17:12.** But I say unto you, That Elias is come already, and they knew him not, but have done unto him whatsoever they listed. Likewise shall also the Son of man suffer of them. **Acts 4:27–28.** For of a truth against thy holy child Jesus, whom thou hast anointed, both Herod, and Pontius Pilate, with the Gentiles, and the people of Israel, were gathered together, for to do whatsoever thy hand and thy counsel determined before to be done. **John 19:11.** Jesus answered, Thou couldest have no power at all against me, except it were given thee from above: therefore he that delivered me unto thee hath the greater sin. **Prov. 16:33.** The lot is cast into the lap; but the whole disposing thereof is of the LORD.

d. **1 Sam. 23:11–12.** Will the men of Keilah deliver me up into his hand? will Saul come down, as thy servant hath heard? O LORD God of Israel, I beseech thee, tell thy servant. And the LORD said, He will come down. Then said David, Will the men of Keilah deliver me and my men into the hand of Saul? And the LORD said, They will deliver thee up. **Matt. 11:21, 23.** Woe unto thee, Chorazin! woe unto thee, Bethsaida! for if the mighty works, which were done in you, had been done in Tyre and Sidon, they would have repented long ago in sackcloth and ashes.... And thou, Capernaum, which art exalted unto heaven, shalt be brought down to hell: for if the mighty works, which have been done in thee, had been done in Sodom, it would have remained until this day.

e. **Rom. 9:11, 13, 16, 18.** ... (for the children being not yet born, neither having done any good or evil, that the purpose of God according to election might stand, not of works, but of him that calleth;) ... As it is written, Jacob have I loved, but Esau have I hated.... So then it is not of him that willeth, nor of him that runneth, but of God that sheweth mercy.... Therefore hath he mercy on whom he will have mercy, and whom he will he hardeneth.

f. **1 Tim. 5:21.** I charge thee before God, and the Lord Jesus Christ, and the elect angels, that thou observe these things without preferring one before another, doing nothing by partiality. **Jude 6.** And the angels which kept not their first estate, but left their own habitation, he hath reserved in everlasting chains under darkness unto the judgment of the great day. **Matt. 25:31, 41.** When the Son of man shall come in his glory, and all the holy angels with him, then shall he sit upon the throne of his glory.... Then shall he say also unto them on the left hand, Depart from me, ye cursed, into everlasting fire, prepared for the devil and his angels.

g. **Eph. 1:5–6.** ... having predestinated us unto the adoption of children by Jesus Christ to himself, according to the good pleasure of his will, to the praise of the glory of his grace, wherein he hath made us accepted in the beloved. **Rom. 9:22–23.** What if God, willing to shew his wrath, and to make his power known, endured with

4. These angels and men, thus predestinated, and foreordained, are particularly and unchangeably designed, and their number so certain and definite, that it cannot be either increased or diminished.[h]

5. Those of mankind that are predestinated unto life, God, before the foundation of the world was laid, according to his eternal and immutable purpose, and the secret counsel and good pleasure of his will, hath chosen, in Christ, unto everlasting glory,[i] out of his mere free grace and love, without any foresight of faith, or good works, or perseverance in either of them, or any other thing in the creature, as conditions, or causes moving him thereunto;[k] and all to the praise of his glorious grace.[l]

much longsuffering the vessels of wrath fitted to destruction: and that he might make known the riches of his glory on the vessels of mercy, which he had afore prepared unto glory. **Prov. 16:4.** The Lord hath made all things for himself: yea, even the wicked for the day of evil.

h. **John 13:18.** I speak not of you all: I know whom I have chosen: but that the scripture may be fulfilled, He that eateth bread with me hath lifted up his heel against me. **2 Tim. 2:19.** Nevertheless the foundation of God standeth sure, having this seal, The Lord knoweth them that are his. And, Let every one that nameth the name of Christ depart from iniquity. **See John 10:14–16, 27–28; 17:2, 6, 9–12.**

i. **Eph. 1:4, 9, 11.** … according as he hath chosen us in him before the foundation of the world, that we should be holy and without blame before him in love.… having made known unto us the mystery of his will, according to his good pleasure which he hath purposed in himself … in whom also we have obtained an inheritance, being predestinated according to the purpose of him who worketh all things after the counsel of his own will. **Rom. 8:28–30.** And we know that all things work together for good to them that love God, to them who are the called according to his purpose. For whom he did foreknow, he also did predestinate to be conformed to the image of his Son, that he might be the firstborn among many brethren. Moreover whom he did predestinate, them he also called: and whom he called, them he also justified: and whom he justified, them he also glorified. **2 Tim. 1:9.** … who hath saved us, and called us with an holy calling, not according to our works, but according to his own purpose and grace, which was given us in Christ Jesus before the world began. **1 Thess. 5:9.** For God hath not appointed us to wrath, but to obtain salvation by our Lord Jesus Christ.

k. **Rom. 9:11, 13, 15–16.** … (for the children being not yet born, neither having done any good or evil, that the purpose of God according to election might stand, not of works, but of him that calleth;) … As it is written, Jacob have I loved, but Esau have I hated.… For he saith to Moses, I will have mercy on whom I will have mercy, and I will have compassion on whom I will have compassion. So then it is not of him that willeth, nor of him that runneth, but of God that sheweth mercy. **Eph. 2:8–9.** For by grace are ye saved through faith; and that not of yourselves: it is the gift of God: not of works, lest any man should boast. **See Eph. 1:5, 9, 11.**

l. **Eph. 1:6, 12.** … to the praise of the glory of his grace, wherein he hath made

6. As God hath appointed the elect unto glory, so hath he, by the eternal and most free purpose of his will, foreordained all the means thereunto.[m] Wherefore, they who are elected, being fallen in Adam, are redeemed by Christ,[n] are effectually called unto faith in Christ by his Spirit working in due season, are justified, adopted, sanctified,[o] and kept by his power, through faith, unto salvation.[p] Neither are any other redeemed by Christ, effectually called, justified, adopted, sanctified, and saved, but the elect only.[q]

us accepted in the beloved.… that we should be to the praise of his glory, who first trusted in Christ.

m. **1 Pet. 1:2.** … elect according to the foreknowledge of God the Father, through sanctification of the Spirit, unto obedience and sprinkling of the blood of Jesus Christ: Grace unto you, and peace, be multiplied. **Eph. 2:10.** For we are his workmanship, created in Christ Jesus unto good works, which God hath before ordained that we should walk in them. **2 Thess. 2:13.** But we are bound to give thanks alway to God for you, brethren beloved of the Lord, because God hath from the beginning chosen you to salvation through sanctification of the Spirit and belief of the truth.

n. **1 Thess. 5:9–10.** For God hath not appointed us to wrath, but to obtain salvation by our Lord Jesus Christ, who died for us, that, whether we wake or sleep, we should live together with him. **Titus 2:14.** … who gave himself for us, that he might redeem us from all iniquity, and purify unto himself a peculiar people, zealous of good works.

o. **Rom. 8:30.** Moreover whom he did predestinate, them he also called: and whom he called, them he also justified: and whom he justified, them he also glorified. **See Eph. 1:5; 2 Thess. 2:13.**

p. **1 Pet. 1:5.** … who are kept by the power of God through faith unto salvation ready to be revealed in the last time.

q. **John 10:14–15, 26.** I am the good shepherd, and know my sheep, and am known of mine. As the Father knoweth me, even so know I the Father: and I lay down my life for the sheep.… But ye believe not, because ye are not of my sheep, as I said unto you. **John 6:64–65.** But there are some of you that believe not. For Jesus knew from the beginning who they were that believed not, and who should betray him. And he said, Therefore said I unto you, that no man can come unto me, except it were given unto him of my Father. **Rom. 8:28–39.** And we know that all things work together for good to them that love God, to them who are the called according to his purpose. For whom he did foreknow, he also did predestinate to be conformed to the image of his Son, that he might be the firstborn among many brethren. Moreover whom he did predestinate, them he also called: and whom he called, them he also justified: and whom he justified, them he also glorified. What shall we then say to these things? If God be for us, who can be against us? He that spared not his own Son, but delivered him up for us all, how shall he not with him also freely give us all things? Who shall lay any thing to the charge of God's elect? It is God that justifieth. Who is he that condemneth? It is Christ that died, yea rather, that is risen again, who is even at the right hand of God, who also maketh intercession for us. Who shall separate us from the love of Christ? shall tribulation, or distress, or persecution, or famine, or

7. The rest of mankind God was pleased, according to the unsearchable counsel of his own will, whereby he extendeth or withholdeth mercy, as he pleaseth, for the glory of his sovereign power over his creatures, to pass by; and to ordain them to dishonor and wrath for their sin, to the praise of his glorious justice.[r]

8. The doctrine of this high mystery of predestination is to be handled with special prudence and care,[s] that men, attending the will of God revealed in his Word, and yielding obedience thereunto, may, from the certainty of their effectual vocation, be assured of their eternal election.[t] So shall this doctrine afford matter of praise, rever-

nakedness, or peril, or sword? As it is written, For thy sake we are killed all the day long; we are accounted as sheep for the slaughter. Nay, in all these things we are more than conquerors through him that loved us. For I am persuaded, that neither death, nor life, nor angels, nor principalities, nor powers, nor things present, nor things to come, nor height, nor depth, nor any other creature, shall be able to separate us from the love of God, which is in Christ Jesus our Lord. **See John 8:47; 17:9; 1 John 2:19.**

r. **Matt. 11:25–26.** At that time Jesus answered and said, I thank thee, O Father, Lord of heaven and earth, because thou hast hid these things from the wise and prudent, and hast revealed them unto babes. Even so, Father: for so it seemed good in thy sight. **Rom. 9:17–18, 21–22.** For the scripture saith unto Pharaoh, Even for this same purpose have I raised thee up, that I might shew my power in thee, and that my name might be declared throughout all the earth. Therefore hath he mercy on whom he will have mercy, and whom he will he hardeneth.… Hath not the potter power over the clay, of the same lump to make one vessel unto honour, and another unto dishonour? What if God, willing to shew his wrath, and to make his power known, endured with much longsuffering the vessels of wrath fitted to destruction. **Jude 4.** For there are certain men crept in unawares, who were before of old ordained to this condemnation, ungodly men, turning the grace of our God into lasciviousness, and denying the only Lord God, and our Lord Jesus Christ. **1 Pet. 2:8.** … and a stone of stumbling, and a rock of offence, even to them which stumble at the word, being disobedient: whereunto also they were appointed. **2 Tim. 2:19–20.** Nevertheless the foundation of God standeth sure, having this seal, The Lord knoweth them that are his. And, Let every one that nameth the name of Christ depart from iniquity. But in a great house there are not only vessels of gold and of silver, but also of wood and of earth; and some to honour, and some to dishonour.

s. **Rom. 9:20.** Nay but, O man, who art thou that repliest against God? Shall the thing formed say to him that formed it, Why hast thou made me thus? **Rom. 11:33.** O the depth of the riches both of the wisdom and knowledge of God! how unsearchable are his judgments, and his ways past finding out! **Deut. 29:29.** The secret things belong unto the LORD our God: but those things which are revealed belong unto us and to our children for ever, that we may do all the words of this law.

t. **2 Pet. 1:10.** Wherefore the rather, brethren, give diligence to make your calling and election sure: for if ye do these things, ye shall never fall. **1 Thess. 1:4–5.**

ence, and admiration of God;[u] and of humility, diligence, and abundant consolation to all that sincerely obey the gospel.[w]

Chapter 4
Of Creation

1. It pleased God the Father, Son, and Holy Ghost,[a] for the manifestation of the glory of his eternal power, wisdom, and goodness,[b] in the beginning, to create, or make of nothing, the world, and all things therein whether visible or invisible, in the space of six days; and all very good.[c]

… knowing, brethren beloved, your election of God. For our gospel came not unto you in word only, but also in power, and in the Holy Ghost, and in much assurance; as ye know what manner of men we were among you for your sake.

u. **Eph. 1:6.** … to the praise of the glory of his grace, wherein he hath made us accepted in the beloved. **See Rom. 11:33.**

w. **Rom. 11:5–6, 20.** Even so then at this present time also there is a remnant according to the election of grace. And if by grace, then is it no more of works: otherwise grace is no more grace. But if it be of works, then is it no more grace: otherwise work is no more work.… Well; because of unbelief they were broken off, and thou standest by faith. Be not highminded, but fear. **Rom. 8:33.** Who shall lay any thing to the charge of God's elect? It is God that justifieth. **Luke 10:20.** Notwithstanding in this rejoice not, that the spirits are subject unto you; but rather rejoice, because your names are written in heaven. **See 2 Pet. 1:10.**

a. **Rom. 11:36.** For of him, and through him, and to him, are all things: to whom be glory for ever. Amen. **1 Cor. 8:6.** But to us there is but one God, the Father, of whom are all things, and we in him; and one Lord Jesus Christ, by whom are all things, and we by him. **Heb. 1:2.** [God] hath in these last days spoken unto us by his Son, whom he hath appointed heir of all things, by whom also he made the worlds. **John 1:2–3.** The same was in the beginning with God. All things were made by him; and without him was not any thing made that was made. **Gen. 1:2.** And the earth was without form, and void; and darkness was upon the face of the deep. And the Spirit of God moved upon the face of the waters. **Job 33:4.** The Spirit of God hath made me, and the breath of the Almighty hath given me life.

b. **Rom. 1:20.** For the invisible things of him from the creation of the world are clearly seen, being understood by the things that are made, even his eternal power and Godhead; so that they are without excuse. **Jer. 10:12.** He hath made the earth by his power, he hath established the world by his wisdom, and hath stretched out the heavens by his discretion. **Ps. 104:24.** O LORD, how manifold are thy works! in wisdom hast thou made them all: the earth is full of thy riches. **Ps. 33:5.** He loveth righteousness and judgment: the earth is full of the goodness of the LORD.

c. **Gen. 1:1–31.** In the beginning God created the heaven and the earth. And

2. After God had made all other creatures, he created man, male and female,[d] with reasonable and immortal souls,[e] endued with knowledge, righteousness, and true holiness, after his own image;[f] having the law of God written in their hearts,[g] and power to fulfill it:[h] and yet under a possibility of transgressing, being left to the liberty of

the earth was without form, and void; and darkness was upon the face of the deep. And the Spirit of God moved upon the face of the waters. And God said, Let there be light: and there was light. And God saw the light, that it was good: and God divided the light from the darkness. And God called the light Day, and the darkness he called Night. And the evening and the morning were the first day…. And God saw every thing that he had made, and, behold, it was very good. And the evening and the morning were the sixth day. **Ps. 33:6.** By the word of the LORD were the heavens made; and all the host of them by the breath of his mouth. **Heb. 11:3.** Through faith we understand that the worlds were framed by the word of God, so that things which are seen were not made of things which do appear. **Col. 1:16.** For by him were all things created, that are in heaven, and that are in earth, visible and invisible, whether they be thrones, or dominions, or principalities, or powers: all things were created by him, and for him. **Acts 17:24.** God that made the world and all things therein, seeing that he is Lord of heaven and earth, dwelleth not in temples made with hands. **Ex. 20:11.** For in six days the LORD made heaven and earth, the sea, and all that in them is, and rested the seventh day: wherefore the LORD blessed the sabbath day, and hallowed it.

d. **Gen. 1:27.** So God created man in his own image, in the image of God created he him; male and female created he them.

e. **Gen. 2:7.** And the LORD God formed man of the dust of the ground, and breathed into his nostrils the breath of life; and man became a living soul. **Eccl. 12:7.** Then shall the dust return to the earth as it was: and the spirit shall return unto God who gave it. **Luke 23:43.** And Jesus said unto him, Verily I say unto thee, To day shalt thou be with me in paradise. **Matt. 10:28.** And fear not them which kill the body, but are not able to kill the soul: but rather fear him which is able to destroy both soul and body in hell.

f. **Gen. 1:26.** And God said, Let us make man in our image, after our likeness: and let them have dominion over the fish of the sea, and over the fowl of the air, and over the cattle, and over all the earth, and over every creeping thing that creepeth upon the earth. **Col. 3:10.** And [ye] have put on the new man, which is renewed in knowledge after the image of him that created him. **Eph. 4:24.** … and that ye put on the new man, which after God is created in righteousness and true holiness.

g. **Rom. 2:14–15.** For when the Gentiles, which have not the law, do by nature the things contained in the law, these, having not the law, are a law unto themselves: which shew the work of the law written in their hearts, their conscience also bearing witness, and their thoughts the mean while accusing or else excusing one another.

h. **Gen. 2:17.** But of the tree of the knowledge of good and evil, thou shalt not eat of it: for in the day that thou eatest thereof thou shalt surely die. **Eccl. 7:29.** Lo, this only have I found, that God hath made man upright; but they have sought out many inventions.

their own will, which was subject unto change.[i] Beside this law written in their hearts, they received a command, not to eat of the tree of the knowledge of good and evil; which while they kept, they were happy in their communion with God,[k] and had dominion over the creatures.[l]

Chapter 5
Of Providence

1. God the great Creator of all things doth uphold,[a] direct, dis-

i. **Gen. 3:6, 17.** And when the woman saw that the tree was good for food, and that it was pleasant to the eyes, and a tree to be desired to make one wise, she took of the fruit thereof, and did eat, and gave also unto her husband with her; and he did eat.… And unto Adam he said, Because thou hast hearkened unto the voice of thy wife, and hast eaten of the tree, of which I commanded thee, saying, Thou shalt not eat of it: cursed is the ground for thy sake; in sorrow shalt thou eat of it all the days of thy life.

k. **Gen. 2:17.** But of the tree of the knowledge of good and evil, thou shalt not eat of it: for in the day that thou eatest thereof thou shalt surely die. **Gen. 2:15–3:24.** And the LORD God took the man, and put him into the garden of Eden to dress it and to keep it. And the LORD God commanded the man, saying, Of every tree of the garden thou mayest freely eat: but of the tree of the knowledge of good and evil, thou shalt not eat of it: for in the day that thou eatest thereof thou shalt surely die.… And when the woman saw that the tree was good for food, and that it was pleasant to the eyes, and a tree to be desired to make one wise, she took of the fruit thereof, and did eat, and gave also unto her husband with her; and he did eat.… And they heard the voice of the LORD God walking in the garden in the cool of the day: and Adam and his wife hid themselves from the presence of the LORD God amongst the trees of the garden.… And unto Adam he said, Because thou hast hearkened unto the voice of thy wife, and hast eaten of the tree, of which I commanded thee, saying, Thou shalt not eat of it: cursed is the ground for thy sake; in sorrow shalt thou eat of it all the days of thy life.… Therefore the LORD God sent him forth from the garden of Eden, to till the ground from whence he was taken.…

l. **Gen. 1:28.** And God blessed them, and God said unto them, Be fruitful, and multiply, and replenish the earth, and subdue it: and have dominion over the fish of the sea, and over the fowl of the air, and over every living thing that moveth upon the earth. **See Gen. 1:29–30; Ps. 8:6–8.**

a. **Neh. 9:6.** Thou, even thou, art LORD alone; thou hast made heaven, the heaven of heavens, with all their host, the earth, and all things that are therein, the seas, and all that is therein, and thou preservest them all; and the host of heaven worshippeth thee. **Ps. 145:14–16.** The LORD upholdeth all that fall, and raiseth up all those that be bowed down. The eyes of all wait upon thee; and thou givest them

pose, and govern all creatures, actions, and things,[b] from the greatest even to the least,[c] by his most wise and holy providence,[d] according to his infallible foreknowledge,[e] and the free and immutable counsel

their meat in due season. Thou openest thine hand, and satisfiest the desire of every living thing. **Heb. 1:3.** … who being the brightness of his glory, and the express image of his person, and upholding all things by the word of his power, when he had by himself purged our sins, sat down on the right hand of the Majesty on high.

b. **Dan. 4:34–35.** And at the end of the days I Nebuchadnezzar lifted up mine eyes unto heaven, and mine understanding returned unto me, and I blessed the most High, and I praised and honoured him that liveth for ever, whose dominion is an everlasting dominion, and his kingdom is from generation to generation: and all the inhabitants of the earth are reputed as nothing: and he doeth according to his will in the army of heaven, and among the inhabitants of the earth: and none can stay his hand, or say unto him, What doest thou? **Ps. 135:6.** Whatsoever the LORD pleased, that did he in heaven, and in earth, in the seas, and all deep places. **Acts 17:25–28.** Neither is [God] worshipped with men's hands, as though he needed any thing, seeing he giveth to all life, and breath, and all things; and hath made of one blood all nations of men for to dwell on all the face of the earth, and hath determined the times before appointed, and the bounds of their habitation; that they should seek the Lord, if haply they might feel after him, and find him, though he be not far from every one of us: for in him we live, and move, and have our being; as certain also of your own poets have said, For we are also his offspring. **Job 38–41.** Then the LORD answered Job out of the whirlwind, and said,… Where wast thou when I laid the foundations of the earth? declare, if thou hast understanding.… Or who shut up the sea with doors, when it brake forth, as if it had issued out of the womb.… Hast thou entered into the springs of the sea? or hast thou walked in the search of the depth? Have the gates of death been opened unto thee? or hast thou seen the doors of the shadow of death.… Canst thou bind the sweet influences of Pleiades, or loose the bands of Orion.… Hast thou given the horse strength? hast thou clothed his neck with thunder.… Hast thou an arm like God? or canst thou thunder with a voice like him? Deck thyself now with majesty and excellency; and array thyself with glory and beauty.… Canst thou draw out leviathan with an hook? or his tongue with a cord which thou lettest down?…

c. **Matt. 10:29–31.** Are not two sparrows sold for a farthing? and one of them shall not fall on the ground without your Father. But the very hairs of your head are all numbered. Fear ye not therefore, ye are of more value than many sparrows. **See Matt. 6:26–32.**

d. **Prov. 15:3.** The eyes of the LORD are in every place, beholding the evil and the good. **2 Chron. 16:9.** For the eyes of the LORD run to and fro throughout the whole earth, to shew himself strong in the behalf of them whose heart is perfect toward him. Herein thou hast done foolishly: therefore from henceforth thou shalt have wars. **Ps. 104:24.** O LORD, how manifold are thy works! in wisdom hast thou made them all: the earth is full of thy riches. **Ps. 145:17.** The LORD is righteous in all his ways, and holy in all his works.

e. **Acts 15:18.** Known unto God are all his works from the beginning of the world. **Isa. 42:9.** Behold, the former things are come to pass, and new things do I declare: before they spring forth I tell you of them. **Ezek. 11:5.** And the Spirit of the

of his own will,[f] to the praise of the glory of his wisdom, power, justice, goodness, and mercy.[g]

2. Although, in relation to the foreknowledge and decree of God, the First Cause, all things come to pass immutably, and infallibly;[h] yet, by the same providence, he ordereth them to fall out, according to the nature of second causes, either necessarily, freely, or contingently.[i]

3. God, in his ordinary providence, maketh use of means,[k] yet is

LORD fell upon me, and said unto me, Speak; Thus saith the LORD; Thus have ye said, O house of Israel: for I know the things that come into your mind, every one of them.

f. **Eph. 1:11.** … in whom also we have obtained an inheritance, being predestinated according to the purpose of him who worketh all things after the counsel of his own will. **Ps. 33:10–11.** The LORD bringeth the counsel of the heathen to nought: he maketh the devices of the people of none effect. The counsel of the LORD standeth for ever, the thoughts of his heart to all generations.

g. **Isa. 63:14.** As a beast goeth down into the valley, the Spirit of the LORD caused him to rest: so didst thou lead thy people, to make thyself a glorious name. **Eph. 3:10.** … to the intent that now unto the principalities and powers in heavenly places might be known by the church the manifold wisdom of God. **Rom. 9:17.** For the scripture saith unto Pharaoh, Even for this same purpose have I raised thee up, that I might shew my power in thee, and that my name might be declared throughout all the earth. **Gen. 45:7.** And God sent me before you to preserve you a posterity in the earth, and to save your lives by a great deliverance. **Ps. 145:7.** They shall abundantly utter the memory of thy great goodness, and shall sing of thy righteousness.

h. **Acts 2:23.** Him, being delivered by the determinate counsel and foreknowledge of God, ye have taken, and by wicked hands have crucified and slain. **See Isa. 14:24, 27.**

i. **Gen. 8:22.** While the earth remaineth, seedtime and harvest, and cold and heat, and summer and winter, and day and night shall not cease. **Jer. 31:35.** Thus saith the LORD, which giveth the sun for a light by day, and the ordinances of the moon and of the stars for a light by night, which divideth the sea when the waves thereof roar; The LORD of hosts is his name. **Isa. 10:6–7.** I will send him against an hypocritical nation, and against the people of my wrath will I give him a charge, to take the spoil, and to take the prey, and to tread them down like the mire of the streets. Howbeit he meaneth not so, neither doth his heart think so; but it is in his heart to destroy and cut off nations not a few. **See Ex. 21:13 and Deut. 19:5; 1 Kings 22:28–34.**

k. **Acts 27:24, 31, 44b.** … saying, Fear not, Paul; thou must be brought before Caesar: and, lo, God hath given thee all them that sail with thee.… Paul said to the centurion and to the soldiers, Except these abide in the ship, ye cannot be saved.… And so it came to pass, that they escaped all safe to land. **Isa. 55:10–11.** For as the rain cometh down, and the snow from heaven, and returneth not thither, but watereth the earth, and maketh it bring forth and bud, that it may give seed to the sower, and bread to the eater: so shall my word be that goeth forth out of my mouth: it shall not return unto me void, but it shall accomplish that which I please, and it shall prosper in

free to work without,[l] above,[m] and against them, at his pleasure.[n]

4. The almighty power, unsearchable wisdom, and infinite goodness of God so far manifest themselves in his providence, that it extendeth itself even to the first fall, and all other sins of angels and men;[o] and that not by a bare permission,[p] but such as hath joined with it a most wise and powerful bounding,[q] and otherwise ordering,

the thing whereto I sent it.

l. **Hos. 1:7.** But I will have mercy upon the house of Judah, and will save them by the LORD their God, and will not save them by bow, nor by sword, nor by battle, by horses, nor by horsemen. **Matt. 4:4.** But he answered and said, It is written, Man shall not live by bread alone, but by every word that proceedeth out of the mouth of God. **Job 34:20.** In a moment shall they die, and the people shall be troubled at midnight, and pass away: and the mighty shall be taken away without hand.

m. **Rom. 4:19–21.** And being not weak in faith, he considered not his own body now dead, when he was about an hundred years old, neither yet the deadness of Sarah's womb: he staggered not at the promise of God through unbelief; but was strong in faith, giving glory to God; and being fully persuaded that, what he had promised, he was able also to perform.

n. **2 Kings 6:6.** And the man of God said, Where fell it? And he shewed him the place. And he cut down a stick, and cast it in thither; and the iron did swim. **Dan. 3:27.** And the princes, governors, and captains, and the king's counsellers, being gathered together, saw these men, upon whose bodies the fire had no power, nor was an hair of their head singed, neither were their coats changed, nor the smell of fire had passed on them.

o. **Isa. 45:7.** I form the light, and create darkness: I make peace, and create evil: I the LORD do all these things. **Rom. 11:32–34.** For God hath concluded them all in unbelief, that he might have mercy upon all. O the depth of the riches both of the wisdom and knowledge of God! how unsearchable are his judgments, and his ways past finding out! For who hath known the mind of the Lord? or who hath been his counsellor? **2 Sam. 16:10.** And the king said, What have I to do with you, ye sons of Zeruiah? so let him curse, because the LORD hath said unto him, Curse David. Who shall then say, Wherefore hast thou done so? **Acts 2:23.** Him, being delivered by the determinate counsel and foreknowledge of God, ye have taken, and by wicked hands have crucified and slain. **Acts 4:27–28.** For of a truth against thy holy child Jesus, whom thou hast anointed, both Herod, and Pontius Pilate, with the Gentiles, and the people of Israel, were gathered together, for to do whatsoever thy hand and thy counsel determined before to be done. **See 2 Sam. 24:1 and 1 Chron. 21:1; 1 Kings 22:22–23; 1 Chron. 10:4, 13–14.**

p. **John 12:40.** He hath blinded their eyes, and hardened their heart; that they should not see with their eyes, nor understand with their heart, and be converted, and I should heal them. **2 Thess. 2:11.** And for this cause God shall send them strong delusion, that they should believe a lie.

q. **Ps. 76:10.** Surely the wrath of man shall praise thee: the remainder of wrath shalt thou restrain. **2 Kings 19:28.** Because thy rage against me and thy tumult is come up into mine ears, therefore I will put my hook in thy nose, and my bridle in thy lips, and I will turn thee back by the way by which thou camest.

and governing of them, in a manifold dispensation, to his own holy ends;[r] yet so, as the sinfulness thereof proceedeth only from the creature, and not from God, who, being most holy and righteous, neither is nor can be the author or approver of sin.[s]

5. The most wise, righteous, and gracious God doth oftentimes leave, for a season, his own children to manifold temptations, and the corruption of their own hearts, to chastise them for their former sins, or to discover unto them the hidden strength of corruption and deceitfulness of their hearts, that they may be humbled;[t] and, to raise them to a more close and constant dependence for their support upon himself, and to make them more watchful against all future occasions

r. **Gen. 50:20.** But as for you, ye thought evil against me; but God meant it unto good, to bring to pass, as it is this day, to save much people alive. **Isa. 10:12.** Wherefore it shall come to pass, that when the Lord hath performed his whole work upon mount Zion and on Jerusalem, I will punish the fruit of the stout heart of the king of Assyria, and the glory of his high looks. **See Isa. 10:6–7, 13–15.**

s. **James 1:13–14, 17.** Let no man say when he is tempted, I am tempted of God: for God cannot be tempted with evil, neither tempteth he any man: but every man is tempted, when he is drawn away of his own lust, and enticed.… Every good gift and every perfect gift is from above, and cometh down from the Father of lights, with whom is no variableness, neither shadow of turning. **1 John 2:16.** For all that is in the world, the lust of the flesh, and the lust of the eyes, and the pride of life, is not of the Father, but is of the world. **Ps. 50:21.** These things hast thou done, and I kept silence; thou thoughtest that I was altogether such an one as thyself: but I will reprove thee, and set them in order before thine eyes.

t. **2 Chron. 32:25–26, 31.** But Hezekiah rendered not again according to the benefit done unto him; for his heart was lifted up: therefore there was wrath upon him, and upon Judah and Jerusalem. Notwithstanding Hezekiah humbled himself for the pride of his heart, both he and the inhabitants of Jerusalem, so that the wrath of the LORD came not upon them in the days of Hezekiah.… Howbeit in the business of the ambassadors of the princes of Babylon, who sent unto him to inquire of the wonder that was done in the land, God left him, to try him, that he might know all that was in his heart. **Deut. 8:2–3, 5.** And thou shalt remember all the way which the LORD thy God led thee these forty years in the wilderness, to humble thee, and to prove thee, to know what was in thine heart, whether thou wouldest keep his commandments, or no. And he humbled thee, and suffered thee to hunger, and fed thee with manna, which thou knewest not, neither did thy fathers know; that he might make thee know that man doth not live by bread only, but by every word that proceedeth out of the mouth of the LORD doth man live.… Thou shalt also consider in thine heart, that, as a man chasteneth his son, so the LORD thy God chasteneth thee. **Luke 22:31–32.** And the Lord said, Simon, Simon, behold, Satan hath desired to have you, that he may sift you as wheat: but I have prayed for thee, that thy faith fail not: and when thou art converted, strengthen thy brethren. **See 2 Sam. 24:1, 25.**

of sin, and for sundry other just and holy ends.[u]

6. As for those wicked and ungodly men whom God, as a righteous Judge, for former sins, doth blind and harden,[w] from them he not only withholdeth his grace whereby they might have been enlightened in their understandings, and wrought upon in their hearts;[x] but sometimes also withdraweth the gifts which they had,[y] and exposeth them to such objects as their corruption makes occasions of sin;[z] and, withal, gives them over to their own lusts, the temptations

u. **2 Cor. 12:7–9.** And lest I should be exalted above measure through the abundance of the revelations, there was given to me a thorn in the flesh, the messenger of Satan to buffet me, lest I should be exalted above measure. For this thing I besought the Lord thrice, that it might depart from me. And he said unto me, My grace is sufficient for thee: for my strength is made perfect in weakness. Most gladly therefore will I rather glory in my infirmities, that the power of Christ may rest upon me. **See Ps. 73:1–28; 77:1–12; Mark 14:66–72; John 21:15–19.**

w. **Rom. 1:24, 26, 28.** Wherefore God also gave them up to uncleanness through the lusts of their own hearts, to dishonour their own bodies between themselves.… For this cause God gave them up unto vile affections: for even their women did change the natural use into that which is against nature.… And even as they did not like to retain God in their knowledge, God gave them over to a reprobate mind, to do those things which are not convenient. **Rom. 11:7–8.** What then? Israel hath not obtained that which he seeketh for; but the election hath obtained it, and the rest were blinded (according as it is written, God hath given them the spirit of slumber, eyes that they should not see, and ears that they should not hear;) unto this day.

x. **Deut. 29:4.** Yet the Lord hath not given you an heart to perceive, and eyes to see, and ears to hear, unto this day. **Mark 4:11–12.** And he said unto them, Unto you it is given to know the mystery of the kingdom of God: but unto them that are without, all these things are done in parables: that seeing they may see, and not perceive; and hearing they may hear, and not understand; lest at any time they should be converted, and their sins should be forgiven them.

y. **Matt. 13:12.** For whosoever hath, to him shall be given, and he shall have more abundance: but whosoever hath not, from him shall be taken away even that he hath. **Matt. 25:29.** For unto every one that hath shall be given, and he shall have abundance: but from him that hath not shall be taken away even that which he hath. **See Acts 13:10–11.**

z. **Gen. 4:8.** And Cain talked with Abel his brother: and it came to pass, when they were in the field, that Cain rose up against Abel his brother, and slew him. **2 Kings 8:12–13.** And Hazael said, Why weepeth my lord? And he answered, Because I know the evil that thou wilt do unto the children of Israel: their strong holds wilt thou set on fire, and their young men wilt thou slay with the sword, and wilt dash their children, and rip up their women with child. And Hazael said, But what, is thy servant a dog, that he should do this great thing? And Elisha answered, The Lord hath shewed me that thou shalt be king over Syria. **See Matt. 26:14–16.**

of the world, and the power of Satan,[a] whereby it comes to pass that they harden themselves, even under those means which God useth for the softening of others.[b]

7. As the providence of God doth, in general, reach to all creatures; so, after a most special manner, it taketh care of his church, and disposeth all things to the good thereof.[c]

a. **Ps. 109:6.** Set thou a wicked man over him: and let Satan stand at his right hand. **Luke 22:3.** Then entered Satan into Judas surnamed Iscariot, being of the number of the twelve. **2 Thess. 2:10–12.** … and with all deceivableness of unrighteousness in them that perish; because they received not the love of the truth, that they might be saved. And for this cause God shall send them strong delusion, that they should believe a lie: that they all might be damned who believed not the truth, but had pleasure in unrighteousness.

b. **Ex. 8:15, 32.** But when Pharaoh saw that there was respite, he hardened his heart, and hearkened not unto them; as the LORD had said.… And Pharaoh hardened his heart at this time also, neither would he let the people go. **2 Cor. 2:15–16.** For we are unto God a sweet savour of Christ, in them that are saved, and in them that perish: to the one we are the savour of death unto death; and to the other the savour of life unto life. And who is sufficient for these things? **Isa. 8:14.** And he shall be for a sanctuary; but for a stone of stumbling and for a rock of offence to both the houses of Israel, for a gin and for a snare to the inhabitants of Jerusalem. **1 Pet. 2:7–8.** Unto you therefore which believe he is precious: but unto them which be disobedient, the stone which the builders disallowed, the same is made the head of the corner, and a stone of stumbling, and a rock of offence, even to them which stumble at the word, being disobedient: whereunto also they were appointed. **See Ex. 7:3; Isa. 6:9–10; Acts 28:26–27.**

c. **1 Tim. 4:10.** For therefore we both labour and suffer reproach, because we trust in the living God, who is the Saviour of all men, specially of those that believe. **Amos 9:8–9.** Behold, the eyes of the Lord GOD are upon the sinful kingdom, and I will destroy it from off the face of the earth; saving that I will not utterly destroy the house of Jacob, saith the LORD. For, lo, I will command, and I will sift the house of Israel among all nations, like as corn is sifted in a sieve, yet shall not the least grain fall upon the earth. **Matt. 16:18.** And I say also unto thee, That thou art Peter, and upon this rock I will build my church; and the gates of hell shall not prevail against it. **Rom. 8:28.** And we know that all things work together for good to them that love God, to them who are the called according to his purpose. **Isa. 43:3–5, 14.** For I am the LORD thy God, the Holy One of Israel, thy Saviour: I gave Egypt for thy ransom, Ethiopia and Seba for thee. Since thou wast precious in my sight, thou hast been honourable, and I have loved thee: therefore will I give men for thee, and people for thy life. Fear not: for I am with thee: I will bring thy seed from the east, and gather thee from the west.… Thus saith the LORD, your redeemer, the Holy One of Israel; For your sake I have sent to Babylon, and have brought down all their nobles, and the Chaldeans, whose cry is in the ships.

Chapter 6
Of the Fall of Man,
of Sin, and of the Punishment Thereof

1. Our first parents, being seduced by the subtilty and temptation of Satan, sinned, in eating the forbidden fruit.[a] This their sin, God was pleased, according to his wise and holy counsel, to permit, having purposed to order it to his own glory.[b]

2. By this sin they fell from their original righteousness and communion with God,[c] and so became dead in sin,[d] and wholly defiled in all the parts and faculties of soul and body.[e]

---

a. **Gen. 3:13.** And the Lord God said unto the woman, What is this that thou hast done? And the woman said, The serpent beguiled me, and I did eat. **2 Cor. 11:3.** But I fear, lest by any means, as the serpent beguiled Eve through his subtilty, so your minds should be corrupted from the simplicity that is in Christ.

b. **See chapter 5, section 4.**

c. **Gen. 3:6–8.** And when the woman saw that the tree was good for food, and that it was pleasant to the eyes, and a tree to be desired to make one wise, she took of the fruit thereof, and did eat, and gave also unto her husband with her; and he did eat. And the eyes of them both were opened, and they knew that they were naked; and they sewed fig leaves together, and made themselves aprons. And they heard the voice of the Lord God walking in the garden in the cool of the day: and Adam and his wife hid themselves from the presence of the Lord God amongst the trees of the garden. **Rom. 3:23.** For all have sinned, and come short of the glory of God.

d. **Gen. 2:17.** But of the tree of the knowledge of good and evil, thou shalt not eat of it: for in the day that thou eatest thereof thou shalt surely die. **Eph. 2:1–3.** And you hath he quickened, who were dead in trespasses and sins; wherein in time past ye walked according to the course of this world, according to the prince of the power of the air, the spirit that now worketh in the children of disobedience: among whom also we all had our conversation in times past in the lusts of our flesh, fulfilling the desires of the flesh and of the mind; and were by nature the children of wrath, even as others. **See Rom. 5:12.**

e. **Gen. 6:5.** And God saw that the wickedness of man was great in the earth, and that every imagination of the thoughts of his heart was only evil continually. **Jer. 17:9.** The heart is deceitful above all things, and desperately wicked: who can know it? **Titus 1:15.** Unto the pure all things are pure: but unto them that are defiled and unbelieving is nothing pure; but even their mind and conscience is defiled. **Rom. 3:10–19.** As it is written, There is none righteous, no, not one: there is none that understandeth, there is none that seeketh after God. They are all gone out of the way, they are together become unprofitable; there is none that doeth good, no, not one. Their throat is an open sepulchre; with their tongues they have used deceit; the poison of asps is under their lips: whose mouth is full of cursing and bitterness: their feet are

3. They being the root of all mankind, the guilt of this sin was imputed;[f] and the same death in sin, and corrupted nature, conveyed to all their posterity descending from them by ordinary generation.[g]

4. From this original corruption, whereby we are utterly indisposed, disabled, and made opposite to all good,[h] and wholly inclined to all evil,[i] do proceed all actual transgressions.[k]

swift to shed blood: destruction and misery are in their ways: and the way of peace have they not known: there is no fear of God before their eyes. Now we know that what things soever the law saith, it saith to them who are under the law: that every mouth may be stopped, and all the world may become guilty before God.

f. **Acts 17:26.** And [God] hath made of one blood all nations of men for to dwell on all the face of the earth, and hath determined the times before appointed, and the bounds of their habitation. **Rom. 5:12, 15–19.** Wherefore, as by one man sin entered into the world, and death by sin; and so death passed upon all men, for that all have sinned: (… But not as the offence, so also is the free gift. For if through the offence of one many be dead, much more the grace of God, and the gift by grace, which is by one man, Jesus Christ, hath abounded unto many. And not as it was by one that sinned, so is the gift: for the judgment was by one to condemnation, but the free gift is of many offences unto justification. For if by one man's offence death reigned by one; much more they which receive abundance of grace and of the gift of righteousness shall reign in life by one, Jesus Christ.) therefore as by the offence of one judgment came upon all men to condemnation; even so by the righteousness of one the free gift came upon all men unto justification of life. For as by one man's disobedience many were made sinners, so by the obedience of one shall many be made righteous. **1 Cor. 15:21–22, 49.** For since by man came death, by man came also the resurrection of the dead. For as in Adam all die, even so in Christ shall all be made alive.… And as we have borne the image of the earthy, we shall also bear the image of the heavenly.

g. **Ps. 51:5.** Behold, I was shapen in iniquity; and in sin did my mother conceive me. **John 3:6.** That which is born of the flesh is flesh; and that which is born of the Spirit is spirit. **Gen. 5:3.** And Adam lived an hundred and thirty years, and begat a son in his own likeness, after his image; and called his name Seth. **Job 15:14.** What is man, that he should be clean? and he which is born of a woman, that he should be righteous?

h. **Rom. 5:6.** For when we were yet without strength, in due time Christ died for the ungodly. **Rom. 7:18.** For I know that in me (that is, in my flesh,) dwelleth no good thing: for to will is present with me; but how to perform that which is good I find not. **Rom. 8:7.** Because the carnal mind is enmity against God: for it is not subject to the law of God, neither indeed can be. **Col. 1:21.** And you, that were sometime alienated and enemies in your mind by wicked works, yet now hath he reconciled.

i. **Gen. 8:21.** And the LORD smelled a sweet savour; and the LORD said in his heart, I will not again curse the ground any more for man's sake; for the imagination of man's heart is evil from his youth; neither will I again smite any more every thing living, as I have done. **See Gen. 6:5; Rom. 3:10–12.**

k. **Matt. 15:19.** For out of the heart proceed evil thoughts, murders, adulteries,

5. This corruption of nature, during this life, doth remain in those that are regenerated;[l] and although it be, through Christ, pardoned, and mortified; yet both itself, and all the motions thereof, are truly and properly sin.[m]

6. Every sin, both original and actual, being a transgression of the righteous law of God, and contrary thereunto,[n] doth, in its own nature, bring guilt upon the sinner,[o] whereby he is bound over to the

---

fornications, thefts, false witness, blasphemies. **James 1:14–15.** But every man is tempted, when he is drawn away of his own lust, and enticed. Then when lust hath conceived, it bringeth forth sin: and sin, when it is finished, bringeth forth death. **Eph. 2:2–3.** … wherein in time past ye walked according to the course of this world, according to the prince of the power of the air, the spirit that now worketh in the children of disobedience: among whom also we all had our conversation in times past in the lusts of our flesh, fulfilling the desires of the flesh and of the mind; and were by nature the children of wrath, even as others.

l. **Prov. 20:9.** Who can say, I have made my heart clean, I am pure from my sin? **Eccl. 7:20.** For there is not a just man upon earth, that doeth good, and sinneth not. **Rom. 7:14, 17–18, 21–23.** For we know that the law is spiritual: but I am carnal, sold under sin.… Now then it is no more I that do it, but sin that dwelleth in me. For I know that in me (that is, in my flesh,) dwelleth no good thing: for to will is present with me; but how to perform that which is good I find not.… I find then a law, that, when I would do good, evil is present with me. For I delight in the law of God after the inward man: but I see another law in my members, warring against the law of my mind, and bringing me into captivity to the law of sin which is in my members. **1 John 1:8, 10.** If we say that we have no sin, we deceive ourselves, and the truth is not in us.… If we say that we have not sinned, we make him a liar, and his word is not in us.

m. **Rom. 7:7–8, 25.** What shall we say then? Is the law sin? God forbid. Nay, I had not known sin, but by the law: for I had not known lust, except the law had said, Thou shalt not covet. But sin, taking occasion by the commandment, wrought in me all manner of concupiscence. For without the law sin was dead.… I thank God through Jesus Christ our Lord. So then with the mind I myself serve the law of God; but with the flesh the law of sin. **Gal. 5:17.** For the flesh lusteth against the Spirit, and the Spirit against the flesh: and these are contrary the one to the other: so that ye cannot do the things that ye would.

n. **1 John 3:4.** Whosoever committeth sin transgresseth also the law: for sin is the transgression of the law.

o. **Rom. 2:15.** … which shew the work of the law written in their hearts, their conscience also bearing witness, and their thoughts the mean while accusing or else excusing one another. **Rom. 3:9, 19.** What then? are we better than they? No, in no wise: for we have before proved both Jews and Gentiles, that they are all under sin.… Now we know that what things soever the law saith, it saith to them who are under the law: that every mouth may be stopped, and all the world may become guilty before God.

wrath of God,[p] and curse of the law,[q] and so made subject to death,[r] with all miseries spiritual,[s] temporal,[t] and eternal.[u]

Chapter 7
Of God's Covenant with Man

1. The distance between God and the creature is so great, that although reasonable creatures do owe obedience unto him as their Creator, yet they could never have any fruition of him as their blessedness and reward, but by some voluntary condescension on God's part, which he hath been pleased to express by way of covenant.[a]

p. **Eph. 2:3.** … among whom also we all had our conversation in times past in the lusts of our flesh, fulfilling the desires of the flesh and of the mind; and were by nature the children of wrath, even as others.

q. **Gal. 3:10.** For as many as are of the works of the law are under the curse: for it is written, Cursed is every one that continueth not in all things which are written in the book of the law to do them.

r. **Rom. 6:23.** For the wages of sin is death; but the gift of God is eternal life through Jesus Christ our Lord.

s. **Eph. 4:18.** … having the understanding darkened, being alienated from the life of God through the ignorance that is in them, because of the blindness of their heart.

t. **Rom. 8:20.** For the creature was made subject to vanity, not willingly, but by reason of him who hath subjected the same in hope. **Lam. 3:39.** Wherefore doth a living man complain, a man for the punishment of his sins?

u. **Matt. 25:41.** Then shall he say also unto them on the left hand, Depart from me, ye cursed, into everlasting fire, prepared for the devil and his angels. **2 Thess. 1:9.** … who shall be punished with everlasting destruction from the presence of the Lord, and from the glory of his power.

a. **Isa. 40:13–17.** Who hath directed the Spirit of the LORD, or being his counseller hath taught him? With whom took he counsel, and who instructed him, and taught him in the path of judgment, and taught him knowledge, and shewed to him the way of understanding? Behold, the nations are as a drop of a bucket, and are counted as the small dust of the balance: behold, he taketh up the isles as a very little thing. And Lebanon is not sufficient to burn, nor the beasts thereof sufficient for a burnt offering. All nations before him are as nothing; and they are counted to him less than nothing, and vanity. **Job 9:32–33.** For he is not a man, as I am, that I should answer him, and we should come together in judgment. Neither is there any daysman betwixt us, that might lay his hand upon us both. **Ps. 113:5–6.** Who is like unto the LORD our God, who dwelleth on high, who humbleth himself to behold the things that are in heaven, and in the earth! **Job 22:2–3.** Can a man be profitable unto God, as he that is wise may be profitable unto himself? Is it any pleasure to the Almighty, that thou art

2. The first covenant made with man was a covenant of works,[b] wherein life was promised to Adam; and in him to his posterity,[c] upon condition of perfect and personal obedience.[d]

3. Man, by his fall, having made himself uncapable of life by that covenant, the Lord was pleased to make a second,[e] commonly called the covenant of grace; wherein he freely offereth unto sinners life

righteous? or is it gain to him, that thou makest thy ways perfect? **Job 35:7–8.** If thou be righteous, what givest thou him? or what receiveth he of thine hand? Thy wickedness may hurt a man as thou art; and thy righteousness may profit the son of man. **Luke 17:10.** So likewise ye, when ye shall have done all those things which are commanded you, say, We are unprofitable servants: we have done that which was our duty to do. **Acts 17:24–25.** God that made the world and all things therein, seeing that he is Lord of heaven and earth, dwelleth not in temples made with hands; neither is worshipped with men's hands, as though he needed any thing, seeing he giveth to all life, and breath, and all things.

b. **Gen. 2:16–17.** And the LORD God commanded the man, saying, Of every tree of the garden thou mayest freely eat: but of the tree of the knowledge of good and evil, thou shalt not eat of it: for in the day that thou eatest thereof thou shalt surely die. **Hos. 6:7.** But they like men have transgressed the covenant: there have they dealt treacherously against me. **Gal. 3:12.** And the law is not of faith: but, The man that doeth them shall live in them.

c. **Gen. 3:22.** And the LORD God said, Behold, the man is become as one of us, to know good and evil: and now, lest he put forth his hand, and take also of the tree of life, and eat, and live for ever … **Rom. 10:5.** For Moses describeth the righteousness which is of the law, That the man which doeth those things shall live by them. **Rom. 5:12–14.** Wherefore, as by one man sin entered into the world, and death by sin; and so death passed upon all men, for that all have sinned: (For until the law sin was in the world: but sin is not imputed when there is no law. Nevertheless death reigned from Adam to Moses, even over them that had not sinned after the similitude of Adam's transgression, who is the figure of him that was to come.…) … **See Rom. 5:15–20.**

d. **Gen. 2:17.** But of the tree of the knowledge of good and evil, thou shalt not eat of it: for in the day that thou eatest thereof thou shalt surely die. **Gal. 3:10.** For as many as are of the works of the law are under the curse: for it is written, Cursed is every one that continueth not in all things which are written in the book of the law to do them.

e. **Gal. 3:21.** Is the law then against the promises of God? God forbid: for if there had been a law given which could have given life, verily righteousness should have been by the law. **Rom. 3:20–21.** Therefore by the deeds of the law there shall no flesh be justified in his sight: for by the law is the knowledge of sin. But now the righteousness of God without the law is manifested, being witnessed by the law and the prophets. **Rom. 8:3.** For what the law could not do, in that it was weak through the flesh, God sending his own Son in the likeness of sinful flesh, and for sin, condemned sin in the flesh. **Gen. 3:15.** And I will put enmity between thee and the woman, and between thy seed and her seed; it shall bruise thy head, and thou shalt bruise his heel. **See Isa. 42:6.**

and salvation by Jesus Christ; requiring of them faith in him, that they may be saved,[f] and promising to give unto all those that are ordained unto eternal life his Holy Spirit, to make them willing, and able to believe.[g]

4. This covenant of grace is frequently set forth in Scripture by the name of a testament, in reference to the death of Jesus Christ the Testator, and to the everlasting inheritance, with all things belonging to it, therein bequeathed.[h]

5. This covenant was differently administered in the time of the law, and in the time of the gospel:[i] under the law, it was administered

f. **John 3:16.** For God so loved the world, that he gave his only begotten Son, that whosoever believeth in him should not perish, but have everlasting life. **Rom. 10:6, 9.** But the righteousness which is of faith speaketh on this wise, Say not in thine heart, Who shall ascend into heaven? (that is, to bring Christ down from above:) … that if thou shalt confess with thy mouth the Lord Jesus, and shalt believe in thine heart that God hath raised him from the dead, thou shalt be saved. **Rev. 22:17.** And the Spirit and the bride say, Come. And let him that heareth say, Come. And let him that is athirst come. And whosoever will, let him take the water of life freely.

g. **Acts 13:48.** And when the Gentiles heard this, they were glad, and glorified the word of the Lord: and as many as were ordained to eternal life believed. **Ezek. 36:26–27.** A new heart also will I give you, and a new spirit will I put within you: and I will take away the stony heart out of your flesh, and I will give you an heart of flesh. And I will put my spirit within you, and cause you to walk in my statutes, and ye shall keep my judgments, and do them. **John 6:37, 44–45.** All that the Father giveth me shall come to me; and him that cometh to me I will in no wise cast out.… No man can come to me, except the Father which hath sent me draw him: and I will raise him up at the last day. It is written in the prophets, And they shall be all taught of God. Every man therefore that hath heard, and hath learned of the Father, cometh unto me. **1 Cor. 12:3.** Wherefore I give you to understand, that no man speaking by the Spirit of God calleth Jesus accursed: and that no man can say that Jesus is the Lord, but by the Holy Ghost.

h. **Heb. 9:15–17.** And for this cause he is the mediator of the new testament, that by means of death, for the redemption of the transgressions that were under the first testament, they which are called might receive the promise of eternal inheritance. For where a testament is, there must also of necessity be the death of the testator. For a testament is of force after men are dead: otherwise it is of no strength at all while the testator liveth.

i. **2 Cor. 3:6–9.** … [God] hath made us able ministers of the new testament; not of the letter, but of the spirit: for the letter killeth, but the spirit giveth life. But if the ministration of death, written and engraven in stones, was glorious, so that the children of Israel could not stedfastly behold the face of Moses for the glory of his countenance; which glory was to be done away: how shall not the ministration of the spirit be rather glorious? For if the ministration of condemnation be glory, much more doth the ministration of righteousness exceed in glory.

by promises, prophecies, sacrifices, circumcision, the paschal lamb, and other types and ordinances delivered to the people of the Jews, all foresignifying Christ to come;[k] which were, for that time, sufficient and efficacious, through the operation of the Spirit, to instruct and build up the elect in faith in the promised Messiah,[l] by whom they had full remission of sins, and eternal salvation; and is called the old testament.[m]

k. **Heb. 8–10.** Now of the things which we have spoken this is the sum: We have such an high priest, who is set on the right hand of the throne of the Majesty in the heavens; a minister of the sanctuary, and of the true tabernacle, which the Lord pitched, and not man.… For if he were on earth, he should not be a priest, seeing that there are priests that offer gifts according to the law: who serve unto the example and shadow of heavenly things, as Moses was admonished of God when he was about to make the tabernacle: for, See, saith he, that thou make all things according to the pattern shewed to thee in the mount. But now hath he obtained a more excellent ministry, by how much also he is the mediator of a better covenant, which was established upon better promises.… But Christ being come an high priest of good things to come, by a greater and more perfect tabernacle, not made with hands, that is to say, not of this building; neither by the blood of goats and calves, but by his own blood he entered in once into the holy place, having obtained eternal redemption for us.… For Christ is not entered into the holy places made with hands, which are the figures of the true; but into heaven itself, now to appear in the presence of God for us.… For the law having a shadow of good things to come, and not the very image of the things, can never with those sacrifices which they offered year by year continually make the comers thereunto perfect.… **Rom. 4:11.** And he received the sign of circumcision, a seal of the righteousness of the faith which he had yet being uncircumcised: that he might be the father of all them that believe, though they be not circumcised; that righteousness might be imputed unto them also. **Col. 2:11–12.** … in whom also ye are circumcised with the circumcision made without hands, in putting off the body of the sins of the flesh by the circumcision of Christ: buried with him in baptism, wherein also ye are risen with him through the faith of the operation of God, who hath raised him from the dead. **1 Cor. 5:7.** Purge out therefore the old leaven, that ye may be a new lump, as ye are unleavened. For even Christ our passover is sacrificed for us.

l. **1 Cor. 10:1–4.** Moreover, brethren, I would not that ye should be ignorant, how that all our fathers were under the cloud, and all passed through the sea; and were all baptized unto Moses in the cloud and in the sea; and did all eat the same spiritual meat; and did all drink the same spiritual drink: for they drank of that spiritual Rock that followed them: and that Rock was Christ. **Heb. 11:13.** These all died in faith, not having received the promises, but having seen them afar off, and were persuaded of them, and embraced them, and confessed that they were strangers and pilgrims on the earth. **John 8:56.** Your father Abraham rejoiced to see my day: and he saw it, and was glad.

m. **Gal. 3:7–9, 14.** Know ye therefore that they which are of faith, the same are the children of Abraham. And the scripture, foreseeing that God would justify the heathen through faith, preached before the gospel unto Abraham, saying, In thee shall

6. Under the gospel, when Christ, the substance,[n] was exhibited, the ordinances in which this covenant is dispensed are the preaching of the Word, and the administration of the sacraments of baptism and the Lord's Supper:[o] which, though fewer in number, and administered with more simplicity, and less outward glory, yet, in them, it is held forth in more fullness, evidence, and spiritual efficacy,[p] to all nations, both Jews and Gentiles;[q] and is called the new

all nations be blessed. So then they which be of faith are blessed with faithful Abraham.... that the blessing of Abraham might come on the Gentiles through Jesus Christ; that we might receive the promise of the Spirit through faith. **Ps. 32:1–2, 5.** Blessed is he whose transgression is forgiven, whose sin is covered. Blessed is the man unto whom the LORD imputeth not iniquity, and in whose spirit there is no guile.... I acknowledged my sin unto thee, and mine iniquity have I not hid. I said, I will confess my transgressions unto the LORD; and thou forgavest the iniquity of my sin. Selah.

n. **Col. 2:17.** ... which are a shadow of things to come; but the body is of Christ.

o. **1 Cor. 1:21.** For after that in the wisdom of God the world by wisdom knew not God, it pleased God by the foolishness of preaching to save them that believe. **Matt. 28:19–20.** Go ye therefore, and teach all nations, baptizing them in the name of the Father, and of the Son, and of the Holy Ghost: teaching them to observe all things whatsoever I have commanded you: and, lo, I am with you alway, even unto the end of the world. Amen. **1 Cor. 11:23–25.** For I have received of the Lord that which also I delivered unto you, That the Lord Jesus the same night in which he was betrayed took bread: and when he had given thanks, he brake it, and said, Take, eat: this is my body, which is broken for you: this do in remembrance of me. After the same manner also he took the cup, when he had supped, saying, This cup is the new testament in my blood: this do ye, as oft as ye drink it, in remembrance of me.

p. **Heb. 12:22–24.** But ye are come unto mount Sion, and unto the city of the living God, the heavenly Jerusalem, and to an innumerable company of angels, to the general assembly and church of the firstborn, which are written in heaven, and to God the Judge of all, and to the spirits of just men made perfect, and to Jesus the mediator of the new covenant, and to the blood of sprinkling, that speaketh better things than that of Abel. **2 Cor. 3:9–11.** For if the ministration of condemnation be glory, much more doth the ministration of righteousness exceed in glory. For even that which was made glorious had no glory in this respect, by reason of the glory that excelleth. For if that which is done away was glorious, much more that which remaineth is glorious. **Jer. 31:33–34.** But this shall be the covenant that I will make with the house of Israel; After those days, saith the LORD, I will put my law in their inward parts, and write it in their hearts; and will be their God, and they shall be my people. And they shall teach no more every man his neighbour, and every man his brother, saying, Know the LORD: for they shall all know me, from the least of them unto the greatest of them, saith the LORD; for I will forgive their iniquity, and I will remember their sin no more.

q. **Luke 2:32.** ... a light to lighten the Gentiles, and the glory of thy people Israel. **Acts 10:34.** Then Peter opened his mouth, and said, Of a truth I perceive that God is no respecter of persons. **Eph. 2:15–19.** ... having abolished in his flesh

testament.[r] There are not therefore two covenants of grace, differing in substance, but one and the same, under various dispensations.[s]

Chapter 8
Of Christ the Mediator

1. It pleased God, in his eternal purpose, to choose and ordain the Lord Jesus, his only begotten Son, to be the Mediator between

the enmity, even the law of commandments contained in ordinances; for to make in himself of twain one new man, so making peace; and that he might reconcile both unto God in one body by the cross, having slain the enmity thereby: and came and preached peace to you which were afar off, and to them that were nigh. For through him we both have access by one Spirit unto the Father. Now therefore ye are no more strangers and foreigners, but fellowcitizens with the saints, and of the household of God.

r. **Luke 22:20.** Likewise also [he took] the cup after supper, saying, This cup is the new testament in my blood, which is shed for you.

s. **Gal. 3:8–9, 14, 16.** And the scripture, foreseeing that God would justify the heathen through faith, preached before the gospel unto Abraham, saying, In thee shall all nations be blessed. So then they which be of faith are blessed with faithful Abraham.… that the blessing of Abraham might come on the Gentiles through Jesus Christ; that we might receive the promise of the Spirit through faith.… Now to Abraham and his seed were the promises made. He saith not, And to seeds, as of many; but as of one, And to thy seed, which is Christ. **Rom. 3:21–22, 30.** But now the righteousness of God without the law is manifested, being witnessed by the law and the prophets; even the righteousness of God which is by faith of Jesus Christ unto all and upon all them that believe: for there is no difference.… seeing it is one God, which shall justify the circumcision by faith, and uncircumcision through faith. **Rom. 4:3, 6–8.** For what saith the scripture? Abraham believed God, and it was counted unto him for righteousness.… Even as David also describeth the blessedness of the man, unto whom God imputeth righteousness without works, saying, Blessed are they whose iniquities are forgiven, and whose sins are covered. Blessed is the man to whom the Lord will not impute sin. **See Gen. 15:6. Ps. 32:1–2.** Blessed is he whose transgression is forgiven, whose sin is covered. Blessed is the man unto whom the LORD imputeth not iniquity, and in whose spirit there is no guile. **Rom. 4:16–17, 23–24.** Therefore it is of faith, that it might be by grace; to the end the promise might be sure to all the seed; not to that only which is of the law, but to that also which is of the faith of Abraham; who is the father of us all, (as it is written, I have made thee a father of many nations,) before him whom he believed, even God, who quickeneth the dead, and calleth those things which be not as though they were.… Now it was not written for his sake alone, that it was imputed to him; but for us also, to whom it shall be imputed, if we believe on him that raised up Jesus our Lord from the dead. **Heb. 4:2.** For unto us was the gospel preached, as well as unto them: but the word preached did not profit them, not being mixed with faith in them that heard it. **See Rom. 10:6–10; 1 Cor. 10:3–4.**

God and man,[a] the Prophet,[b] Priest,[c] and King,[d] the Head and Savior of his church,[e] the Heir of all things,[f] and Judge of the world:[g] unto whom he did from all eternity give a people, to be his seed,[h] and to be by him in time redeemed, called, justified, sanctified, and glorified.[i]

a. **Isa. 42:1.** Behold my servant, whom I uphold; mine elect, in whom my soul delighteth; I have put my spirit upon him: he shall bring forth judgment to the Gentiles. **1 Pet. 1:19–20.** But [ye were redeemed] with the precious blood of Christ, as of a lamb without blemish and without spot: who verily was foreordained before the foundation of the world, but was manifest in these last times for you. **John 3:16.** For God so loved the world, that he gave his only begotten Son, that whosoever believeth in him should not perish, but have everlasting life. **1 Tim. 2:5.** For there is one God, and one mediator between God and men, the man Christ Jesus.

b. **Acts 3:20, 22.** And he shall send Jesus Christ, which before was preached unto you.… For Moses truly said unto the fathers, A prophet shall the Lord your God raise up unto you of your brethren, like unto me; him shall ye hear in all things whatsoever he shall say unto you. **See Deut. 18:15.**

c. **Heb. 5:5–6.** So also Christ glorified not himself to be made an high priest; but he that said unto him, Thou art my Son, to day have I begotten thee. As he saith also in another place, Thou art a priest for ever after the order of Melchisedec.

d. **Ps. 2:6.** Yet have I set my king upon my holy hill of Zion. **Luke 1:33.** And he shall reign over the house of Jacob for ever; and of his kingdom there shall be no end. **See Isa. 9:5–6; Acts 2:29–36; Col. 1:13.**

e. **Eph. 5:23.** For the husband is the head of the wife, even as Christ is the head of the church: and he is the saviour of the body.

f. **Heb. 1:2.** [God] hath in these last days spoken unto us by his Son, whom he hath appointed heir of all things, by whom also he made the worlds.

g. **Acts 17:31.** … because he hath appointed a day, in the which he will judge the world in righteousness by that man whom he hath ordained; whereof he hath given assurance unto all men, in that he hath raised him from the dead.

h. **John 17:6.** I have manifested thy name unto the men which thou gavest me out of the world: thine they were, and thou gavest them me; and they have kept thy word. **Ps. 22:30.** A seed shall serve him; it shall be accounted to the Lord for a generation. **Isa. 53:10.** Yet it pleased the LORD to bruise him; he hath put him to grief: when thou shalt make his soul an offering for sin, he shall see his seed, he shall prolong his days, and the pleasure of the LORD shall prosper in his hand. **Eph. 1:4.** … according as he hath chosen us in him before the foundation of the world, that we should be holy and without blame before him in love.

i. **1 Tim. 2:6.** … who gave himself a ransom for all, to be testified in due time. **Isa. 55:4–5.** Behold, I have given him for a witness to the people, a leader and commander to the people. Behold, thou shalt call a nation that thou knowest not, and nations that knew not thee shall run unto thee because of the LORD thy God, and for the Holy One of Israel; for he hath glorified thee. **1 Cor. 1:30.** But of him are ye in Christ Jesus, who of God is made unto us wisdom, and righteousness, and sanctification, and redemption. **Rom. 8:30.** Moreover whom he did predestinate, them he also called: and whom he called, them he also justified: and whom he justified, them he also glorified.

2. The Son of God, the second person in the Trinity, being very and eternal God, of one substance and equal with the Father, did, when the fullness of time was come, take upon him man's nature,ᵏ with all the essential properties, and common infirmities thereof, yet without sin;ˡ being conceived by the power of the Holy Ghost, in the womb of the virgin Mary, of her substance.ᵐ So that two whole, perfect, and distinct natures, the Godhead and the manhood, were inseparably joined together in one person, without conversion, composition, or confusion.ⁿ Which person is very God, and very man, yet

k. **John 1:1, 14.** In the beginning was the Word, and the Word was with God, and the Word was God.... And the Word was made flesh, and dwelt among us, (and we beheld his glory, the glory as of the only begotten of the Father,) full of grace and truth. **1 John 5:20.** And we know that the Son of God is come, and hath given us an understanding, that we may know him that is true, and we are in him that is true, even in his Son Jesus Christ. This is the true God, and eternal life. **Phil. 2:6.** ... who, being in the form of God, thought it not robbery to be equal with God. **Gal. 4:4.** But when the fulness of the time was come, God sent forth his Son, made of a woman, made under the law.

l. **Phil. 2:7.** ... but made himself of no reputation, and took upon him the form of a servant, and was made in the likeness of men. **Heb. 2:14, 16–17.** Forasmuch then as the children are partakers of flesh and blood, he also himself likewise took part of the same; that through death he might destroy him that had the power of death, that is, the devil.... For verily he took not on him the nature of angels; but he took on him the seed of Abraham. Wherefore in all things it behoved him to be made like unto his brethren, that he might be a merciful and faithful high priest in things pertaining to God, to make reconciliation for the sins of the people. **Heb. 4:15.** For we have not an high priest which cannot be touched with the feeling of our infirmities; but was in all points tempted like as we are, yet without sin.

m. **Luke 1:27, 31, 35.** To a virgin espoused to a man whose name was Joseph, of the house of David; and the virgin's name was Mary.... And, behold, thou shalt conceive in thy womb, and bring forth a son, and shalt call his name JESUS.... And the angel answered and said unto her, The Holy Ghost shall come upon thee, and the power of the Highest shall overshadow thee: therefore also that holy thing which shall be born of thee shall be called the Son of God. **Gal. 4:4.** But when the fulness of the time was come, God sent forth his Son, made of a woman, made under the law. **See Matt. 1:18, 20–21.**

n. **Matt. 16:16.** And Simon Peter answered and said, Thou art the Christ, the Son of the living God. **Col. 2:9.** For in him dwelleth all the fulness of the Godhead bodily. **Rom. 9:5.** ... whose are the fathers, and of whom as concerning the flesh Christ came, who is over all, God blessed for ever. Amen. **1 Tim. 3:16.** And without controversy great is the mystery of godliness: God was manifest in the flesh, justified in the Spirit, seen of angels, preached unto the Gentiles, believed on in the world, received up into glory.

one Christ, the only Mediator between God and man.[o]

3. The Lord Jesus, in his human nature thus united to the divine, was sanctified, and anointed with the Holy Spirit, above measure,[p] having in him all the treasures of wisdom and knowledge;[q] in whom it pleased the Father that all fullness should dwell;[r] to the end that, being holy, harmless, undefiled, and full of grace and truth,[s] he might be thoroughly furnished to execute the office of a mediator, and surety.[t] Which office he took not unto himself, but was thereunto called by his Father,[u] who put all power and judgment into his hand, and gave him commandment to execute the same.[w]

4. This office the Lord Jesus did most willingly undertake;[x]

o. **Rom. 1:3–4.** … concerning his Son Jesus Christ our Lord, which was made of the seed of David according to the flesh; and declared to be the Son of God with power, according to the spirit of holiness, by the resurrection from the dead. **1 Tim. 2:5.** For there is one God, and one mediator between God and men, the man Christ Jesus.

p. **Ps. 45:7.** Thou lovest righteousness, and hatest wickedness: therefore God, thy God, hath anointed thee with the oil of gladness above thy fellows. **John 3:34.** For he whom God hath sent speaketh the words of God: for God giveth not the Spirit by measure unto him. **See Isa. 61:1; Luke 4:18; Heb. 1:8–9.**

q. **Col. 2:3.** … in whom are hid all the treasures of wisdom and knowledge.

r. **Col. 1:19.** For it pleased the Father that in him should all fulness dwell.

s. **Heb. 7:26.** For such an high priest became us, who is holy, harmless, undefiled, separate from sinners, and made higher than the heavens. **John 1:14.** And the Word was made flesh, and dwelt among us, (and we beheld his glory, the glory as of the only begotten of the Father,) full of grace and truth.

t. **Acts 10:38.** … how God anointed Jesus of Nazareth with the Holy Ghost and with power: who went about doing good, and healing all that were oppressed of the devil; for God was with him. **Heb. 12:24.** … and to Jesus the mediator of the new covenant, and to the blood of sprinkling, that speaketh better things than that of Abel. **Heb. 7:22.** … by so much was Jesus made a surety of a better testament.

u. **Heb. 5:4–5.** And no man taketh this honour unto himself, but he that is called of God, as was Aaron. So also Christ glorified not himself to be made an high priest; but he that said unto him, Thou art my Son, to day have I begotten thee.

w. **John 5:22, 27.** For the Father judgeth no man, but hath committed all judgment unto the Son.… and hath given him authority to execute judgment also, because he is the Son of man. **Matt. 28:18.** And Jesus came and spake unto them, saying, All power is given unto me in heaven and in earth. **Acts 2:36.** Therefore let all the house of Israel know assuredly, that God hath made that same Jesus, whom ye have crucified, both Lord and Christ.

x. **Ps. 40:7–8.** Then said I, Lo, I come: in the volume of the book it is written of me, I delight to do thy will, O my God: yea, thy law is within my heart. **See Heb. 10:5–10. John 4:34.** Jesus saith unto them, My meat is to do the will of him that sent me, and to finish his work. **John 10:18.** No man taketh it from me, but I lay it down

which that he might discharge, he was made under the law,[y] and did perfectly fulfill it;[z] endured most grievous torments immediately in his soul,[a] and most painful sufferings in his body;[b] was crucified, and died,[c] was buried, and remained under the power of death, yet saw no corruption.[d] On the third day he arose from the

of myself. I have power to lay it down, and I have power to take it again. This commandment have I received of my Father. **Phil. 2:8.** And being found in fashion as a man, he humbled himself, and became obedient unto death, even the death of the cross.

y. **Gal. 4:4.** But when the fulness of the time was come, God sent forth his Son, made of a woman, made under the law.

z. **Matt. 3:15.** And Jesus answering said unto him, Suffer it to be so now: for thus it becometh us to fulfil all righteousness. Then he suffered him. **Matt. 5:17.** Think not that I am come to destroy the law, or the prophets: I am not come to destroy, but to fulfil. **Heb. 5:8–9.** Though he were a Son, yet learned he obedience by the things which he suffered; and being made perfect, he became the author of eternal salvation unto all them that obey him.

a. **Matt. 26:37–38.** And he took with him Peter and the two sons of Zebedee, and began to be sorrowful and very heavy. Then saith he unto them, My soul is exceeding sorrowful, even unto death: tarry ye here, and watch with me. **Luke 22:44.** And being in an agony he prayed more earnestly: and his sweat was as it were great drops of blood falling down to the ground. **Matt. 27:46.** And about the ninth hour Jesus cried with a loud voice, saying, Eli, Eli, lama sabachthani? that is to say, My God, my God, why hast thou forsaken me?

b. **Matt. 26:67–68.** Then did they spit in his face, and buffeted him; and others smote him with the palms of their hands. **Matt. 27:27–50.** Then the soldiers of the governor took Jesus into the common hall, and gathered unto him the whole band of soldiers. And they stripped him, and put on him a scarlet robe. And when they had platted a crown of thorns, they put it upon his head, and a reed in his right hand: and they bowed the knee before him, and mocked him, saying, Hail, King of the Jews! And they spit upon him, and took the reed, and smote him on the head. And after that they had mocked him, they took the robe off from him, and put his own raiment on him, and led him away to crucify him.… Jesus, when he had cried again with a loud voice, yielded up the ghost.

c. **Mark 15:24, 37.** And when they had crucified him, they parted his garments, casting lots upon them, what every man should take.… And Jesus cried with a loud voice, and gave up the ghost. **Phil. 2:8.** And being found in fashion as a man, he humbled himself, and became obedient unto death, even the death of the cross.

d. **Matt. 27:60.** … and laid it in his own new tomb, which he had hewn out in the rock: and he rolled a great stone to the door of the sepulchre, and departed. **Acts 2:24, 27.** … whom God hath raised up, having loosed the pains of death: because it was not possible that he should be holden of it.… because thou wilt not leave my soul in hell, neither wilt thou suffer thine Holy One to see corruption. **Acts 13:29, 37.** And when they had fulfilled all that was written of him, they took him down from the tree, and laid him in a sepulchre.… But he, whom God raised again, saw no corruption. **Rom. 6:9.** … knowing that Christ being raised from the dead dieth no more; death hath no more dominion over him.

dead,[e] with the same body in which he suffered,[f] with which also he ascended into heaven, and there sitteth at the right hand of his Father,[g] making intercession,[h] and shall return, to judge men and angels, at the end of the world.[i]

5. The Lord Jesus, by his perfect obedience, and sacrifice of himself, which he, through the eternal Spirit, once offered up unto God, hath fully satisfied the justice of his Father;[k] and purchased, not only

e. **1 Cor. 15:3–4.** For I delivered unto you first of all that which I also received, how that Christ died for our sins according to the scriptures; and that he was buried, and that he rose again the third day according to the scriptures.

f. **Luke 24:39.** Behold my hands and my feet, that it is I myself: handle me, and see; for a spirit hath not flesh and bones, as ye see me have. **John 20:25, 27.** The other disciples therefore said unto him, We have seen the Lord. But he said unto them, Except I shall see in his hands the print of the nails, and put my finger into the print of the nails, and thrust my hand into his side, I will not believe.… Then saith he to Thomas, reach hither thy finger, and behold my hands; and reach hither thy hand, and thrust it into my side: and be not faithless, but believing.

g. **Luke 24:50–51.** And he led them out as far as to Bethany, and he lifted up his hands, and blessed them. And it came to pass, while he blessed them, he was parted from them, and carried up into heaven. **1 Pet. 3:22.** … who is gone into heaven, and is on the right hand of God; angels and authorities and powers being made subject unto him.

h. **Rom. 8:34.** Who is he that condemneth? It is Christ that died, yea rather, that is risen again, who is even at the right hand of God, who also maketh intercession for us. **Heb. 7:25.** Wherefore he is able also to save them to the uttermost that come unto God by him, seeing he ever liveth to make intercession for them. **See Heb. 9:24.**

i. **Acts 1:11.** … which also said, Ye men of Galilee, why stand ye gazing up into heaven? this same Jesus, which is taken up from you into heaven, shall so come in like manner as ye have seen him go into heaven. **John 5:28–29.** Marvel not at this: for the hour is coming, in the which all that are in the graves shall hear his voice, and shall come forth; they that have done good, unto the resurrection of life; and they that have done evil, unto the resurrection of damnation. **Rom. 14:10b.** … for we shall all stand before the judgment seat of Christ. **Acts 10:42.** And he commanded us to preach unto the people, and to testify that it is he which was ordained of God to be the Judge of quick and dead. **Matt. 13:40–42.** As therefore the tares are gathered and burned in the fire; so shall it be in the end of this world. The Son of man shall send forth his angels, and they shall gather out of his kingdom all things that offend, and them which do iniquity; and shall cast them into a furnace of fire: there shall be wailing and gnashing of teeth. **Jude 6.** And the angels which kept not their first estate, but left their own habitation, he hath reserved in everlasting chains under darkness unto the judgment of the great day. **See 2 Pet. 2:4.**

k. **Rom. 5:19.** For as by one man's disobedience many were made sinners, so by the obedience of one shall many be made righteous. **Heb. 9:14.** How much more shall the blood of Christ, who through the eternal Spirit offered himself without spot

reconciliation, but an everlasting inheritance in the kingdom of heaven, for all those whom the Father hath given unto him.[l]

6. Although the work of redemption was not actually wrought by Christ till after his incarnation, yet the virtue, efficacy, and benefits thereof were communicated unto the elect, in all ages successively from the beginning of the world, in and by those promises, types, and sacrifices, wherein he was revealed, and signified to be the seed of the woman which should bruise the serpent's head; and the Lamb slain from the beginning of the world; being yesterday and today the same, and forever.[m]

to God, purge your conscience from dead works to serve the living God? **Heb. 10:14.** For by one offering he hath perfected for ever them that are sanctified. **Eph. 5:2.** … and walk in love, as Christ also hath loved us, and hath given himself for us an offering and a sacrifice to God for a sweetsmelling savour. **Rom. 3:25–26.** … whom God hath set forth to be a propitiation through faith in his blood, to declare his righteousness for the remission of sins that are past, through the forbearance of God; to declare, I say, at this time his righteousness: that he might be just, and the justifier of him which believeth in Jesus.

l. **Dan. 9:24.** Seventy weeks are determined upon thy people and upon thy holy city, to finish the transgression, and to make an end of sins, and to make reconciliation for iniquity, and to bring in everlasting righteousness, and to seal up the vision and prophecy, and to anoint the most Holy. **2 Cor. 5:18.** And all things are of God, who hath reconciled us to himself by Jesus Christ, and hath given to us the ministry of reconciliation. **Col. 1:20.** … and, having made peace through the blood of his cross, by him to reconcile all things unto himself; by him, I say, whether they be things in earth, or things in heaven. **Eph. 1:11, 14.** … in whom also we have obtained an inheritance, being predestinated according to the purpose of him who worketh all things after the counsel of his own will.… which is the earnest of our inheritance until the redemption of the purchased possession, unto the praise of his glory. **Heb. 9:12, 15.** Neither by the blood of goats and calves, but by his own blood he entered in once into the holy place, having obtained eternal redemption for us.… And for this cause he is the mediator of the new testament, that by means of death, for the redemption of the transgressions that were under the first testament, they which are called might receive the promise of eternal inheritance. **John 17:2.** … as thou hast given him power over all flesh, that he should give eternal life to as many as thou hast given him.

m. **Gal. 4:4–5.** But when the fulness of the time was come, God sent forth his Son, made of a woman, made under the law, to redeem them that were under the law, that we might receive the adoption of sons. **Gen. 3:15.** And I will put enmity between thee and the woman, and between thy seed and her seed; it shall bruise thy head, and thou shalt bruise his heel. **1 Cor. 10:4.** And [our fathers] did all drink the same spiritual drink: for they drank of that spiritual Rock that followed them: and that Rock was Christ. **Rev. 13:8.** And all that dwell upon the earth shall worship him, whose names are not written in the book of life of the Lamb slain from the foundation of the world. **Heb. 13:8.** Jesus Christ the same yesterday, and to day, and for ever. **See Rom. 3:25; Heb. 9:15.**

7. Christ, in the work of mediation, acts according to both natures, by each nature doing that which is proper to itself;[n] yet, by reason of the unity of the person, that which is proper to one nature is sometimes in Scripture attributed to the person denominated by the other nature.[o]

8. To all those for whom Christ hath purchased redemption, he doth certainly and effectually apply and communicate the same;[p] making intercession for them,[q] and revealing unto them, in and by the Word, the mysteries of salvation;[r] effectually persuading them by his Spirit to believe and obey, and governing their hearts by his Word

n. **John 10:17–18.** Therefore doth my Father love me, because I lay down my life, that I might take it again. No man taketh it from me, but I lay it down of myself. I have power to lay it down, and I have power to take it again. This commandment have I received of my Father. **1 Pet. 3:18.** For Christ also hath once suffered for sins, the just for the unjust, that he might bring us to God, being put to death in the flesh, but quickened by the Spirit. **Heb. 1:3.** … who being the brightness of his glory, and the express image of his person, and upholding all things by the word of his power, when he had by himself purged our sins, sat down on the right hand of the Majesty on high. **See Heb. 9:14.**

o. **Acts 20:28.** Take heed therefore unto yourselves, and to all the flock, over the which the Holy Ghost hath made you overseers, to feed the church of God, which he hath purchased with his own blood. **Luke 1:43.** And whence is this to me, that the mother of my Lord should come to me? **See Rom. 9:5.**

p. **John 6:37, 39.** All that the Father giveth me shall come to me; and him that cometh to me I will in no wise cast out.… And this is the Father's will which hath sent me, that of all which he hath given me I should lose nothing, but should raise it up again at the last day. **John 10:15–16, 27–28.** As the Father knoweth me, even so know I the Father: and I lay down my life for the sheep. And other sheep I have, which are not of this fold: them also I must bring, and they shall hear my voice; and there shall be one fold, and one shepherd.… My sheep hear my voice, and I know them, and they follow me: and I give unto them eternal life; and they shall never perish, neither shall any man pluck them out of my hand.

q. **1 John 2:1.** My little children, these things write I unto you, that ye sin not. And if any man sin, we have an advocate with the Father, Jesus Christ the righteous. **Rom. 8:34.** Who is he that condemneth? It is Christ that died, yea rather, that is risen again, who is even at the right hand of God, who also maketh intercession for us.

r. **John 15:15.** Henceforth I call you not servants; for the servant knoweth not what his lord doeth: but I have called you friends; for all things that I have heard of my Father I have made known unto you. **Eph. 1:9.** … having made known unto us the mystery of his will, according to his good pleasure which he hath purposed in himself. **John 17:6.** I have manifested thy name unto the men which thou gavest me out of the world: thine they were, and thou gavest them me; and they have kept thy word.

and Spirit;[s] overcoming all their enemies by his almighty power and wisdom, in such manner, and ways, as are most consonant to his wonderful and unsearchable dispensation.[t]

Chapter 9
Of Free Will

1. God hath endued the will of man with that natural liberty, that it is neither forced, nor, by any absolute necessity of nature, determined to good, or evil.[a]

2. Man, in his state of innocency, had freedom, and power to will

---

s. **John 14:26.** But the Comforter, which is the Holy Ghost, whom the Father will send in my name, he shall teach you all things, and bring all things to your remembrance, whatsoever I have said unto you. **2 Cor. 4:13.** We having the same spirit of faith, according as it is written, I believed, and therefore have I spoken; we also believe, and therefore speak. **Rom. 8:9, 14.** But ye are not in the flesh, but in the Spirit, if so be that the Spirit of God dwell in you. Now if any man have not the Spirit of Christ, he is none of his.… For as many as are led by the Spirit of God, they are the sons of God. **Rom. 15:18–19.** For I will not dare to speak of any of those things which Christ hath not wrought by me, to make the Gentiles obedient, by word and deed, through mighty signs and wonders, by the power of the Spirit of God; so that from Jerusalem, and round about unto Illyricum, I have fully preached the gospel of Christ. **John 17:17.** Sanctify them through thy truth: thy word is truth.

t. **Ps. 110:1.** The Lord said unto my Lord, Sit thou at my right hand, until I make thine enemies thy footstool. **1 Cor. 15:25–26.** For he must reign, till he hath put all enemies under his feet. The last enemy that shall be destroyed is death. **Col. 2:15.** And having spoiled principalities and powers, he made a shew of them openly, triumphing over them in it. **Luke 10:19.** Behold, I give unto you power to tread on serpents and scorpions, and over all the power of the enemy: and nothing shall by any means hurt you.

a. **James 1:13–14.** Let no man say when he is tempted, I am tempted of God: for God cannot be tempted with evil, neither tempteth he any man: but every man is tempted, when he is drawn away of his own lust, and enticed. **Deut. 30:19.** I call heaven and earth to record this day against you, that I have set before you life and death, blessing and cursing: therefore choose life, that both thou and thy seed may live. **Isa. 7:11–12.** Ask thee a sign of the Lord thy God; ask it either in the depth, or in the height above. But Ahaz said, I will not ask, neither will I tempt the Lord. **Matt. 17:12.** But I say unto you, That Elias is come already, and they knew him not, but have done unto him whatsoever they listed. Likewise shall also the Son of man suffer of them. **John 5:40.** And ye will not come to me, that ye might have life. **James 4:7.** Submit yourselves therefore to God. Resist the devil, and he will flee from you.

and to do that which was good and well pleasing to God;[b] but yet, mutably, so that he might fall from it.[c]

3. Man, by his fall into a state of sin, hath wholly lost all ability of will to any spiritual good accompanying salvation:[d] so as, a natural man, being altogether averse from that good,[e] and dead in sin,[f] is not able, by his own strength, to convert himself, or to prepare himself thereunto.[g]

b. **Eccl. 7:29.** Lo, this only have I found, that God hath made man upright; but they have sought out many inventions. **Gen. 1:26, 31.** And God said, Let us make man in our image, after our likeness: and let them have dominion over the fish of the sea, and over the fowl of the air, and over the cattle, and over all the earth, and over every creeping thing that creepeth upon the earth.... And God saw every thing that he had made, and, behold, it was very good. And the evening and the morning were the sixth day. **Col. 3:10.** And [ye] have put on the new man, which is renewed in knowledge after the image of him that created him.

c. **Gen. 2:16–17.** And the LORD God commanded the man, saying, Of every tree of the garden thou mayest freely eat: but of the tree of the knowledge of good and evil, thou shalt not eat of it: for in the day that thou eatest thereof thou shalt surely die. **Gen. 3:6, 17.** And when the woman saw that the tree was good for food, and that it was pleasant to the eyes, and a tree to be desired to make one wise, she took of the fruit thereof, and did eat, and gave also unto her husband with her; and he did eat.... And unto Adam he said, Because thou hast hearkened unto the voice of thy wife, and hast eaten of the tree, of which I commanded thee, saying, Thou shalt not eat of it: cursed is the ground for thy sake; in sorrow shalt thou eat of it all the days of thy life.

d. **Rom. 8:7–8.** Because the carnal mind is enmity against God: for it is not subject to the law of God, neither indeed can be. So then they that are in the flesh cannot please God. **John 6:44, 65.** No man can come to me, except the Father which hath sent me draw him: and I will raise him up at the last day.... And he said, Therefore said I unto you, that no man can come unto me, except it were given unto him of my Father. **John 15:5.** I am the vine, ye are the branches: He that abideth in me, and I in him, the same bringeth forth much fruit: for without me ye can do nothing. **Rom. 5:5.** And hope maketh not ashamed; because the love of God is shed abroad in our hearts by the Holy Ghost which is given unto us.

e. **Rom. 3:9–10, 12, 23.** What then? are we better than they? No, in no wise: for we have before proved both Jews and Gentiles, that they are all under sin; as it is written, There is none righteous, no, not one.... They are all gone out of the way, they are together become unprofitable; there is none that doeth good, no, not one.... For all have sinned, and come short of the glory of God.

f. **Eph. 2:1, 5.** And you hath he quickened, who were dead in trespasses and sins.... Even when we were dead in sins, [God] hath quickened us together with Christ, (by grace ye are saved;) ... **Col. 2:13.** And you, being dead in your sins and the uncircumcision of your flesh, hath he quickened together with him, having forgiven you all trespasses.

g. **John 6:44, 65.** No man can come to me, except the Father which hath sent me

4. When God converts a sinner, and translates him into the state of grace, he freeth him from his natural bondage under sin;[h] and, by his grace alone, enables him freely to will and to do that which is spiritually good;[i] yet so, as that by reason of his remaining corruption, he doth not perfectly, nor only, will that which is good, but doth also will that which is evil.[k]

draw him: and I will raise him up at the last day.... And he said, Therefore said I unto you, that no man can come unto me, except it were given unto him of my Father. **John 3:3, 5–6.** Jesus answered and said unto him, Verily, verily, I say unto thee, Except a man be born again, he cannot see the kingdom of God.... Jesus answered, Verily, verily, I say unto thee, Except a man be born of water and of the Spirit, he cannot enter into the kingdom of God. That which is born of the flesh is flesh; and that which is born of the Spirit is spirit. **1 Cor. 2:14.** But the natural man receiveth not the things of the Spirit of God: for they are foolishness unto him: neither can he know them, because they are spiritually discerned. **Titus 3:3–5.** For we ourselves also were sometimes foolish, disobedient, deceived, serving divers lusts and pleasures, living in malice and envy, hateful, and hating one another. But after that the kindness and love of God our Saviour toward man appeared, not by works of righteousness which we have done, but according to his mercy he saved us, by the washing of regeneration, and renewing of the Holy Ghost.

h. **Col. 1:13.** ... who hath delivered us from the power of darkness, and hath translated us into the kingdom of his dear Son. **John 8:34, 36.** Jesus answered them, Verily, verily, I say unto you, Whosoever committeth sin is the servant of sin.... If the Son therefore shall make you free, ye shall be free indeed. **Rom. 6:6–7.** ... knowing this, that our old man is crucified with him, that the body of sin might be destroyed, that henceforth we should not serve sin. For he that is dead is freed from sin.

i. **Phil. 2:13.** For it is God which worketh in you both to will and to do of his good pleasure. **Rom. 6:14, 17–19, 22.** For sin shall not have dominion over you: for ye are not under the law, but under grace.... But God be thanked, that ye were the servants of sin, but ye have obeyed from the heart that form of doctrine which was delivered you. Being then made free from sin, ye became the servants of righteousness. I speak after the manner of men because of the infirmity of your flesh: for as ye have yielded your members servants to uncleanness and to iniquity unto iniquity; even so now yield your members servants to righteousness unto holiness.... But now being made free from sin, and become servants to God, ye have your fruit unto holiness, and the end everlasting life.

k. **Gal. 5:17.** For the flesh lusteth against the Spirit, and the Spirit against the flesh: and these are contrary the one to the other: so that ye cannot do the things that ye would. **Rom. 7:14–25.** For we know that the law is spiritual: but I am carnal, sold under sin. For that which I do I allow not: for what I would, that do I not; but what I hate, that do I. If then I do that which I would not, I consent unto the law that it is good. Now then it is no more I that do it, but sin that dwelleth in me. For I know that in me (that is, in my flesh,) dwelleth no good thing: for to will is present with me; but how to perform that which is good I find not. For the good that I would I do not: but the evil which I would not, that I do. Now if I do that I would not, it is no more I that

5. The will of man is made perfectly and immutably free to good alone, in the state of glory only.[l]

Chapter 10
Of Effectual Calling

1. All those whom God hath predestinated unto life, and those only, he is pleased, in his appointed and accepted time, effectually to call,[a]

do it, but sin that dwelleth in me. I find then a law, that, when I would do good, evil is present with me. For I delight in the law of God after the inward man: but I see another law in my members, warring against the law of my mind, and bringing me into captivity to the law of sin which is in my members. O wretched man that I am! who shall deliver me from the body of this death? I thank God through Jesus Christ our Lord. So then with the mind I myself serve the law of God; but with the flesh the law of sin. **1 John 1:8, 10.** If we say that we have no sin, we deceive ourselves, and the truth is not in us.… If we say that we have not sinned, we make him a liar, and his word is not in us.

l. **Heb. 12:23.** … to the general assembly and church of the firstborn, which are written in heaven, and to God the Judge of all, and to the spirits of just men made perfect. **1 John 3:2.** Beloved, now are we the sons of God, and it doth not yet appear what we shall be: but we know that, when he shall appear, we shall be like him; for we shall see him as he is. **Jude 24.** Now unto him that is able to keep you from falling, and to present you faultless before the presence of his glory with exceeding joy … **Rev. 21:27.** And there shall in no wise enter into it any thing that defileth, neither whatsoever worketh abomination, or maketh a lie: but they which are written in the Lamb's book of life.

a. **Acts 13:48.** And when the Gentiles heard this, they were glad, and glorified the word of the Lord: and as many as were ordained to eternal life believed. **Rom. 8:28, 30.** And we know that all things work together for good to them that love God, to them who are the called according to his purpose.… Moreover whom he did pre-destinate, them he also called: and whom he called, them he also justified: and whom he justified, them he also glorified. **Rom. 11:7.** What then? Israel hath not obtained that which he seeketh for; but the election hath obtained it, and the rest were blinded. **Eph. 1:5, 11.** … having predestinated us unto the adoption of children by Jesus Christ to himself, according to the good pleasure of his will.… in whom also we have obtained an inheritance, being predestinated according to the purpose of him who worketh all things after the counsel of his own will. **2 Tim. 1:9–10.** … who hath saved us, and called us with an holy calling, not according to our works, but according to his own purpose and grace, which was given us in Christ Jesus before the world began, but is now made manifest by the appearing of our Saviour Jesus Christ, who hath abolished death, and hath brought life and immortality to light through the gospel.

by his Word and Spirit,[b] out of that state of sin and death, in which they are by nature, to grace and salvation, by Jesus Christ;[c] enlightening their minds spiritually and savingly to understand the things of God,[d] taking away their heart of stone, and giving unto them a heart

b. **2 Thess. 2:13–14.** But we are bound to give thanks alway to God for you, brethren beloved of the Lord, because God hath from the beginning chosen you to salvation through sanctification of the Spirit and belief of the truth: whereunto he called you by our gospel, to the obtaining of the glory of our Lord Jesus Christ. **James 1:18.** Of his own will begat he us with the word of truth, that we should be a kind of firstfruits of his creatures. **2 Cor. 3:3, 6.** Forasmuch as ye are manifestly declared to be the epistle of Christ ministered by us, written not with ink, but with the Spirit of the living God; not in tables of stone, but in fleshy tables of the heart.… who also hath made us able ministers of the new testament; not of the letter, but of the spirit: for the letter killeth, but the spirit giveth life. **1 Cor. 2:12.** Now we have received, not the spirit of the world, but the spirit which is of God; that we might know the things that are freely given to us of God.

c. **2 Tim. 1:9–10.** … who hath saved us, and called us with an holy calling, not according to our works, but according to his own purpose and grace, which was given us in Christ Jesus before the world began, but is now made manifest by the appearing of our Saviour Jesus Christ, who hath abolished death, and hath brought life and immortality to light through the gospel. **1 Pet. 2:9.** But ye are a chosen generation, a royal priesthood, an holy nation, a peculiar people; that ye should shew forth the praises of him who hath called you out of darkness into his marvellous light. **Rom. 8:2.** For the law of the Spirit of life in Christ Jesus hath made me free from the law of sin and death. **Eph. 2:1–10.** And you hath he quickened, who were dead in trespasses and sins; wherein in time past ye walked according to the course of this world, according to the prince of the power of the air, the spirit that now worketh in the children of disobedience: among whom also we all had our conversation in times past in the lusts of our flesh, fulfilling the desires of the flesh and of the mind; and were by nature the children of wrath, even as others. But God, who is rich in mercy, for his great love wherewith he loved us, even when we were dead in sins, hath quickened us together with Christ, (by grace ye are saved;) and hath raised us up together, and made us sit together in heavenly places in Christ Jesus: that in the ages to come he might shew the exceeding riches of his grace in his kindness toward us through Christ Jesus. For by grace are ye saved through faith; and that not of yourselves: it is the gift of God: not of works, lest any man should boast. For we are his workmanship, created in Christ Jesus unto good works, which God hath before ordained that we should walk in them.

d. **Acts 26:18.** [I send thee] to open their eyes, and to turn them from darkness to light, and from the power of Satan unto God, that they may receive forgiveness of sins, and inheritance among them which are sanctified by faith that is in me. **1 Cor. 2:10, 12.** But God hath revealed them unto us by his Spirit: for the Spirit searcheth all things, yea, the deep things of God.… Now we have received, not the spirit of the world, but the spirit which is of God; that we might know the things that are freely given to us of God. **Eph. 1:17–18.** … that the God of our Lord Jesus Christ, the Father of glory, may give unto you the spirit of wisdom and revelation in the knowl-

of flesh;[e] renewing their wills, and, by his almighty power, determining them to that which is good,[f] and effectually drawing them to Jesus Christ:[g] yet so, as they come most freely, being made willing by his grace.[h]

2. This effectual call is of God's free and special grace alone, not

edge of him: the eyes of your understanding being enlightened; that ye may know what is the hope of his calling, and what the riches of the glory of his inheritance in the saints. **2 Cor. 4:6.** For God, who commanded the light to shine out of darkness, hath shined in our hearts, to give the light of the knowledge of the glory of God in the face of Jesus Christ.

e. **Ezek. 36:26.** A new heart also will I give you, and a new spirit will I put within you: and I will take away the stony heart out of your flesh, and I will give you an heart of flesh.

f. **Ezek. 11:19.** And I will give them one heart, and I will put a new spirit within you; and I will take the stony heart out of their flesh, and will give them an heart of flesh. **Deut. 30:6.** And the LORD thy God will circumcise thine heart, and the heart of thy seed, to love the LORD thy God with all thine heart, and with all thy soul, that thou mayest live. **Ezek. 36:27.** And I will put my spirit within you, and cause you to walk in my statutes, and ye shall keep my judgments, and do them. **John 3:5.** Jesus answered, Verily, verily, I say unto thee, Except a man be born of water and of the Spirit, he cannot enter into the kingdom of God. **Titus 3:5.** Not by works of righteousness which we have done, but according to his mercy he saved us, by the washing of regeneration, and renewing of the Holy Ghost. **1 Pet. 1:23.** … being born again, not of corruptible seed, but of incorruptible, by the word of God, which liveth and abideth for ever.

g. **John 6:44–45.** No man can come to me, except the Father which hath sent me draw him: and I will raise him up at the last day. It is written in the prophets, And they shall be all taught of God. Every man therefore that hath heard, and hath learned of the Father, cometh unto me. **Acts 16:14.** And a certain woman named Lydia, a seller of purple, of the city of Thyatira, which worshipped God, heard us: whose heart the Lord opened, that she attended unto the things which were spoken of Paul.

h. **Ps. 110:3.** Thy people shall be willing in the day of thy power, in the beauties of holiness from the womb of the morning: thou hast the dew of thy youth. **John 6:37.** All that the Father giveth me shall come to me; and him that cometh to me I will in no wise cast out. **Matt. 11:28.** Come unto me, all ye that labour and are heavy laden, and I will give you rest. **Rev. 22:17.** And the Spirit and the bride say, Come. And let him that heareth say, Come. And let him that is athirst come. And whosoever will, let him take the water of life freely. **Rom. 6:16–18.** Know ye not, that to whom ye yield yourselves servants to obey, his servants ye are to whom ye obey; whether of sin unto death, or of obedience unto righteousness? But God be thanked, that ye were the servants of sin, but ye have obeyed from the heart that form of doctrine which was delivered you. Being then made free from sin, ye became the servants of righteousness. **Eph. 2:8.** For by grace are ye saved through faith; and that not of yourselves: it is the gift of God. **Phil. 1:29.** For unto you it is given in the behalf of Christ, not only to believe on him, but also to suffer for his sake.

from anything at all foreseen in man,[i] who is altogether passive therein, until, being quickened and renewed by the Holy Spirit,[k] he is thereby enabled to answer this call, and to embrace the grace offered and conveyed in it.[l]

3. Elect infants, dying in infancy, are regenerated, and saved by Christ, through the Spirit,[m] who worketh when, and where, and how he pleaseth:[n] so also are all other elect persons who are uncapable of

i. **2 Tim. 1:9.** … who hath saved us, and called us with an holy calling, not according to our works, but according to his own purpose and grace, which was given us in Christ Jesus before the world began. **Eph. 2:8–9.** For by grace are ye saved through faith; and that not of yourselves: it is the gift of God: not of works, lest any man should boast. **Rom. 9:11.** … (for the children being not yet born, neither having done any good or evil, that the purpose of God according to election might stand, not of works, but of him that calleth;) …

k. **1 Cor. 2:14.** But the natural man receiveth not the things of the Spirit of God: for they are foolishness unto him: neither can he know them, because they are spiritually discerned. **Rom. 8:7–9.** Because the carnal mind is enmity against God: for it is not subject to the law of God, neither indeed can be. So then they that are in the flesh cannot please God. But ye are not in the flesh, but in the Spirit, if so be that the Spirit of God dwell in you. Now if any man have not the Spirit of Christ, he is none of his. **Titus 3:4–5.** But after that the kindness and love of God our Saviour toward man appeared, not by works of righteousness which we have done, but according to his mercy he saved us, by the washing of regeneration, and renewing of the Holy Ghost.

l. **John 6:37.** All that the Father giveth me shall come to me; and him that cometh to me I will in no wise cast out. **Ezek. 36:27.** And I will put my spirit within you, and cause you to walk in my statutes, and ye shall keep my judgments, and do them. **1 John 5:1.** Whosoever believeth that Jesus is the Christ is born of God: and every one that loveth him that begat loveth him also that is begotten of him. **Cf. 1 John 3:9.**

m. **Gen. 17:7.** And I will establish my covenant between me and thee and thy seed after thee in their generations for an everlasting covenant, to be a God unto thee, and to thy seed after thee. **Luke 18:15–16.** And they brought unto him also infants, that he would touch them: but when his disciples saw it, they rebuked them. But Jesus called them unto him, and said, Suffer little children to come unto me, and forbid them not: for of such is the kingdom of God. **Acts 2:39.** For the promise is unto you, and to your children, and to all that are afar off, even as many as the Lord our God shall call. **John 3:3, 5.** Jesus answered and said unto him, Verily, verily, I say unto thee, Except a man be born again, he cannot see the kingdom of God.… Jesus answered, Verily, verily, I say unto thee, Except a man be born of water and of the Spirit, he cannot enter into the kingdom of God. **1 John 5:12.** He that hath the Son hath life; and he that hath not the Son of God hath not life. **See Luke 1:15.**

n. **John 3:8.** The wind bloweth where it listeth, and thou hearest the sound thereof, but canst not tell whence it cometh, and whither it goeth: so is every one that is born of the Spirit.

being outwardly called by the ministry of the Word.°

4. Others, not elected, although they may be called by the ministry of the Word,ᵖ and may have some common operations of the
Spirit, q yet they never truly come unto Christ, and therefore cannot
be saved:ʳ much less can men, not professing the Christian religion,
be saved in any other way whatsoever, be they never so diligent to
frame their lives according to the light of nature, and the laws of that
religion they do profess.ˢ And, to assert and maintain that they may,

o. **John 16:7–8.** Nevertheless I tell you the truth; It is expedient for you that I go
away: for if I go not away, the Comforter will not come unto you; but if I depart, I will
send him unto you. And when he is come, he will reprove the world of sin, and of
righteousness, and of judgment. **1 John 5:12.** He that hath the Son hath life; and he
that hath not the Son of God hath not life. **Acts 4:12.** Neither is there salvation in
any other: for there is none other name under heaven given among men, whereby we
must be saved.

p. **Matt. 13:14–15.** And in them is fulfilled the prophecy of Esaias, which saith,
By hearing ye shall hear, and shall not understand; and seeing ye shall see, and shall
not perceive. **Acts 28:24.** And some believed the things which were spoken, and
some believed not. **Cf. Acts 13:48. Matt. 22:14.** For many are called, but few are
chosen.

q. **Matt. 13:20–21.** But he that received the seed into stony places, the same is
he that heareth the word, and anon with joy receiveth it; yet hath he not root in himself, but dureth for a while: for when tribulation or persecution ariseth because of the
word, by and by he is offended. **Matt. 7:22.** Many will say to me in that day, Lord,
Lord, have we not prophesied in thy name? and in thy name have cast out devils? and
in thy name done many wonderful works? **Heb. 6:4–5.** For it is impossible for those
who were once enlightened, and have tasted of the heavenly gift, and were made
partakers of the Holy Ghost, and have tasted the good word of God, and the powers
of the world to come …

r. **John 6:37, 64–66.** All that the Father giveth me shall come to me; and him
that cometh to me I will in no wise cast out.… But there are some of you that believe
not. For Jesus knew from the beginning who they were that believed not, and who
should betray him. And he said, Therefore said I unto you, that no man can come
unto me, except it were given unto him of my Father. From that time many of his
disciples went back, and walked no more with him. **John 8:44.** Ye are of your father
the devil, and the lusts of your father ye will do. He was a murderer from the beginning, and abode not in the truth, because there is no truth in him. When he speaketh
a lie, he speaketh of his own: for he is a liar, and the father of it. **John 13:18.** I speak
not of you all: I know whom I have chosen: but that the scripture may be fulfilled, He
that eateth bread with me hath lifted up his heel against me. **Cf. John 17:12.**

s. **Acts 4:12.** Neither is there salvation in any other: for there is none other name
under heaven given among men, whereby we must be saved. **1 John 4:2–3.** Hereby
know ye the Spirit of God: Every spirit that confesseth that Jesus Christ is come in the
flesh is of God: and every spirit that confesseth not that Jesus Christ is come in the
flesh is not of God: and this is that spirit of antichrist, whereof ye have heard that it

is very pernicious, and to be detested.[t]

Chapter 11
Of Justification

1. Those whom God effectually calleth, he also freely justifieth:[a] not by infusing righteousness into them, but by pardoning their sins,

should come; and even now already is it in the world. **2 John 9.** Whosoever transgresseth, and abideth not in the doctrine of Christ, hath not God. He that abideth in the doctrine of Christ, he hath both the Father and the Son. **John 14:6.** Jesus saith unto him, I am the way, the truth, and the life: no man cometh unto the Father, but by me. **Eph. 2:12–13.** … that at that time ye were without Christ, being aliens from the commonwealth of Israel, and strangers from the covenants of promise, having no hope, and without God in the world: but now in Christ Jesus ye who sometimes were far off are made nigh by the blood of Christ. **John 4:22.** Ye worship ye know not what: we know what we worship: for salvation is of the Jews. **John 17:3.** And this is life eternal, that they might know thee the only true God, and Jesus Christ, whom thou hast sent. **Rom. 10:13–17.** For whosoever shall call upon the name of the Lord shall be saved. How then shall they call on him in whom they have not believed? and how shall they believe in him of whom they have not heard? and how shall they hear without a preacher? And how shall they preach, except they be sent? as it is written, How beautiful are the feet of them that preach the gospel of peace, and bring glad tidings of good things! But they have not all obeyed the gospel. For Esaias saith, Lord, who hath believed our report? So then faith cometh by hearing, and hearing by the word of God.

t. **2 John 9–11.** Whosoever transgresseth, and abideth not in the doctrine of Christ, hath not God. He that abideth in the doctrine of Christ, he hath both the Father and the Son. If there come any unto you, and bring not this doctrine, receive him not into your house, neither bid him God speed: for he that biddeth him God speed is partaker of his evil deeds. **1 Cor. 16:22.** If any man love not the Lord Jesus Christ, let him be Anathema Maranatha. **Gal. 1:6–8.** I marvel that ye are so soon removed from him that called you into the grace of Christ unto another gospel: which is not another; but there be some that trouble you, and would pervert the gospel of Christ. But though we, or an angel from heaven, preach any other gospel unto you than that which we have preached unto you, let him be accursed.

a. **Rom. 8:30.** Moreover whom he did predestinate, them he also called: and whom he called, them he also justified: and whom he justified, them he also glorified. **Rom. 3:24.** … being justified freely by his grace through the redemption that is in Christ Jesus. **Rom. 5:15–16.** But not as the offence, so also is the free gift. For if through the offence of one many be dead, much more the grace of God, and the gift by grace, which is by one man, Jesus Christ, hath abounded unto many. And not as it was by one that sinned, so is the gift: for the judgment was by one to condemnation, but the free gift is of many offences unto justification.

and by accounting and accepting their persons as righteous; not for anything wrought in them, or done by them, but for Christ's sake alone; nor by imputing faith itself, the act of believing, or any other evangelical obedience to them, as their righteousness; but by imputing the obedience and satisfaction of Christ unto them,[b] they receiving and resting on him and his righteousness, by faith; which faith they have not of themselves, it is the gift of God.[c]

b. **Rom. 4:5–8.** But to him that worketh not, but believeth on him that justifieth the ungodly, his faith is counted for righteousness. Even as David also describeth the blessedness of the man, unto whom God imputeth righteousness without works, saying, Blessed are they whose iniquities are forgiven, and whose sins are covered. Blessed is the man to whom the Lord will not impute sin. Cometh this blessedness then upon the circumcision only, or upon the uncircumcision also? for we say that faith was reckoned to Abraham for righteousness. **2 Cor. 5:19, 21.** … to wit, that God was in Christ, reconciling the world unto himself, not imputing their trespasses unto them; and hath committed unto us the word of reconciliation.… For he hath made him to be sin for us, who knew no sin; that we might be made the righteousness of God in him. **Rom. 3:22–28.** … even the righteousness of God which is by faith of Jesus Christ unto all and upon all them that believe: for there is no difference: for all have sinned, and come short of the glory of God; being justified freely by his grace through the redemption that is in Christ Jesus: whom God hath set forth to be a propitiation through faith in his blood, to declare his righteousness for the remission of sins that are past, through the forbearance of God; to declare, I say, at this time his righteousness: that he might be just, and the justifier of him which believeth in Jesus. Where is boasting then? It is excluded. By what law? of works? Nay: but by the law of faith. Therefore we conclude that a man is justified by faith without the deeds of the law. **Titus 3:5, 7.** Not by works of righteousness which we have done, but according to his mercy he saved us, by the washing of regeneration, and renewing of the Holy Ghost;… that being justified by his grace, we should be made heirs according to the hope of eternal life. **Eph. 1:7.** … in whom we have redemption through his blood, the forgiveness of sins, according to the riches of his grace. **Jer. 23:6.** In his days Judah shall be saved, and Israel shall dwell safely: and this is his name whereby he shall be called, THE LORD OUR RIGHTEOUSNESS. **1 Cor. 1:30–31.** But of him are ye in Christ Jesus, who of God is made unto us wisdom, and righteousness, and sanctification, and redemption: that, according as it is written, He that glorieth, let him glory in the Lord. **Rom. 5:17–19.** … (For if by one man's offence death reigned by one; much more they which receive abundance of grace and of the gift of righteousness shall reign in life by one, Jesus Christ.) therefore as by the offence of one judgment came upon all men to condemnation; even so by the righteousness of one the free gift came upon all men unto justification of life. For as by one man's disobedience many were made sinners, so by the obedience of one shall many be made righteous.

c. **John 1:12.** But as many as received him, to them gave he power to become the sons of God, even to them that believe on his name. **Acts 10:43.** To him give all the prophets witness, that through his name whosoever believeth in him shall receive remission of sins. **Acts 13:38–39.** Be it known unto you therefore, men and brethren,

2. Faith, thus receiving and resting on Christ and his righteousness, is the alone instrument of justification:[d] yet is it not alone in the person justified, but is ever accompanied with all other saving graces, and is no dead faith, but worketh by love.[e]

3. Christ, by his obedience and death, did fully discharge the debt of all those that are thus justified, and did make a proper, real, and full satisfaction to his Father's justice in their behalf.[f] Yet, inas-

that through this man is preached unto you the forgiveness of sins: and by him all that believe are justified from all things, from which ye could not be justified by the law of Moses. **Phil. 3:9.** … and be found in him, not having mine own righteousness, which is of the law, but that which is through the faith of Christ, the righteousness which is of God by faith. **Eph. 2:7–8.** … that in the ages to come he might shew the exceeding riches of his grace in his kindness toward us through Christ Jesus. For by grace are ye saved through faith; and that not of yourselves: it is the gift of God. **John 6:44–45, 65.** No man can come to me, except the Father which hath sent me draw him: and I will raise him up at the last day. It is written in the prophets, And they shall be all taught of God. Every man therefore that hath heard, and hath learned of the Father, cometh unto me.… And he said, Therefore said I unto you, that no man can come unto me, except it were given unto him of my Father. **Phil. 1:29.** For unto you it is given in the behalf of Christ, not only to believe on him, but also to suffer for his sake.

d. **John 3:18, 36.** He that believeth on him is not condemned: but he that believeth not is condemned already, because he hath not believed in the name of the only begotten Son of God.… He that believeth on the Son hath everlasting life: and he that believeth not the Son shall not see life; but the wrath of God abideth on him. **Rom. 3:28.** Therefore we conclude that a man is justified by faith without the deeds of the law. **Rom. 5:1.** Therefore being justified by faith, we have peace with God through our Lord Jesus Christ.

e. **James 2:17, 22, 26.** Even so faith, if it hath not works, is dead, being alone.… Seest thou how faith wrought with his works, and by works was faith made perfect?… For as the body without the spirit is dead, so faith without works is dead also. **Gal. 5:6.** For in Jesus Christ neither circumcision availeth anything, nor uncircumcision; but faith which worketh by love.

f. **Mark 10:45.** For even the Son of man came not to be ministered unto, but to minister, and to give his life a ransom for many. **Rom. 5:8–10, 18–19.** But God commendeth his love toward us, in that, while we were yet sinners, Christ died for us. Much more then, being now justified by his blood, we shall be saved from wrath through him. For if, when we were enemies, we were reconciled to God by the death of his Son, much more, being reconciled, we shall be saved by his life.… Therefore as by the offence of one judgment came upon all men to condemnation; even so by the righteousness of one the free gift came upon all men unto justification of life. For as by one man's disobedience many were made sinners, so by the obedience of one shall many be made righteous. **Gal. 3:13.** Christ hath redeemed us from the curse of the law, being made a curse for us: for it is written, Cursed is every one that hangeth on a tree. **1 Tim. 2:5–6.** For there is one God, and one mediator between God and men, the man Christ Jesus; who gave himself a ransom for all, to be testified in due time.

much as he was given by the Father for them;^g and his obedience and satisfaction accepted in their stead;^h and both, freely, not for anything in them; their justification is only of free grace;ⁱ that both the exact justice and rich grace of God might be glorified in the justification of sinners.^k

Heb. 1:3. … who being the brightness of his glory, and the express image of his person, and upholding all things by the word of his power, when he had by himself purged our sins, sat down on the right hand of the Majesty on high. **Heb. 10:10, 14.** By the which will we are sanctified through the offering of the body of Jesus Christ once for all.… For by one offering he hath perfected for ever them that are sanctified. **Dan. 9:24, 26.** Seventy weeks are determined upon thy people and upon thy holy city, to finish the transgression, and to make an end of sins, and to make reconciliation for iniquity, and to bring in everlasting righteousness, and to seal up the vision and prophecy, and to anoint the most Holy.… And after threescore and two weeks shall Messiah be cut off, but not for himself: and the people of the prince that shall come shall destroy the city and the sanctuary; and the end thereof shall be with a flood, and unto the end of the war desolations are determined. **See Isa. 52:13–53:12.**

g. **Rom. 8:32.** He that spared not his own Son, but delivered him up for us all, how shall he not with him also freely give us all things? **John 3:16.** For God so loved the world, that he gave his only begotten Son, that whosoever believeth in him should not perish, but have everlasting life.

h. **2 Cor. 5:21.** For he hath made him to be sin for us, who knew no sin; that we might be made the righteousness of God in him. **Eph. 5:2.** … and walk in love, as Christ also hath loved us, and hath given himself for us an offering and a sacrifice to God for a sweetsmelling savour. **Phil. 2:6–9.** … who, being in the form of God, thought it not robbery to be equal with God: but made himself of no reputation, and took upon him the form of a servant, and was made in the likeness of men: and being found in fashion as a man, he humbled himself, and became obedient unto death, even the death of the cross. Wherefore God also hath highly exalted him, and given him a name which is above every name. **Isa. 53:10–11.** Yet it pleased the LORD to bruise him; he hath put him to grief: when thou shalt make his soul an offering for sin, he shall see his seed, he shall prolong his days, and the pleasure of the LORD shall prosper in his hand. He shall see of the travail of his soul, and shall be satisfied: by his knowledge shall my righteous servant justify many; for he shall bear their iniquities.

i. **Rom. 3:24.** … being justified freely by his grace through the redemption that is in Christ Jesus. **Eph. 1:7.** … in whom we have redemption through his blood, the forgiveness of sins, according to the riches of his grace.

k. **Rom. 3:26.** … to declare, I say, at this time his righteousness: that he might be just, and the justifier of him which believeth in Jesus. **Eph. 2:7.** … that in the ages to come he might shew the exceeding riches of his grace in his kindness toward us through Christ Jesus. **Zech. 9:9.** Rejoice greatly, O daughter of Zion; shout, O daughter of Jerusalem: behold, thy King cometh unto thee: he is just, and having salvation; lowly, and riding upon an ass, and upon a colt the foal of an ass. **Isa. 45:21.** Tell ye, and bring them near; yea, let them take counsel together: who hath declared this from ancient time? who hath told it from that time? have not I the LORD? and there is no God else beside me; a just God and a Saviour; there is none beside me.

4. God did, from all eternity, decree to justify all the elect,[l] and Christ did, in the fullness of time, die for their sins, and rise again for their justification:[m] nevertheless, they are not justified, until the Holy Spirit doth, in due time, actually apply Christ unto them.[n]

5. God doth continue to forgive the sins of those that are justified;[o] and, although they can never fall from the state of justification,[p] yet

l. **Rom. 8:29–30.** For whom he did foreknow, he also did predestinate to be conformed to the image of his Son, that he might be the firstborn among many brethren. Moreover whom he did predestinate, them he also called: and whom he called, them he also justified: and whom he justified, them he also glorified. **Gal. 3:8.** And the scripture, foreseeing that God would justify the heathen through faith, preached before the gospel unto Abraham, saying, In thee shall all nations be blessed. **1 Pet. 1:2, 19–20.** … elect according to the foreknowledge of God the Father, through sanctification of the Spirit, unto obedience and sprinkling of the blood of Jesus Christ: Grace unto you, and peace, be multiplied.… But [ye were redeemed] with the precious blood of Christ, as of a lamb without blemish and without spot: who verily was foreordained before the foundation of the world, but was manifest in these last times for you.

m. **Gal. 4:4.** But when the fulness of the time was come, God sent forth his Son, made of a woman, made under the law. **1 Tim. 2:6.** … who gave himself a ransom for all, to be testified in due time. **Rom. 4:25.** … who was delivered for our offences, and was raised again for our justification.

n. **Eph. 2:3.** … among whom also we all had our conversation in times past in the lusts of our flesh, fulfilling the desires of the flesh and of the mind; and were by nature the children of wrath, even as others. **Titus 3:3–7.** For we ourselves also were sometimes foolish, disobedient, deceived, serving divers lusts and pleasures, living in malice and envy, hateful, and hating one another. But after that the kindness and love of God our Saviour toward man appeared, not by works of righteousness which we have done, but according to his mercy he saved us, by the washing of regeneration, and renewing of the Holy Ghost; which he shed on us abundantly through Jesus Christ our Saviour; that being justified by his grace, we should be made heirs according to the hope of eternal life. **Gal. 2:16.** … knowing that a man is not justified by the works of the law, but by the faith of Jesus Christ, even we have believed in Jesus Christ, that we might be justified by the faith of Christ, and not by the works of the law: for by the works of the law shall no flesh be justified. **Cf. Col. 1:21–22.**

o. **Matt. 6:12.** And forgive us our debts, as we forgive our debtors. **1 John 1:7, 9.** But if we walk in the light, as he is in the light, we have fellowship one with another, and the blood of Jesus Christ his Son cleanseth us from all sin.… If we confess our sins, he is faithful and just to forgive us our sins, and to cleanse us from all unrighteousness. **1 John 2:1–2.** My little children, these things write I unto you, that ye sin not. And if any man sin, we have an advocate with the Father, Jesus Christ the righteous: and he is the propitiation for our sins: and not for ours only, but also for the sins of the whole world.

p. **Rom. 5:1–5.** Therefore being justified by faith, we have peace with God through our Lord Jesus Christ: by whom also we have access by faith into this grace

they may, by their sins, fall under God's fatherly displeasure, and not have the light of his countenance restored unto them, until they humble themselves, confess their sins, beg pardon, and renew their faith and repentance.[q]

6. The justification of believers under the old testament was, in all these respects, one and the same with the justification of believers

wherein we stand, and rejoice in hope of the glory of God. And not only so, but we glory in tribulations also: knowing that tribulation worketh patience; and patience, experience; and experience, hope: and hope maketh not ashamed; because the love of God is shed abroad in our hearts by the Holy Ghost which is given unto us. **Rom. 8:30–39.** Moreover whom he did predestinate, them he also called: and whom he called, them he also justified: and whom he justified, them he also glorified. What shall we then say to these things? If God be for us, who can be against us? He that spared not his own Son, but delivered him up for us all, how shall he not with him also freely give us all things? Who shall lay any thing to the charge of God's elect? It is God that justifieth. Who is he that condemneth? It is Christ that died, yea rather, that is risen again, who is even at the right hand of God, who also maketh intercession for us. Who shall separate us from the love of Christ? shall tribulation, or distress, or persecution, or famine, or nakedness, or peril, or sword? As it is written, For thy sake we are killed all the day long; we are accounted as sheep for the slaughter. Nay, in all these things we are more than conquerors through him that loved us. For I am persuaded, that neither death, nor life, nor angels, nor principalities, nor powers, nor things present, nor things to come, nor height, nor depth, nor any other creature, shall be able to separate us from the love of God, which is in Christ Jesus our Lord. **Heb. 10:14.** For by one offering he hath perfected for ever them that are sanctified. **Cf. Luke 22:32; John 10:28.**

q. **Ps. 89:30–33.** If his children forsake my law, and walk not in my judgments; if they break my statutes, and keep not my commandments; then will I visit their transgression with the rod, and their iniquity with stripes. Nevertheless my lovingkindness will I not utterly take from him, nor suffer my faithfulness to fail. **Ps. 51.** Have mercy upon me, O God, according to thy lovingkindness: according unto the multitude of thy tender mercies blot out my transgressions. Wash me throughly from mine iniquity, and cleanse me from my sin. For I acknowledge my transgressions: and my sin is ever before me.... Create in me a clean heart, O God; and renew a right spirit within me.... Restore unto me the joy of thy salvation; and uphold me with thy free spirit.... **Ps. 32:5.** I acknowledged my sin unto thee, and mine iniquity have I not hid. I said, I will confess my transgressions unto the LORD; and thou forgavest the iniquity of my sin. Selah. **Matt. 26:75.** And Peter remembered the word of Jesus, which said unto him, Before the cock crow, thou shalt deny me thrice. And he went out, and wept bitterly. **Luke 1:20.** And, behold, thou shalt be dumb, and not able to speak, until the day that these things shall be performed, because thou believest not my words, which shall be fulfilled in their season. **1 Cor. 11:30, 32.** For this cause many are weak and sickly among you, and many sleep.... But when we are judged, we are chastened of the Lord, that we should not be condemned with the world.

under the new testament.[r]

Chapter 12
Of Adoption

1. All those that are justified, God vouchsafeth, in and for his only Son Jesus Christ, to make partakers of the grace of adoption,[a] by which they are taken into the number, and enjoy the liberties and privileges of the children of God,[b] have his name put upon them,[c]

r. **Gal. 3:9, 13–14.** So then they which be of faith are blessed with faithful Abraham.… Christ hath redeemed us from the curse of the law, being made a curse for us: for it is written, Cursed is every one that hangeth on a tree: that the blessing of Abraham might come on the Gentiles through Jesus Christ; that we might receive the promise of the Spirit through faith. **Rom. 4:6–8, 22–24.** Even as David also describeth the blessedness of the man, unto whom God imputeth righteousness without works, saying, Blessed are they whose iniquities are forgiven, and whose sins are covered. Blessed is the man to whom the Lord will not impute sin.… And therefore it was imputed to him for righteousness. Now it was not written for his sake alone, that it was imputed to him; but for us also, to whom it shall be imputed, if we believe on him that raised up Jesus our Lord from the dead. **Rom. 10:6–13.** But the righteousness which is of faith speaketh on this wise, Say not in thine heart, Who shall ascend into heaven? (that is, to bring Christ down from above:) or, Who shall descend into the deep? (that is, to bring up Christ again from the dead.) But what saith it? The word is nigh thee, even in thy mouth, and in thy heart: that is, the word of faith, which we preach; that if thou shalt confess with thy mouth the Lord Jesus, and shalt believe in thine heart that God hath raised him from the dead, thou shalt be saved. For with the heart man believeth unto righteousness; and with the mouth confession is made unto salvation. For the scripture saith, Whosoever believeth on him shall not be ashamed. For there is no difference between the Jew and the Greek: for the same Lord over all is rich unto all that call upon him. For whosoever shall call upon the name of the Lord shall be saved. **Heb. 13:8.** Jesus Christ the same yesterday, and to day, and for ever.

a. **Eph. 1:5.** … having predestinated us unto the adoption of children by Jesus Christ to himself, according to the good pleasure of his will. **Gal. 4:4–5.** But when the fulness of the time was come, God sent forth his Son, made of a woman, made under the law, to redeem them that were under the law, that we might receive the adoption of sons.

b. **Rom. 8:17.** … and if children, then heirs; heirs of God, and joint-heirs with Christ; if so be that we suffer with him, that we may be also glorified together. **John 1:12.** But as many as received him, to them gave he power to become the sons of God, even to them that believe on his name.

c. **Num. 6:24–26.** The LORD bless thee, and keep thee: the LORD make his face shine upon thee, and be gracious unto thee: the LORD lift up his countenance upon

receive the Spirit of adoption,[d] have access to the throne of grace with boldness,[e] are enabled to cry, Abba, Father,[f] are pitied,[g] protected,[h] provided for,[i] and chastened by him, as by a father:[k] yet never cast off,[l] but sealed to the day of redemption;[m] and inherit the promises,[n] as heirs of everlasting salvation.[o]

thee, and give thee peace. **Jer. 14:9.** Why shouldest thou be as a man astonied, as a mighty man that cannot save? yet thou, O LORD, art in the midst of us, and we are called by thy name; leave us not. **Amos 9:12.** … that they may possess the remnant of Edom, and of all the heathen, which are called by my name, saith the LORD that doeth this. **Acts 15:17.** … that the residue of men might seek after the Lord, and all the Gentiles, upon whom my name is called, saith the Lord, who doeth all these things. **2 Cor. 6:18.** … and will be a Father unto you, and ye shall be my sons and daughters, saith the Lord Almighty. **Rev. 3:12.** Him that overcometh will I make a pillar in the temple of my God, and he shall go no more out: and I will write upon him the name of my God, and the name of the city of my God, which is new Jerusalem, which cometh down out of heaven from my God: and I will write upon him my new name.

d. **Rom. 8:15.** For ye have not received the spirit of bondage again to fear; but ye have received the Spirit of adoption, whereby we cry, Abba, Father.

e. **Eph. 3:12.** … in whom we have boldness and access with confidence by the faith of him. **See Heb. 4:16.**

f. **Rom. 8:15.** For ye have not received the spirit of bondage again to fear; but ye have received the Spirit of adoption, whereby we cry, Abba, Father. **See Gal. 4:6; Rom. 8:16.**

g. **Ps. 103:13.** Like as a father pitieth his children, so the LORD pitieth them that fear him.

h. **Prov. 14:26.** In the fear of the LORD is strong confidence: and his children shall have a place of refuge.

i. **Matt. 6:30, 32.** Wherefore, if God so clothe the grass of the field, which to day is, and to morrow is cast into the oven, shall he not much more clothe you, O ye of little faith?… (for after all these things do the Gentiles seek:) for your heavenly Father knoweth that ye have need of all these things. **1 Pet. 5:7.** … casting all your care upon him; for he careth for you.

k. **Heb. 12:6.** For whom the Lord loveth he chasteneth, and scourgeth every son whom he receiveth.

l. **Lam. 3:31–32.** For the Lord will not cast off for ever: but though he cause grief, yet will he have compassion according to the multitude of his mercies. **See Ps. 89:30–35.**

m. **Eph. 4:30.** And grieve not the holy Spirit of God, whereby ye are sealed unto the day of redemption.

n. **Heb. 6:12.** … that ye be not slothful, but followers of them who through faith and patience inherit the promises.

o. **1 Pet. 1:3–4.** Blessed be the God and Father of our Lord Jesus Christ, which according to his abundant mercy hath begotten us again unto a lively hope by the resurrection of Jesus Christ from the dead, to an inheritance incorruptible, and undefiled, and that fadeth not away, reserved in heaven for you. **Heb. 1:14.** Are they not all ministering spirits, sent forth to minister for them who shall be heirs of salvation?

Chapter 13
Of Sanctification

1. They, who are once effectually called, and regenerated, having a new heart, and a new spirit created in them, are further sanctified, really and personally, through the virtue of Christ's death and resurrection,[a] by his Word and Spirit dwelling in them:[b] the domin-

a. **1 Thess. 5:23–24.** And the very God of peace sanctify you wholly; and I pray God your whole spirit and soul and body be preserved blameless unto the coming of our Lord Jesus Christ. Faithful is he that calleth you, who also will do it. **2 Thess. 2:13–14.** But we are bound to give thanks alway to God for you, brethren beloved of the Lord, because God hath from the beginning chosen you to salvation through sanctification of the Spirit and belief of the truth: whereunto he called you by our gospel, to the obtaining of the glory of our Lord Jesus Christ. **Ezek. 36:22–28.** Therefore say unto the house of Israel, Thus saith the Lord GOD; I do not this for your sakes, O house of Israel, but for mine holy name's sake, which ye have profaned among the heathen, whither ye went. And I will sanctify my great name, which was profaned among the heathen, which ye have profaned in the midst of them; and the heathen shall know that I am the LORD, saith the Lord GOD, when I shall be sanctified in you before their eyes. For I will take you from among the heathen, and gather you out of all countries, and will bring you into your own land. Then will I sprinkle clean water upon you, and ye shall be clean: from all your filthiness, and from all your idols, will I cleanse you. A new heart also will I give you, and a new spirit will I put within you: and I will take away the stony heart out of your flesh, and I will give you an heart of flesh. And I will put my spirit within you, and cause you to walk in my statutes, and ye shall keep my judgments, and do them. And ye shall dwell in the land that I gave to your fathers; and ye shall be my people, and I will be your God. **Titus 3:5.** Not by works of righteousness which we have done, but according to his mercy he saved us, by the washing of regeneration, and renewing of the Holy Ghost. **Acts 20:32.** And now, brethren, I commend you to God, and to the word of his grace, which is able to build you up, and to give you an inheritance among all them which are sanctified. **Phil. 3:10.** … that I may know him, and the power of his resurrection, and the fellowship of his sufferings, being made conformable unto his death. **Rom. 6:5–6.** For if we have been planted together in the likeness of his death, we shall be also in the likeness of his resurrection: knowing this, that our old man is crucified with him, that the body of sin might be destroyed, that henceforth we should not serve sin.

b. **John 17:17, 19.** Sanctify them through thy truth: thy word is truth.… And for their sakes I sanctify myself, that they also might be sanctified through the truth. **Eph. 5:26.** … that he might sanctify and cleanse it with the washing of water by the word. **Rom. 8:13–14.** For if ye live after the flesh, ye shall die: but if ye through the Spirit do mortify the deeds of the body, ye shall live. For as many as are led by the Spirit of God, they are the sons of God. **2 Thess. 2:13.** But we are bound to give thanks alway to God for you, brethren beloved of the Lord, because God hath from the beginning chosen you to salvation through sanctification of the Spirit and belief of the truth.

ion of the whole body of sin is destroyed,[c] and the several lusts thereof are more and more weakened and mortified;[d] and they more and more quickened and strengthened in all saving graces,[e] to the practice of true holiness, without which no man shall see the Lord.[f]

2. This sanctification is throughout, in the whole man;[g] yet imperfect in this life, there abiding still some remnants of corruption in every part;[h] whence ariseth a continual and irreconcilable war, the

c. **Rom. 6:6, 14.** … knowing this, that our old man is crucified with him, that the body of sin might be destroyed, that henceforth we should not serve sin.… For sin shall not have dominion over you: for ye are not under the law, but under grace.

d. **Gal. 5:24.** And they that are Christ's have crucified the flesh with the affections and lusts. **Rom. 8:13.** For if ye live after the flesh, ye shall die: but if ye through the Spirit do mortify the deeds of the body, ye shall live.

e. **Col. 1:10–11.** … that ye might walk worthy of the Lord unto all pleasing, being fruitful in every good work, and increasing in the knowledge of God; strengthened with all might, according to his glorious power, unto all patience and longsuffering with joyfulness. **Eph. 3:16–19.** … that he would grant you, according to the riches of his glory, to be strengthened with might by his Spirit in the inner man; that Christ may dwell in your hearts by faith; that ye, being rooted and grounded in love, may be able to comprehend with all saints what is the breadth, and length, and depth, and height; and to know the love of Christ, which passeth knowledge, that ye might be filled with all the fulness of God.

f. **2 Cor. 7:1.** Having therefore these promises, dearly beloved, let us cleanse ourselves from all filthiness of the flesh and spirit, perfecting holiness in the fear of God. **Col. 1:28.** … whom we preach, warning every man, and teaching every man in all wisdom; that we may present every man perfect in Christ Jesus. **Col. 4:12.** Epaphras, who is one of you, a servant of Christ, saluteth you, always labouring fervently for you in prayers, that ye may stand perfect and complete in all the will of God. **Heb. 12:14.** Follow peace with all men, and holiness, without which no man shall see the Lord.

g. **1 Thess. 5:23.** And the very God of peace sanctify you wholly; and I pray God your whole spirit and soul and body be preserved blameless unto the coming of our Lord Jesus Christ. **Rom. 12:1–2.** I beseech you therefore, brethren, by the mercies of God, that ye present your bodies a living sacrifice, holy, acceptable unto God, which is your reasonable service. And be not conformed to this world: but be ye transformed by the renewing of your mind, that ye may prove what is that good, and acceptable, and perfect, will of God.

h. **1 John 1:8–10.** If we say that we have no sin, we deceive ourselves, and the truth is not in us. If we confess our sins, he is faithful and just to forgive us our sins, and to cleanse us from all unrighteousness. If we say that we have not sinned, we make him a liar, and his word is not in us. **Rom. 7:14–25.** For we know that the law is spiritual: but I am carnal, sold under sin. For that which I do I allow not: for what I would, that do I not; but what I hate, that do I.… For I know that in me (that is, in my flesh,) dwelleth no good thing: for to will is present with me; but how to perform that which is good I find not.… O wretched man that I am! who shall deliver me from the body of

flesh lusting against the Spirit, and the Spirit against the flesh.[i]

3. In which war, although the remaining corruption, for a time, may much prevail;[k] yet, through the continual supply of strength from the sanctifying Spirit of Christ, the regenerate part doth overcome;[l] and so, the saints grow in grace,[m] perfecting holiness in the fear of God.[n]

Chapter 14
Of Saving Faith

1. The grace of faith, whereby the elect are enabled to believe to the saving of their souls,[a] is the work of the Spirit of Christ in their

this death? I thank God through Jesus Christ our Lord. So then with the mind I myself serve the law of God; but with the flesh the law of sin. **Phil. 3:12.** Not as though I had already attained, either were already perfect: but I follow after, if that I may apprehend that for which also I am apprehended of Christ Jesus.

i. **Gal. 5:17.** For the flesh lusteth against the Spirit, and the Spirit against the flesh: and these are contrary the one to the other: so that ye cannot do the things that ye would.

k. **Rom. 7:23.** But I see another law in my members, warring against the law of my mind, and bringing me into captivity to the law of sin which is in my members.

l. **Rom. 6:14.** For sin shall not have dominion over you: for ye are not under the law, but under grace. **1 John 5:4.** For whatsoever is born of God overcometh the world: and this is the victory that overcometh the world, even our faith. **Eph. 4:15–16.** … but speaking the truth in love, may grow up into him in all things, which is the head, even Christ: from whom the whole body fitly joined together and compacted by that which every joint supplieth, according to the effectual working in the measure of every part, maketh increase of the body unto the edifying of itself in love. **See Rom. 8:2.**

m. **2 Pet. 3:18.** But grow in grace, and in the knowledge of our Lord and Saviour Jesus Christ. To him be glory both now and for ever. Amen. **2 Cor. 3:18.** But we all, with open face beholding as in a glass the glory of the Lord, are changed into the same image from glory to glory, even as by the Spirit of the Lord.

n. **2 Cor. 7:1.** Having therefore these promises, dearly beloved, let us cleanse ourselves from all filthiness of the flesh and spirit, perfecting holiness in the fear of God.

a. **Titus 1:1.** Paul, a servant of God, and an apostle of Jesus Christ, according to the faith of God's elect, and the acknowledging of the truth which is after godliness. **Heb. 10:39.** But we are not of them who draw back unto perdition; but of them that believe to the saving of the soul.

hearts,[b] and is ordinarily wrought by the ministry of the Word,[c] by which also, and by the administration of the sacraments, and prayer, it is increased and strengthened.[d]

b. **1 Cor. 12:3.** Wherefore I give you to understand, that no man speaking by the Spirit of God calleth Jesus accursed: and that no man can say that Jesus is the Lord, but by the Holy Ghost. **John 3:5.** Jesus answered, Verily, verily, I say unto thee, Except a man be born of water and of the Spirit, he cannot enter into the kingdom of God. **Titus 3:5.** Not by works of righteousness which we have done, but according to his mercy he saved us, by the washing of regeneration, and renewing of the Holy Ghost. **John 6:44–45, 65.** No man can come to me, except the Father which hath sent me draw him: and I will raise him up at the last day. It is written in the prophets, And they shall be all taught of God. Every man therefore that hath heard, and hath learned of the Father, cometh unto me.… And he said, Therefore said I unto you, that no man can come unto me, except it were given unto him of my Father. **Eph. 2:8.** For by grace are ye saved through faith; and that not of yourselves: it is the gift of God. **Phil. 1:29.** For unto you it is given in the behalf of Christ, not only to believe on him, but also to suffer for his sake. **2 Pet. 1:1.** Simon Peter, a servant and an apostle of Jesus Christ, to them that have obtained like precious faith with us through the righteousness of God and our Saviour Jesus Christ. **See 1 Pet. 1:2.**

c. **Matt. 28:19–20.** Go ye therefore, and teach all nations, baptizing them in the name of the Father, and of the Son, and of the Holy Ghost: teaching them to observe all things whatsoever I have commanded you: and, lo, I am with you alway, even unto the end of the world. Amen. **Rom. 10:14, 17.** How then shall they call on him in whom they have not believed? and how shall they believe in him of whom they have not heard? and how shall they hear without a preacher.… So then faith cometh by hearing, and hearing by the word of God. **1 Cor. 1:21.** For after that in the wisdom of God the world by wisdom knew not God, it pleased God by the foolishness of preaching to save them that believe.

d. **1 Pet. 2:2.** As newborn babes, desire the sincere milk of the word, that ye may grow thereby. **Acts 20:32.** And now, brethren, I commend you to God, and to the word of his grace, which is able to build you up, and to give you an inheritance among all them which are sanctified. **Rom. 1:16–17.** For I am not ashamed of the gospel of Christ: for it is the power of God unto salvation to every one that believeth; to the Jew first, and also to the Greek. For therein is the righteousness of God revealed from faith to faith: as it is written, The just shall live by faith. **Matt. 28:19.** Go ye therefore, and teach all nations, baptizing them in the name of the Father, and of the Son, and of the Holy Ghost. **See Acts 2:38. 1 Cor. 10:16.** The cup of blessing which we bless, is it not the communion of the blood of Christ? The bread which we break, is it not the communion of the body of Christ? **1 Cor. 11:23–29.** For I have received of the Lord that which also I delivered unto you, That the Lord Jesus the same night in which he was betrayed took bread: and when he had given thanks, he brake it, and said, Take, eat: this is my body, which is broken for you: this do in remembrance of me. After the same manner also he took the cup, when he had supped, saying, This cup is the new testament in my blood: this do ye, as oft as ye drink it, in remembrance of me. For as often as ye eat this bread, and drink this cup, ye do shew the Lord's death till he come. Wherefore whosoever shall eat this bread, and drink this cup of the Lord, un-

2. By this faith, a Christian believeth to be true whatsoever is revealed in the Word, for the authority of God himself speaking therein;[e] and acteth differently upon that which each particular passage thereof containeth; yielding obedience to the commands,[f] trembling at the threatenings,[g] and embracing the promises of God for this life, and that which is to come.[h] But the principal acts of saving

worthily, shall be guilty of the body and blood of the Lord. But let a man examine himself, and so let him eat of that bread, and drink of that cup. For he that eateth and drinketh unworthily, eateth and drinketh damnation to himself, not discerning the Lord's body. **Luke 17:5.** And the apostles said unto the Lord, Increase our faith. **Phil. 4:6–7.** Be careful for nothing; but in every thing by prayer and supplication with thanksgiving let your requests be made known unto God. And the peace of God, which passeth all understanding, shall keep your hearts and minds through Christ Jesus.

e. **2 Pet. 1:20–21.** … knowing this first, that no prophecy of the scripture is of any private interpretation. For the prophecy came not in old time by the will of man: but holy men of God spake as they were moved by the Holy Ghost. **John 4:42.** And [they] said unto the woman, Now we believe, not because of thy saying: for we have heard him ourselves, and know that this is indeed the Christ, the Saviour of the world. **1 Thess. 2:13.** For this cause also thank we God without ceasing, because, when ye received the word of God which ye heard of us, ye received it not as the word of men, but as it is in truth, the word of God, which effectually worketh also in you that believe. **1 John 5:9–10.** If we receive the witness of men, the witness of God is greater: for this is the witness of God which he hath testified of his Son. He that believeth on the Son of God hath the witness in himself: he that believeth not God hath made him a liar; because he believeth not the record that God gave of his Son. **Acts 24:14.** But this I confess unto thee, that after the way which they call heresy, so worship I the God of my fathers, believing all things which are written in the law and in the prophets.

f. **Ps. 119:10–11, 48, 97–98, 167–168.** With my whole heart have I sought thee: O let me not wander from thy commandments. Thy word have I hid in mine heart, that I might not sin against thee.… My hands also will I lift up unto thy commandments, which I have loved; and I will meditate in thy statutes.… O how love I thy law! it is my meditation all the day. Thou through thy commandments hast made me wiser than mine enemies: for they are ever with me.… My soul hath kept thy testimonies; and I love them exceedingly. I have kept thy precepts and thy testimonies: for all my ways are before thee. **John 14:15.** If ye love me, keep my commandments.

g. **Ezra 9:4.** Then were assembled unto me every one that trembled at the words of the God of Israel, because of the transgression of those that had been carried away; and I sat astonied until the evening sacrifice. **Isa. 66:2.** For all those things hath mine hand made, and all those things have been, saith the LORD: but to this man will I look, even to him that is poor and of a contrite spirit, and trembleth at my word. **Heb. 4:1.** Let us therefore fear, lest, a promise being left us of entering into his rest, any of you should seem to come short of it.

h. **Heb. 11:13.** These all died in faith, not having received the promises, but having seen them afar off, and were persuaded of them, and embraced them, and confessed that they were strangers and pilgrims on the earth. **1 Tim. 4:8.** For bodily exercise profiteth little: but godliness is profitable unto all things, having promise of

faith are accepting, receiving, and resting upon Christ alone for justification, sanctification, and eternal life, by virtue of the covenant of
grace.[i]

3. This faith is different in degrees, weak or strong;[k] may be often
and many ways assailed, and weakened, but gets the victory:[l] growing up in many to the attainment of a full assurance, through Christ,[m]

the life that now is, and of that which is to come.

i. **John 1:12.** But as many as received him, to them gave he power to become the
sons of God, even to them that believe on his name. **Acts 16:31.** And they said,
Believe on the Lord Jesus Christ, and thou shalt be saved, and thy house. **Gal. 2:20.**
I am crucified with Christ: nevertheless I live; yet not I, but Christ liveth in me: and the
life which I now live in the flesh I live by the faith of the Son of God, who loved me,
and gave himself for me. **Acts 15:11.** But we believe that through the grace of the
Lord Jesus Christ we shall be saved, even as they. **2 Tim. 1:9–10.** … who hath saved
us, and called us with an holy calling, not according to our works, but according to his
own purpose and grace, which was given us in Christ Jesus before the world began,
but is now made manifest by the appearing of our Saviour Jesus Christ, who hath
abolished death, and hath brought life and immortality to light through the gospel.

k. **Heb. 5:13–14.** For every one that useth milk is unskilful in the word of righteousness: for he is a babe. But strong meat belongeth to them that are of full age, even
those who by reason of use have their senses exercised to discern both good and evil.
Rom. 14:1–2. Him that is weak in the faith receive ye, but not to doubtful disputa-
tions. For one believeth that he may eat all things: another, who is weak, eateth herbs.
Matt. 6:30. Wherefore, if God so clothe the grass of the field, which to day is, and to
morrow is cast into the oven, shall he not much more clothe you, O ye of little faith?
Rom. 4:19–20. And being not weak in faith, he considered not his own body now
dead, when he was about an hundred years old, neither yet the deadness of Sarah's
womb: he staggered not at the promise of God through unbelief; but was strong in
faith, giving glory to God. **Matt. 8:10.** When Jesus heard it, he marvelled, and said
to them that followed, Verily I say unto you, I have not found so great faith, no, not in
Israel.

l. **Luke 22:31–32.** And the Lord said, Simon, Simon, behold, Satan hath desired to have you, that he may sift you as wheat: but I have prayed for thee, that thy
faith fail not: and when thou art converted, strengthen thy brethren. **Eph. 6:16.**
… above all, taking the shield of faith, wherewith ye shall be able to quench all the
fiery darts of the wicked. **1 John 5:4–5.** For whatsoever is born of God overcometh
the world: and this is the victory that overcometh the world, even our faith. Who is he
that overcometh the world, but he that believeth that Jesus is the Son of God?

m. **Heb. 6:11–12.** And we desire that every one of you do shew the same diligence to the full assurance of hope unto the end: that ye be not slothful, but followers
of them who through faith and patience inherit the promises. **Heb. 10:22.** Let us
draw near with a true heart in full assurance of faith, having our hearts sprinkled from
an evil conscience, and our bodies washed with pure water. **Col. 2:2.** … that their
hearts might be comforted, being knit together in love, and unto all riches of the full
assurance of understanding, to the acknowledgement of the mystery of God, and of
the Father, and of Christ.

who is both the author and finisher of our faith.[n]

Chapter 15
Of Repentance unto Life

1. Repentance unto life is an evangelical grace,[a] the doctrine whereof is to be preached by every minister of the gospel, as well as that of faith in Christ.[b]

2. By it, a sinner, out of the sight and sense not only of the danger, but also of the filthiness and odiousness of his sins, as contrary to the holy nature, and righteous law of God; and upon the apprehension of his mercy in Christ to such as are penitent, so grieves for, and hates his sins, as to turn from them all unto God,[c] purposing and

n. **Heb. 12:2.** … looking unto Jesus the author and finisher of our faith; who for the joy that was set before him endured the cross, despising the shame, and is set down at the right hand of the throne of God.

a. **Acts 11:18.** When they heard these things, they held their peace, and glorified God, saying, Then hath God also to the Gentiles granted repentance unto life. **2 Cor. 7:10.** For godly sorrow worketh repentance to salvation not to be repented of: but the sorrow of the world worketh death. **Zech. 12:10.** And I will pour upon the house of David, and upon the inhabitants of Jerusalem, the spirit of grace and of supplications: and they shall look upon me whom they have pierced, and they shall mourn for him, as one mourneth for his only son, and shall be in bitterness for him, as one that is in bitterness for his firstborn.

b. **Luke 24:47.** … and that repentance and remission of sins should be preached in his name among all nations, beginning at Jerusalem. **Mark 1:15.** … and saying, The time is fulfilled, and the kingdom of God is at hand: repent ye, and believe the gospel. **Acts 20:21.** … testifying both to the Jews, and also to the Greeks, repentance toward God, and faith toward our Lord Jesus Christ.

c. **Ezek. 18:30–31.** Therefore I will judge you, O house of Israel, every one according to his ways, saith the Lord GOD. Repent, and turn yourselves from all your transgressions; so iniquity shall not be your ruin. Cast away from you all your transgressions, whereby ye have transgressed; and make you a new heart and a new spirit: for why will ye die, O house of Israel? **Ezek. 36:31.** Then shall ye remember your own evil ways, and your doings that were not good, and shall lothe yourselves in your own sight for your iniquities and for your abominations. **Isa. 30:22.** Ye shall defile also the covering of thy graven images of silver, and the ornament of thy molten images of gold: thou shalt cast them away as a menstruous cloth; thou shalt say unto it, Get thee hence. **Ps. 51:4.** Against thee, thee only, have I sinned, and done this evil in thy sight: that thou mightest be justified when thou speakest, and be clear when thou judgest. **Jer. 31:18–19.** I have surely heard Ephraim bemoaning himself thus; Thou hast chastised me, and I was chastised, as a bullock unaccustomed to the yoke: turn

endeavoring to walk with him in all the ways of his commandments.[d]

3. Although repentance be not to be rested in, as any satisfaction for sin, or any cause of the pardon thereof,[e] which is the act of God's free grace in Christ;[f] yet it is of such necessity to all sinners, that none may expect pardon without it.[g]

thou me, and I shall be turned; for thou art the LORD my God. **Joel 2:12–13.** Therefore also now, saith the LORD, turn ye even to me with all your heart, and with fasting, and with weeping, and with mourning: and rend your heart, and not your garments, and turn unto the LORD your God: for he is gracious and merciful, slow to anger, and of great kindness, and repenteth him of the evil. **Amos 5:15.** Hate the evil, and love the good, and establish judgment in the gate: it may be that the LORD God of hosts will be gracious unto the remnant of Joseph. **Ps. 119:128.** Therefore I esteem all thy precepts concerning all things to be right; and I hate every false way. **2 Cor. 7:11.** For behold this selfsame thing, that ye sorrowed after a godly sort, what carefulness it wrought in you, yea, what clearing of yourselves, yea, what indignation, yea, what fear, yea, what vehement desire, yea, what zeal, yea, what revenge! In all things ye have approved yourselves to be clear in this matter. **1 Thess. 1:9.** For they themselves shew of us what manner of entering in we had unto you, and how ye turned to God from idols to serve the living and true God.

d. **Ps. 119:6, 59, 106.** Then shall I not be ashamed, when I have respect unto all thy commandments.… I thought on my ways, and turned my feet unto thy testimonies.… I have sworn, and I will perform it, that I will keep thy righteous judgments. **2 Kings 23:25.** And like unto him was there no king before him, that turned to the LORD with all his heart, and with all his soul, and with all his might, according to all the law of Moses; neither after him arose there any like him. **See Luke 1:6.**

e. **Ezek. 36:31–32.** Then shall ye remember your own evil ways, and your doings that were not good, and shall lothe yourselves in your own sight for your iniquities and for your abominations. Not for your sakes do I this, saith the Lord GOD, be it known unto you: be ashamed and confounded for your own ways, O house of Israel. **Ezek. 16:61–63.** Then thou shalt remember thy ways, and be ashamed, when thou shalt receive thy sisters, thine elder and thy younger: and I will give them unto thee for daughters, but not by thy covenant. And I will establish my covenant with thee; and thou shalt know that I am the LORD: that thou mayest remember, and be confounded, and never open thy mouth any more because of thy shame, when I am pacified toward thee for all that thou hast done, saith the Lord GOD. **Isa. 43:25.** I, even I, am he that blotteth out thy transgressions for mine own sake, and will not remember thy sins.

f. **Hos. 14:2, 4.** Take with you words, and turn to the LORD: say unto him, Take away all iniquity, and receive us graciously: so will we render the calves of our lips.… I will heal their backsliding, I will love them freely: for mine anger is turned away from him. **Rom. 3:24.** … being justified freely by his grace through the redemption that is in Christ Jesus. **Eph. 1:7.** … in whom we have redemption through his blood, the forgiveness of sins, according to the riches of his grace.

g. **Luke 13:3, 5.** I tell you, Nay: but, except ye repent, ye shall all likewise perish.… I tell you, Nay: but, except ye repent, ye shall all likewise perish. **Mark 1:4.** John did baptize in the wilderness, and preach the baptism of repentance for the

4. As there is no sin so small, but it deserves damnation;[h] so there is no sin so great, that it can bring damnation upon those who truly repent.[i]

5. Men ought not to content themselves with a general repentance, but it is every man's duty to endeavor to repent of his particular sins, particularly.[k]

6. As every man is bound to make private confession of his sins to God, praying for the pardon thereof;[l] upon which, and the forsaking

remission of sins. **Acts 17:30–31.** And the times of this ignorance God winked at; but now commandeth all men every where to repent: because he hath appointed a day, in the which he will judge the world in righteousness by that man whom he hath ordained; whereof he hath given assurance unto all men, in that he hath raised him from the dead.

h. **Rom. 6:23.** For the wages of sin is death; but the gift of God is eternal life through Jesus Christ our Lord. **Gal. 3:10.** For as many as are of the works of the law are under the curse: for it is written, Cursed is every one that continueth not in all things which are written in the book of the law to do them. **Matt. 12:36.** But I say unto you, That every idle word that men shall speak, they shall give account thereof in the day of judgment.

i. **Isa. 55:7.** Let the wicked forsake his way, and the unrighteous man his thoughts: and let him return unto the LORD, and he will have mercy upon him; and to our God, for he will abundantly pardon. **Rom. 8:1.** There is therefore now no condemnation to them which are in Christ Jesus, who walk not after the flesh, but after the Spirit. **Isa. 1:16–18.** Wash you, make you clean; put away the evil of your doings from before mine eyes; cease to do evil; learn to do well; seek judgment, relieve the oppressed, judge the fatherless, plead for the widow. Come now, and let us reason together, saith the LORD: though your sins be as scarlet, they shall be as white as snow; though they be red like crimson, they shall be as wool.

k. **Ps. 19:13.** Keep back thy servant also from presumptuous sins; let them not have dominion over me: then shall I be upright, and I shall be innocent from the great transgression. **Matt. 26:75.** And Peter remembered the word of Jesus, which said unto him, Before the cock crow, thou shalt deny me thrice. And he went out, and wept bitterly. **Luke 19:8.** And Zacchaeus stood, and said unto the Lord; Behold, Lord, the half of my goods I give to the poor; and if I have taken any thing from any man by false accusation, I restore him fourfold. **1 Tim. 1:13, 15.** … who was before a blasphemer, and a persecutor, and injurious: but I obtained mercy, because I did it ignorantly in unbelief.… This is a faithful saying, and worthy of all acceptation, that Christ Jesus came into the world to save sinners; of whom I am chief.

l. **Ps. 32:5–6.** I acknowledged my sin unto thee, and mine iniquity have I not hid. I said, I will confess my transgressions unto the LORD; and thou forgavest the iniquity of my sin. Selah. For this shall every one that is godly pray unto thee in a time when thou mayest be found: surely in the floods of great waters they shall not come nigh unto him. **Ps. 51:1–14.** Have mercy upon me, O God, according to thy lovingkindness: according unto the multitude of thy tender mercies blot out my transgressions. Wash me throughly from mine iniquity, and cleanse me from my sin. For I ac-

of them, he shall find mercy;[m] so, he that scandalizeth his brother, or the church of Christ, ought to be willing, by a private or public confession, and sorrow for his sin, to declare his repentance to those that are offended,[n] who are thereupon to be reconciled to him, and in love to receive him.[o]

Chapter 16
Of Good Works

1. Good works are only such as God hath commanded in his holy Word,[a] and not such as, without the warrant thereof, are devised by men, out of blind zeal, or upon any pretense of good intention.[b]

knowledge my transgressions: and my sin is ever before me.... Hide thy face from my sins, and blot out all mine iniquities.... Deliver me from bloodguiltiness, O God, thou God of my salvation: and my tongue shall sing aloud of thy righteousness.

m. **Prov. 28:13.** He that covereth his sins shall not prosper: but whoso confesseth and forsaketh them shall have mercy. **Isa. 55:7.** Let the wicked forsake his way, and the unrighteous man his thoughts: and let him return unto the Lord, and he will have mercy upon him; and to our God, for he will abundantly pardon. **1 John 1:9.** If we confess our sins, he is faithful and just to forgive us our sins, and to cleanse us from all unrighteousness.

n. **James 5:16.** Confess your faults one to another, and pray one for another, that ye may be healed. The effectual fervent prayer of a righteous man availeth much. **Luke 17:3–4.** Take heed to yourselves: If thy brother trespass against thee, rebuke him; and if he repent, forgive him. And if he trespass against thee seven times in a day, and seven times in a day turn again to thee, saying, I repent; thou shalt forgive him. **Josh. 7:19.** And Joshua said unto Achan, My son, give, I pray thee, glory to the Lord God of Israel, and make confession unto him; and tell me now what thou hast done; hide it not from me. **See Matt. 18:15–18.**

o. **2 Cor. 2:7–8.** So that contrariwise ye ought rather to forgive him, and comfort him, lest perhaps such a one should be swallowed up with overmuch sorrow. Wherefore I beseech you that ye would confirm your love toward him. **See Gal. 6:1–2.**

a. **Mic. 6:8.** He hath shewed thee, O man, what is good; and what doth the Lord require of thee, but to do justly, and to love mercy, and to walk humbly with thy God? **Rom. 12:2.** And be not conformed to this world: but be ye transformed by the renewing of your mind, that ye may prove what is that good, and acceptable, and perfect, will of God. **Heb. 13:21.** ... make you perfect in every good work to do his will, working in you that which is wellpleasing in his sight, through Jesus Christ; to whom be glory for ever and ever. Amen.

b. **Matt. 15:9.** But in vain they do worship me, teaching for doctrines the commandments of men. **Isa. 29:13.** Wherefore the Lord said, Forasmuch as this people draw near me with their mouth, and with their lips do honour me, but have removed

2. These good works, done in obedience to God's command-ments, are the fruits and evidences of a true and lively faith:[c] and by them believers manifest their thankfulness,[d] strengthen their assurance,[e] edify their brethren,[f] adorn the profession of the gospel,[g]

their heart far from me, and their fear toward me is taught by the precept of men … **1 Pet. 1:18.** … forasmuch as ye know that ye were not redeemed with corruptible things, as silver and gold, from your vain conversation received by tradition from your fathers. **John 16:2.** They shall put you out of the synagogues: yea, the time cometh, that whosoever killeth you will think that he doeth God service. **Rom. 10:2.** For I bear them record that they have a zeal of God, but not according to knowledge. **1 Sam. 15:21–23.** But the people took of the spoil, sheep and oxen, the chief of the things which should have been utterly destroyed, to sacrifice unto the LORD thy God in Gilgal. And Samuel said, Hath the LORD as great delight in burnt offerings and sacri-fices, as in obeying the voice of the LORD? Behold, to obey is better than sacrifice, and to hearken than the fat of rams. For rebellion is as the sin of witchcraft, and stubborn-ness is as iniquity and idolatry. Because thou hast rejected the word of the LORD, he hath also rejected thee from being king. **Deut. 10:12–13.** And now, Israel, what doth the LORD thy God require of thee, but to fear the LORD thy God, to walk in all his ways, and to love him, and to serve the LORD thy God with all thy heart and with all thy soul, to keep the commandments of the LORD, and his statutes, which I command thee this day for thy good? **Col. 2:16–17, 20–23.** Let no man therefore judge you in meat, or in drink, or in respect of an holyday, or of the new moon, or of the sabbath days: which are a shadow of things to come; but the body is of Christ.… Wherefore if ye be dead with Christ from the rudiments of the world, why, as though living in the world, are ye subject to ordinances, (touch not; taste not; handle not; which all are to perish with the using;) after the commandments and doctrines of men? Which things have indeed a shew of wisdom in will worship, and humility, and neglecting of the body; not in any honour to the satisfying of the flesh.

c. **James 2:18, 22.** Yea, a man may say, Thou hast faith, and I have works: shew me thy faith without thy works, and I will shew thee my faith by my works.… Seest thou how faith wrought with his works, and by works was faith made perfect?

d. **Ps. 116:12–14.** What shall I render unto the LORD for all his benefits toward me? I will take the cup of salvation, and call upon the name of the LORD. I will pay my vows unto the LORD now in the presence of all his people. **Col. 3:15–17.** And let the peace of God rule in your hearts, to the which also ye are called in one body; and be ye thankful. Let the word of Christ dwell in you richly in all wisdom; teaching and ad-monishing one another in psalms and hymns and spiritual songs, singing with grace in your hearts to the Lord. And whatsoever ye do in word or deed, do all in the name of the Lord Jesus, giving thanks to God and the Father by him. **1 Pet. 2:9.** But ye are a chosen generation, a royal priesthood, an holy nation, a peculiar people; that ye should shew forth the praises of him who hath called you out of darkness into his marvellous light.

e. **1 John 2:3, 5.** And hereby we do know that we know him, if we keep his commandments.… But whoso keepeth his word, in him verily is the love of God per-fected: hereby know we that we are in him. **2 Pet. 1:5–10.** And beside this, giving all diligence, add to your faith virtue; and to virtue knowledge; and to knowledge temper-

stop the mouths of the adversaries,[h] and glorify God,[i] whose work-manship they are, created in Christ Jesus thereunto,[k] that, having their fruit unto holiness, they may have the end, eternal life.[l]

3. Their ability to do good works is not at all of themselves, but wholly from the Spirit of Christ.[m] And that they may be enabled

ance; and to temperance patience; and to patience godliness; and to godliness broth-erly kindness; and to brotherly kindness charity. For if these things be in you, and abound, they make you that ye shall neither be barren nor unfruitful in the knowledge of our Lord Jesus Christ. But he that lacketh these things is blind, and cannot see afar off, and hath forgotten that he was purged from his old sins. Wherefore the rather, brethren, give diligence to make your calling and election sure: for if ye do these things, ye shall never fall.

f. **2 Cor. 9:2.** For I know the forwardness of your mind, for which I boast of you to them of Macedonia, that Achaia was ready a year ago; and your zeal hath provoked very many. **Matt. 5:16.** Let your light so shine before men, that they may see your good works, and glorify your Father which is in heaven. **1 Tim. 4:12.** Let no man despise thy youth; but be thou an example of the believers, in word, in conversation, in charity, in spirit, in faith, in purity.

g. **Titus 2:5, 9–12.** … to be discreet, chaste, keepers at home, good, obedient to their own husbands, that the word of God be not blasphemed.… Exhort servants to be obedient unto their own masters, and to please them well in all things; not answer-ing again; not purloining, but shewing all good fidelity; that they may adorn the doc-trine of God our Saviour in all things. For the grace of God that bringeth salvation hath appeared to all men, teaching us that, denying ungodliness and worldly lusts, we should live soberly, righteously, and godly, in this present world. **1 Tim. 6:1.** Let as many servants as are under the yoke count their own masters worthy of all honour, that the name of God and his doctrine be not blasphemed.

h. **1 Pet. 2:15.** For so is the will of God, that with well doing ye may put to silence the ignorance of foolish men.

i. **1 Pet. 2:12.** … having your conversation honest among the Gentiles: that, whereas they speak against you as evildoers, they may by your good works, which they shall behold, glorify God in the day of visitation. **Phil. 1:11.** … being filled with the fruits of righteousness, which are by Jesus Christ, unto the glory and praise of God. **John 15:8.** Herein is my Father glorified, that ye bear much fruit; so shall ye be my disciples.

k. **Eph. 2:10.** For we are his workmanship, created in Christ Jesus unto good works, which God hath before ordained that we should walk in them.

l. **Rom. 6:22.** But now being made free from sin, and become servants to God, ye have your fruit unto holiness, and the end everlasting life.

m. **John 15:4–6.** Abide in me, and I in you. As the branch cannot bear fruit of itself, except it abide in the vine; no more can ye, except ye abide in me. I am the vine, ye are the branches: He that abideth in me, and I in him, the same bringeth forth much fruit: for without me ye can do nothing. If a man abide not in me, he is cast forth as a branch, and is withered; and men gather them, and cast them into the fire, and they are burned. **Rom. 8:4–14.** … that the righteousness of the law might be ful-filled in us, who walk not after the flesh, but after the Spirit. For they that are after the

thereunto, beside the graces they have already received, there is required an actual influence of the same Holy Spirit, to work in them to will, and to do, of his good pleasure:[n] yet are they not hereupon to grow negligent, as if they were not bound to perform any duty unless upon a special motion of the Spirit; but they ought to be diligent in stirring up the grace of God that is in them.[o]

4. They who, in their obedience, attain to the greatest height which is possible in this life, are so far from being able to supererogate, and to do more than God requires, as that they fall short of much

flesh do mind the things of the flesh; but they that are after the Spirit the things of the Spirit.... But ye are not in the flesh, but in the Spirit, if so be that the Spirit of God dwell in you. Now if any man have not the Spirit of Christ, he is none of his. And if Christ be in you, the body is dead because of sin; but the Spirit is life because of righteousness.... For as many as are led by the Spirit of God, they are the sons of God. **Ezek. 36:26–27.** A new heart also will I give you, and a new spirit will I put within you: and I will take away the stony heart out of your flesh, and I will give you an heart of flesh. And I will put my spirit within you, and cause you to walk in my statutes, and ye shall keep my judgments, and do them.

n. **Phil. 2:13.** For it is God which worketh in you both to will and to do of his good pleasure. **Phil. 4:13.** I can do all things through Christ which strengtheneth me. **2 Cor. 3:5.** Not that we are sufficient of ourselves to think any thing as of ourselves; but our sufficiency is of God. **Eph. 3:16.** ... that he would grant you, according to the riches of his glory, to be strengthened with might by his Spirit in the inner man.

o. **Phil. 2:12.** Wherefore, my beloved, as ye have always obeyed, not as in my presence only, but now much more in my absence, work out your own salvation with fear and trembling. **Heb. 6:11–12.** And we desire that every one of you do shew the same diligence to the full assurance of hope unto the end: that ye be not slothful, but followers of them who through faith and patience inherit the promises. **2 Pet. 1:3, 5, 10–11.** ... according as his divine power hath given unto us all things that pertain unto life and godliness, through the knowledge of him that hath called us to glory and virtue.... And beside this, giving all diligence, add to your faith virtue; and to virtue knowledge.... Wherefore the rather, brethren, give diligence to make your calling and election sure: for if ye do these things, ye shall never fall: for so an entrance shall be ministered unto you abundantly into the everlasting kingdom of our Lord and Saviour Jesus Christ. **Isa. 64:7.** And there is none that calleth upon thy name, that stirreth up himself to take hold of thee: for thou hast hid thy face from us, and hast consumed us, because of our iniquities. **2 Tim. 1:6.** Wherefore I put thee in remembrance that thou stir up the gift of God, which is in thee by the putting on of my hands. **Acts 26:6–7.** And now I stand and am judged for the hope of the promise made of God unto our fathers: unto which promise our twelve tribes, instantly serving God day and night, hope to come. For which hope's sake, king Agrippa, I am accused of the Jews. **Jude 20–21.** But ye, beloved, building up yourselves on your most holy faith, praying in the Holy Ghost, keep yourselves in the love of God, looking for the mercy of our Lord Jesus Christ unto eternal life.

which in duty they are bound to do.ᵖ

5. We cannot by our best works merit pardon of sin, or eternal life at the hand of God, by reason of the great disproportion that is between them and the glory to come; and the infinite distance that is between us and God, whom, by them, we can neither profit, nor satisfy for the debt of our former sins, q but when we have done all we

p. **Luke 17:10.** So likewise ye, when ye shall have done all those things which are commanded you, say, We are unprofitable servants: we have done that which was our duty to do. **Neh. 13:22.** And I commanded the Levites that they should cleanse themselves, and that they should come and keep the gates, to sanctify the sabbath day. Remember me, O my God, concerning this also, and spare me according to the greatness of thy mercy. **Rom. 8:21–25.** Because the creature itself also shall be delivered from the bondage of corruption into the glorious liberty of the children of God. For we know that the whole creation groaneth and travaileth in pain together until now. And not only they, but ourselves also, which have the firstfruits of the Spirit, even we ourselves groan within ourselves, waiting for the adoption, to wit, the redemption of our body. For we are saved by hope: but hope that is seen is not hope: for what a man seeth, why doth he yet hope for? But if we hope for that we see not, then do we with patience wait for it. **Gal. 5:17.** For the flesh lusteth against the Spirit, and the Spirit against the flesh: and these are contrary the one to the other: so that ye cannot do the things that ye would.

q. **Rom. 3:20.** Therefore by the deeds of the law there shall no flesh be justified in his sight: for by the law is the knowledge of sin. **Rom. 4:2, 4, 6.** For if Abraham were justified by works, he hath whereof to glory; but not before God.… Now to him that worketh is the reward not reckoned of grace, but of debt.… Even as David also describeth the blessedness of the man, unto whom God imputeth righteousness without works. **Eph. 2:8–9.** For by grace are ye saved through faith; and that not of yourselves: it is the gift of God: not of works, lest any man should boast. **Titus 3:5– 7.** Not by works of righteousness which we have done, but according to his mercy he saved us, by the washing of regeneration, and renewing of the Holy Ghost; which he shed on us abundantly through Jesus Christ our Saviour; that being justified by his grace, we should be made heirs according to the hope of eternal life. **Rom. 8:18, 22–24.** For I reckon that the sufferings of this present time are not worthy to be compared with the glory which shall be revealed in us.… For we know that the whole creation groaneth and travaileth in pain together until now. And not only they, but ourselves also, which have the firstfruits of the Spirit, even we ourselves groan within ourselves, waiting for the adoption, to wit, the redemption of our body. For we are saved by hope: but hope that is seen is not hope: for what a man seeth, why doth he yet hope for? **Ps. 16:2.** O my soul, thou hast said unto the LORD, Thou art my Lord: my goodness extendeth not to thee. **Job 22:2–3.** Can a man be profitable unto God, as he that is wise may be profitable unto himself? Is it any pleasure to the Almighty, that thou art righteous? or is it gain to him that thou makest thy ways perfect? **Job 35:7–8.** If thou be righteous, what givest thou him? or what receiveth he of thine hand? Thy wickedness may hurt a man as thou art; and thy righteousness may profit the son of man.

can, we have done but our duty, and are unprofitable servants:[r] and because, as they are good, they proceed from his Spirit;[s] and as they are wrought by us, they are defiled, and mixed with so much weakness and imperfection, that they cannot endure the severity of God's judgment.[t]

6. Notwithstanding, the persons of believers being accepted through Christ, their good works also are accepted in him;[u] not as though they were in this life wholly unblamable and unreprovable in God's sight;[w] but that he, looking upon them in his Son, is pleased to accept and reward that which is sincere, although accompanied with many weaknesses and imperfections.[x]

r. **Luke 17:10.** So likewise ye, when ye shall have done all those things which are commanded you, say, We are unprofitable servants: we have done that which was our duty to do.

s. **Rom. 8:13–14.** For if ye live after the flesh, ye shall die: but if ye through the Spirit do mortify the deeds of the body, ye shall live. For as many as are led by the Spirit of God, they are the sons of God. **Gal. 5:22–23.** But the fruit of the Spirit is love, joy, peace, longsuffering, gentleness, goodness, faith, meekness, temperance: against such there is no law.

t. **Isa. 64:6.** But we are all as an unclean thing, and all our righteousnesses are as filthy rags; and we all do fade as a leaf; and our iniquities, like the wind, have taken us away. **Gal. 5:17.** For the flesh lusteth against the Spirit, and the Spirit against the flesh: and these are contrary the one to the other: so that ye cannot do the things that ye would. **Rom. 7:15, 18.** For that which I do I allow not: for what I would, that do I not; but what I hate, that do I.… For I know that in me (that is, in my flesh,) dwelleth no good thing: for to will is present with me; but how to perform that which is good I find not. **Ps. 143:2.** And enter not into judgment with thy servant: for in thy sight shall no man living be justified. **Ps. 130:3.** If thou, Lord, shouldest mark iniquities, O Lord, who shall stand?

u. **Eph. 1:6.** … to the praise of the glory of his grace, wherein he hath made us accepted in the beloved. **1 Pet. 2:5.** Ye also, as lively stones, are built up a spiritual house, an holy priesthood, to offer up spiritual sacrifices, acceptable to God by Jesus Christ. **See Ex. 28:38; Gen. 4:4; Heb. 11:4.**

w. **Job 9:20.** If I justify myself, mine own mouth shall condemn me: if I say, I am perfect, it shall also prove me perverse. **Ps. 143:2.** And enter not into judgment with thy servant: for in thy sight shall no man living be justified. **1 John 1:8.** If we say that we have no sin, we deceive ourselves, and the truth is not in us.

x. **Heb. 13:20–21.** Now the God of peace, that brought again from the dead our Lord Jesus, that great shepherd of the sheep, through the blood of the everlasting covenant, make you perfect in every good work to do his will, working in you that which is wellpleasing in his sight, through Jesus Christ; to whom be glory for ever and ever. Amen. **2 Cor. 8:12.** For if there be first a willing mind, it is accepted according to that a man hath, and not according to that he hath not. **Heb. 6:10.** For God is not unrighteous to forget your work and labour of love, which ye have shewed toward his

7. Works done by unregenerate men, although for the matter of them they may be things which God commands; and of good use both to themselves and others:[y] yet, because they proceed not from an heart purified by faith;[z] nor are done in a right manner, according to the Word;[a] nor to a right end, the glory of God,[b] they

name, in that ye have ministered to the saints, and do minister. **Matt. 25:21, 23.** His lord said unto him, Well done, thou good and faithful servant: thou hast been faithful over a few things, I will make thee ruler over many things: enter thou into the joy of thy lord.... His lord said unto him, Well done, good and faithful servant; thou hast been faithful over a few things, I will make thee ruler over many things: enter thou into the joy of thy lord. **1 Cor. 3:14.** If any man's work abide which he hath built thereupon, he shall receive a reward. **1 Cor. 4:5.** Therefore judge nothing before the time, until the Lord come, who both will bring to light the hidden things of darkness, and will make manifest the counsels of the hearts: and then shall every man have praise of God.

y. **2 Kings 10:30–31.** And the LORD said unto Jehu, Because thou hast done well in executing that which is right in mine eyes, and hast done unto the house of Ahab according to all that was in mine heart, thy children of the fourth generation shall sit on the throne of Israel. But Jehu took no heed to walk in the law of the LORD God of Israel with all his heart: for he departed not from the sins of Jeroboam, which made Israel to sin. **1 Kings 21:27, 29.** And it came to pass, when Ahab heard those words, that he rent his clothes, and put sackcloth upon his flesh, and fasted, and lay in sackcloth, and went softly.... Seest thou how Ahab humbleth himself before me? because he humbleth himself before me, I will not bring the evil in his days: but in his son's days will I bring the evil upon his house. **Luke 6:32–34.** For if ye love them which love you, what thank have ye? for sinners also love those that love them. And if ye do good to them which do good to you, what thank have ye? for sinners also do even the same. And if ye lend to them of whom ye hope to receive, what thank have ye? for sinners also lend to sinners, to receive as much again. **Luke 18:2–7.** ... saying, There was in a city a judge, which feared not God, neither regarded man: and there was a widow in that city; and she came unto him, saying, Avenge me of mine adversary. And he would not for a while: but afterward he said within himself, Though I fear not God, nor regard man; yet because this widow troubleth me, I will avenge her, lest by her continual coming she weary me. And the Lord said, Hear what the unjust judge saith. And shall not God avenge his own elect, which cry day and night unto him, though he bear long with them? **See Rom. 13:4.**

z. **Heb. 11:4, 6.** By faith Abel offered unto God a more excellent sacrifice than Cain, by which he obtained witness that he was righteous, God testifying of his gifts: and by it he being dead yet speaketh.... But without faith it is impossible to please him: for he that cometh to God must believe that he is, and that he is a rewarder of them that diligently seek him. **See Gen. 4:3–5.**

a. **1 Cor. 13:3.** And though I bestow all my goods to feed the poor, and though I give my body to be burned, and have not charity, it profiteth me nothing. **Isa. 1:12.** When ye come to appear before me, who hath required this at your hand, to tread my courts?

b. **Matt. 6:2, 5, 16.** Therefore when thou doest thine alms, do not sound a

are therefore sinful, and cannot please God, or make a man meet to receive grace from God:[c] and yet, their neglect of them is more sinful and displeasing unto God.[d]

Chapter 17
Of the Perseverance of the Saints

1. They, whom God hath accepted in his Beloved, effectually called, and sanctified by his Spirit, can neither totally nor finally fall away from the state of grace, but shall certainly persevere therein to

trumpet before thee, as the hypocrites do in the synagogues and in the streets, that they may have glory of men. Verily I say unto you, They have their reward.… And when thou prayest, thou shalt not be as the hypocrites are: for they love to pray standing in the synagogues and in the corners of the streets, that they may be seen of men. Verily I say unto you, They have their reward.… Moreover when ye fast, be not, as the hypocrites, of a sad countenance: for they disfigure their faces, that they may appear unto men to fast. Verily I say unto you, They have their reward. **1 Cor. 10:31.** Whether therefore ye eat, or drink, or whatsoever ye do, do all to the glory of God.

c. **Prov. 21:27.** The sacrifice of the wicked is abomination: how much more, when he bringeth it with a wicked mind? **Hag. 2:14.** Then answered Haggai, and said, So is this people, and so is this nation before me, saith the Lord; and so is every work of their hands; and that which they offer there is unclean. **Titus 1:15.** Unto the pure all things are pure: but unto them that are defiled and unbelieving is nothing pure; but even their mind and conscience is defiled. **Amos 5:21–22.** I hate, I despise your feast days, and I will not smell in your solemn assemblies. Though ye offer me burnt offerings and your meat offerings, I will not accept them: neither will I regard the peace offerings of your fat beasts. **Mark 7:6–7.** He answered and said unto them, Well hath Esaias prophesied of you hypocrites, as it is written, This people honoureth me with their lips, but their heart is far from me. Howbeit in vain do they worship me, teaching for doctrines the commandments of men. **Hos. 1:4.** And the Lord said unto him, Call his name Jezreel; for yet a little while, and I will avenge the blood of Jezreel upon the house of Jehu, and will cause to cease the kingdom of the house of Israel. **Rom. 9:16.** So then it is not of him that willeth, nor of him that runneth, but of God that sheweth mercy. **Titus 3:5.** Not by works of righteousness which we have done, but according to his mercy he saved us, by the washing of regeneration, and renewing of the Holy Ghost.

d. **Ps. 14:4.** Have all the workers of iniquity no knowledge? who eat up my people as they eat bread, and call not upon the Lord. **Ps. 36:3.** The words of his mouth are iniquity and deceit: he hath left off to be wise, and to do good. **Matt. 25:41–45.** Then shall he say also unto them on the left hand, Depart from me, ye cursed, into everlasting fire, prepared for the devil and his angels: for I was an hungred, and ye gave me no meat: I was thirsty, and ye gave me no drink: I was a stranger, and ye took me not in: naked, and ye clothed me not: sick, and in prison, and ye visited me

the end, and be eternally saved.^a

2. This perseverance of the saints depends not upon their own free will, but upon the immutability of the decree of election, flowing from the free and unchangeable love of God the Father;^b upon the efficacy of the merit and intercession of Jesus Christ,^c the

not. Then shall they also answer him, saying, Lord, when saw we thee an hungred, or athirst, or a stranger, or naked, or sick, or in prison, and did not minister unto thee? Then shall he answer them, saying, Verily I say unto you, Inasmuch as ye did it not to one of the least of these, ye did it not to me. **Matt. 23:23.** Woe unto you, scribes and Pharisees, hypocrites! for ye pay tithe of mint and anise and cummin, and have omitted the weightier matters of the law, judgment, mercy, and faith: these ought ye to have done, and not to leave the other undone. **See Rom. 1:21–32.**

a. **Phil. 1:6.** … being confident of this very thing, that he which hath begun a good work in you will perform it until the day of Jesus Christ. **2 Pet. 1:10.** Wherefore the rather, brethren, give diligence to make your calling and election sure: for if ye do these things, ye shall never fall. **Rom. 8:28–30.** And we know that all things work together for good to them that love God, to them who are the called according to his purpose. For whom he did foreknow, he also did predestinate to be conformed to the image of his Son, that he might be the firstborn among many brethren. Moreover whom he did predestinate, them he also called: and whom he called, them he also justified: and whom he justified, them he also glorified. **John 10:28–29.** And I give unto them eternal life; and they shall never perish, neither shall any man pluck them out of my hand. My Father, which gave them me, is greater than all; and no man is able to pluck them out of my Father's hand. **1 John 3:9.** Whosoever is born of God doth not commit sin; for his seed remaineth in him: and he cannot sin, because he is born of God. **1 John 5:18.** We know that whosoever is born of God sinneth not; but he that is begotten of God keepeth himself, and that wicked one toucheth him not. **1 Pet. 1:5, 9.** … who are kept by the power of God through faith unto salvation ready to be revealed in the last time.… receiving the end of your faith, even the salvation of your souls.

b. **Ps. 89:3–4, 28–33.** I have made a covenant with my chosen, I have sworn unto David my servant, Thy seed will I establish for ever, and build up thy throne to all generations. Selah.… My mercy will I keep for him for evermore, and my covenant shall stand fast with him. His seed also will I make to endure for ever, and his throne as the days of heaven. If his children forsake my law, and walk not in my judgments; if they break my statutes, and keep not my commandments; then will I visit their transgression with the rod, and their iniquity with stripes. Nevertheless my lovingkindness will I not utterly take from him, nor suffer my faithfulness to fail. **2 Tim. 2:18–19.** … who concerning the truth have erred, saying that the resurrection is past already; and overthrow the faith of some. Nevertheless the foundation of God standeth sure, having this seal, The Lord knoweth them that are his. And, Let every one that nameth the name of Christ depart from iniquity. **Jer. 31:3.** The Lord hath appeared of old unto me, saying, Yea, I have loved thee with an everlasting love: therefore with lovingkindness have I drawn thee.

c. **Heb. 10:10, 14.** By the which will we are sanctified through the offering of

abiding of the Spirit, and of the seed of God within them,[d] and the nature of the covenant of grace:[e] from all which ariseth also the

the body of Jesus Christ once for all.... For by one offering he hath perfected for ever them that are sanctified. **Heb. 13:20–21.** Now the God of peace, that brought again from the dead our Lord Jesus, that great shepherd of the sheep, through the blood of the everlasting covenant, make you perfect in every good work to do his will, working in you that which is wellpleasing in his sight, through Jesus Christ; to whom be glory for ever and ever. Amen. **Heb. 9:12–15.** Neither by the blood of goats and calves, but by his own blood he entered in once into the holy place, having obtained eternal redemption for us. For if the blood of bulls and of goats, and the ashes of an heifer sprinkling the unclean, sanctifieth to the purifying of the flesh: how much more shall the blood of Christ, who through the eternal Spirit offered himself without spot to God, purge your conscience from dead works to serve the living God? And for this cause he is the mediator of the new testament, that by means of death, for the redemption of the transgressions that were under the first testament, they which are called might receive the promise of eternal inheritance. **Rom. 8:33–39.** Who shall lay any thing to the charge of God's elect? It is God that justifieth. Who is he that condemneth? It is Christ that died, yea rather, that is risen again, who is even at the right hand of God, who also maketh intercession for us. Who shall separate us from the love of Christ? shall tribulation, or distress, or persecution, or famine, or nakedness, or peril, or sword? As it is written, For thy sake we are killed all the day long; we are accounted as sheep for the slaughter. Nay, in all these things we are more than conquerors through him that loved us. For I am persuaded, that neither death, nor life, nor angels, nor principalities, nor powers, nor things present, nor things to come, nor height, nor depth, nor any other creature, shall be able to separate us from the love of God, which is in Christ Jesus our Lord. **John 17:11, 24.** And now I am no more in the world, but these are in the world, and I come to thee. Holy Father, keep through thine own name those whom thou hast given me, that they may be one, as we are.... Father, I will that they also, whom thou hast given me, be with me where I am; that they may behold my glory, which thou hast given me: for thou lovedst me before the foundation of the world. **Luke 22:32.** But I have prayed for thee, that thy faith fail not: and when thou art converted, strengthen thy brethren. **Heb. 7:25.** Wherefore he is able also to save them to the uttermost that come unto God by him, seeing he ever liveth to make intercession for them.

d. **John 14:16–17.** And I will pray the Father, and he shall give you another Comforter, that he may abide with you for ever; even the Spirit of truth; whom the world cannot receive, because it seeth him not, neither knoweth him: but ye know him; for he dwelleth with you, and shall be in you. **1 John 2:27.** But the anointing which ye have received of him abideth in you, and ye need not that any man teach you: but as the same anointing teacheth you of all things, and is truth, and is no lie, and even as it hath taught you, ye shall abide in him. **1 John 3:9.** Whosoever is born of God doth not commit sin; for his seed remaineth in him: and he cannot sin, because he is born of God.

e. **Jer. 32:40.** And I will make an everlasting covenant with them, that I will not turn away from them, to do them good; but I will put my fear in their hearts, that they shall not depart from me. **Ps. 89:34–37.** My covenant will I not break, nor alter the

certainty and infallibility thereof.[f]

3. Nevertheless, they may, through the temptations of Satan and of the world, the prevalency of corruption remaining in them, and the neglect of the means of their preservation, fall into grievous sins;[g] and, for a time, continue therein:[h] whereby they incur God's

thing that is gone out of my lips. Once have I sworn by my holiness that I will not lie unto David. His seed shall endure for ever, and his throne as the sun before me. It shall be established for ever as the moon, and as a faithful witness in heaven. Selah. **See Jer. 31:31–34.**

f. **John 6:38–40.** For I came down from heaven, not to do mine own will, but the will of him that sent me. And this is the Father's will which hath sent me, that of all which he hath given me I should lose nothing, but should raise it up again at the last day. And this is the will of him that sent me, that every one which seeth the Son, and believeth on him, may have everlasting life: and I will raise him up at the last day. **John 10:28.** And I give unto them eternal life; and they shall never perish, neither shall any man pluck them out of my hand. **2 Thess. 3:3.** But the Lord is faithful, who shall stablish you, and keep you from evil. **1 John 2:19.** They went out from us, but they were not of us; for if they had been of us, they would no doubt have continued with us: but they went out, that they might be made manifest that they were not all of us.

g. **Ex. 32:21.** And Moses said unto Aaron, What did this people unto thee, that thou hast brought so great a sin upon them? **Jonah 1:3, 10.** But Jonah rose up to flee unto Tarshish from the presence of the LORD, and went down to Joppa; and he found a ship going to Tarshish: so he paid the fare thereof, and went down into it, to go with them unto Tarshish from the presence of the LORD.… Then were the men exceedingly afraid, and said unto him, Why hast thou done this? For the men knew that he fled from the presence of the LORD, because he had told them. **Ps. 51:14.** Deliver me from bloodguiltiness, O God, thou God of my salvation: and my tongue shall sing aloud of thy righteousness. **Matt. 26:70, 72, 74.** But he denied before them all, saying, I know not what thou sayest.… And again he denied with an oath, I do not know the man.… Then began he to curse and to swear, saying, I know not the man. And immediately the cock crew.

h. **2 Sam. 12:9, 13.** Wherefore hast thou despised the commandment of the LORD, to do evil in his sight? thou hast killed Uriah the Hittite with the sword, and hast taken his wife to be thy wife, and hast slain him with the sword of the children of Ammon.… And David said unto Nathan, I have sinned against the LORD. And Nathan said unto David, The LORD also hath put away thy sin; thou shalt not die. **Gal. 2:11–14.** But when Peter was come to Antioch, I withstood him to the face, because he was to be blamed. For before that certain came from James, he did eat with the Gentiles: but when they were come, he withdrew and separated himself, fearing them which were of the circumcision. And the other Jews dissembled likewise with him; insomuch that Barnabas also was carried away with their dissimulation. But when I saw that they walked not uprightly according to the truth of the gospel, I said unto Peter before them all, If thou, being a Jew, livest after the manner of Gentiles, and not as do the Jews, why compellest thou the Gentiles to live as do the Jews?

displeasure,[i] and grieve his Holy Spirit,[k] come to be deprived of some measure of their graces and comforts,[l] have their hearts hardened,[m] and their consciences wounded;[n] hurt and scandalize others,[o] and bring temporal judgments upon themselves.[p]

i. **Num. 20:12.** And the LORD spake unto Moses and Aaron, Because ye believed me not, to sanctify me in the eyes of the children of Israel, therefore ye shall not bring this congregation into the land which I have given them. **2 Sam. 11:27.** And when the mourning was past, David sent and fetched her to his house, and she became his wife, and bare him a son. But the thing that David had done displeased the LORD. **Isa. 64:7, 9.** And there is none that calleth upon thy name, that stirreth up himself to take hold of thee: for thou hast hid thy face from us, and hast consumed us, because of our iniquities.... Be not wroth very sore, O LORD, neither remember iniquity for ever: behold, see, we beseech thee, we are all thy people.

k. **Eph. 4:30.** And grieve not the holy Spirit of God, whereby ye are sealed unto the day of redemption.

l. **Ps. 51:8, 10, 12.** Make me to hear joy and gladness; that the bones which thou hast broken may rejoice.... Create in me a clean heart, O God; and renew a right spirit within me.... Restore unto me the joy of thy salvation; and uphold me with thy free spirit. **Rev. 2:4.** Nevertheless I have somewhat against thee, because thou hast left thy first love. **Matt. 26:75.** And Peter remembered the word of Jesus, which said unto him, Before the cock crow, thou shalt deny me thrice. And he went out, and wept bitterly.

m. **Isa. 63:17.** O LORD, why hast thou made us to err from thy ways, and hardened our heart from thy fear? Return for thy servants' sake, the tribes of thine inheritance.

n. **Ps. 32:3–4.** When I kept silence, my bones waxed old through my roaring all the day long. For day and night thy hand was heavy upon me: my moisture is turned into the drought of summer. Selah. **Ps. 51:8.** Make me to hear joy and gladness; that the bones which thou hast broken may rejoice.

o. **Gen. 12:10–20.** And there was a famine in the land: and Abram went down into Egypt to sojourn there.... And ... he said unto Sarai his wife, Behold now ... it shall come to pass, when the Egyptians shall see thee, that they shall say, This is his wife: and they will kill me, but they will save thee alive. Say, I pray thee, thou art my sister: that it may be well with me for thy sake; and my soul shall live because of thee.... The princes also of Pharaoh saw her, and commended her before Pharaoh: and the woman was taken into Pharaoh's house.... And the LORD plagued Pharaoh and his house with great plagues because of Sarai Abram's wife. And Pharaoh called Abram, and said, What is this that thou hast done unto me.... I might have taken her to me to wife: now therefore behold thy wife, take her, and go thy way.... **2 Sam. 12:14.** Howbeit, because by this deed thou hast given great occasion to the enemies of the LORD to blaspheme, the child also that is born unto thee shall surely die. **Gal. 2:13.** And the other Jews dissembled likewise with him; insomuch that Barnabas also was carried away with their dissimulation.

p. **Ps. 89:31–32.** If they break my statutes, and keep not my commandments; then will I visit their transgression with the rod, and their iniquity with stripes. **1 Cor. 11:32.** But when we are judged, we are chastened of the Lord, that we should not be condemned with the world.

Chapter 18
Of the Assurance of Grace and Salvation

1. Although hypocrites and other unregenerate men may vainly deceive themselves with false hopes and carnal presumptions of being in the favor of God, and estate of salvation[a] (which hope of theirs shall perish[b]): yet such as truly believe in the Lord Jesus, and love him in sincerity, endeavoring to walk in all good conscience before him, may, in this life, be certainly assured that they are in the state of grace,[c] and may rejoice in the hope of the glory of God, which hope shall never make them ashamed.[d]

2. This certainty is not a bare conjectural and probable persuasion grounded upon a fallible hope;[e] but an infallible assurance of

a. **Mic. 3:11.** The heads thereof judge for reward, and the priests thereof teach for hire, and the prophets thereof divine for money: yet will they lean upon the LORD, and say, Is not the LORD among us? none evil can come upon us. **Deut. 29:19.** … and it come to pass, when he heareth the words of this curse, that he bless himself in his heart, saying, I shall have peace, though I walk in the imagination of mine heart, to add drunkenness to thirst. **John 8:41.** Ye do the deeds of your father. Then said they to him, We be not born of fornication; we have one Father, even God.

b. **Amos 9:10.** All the sinners of my people shall die by the sword, which say, The evil shall not overtake nor prevent us. **Matt. 7:22–23.** Many will say to me in that day, Lord, Lord, have we not prophesied in thy name? and in thy name have cast out devils? and in thy name done many wonderful works? And then will I profess unto them, I never knew you: depart from me, ye that work iniquity.

c. **1 John 5:13.** These things have I written unto you that believe on the name of the Son of God; that ye may know that ye have eternal life, and that ye may believe on the name of the Son of God. **1 John 2:3.** And hereby we do know that we know him, if we keep his commandments. **1 John 3:14, 18–19, 21, 24.** We know that we have passed from death unto life, because we love the brethren. He that loveth not his brother abideth in death.… My little children, let us not love in word, neither in tongue; but in deed and in truth.… And hereby we know that we are of the truth, and shall assure our hearts before him.… Beloved, if our heart condemn us not, then have we confidence toward God.… And he that keepeth his commandments dwelleth in him, and he in him. And hereby we know that he abideth in us, by the Spirit which he hath given us.

d. **Rom. 5:2, 5.** … by whom also we have access by faith into this grace wherein we stand, and rejoice in hope of the glory of God.… And hope maketh not ashamed; because the love of God is shed abroad in our hearts by the Holy Ghost which is given unto us.

e. **Heb. 6:11, 19.** And we desire that every one of you do shew the same diligence to the full assurance of hope unto the end.… which hope we have as an anchor of the soul, both sure and stedfast, and which entereth into that within the veil.

faith founded upon the divine truth of the promises of salvation,[f] the inward evidence of those graces unto which these promises are made,[g] the testimony of the Spirit of adoption witnessing with our spirits that we are the children of God,[h] which Spirit is the earnest of our inheritance, whereby we are sealed to the day of redemption.[i]

3. This infallible assurance doth not so belong to the essence of faith, but that a true believer may wait long, and conflict with many difficulties, before he be partaker of it:[k] yet, being enabled by the Spirit to know the things which are freely given him of God, he may,

f. **Heb. 6:17–18.** Wherein God, willing more abundantly to shew unto the heirs of promise the immutability of his counsel, confirmed it by an oath: that by two immutable things, in which it was impossible for God to lie, we might have a strong consolation, who have fled for refuge to lay hold upon the hope set before us.

g. **2 Pet. 1:4–11.** … whereby are given unto us exceeding great and precious promises: that by these ye might be partakers of the divine nature, having escaped the corruption that is in the world through lust. And beside this, giving all diligence, add to your faith virtue; and to virtue knowledge; and to knowledge temperance; and to temperance patience; and to patience godliness; and to godliness brotherly kindness; and to brotherly kindness charity. For if these things be in you, and abound, they make you that ye shall neither be barren nor unfruitful in the knowledge of our Lord Jesus Christ. But he that lacketh these things is blind, and cannot see afar off, and hath forgotten that he was purged from his old sins. Wherefore the rather, brethren, give diligence to make your calling and election sure: for if ye do these things, ye shall never fall: for so an entrance shall be ministered unto you abundantly into the everlasting kingdom of our Lord and Saviour Jesus Christ. **1 John 2:3.** And hereby we do know that we know him, if we keep his commandments. **1 John 3:14.** We know that we have passed from death unto life, because we love the brethren. He that loveth not his brother abideth in death. **2 Cor. 1:12.** For our rejoicing is this, the testimony of our conscience, that in simplicity and godly sincerity, not with fleshly wisdom, but by the grace of God, we have had our conversation in the world, and more abundantly to you-ward.

h. **Rom. 8:15–16.** For ye have not received the spirit of bondage again to fear; but ye have received the Spirit of adoption, whereby we cry, Abba, Father. The Spirit itself beareth witness with our spirit, that we are the children of God.

i. **Eph. 1:13–14.** … in whom ye also trusted, after that ye heard the word of truth, the gospel of your salvation: in whom also after that ye believed, ye were sealed with that holy Spirit of promise, which is the earnest of our inheritance until the redemption of the purchased possession, unto the praise of his glory. **Eph. 4:30.** And grieve not the holy Spirit of God, whereby ye are sealed unto the day of redemption. **2 Cor. 1:21–22.** Now he which stablisheth us with you in Christ, and hath anointed us, is God; who hath also sealed us, and given the earnest of the Spirit in our hearts.

k. **1 John 5:13.** These things have I written unto you that believe on the name of the Son of God; that ye may know that ye have eternal life, and that ye may believe on the name of the Son of God.

without extraordinary revelation, in the right use of ordinary means, attain thereunto.[l] And therefore it is the duty of everyone to give all diligence to make his calling and election sure,[m] that thereby his heart may be enlarged in peace and joy in the Holy Ghost, in love and thankfulness to God, and in strength and cheerfulness in the duties of obedience, the proper fruits of this assurance;[n] so far is it from inclining men to looseness.[o]

l. **1 Cor. 2:12.** Now we have received, not the spirit of the world, but the spirit which is of God; that we might know the things that are freely given to us of God. **1 John 4:13.** Hereby know we that we dwell in him, and he in us, because he hath given us of his Spirit. **Heb. 6:11–12.** And we desire that every one of you do shew the same diligence to the full assurance of hope unto the end: that ye be not slothful, but followers of them who through faith and patience inherit the promises. **Eph. 3:17–18.** … that Christ may dwell in your hearts by faith; that ye, being rooted and grounded in love, may be able to comprehend with all saints what is the breadth, and length, and depth, and height.

m. **2 Pet. 1:10.** Wherefore the rather, brethren, give diligence to make your calling and election sure: for if ye do these things, ye shall never fall.

n. **Rom. 5:1–2, 5.** Therefore being justified by faith, we have peace with God through our Lord Jesus Christ: by whom also we have access by faith into this grace wherein we stand, and rejoice in hope of the glory of God.… And hope maketh not ashamed; because the love of God is shed abroad in our hearts by the Holy Ghost which is given unto us. **Rom. 14:17.** For the kingdom of God is not meat and drink; but righteousness, and peace, and joy in the Holy Ghost. **Rom. 15:13.** Now the God of hope fill you with all joy and peace in believing, that ye may abound in hope, through the power of the Holy Ghost. **Eph. 1:3–4.** Blessed be the God and Father of our Lord Jesus Christ, who hath blessed us with all spiritual blessings in heavenly places in Christ: according as he hath chosen us in him before the foundation of the world, that we should be holy and without blame before him in love. **Ps. 4:6–7.** There be many that say, Who will shew us any good? LORD, lift thou up the light of thy countenance upon us.… Thou hast put gladness in my heart, more than in the time that their corn and their wine increased. **Ps. 119:32.** I will run the way of thy commandments, when thou shalt enlarge my heart.

o. **1 John 2:1–2.** My little children, these things write I unto you, that ye sin not. And if any man sin, we have an advocate with the Father, Jesus Christ the righteous: and he is the propitiation for our sins: and not for ours only, but also for the sins of the whole world. **Rom. 6:1–2.** What shall we say then? Shall we continue in sin, that grace may abound? God forbid. How shall we, that are dead to sin, live any longer therein? **Titus 2:11–12, 14.** For the grace of God that bringeth salvation hath appeared to all men, teaching us that, denying ungodliness and worldly lusts, we should live soberly, righteously, and godly, in this present world.… who gave himself for us, that he might redeem us from all iniquity, and purify unto himself a peculiar people, zealous of good works. **2 Cor. 7:1.** Having therefore these promises, dearly beloved, let us cleanse ourselves from all filthiness of the flesh and spirit, perfecting holiness in the fear of God. **Rom. 8:1, 12.** There is therefore now no condemnation to them

4. True believers may have the assurance of their salvation divers ways shaken, diminished, and intermitted; as, by negligence in preserving of it, by falling into some special sin which woundeth the conscience and grieveth the Spirit; by some sudden or vehement temptation, by God's withdrawing the light of his countenance, and suffering even such as fear him to walk in darkness and to have no light:[p] yet are they never utterly destitute of that seed of God, and life of faith, that love of Christ and the brethren, that sincerity of heart, and conscience of duty, out of which, by the operation of the Spirit, this assurance may, in due time, be revived;[q] and by the which, in the meantime, they are supported from utter despair.[r]

which are in Christ Jesus, who walk not after the flesh, but after the Spirit.... Therefore, brethren, we are debtors, not to the flesh, to live after the flesh. **1 John 3:2–3.** Beloved, now are we the sons of God, and it doth not yet appear what we shall be: but we know that, when he shall appear, we shall be like him; for we shall see him as he is. And every man that hath this hope in him purifieth himself, even as he is pure. **Ps. 130:4.** But there is forgiveness with thee, that thou mayest be feared. **1 John 1:6–7.** If we say that we have fellowship with him, and walk in darkness, we lie, and do not the truth: but if we walk in the light, as he is in the light, we have fellowship one with another, and the blood of Jesus Christ his Son cleanseth us from all sin.

p. **Ps. 51:8, 12, 14.** Make me to hear joy and gladness; that the bones which thou hast broken may rejoice.... Restore unto me the joy of thy salvation; and uphold me with thy free spirit.... Deliver me from bloodguiltiness, O God, thou God of my salvation: and my tongue shall sing aloud of thy righteousness. **Eph. 4:30–31.** And grieve not the holy Spirit of God, whereby ye are sealed unto the day of redemption. Let all bitterness, and wrath, and anger, and clamour, and evil speaking, be put away from you, with all malice. **Ps. 77:1–10.** I cried unto God with my voice, even unto God with my voice; and he gave ear unto me.... Will the Lord cast off for ever? and will he be favourable no more? Is his mercy clean gone for ever? doth his promise fail for evermore? Hath God forgotten to be gracious? hath he in anger shut up his tender mercies? Selah. And I said, This is my infirmity: but I will remember the years of the right hand of the most High. **Ps. 31:22.** For I said in my haste, I am cut off from before thine eyes: nevertheless thou heardest the voice of my supplications when I cried unto thee. **Cf. Matt. 26:69–72 and Luke 22:31–34.**

q. **1 John 3:9.** Whosoever is born of God doth not commit sin; for his seed remaineth in him: and he cannot sin, because he is born of God. **Luke 22:32.** But I have prayed for thee, that thy faith fail not: and when thou art converted, strengthen thy brethren. **Ps. 51:8, 12.** Make me to hear joy and gladness; that the bones which thou hast broken may rejoice.... Restore unto me the joy of thy salvation; and uphold me with thy free spirit. **See Ps. 73:15.**

r. **Mic. 7:7–9.** Therefore I will look unto the LORD; I will wait for the God of my salvation: my God will hear me. Rejoice not against me, O mine enemy: when I fall, I shall arise; when I sit in darkness, the LORD shall be a light unto me. I will bear the indignation of the LORD, because I have sinned against him, until he plead my cause,

Chapter 19
Of the Law of God

1. God gave to Adam a law, as a covenant of works, by which he bound him and all his posterity to personal, entire, exact, and perpetual obedience, promised life upon the fulfilling, and threatened death upon the breach of it, and endued him with power and ability to keep it.[a]

and execute judgment for me: he will bring me forth to the light, and I shall behold his righteousness. **Jer. 32:40.** And I will make an everlasting covenant with them, that I will not turn away from them, to do them good; but I will put my fear in their hearts, that they will not depart from me. **Isa. 54:7–14.** For a small moment have I forsaken thee; but with great mercies will I gather thee. In a little wrath I hid my face from thee for a moment; but with everlasting kindness will I have mercy on thee, saith the LORD thy Redeemer.… For the mountains shall depart, and the hills be removed; but my kindness shall not depart from thee, neither shall the covenant of my peace be removed, saith the LORD that hath mercy on thee.… In righteousness shalt thou be established: thou shalt be far from oppression; for thou shalt not fear: and from terror; for it shall not come near thee. **2 Cor. 4:8–10.** We are troubled on every side, yet not distressed; we are perplexed, but not in despair; persecuted, but not forsaken; cast down, but not destroyed; always bearing about in the body the dying of the Lord Jesus, that the life also of Jesus might be made manifest in our body.

a. **Gen. 1:26–27.** And God said, Let us make man in our image, after our likeness: and let them have dominion over the fish of the sea, and over the fowl of the air, and over the cattle, and over all the earth, and over every creeping thing that creepeth upon the earth. So God created man in his own image, in the image of God created he him; male and female created he them. **Gen. 2:17.** But of the tree of the knowledge of good and evil, thou shalt not eat of it: for in the day that thou eatest thereof thou shalt surely die. **Eph. 4:24.** … and that ye put on the new man, which after God is created in righteousness and true holiness. **Rom. 2:14–15.** For when the Gentiles, which have not the law, do by nature the things contained in the law, these, having not the law, are a law unto themselves: which shew the work of the law written in their hearts, their conscience also bearing witness, and their thoughts the mean while accusing or else excusing one another. **Rom. 10:5.** For Moses describeth the righteousness which is of the law, That the man which doeth those things shall live by them. **Rom. 5:12, 19.** Wherefore, as by one man sin entered into the world, and death by sin; and so death passed upon all men, for that all have sinned … For as by one man's disobedience many were made sinners, so by the obedience of one shall many be made righteous. **Gal. 3:10, 12.** For as many as are of the works of the law are under the curse: for it is written, Cursed is every one that continueth not in all things which are written in the book of the law to do them.… And the law is not of faith: but, The man that doeth them shall live in them. **Eccl. 7:29.** Lo, this only have I found, that God hath made man upright; but they have sought out many inventions.

2. This law, after his fall, continued to be a perfect rule of righteousness; and, as such, was delivered by God upon Mount Sinai, in ten commandments, and written in two tables:[b] the first four commandments containing our duty towards God; and the other six, our duty to man.[c]

b. **James 1:25.** But whoso looketh into the perfect law of liberty, and continueth therein, he being not a forgetful hearer, but a doer of the work, this man shall be blessed in his deed. **James 2:8, 10–12.** If ye fulfil the royal law according to the scripture, Thou shalt love thy neighbour as thyself, ye do well.... For whosoever shall keep the whole law, and yet offend in one point, he is guilty of all. For he that said, Do not commit adultery, said also, Do not kill. Now if thou commit no adultery, yet if thou kill, thou art become a transgressor of the law. So speak ye, and so do, as they that shall be judged by the law of liberty. **Rom. 3:19.** Now we know that what things soever the law saith, it saith to them who are under the law: that every mouth may be stopped, and all the world may become guilty before God. **Rom. 13:8–9.** Owe no man any thing, but to love one another: for he that loveth another hath fulfilled the law. For this, Thou shalt not commit adultery, Thou shalt not kill, Thou shalt not steal, Thou shalt not bear false witness, Thou shalt not covet; and if there be any other commandment, it is briefly comprehended in this saying, namely, Thou shalt love thy neighbour as thyself. **Deut. 5:32.** Ye shall observe to do therefore as the LORD your God hath commanded you: ye shall not turn aside to the right hand or to the left. **Deut. 10:4.** And he wrote on the tables, according to the first writing, the ten commandments, which the LORD spake unto you in the mount out of the midst of the fire in the day of the assembly: and the LORD gave them unto me. **Ex. 34:1.** And the LORD said unto Moses, Hew thee two tables of stone like unto the first: and I will write upon these tables the words that were in the first tables, which thou brakest.

c. **Ex. 20:3–17.** Thou shalt have no other gods before me. Thou shalt not make unto thee any graven image, or any likeness of any thing that is in heaven above, or that is in the earth beneath, or that is in the water under the earth: thou shalt not bow down thyself to them, nor serve them: for I the LORD thy God am a jealous God, visiting the iniquity of the fathers upon the children unto the third and fourth generation of them that hate me; and shewing mercy unto thousands of them that love me, and keep my commandments. Thou shalt not take the name of the LORD thy God in vain; for the LORD will not hold him guiltless that taketh his name in vain. Remember the sabbath day, to keep it holy. Six days shalt thou labour, and do all thy work: but the seventh day is the sabbath of the LORD thy God: in it thou shalt not do any work, thou, nor thy son, nor thy daughter, thy manservant, nor thy maidservant, nor thy cattle, nor thy stranger that is within thy gates: for in six days the LORD made heaven and earth, the sea, and all that in them is, and rested the seventh day: wherefore the LORD blessed the sabbath day, and hallowed it. Honour thy father and thy mother: that thy days may be long upon the land which the LORD thy God giveth thee. Thou shalt not kill. Thou shalt not commit adultery. Thou shalt not steal. Thou shalt not bear false witness against thy neighbour. Thou shalt not covet thy neighbour's house, thou shalt not covet thy neighbour's wife, nor his manservant, nor his maidservant, nor his ox, nor his ass, nor any thing that is thy neighbour's. **Matt. 22:37–40.** Jesus said unto him, Thou shalt love the Lord thy God with all thy heart, and with all thy soul, and with all

3. Beside this law, commonly called moral, God was pleased to give to the people of Israel, as a church under age, ceremonial laws, containing several typical ordinances, partly of worship, prefiguring Christ, his graces, actions, sufferings, and benefits;[d] and partly, holding forth divers instructions of moral duties.[e] All which ceremonial

thy mind. This is the first and great commandment. And the second is like unto it, Thou shalt love thy neighbour as thyself. On these two commandments hang all the law and the prophets.

d. **Heb. 10:1.** For the law having a shadow of good things to come, and not the very image of the things, can never with those sacrifices which they offered year by year continually make the comers thereunto perfect. **Gal. 4:1–3.** Now I say, That the heir, as long as he is a child, differeth nothing from a servant, though he be lord of all; but is under tutors and governors until the time appointed of the father. Even so we, when we were children, were in bondage under the elements of the world. **Col. 2:17.** … which are a shadow of things to come; but the body is of Christ. **Heb. 9:1–28.** Then verily the first covenant had also ordinances of divine service, and a worldly sanctuary. For there was a tabernacle made; the first, wherein was the candlestick, and the table, and the shewbread; which is called the sanctuary. And after the second veil, the tabernacle which is called the Holiest of all.… Now when these things were thus ordained, the priests went always into the first tabernacle, accomplishing the service of God. But into the second went the high priest alone once every year, not without blood, which he offered for himself, and for the errors of the people: the Holy Ghost this signifying, that the way into the holiest of all was not yet made manifest, while as the first tabernacle was yet standing: which was a figure for the time then present, in which were offered both gifts and sacrifices, that could not make him that did the service perfect, as pertaining to the conscience; which stood only in meats and drinks, and divers washings, and carnal ordinances, imposed on them until the time of reformation. But Christ being come an high priest of good things to come, by a greater and more perfect tabernacle, not made with hands, that is to say, not of this building; neither by the blood of goats and calves, but by his own blood he entered in once into the holy place, having obtained eternal redemption for us.… It was therefore necessary that the patterns of things in the heavens should be purified with these; but the heavenly things themselves with better sacrifices than these. For Christ is not entered into the holy places made with hands, which are the figures of the true; but into heaven itself, now to appear in the presence of God for us.…

e. **Lev. 19:9–10, 19, 23, 27.** And when ye reap the harvest of your land, thou shalt not wholly reap the corners of thy field, neither shalt thou gather the gleanings of thy harvest. And thou shalt not glean thy vineyard, neither shalt thou gather every grape of thy vineyard; thou shalt leave them for the poor and stranger: I am the LORD your God.… Ye shall keep my statutes. Thou shalt not let thy cattle gender with a diverse kind: thou shalt not sow thy field with mingled seed: neither shall a garment mingled of linen and woollen come upon thee.… And when ye shall come into the land, and shall have planted all manner of trees for food, then ye shall count the fruit thereof as uncircumcised: three years shall it be as uncircumcised unto you: it shall not be eaten of.… Ye shall not round the corners of your heads, neither shalt thou mar the

laws are now abrogated, under the new testament.[f]

4. To them also, as a body politic, he gave sundry judicial laws, which expired together with the State of that people; not obliging

corners of thy beard. **Deut. 24:19–21.** When thou cuttest down thine harvest in thy field, and hast forgot a sheaf in the field, thou shalt not go again to fetch it: it shall be for the stranger, for the fatherless, and for the widow: that the LORD thy God may bless thee in all the work of thine hands. When thou beatest thine olive tree, thou shalt not go over the boughs again: it shall be for the stranger, for the fatherless, and for the widow. When thou gatherest the grapes of thy vineyard, thou shalt not glean it afterward: it shall be for the stranger, for the fatherless, and for the widow. **See 1 Cor. 5:7; 2 Cor. 6:17; Jude 23.**

f. **Col. 2:14, 16–17.** … blotting out the handwriting of ordinances that was against us, which was contrary to us, and took it out of the way, nailing it to his cross.… Let no man therefore judge you in meat, or in drink, or in respect of an holyday, or of the new moon, or of the sabbath days: which are a shadow of things to come; but the body is of Christ. **Dan. 9:27.** And he shall confirm the covenant with many for one week: and in the midst of the week he shall cause the sacrifice and the oblation to cease, and for the overspreading of abominations he shall make it desolate, even until the consummation, and that determined shall be poured upon the desolate. **Eph. 2:15–16.** … having abolished in his flesh the enmity, even the law of commandments contained in ordinances; for to make in himself of twain one new man, so making peace; and that he might reconcile both unto God in one body by the cross, having slain the enmity thereby. **Heb. 9:10.** … which stood only in meats and drinks, and divers washings, and carnal ordinances, imposed on them until the time of reformation. **Acts 10:9–16.** On the morrow, as they went on their journey, and drew nigh unto the city, Peter went up upon the housetop to pray about the sixth hour: and he became very hungry, and would have eaten: but while they made ready, he fell into a trance, and saw heaven opened, and a certain vessel descending unto him, as it had been a great sheet knit at the four corners, and let down to the earth: wherein were all manner of fourfooted beasts of the earth, and wild beasts, and creeping things, and fowls of the air. And there came a voice to him, Rise, Peter; kill, and eat. But Peter said, Not so, Lord; for I have never eaten any thing that is common or unclean. And the voice spake unto him again the second time, What God hath cleansed, that call not thou common. This was done thrice: and the vessel was received up again into heaven. **Acts 11:2–10.** And when Peter was come up to Jerusalem, they that were of the circumcision contended with him, saying, Thou wentest in to men uncircumcised, and didst eat with them. But Peter rehearsed the matter from the beginning, and expounded it by order unto them, saying, I was in the city of Joppa praying: and in a trance I saw a vision, A certain vessel descend, as it had been a great sheet, let down from heaven by four corners; and it came even to me: upon the which when I had fastened mine eyes, I considered, and saw fourfooted beasts of the earth, and wild beasts, and creeping things, and fowls of the air. And I heard a voice saying unto me, Arise, Peter; slay and eat. But I said, Not so, Lord: for nothing common or unclean hath at any time entered into my mouth. But the voice answered me again from heaven, What God hath cleansed, that call not thou common. And this was done three times: and all were drawn up again into heaven.

any other now, further than the general equity thereof may require.[g]

5. The moral law doth forever bind all, as well justified persons as others, to the obedience thereof;[h] and that, not only in regard of the matter contained in it, but also in respect of the authority of God the

---

g. **Ex. 21:1–23:19.** Now these are the judgments which thou shalt set before them. If thou buy an Hebrew servant, six years he shall serve: and in the seventh he shall go out free for nothing.… He that smiteth a man, so that he die, shall be surely put to death.… And he that curseth his father, or his mother, shall surely be put to death.… If an ox gore a man or a woman, that they die: then the ox shall be surely stoned, and his flesh shall not be eaten; but the owner of the ox shall be quit.… If a man shall steal an ox, or a sheep, and kill it, or sell it; he shall restore five oxen for an ox, and four sheep for a sheep.… And if a man entice a maid that is not betrothed, and lie with her, he shall surely endow her to be his wife.… Thou shalt not suffer a witch to live.… Ye shall not afflict any widow, or fatherless child.… And ye shall be holy men unto me: neither shall ye eat any flesh that is torn of beasts in the field; ye shall cast it to the dogs. Thou shalt not raise a false report: put not thine hand with the wicked to be an unrighteous witness.… Three times thou shalt keep a feast unto me in the year.… The first of the firstfruits of thy land thou shalt bring into the house of the LORD thy God. Thou shalt not seethe a kid in his mother's milk. **Cf. Gen. 49:10 with 1 Pet. 2:13–14. 1 Cor. 9:8–10.** Say I these things as a man? or saith not the law the same also? For it is written in the law of Moses, Thou shalt not muzzle the mouth of the ox that treadeth out the corn. Doth God take care for oxen? Or saith he it altogether for our sakes? For our sakes, no doubt, this is written: that he that ploweth should plow in hope; and that he that thresheth in hope should be partaker of his hope.

h. **Rom. 13:8–10.** Owe no man any thing, but to love one another: for he that loveth another hath fulfilled the law. For this, Thou shalt not commit adultery, Thou shalt not kill, Thou shalt not steal, Thou shalt not bear false witness, Thou shalt not covet; and if there be any other commandment, it is briefly comprehended in this saying, namely, Thou shalt love thy neighbour as thyself. Love worketh no ill to his neighbour: therefore love is the fulfilling of the law. **Rom. 3:31.** Do we then make void the law through faith? God forbid: yea, we establish the law. **Rom. 7:25.** I thank God through Jesus Christ our Lord. So then with the mind I myself serve the law of God; but with the flesh the law of sin. **1 Cor. 9:21.** [I became] to them that are without law, as without law, (being not without law to God, but under the law to Christ,) that I might gain them that are without law. **Gal. 5:14.** For all the law is fulfilled in one word, even in this; Thou shalt love thy neighbour as thyself. **Eph. 6:2–3.** Honour thy father and mother; (which is the first commandment with promise;) that it may be well with thee, and thou mayest live long on the earth. **1 John 2:3–4, 7.** And hereby we do know that we know him, if we keep his commandments. He that saith, I know him, and keepeth not his commandments, is a liar, and the truth is not in him.… Brethren, I write no new commandment unto you, but an old commandment which ye had from the beginning. The old commandment is the word which ye have heard from the beginning. **Cf. Rom. 3:20; Rom. 7:7–8 and 1 John 3:4 with Rom. 6:15.**

Creator, who gave it.[i] Neither doth Christ, in the gospel, any way dissolve, but much strengthen this obligation.[k]

6. Although true believers be not under the law, as a covenant of works, to be thereby justified, or condemned;[l] yet is it of great use to

i. **Deut. 6:4–5.** Hear, O Israel: The LORD our God is one LORD: and thou shalt love the LORD thy God with all thine heart, and with all thy soul, and with all thy might. **Ex. 20:11.** For in six days the LORD made heaven and earth, the sea, and all that in them is, and rested the seventh day: wherefore the LORD blessed the sabbath day, and hallowed it. **Rom. 3:19.** Now we know that what things soever the law saith, it saith to them who are under the law: that every mouth may be stopped, and all the world may become guilty before God. **James 2:8, 10–11.** If ye fulfil the royal law according to the scripture, Thou shalt love thy neighbour as thyself, ye do well.… For whosoever shall keep the whole law, and yet offend in one point, he is guilty of all. For he that said, Do not commit adultery, said also, Do not kill. Now if thou commit no adultery, yet if thou kill, thou art become a transgressor of the law. **Matt. 19:4–6.** And he answered and said unto them, Have ye not read, that he which made them at the beginning made them male and female, and said, For this cause shall a man leave father and mother, and shall cleave to his wife: and they twain shall be one flesh? Wherefore they are no more twain, but one flesh. What therefore God hath joined together, let not man put asunder. **Gen. 17:1.** And when Abram was ninety years old and nine, the LORD appeared to Abram, and said unto him, I am the Almighty God; walk before me, and be thou perfect.

k. **Matt. 5:17–19.** Think not that I am come to destroy the law, or the prophets: I am not come to destroy, but to fulfil. For verily I say unto you, Till heaven and earth pass, one jot or one tittle shall in no wise pass from the law, till all be fulfilled. Whosoever therefore shall break one of these least commandments, and shall teach men so, he shall be called the least in the kingdom of heaven: but whosoever shall do and teach them, the same shall be called great in the kingdom of heaven. **Rom. 3:31.** Do we then make void the law through faith? God forbid: yea, we establish the law. **1 Cor. 9:21.** [I became] to them that are without law, as without law, (being not without law to God, but under the law to Christ,) that I might gain them that are without law. **Luke 16:17–18.** And it is easier for heaven and earth to pass, than one tittle of the law to fail. Whosoever putteth away his wife, and marrieth another, committeth adultery: and whosoever marrieth her that is put away from her husband committeth adultery.

l. **Rom. 6:14.** For sin shall not have dominion over you: for ye are not under the law, but under grace. **Rom.7:4.** Wherefore, my brethren, ye also are become dead to the law by the body of Christ; that ye should be married to another, even to him who is raised from the dead, that we should bring forth fruit unto God. **Gal. 2:16.** … knowing that a man is not justified by the works of the law, but by the faith of Jesus Christ, even we have believed in Jesus Christ, that we might be justified by the faith of Christ, and not by the works of the law: for by the works of the law shall no flesh be justified. **Gal. 3:13.** Christ hath redeemed us from the curse of the law, being made a curse for us: for it is written, Cursed is every one that hangeth on a tree. **Gal. 4:4–5.** But when the fulness of the time was come, God sent forth his Son, made of a woman, made under the law, to redeem them that were under the law, that we might receive

them, as well as to others; in that, as a rule of life informing them of the will of God, and their duty, it directs and binds them to walk accordingly;[m] discovering also the sinful pollutions of their nature, hearts, and lives;[n] so as, examining themselves thereby, they may come to further conviction of, humiliation for, and hatred against sin,[o]

the adoption of sons. **Acts 13:38–39.** Be it known unto you therefore, men and brethren, that through this man is preached unto you the forgiveness of sins: and by him all that believe are justified from all things, from which ye could not be justified by the law of Moses. **Rom. 8:1, 33.** There is therefore now no condemnation to them which are in Christ Jesus, who walk not after the flesh, but after the Spirit.… Who shall lay any thing to the charge of God's elect? It is God that justifieth.

m. **Rom. 7:12, 22, 25.** Wherefore the law is holy, and the commandment holy, and just, and good.… For I delight in the law of God after the inward man.… I thank God through Jesus Christ our Lord. So then with the mind I myself serve the law of God; but with the flesh the law of sin. **Ps. 119:1–6.** Blessed are the undefiled in the way, who walk in the law of the LORD. Blessed are they that keep his testimonies, and that seek him with the whole heart. They also do no iniquity: they walk in his ways. Thou hast commanded us to keep thy precepts diligently. O that my ways were directed to keep thy statutes! Then shall I not be ashamed, when I have respect unto all thy commandments. **1 Cor. 7:19.** Circumcision is nothing, and uncircumcision is nothing, but the keeping of the commandments of God. **Gal. 5:14–23.** For all the law is fulfilled in one word, even in this; Thou shalt love thy neighbour as thyself. But if ye bite and devour one another, take heed that ye be not consumed one of another. This I say then, Walk in the Spirit, and ye shall not fulfil the lust of the flesh. For the flesh lusteth against the Spirit, and the Spirit against the flesh: and these are contrary the one to the other: so that ye cannot do the things that ye would. But if ye be led of the Spirit, ye are not under the law. Now the works of the flesh are manifest, which are these; Adultery, fornication, uncleanness, lasciviousness, idolatry, witchcraft, hatred, variance, emulations, wrath, strife, seditions, heresies, envyings, murders, drunkenness, revellings, and such like: of the which I tell you before, as I have also told you in time past, that they which do such things shall not inherit the kingdom of God. But the fruit of the Spirit is love, joy, peace, longsuffering, gentleness, goodness, faith, meekness, temperance: against such there is no law.

n. **Rom. 7:7, 13.** What shall we say then? Is the law sin? God forbid. Nay, I had not known sin, but by the law: for I had not known lust, except the law had said, Thou shalt not covet.… Was then that which is good made death unto me? God forbid. But sin, that it might appear sin, working death in me by that which is good; that sin by the commandment might become exceeding sinful. **Rom. 3:20.** Therefore by the deeds of the law there shall no flesh be justified in his sight: for by the law is the knowledge of sin.

o. **James 1:23–25.** For if any be a hearer of the word, and not a doer, he is like unto a man beholding his natural face in a glass: for he beholdeth himself, and goeth his way, and straightway forgetteth what manner of man he was. But whoso looketh into the perfect law of liberty, and continueth therein, he being not a forgetful hearer, but a doer of the work, this man shall be blessed in his deed. **Rom. 7:9, 14, 24.** For I was alive without the law once: but when the commandment came, sin revived, and

together with a clearer sight of the need they have of Christ, and the perfection of his obedience.[p] It is likewise of use to the regenerate, to restrain their corruptions, in that it forbids sin:[q] and the threatenings of it serve to show what even their sins deserve; and what afflictions, in this life, they may expect for them, although freed from the curse thereof threatened in the law.[r] The promises of it, in like manner, show them God's approbation of obedience, and what blessings they may expect upon the performance thereof:[s] although not as due to

I died.... For we know that the law is spiritual: but I am carnal, sold under sin.... O wretched man that I am! who shall deliver me from the body of this death?

p. **Gal. 3:24.** Wherefore the law was our schoolmaster to bring us unto Christ, that we might be justified by faith. **Rom. 7:24–25.** O wretched man that I am! who shall deliver me from the body of this death? I thank God through Jesus Christ our Lord. So then with the mind I myself serve the law of God; but with the flesh the law of sin. **Rom. 8:3–4.** For what the law could not do, in that it was weak through the flesh, God sending his own Son in the likeness of sinful flesh, and for sin, condemned sin in the flesh: that the righteousness of the law might be fulfilled in us, who walk not after the flesh, but after the Spirit.

q. **James 2:11–12.** For he that said, Do not commit adultery, said also, Do not kill. Now if thou commit no adultery, yet if thou kill, thou art become a transgressor of the law. So speak ye, and so do, as they that shall be judged by the law of liberty. **Ps. 119:101, 104, 128.** I have refrained my feet from every evil way, that I might keep thy word.... Through thy precepts I get understanding: therefore I hate every false way.... Therefore I esteem all thy precepts concerning all things to be right; and I hate every false way.

r. **Ezra 9:13–14.** And after all that is come upon us for our evil deeds, and for our great trespass, seeing that thou our God hast punished us less than our iniquities deserve, and hast given us such deliverance as this; should we again break thy commandments, and join in affinity with the people of these abominations? wouldest not thou be angry with us till thou hadst consumed us, so that there should be no remnant nor escaping? **Ps. 89:30–34.** If his children forsake my law, and walk not in my judgments; if they break my statutes, and keep not my commandments; then will I visit their transgression with the rod, and their iniquity with stripes. Nevertheless my lovingkindness will I not utterly take from him, nor suffer my faithfulness to fail. My covenant will I not break, nor alter the thing that is gone out of my lips. **Gal. 3:13.** Christ hath redeemed us from the curse of the law, being made a curse for us: for it is written, Cursed is every one that hangeth on a tree.

s. **Ex. 19:5–6.** Now therefore, if ye will obey my voice indeed, and keep my covenant, then ye shall be a peculiar treasure unto me above all people: for all the earth is mine: and ye shall be unto me a kingdom of priests, and an holy nation. These are the words which thou shalt speak unto the children of Israel. **Deut. 5:33.** Ye shall walk in all the ways which the Lord your God hath commanded you, that ye may live, and that it may be well with you, and that ye may prolong your days in the land which ye shall possess. **Lev. 18:5.** Ye shall therefore keep my statutes, and my judgments: which if a man do, he shall live in them: I am the Lord. **Matt. 19:17.** And he said

them by the law as a covenant of works.^t So as, a man's doing good, and refraining from evil, because the law encourageth to the one, and deterreth from the other, is no evidence of his being under the law; and, not under grace.^u

unto him, Why callest thou me good? there is none good but one, that is, God: but if thou wilt enter into life, keep the commandments. **Lev. 26:1–13.** … If ye walk in my statutes, and keep my commandments, and do them; then I will give you rain in due season, and the land shall yield her increase, and the trees of the field shall yield their fruit. And your threshing shall reach unto the vintage, and the vintage shall reach unto the sowing time: and ye shall eat your bread to the full, and dwell in your land safely. And I will give peace in the land, and ye shall lie down, and none shall make you afraid: and I will rid evil beasts out of the land, neither shall the sword go through your land. And ye shall chase your enemies, and they shall fall before you by the sword.… For I will have respect unto you, and make you fruitful, and multiply you, and establish my covenant with you.… And I will walk among you, and will be your God, and ye shall be my people.… **2 Cor. 6:16.** And what agreement hath the temple of God with idols? for ye are the temple of the living God; as God hath said, I will dwell in them, and walk in them; and I will be their God, and they shall be my people. **Eph. 6:2–3.** Honour thy father and mother; (which is the first commandment with promise;) that it may be well with thee, and thou mayest live long on the earth. **Ps. 19:11.** Moreover by them is thy servant warned: and in keeping of them there is great reward. **Ps. 37:11.** But the meek shall inherit the earth; and shall delight themselves in the abundance of peace. **Matt. 5:5.** Blessed are the meek: for they shall inherit the earth.

t. **Gal. 2:16.** … knowing that a man is not justified by the works of the law, but by the faith of Jesus Christ, even we have believed in Jesus Christ, that we might be justified by the faith of Christ, and not by the works of the law: for by the works of the law shall no flesh be justified. **Luke 17:10.** So likewise ye, when ye shall have done all those things which are commanded you, say, We are unprofitable servants: we have done that which was our duty to do.

u. **Rom. 6:12–15.** Let not sin therefore reign in your mortal body, that ye should obey it in the lusts thereof. Neither yield ye your members as instruments of unrighteousness unto sin: but yield yourselves unto God, as those that are alive from the dead, and your members as instruments of righteousness unto God. For sin shall not have dominion over you: for ye are not under the law, but under grace. What then? shall we sin, because we are not under the law, but under grace? God forbid. **1 Pet. 3:8–12.** Finally, be ye all of one mind, having compassion one of another, love as brethren, be pitiful, be courteous: not rendering evil for evil, or railing for railing: but contrariwise blessing; knowing that ye are thereunto called, that ye should inherit a blessing. For he that will love life, and see good days, let him refrain his tongue from evil, and his lips that they speak no guile: let him eschew evil, and do good; let him seek peace, and ensue it. For the eyes of the Lord are over the righteous, and his ears are open unto their prayers: but the face of the Lord is against them that do evil. And who is he that will harm you, if ye be followers of that which is good? **With Ps. 34:12– 16.** What man is he that desireth life, and loveth many days, that he may see good? Keep thy tongue from evil, and thy lips from speaking guile. Depart from evil, and do

7. Neither are the forementioned uses of the law contrary to the grace of the gospel, but do sweetly comply with it;[w] the Spirit of Christ subduing and enabling the will of man to do that freely, and cheerfully, which the will of God, revealed in the law, requireth to be done.[x]

Chapter 20
Of Christian Liberty
and Liberty of Conscience

1. The liberty which Christ hath purchased for believers under the gospel consists in their freedom from the guilt of sin, the condemning wrath of God, the curse of the moral law;[a] and, in their

good; seek peace, and pursue it. The eyes of the LORD are upon the righteous, and his ears are open unto their cry. The face of the LORD is against them that do evil, to cut off the remembrance of them from the earth. **Heb. 12:28–29.** Wherefore we receiving a kingdom which cannot be moved, let us have grace, whereby we may serve God acceptably with reverence and godly fear: for our God is a consuming fire.

w. **Rom. 3:31.** Do we then make void the law through faith? God forbid: yea, we establish the law. **Gal. 3:21.** Is the law then against the promises of God? God forbid: for if there had been a law given which could have given life, verily righteousness should have been by the law. **Titus 2:11–14.** For the grace of God that bringeth salvation hath appeared to all men, teaching us that, denying ungodliness and worldly lusts, we should live soberly, righteously, and godly, in this present world; looking for that blessed hope, and the glorious appearing of the great God and our Saviour Jesus Christ; who gave himself for us, that he might redeem us from all iniquity, and purify unto himself a peculiar people, zealous of good works.

x. **Ezek. 36:27.** And I will put my spirit within you, and cause you to walk in my statutes, and ye shall keep my judgments, and do them. **Heb. 8:10.** For this is the covenant that I will make with the house of Israel after those days, saith the Lord; I will put my laws into their mind, and write them in their hearts: and I will be to them a God, and they shall be to me a people. **With Jer. 31:33.** But this shall be the covenant that I will make with the house of Israel; After those days, saith the LORD, I will put my law in their inward parts, and write it in their hearts; and will be their God, and they shall be my people. **Ps. 119:35, 47.** Make me to go in the path of thy commandments; for therein do I delight.… And I will delight myself in thy commandments, which I have loved. **Rom. 7:22.** For I delight in the law of God after the inward man.

a. **Titus 2:14.** … who gave himself for us, that he might redeem us from all iniquity, and purify unto himself a peculiar people, zealous of good works. **1 Thess. 1:10.** … and to wait for his Son from heaven, whom he raised from the dead, even

being delivered from this present evil world, bondage to Satan, and dominion of sin;[b] from the evil of afflictions, the sting of death, the victory of the grave, and everlasting damnation;[c] as also, in their free access to God,[d] and their yielding obedience unto him, not out of slavish fear, but a childlike love and willing mind.[e] All which were common also to believers under the law.[f] But, under the new testa-

Jesus, which delivered us from the wrath to come. **Gal. 3:13.** Christ hath redeemed us from the curse of the law, being made a curse for us: for it is written, Cursed is every one that hangeth on a tree.

b. **Gal. 1:4.** … who gave himself for our sins, that he might deliver us from this present evil world, according to the will of God and our Father. **Col. 1:13.** … who hath delivered us from the power of darkness, and hath translated us into the kingdom of his dear Son. **Acts 26:18.** [I send thee] to open their eyes, and to turn them from darkness to light, and from the power of Satan unto God, that they may receive forgiveness of sins, and inheritance among them which are sanctified by faith that is in me. **Rom. 6:14.** For sin shall not have dominion over you: for ye are not under the law, but under grace.

c. **Rom. 8:28.** And we know that all things work together for good to them that love God, to them who are the called according to his purpose. **Ps. 119:71.** It is good for me that I have been afflicted; that I might learn thy statutes. **2 Cor. 4:15–18.** For all things are for your sakes, that the abundant grace might through the thanksgiving of many redound to the glory of God. For which cause we faint not; but though our outward man perish, yet the inward man is renewed day by day. For our light affliction, which is but for a moment, worketh for us a far more exceeding and eternal weight of glory; while we look not at the things which are seen, but at the things which are not seen: for the things which are seen are temporal; but the things which are not seen are eternal. **1 Cor. 15:54–57.** So when this corruptible shall have put on incorruption, and this mortal shall have put on immortality, then shall be brought to pass the saying that is written, Death is swallowed up in victory. O death, where is thy sting? O grave, where is thy victory? The sting of death is sin; and the strength of sin is the law. But thanks be to God, which giveth us the victory through our Lord Jesus Christ. **Rom. 5:9.** Much more then, being now justified by his blood, we shall be saved from wrath through him. **Rom. 8:1.** There is therefore now no condemnation to them which are in Christ Jesus, who walk not after the flesh, but after the Spirit. **See 1 Thess. 1:10.**

d. **Rom. 5:1–2.** Therefore being justified by faith, we have peace with God through our Lord Jesus Christ: by whom also we have access by faith into this grace wherein we stand, and rejoice in hope of the glory of God.

e. **Rom. 8:14–15.** For as many as are led by the Spirit of God, they are the sons of God. For ye have not received the spirit of bondage again to fear; but ye have received the Spirit of adoption, whereby we cry, Abba, Father. **Gal. 4:6.** And because ye are sons, God hath sent forth the Spirit of his Son into your hearts, crying, Abba, Father. **1 John 4:18.** There is no fear in love; but perfect love casteth out fear: because fear hath torment. He that feareth is not made perfect in love.

f. **Gal. 3:8–9, 14.** And the scripture, foreseeing that God would justify the heathen through faith, preached before the gospel unto Abraham, saying, In thee shall all

ment, the liberty of Christians is further enlarged, in their freedom from the yoke of the ceremonial law, to which the Jewish church was subjected;g and in greater boldness of access to the throne of grace,h

nations be blessed. So then they which be of faith are blessed with faithful Abraham.… that the blessing of Abraham might come on the Gentiles through Jesus Christ; that we might receive the promise of the Spirit through faith. **Rom. 4:6–8.** Even as David also describeth the blessedness of the man, unto whom God imputeth righteousness without works, saying, Blessed are they whose iniquities are forgiven, and whose sins are covered. Blessed is the man to whom the Lord will not impute sin. **1 Cor. 10:3–4.** And [our fathers] did all eat the same spiritual meat; and did all drink the same spiritual drink: for they drank of that spiritual Rock that followed them: and that Rock was Christ. **Heb. 11:1–40.** Now faith is the substance of things hoped for, the evidence of things not seen. For by it the elders obtained a good report.… By faith Abel offered unto God a more excellent sacrifice than Cain, by which he obtained witness that he was righteous, God testifying of his gifts: and by it he being dead yet speaketh.… By faith Noah, being warned of God of things not seen as yet, moved with fear, prepared an ark to the saving of his house; by the which he condemned the world, and became heir of the righteousness which is by faith. By faith Abraham, when he was called to go out into a place which he should after receive for an inheritance, obeyed; and he went out, not knowing whither he went.… By faith Moses, when he was come to years, refused to be called the son of Pharaoh's daughter; choosing rather to suffer affliction with the people of God, than to enjoy the pleasures of sin for a season; esteeming the reproach of Christ greater riches than the treasures in Egypt: for he had respect unto the recompence of the reward.… And these all, having obtained a good report through faith, received not the promise: God having provided some better thing for us, that they without us should not be made perfect.

g. **Gal. 4:1–7.** Now I say, That the heir, as long as he is a child, differeth nothing from a servant, though he be lord of all; but is under tutors and governors until the time appointed of the father. Even so we, when we were children, were in bondage under the elements of the world: but when the fulness of the time was come, God sent forth his Son, made of a woman, made under the law, to redeem them that were under the law, that we might receive the adoption of sons. And because ye are sons, God hath sent forth the Spirit of his Son into your hearts, crying, Abba, Father. Wherefore thou art no more a servant, but a son; and if a son, then an heir of God through Christ. **Gal. 5:1.** Stand fast therefore in the liberty wherewith Christ hath made us free, and be not entangled again with the yoke of bondage. **Acts 15:10–11.** Now therefore why tempt ye God, to put a yoke upon the neck of the disciples, which neither our fathers nor we were able to bear? But we believe that through the grace of the Lord Jesus Christ we shall be saved, even as they.

h. **Heb. 4:14–16.** Seeing then that we have a great high priest, that is passed into the heavens, Jesus the Son of God, let us hold fast our profession. For we have not an high priest which cannot be touched with the feeling of our infirmities; but was in all points tempted like as we are, yet without sin. Let us therefore come boldly unto the throne of grace, that we may obtain mercy, and find grace to help in time of need. **Heb. 10:19–22.** Having therefore, brethren, boldness to enter into the holiest by the blood of Jesus, by a new and living way, which he hath consecrated for us, through the

and in fuller communications of the free Spirit of God, than believers under the law did ordinarily partake of.[i]

2. God alone is Lord of the conscience,[k] and hath left it free from the doctrines and commandments of men, which are, in anything, contrary to his Word; or beside it, if matters of faith, or worship.[l] So

veil, that is to say, his flesh; and having an high priest over the house of God; let us draw near with a true heart in full assurance of faith, having our hearts sprinkled from an evil conscience, and our bodies washed with pure water.

i. **John 7:38–39.** He that believeth on me, as the scripture hath said, out of his belly shall flow rivers of living water. (But this spake he of the Spirit, which they that believe on him should receive: for the Holy Ghost was not yet given; because that Jesus was not yet glorified.) **Acts 2:17–18.** And it shall come to pass in the last days, saith God, I will pour out of my Spirit upon all flesh: and your sons and your daughters shall prophesy, and your young men shall see visions, and your old men shall dream dreams: and on my servants and on my handmaidens I will pour out in those days of my Spirit; and they shall prophesy. **2 Cor. 3:8, 13, 17–18.** How shall not the ministration of the spirit be rather glorious?… And not as Moses, which put a vail over his face, that the children of Israel could not stedfastly look to the end of that which is abolished.… Now the Lord is that Spirit: and where the Spirit of the Lord is, there is liberty. But we all, with open face beholding as in a glass the glory of the Lord, are changed into the same image from glory to glory, even as by the Spirit of the Lord. **See Jer. 31:31–34.**

k. **James 4:12.** There is one lawgiver, who is able to save and to destroy: who art thou that judgest another? **Rom. 14:4, 10.** Who art thou that judgest another man's servant? to his own master he standeth or falleth. Yea, he shall be holden up: for God is able to make him stand.… But why dost thou judge thy brother? or why dost thou set at nought thy brother? for we shall all stand before the judgment seat of Christ. **1 Cor. 10:29.** Conscience, I say, not thine own, but of the other: for why is my liberty judged of another man's conscience?

l. **Acts 4:19.** But Peter and John answered and said unto them, Whether it be right in the sight of God to hearken unto you more than unto God, judge ye. **Acts 5:29.** Then Peter and the other apostles answered and said, We ought to obey God rather than men. **1 Cor. 7:22–23.** For he that is called in the Lord, being a servant, is the Lord's freeman: likewise also he that is called, being free, is Christ's servant. Ye are bought with a price; be not ye the servants of men. **Matt. 15:1–6.** Then came to Jesus scribes and Pharisees, which were of Jerusalem, saying, Why do thy disciples transgress the tradition of the elders? for they wash not their hands when they eat bread. But he answered and said unto them, Why do ye also transgress the commandment of God by your tradition? For God commanded, saying, Honour thy father and mother: and, He that curseth father or mother, let him die the death. But ye say, Whosoever shall say to his father or his mother, It is a gift, by whatsoever thou mightest be profited by me; and honour not his father or his mother, he shall be free. Thus have ye made the commandment of God of none effect by your tradition. **Matt. 23:8–10.** But be not ye called Rabbi: for one is your Master, even Christ; and all ye are brethren. And call no man your father upon the earth: for one is your Father, which is in heaven. Neither be ye called masters: for one is your Master, even Christ.

that, to believe such doctrines, or to obey such commands, out of conscience, is to betray true liberty of conscience:[m] and the requiring of an implicit faith, and an absolute and blind obedience, is to destroy liberty of conscience, and reason also.[n]

3. They who, upon pretense of Christian liberty, do practice any sin, or cherish any lust, do thereby destroy the end of Christian liberty, which is, that being delivered out of the hands of our enemies, we might serve the Lord without fear, in holiness and righteousness before him, all the days of our life.[o]

2 Cor. 1:24. Not for that we have dominion over your faith, but are helpers of your joy: for by faith ye stand. **Matt. 15:9.** But in vain they do worship me, teaching for doctrines the commandments of men.

m. **Col. 2:20–23.** Wherefore if ye be dead with Christ from the rudiments of the world, why, as though living in the world, are ye subject to ordinances, (touch not; taste not; handle not; which all are to perish with the using;) after the commandments and doctrines of men? Which things have indeed a shew of wisdom in will worship, and humility, and neglecting of the body; not in any honour to the satisfying of the flesh. **Gal. 1:10.** For do I now persuade men, or God? or do I seek to please men? for if I yet pleased men, I should not be the servant of Christ. **Gal. 2:4–5.** … and that because of false brethren unawares brought in, who came in privily to spy out our liberty which we have in Christ Jesus, that they might bring us into bondage: to whom we gave place by subjection, no, not for an hour; that the truth of the gospel might continue with you. **Gal. 4:9–10.** But now, after that ye have known God, or rather are known of God, how turn ye again to the weak and beggarly elements, whereunto ye desire again to be in bondage? Ye observe days, and months, and times, and years. **Gal. 5:1.** Stand fast therefore in the liberty wherewith Christ hath made us free, and be not entangled again with the yoke of bondage.

n. **Rom. 10:17.** So then faith cometh by hearing, and hearing by the word of God. **Isa. 8:20.** To the law and to the testimony: if they speak not according to this word, it is because there is no light in them. **Acts 17:11.** These were more noble than those in Thessalonica, in that they received the word with all readiness of mind, and searched the scriptures daily, whether those things were so. **John 4:22.** Ye worship ye know not what: we know what we worship: for salvation is of the Jews. **Rev. 13:12, 16–17.** And he exerciseth all the power of the first beast before him, and causeth the earth and them which dwell therein to worship the first beast, whose deadly wound was healed.… And he causeth all, both small and great, rich and poor, free and bond, to receive a mark in their right hand, or in their foreheads: and that no man might buy or sell, save he that had the mark, or the name of the beast, or the number of his name. **Jer. 8:9.** The wise men are ashamed, they are dismayed and taken: lo, they have rejected the word of the LORD; and what wisdom is in them? **1 Pet. 3:15.** But sanctify the Lord God in your hearts: and be ready always to give an answer to every man that asketh you a reason of the hope that is in you with meekness and fear.

o. **Gal. 5:13.** For, brethren, ye have been called unto liberty; only use not liberty for an occasion to the flesh, but by love serve one another. **1 Pet. 2:16.** … as free, and not using your liberty for a cloke of maliciousness, but as the servants of God.

4. And because the powers which God hath ordained, and the liberty which Christ hath purchased, are not intended by God to destroy, but mutually to uphold and preserve one another, they who, upon pretense of Christian liberty, shall oppose any lawful power, or the lawful exercise of it, whether it be civil or ecclesiastical, resist the ordinance of God.ᵖ And, for their publishing of such opinions, or maintaining of such practices, as are contrary to the light of nature, or to the known principles of Christianity (whether concerning faith, worship, or conversation), or to the power of godliness; or, such erroneous opinions or practices, as either in their own nature, or in the manner of publishing or maintaining them, are destructive to the external peace and order which Christ hath established in the church, they may lawfully be called to account, and proceeded against, by

2 Pet. 2:19. While they promise them liberty, they themselves are the servants of corruption: for of whom a man is overcome, of the same is he brought in bondage. **Rom. 6:15.** What then? shall we sin, because we are not under the law, but under grace? God forbid. **John 8:34.** Jesus answered them, Verily, verily, I say unto you, Whosoever committeth sin is the servant of sin. **Luke 1:74–75.** ... that he would grant unto us, that we being delivered out of the hand of our enemies might serve him without fear, in holiness and righteousness before him, all the days of our life.

p. **1 Pet. 2:13–14, 16.** Submit yourselves to every ordinance of man for the Lord's sake: whether it be to the king, as supreme; or unto governors, as unto them that are sent by him for the punishment of evildoers, and for the praise of them that do well.... as free, and not using your liberty for a cloke of maliciousness, but as the servants of God. **Rom. 13:1–8.** Let every soul be subject unto the higher powers. For there is no power but of God: the powers that be are ordained of God. Whosoever therefore resisteth the power, resisteth the ordinance of God: and they that resist shall receive to themselves damnation. For rulers are not a terror to good works, but to the evil. Wilt thou then not be afraid of the power? do that which is good, and thou shalt have praise of the same: for he is the minister of God to thee for good. But if thou do that which is evil, be afraid; for he beareth not the sword in vain: for he is the minister of God, a revenger to execute wrath upon him that doeth evil. Wherefore ye must needs be subject, not only for wrath, but also for conscience sake. For for this cause pay ye tribute also: for they are God's ministers, attending continually upon this very thing. Render therefore to all their dues: tribute to whom tribute is due; custom to whom custom; fear to whom fear; honour to whom honour. Owe no man any thing, but to love one another: for he that loveth another hath fulfilled the law. **Heb. 13:17.** Obey them that have the rule over you, and submit yourselves: for they watch for your souls, as they that must give account, that they may do it with joy, and not with grief: for that is unprofitable for you. **1 Thess. 5:12–13.** And we beseech you, brethren, to know them which labour among you, and are over you in the Lord, and admonish you; and to esteem them very highly in love for their work's sake. And be at peace among yourselves.

the censures of the church.[q]

q. **Rom. 1:32.** … who knowing the judgment of God, that they which commit such things are worthy of death, not only do the same, but have pleasure in them that do them. **1 Cor. 5:1, 5, 11–13.** It is reported commonly that there is fornication among you, and such fornication as is not so much as named among the Gentiles, that one should have his father's wife.… to deliver such an one unto Satan for the destruction of the flesh, that the spirit may be saved in the day of the Lord Jesus.… But now I have written unto you not to keep company, if any man that is called a brother be a fornicator, or covetous, or an idolater, or a railer, or a drunkard, or an extortioner; with such an one no not to eat. For what have I to do to judge them also that are without? do not ye judge them that are within? But them that are without God judgeth. Therefore put away from among yourselves that wicked person. **2 John 10–11.** If there come any unto you, and bring not this doctrine, receive him not into your house, neither bid him God speed: for he that biddeth him God speed is partaker of his evil deeds. **2 Thess. 3:6, 14.** Now we command you, brethren, in the name of our Lord Jesus Christ, that ye withdraw yourselves from every brother that walketh disorderly, and not after the tradition which he received of us.… And if any man obey not our word by this epistle, note that man, and have no company with him, that he may be ashamed. **1 Tim. 6:3–4.** If any man teach otherwise, and consent not to wholesome words, even the words of our Lord Jesus Christ, and to the doctrine which is according to godliness; he is proud, knowing nothing, but doting about questions and strifes of words, whereof cometh envy, strife, railings, evil surmisings. **Titus 1:10–11, 13–14.** For there are many unruly and vain talkers and deceivers, specially they of the circumcision: whose mouths must be stopped, who subvert whole houses, teaching things which they ought not, for filthy lucre's sake.… This witness is true. Wherefore rebuke them sharply, that they may be sound in the faith; not giving heed to Jewish fables, and commandments of men, that turn from the truth. **Titus 3:10.** A man that is an heretick after the first and second admonition reject. **Rom. 16:17.** Now I beseech you, brethren, mark them which cause divisions and offences contrary to the doctrine which ye have learned; and avoid them. **Matt. 18:15–17.** Moreover if thy brother shall trespass against thee, go and tell him his fault between thee and him alone: if he shall hear thee, thou hast gained thy brother. But if he will not hear thee, then take with thee one or two more, that in the mouth of two or three witnesses every word may be established. And if he shall neglect to hear them, tell it unto the church: but if he neglect to hear the church, let him be unto thee as an heathen man and a publican. **1 Tim. 1:19–20.** … holding faith, and a good conscience; which some having put away concerning faith have made shipwreck: of whom is Hymenaeus and Alexander; whom I have delivered unto Satan, that they may learn not to blaspheme. **Rev. 2:2, 14–15, 20.** I know thy works, and thy labour, and thy patience, and how thou canst not bear them which are evil: and thou hast tried them which say they are apostles, and are not, and hast found them liars.… But I have a few things against thee, because thou hast there them that hold the doctrine of Balaam, who taught Balac to cast a stumblingblock before the children of Israel, to eat things sacrificed unto idols, and to commit fornication. So hast thou also them that hold the doctrine of the Nicolaitanes, which thing I hate.… Notwithstanding I have a few things against thee, because thou sufferest that woman Jezebel, which calleth herself a prophetess, to teach and to seduce my servants to commit fornication, and to eat things sacrificed unto idols.

Chapter 21
Of Religious Worship and the Sabbath Day

1. The light of nature showeth that there is a God, who hath lordship and sovereignty over all, is good, and doth good unto all, and is therefore to be feared, loved, praised, called upon, trusted in, and served, with all the heart, and with all the soul, and with all the might.[a] But the acceptable way of worshiping the true God is

a. **Rom. 1:20.** For the invisible things of him from the creation of the world are clearly seen, being understood by the things that are made, even his eternal power and Godhead; so that they are without excuse. **Ps. 19:1–4a.** The heavens declare the glory of God; and the firmament sheweth his handywork. Day unto day uttereth speech, and night unto night sheweth knowledge. There is no speech nor language, where their voice is not heard. Their line is gone out through all the earth, and their words to the end of the world. **Ps. 50:6.** And the heavens shall declare his righteousness: for God is judge himself. Selah. **Ps. 97:6.** The heavens declare his righteousness, and all the people see his glory. **Ps. 145:9–12.** The LORD is good to all: and his tender mercies are over all his works. All thy works shall praise thee, O LORD; and thy saints shall bless thee. They shall speak of the glory of thy kingdom, and talk of thy power; to make known to the sons of men his mighty acts, and the glorious majesty of his kingdom. **Acts 14:17.** Nevertheless he left not himself without witness, in that he did good, and gave us rain from heaven, and fruitful seasons, filling our hearts with food and gladness. **Ps. 104:1–35.** Bless the LORD, O my soul. O LORD my God, thou art very great; thou art clothed with honour and majesty.… Who laid the foundations of the earth, that it should not be removed for ever.… He causeth the grass to grow for the cattle, and herb for the service of man: that he may bring forth food out of the earth.… O LORD, how manifold are thy works! in wisdom hast thou made them all: the earth is full of thy riches.… The glory of the LORD shall endure for ever: the LORD shall rejoice in his works. He looketh on the earth, and it trembleth: he toucheth the hills, and they smoke. I will sing unto the LORD as long as I live: I will sing praise to my God while I have my being. My meditation of him shall be sweet: I will be glad in the LORD.… **Ps. 86:8–10.** Among the gods there is none like unto thee, O Lord; neither are there any works like unto thy works. All nations whom thou hast made shall come and worship before thee, O Lord; and shall glorify thy name. For thou art great, and doest wondrous things: thou art God alone. **Ps. 95:1–6.** O come, let us sing unto the LORD: let us make a joyful noise to the rock of our salvation. Let us come before his presence with thanksgiving, and make a joyful noise unto him with psalms. For the LORD is a great God, and a great King above all gods. In his hand are the deep places of the earth: the strength of the hills is his also. The sea is his, and he made it: and his hands formed the dry land. O come, let us worship and bow down: let us kneel before the LORD our maker. **Ps. 89:5–7.** And the heavens shall praise thy wonders, O LORD: thy faithfulness also in the congregation of the saints. For who in the heaven can be compared unto the LORD? who among the sons of the mighty can be likened unto the LORD? God is greatly to be feared in the assembly of the saints, and to be had in reverence of all them that are about him. **Deut. 6:4–5.** Hear, O Israel: The LORD

instituted by himself, and so limited by his own revealed will, that he may not be worshiped according to the imaginations and devices of men, or the suggestions of Satan, under any visible representation, or any other way not prescribed in the Holy Scripture.[b]

our God is one LORD: and thou shalt love the LORD thy God with all thine heart, and with all thy soul, and with all thy might.

    b. **Deut. 12:32.** What thing soever I command you, observe to do it: thou shalt not add thereto, nor diminish from it. **Matt. 15:9.** But in vain they do worship me, teaching for doctrines the commandments of men. **Acts 17:23–25.** For as I passed by, and beheld your devotions, I found an altar with this inscription, TO THE UNKNOWN GOD. Whom therefore ye ignorantly worship, him declare I unto you. God that made the world and all things therein, seeing that he is Lord of heaven and earth, dwelleth not in temples made with hands; neither is worshipped with men's hands, as though he needed any thing, seeing he giveth to all life, and breath, and all things. **Matt. 4:9–10.** And [the devil] saith unto him, All these things will I give thee, if thou wilt fall down and worship me. Then saith Jesus unto him, Get thee hence, Satan: for it is written, Thou shalt worship the Lord thy God, and him only shalt thou serve. **Deut. 4:15–20.** Take ye therefore good heed unto yourselves; for ye saw no manner of similitude on the day that the LORD spake unto you in Horeb out of the midst of the fire: lest ye corrupt yourselves, and make you a graven image, the similitude of any figure, the likeness of male or female, the likeness of any beast that is on the earth, the likeness of any winged fowl that flieth in the air, the likeness of any thing that creepeth on the ground, the likeness of any fish that is in the waters beneath the earth: and lest thou lift up thine eyes unto heaven, and when thou seest the sun, and the moon, and the stars, even all the host of heaven, shouldest be driven to worship them, and serve them, which the LORD thy God hath divided unto all nations under the whole heaven. But the LORD hath taken you, and brought you forth out of the iron furnace, even out of Egypt, to be unto him a people of inheritance, as ye are this day. **Ex. 20:4–6.** Thou shalt not make unto thee any graven image, or any likeness of any thing that is in heaven above, or that is in the earth beneath, or that is in the water under the earth: thou shalt not bow down thyself to them, nor serve them: for I the LORD thy God am a jealous God, visiting the iniquity of the fathers upon the children unto the third and fourth generation of them that hate me; and shewing mercy unto thousands of them that love me, and keep my commandments. **John 4:23–24.** But the hour cometh, and now is, when the true worshippers shall worship the Father in spirit and in truth: for the Father seeketh such to worship him. God is a Spirit: and they that worship him must worship him in spirit and in truth. **Col. 2:18–23.** Let no man beguile you of your reward in a voluntary humility and worshipping of angels, intruding into those things which he hath not seen, vainly puffed up by his fleshly mind, and not holding the Head, from which all the body by joints and bands having nourishment ministered, and knit together, increaseth with the increase of God. Wherefore if ye be dead with Christ from the rudiments of the world, why, as though living in the world, are ye subject to ordinances, (touch not; taste not; handle not; which all are to perish with the using;) after the commandments and doctrines of men? Which things have indeed a shew of wisdom in will worship, and humility, and neglecting of the body; not in any honour to the satisfying of the flesh.

2. Religious worship is to be given to God, the Father, Son, and Holy Ghost; and to him alone;[c] not to angels, saints, or any other creature:[d] and, since the fall, not without a Mediator; nor in the mediation of any other but of Christ alone.[e]

3. Prayer, with thanksgiving, being one special part of religious worship,[f] is by God required of all men:[g] and, that it may be

c. **John 5:23.** … that all men should honour the Son, even as they honour the Father. He that honoureth not the Son honoureth not the Father which hath sent him. **Matt. 28:19.** Go ye therefore, and teach all nations, baptizing them in the name of the Father, and of the Son, and of the Holy Ghost. **2 Cor. 13:14.** The grace of the Lord Jesus Christ, and the love of God, and the communion of the Holy Ghost, be with you all. Amen. **Eph. 3:14.** For this cause I bow my knees unto the Father of our Lord Jesus Christ. **Rev. 5:11–14.** And I beheld, and I heard the voice of many angels round about the throne and the beasts and the elders: and the number of them was ten thousand times ten thousand, and thousands of thousands; saying with a loud voice, Worthy is the Lamb that was slain to receive power, and riches, and wisdom, and strength, and honour, and glory, and blessing. And every creature which is in heaven, and on the earth, and under the earth, and such as are in the sea, and all that are in them, heard I saying, Blessing, and honour, and glory, and power, be unto him that sitteth upon the throne, and unto the Lamb for ever and ever. And the four beasts said, Amen. And the four and twenty elders fell down and worshipped him that liveth for ever and ever. **Acts 10:25–26.** And as Peter was coming in, Cornelius met him, and fell down at his feet, and worshipped him. But Peter took him up, saying, Stand up; I myself also am a man.

d. **Col. 2:18.** Let no man beguile you of your reward in a voluntary humility and worshipping of angels, intruding into those things which he hath not seen, vainly puffed up by his fleshly mind. **Rev. 19:10.** And I fell at his feet to worship him. And he said unto me, See thou do it not: I am thy fellowservant, and of thy brethren that have the testimony of Jesus: worship God: for the testimony of Jesus is the spirit of prophecy. **Rom. 1:25.** … who changed the truth of God into a lie, and worshipped and served the creature more than the Creator, who is blessed for ever. Amen.

e. **John 14:6.** Jesus saith unto him, I am the way, the truth, and the life: no man cometh unto the Father, but by me. **1 Tim. 2:5.** For there is one God, and one mediator between God and men, the man Christ Jesus. **Eph. 2:18.** For through him we both have access by one Spirit unto the Father. **Col. 3:17.** And whatsoever ye do in word or deed, do all in the name of the Lord Jesus, giving thanks to God and the Father by him.

f. **Phil. 4:6.** Be careful for nothing; but in every thing by prayer and supplication with thanksgiving let your requests be made known unto God. **1 Tim. 2:1.** I exhort therefore, that, first of all, supplications, prayers, intercessions, and giving of thanks, be made for all men. **Col. 4:2.** Continue in prayer, and watch in the same with thanksgiving.

g. **Ps. 65:2.** O thou that hearest prayer, unto thee shall all flesh come. **Ps. 67:3.** Let the people praise thee, O God; let all the people praise thee. **Ps. 96:7–8.** Give unto the LORD, O ye kindreds of the people, give unto the LORD glory and strength.

accepted, it is to be made in the name of the Son,[h] by the help of his Spirit,[i] according to his will,[k] with understanding, reverence, humility, fervency, faith, love, and perseverance;[l] and, if vocal, in a known tongue.[m]

Give unto the LORD the glory due unto his name: bring an offering, and come into his courts. **Ps. 148:11–13.** Kings of the earth, and all people; princes, and all judges of the earth: both young men, and maidens; old men, and children: let them praise the name of the LORD: for his name alone is excellent; his glory is above the earth and heaven. **Isa. 55:6–7.** Seek ye the LORD while he may be found, call ye upon him while he is near: let the wicked forsake his way, and the unrighteous man his thoughts: and let him return unto the LORD, and he will have mercy upon him; and to our God, for he will abundantly pardon.

h. **John 14:13–14.** And whatsoever ye shall ask in my name, that will I do, that the Father may be glorified in the Son. If ye shall ask any thing in my name, I will do it. **1 Pet. 2:5.** Ye also, as lively stones, are built up a spiritual house, an holy priesthood, to offer up spiritual sacrifices, acceptable to God by Jesus Christ.

i. **Rom. 8:26.** Likewise the Spirit also helpeth our infirmities: for we know not what we should pray for as we ought: but the Spirit itself maketh intercession for us with groanings which cannot be uttered. **Eph. 6:18.** … praying always with all prayer and supplication in the Spirit, and watching thereunto with all perseverance and supplication for all saints.

k. **1 John 5:14.** And this is the confidence that we have in him, that, if we ask any thing according to his will, he heareth us.

l. **Ps. 47:7.** For God is the King of all the earth: sing ye praises with understanding. **Eccl. 5:1–2.** Keep thy foot when thou goest to the house of God, and be more ready to hear, than to give the sacrifice of fools: for they consider not that they do evil. Be not rash with thy mouth, and let not thine heart be hasty to utter any thing before God: for God is in heaven, and thou upon earth: therefore let thy words be few. **Heb. 12:28.** Wherefore we receiving a kingdom which cannot be moved, let us have grace, whereby we may serve God acceptably with reverence and godly fear. **Gen. 18:27.** And Abraham answered and said, Behold now, I have taken upon me to speak unto the Lord, which am but dust and ashes. **James 5:16.** Confess your faults one to another, and pray one for another, that ye may be healed. The effectual fervent prayer of a righteous man availeth much. **James 1:6–7.** But let him ask in faith, nothing wavering. For he that wavereth is like a wave of the sea driven with the wind and tossed. For let not that man think that he shall receive any thing of the Lord. **Mark 11:24.** Therefore I say unto you, What things soever ye desire, when ye pray, believe that ye receive them, and ye shall have them. **Matt. 6:12, 14–15.** And forgive us our debts, as we forgive our debtors.… For if ye forgive men their trespasses, your heavenly Father will also forgive you: but if ye forgive not men their trespasses, neither will your Father forgive your trespasses. **Col. 4:2.** Continue in prayer, and watch in the same with thanksgiving. **Eph. 6:18.** … praying always with all prayer and supplication in the Spirit, and watching thereunto with all perseverance and supplication for all saints.

m. **1 Cor. 14:14.** For if I pray in an unknown tongue, my spirit prayeth, but my understanding is unfruitful.

4. Prayer is to be made for things lawful;[n] and for all sorts of men living, or that shall live hereafter:[o] but not for the dead,[p] nor for those

n. **1 John 5:14, 16.** And this is the confidence that we have in him, that, if we ask any thing according to his will, he heareth us.… If any man see his brother sin a sin which is not unto death, he shall ask, and he shall give him life for them that sin not unto death. There is a sin unto death: I do not say that he shall pray for it. **John 15:7.** If ye abide in me, and my words abide in you, ye shall ask what ye will, and it shall be done unto you.

o. **1 Tim. 2:1–2.** I exhort therefore, that, first of all, supplications, prayers, intercessions, and giving of thanks, be made for all men; for kings, and for all that are in authority; that we may lead a quiet and peaceable life in all godliness and honesty. **John 17:20.** Neither pray I for these alone, but for them also which shall believe on me through their word. **2 Sam. 7:29.** Therefore now let it please thee to bless the house of thy servant, that it may continue for ever before thee: for thou, O Lord GOD, hast spoken it: and with thy blessing let the house of thy servant be blessed for ever. **2 Chron. 6:14–42.** And said, O LORD God of Israel, there is no God like thee in the heaven, nor in the earth; which keepest covenant, and shewest mercy unto thy servants, that walk before thee with all their hearts.… Now therefore, O LORD God of Israel, keep with thy servant David my father that which thou hast promised him, saying, There shall not fail thee a man in my sight to sit upon the throne of Israel; yet so that thy children take heed to their way to walk in my law, as thou hast walked before me.… Hearken therefore unto the supplications of thy servant, and of thy people Israel, which they shall make toward this place: hear thou from thy dwelling place, even from heaven; and when thou hearest, forgive.… Moreover concerning the stranger, which is not of thy people Israel, but is come from a far country for thy great name's sake, and thy mighty hand, and thy stretched out arm; if they come and pray in this house; then hear thou from the heavens, even from thy dwelling place, and do according to all that the stranger calleth to thee for; that all people of the earth may know thy name, and fear thee, as doth thy people Israel, and may know that this house which I have built is called by thy name.…

p. **Luke 16:25–26.** But Abraham said, Son, remember that thou in thy lifetime receivedst thy good things, and likewise Lazarus evil things: but now he is comforted, and thou art tormented. And beside all this, between us and you there is a great gulf fixed: so that they which would pass from hence to you cannot; neither can they pass to us, that would come from thence. **Isa. 57:1–2.** The righteous perisheth, and no man layeth it to heart: and merciful men are taken away, none considering that the righteous is taken away from the evil to come. He shall enter into peace: they shall rest in their beds, each one walking in his uprightness. **Ps. 73:24.** Thou shalt guide me with thy counsel, and afterward receive me to glory. **2 Cor. 5:8, 10.** We are confident, I say, and willing rather to be absent from the body, and to be present with the Lord.… For we must all appear before the judgment seat of Christ; that every one may receive the things done in his body, according to that he hath done, whether it be good or bad. **Phil. 1:21–24.** For to me to live is Christ, and to die is gain. But if I live in the flesh, this is the fruit of my labour: yet what I shall choose I wot not. For I am in a strait betwixt two, having a desire to depart, and to be with Christ; which is far better: nevertheless to abide in the flesh is more needful for you. **Rev. 14:13.** And I heard a

of whom it may be known that they have sinned the sin unto death.^q

5. The reading of the Scriptures with godly fear,^r the sound preaching^s and conscionable hearing of the Word, in obedience unto God, with understanding, faith, and reverence,^t singing of psalms with grace in the heart;^u as also, the due administration and worthy receiving of the sacraments instituted by Christ, are all parts of the

voice from heaven saying unto me, Write, Blessed are the dead which die in the Lord from henceforth: Yea, saith the Spirit, that they may rest from their labours; and their works do follow them.

q. **1 John 5:16.** If any man see his brother sin a sin which is not unto death, he shall ask, and he shall give him life for them that sin not unto death. There is a sin unto death: I do not say that he shall pray for it.

r. **Luke 4:16–17.** And he came to Nazareth, where he had been brought up: and, as his custom was, he went into the synagogue on the sabbath day, and stood up for to read. And there was delivered unto him the book of the prophet Esaias. And when he had opened the book, he found the place where it was written … **Acts 15:21.** For Moses of old time hath in every city them that preach him, being read in the synagogues every sabbath day. **Col. 4:16.** And when this epistle is read among you, cause that it be read also in the church of the Laodiceans; and that ye likewise read the epistle from Laodicea. **1 Thess. 5:27.** I charge you by the Lord that this epistle be read unto all the holy brethren. **Rev. 1:3.** Blessed is he that readeth, and they that hear the words of this prophecy, and keep those things which are written therein: for the time is at hand.

s. **2 Tim. 4:2.** Preach the word; be instant in season, out of season; reprove, rebuke, exhort with all longsuffering and doctrine. **Acts 5:42.** And daily in the temple, and in every house, they ceased not to teach and preach Jesus Christ.

t. **James 1:22.** But be ye doers of the word, and not hearers only, deceiving your own selves. **Acts 10:33.** Immediately therefore I sent to thee; and thou hast well done that thou art come. Now therefore are we all here present before God, to hear all things that are commanded thee of God. **Matt. 13:19.** When any one heareth the word of the kingdom, and understandeth it not, then cometh the wicked one, and catcheth away that which was sown in his heart. This is he which received seed by the way side. **Heb. 4:2.** For unto us was the gospel preached, as well as unto them: but the word preached did not profit them, not being mixed with faith in them that heard it. **Isa. 66:2.** For all those things hath mine hand made, and all those things have been, saith the Lord: but to this man will I look, even to him that is poor and of a contrite spirit, and trembleth at my word.

u. **Col. 3:16.** Let the word of Christ dwell in you richly in all wisdom; teaching and admonishing one another in psalms and hymns and spiritual songs, singing with grace in your hearts to the Lord. **Eph. 5:19.** Speaking to yourselves in psalms and hymns and spiritual songs, singing and making melody in your heart to the Lord. **James 5:13.** Is any among you afflicted? let him pray. Is any merry? let him sing psalms. **1 Cor. 14:15.** What is it then? I will pray with the spirit, and I will pray with the understanding also: I will sing with the spirit, and I will sing with the understanding also.

ordinary religious worship of God:[w] beside religious oaths,[x] vows,[y] solemn fastings,[z] and thanksgivings upon special occasions,[a] which

w. **Matt. 28:19.** Go ye therefore, and teach all nations, baptizing them in the name of the Father, and of the Son, and of the Holy Ghost. **1 Cor. 11:23–29.** For I have received of the Lord that which also I delivered unto you, That the Lord Jesus the same night in which he was betrayed took bread: and when he had given thanks, he brake it, and said, Take, eat: this is my body, which is broken for you: this do in remembrance of me. After the same manner also he took the cup, when he had supped, saying, This cup is the new testament in my blood: this do ye, as oft as ye drink it, in remembrance of me. For as often as ye eat this bread, and drink this cup, ye do shew the Lord's death till he come. Wherefore whosoever shall eat this bread, and drink this cup of the Lord, unworthily, shall be guilty of the body and blood of the Lord. But let a man examine himself, and so let him eat of that bread, and drink of that cup. For he that eateth and drinketh unworthily, eateth and drinketh damnation to himself, not discerning the Lord's body. **Acts 2:42.** And they continued stedfastly in the apostles' doctrine and fellowship, and in breaking of bread, and in prayers.

x. **Deut. 6:13.** Thou shalt fear the LORD thy God, and serve him, and shalt swear by his name. **Neh. 10:29.** They clave to their brethren, their nobles, and entered into a curse, and into an oath, to walk in God's law, which was given by Moses the servant of God, and to observe and do all the commandments of the LORD our Lord, and his judgments and his statutes. **2 Cor. 1:23.** Moreover I call God for a record upon my soul, that to spare you I came not as yet unto Corinth.

y. **Ps. 116:14.** I will pay my vows unto the LORD now in the presence of all his people. **Isa. 19:21.** And the LORD shall be known to Egypt, and the Egyptians shall know the LORD in that day, and shall do sacrifice and oblation; yea, they shall vow a vow unto the LORD, and perform it. **Eccl. 5:4–5.** When thou vowest a vow unto God, defer not to pay it; for he hath no pleasure in fools: pay that which thou hast vowed. Better is it that thou shouldest not vow, than that thou shouldest vow and not pay.

z. **Joel 2:12.** Therefore also now, saith the LORD, turn ye even to me with all your heart, and with fasting, and with weeping, and with mourning. **Est. 4:16.** Go, gather together all the Jews that are present in Shushan, and fast ye for me, and neither eat nor drink three days, night or day: I also and my maidens will fast likewise; and so will I go in unto the king, which is not according to the law: and if I perish, I perish. **Matt. 9:15.** And Jesus said unto them, Can the children of the bridechamber mourn, as long as the bridegroom is with them? but the days will come, when the bridegroom shall be taken from them, and then shall they fast. **Acts 14:23.** And when they had ordained them elders in every church, and had prayed with fasting, they commended them to the Lord, on whom they believed.

a. **Ex. 15:1–21.** Then sang Moses and the children of Israel this song unto the LORD, and spake, saying, I will sing unto the LORD, for he hath triumphed gloriously: the horse and his rider hath he thrown into the sea. The LORD is my strength and song, and he is become my salvation: he is my God, and I will prepare him an habitation; my father's God, and I will exalt him. The LORD is a man of war: the LORD is his name. Pharaoh's chariots and his host hath he cast into the sea: his chosen captains also are drowned in the Red sea.… And Miriam the prophetess, the sister of Aaron, took a timbrel in her hand; and all the women went out after her with timbrels and

are, in their several times and seasons, to be used in an holy and religious manner.[b]

6. Neither prayer, nor any other part of religious worship, is now, under the gospel, either tied unto, or made more acceptable by any place in which it is performed, or towards which it is directed:[c] but God is to be worshiped everywhere,[d] in spirit and truth;[e] as, in private families[f] daily,[g] and in secret, each one by himself;[h] so, more

with dances. And Miriam answered them, Sing ye to the LORD, for he hath triumphed gloriously; the horse and his rider hath he thrown into the sea. **Ps. 107:1–43.** O give thanks unto the LORD, for he is good: for his mercy endureth for ever. Let the redeemed of the LORD say so, whom he hath redeemed from the hand of the enemy; and gathered them out of the lands, from the east, and from the west, from the north, and from the south.… Then they cried unto the LORD in their trouble, and he delivered them out of their distresses.… Oh that men would praise the LORD for his goodness, and for his wonderful works to the children of men.… **Neh. 12:27–43.** And at the dedication of the wall of Jerusalem they sought the Levites out of all their places, to bring them to Jerusalem, to keep the dedication with gladness, both with thanksgivings, and with singing, with cymbals, psalteries, and with harps. And the sons of the singers gathered themselves together, both out of the plain country round about Jerusalem, and from the villages of Netophathi.… So stood the two companies of them that gave thanks in the house of God, and I, and the half of the rulers with me.… Also that day they offered great sacrifices, and rejoiced: for God had made them rejoice with great joy: the wives also and the children rejoiced: so that the joy of Jerusalem was heard even afar off. **Est. 9:20–22.** And Mordecai wrote these things, and sent letters unto all the Jews that were in all the provinces of the king Ahasuerus, both nigh and far, to stablish this among them, that they should keep the fourteenth day of the month Adar, and the fifteenth day of the same, yearly, as the days wherein the Jews rested from their enemies, and the month which was turned unto them from sorrow to joy, and from mourning into a good day: that they should make them days of feasting and joy, and of sending portions one to another, and gifts to the poor.

b. **Heb. 12:28.** Wherefore we receiving a kingdom which cannot be moved, let us have grace, whereby we may serve God acceptably with reverence and godly fear.

c. **John 4:21.** Jesus saith unto her, Woman, believe me, the hour cometh, when ye shall neither in this mountain, nor yet at Jerusalem, worship the Father.

d. **Mal. 1:11.** For from the rising of the sun even unto the going down of the same my name shall be great among the Gentiles; and in every place incense shall be offered unto my name, and a pure offering: for my name shall be great among the heathen, saith the LORD of hosts. **1 Tim. 2:8.** I will therefore that men pray every where, lifting up holy hands, without wrath and doubting.

e. **John 4:23–24.** But the hour cometh, and now is, when the true worshippers shall worship the Father in spirit and in truth: for the Father seeketh such to worship him. God is a Spirit: and they that worship him must worship him in spirit and in truth.

f. **Jer. 10:25.** Pour out thy fury upon the heathen that know thee not, and upon the families that call not on thy name: for they have eaten up Jacob, and devoured him, and consumed him, and have made his habitation desolate. **Deut. 6:6–7.** And

solemnly in the public assemblies, which are not carelessly or willfully to be neglected, or forsaken, when God, by his Word or providence, calleth thereunto.[i]

these words, which I command thee this day, shall be in thine heart: and thou shalt teach them diligently unto thy children, and shalt talk of them when thou sittest in thine house, and when thou walkest by the way, and when thou liest down, and when thou risest up. **Job 1:5.** And it was so, when the days of their feasting were gone about, that Job sent and sanctified them, and rose up early in the morning, and offered burnt offerings according to the number of them all: for Job said, It may be that my sons have sinned, and cursed God in their hearts. Thus did Job continually. **2 Sam. 6:18, 20.** And as soon as David had made an end of offering burnt offerings and peace offerings, he blessed the people in the name of the LORD of hosts.… Then David returned to bless his household.…

g. **Matt. 6:11.** Give us this day our daily bread. **See Job 1:5.**

h. **Matt. 6:6, 16–18.** But thou, when thou prayest, enter into thy closet, and when thou hast shut thy door, pray to thy Father which is in secret; and thy Father which seeth in secret shall reward thee openly.… Moreover when ye fast, be not, as the hypocrites, of a sad countenance: for they disfigure their faces, that they may appear unto men to fast. Verily I say unto you, They have their reward. But thou, when thou fastest, anoint thine head, and wash thy face; that thou appear not unto men to fast, but unto thy Father which is in secret: and thy Father, which seeth in secret, shall reward thee openly. **Neh. 1:4–11.** And it came to pass, when I heard these words, that I sat down and wept, and mourned certain days, and fasted, and prayed before the God of heaven, and said, … O Lord, I beseech thee, let now thine ear be attentive to the prayer of thy servant, and to the prayer of thy servants, who desire to fear thy name: and prosper, I pray thee, thy servant this day, and grant him mercy in the sight of this man. For I was the king's cupbearer. **Dan. 9:3–4a.** And I set my face unto the Lord God, to seek by prayer and supplication, with fasting, and sackcloth, and ashes: and I prayed unto the LORD my God, and made my confession.…

i. **Isa. 56:6–7.** Also the sons of the stranger, that join themselves to the LORD, to serve him, and to love the name of the LORD, to be his servants, every one that keepeth the sabbath from polluting it, and taketh hold of my covenant; even them will I bring to my holy mountain, and make them joyful in my house of prayer: their burnt offerings and their sacrifices shall be accepted upon mine altar; for mine house shall be called an house of prayer for all people. **Heb. 10:25.** Not forsaking the assembling of ourselves together, as the manner of some is; but exhorting one another: and so much the more, as ye see the day approaching. **Ps. 100:4.** Enter into his gates with thanksgiving, and into his courts with praise: be thankful unto him, and bless his name. **Ps. 122:1.** I was glad when they said unto me, Let us go into the house of the LORD. **Ps. 84:1–12.** How amiable are thy tabernacles, O LORD of hosts! My soul longeth, yea, even fainteth for the courts of the LORD: my heart and my flesh crieth out for the living God.… For a day in thy courts is better than a thousand. I had rather be a doorkeeper in the house of my God, than to dwell in the tents of wickedness.… O LORD of hosts, blessed is the man that trusteth in thee. **Luke 4:16.** And he came to Nazareth, where he had been brought up: and, as his custom was, he went into the synagogue on the sabbath day, and stood up for to read. **Acts 13:42, 44.** And when the Jews were gone out of the synagogue, the Gentiles besought that these words

7. As it is the law of nature, that, in general, a due proportion of time be set apart for the worship of God; so, in his Word, by a positive, moral, and perpetual commandment binding all men in all ages, he hath particularly appointed one day in seven, for a Sabbath, to be kept holy unto him:[k] which, from the beginning of the world to the resurrection of Christ, was the last day of the week; and, from the resurrection of Christ, was changed into the first day of the week,[l] which, in Scripture, is called the Lord's Day,[m] and is to be continued to the end of the world, as the Christian Sabbath.[n]

might be preached to them the next sabbath…. And the next sabbath day came almost the whole city together to hear the word of God. **Acts 2:42.** And they continued stedfastly in the apostles' doctrine and fellowship, and in breaking of bread, and in prayers.

k. **Ex. 20:8–11.** Remember the sabbath day, to keep it holy. Six days shalt thou labour, and do all thy work: but the seventh day is the sabbath of the LORD thy God: in it thou shalt not do any work, thou, nor thy son, nor thy daughter, thy manservant, nor thy maidservant, nor thy cattle, nor thy stranger that is within thy gates: for in six days the LORD made heaven and earth, the sea, and all that in them is, and rested the seventh day: wherefore the LORD blessed the sabbath day, and hallowed it. **Isa. 56:2–7.** Blessed is the man that doeth this, and the son of man that layeth hold on it; that keepeth the sabbath from polluting it, and keepeth his hand from doing any evil. Neither let the son of the stranger, that hath joined himself to the LORD, speak, saying, The LORD hath utterly separated me from his people: neither let the eunuch say, Behold, I am a dry tree. For thus saith the LORD unto the eunuchs that keep my sabbaths, and choose the things that please me, and take hold of my covenant; even unto them will I give in mine house and within my walls a place and a name better than of sons and of daughters: I will give them an everlasting name, that shall not be cut off. Also the sons of the stranger, that join themselves to the LORD, to serve him, and to love the name of the LORD, to be his servants, every one that keepeth the sabbath from polluting it, and taketh hold of my covenant; even them will I bring to my holy mountain, and make them joyful in my house of prayer: their burnt offerings and their sacrifices shall be accepted upon mine altar; for mine house shall be called an house of prayer for all people.

l. **Gen. 2:2–3.** And on the seventh day God ended his work which he had made; and he rested on the seventh day from all his work which he had made. And God blessed the seventh day, and sanctified it: because that in it he had rested from all his work which God created and made. **1 Cor. 16:1–2.** Now concerning the collection for the saints, as I have given order to the churches of Galatia, even so do ye. Upon the first day of the week let every one of you lay by him in store, as God hath prospered him, that there be no gatherings when I come. **Acts 20:7.** And upon the first day of the week, when the disciples came together to break bread, Paul preached unto them, ready to depart on the morrow; and continued his speech until midnight.

m. **Rev. 1:10.** I was in the Spirit on the Lord's day, and heard behind me a great voice, as of a trumpet.

n. **Matt. 5:17–18.** Think not that I am come to destroy the law, or the prophets:

8. This Sabbath is then kept holy unto the Lord, when men, after a due preparing of their hearts, and ordering of their common affairs beforehand, do not only observe an holy rest, all the day, from their own works, words, and thoughts about their worldly employments and recreations,º but also are taken up, the whole time, in the

I am not come to destroy, but to fulfil. For verily I say unto you, Till heaven and earth pass, one jot or one tittle shall in no wise pass from the law, till all be fulfilled. **Mark 2:27–28.** And he said unto them, The sabbath was made for man, and not man for the sabbath: therefore the Son of man is Lord also of the sabbath. **Rom. 13:8–10.** Owe no man any thing, but to love one another: for he that loveth another hath fulfilled the law. For this, Thou shalt not commit adultery, Thou shalt not kill, Thou shalt not steal, Thou shalt not bear false witness, Thou shalt not covet; and if there be any other commandment, it is briefly comprehended in this saying, namely, Thou shalt love thy neighbour as thyself. Love worketh no ill to his neighbour: therefore love is the fulfilling of the law. **James 2:8–12.** If ye fulfil the royal law according to the scripture, Thou shalt love thy neighbour as thyself, ye do well: but if ye have respect to persons, ye commit sin, and are convinced of the law as transgressors. For whosoever shall keep the whole law, and yet offend in one point, he is guilty of all. For he that said, Do not commit adultery, said also, Do not kill. Now if thou commit no adultery, yet if thou kill, thou art become a transgressor of the law. So speak ye, and so do, as they that shall be judged by the law of liberty.

o. **Ex. 20:8.** Remember the sabbath day, to keep it holy. **Ex. 16:23–30.** And he said unto them, This is that which the Lᴏʀᴅ hath said, To morrow is the rest of the holy sabbath unto the Lᴏʀᴅ: bake that which ye will bake to day, and seethe that ye will seethe; and that which remaineth over lay up for you to be kept until the morning. And they laid it up till the morning, as Moses bade: and it did not stink, neither was there any worm therein. And Moses said, Eat that to day; for to day is a sabbath unto the Lᴏʀᴅ: to day ye shall not find it in the field. Six days ye shall gather it; but on the seventh day, which is the sabbath, in it there shall be none. And it came to pass, that there went out some of the people on the seventh day for to gather, and they found none. And the Lᴏʀᴅ said unto Moses, How long refuse ye to keep my commandments and my laws? See, for that the Lᴏʀᴅ hath given you the sabbath, therefore he giveth you on the sixth day the bread of two days; abide ye every man in his place, let no man go out of his place on the seventh day. So the people rested on the seventh day. **Ex. 31:15–17.** Six days may work be done; but in the seventh is the sabbath of rest, holy to the Lᴏʀᴅ: whosoever doeth any work in the sabbath day, he shall surely be put to death. Wherefore the children of Israel shall keep the sabbath, to observe the sabbath throughout their generations, for a perpetual covenant. It is a sign between me and the children of Israel for ever: for in six days the Lᴏʀᴅ made heaven and earth, and on the seventh day he rested, and was refreshed. **Isa. 58:13–14.** If thou turn away thy foot from the sabbath, from doing thy pleasure on my holy day; and call the sabbath a delight, the holy of the Lᴏʀᴅ, honourable; and shalt honour him, not doing thine own ways, nor finding thine own pleasure, nor speaking thine own words: then shalt thou delight thyself in the Lᴏʀᴅ; and I will cause thee to ride upon the high places of the earth, and feed thee with the heritage of Jacob thy father: for the mouth of the Lᴏʀᴅ hath spoken it. **Neh. 13:15–22.** In those days saw I in Judah some treading wine

public and private exercises of his worship, and in the duties of necessity and mercy.ᴾ

presses on the sabbath, and bringing in sheaves, and lading asses; as also wine, grapes, and figs, and all manner of burdens, which they brought into Jerusalem on the sabbath day: and I testified against them in the day wherein they sold victuals. There dwelt men of Tyre also therein, which brought fish, and all manner of ware, and sold on the sabbath unto the children of Judah, and in Jerusalem. Then I contended with the nobles of Judah, and said unto them, What evil thing is this that ye do, and profane the sabbath day? Did not your fathers thus, and did not our God bring all this evil upon us, and upon this city? yet ye bring more wrath upon Israel by profaning the sabbath. And it came to pass, that when the gates of Jerusalem began to be dark before the sabbath, I commanded that the gates should be shut, and charged that they should not be opened till after the sabbath: and some of my servants set I at the gates, that there should no burden be brought in on the sabbath day. So the merchants and sellers of all kind of ware lodged without Jerusalem once or twice. Then I testified against them, and said unto them, Why lodge ye about the wall? if ye do so again, I will lay hands on you. From that time forth came they no more on the sabbath. And I commanded the Levites that they should cleanse themselves, and that they should come and keep the gates, to sanctify the sabbath day. Remember me, O my God, concerning this also, and spare me according to the greatness of thy mercy.

p. **Isa. 58:13–14.** If thou turn away thy foot from the sabbath, from doing thy pleasure on my holy day; and call the sabbath a delight, the holy of the LORD, honourable; and shalt honour him, not doing thine own ways, nor finding thine own pleasure, nor speaking thine own words: then shalt thou delight thyself in the LORD; and I will cause thee to ride upon the high places of the earth, and feed thee with the heritage of Jacob thy father: for the mouth of the LORD hath spoken it. **Luke 4:16.** And he came to Nazareth, where he had been brought up: and, as his custom was, he went into the synagogue on the sabbath day, and stood up for to read. **Matt. 12:1–13.** At that time Jesus went on the sabbath day through the corn; and his disciples were an hungred, and began to pluck the ears of corn, and to eat. But when the Pharisees saw it, they said unto him, Behold, thy disciples do that which is not lawful to do upon the sabbath day. But he said unto them, Have ye not read what David did, when he was an hungred, and they that were with him; how he entered into the house of God, and did eat the shewbread, which was not lawful for him to eat, neither for them which were with him, but only for the priests? Or have ye not read in the law, how that on the sabbath days the priests in the temple profane the sabbath, and are blameless? But I say unto you, That in this place is one greater than the temple. But if ye had known what this meaneth, I will have mercy, and not sacrifice, ye would not have condemned the guiltless. For the Son of man is Lord even of the sabbath day. And when he was departed thence, he went into their synagogue: and, behold, there was a man which had his hand withered. And they asked him, saying, Is it lawful to heal on the sabbath days? that they might accuse him. And he said unto them, What man shall there be among you, that shall have one sheep, and if it fall into a pit on the sabbath day, will he not lay hold on it, and lift it out? How much then is a man better than a sheep? Wherefore it is lawful to do well on the sabbath days. Then saith he to the man, Stretch forth thine hand. And he stretched it forth; and it was restored whole, like as the other. **Mark 3:1–5.** And he entered again into the synagogue; and there

Chapter 22
Of Lawful Oaths and Vows

1. A lawful oath is a part of religious worship,[a] wherein, upon just occasion, the person swearing solemnly calleth God to witness what he asserteth, or promiseth, and to judge him according to the truth or falsehood of what he sweareth.[b]

2. The name of God only is that by which men ought to swear, and therein it is to be used with all holy fear and reverence.[c] Therefore, to swear vainly, or rashly, by that glorious and dreadful Name;

was a man there which had a withered hand. And they watched him, whether he would heal him on the sabbath day; that they might accuse him. And he saith unto the man which had the withered hand, Stand forth. And he saith unto them, Is it lawful to do good on the sabbath days, or to do evil? to save life, or to kill? But they held their peace. And when he had looked round about on them with anger, being grieved for the hardness of their hearts, he saith unto the man, Stretch forth thine hand. And he stretched it out: and his hand was restored whole as the other.

a. **Deut. 10:20.** Thou shalt fear the LORD thy God; him shalt thou serve, and to him shalt thou cleave, and swear by his name. **Isa. 45:23.** I have sworn by myself, the word is gone out of my mouth in righteousness, and shall not return, That unto me every knee shall bow, every tongue shall swear. **Rom. 14:11.** For it is written, As I live, saith the Lord, every knee shall bow to me, and every tongue shall confess to God. **Phil. 2:10–11.** That at the name of Jesus every knee should bow, of things in heaven, and things in earth, and things under the earth; and that every tongue should confess that Jesus Christ is Lord, to the glory of God the Father.

b. **Ex. 20:7.** Thou shalt not take the name of the LORD thy God in vain; for the LORD will not hold him guiltless that taketh his name in vain. **Lev. 19:12.** And ye shall not swear by my name falsely, neither shalt thou profane the name of thy God: I am the LORD. **Rom. 1:9.** For God is my witness, whom I serve with my spirit in the gospel of his Son, that without ceasing I make mention of you always in my prayers. **2 Cor. 1:23.** Moreover I call God for a record upon my soul, that to spare you I came not as yet unto Corinth. **2 Cor. 11:31.** The God and Father of our Lord Jesus Christ, which is blessed for evermore, knoweth that I lie not. **Gal. 1:20.** Now the things which I write unto you, behold, before God, I lie not. **2 Chron. 6:22–23.** If a man sin against his neighbour, and an oath be laid upon him to make him swear, and the oath come before thine altar in this house; then hear thou from heaven, and do, and judge thy servants, by requiting the wicked, by recompensing his way upon his own head; and by justifying the righteous, by giving him according to his righteousness.

c. **Deut. 6:13.** Thou shalt fear the LORD thy God, and serve him, and shalt swear by his name. **Josh. 23:7.** … that ye come not among these nations, these that remain among you; neither make mention of the name of their gods, nor cause to swear by them, neither serve them, nor bow yourselves unto them.

or, to swear at all by any other thing, is sinful, and to be abhorred.[d]
Yet, as in matters of weight and moment, an oath is warranted by the
Word of God, under the new testament as well as under the old;[e] so
a lawful oath, being imposed by lawful authority, in such matters,
ought to be taken.[f]

3. Whosoever taketh an oath ought duly to consider the weightiness of so solemn an act, and therein to avouch nothing but what he
is fully persuaded is the truth:[g] neither may any man bind himself by
oath to anything but what is good and just, and what he believeth so
to be, and what he is able and resolved to perform.[h]

d. **Ex. 20:7.** Thou shalt not take the name of the Lord thy God in vain; for the
Lord will not hold him guiltless that taketh his name in vain. **Jer. 5:7.** How shall I
pardon thee for this? thy children have forsaken me, and sworn by them that are no
gods: when I had fed them to the full, they then committed adultery, and assembled
themselves by troops in the harlots' houses. **Matt. 5:33–37.** Again, ye have heard
that it hath been said by them of old time, Thou shalt not forswear thyself, but shalt
perform unto the Lord thine oaths: but I say unto you, Swear not at all; neither by
heaven; for it is God's throne: nor by the earth; for it is his footstool: neither by Jerusalem; for it is the city of the great King. Neither shalt thou swear by thy head, because
thou canst not make one hair white or black. But let your communication be, Yea,
yea; Nay, nay: for whatsoever is more than these cometh of evil. **James 5:12.** But
above all things, my brethren, swear not, neither by heaven, neither by the earth,
neither by any other oath: but let your yea be yea; and your nay, nay; lest ye fall into
condemnation.

e. **Heb. 6:16.** For men verily swear by the greater: and an oath for confirmation
is to them an end of all strife. **2 Cor. 1:23.** Moreover I call God for a record upon my
soul, that to spare you I came not as yet unto Corinth. **Isa. 65:16.** … that he who
blesseth himself in the earth shall bless himself in the God of truth; and he that sweareth
in the earth shall swear by the God of truth; because the former troubles are forgotten,
and because they are hid from mine eyes.

f. **1 Kings 8:31.** If any man trespass against his neighbour, and an oath be laid
upon him to cause him to swear, and the oath come before thine altar in this house …
Neh. 13:25. And I contended with them, and cursed them, and smote certain of
them, and plucked off their hair, and made them swear by God, saying, Ye shall not
give your daughters unto their sons, nor take their daughters unto your sons, or for
yourselves. **Ezra 10:5.** Then arose Ezra, and made the chief priests, the Levites, and
all Israel, to swear that they should do according to this word. And they sware.

g. **Ex. 20:7.** Thou shalt not take the name of the Lord thy God in vain; for the
Lord will not hold him guiltless that taketh his name in vain. **Lev. 19:12.** And ye
shall not swear by my name falsely, neither shalt thou profane the name of thy God: I
am the Lord. **Jer. 4:2.** And thou shalt swear, The Lord liveth, in truth, in judgment,
and in righteousness; and the nations shall bless themselves in him, and in him shall
they glory. **Hos. 10:4.** They have spoken words, swearing falsely in making a covenant: thus judgment springeth up as hemlock in the furrows of the field.

h. **Gen. 24:2–9.** And Abraham said unto his eldest servant of his house, that

4. An oath is to be taken in the plain and common sense of the words, without equivocation, or mental reservation.[i] It cannot oblige to sin; but in anything not sinful, being taken, it binds to performance, although to a man's own hurt.[k] Nor is it to be violated, although made to heretics, or infidels.[l]

ruled over all that he had, Put, I pray thee, thy hand under my thigh: and I will make thee swear by the LORD, the God of heaven, and the God of the earth, that thou shalt not take a wife unto my son of the daughters of the Canaanites, among whom I dwell.… And the servant put his hand under the thigh of Abraham his master, and sware to him concerning that matter. **Neh. 5:12–13.** Then said they, We will restore them, and will require nothing of them; so will we do as thou sayest. Then I called the priests, and took an oath of them, that they should do according to this promise. Also I shook my lap, and said, So God shake out every man from his house, and from his labour, that performeth not this promise, even thus be he shaken out, and emptied. And all the congregation said, Amen, and praised the LORD. And the people did according to this promise. **Eccl. 5:2, 5.** Be not rash with thy mouth, and let not thine heart be hasty to utter any thing before God: for God is in heaven, and thou upon earth: therefore let thy words be few.… Better is it that thou shouldest not vow, than that thou shouldest vow and not pay.

i. **Jer. 4:2.** And thou shalt swear, The LORD liveth, in truth, in judgment, and in righteousness; and the nations shall bless themselves in him, and in him shall they glory. **Ps. 24:4.** He that hath clean hands, and a pure heart; who hath not lifted up his soul unto vanity, nor sworn deceitfully.

k. **1 Sam. 25:22, 32–34.** So and more also do God unto the enemies of David, if I leave of all that pertain to him by the morning light any that pisseth against the wall.… And David said to Abigail, Blessed be the LORD God of Israel, which sent thee this day to meet me: and blessed be thy advice, and blessed be thou, which hast kept me this day from coming to shed blood, and from avenging myself with mine own hand. For in very deed, as the LORD God of Israel liveth, which hath kept me back from hurting thee, except thou hadst hasted and come to meet me, surely there had not been left unto Nabal by the morning light any that pisseth against the wall. **Ps. 15:4.** … He that sweareth to his own hurt, and changeth not.

l. **Ezek. 17:16–19.** As I live, saith the Lord GOD, surely in the place where the king dwelleth that made him king, whose oath he despised, and whose covenant he brake, even with him in the midst of Babylon he shall die. Neither shall Pharaoh with his mighty army and great company make for him in the war, by casting up mounts, and building forts, to cut off many persons: seeing he despised the oath by breaking the covenant, when, lo, he had given his hand, and hath done all these things, he shall not escape. Therefore thus saith the Lord GOD; As I live, surely mine oath that he hath despised, and my covenant that he hath broken, even it will I recompense upon his own head. **Josh. 9:18–19.** And the children of Israel smote them not, because the princes of the congregation had sworn unto them by the LORD God of Israel. And all the congregation murmured against the princes. But all the princes said unto all the congregation, We have sworn unto them by the LORD God of Israel: now therefore we may not touch them. **2 Sam. 21:1.** Then there was a famine in the days of David

5. A vow is of the like nature with a promissory oath, and ought to be made with the like religious care, and to be performed with the like faithfulness.[m]

6. It is not to be made to any creature, but to God alone:[n] and, that it may be accepted, it is to be made voluntarily, out of faith, and conscience of duty, in way of thankfulness for mercy received, or for the obtaining of what we want, whereby we more strictly bind ourselves to necessary duties; or, to other things, so far and so long as they may fitly conduce thereunto.[o]

three years, year after year; and David inquired of the LORD. And the LORD answered, It is for Saul, and for his bloody house, because he slew the Gibeonites.

m. **Num. 30:2.** If a man vow a vow unto the LORD, or swear an oath to bind his soul with a bond; he shall not break his word, he shall do according to all that proceedeth out of his mouth. **Isa. 19:21.** And the LORD shall be known to Egypt, and the Egyptians shall know the LORD in that day, and shall do sacrifice and oblation; yea, they shall vow a vow unto the LORD, and perform it. **Eccl. 5:4–6.** When thou vowest a vow unto God, defer not to pay it; for he hath no pleasure in fools: pay that which thou hast vowed. Better is it that thou shouldest not vow, than that thou shouldest vow and not pay. Suffer not thy mouth to cause thy flesh to sin; neither say thou before the angel, that it was an error: wherefore should God be angry at thy voice, and destroy the work of thine hands? **Ps. 61:8.** So will I sing praise unto thy name for ever, that I may daily perform my vows. **Ps. 66:13–14.** I will go into thy house with burnt offerings: I will pay thee my vows, which my lips have uttered, and my mouth hath spoken, when I was in trouble.

n. **Ps. 50:14.** Offer unto God thanksgiving; and pay thy vows unto the most High. **Ps. 76:11.** Vow, and pay unto the LORD your God: let all that be round about him bring presents unto him that ought to be feared. **Ps. 116:14.** I will pay my vows unto the LORD now in the presence of all his people.

o. **Deut. 23:21–23.** When thou shalt vow a vow unto the LORD thy God, thou shalt not slack to pay it: for the LORD thy God will surely require it of thee; and it would be sin in thee. But if thou shalt forbear to vow, it shall be no sin in thee. That which is gone out of thy lips thou shalt keep and perform; even a freewill offering, according as thou hast vowed unto the LORD thy God, which thou hast promised with thy mouth. **Gen. 28:20–22.** And Jacob vowed a vow, saying, If God will be with me, and will keep me in this way that I go, and will give me bread to eat, and raiment to put on, so that I come again to my father's house in peace; then shall the LORD be my God: and this stone, which I have set for a pillar, shall be God's house: and of all that thou shalt give me I will surely give the tenth unto thee. **1 Sam. 1:11.** And she vowed a vow, and said, O LORD of hosts, if thou wilt indeed look on the affliction of thine handmaid, and remember me, and not forget thine handmaid, but wilt give unto thine handmaid a man child, then I will give him unto the LORD all the days of his life, and there shall no rasor come upon his head. **Ps. 66:13–14.** I will go into thy house with burnt offerings: I will pay thee my vows, which my lips have uttered, and my mouth hath spoken, when I was in trouble. **Ps. 132:2–5.** ... how he sware unto the LORD,

7. No man may vow to do anything forbidden in the Word of God, or what would hinder any duty therein commanded, or which is not in his own power, and for the performance whereof he hath no promise of ability from God.[p] In which respects, popish monastical vows of perpetual single life, professed poverty, and regular obedience, are so far from being degrees of higher perfection, that they are superstitious and sinful snares, in which no Christian may entangle himself.[q]

and vowed unto the mighty God of Jacob; surely I will not come into the tabernacle of my house, nor go up into my bed; I will not give sleep to mine eyes, or slumber to mine eyelids, until I find out a place for the LORD, an habitation for the mighty God of Jacob.

p. **Acts 23:12–14.** And when it was day, certain of the Jews banded together, and bound themselves under a curse, saying that they would neither eat nor drink till they had killed Paul. And they were more than forty which had made this conspiracy. And they came to the chief priests and elders, and said, We have bound ourselves under a great curse, that we will eat nothing until we have slain Paul. **Mark 6:26.** And the king was exceeding sorry; yet for his oath's sake, and for their sakes which sat with him, he would not reject her. **Num. 30:5, 8, 12–13.** But if her father disallow her in the day that he heareth; not any of her vows, or of her bonds wherewith she hath bound her soul, shall stand: and the LORD shall forgive her, because her father disallowed her.... But if her husband disallowed her on the day that he heard it; then he shall make her vow which she vowed, and that which she uttered with her lips, wherewith she bound her soul, of none effect: and the LORD shall forgive her.... But if her husband hath utterly made them void on the day he heard them; then whatsoever proceeded out of her lips concerning her vows, or concerning the bond of her soul, shall not stand: her husband hath made them void; and the LORD shall forgive her. Every vow, and every binding oath to afflict the soul, her husband may establish it, or her husband may make it void.

q. **Matt. 19:11–12.** But he said unto them, All men cannot receive this saying, save they to whom it is given. For there are some eunuchs, which were so born from their mother's womb: and there are some eunuchs, which were made eunuchs of men: and there be eunuchs, which have made themselves eunuchs for the kingdom of heaven's sake. He that is able to receive it, let him receive it. **1 Cor. 7:2, 9.** Nevertheless, to avoid fornication, let every man have his own wife, and let every woman have her own husband.... But if they cannot contain, let them marry: for it is better to marry than to burn. **Heb. 13:4.** Marriage is honourable in all, and the bed undefiled: but whoremongers and adulterers God will judge. **Eph. 4:28.** Let him that stole steal no more: but rather let him labour, working with his hands the thing which is good, that he may have to give to him that needeth. **1 Thess. 4:11–12.** ... and that ye study to be quiet, and to do your own business, and to work with your own hands, as we commanded you; that ye may walk honestly toward them that are without, and that ye may have lack of nothing. **1 Cor. 7:23.** Ye are bought with a price; be not ye the servants of men.

Chapter 23
Of the Civil Magistrate

1. God, the supreme Lord and King of all the world, hath ordained civil magistrates, to be, under him, over the people, for his
own glory, and the public good: and, to this end, hath armed them
with the power of the sword, for the defense and encouragement of
them that are good, and for the punishment of evildoers.ª

2. It is lawful for Christians to accept and execute the office of a
magistrate, when called thereunto:ᵇ in the managing whereof, as they

a. **Rom. 13:1–4.** Let every soul be subject unto the higher powers. For there is
no power but of God: the powers that be are ordained of God. Whosoever therefore
resisteth the power, resisteth the ordinance of God: and they that resist shall receive to
themselves damnation. For rulers are not a terror to good works, but to the evil. Wilt
thou then not be afraid of the power? do that which is good, and thou shalt have
praise of the same: for he is the minister of God to thee for good. But if thou do that
which is evil, be afraid; for he beareth not the sword in vain: for he is the minister of
God, a revenger to execute wrath upon him that doeth evil. **1 Pet. 2:13–14.** Submit
yourselves to every ordinance of man for the Lord's sake: whether it be to the king, as
supreme; or unto governors, as unto them that are sent by him for the punishment of
evildoers, and for the praise of them that do well.

b. **Gen. 41:39–43.** And Pharaoh said unto Joseph, Forasmuch as God hath
shewed thee all this, there is none so discreet and wise as thou art: thou shalt be over
my house, and according unto thy word shall all my people be ruled: only in the throne
will I be greater than thou. And Pharaoh said unto Joseph, See, I have set thee over all
the land of Egypt. And Pharaoh took off his ring from his hand, and put it upon
Joseph's hand, and arrayed him in vestures of fine linen, and put a gold chain about
his neck; and he made him to ride in the second chariot which he had; and they cried
before him, Bow the knee: and he made him ruler over all the land of Egypt. **Neh.
12:26.** These were in the days of Joiakim the son of Jeshua, the son of Jozadak, and
in the days of Nehemiah the governor, and of Ezra the priest, the scribe. **Neh. 13:15–
31.** In those days saw I in Judah some treading wine presses on the sabbath, and
bringing in sheaves, and lading asses; as also wine, grapes, and figs, and all manner of
burdens, which they brought into Jerusalem on the sabbath day: and I testified against
them in the day wherein they sold victuals.… And it came to pass, that when the gates
of Jerusalem began to be dark before the sabbath, I commanded that the gates should
be shut, and charged that they should not be opened till after the sabbath: and some of
my servants set I at the gates, that there should no burden be brought in on the sabbath day.… **Dan. 2:48–49.** Then the king made Daniel a great man, and gave him
many great gifts, and made him ruler over the whole province of Babylon, and chief
of the governors over all the wise men of Babylon. Then Daniel requested of the king,
and he set Shadrach, Meshach, and Abed-nego, over the affairs of the province of
Babylon: but Daniel sat in the gate of the king. **Prov. 8:15–16.** By me kings reign,
and princes decree justice. By me princes rule, and nobles, even all the judges of the

ought especially to maintain piety, justice, and peace, according to the wholesome laws of each commonwealth;[c] so, for that end, they may lawfully, now under the new testament, wage war, upon just and necessary occasion.[d]

3. Civil magistrates may not assume to themselves the administration of the Word and sacraments; or the power of the keys of the kingdom of heaven;[e] or, in the least, interfere in matters of

earth. **Rom. 13:1–4.** Let every soul be subject unto the higher powers. For there is no power but of God: the powers that be are ordained of God. Whosoever therefore resisteth the power, resisteth the ordinance of God: and they that resist shall receive to themselves damnation. For rulers are not a terror to good works, but to the evil. Wilt thou then not be afraid of the power? do that which is good, and thou shalt have praise of the same: for he is the minister of God to thee for good. But if thou do that which is evil, be afraid; for he beareth not the sword in vain: for he is the minister of God, a revenger to execute wrath upon him that doeth evil.

c. **Ps. 2:10–12.** Be wise now therefore, O ye kings: be instructed, ye judges of the earth. Serve the LORD with fear, and rejoice with trembling. Kiss the Son, lest he be angry, and ye perish from the way, when his wrath is kindled but a little. Blessed are all they that put their trust in him. **1 Tim. 2:2.** [Pray] for kings, and for all that are in authority; that we may lead a quiet and peaceable life in all godliness and honesty. **Ps. 82:3–4.** Defend the poor and fatherless: do justice to the afflicted and needy. Deliver the poor and needy: rid them out of the hand of the wicked. **2 Sam. 23:3.** The God of Israel said, the Rock of Israel spake to me, He that ruleth over men must be just, ruling in the fear of God. **1 Pet. 2:13.** Submit yourselves to every ordinance of man for the Lord's sake....

d. **Luke 3:14.** And the soldiers likewise demanded of him, saying, And what shall we do? And he said unto them, Do violence to no man, neither accuse any falsely; and be content with your wages. **Rom. 13:4.** For he is the minister of God to thee for good. But if thou do that which is evil, be afraid; for he beareth not the sword in vain: for he is the minister of God, a revenger to execute wrath upon him that doeth evil. **Matt. 8:9–10.** For I am a man under authority, having soldiers under me: and I say to this man, Go, and he goeth; and to another, Come, and he cometh; and to my servant, Do this, and he doeth it. When Jesus heard it, he marvelled, and said to them that followed, Verily I say unto you, I have not found so great faith, no, not in Israel. **Acts 10:1–2.** There was a certain man in Caesarea called Cornelius, a centurion of the band called the Italian band, a devout man, and one that feared God with all his house, which gave much alms to the people, and prayed to God alway.

e. **2 Chron. 26:18.** And they withstood Uzziah the king, and said unto him, It appertaineth not unto thee, Uzziah, to burn incense unto the LORD, but to the priests the sons of Aaron, that are consecrated to burn incense: go out of the sanctuary; for thou hast trespassed; neither shall it be for thine honour from the LORD God. **Matt. 18:17.** And if he shall neglect to hear them, tell it unto the church: but if he neglect to hear the church, let him be unto thee as an heathen man and a publican. **Matt. 16:19.** And I will give unto thee the keys of the kingdom of heaven: and whatsoever thou shalt bind on earth shall be bound in heaven: and whatsoever thou shalt loose on

faith.[f] Yet, as nursing fathers, it is the duty of civil magistrates to protect the church of our common Lord, without giving the preference to any denomination of Christians above the rest, in such a manner that all ecclesiastical persons whatever shall enjoy the full, free, and unquestioned liberty of discharging every part of their sacred functions, without violence or danger.[g] And, as Jesus Christ hath appointed a regular government and discipline in his church, no law of any commonwealth should interfere with, let, or hinder, the due exercise thereof, among the voluntary members of *any* denomination of Christians, according to their own profession and belief.[h] It is the

earth shall be loosed in heaven. **1 Cor. 12:28–29.** And God hath set some in the church, first apostles, secondarily prophets, thirdly teachers, after that miracles, then gifts of healings, helps, governments, diversities of tongues. Are all apostles? are all prophets? are all teachers? are all workers of miracles? **Eph. 4:11–12.** And he gave some, apostles; and some, prophets; and some, evangelists; and some, pastors and teachers; for the perfecting of the saints, for the work of the ministry, for the edifying of the body of Christ. **1 Cor. 4:1–2.** Let a man so account of us, as of the ministers of Christ, and stewards of the mysteries of God. Moreover it is required in stewards, that a man be found faithful. **Rom. 10:15.** And how shall they preach, except they be sent? as it is written, How beautiful are the feet of them that preach the gospel of peace, and bring glad tidings of good things! **Heb. 5:4.** And no man taketh this honour unto himself, but he that is called of God, as was Aaron.

f. **John 18:36.** Jesus answered, My kingdom is not of this world: if my kingdom were this world, then would my servants fight, that I should not be delivered to the Jews: but now is my kingdom not from hence. **Acts 5:29.** Then Peter and the other apostles answered and said, We ought to obey God rather than men. **Eph. 4:11–12.** And he gave some, apostles; and some, prophets; and some, evangelists; and some, pastors and teachers; for the perfecting of the saints, for the work of the ministry, for the edifying of the body of Christ.

g. **Isa. 49:23.** And kings shall be thy nursing fathers, and their queens thy nursing mothers: they shall bow down to thee with their face toward the earth, and lick up the dust of thy feet; and thou shalt know that I am the LORD: for they shall not be ashamed that wait for me. **Rom. 13:1–6.** Let every soul be subject unto the higher powers. For there is no power but of God: the powers that be are ordained of God. Whosoever therefore resisteth the power, resisteth the ordinance of God: and they that resist shall receive to themselves damnation. For rulers are not a terror to good works, but to the evil. Wilt thou then not be afraid of the power? do that which is good, and thou shalt have praise of the same: for he is the minister of God to thee for good. But if thou do that which is evil, be afraid; for he beareth not the sword in vain: for he is the minister of God, a revenger to execute wrath upon him that doeth evil. Wherefore ye must needs be subject, not only for wrath, but also for conscience sake. For for this cause pay ye tribute also: for they are God's ministers, attending continually upon this very thing.

h. **Ps. 105:15.** … saying, Touch not mine anointed, and do my prophets no harm.

duty of civil magistrates to protect the person and good name of all their people, in such an effectual manner as that no person be suffered, either upon pretense of religion or of infidelity, to offer any indignity, violence, abuse, or injury to any other person whatsoever: and to take order, that all religious and ecclesiastical assemblies be held without molestation or disturbance.[i]

4. It is the duty of people to pray for magistrates,[k] to honor their persons,[l] to pay them tribute or other dues,[m] to obey their lawful commands, and to be subject to their authority, for conscience' sake.[n] Infidelity, or difference in religion, doth not make void the magistrates' just and legal authority, nor free the people from their due obedience to them:[o] from which ecclesiastical persons are not exempted,[p] much less hath the pope any power and jurisdiction over

i. **Rom. 13:4.** For he is the minister of God to thee for good. But if thou do that which is evil, be afraid; for he beareth not the sword in vain: for he is the minister of God, a revenger to execute wrath upon him that doeth evil. **1 Tim. 2:2.** [Pray] for kings, and for all that are in authority; that we may lead a quiet and peaceable life in all godliness and honesty.

k. **1 Tim. 2:1–3.** I exhort therefore, that, first of all, supplications, prayers, intercessions, and giving of thanks, be made for all men; for kings, and for all that are in authority; that we may lead a quiet and peaceable life in all godliness and honesty. For this is good and acceptable in the sight of God our Saviour.

l. **1 Pet. 2:17.** Honour all men. Love the brotherhood. Fear God. Honour the king.

m. **Matt. 22:21.** They say unto him, Caesar's. Then saith he unto them, Render therefore unto Caesar the things which are Caesar's; and unto God the things that are God's. **Rom. 13:6–7.** For for this cause pay ye tribute also: for they are God's ministers, attending continually upon this very thing. Render therefore to all their dues: tribute to whom tribute is due; custom to whom custom; fear to whom fear; honour to whom honour.

n. **Rom. 13:5.** Wherefore ye must needs be subject, not only for wrath, but also for conscience sake. **Titus 3:1.** Put them in mind to be subject to principalities and powers, to obey magistrates, to be ready to every good work.

o. **1 Pet. 2:13–16.** Submit yourselves to every ordinance of man for the Lord's sake: whether it be to the king, as supreme; or unto governors, as unto them that are sent by him for the punishment of evildoers, and for the praise of them that do well. For so is the will of God, that with well doing ye may put to silence the ignorance of foolish men: as free, and not using your liberty for a cloke of maliciousness, but as the servants of God.

p. **Rom. 13:1.** Let every soul be subject unto the higher powers. For there is no power but of God: the powers that be are ordained of God. **Acts 25:9–11.** But Festus, willing to do the Jews a pleasure, answered Paul, and said, Wilt thou go up to Jerusalem, and there be judged of these things before me? Then said Paul, I stand at Caesar's judgment seat, where I ought to be judged: to the Jews have I done no wrong,

them in their dominions, or over any of their people; and, least of all, to deprive them of their dominions, or lives, if he shall judge them to be heretics, or upon any other pretense whatsoever.[q]

Chapter 24
Of Marriage and Divorce

1. Marriage is to be between one man and one woman: neither is it lawful for any man to have more than one wife, nor for any woman to have more than one husband, at the same time.[a]

as thou very well knowest. For if I be an offender, or have committed any thing worthy of death, I refuse not to die: but if there be none of these things whereof these accuse me, no man may deliver me unto them. I appeal unto Caesar. **2 Pet. 2:1, 10–11.** But there were false prophets also among the people, even as there shall be false teachers among you, who privily shall bring in damnable heresies, even denying the Lord that bought them, and bring upon themselves swift destruction.... But chiefly them that walk after the flesh in the lust of uncleanness, and despise government. Presumptuous are they, selfwilled, they are not afraid to speak evil of dignities. Whereas angels, which are greater in power and might, bring not railing accusation against them before the Lord. **Jude 8–11.** Likewise also these filthy dreamers defile the flesh, despise dominion, and speak evil of dignities. Yet Michael the archangel, when contending with the devil he disputed about the body of Moses, durst not bring against him a railing accusation, but said, The Lord rebuke thee. But these speak evil of those things which they know not: but what they know naturally, as brute beasts, in those things they corrupt themselves. Woe unto them! for they have gone in the way of Cain, and ran greedily after the error of Balaam for reward, and perished in the gainsaying of Core.

q. **Mark 10:42–44.** But Jesus called them to him, and saith unto them, Ye know that they which are accounted to rule over the Gentiles exercise lordship over them; and their great ones exercise authority upon them. But so shall it not be among you: but whosoever will be great among you, shall be your minister: and whosoever of you will be the chiefest, shall be servant of all. **Matt. 23:8–12.** But be not ye called Rabbi: for one is your Master, even Christ; and all ye are brethren. And call no man your father upon the earth: for one is your Father, which is in heaven. Neither be ye called masters: for one is your Master, even Christ. But he that is greatest among you shall be your servant. And whosoever shall exalt himself shall be abased; and he that shall humble himself shall be exalted. **2 Tim. 2:24.** And the servant of the Lord must not strive; but be gentle unto all men, apt to teach, patient. **1 Pet. 5:3.** ... neither as being lords over God's heritage, but being ensamples to the flock.

a. **Gen. 2:24.** Therefore shall a man leave his father and his mother, and shall cleave unto his wife: and they shall be one flesh. **Matt. 19:4–6.** And he answered and said unto them, Have ye not read, that he which made them at the beginning made them male and female, and said, For this cause shall a man leave father and mother, and shall cleave to his wife: and they twain shall be one flesh? Wherefore they are no

2. Marriage was ordained for the mutual help of husband and wife,[b] for the increase of mankind with legitimate issue, and of the church with an holy seed;[c] and for preventing of uncleanness.[d]

3. It is lawful for all sorts of people to marry, who are able with judgment to give their consent.[e] Yet it is the duty of Christians to marry only in the Lord.[f] And therefore such as profess the true reformed religion should not marry with infidels, papists, or other idolaters: neither should such as are godly be unequally yoked, by marrying with such as are notoriously wicked in their life, or maintain

more twain, but one flesh. What therefore God hath joined together, let not man put asunder. **Rom. 7:3.** So then if, while her husband liveth, she be married to another man, she shall be called an adulteress: but if her husband be dead, she is free from that law; so that she is no adulteress, though she be married to another man. **Prov. 2:17.** … which forsaketh the guide of her youth, and forgetteth the covenant of her God.

b. **Gen. 2:18.** And the LORD God said, It is not good that the man should be alone; I will make him an help meet for him. **Eph. 5:28.** So ought men to love their wives as their own bodies. He that loveth his wife loveth himself. **1 Pet. 3:7.** Likewise, ye husbands, dwell with them according to knowledge, giving honour unto the wife, as unto the weaker vessel, and as being heirs together of the grace of life; that your prayers be not hindered.

c. **Gen. 1:28.** And God blessed them, and God said unto them, Be fruitful, and multiply, and replenish the earth, and subdue it: and have dominion over the fish of the sea, and over the fowl of the air, and over every living thing that moveth upon the earth. **Gen. 9:1.** And God blessed Noah and his sons, and said unto them, Be fruitful, and multiply, and replenish the earth. **Mal. 2:15.** And did not he make one? Yet had he the residue of the spirit. And wherefore one? That he might seek a godly seed. Therefore take heed to your spirit, and let none deal treacherously against the wife of his youth.

d. **1 Cor. 7:2, 9.** Nevertheless, to avoid fornication, let every man have his own wife, and let every woman have her own husband.… But if they cannot contain, let them marry: for it is better to marry than to burn.

e. **Heb. 13:4.** Marriage is honourable in all, and the bed undefiled: but whoremongers and adulterers God will judge. **1 Tim. 4:3.** … forbidding to marry, and commanding to abstain from meats, which God hath created to be received with thanksgiving of them which believe and know the truth. **1 Cor. 7:36–38.** But if any man think that he behaveth himself uncomely toward his virgin, if she pass the flower of her age, and need so require, let him do what he will, he sinneth not: let them marry. Nevertheless he that standeth stedfast in his heart, having no necessity, but hath power over his own will, and hath so decreed in his heart that he will keep his virgin, doeth well. So then he that giveth her in marriage doeth well; but he that giveth her not in marriage doeth better. **Gen. 24:57–58.** And they said, We will call the damsel, and inquire at her mouth. And they called Rebekah, and said unto her, Wilt thou go with this man? And she said, I will go.

f. **1 Cor. 7:39.** The wife is bound by the law as long as her husband liveth; but if her husband be dead, she is at liberty to be married to whom she will; only in the Lord.

damnable heresies.[g]

4. Marriage ought not to be within the degrees of consanguinity or affinity forbidden by the Word.[h] Nor can such incestuous marriages ever be made lawful by any law of man or consent of parties, so as those persons may live together as man and wife.[i]

5. Adultery or fornication committed after a contract, being detected before marriage, giveth just occasion to the innocent party to dissolve that contract.[k] In the case of adultery after marriage, it is

g. **Gen. 34:14.** And they said unto them, We cannot do this thing, to give our sister to one that is uncircumcised; for that were a reproach unto us. **Ex. 34:16.** And thou take of their daughters unto thy sons, and their daughters go a whoring after their gods, and make thy sons go a whoring after their gods. **2 Cor. 6:14.** Be ye not unequally yoked together with unbelievers: for what fellowship hath righteousness with unrighteousness? and what communion hath light with darkness? **See Deut. 7:3–4; 1 Kings 11:4; Neh. 13:25–27; Mal. 2:11–12.**

h. **Lev. 18:6–17, 24–30.** None of you shall approach to any that is near of kin to him, to uncover their nakedness: I am the LORD. The nakedness of thy father, or the nakedness of thy mother, shalt thou not uncover: she is thy mother; thou shalt not uncover her nakedness. The nakedness of thy father's wife shalt thou not uncover: it is thy father's nakedness. The nakedness of thy sister, the daughter of thy father, or daughter of thy mother, whether she be born at home, or born abroad, even their nakedness thou shalt not uncover.... Therefore shall ye keep mine ordinance, that ye commit not any one of these abominable customs, which were committed before you, and that ye defile not yourselves therein: I am the LORD your God. **Lev. 20:19.** And thou shalt not uncover the nakedness of thy mother's sister, nor of thy father's sister: for he uncovereth his near kin: they shall bear their iniquity. **1 Cor. 5:1.** It is reported commonly that there is fornication among you, and such fornication as is not so much as named among the Gentiles, that one should have his father's wife. **Amos 2:7.** ... that pant after the dust of the earth on the head of the poor, and turn aside the way of the meek: and a man and his father will go in unto the same maid, to profane my holy name.

i. **Mark 6:18.** For John had said unto Herod, It is not lawful for thee to have thy brother's wife. **Lev. 18:24–28.** Defile not ye yourselves in any of these things: for in all these the nations are defiled which I cast out before you: and the land is defiled: therefore I do visit the iniquity thereof upon it, and the land itself vomiteth out her inhabitants. Ye shall therefore keep my statutes and my judgments, and shall not commit any of these abominations; neither any of your own nation, nor any stranger that sojourneth among you....

k. **Matt. 1:18–20.** Now the birth of Jesus Christ was on this wise: When as his mother Mary was espoused to Joseph, before they came together, she was found with child of the Holy Ghost. Then Joseph her husband, being a just man, and not willing to make her a publick example, was minded to put her away privily. But while he thought on these things, behold, the angel of the Lord appeared unto him in a dream, saying, Joseph, thou son of David, fear not to take unto thee Mary thy wife: for that which is conceived in her is of the Holy Ghost. **See Deut. 22:23–24.**

lawful for the innocent party to sue out a divorce:[l] and, after the divorce, to marry another, as if the offending party were dead.[m]

6. Although the corruption of man be such as is apt to study arguments unduly to put asunder those whom God hath joined together in marriage: yet, nothing but adultery, or such willful desertion as can no way be remedied by the church, or civil magistrate, is cause sufficient of dissolving the bond of marriage:[n] wherein, a public and orderly course of proceeding is to be observed; and the persons concerned in it not left to their own wills, and discretion, in their own case.[o]

Chapter 25
Of the Church

1. The catholic or universal church, which is invisible, consists of the whole number of the elect, that have been, are, or shall be gath-

l. **Matt. 5:31–32.** It hath been said, Whosoever shall put away his wife, let him give her a writing of divorcement: but I say unto you, That whosoever shall put away his wife, saving for the cause of fornication, causeth her to commit adultery: and whosoever shall marry her that is divorced committeth adultery.

m. **Matt. 19:9.** And I say unto you, Whosoever shall put away his wife, except it be for fornication, and shall marry another, committeth adultery: and whoso marrieth her which is put away doth commit adultery. **Rom. 7:2–3.** For the woman which hath an husband is bound by the law to her husband so long as he liveth; but if the husband be dead, she is loosed from the law of her husband. So then if, while her husband liveth, she be married to another man, she shall be called an adulteress: but if her husband be dead, she is free from that law; so that she is no adulteress, though she be married to another man.

n. **Matt. 19:8–9.** He saith unto them, Moses because of the hardness of your hearts suffered you to put away your wives: but from the beginning it was not so. And I say unto you, Whosoever shall put away his wife, except it be for fornication, and shall marry another, committeth adultery: and whoso marrieth her which is put away doth commit adultery. **1 Cor. 7:15.** But if the unbelieving depart, let him depart. A brother or a sister is not under bondage in such cases: but God hath called us to peace. **Matt. 19:6.** Wherefore they are no more twain, but one flesh. What therefore God hath joined together, let not man put asunder.

o. **Deut. 24:1–4.** When a man hath taken a wife, and married her, and it come to pass that she find no favour in his eyes, because he hath found some uncleanness in her: then let him write her a bill of divorcement, and give it in her hand, and send her out of his house. And when she is departed out of his house, she may go and be another man's wife. And if the latter husband hate her, and write her a bill of divorcement, and giveth it in her hand, and sendeth her out of his house; or if the latter

ered into one, under Christ the Head thereof; and is the spouse, the body, the fullness of him that filleth all in all.[a]

2. The visible church, which is also catholic or universal under the gospel (not confined to one nation, as before under the law), consists of all those throughout the world that profess the true religion;[b] and of their children:[c] and is the kingdom of the Lord Jesus

husband die, which took her to be his wife; her former husband, which sent her away, may not take her again to be his wife, after that she is defiled; for that is abomination before the LORD: and thou shalt not cause the land to sin, which the LORD thy God giveth thee for an inheritance.

a. **Eph. 1:10, 22–23.** … that in the dispensation of the fulness of times he might gather together in one all things in Christ, both which are in heaven, and which are on earth; even in him.… and hath put all things under his feet, and gave him to be the head over all things to the church, which is his body, the fulness of him that filleth all in all. **Eph. 5:23, 27, 32.** For the husband is the head of the wife, even as Christ is the head of the church: and he is the saviour of the body.… that he might present it to himself a glorious church, not having spot, or wrinkle, or any such thing; but that it should be holy and without blemish.… This is a great mystery: but I speak concerning Christ and the church. **Col. 1:18.** And he is the head of the body, the church: who is the beginning, the firstborn from the dead; that in all things he might have the preeminence.

b. **1 Cor. 1:2.** … unto the church of God which is at Corinth, to them that are sanctified in Christ Jesus, called to be saints, with all that in every place call upon the name of Jesus Christ our Lord, both theirs and ours. **1 Cor. 12:12–13.** For as the body is one, and hath many members, and all the members of that one body, being many, are one body: so also is Christ. For by one Spirit are we all baptized into one body, whether we be Jews or Gentiles, whether we be bond or free; and have been all made to drink into one Spirit. **Ps. 2:8.** Ask of me, and I shall give thee the heathen for thine inheritance, and the uttermost parts of the earth for thy possession. **Rev. 7:9.** After this I beheld, and, lo, a great multitude, which no man could number, of all nations, and kindreds, and people, and tongues, stood before the throne, and before the Lamb, clothed with white robes, and palms in their hands. **Rom. 15:9–12.** … and that the Gentiles might glorify God for his mercy; as it is written, For this cause I will confess to thee among the Gentiles, and sing unto thy name. And again he saith, Rejoice, ye Gentiles, with his people. And again, Praise the Lord, all ye Gentiles; and laud him, all ye people. And again, Esaias saith, There shall be a root of Jesse, and he that shall rise to reign over the Gentiles; in him shall the Gentiles trust.

c. **1 Cor. 7:14.** For the unbelieving husband is sanctified by the wife, and the unbelieving wife is sanctified by the husband: else were your children unclean; but now are they holy. **Acts 2:39.** For the promise is unto you, and to your children, and to all that are afar off, even as many as the Lord our God shall call. **Gen. 17:7–12.** And I will establish my covenant between me and thee and thy seed after thee in their generations for an everlasting covenant, to be a God unto thee, and to thy seed after thee. And I will give unto thee, and to thy seed after thee, the land wherein thou art a stranger, all the land of Canaan, for an everlasting possession; and I will be their God.

Christ,^d the house and family of God,^e out of which there is no ordinary possibility of salvation.^f

3. Unto this catholic visible church Christ hath given the ministry, oracles, and ordinances of God, for the gathering and perfecting of the saints, in this life, to the end of the world: and doth, by his own presence and Spirit, according to his promise, make them effectual thereunto.^g

And God said unto Abraham, Thou shalt keep my covenant therefore, thou, and thy seed after thee in their generations. This is my covenant, which ye shall keep, between me and you and thy seed after thee; Every man child among you shall be circumcised. And ye shall circumcise the flesh of your foreskin; and it shall be a token of the covenant betwixt me and you. And he that is eight days old shall be circumcised among you, every man child in your generations, he that is born in the house, or bought with money of any stranger, which is not of thy seed. **Ezek. 16:20–21.** Moreover thou hast taken thy sons and thy daughters, whom thou hast borne unto me, and these hast thou sacrificed unto them to be devoured. Is this of thy whoredoms a small matter, that thou hast slain my children, and delivered them to cause them to pass through the fire for them? **Rom. 11:16.** For if the firstfruit be holy, the lump is also holy: and if the root be holy, so are the branches. **See Gal. 3:7, 9, 14; Rom. 4:12, 16, 24.**

d. **Matt. 13:47.** Again, the kingdom of heaven is like unto a net, that was cast into the sea, and gathered of every kind. **Isa. 9:7.** Of the increase of his government and peace there shall be no end, upon the throne of David, and upon his kingdom, to order it, and to establish it with judgment and with justice from henceforth even for ever. The zeal of the LORD of hosts will perform this. **Luke 1:32–33.** He shall be great, and shall be called the Son of the Highest: and the Lord God shall give unto him the throne of his father David: and he shall reign over the house of Jacob for ever; and of his kingdom there shall be no end. **Acts 2:30–36.** Therefore being a prophet, and knowing that God had sworn with an oath to him, that of the fruit of his loins, according to the flesh, he would raise up Christ to sit on his throne; he seeing this before spake of the resurrection of Christ, that his soul was not left in hell, neither his flesh did see corruption. This Jesus hath God raised up, whereof we all are witnesses. Therefore being by the right hand of God exalted, and having received of the Father the promise of the Holy Ghost, he hath shed forth this, which ye now see and hear. For David is not ascended into the heavens: but he saith himself, The LORD said unto my Lord, Sit thou on my right hand, until I make thy foes thy footstool. Therefore let all the house of Israel know assuredly, that God hath made that same Jesus, whom ye have crucified, both Lord and Christ. **Col. 1:13.** … who hath delivered us from the power of darkness, and hath translated us into the kingdom of his dear Son.

e. **Eph. 2:19.** Now therefore ye are no more strangers and foreigners, but fellow-citizens with the saints, and of the household of God. **Eph. 3:15.** … [the Father of our Lord Jesus Christ,] of whom the whole family in heaven and earth is named.

f. **Acts 2:47.** [All that believed were] praising God, and having favour with all the people. And the Lord added to the church daily such as should be saved.

g. **1 Cor. 12:28.** And God hath set some in the church, first apostles, secondarily prophets, thirdly teachers, after that miracles, then gifts of healings, helps, governments, diversities of tongues. **Eph. 4:11–13.** And he gave some, apostles; and some,

4. This catholic church hath been sometimes more, sometimes less visible.[h] And particular churches, which are members thereof, are more or less pure, according as the doctrine of the gospel is taught and embraced, ordinances administered, and public worship performed more or less purely in them.[i]

prophets; and some, evangelists; and some, pastors and teachers; for the perfecting of the saints, for the work of the ministry, for the edifying of the body of Christ: till we all come in the unity of the faith, and of the knowledge of the Son of God, unto a perfect man, unto the measure of the stature of the fulness of Christ. **Matt. 28:19–20.** Go ye therefore, and teach all nations, baptizing them in the name of the Father, and of the Son, and of the Holy Ghost: teaching them to observe all things whatsoever I have commanded you: and, lo, I am with you alway, even unto the end of the world. Amen. **Isa. 59:12.** For our transgressions are multiplied before thee, and our sins testify against us: for our transgressions are with us; and as for our iniquities, we know them.

h. **Rom. 11:3–5.** … Lord, they have killed thy prophets, and digged down thine altars; and I am left alone, and they seek my life. But what saith the answer of God unto him? I have reserved to myself seven thousand men, who have not bowed the knee to the image of Baal. Even so then at this present time also there is a remnant according to the election of grace. **Acts 9:31.** Then had the churches rest throughout all Judaea and Galilee and Samaria, and were edified; and walking in the fear of the Lord, and in the comfort of the Holy Ghost, were multiplied. **Acts 2:41, 47.** Then they that gladly received his word were baptized: and the same day there were added unto them about three thousand souls.… [All that believed were] praising God, and having favour with all the people. And the Lord added to the church daily such as should be saved. **Acts 18:8–10.** And Crispus, the chief ruler of the synagogue, believed on the Lord with all his house; and many of the Corinthians hearing believed, and were baptized. Then spake the Lord to Paul in the night by a vision, Be not afraid, but speak, and hold not thy peace: for I am with thee, and no man shall set on thee to hurt thee: for I have much people in this city.

i. **Acts 2:41–42.** Then they that gladly received his word were baptized: and the same day there were added unto them about three thousand souls. And they continued stedfastly in the apostles' doctrine and fellowship, and in breaking of bread, and in prayers. **1 Cor. 5:6–7.** Your glorying is not good. Know ye not that a little leaven leaveneth the whole lump? Purge out therefore the old leaven, that ye may be a new lump, as ye are unleavened. For even Christ our passover is sacrificed for us. **Rev. 2–3.** Unto the angel of the church of Ephesus write … I know thy works, and thy labour, and thy patience, and how thou canst not bear them which are evil: and thou hast tried them which say they are apostles, and are not, and hast found them liars.… Nevertheless I have somewhat against thee, because thou hast left thy first love.… And unto the angel of the church in Smyrna write … I know thy works, and tribulation, and poverty, (but thou art rich).… And to the angel of the church in Pergamos write … I have a few things against thee, because thou hast there them that hold the doctrine of Balaam.… And unto the angel of the church in Thyatira write … I have a few things against thee, because thou sufferest that woman Jezebel, which calleth herself a prophetess, to teach and to seduce my servants to commit fornication, and to eat things sacrificed unto idols.… And unto the angel of the church in Sardis write …

5. The purest churches under heaven are subject both to mixture and error;[k] and some have so degenerated, as to become no churches of Christ, but synagogues of Satan.[l] Nevertheless, there shall be always a church on earth, to worship God according to his will.[m]

Remember therefore how thou hast received and heard, and hold fast, and repent.… And to the angel of the church in Philadelphia write … I know thy works.… thou hast a little strength, and hast kept my word, and hast not denied my name.… And unto the angel of the church of the Laodiceans write … I know thy works, that thou art neither cold nor hot.…

k. **1 Cor. 13:12.** For now we see through a glass, darkly; but then face to face: now I know in part; but then shall I know even as also I am known. **Rev. 2–3. See footnote *i* above. Matt. 13:24–30, 47.** Another parable put he forth unto them, saying, The kingdom of heaven is likened unto a man which sowed good seed in his field: but while men slept, his enemy came and sowed tares among the wheat, and went his way. But when the blade was sprung up, and brought forth fruit, then appeared the tares also. So the servants of the householder came and said unto him, Sir, didst not thou sow good seed in thy field? from whence then hath it tares? He said unto them, An enemy hath done this. The servants said unto him, Wilt thou then that we go and gather them up? But he said, Nay; lest while ye gather up the tares, ye root up also the wheat with them. Let both grow together until the harvest: and in the time of harvest I will say to the reapers, Gather ye together first the tares, and bind them in bundles to burn them: but gather the wheat into my barn.… Again, the kingdom of heaven is like unto a net, that was cast into the sea, and gathered of every kind.

l. **Matt. 23:37–39.** O Jerusalem, Jerusalem, thou that killest the prophets, and stonest them which are sent unto thee, how often would I have gathered thy children together, even as a hen gathereth her chickens under her wings, and ye would not! Behold, your house is left unto you desolate. For I say unto you, Ye shall not see me henceforth, till ye shall say, Blessed is he that cometh in the name of the Lord. **Rom. 11:18–22.** Boast not against the branches. But if thou boast, thou bearest not the root, but the root thee. Thou wilt say then, The branches were broken off, that I might be graffed in. Well; because of unbelief they were broken off, and thou standest by faith. Be not highminded, but fear: for if God spared not the natural branches, take heed lest he also spare not thee. Behold therefore the goodness and severity of God: on them which fell, severity; but toward thee, goodness, if thou continue in his goodness: otherwise thou also shalt be cut off.

m. **Matt. 16:18.** And I say also unto thee, That thou art Peter, and upon this rock I will build my church; and the gates of hell shall not prevail against it. **Ps. 45:16–17.** Instead of thy fathers shall be thy children, whom thou mayest make princes in all the earth. I will make thy name to be remembered in all generations: therefore shall the people praise thee for ever and ever. **Ps. 72:17.** His name shall endure for ever: his name shall be continued as long as the sun: and men shall be blessed in him: all nations shall call him blessed. **Matt. 28:19–20.** Go ye therefore, and teach all nations, baptizing them in the name of the Father, and of the Son, and of the Holy Ghost: teaching them to observe all things whatsoever I have commanded you: and, lo, I am with you alway, even unto the end of the world. Amen. **1 Cor. 15:51–52.** Behold, I shew you a mystery; We shall not all sleep, but we shall all be changed, in a

6. There is no other head of the church but the Lord Jesus Christ.[n] Nor can the pope of Rome, in any sense, be head thereof.[o]

Chapter 26
Of the Communion of Saints

1. All saints, that are united to Jesus Christ their Head, by his Spirit, and by faith, have fellowship with him in his graces, sufferings, death, resurrection, and glory:[a] and, being united to one another in

moment, in the twinkling of an eye, at the last trump: for the trumpet shall sound, and the dead shall be raised incorruptible, and we shall be changed. **1 Thess. 4:17.** Then we which are alive and remain shall be caught up together with them in the clouds, to meet the Lord in the air: and so shall we ever be with the Lord.

n. **Col. 1:18.** And he is the head of the body, the church: who is the beginning, the firstborn from the dead; that in all things he might have the preeminence. **Eph. 1:22.** ... and hath put all things under his feet, and gave him to be the head over all things to the church.

o. **Matt. 23:8–10.** But be not ye called Rabbi: for one is your Master, even Christ; and all ye are brethren. And call no man your father upon the earth: for one is your Father, which is in heaven. Neither be ye called masters: for one is your Master, even Christ. **1 Pet. 5:2–4.** Feed the flock of God which is among you, taking the oversight thereof, not by constraint, but willingly; not for filthy lucre, but of a ready mind; neither as being lords over God's heritage, but being ensamples to the flock. And when the chief Shepherd shall appear, ye shall receive a crown of glory that fadeth not away.

a. **1 John 1:3.** That which we have seen and heard declare we unto you, that ye also may have fellowship with us: and truly our fellowship is with the Father, and with his Son Jesus Christ. **Eph. 3:16–18.** ... that he would grant you, according to the riches of his glory, to be strengthened with might by his Spirit in the inner man; that Christ may dwell in your hearts by faith; that ye, being rooted and grounded in love, may be able to comprehend with all saints what is the breadth, and length, and depth, and height. **John 1:16.** And of his fulness have all we received, and grace for grace. **Eph. 2:5–6.** Even when we were dead in sins, [God] hath quickened us together with Christ, (by grace ye are saved;) and hath raised us up together, and made us sit together in heavenly places in Christ Jesus. **Phil. 3:10.** ...that I may know him, and the power of his resurrection, and the fellowship of his sufferings, being made conformable unto his death. **Rom. 6:5–6.** For if we have been planted together in the likeness of his death, we shall be also in the likeness of his resurrection: knowing this, that our old man is crucified with him, that the body of sin might be destroyed, that henceforth we should not serve sin. **Rom. 8:17.** ... and if children, then heirs; heirs of God, and joint-heirs with Christ; if so be that we suffer with him, that we may be also glorified together. **2 Tim. 2:12.** If we suffer, we shall also reign with him: if we deny him, he also will deny us.

love, they have communion in each other's gifts and graces,[b] and are obliged to the performance of such duties, public and private, as do conduce to their mutual good, both in the inward and outward man.[c]

2. Saints by profession are bound to maintain an holy fellowship and communion in the worship of God, and in performing such other spiritual services as tend to their mutual edification;[d] as also in relieving each other in outward things, according to their several abilities and necessities. Which communion, as God offereth opportunity, is to be extended unto all those who, in every place, call upon the name

b. **Eph. 4:15–16.** … but speaking the truth in love, may grow up into him in all things, which is the head, even Christ: from whom the whole body fitly joined together and compacted by that which every joint supplieth, according to the effectual working in the measure of every part, maketh increase of the body unto the edifying of itself in love. **1 Cor. 12:7, 12.** But the manifestation of the Spirit is given to every man to profit withal.… For as the body is one, and hath many members, and all the members of that one body, being many, are one body: so also is Christ. **1 Cor. 3:21–23.** Therefore let no man glory in men. For all things are yours; whether Paul, or Apollos, or Cephas, or the world, or life, or death, or things present, or things to come; all are yours; and ye are Christ's; and Christ is God's. **Col. 2:19.** … and not holding the Head, from which all the body by joints and bands having nourishment ministered, and knit together, increaseth with the increase of God.

c. **1 Thess. 5:11, 14.** Wherefore comfort yourselves together, and edify one another, even as also ye do.… Now we exhort you, brethren, warn them that are unruly, comfort the feebleminded, support the weak, be patient toward all men. **Rom. 1:11–12, 14.** For I long to see you, that I may impart unto you some spiritual gift, to the end ye may be established; that is, that I may be comforted together with you by the mutual faith both of you and me.… I am debtor both to the Greeks, and to the Barbarians; both to the wise, and to the unwise. **1 John 3:16–18.** Hereby perceive we the love of God, because he laid down his life for us: and we ought to lay down our lives for the brethren. But whoso hath this world's good, and seeth his brother have need, and shutteth up his bowels of compassion from him, how dwelleth the love of God in him? My little children, let us not love in word, neither in tongue; but in deed and in truth. **Gal. 6:10.** As we have therefore opportunity, let us do good unto all men, especially unto them who are of the household of faith.

d. **Heb. 10:24–25.** And let us consider one another to provoke unto love and to good works: not forsaking the assembling of ourselves together, as the manner of some is; but exhorting one another: and so much the more, as ye see the day approaching. **Acts 2:42, 46.** And they continued stedfastly in the apostles' doctrine and fellowship, and in breaking of bread, and in prayers.… And they, continuing daily with one accord in the temple, and breaking bread from house to house, did eat their meat with gladness and singleness of heart. **Isa. 2:3.** And many people shall go and say, Come ye, and let us go up to the mountain of the LORD, to the house of the God of Jacob; and he will teach us of his ways, and we will walk in his paths: for out of Zion shall go forth the law, and the word of the LORD from Jerusalem. **1 Cor. 11:20.** When ye come together therefore into one place, this is not to eat the Lord's supper.

of the Lord Jesus.[e]

3. This communion which the saints have with Christ, doth not make them in any wise partakers of the substance of his Godhead; or to be equal with Christ in any respect: either of which to affirm is impious and blasphemous.[f] Nor doth their communion one with another, as saints, take away, or infringe the title or propriety which each man hath in his goods and possessions.[g]

e. **1 John 3:17.** But whoso hath this world's good, and seeth his brother have need, and shutteth up his bowels of compassion from him, how dwelleth the love of God in him? **2 Cor. 8–9.** Moreover, brethren, we do you to wit of the grace of God bestowed on the churches of Macedonia; how that in a great trial of affliction the abundance of their joy and their deep poverty abounded unto the riches of their liberality.… Therefore, as ye abound in every thing, in faith, and utterance, and knowledge, and in all diligence, and in your love to us, see that ye abound in this grace also.… For I mean not that other men be eased, and ye burdened: but by an equality, that now at this time your abundance may be a supply for their want, that their abundance also may be a supply for your want: that there may be equality.… For the administration of this service not only supplieth the want of the saints, but is abundant also by many thanksgivings unto God; whiles by the experiment of this ministration they glorify God for your professed subjection unto the gospel of Christ, and for your liberal distribution unto them, and unto all men. **Acts 11:29–30.** Then the disciples, every man according to his ability, determined to send relief unto the brethren which dwelt in Judaea: which also they did, and sent it to the elders by the hands of Barnabas and Saul. **See Acts 2:44–45.**

f. **Col. 1:18–19.** And he is the head of the body, the church: who is the beginning, the firstborn from the dead; that in all things he might have the preeminence. For it pleased the Father that in him should all fulness dwell. **1 Cor. 8:6.** But to us there is but one God, the Father, of whom are all things, and we in him; and one Lord Jesus Christ, by whom are all things, and we by him. **Ps. 45:6–7.** Thy throne, O God, is for ever and ever: the sceptre of thy kingdom is a right sceptre. Thou lovest righteousness, and hatest wickedness: therefore God, thy God, hath anointed thee with the oil of gladness above thy fellows. **Heb. 1:6–9.** And again, when he bringeth in the firstbegotten into the world, he saith, And let all the angels of God worship him. And of the angels he saith, Who maketh his angels spirits, and his ministers a flame of fire. But unto the Son he saith, Thy throne, O God, is for ever and ever: a sceptre of righteousness is the sceptre of thy kingdom. Thou hast loved righteousness, and hated iniquity; therefore God, even thy God, hath anointed thee with the oil of gladness above thy fellows. **John 1:14.** And the Word was made flesh, and dwelt among us, (and we beheld his glory, the glory as of the only begotten of the Father,) full of grace and truth. **John 20:17.** Jesus saith unto her, Touch me not; for I am not yet ascended to my Father: but go to my brethren, and say unto them, I ascend unto my Father, and your Father; and to my God, and your God.

g. **Ex. 20:15.** Thou shalt not steal. **Eph. 4:28.** Let him that stole steal no more: but rather let him labour, working with his hands the thing which is good, that he may have to give to him that needeth. **Acts 5:4.** Whiles it remained, was it not thine own? and after it was sold, was it not in thine own power? why hast thou conceived this thing

Chapter 27
Of the Sacraments

1. Sacraments are holy signs and seals of the covenant of grace,[a] immediately instituted by God,[b] to represent Christ, and his benefits; and to confirm our interest in him:[c] as also, to put a visible difference between those that belong unto the church, and the rest of the world;[d] and solemnly to engage them to the service of God in Christ, according to his Word.[e]

in thine heart? thou hast not lied unto men, but unto God.

a. **Rom. 4:11.** And he received the sign of circumcision, a seal of the righteousness of the faith which he had yet being uncircumcised: that he might be the father of all them that believe, though they be not circumcised; that righteousness might be imputed unto them also. **Gen. 17:7, 10–11.** And I will establish my covenant between me and thee and thy seed after thee in their generations for an everlasting covenant, to be a God unto thee, and to thy seed after thee.... This is my covenant, which ye shall keep, between me and you and thy seed after thee; Every man child among you shall be circumcised. And ye shall circumcise the flesh of your foreskin; and it shall be a token of the covenant betwixt me and you.

b. **Matt. 28:19.** Go ye therefore, and teach all nations, baptizing them in the name of the Father, and of the Son, and of the Holy Ghost. **1 Cor. 11:23.** For I have received of the Lord that which also I delivered unto you, That the Lord Jesus the same night in which he was betrayed took bread.

c. **Rom. 6:3–4.** Know ye not, that so many of us as were baptized into Jesus Christ were baptized into his death? Therefore we are buried with him by baptism into death: that like as Christ was raised up from the dead by the glory of the Father, even so we also should walk in newness of life. **Col. 2:12.** ... buried with him in baptism, wherein also ye are risen with him through the faith of the operation of God, who hath raised him from the dead. **1 Cor. 10:16.** The cup of blessing which we bless, is it not the communion of the blood of Christ? The bread which we break, is it not the communion of the body of Christ? **1 Cor. 11:25–26.** After the same manner also he took the cup, when he had supped, saying, This cup is the new testament in my blood: this do ye, as oft as ye drink it, in remembrance of me. For as often as ye eat this bread, and drink this cup, ye do shew the Lord's death till he come. **Gal. 3:27.** For as many of you as have been baptized into Christ have put on Christ.

d. **Ex. 12:48.** And when a stranger shall sojourn with thee, and will keep the passover to the Lord, let all his males be circumcised, and then let him come near and keep it; and he shall be as one that is born in the land: for no uncircumcised person shall eat thereof. **Gen. 34:14.** And they said unto them, We cannot do this thing, to give our sister to one that is uncircumcised; for that were a reproach unto us. **1 Cor. 10:21.** Ye cannot drink the cup of the Lord, and the cup of devils: ye cannot be partakers of the Lord's table, and of the table of devils.

e. **Rom. 6:3–4.** Know ye not, that so many of us as were baptized into Jesus

2. There is, in every sacrament, a spiritual relation, or sacramental union, between the sign and the thing signified: whence it comes to pass, that the names and effects of the one are attributed to the other.[f]

3. The grace which is exhibited in or by the sacraments rightly used, is not conferred by any power in them; neither doth the efficacy of a sacrament depend upon the piety or intention of him that doth administer it:[g] but upon the work of the Spirit,[h] and the word of institution, which contains, together with a precept authorizing the use thereof, a promise of benefit to worthy receivers.[i]

Christ were baptized into his death? Therefore we are buried with him by baptism into death: that like as Christ was raised up from the dead by the glory of the Father, even so we also should walk in newness of life. **Gal. 3:27.** For as many of you as have been baptized into Christ have put on Christ. **1 Pet. 3:21.** The like figure whereunto even baptism doth also now save us (not the putting away of the filth of the flesh, but the answer of a good conscience toward God,) by the resurrection of Jesus Christ. **1 Cor. 10:16.** The cup of blessing which we bless, is it not the communion of the blood of Christ? The bread which we break, is it not the communion of the body of Christ? **See 1 Cor. 5:7–8.**

f. **Gen. 17:10.** This is my covenant, which ye shall keep, between me and you and thy seed after thee; Every man child among you shall be circumcised. **Matt. 26:27–28.** And he took the cup, and gave thanks, and gave it to them, saying, Drink ye all of it; for this is my blood of the new testament, which is shed for many for the remission of sins. **1 Cor. 10:16–18.** The cup of blessing which we bless, is it not the communion of the blood of Christ? The bread which we break, is it not the communion of the body of Christ? For we being many are one bread, and one body: for we are all partakers of that one bread. Behold Israel after the flesh: are not they which eat of the sacrifices partakers of the altar?

g. **Rom. 2:28–29.** For he is not a Jew, which is one outwardly; neither is that circumcision, which is outward in the flesh: but he is a Jew, which is one inwardly; and circumcision is that of the heart, in the spirit, and not in the letter; whose praise is not of men, but of God. **1 Pet. 3:21.** The like figure whereunto even baptism doth also now save us (not the putting away of the filth of the flesh, but the answer of a good conscience toward God,) by the resurrection of Jesus Christ.

h. **1 Cor. 12:13.** For by one Spirit are we all baptized into one body, whether we be Jews or Gentiles, whether we be bond or free; and have been all made to drink into one Spirit.

i. **Matt. 26:26–28.** And as they were eating, Jesus took bread, and blessed it, and brake it, and gave it to the disciples, and said, Take, eat; this is my body. And he took the cup, and gave thanks, and gave it to them, saying, Drink ye all of it; for this is my blood of the new testament, which is shed for many for the remission of sins. **Luke 22:19–20.** And he took bread, and gave thanks, and brake it, and gave unto them, saying, This is my body which is given for you: this do in remembrance of me. Likewise also the cup after supper, saying, This cup is the new testament in my blood,

4. There be only two sacraments ordained by Christ our Lord in the gospel; that is to say, baptism, and the Supper of the Lord: neither of which may be dispensed by any, but by a minister of the Word lawfully ordained.[k]

5. The sacraments of the old testament, in regard of the spiritual things thereby signified and exhibited, were, for substance, the same with those of the new.[l]

Chapter 28
Of Baptism

1. Baptism is a sacrament of the new testament, ordained by Jesus Christ,[a] not only for the solemn admission of the party bap-

which is shed for you. **Matt. 28:19–20.** Go ye therefore, and teach all nations, baptizing them in the name of the Father, and of the Son, and of the Holy Ghost: teaching them to observe all things whatsoever I have commanded you: and, lo, I am with you alway, even unto the end of the world. Amen. **1 Cor. 11:26.** For as often as ye eat this bread, and drink this cup, ye do shew the Lord's death till he come.

k. **Matt. 28:19.** Go ye therefore, and teach all nations, baptizing them in the name of the Father, and of the Son, and of the Holy Ghost. **1 Cor. 11:20, 23.** When ye come together therefore into one place, this is not to eat the Lord's supper.... For I have received of the Lord that which also I delivered unto you, That the Lord Jesus the same night in which he was betrayed took bread. **1 Cor. 4:1.** Let a man so account of us, as of the ministers of Christ, and stewards of the mysteries of God. **Eph. 4:11–12.** And he gave some, apostles; and some, prophets; and some, evangelists; and some, pastors and teachers; for the perfecting of the saints, for the work of the ministry, for the edifying of the body of Christ.

l. **1 Cor. 10:1–4.** Moreover, brethren, I would not that ye should be ignorant, how that all our fathers were under the cloud, and all passed through the sea; and were all baptized unto Moses in the cloud and in the sea; and did all eat the same spiritual meat; and did all drink the same spiritual drink: for they drank of that spiritual Rock that followed them: and that Rock was Christ. **Rom. 4:11.** And he received the sign of circumcision, a seal of the righteousness of the faith which he had yet being uncircumcised: that he might be the father of all them that believe, though they be not circumcised; that righteousness might be imputed unto them also. **Col. 2:11–12.** ... in whom also ye are circumcised with the circumcision made without hands, in putting off the body of the sins of the flesh by the circumcision of Christ: buried with him in baptism, wherein also ye are risen with him through the faith of the operation of God, who hath raised him from the dead.

a. **Matt. 28:19.** Go ye therefore, and teach all nations, baptizing them in the name of the Father, and of the Son, and of the Holy Ghost.

tized into the visible church;[b] but also, to be unto him a sign and seal of the covenant of grace,[c] of his ingrafting into Christ,[d] of regeneration,[e] of remission of sins,[f] and of his giving up unto God, through Jesus Christ, to walk in newness of life.[g] Which sacrament is, by Christ's own appointment, to be continued in his church until the end of the world.[h]

2. The outward element to be used in this sacrament is water, wherewith the party is to be baptized, in the name of the Father, and of the Son, and of the Holy Ghost, by a minister of the gospel, lawfully called thereunto.[i]

b. **1 Cor. 12:13.** For by one Spirit are we all baptized into one body, whether we be Jews or Gentiles, whether we be bond or free; and have been all made to drink into one Spirit. **Gal. 3:27–28.** For as many of you as have been baptized into Christ have put on Christ. There is neither Jew nor Greek, there is neither bond nor free, there is neither male nor female: for ye are all one in Christ Jesus.

c. **Rom. 4:11.** And he received the sign of circumcision, a seal of the righteousness of the faith which he had yet being uncircumcised: that he might be the father of all them that believe, though they be not circumcised; that righteousness might be imputed unto them also. **Col. 2:11–12.** … in whom also ye are circumcised with the circumcision made without hands, in putting off the body of the sins of the flesh by the circumcision of Christ: buried with him in baptism, wherein also ye are risen with him through the faith of the operation of God, who hath raised him from the dead.

d. **Gal. 3:27.** For as many of you as have been baptized into Christ have put on Christ. **Rom. 6:5.** For if we have been planted together in the likeness of his death, we shall be also in the likeness of his resurrection.

e. **John 3:5.** Jesus answered, Verily, verily, I say unto thee, Except a man be born of water and of the Spirit, he cannot enter into the kingdom of God. **Titus 3:5.** Not by works of righteousness which we have done, but according to his mercy he saved us, by the washing of regeneration, and renewing of the Holy Ghost.

f. **Mark 1:4.** John did baptize in the wilderness, and preach the baptism of repentance for the remission of sins. **Acts 2:38.** Then Peter said unto them, Repent, and be baptized every one of you in the name of Jesus Christ for the remission of sins, and ye shall receive the gift of the Holy Ghost. **Acts 22:16.** And now why tarriest thou? arise, and be baptized, and wash away thy sins, calling on the name of the Lord.

g. **Rom. 6:3–4.** Know ye not, that so many of us as were baptized into Jesus Christ were baptized into his death? Therefore we are buried with him by baptism into death: that like as Christ was raised up from the dead by the glory of the Father, even so we also should walk in newness of life.

h. **Matt. 28:19–20.** Go ye therefore, and teach all nations, baptizing them in the name of the Father, and of the Son, and of the Holy Ghost: teaching them to observe all things whatsoever I have commanded you: and, lo, I am with you alway, even unto the end of the world. Amen.

i. **Acts 10:47.** Can any man forbid water, that these should not be baptized, which have received the Holy Ghost as well as we? **Acts 8:36, 38.** And as they went on their way, they came unto a certain water: and the eunuch said, See, here is water;

3. Dipping of the person into the water is not necessary; but baptism is rightly administered by pouring, or sprinkling water upon the person.[k]

4. Not only those that do actually profess faith in and obedience unto Christ,[l] but also the infants of one, or both, believing parents, are to be baptized.[m]

what doth hinder me to be baptized?… And he commanded the chariot to stand still: and they went down both into the water, both Philip and the eunuch; and he baptized him. **Matt. 28:19.** Go ye therefore, and teach all nations, baptizing them in the name of the Father, and of the Son, and of the Holy Ghost.

k. **Heb. 9:10, 13, 19, 21.** … which stood only in meats and drinks, and divers washings, and carnal ordinances, imposed on them until the time of reformation.… For if the blood of bulls and of goats, and the ashes of an heifer sprinkling the unclean, sanctifieth to the purifying of the flesh … For when Moses had spoken every precept to all the people according to the law, he took the blood of calves and of goats, with water, and scarlet wool, and hyssop, and sprinkled both the book, and all the people.… Moreover he sprinkled with blood both the tabernacle, and all the vessels of the ministry. **Mark 7:2–4.** And when they saw some of his disciples eat bread with defiled, that is to say, with unwashen, hands, they found fault. For the Pharisees, and all the Jews, except they wash their hands oft, eat not, holding the tradition of the elders. And when they come from the market, except they wash, they eat not. And many other things there be, which they have received to hold, as the washing of cups, and pots, brasen vessels, and of tables. **Luke 11:38.** And when the Pharisee saw it, he marvelled that he had not first washed before dinner.

l. **Acts 2:41.** Then they that gladly received his word were baptized: and the same day there were added unto them about three thousand souls. **Acts 8:12–13.** But when they believed Philip preaching the things concerning the kingdom of God, and the name of Jesus Christ, they were baptized, both men and women. Then Simon himself believed also: and when he was baptized, he continued with Philip, and wondered, beholding the miracles and signs which were done. **Acts 16:14–15.** And a certain woman named Lydia, a seller of purple, of the city of Thyatira, which worshipped God, heard us: whose heart the Lord opened, that she attended unto the things which were spoken of Paul. And when she was baptized, and her household, she besought us, saying, If ye have judged me to be faithful to the Lord, come into my house, and abide there. And she constrained us.

m. **Gen. 17:7–14.** And I will establish my covenant between me and thee and thy seed after thee in their generations for an everlasting covenant, to be a God unto thee, and to thy seed after thee.… This is my covenant, which ye shall keep, between me and you and thy seed after thee; Every man child among you shall be circumcised. And ye shall circumcise the flesh of your foreskin; and it shall be a token of the covenant betwixt me and you.… And the uncircumcised man child whose flesh of his foreskin is not circumcised, that soul shall be cut off from his people; he hath broken my covenant. **Gal. 3:9, 14.** So then they which be of faith are blessed with faithful Abraham.… that the blessing of Abraham might come on the Gentiles through Jesus Christ; that we might receive the promise of the Spirit through faith. **Col. 2:11–12.** … in whom also ye are circumcised with the circumcision made without hands, in

5. Although it be a great sin to contemn or neglect this ordinance,[n] yet grace and salvation are not so inseparably annexed unto it, as that no person can be regenerated, or saved, without it;[o] or, that all

putting off the body of the sins of the flesh by the circumcision of Christ: buried with him in baptism, wherein also ye are risen with him through the faith of the operation of God, who hath raised him from the dead. **Acts 2:38–39.** Then Peter said unto them, Repent, and be baptized every one of you in the name of Jesus Christ for the remission of sins, and ye shall receive the gift of the Holy Ghost. For the promise is unto you, and to your children, and to all that are afar off, even as many as the Lord our God shall call. **Rom. 4:11–12.** And he received the sign of circumcision, a seal of the righteousness of the faith which he had yet being uncircumcised: that he might be the father of all them that believe, though they be not circumcised; that righteousness might be imputed unto them also: and the father of circumcision to them who are not of the circumcision only, but who also walk in the steps of that faith of our father Abraham, which he had being yet uncircumcised. **Matt. 19:13.** Then were there brought unto him little children, that he should put his hands on them, and pray: and the disciples rebuked them. **Mark 10:13–16.** And they brought young children to him, that he should touch them: and his disciples rebuked those that brought them. But when Jesus saw it, he was much displeased, and said unto them, Suffer the little children to come unto me, and forbid them not: for of such is the kingdom of God. Verily I say unto you, Whosoever shall not receive the kingdom of God as a little child, he shall not enter therein. And he took them up in his arms, put his hands upon them, and blessed them. **Luke 18:15–17.** And they brought unto him also infants, that he would touch them: but when his disciples saw it, they rebuked them. But Jesus called them unto him, and said, Suffer little children to come unto me, and forbid them not: for of such is the kingdom of God. Verily I say unto you, Whosoever shall not receive the kingdom of God as a little child shall in no wise enter therein. **Matt. 28:19.** Go ye therefore, and teach all nations, baptizing them in the name of the Father, and of the Son, and of the Holy Ghost. **1 Cor. 7:14.** For the unbelieving husband is sanctified by the wife, and the unbelieving wife is sanctified by the husband: else were your children unclean; but now are they holy.

n. **Gen. 17:14.** And the uncircumcised man child whose flesh of his foreskin is not circumcised, that soul shall be cut off from his people; he hath broken my covenant. **Matt. 28:19.** Go ye therefore, and teach all nations, baptizing them in the name of the Father, and of the Son, and of the Holy Ghost. **Acts 2:38.** Then Peter said unto them, Repent, and be baptized every one of you in the name of Jesus Christ for the remission of sins, and ye shall receive the gift of the Holy Ghost. **See Luke 7:30.**

o. **Rom. 4:11.** And he received the sign of circumcision, a seal of the righteousness of the faith which he had yet being uncircumcised: that he might be the father of all them that believe, though they be not circumcised; that righteousness might be imputed unto them also. **Acts 10:2, 4, 22, 31, 45, 47.** … a devout man, and one that feared God with all his house, which gave much alms to the people, and prayed to God alway.… And when he looked on him, he was afraid, and said, What is it, Lord? And he said unto him, Thy prayers and thine alms are come up for a memorial before God.… And they said, Cornelius the centurion, a just man, and one that feareth God,

that are baptized are undoubtedly regenerated.[p]

6. The efficacy of baptism is not tied to that moment of time wherein it is administered;[q] yet, notwithstanding, by the right use of this ordinance, the grace promised is not only offered, but really exhibited, and conferred, by the Holy Ghost, to such (whether of age or infants) as that grace belongeth unto, according to the counsel of God's own will, in his appointed time.[r]

7. The sacrament of baptism is but once to be administered unto any person.[s]

and of good report among all the nation of the Jews, was warned from God by an holy angel to send for thee into his house, and to hear words of thee.... And said, Cornelius, thy prayer is heard, and thine alms are had in remembrance in the sight of God.... And they of the circumcision which believed were astonished, as many as came with Peter, because that on the Gentiles also was poured out the gift of the Holy Ghost.... Can any man forbid water, that these should not be baptized, which have received the Holy Ghost as well as we?

p. **Acts 8:13, 23.** Then Simon himself believed also: and when he was baptized, he continued with Philip, and wondered, beholding the miracles and signs which were done.... For I perceive that thou art in the gall of bitterness, and in the bond of iniquity.

q. **John 3:5, 8.** Jesus answered, Verily, verily, I say unto thee, Except a man be born of water and of the Spirit, he cannot enter into the kingdom of God.... The wind bloweth where it listeth, and thou hearest the sound thereof, but canst not tell whence it cometh, and whither it goeth: so is every one that is born of the Spirit.

r. **Rom. 6:3–6.** Know ye not, that so many of us as were baptized into Jesus Christ were baptized into his death? Therefore we are buried with him by baptism into death: that like as Christ was raised up from the dead by the glory of the Father, even so we also should walk in newness of life. For if we have been planted together in the likeness of his death, we shall be also in the likeness of his resurrection: knowing this, that our old man is crucified with him, that the body of sin might be destroyed, that henceforth we should not serve sin. **Gal. 3:27.** For as many of you as have been baptized into Christ have put on Christ. **1 Pet. 3:21.** The like figure whereunto even baptism doth also now save us (not the putting away of the filth of the flesh, but the answer of a good conscience toward God,) by the resurrection of Jesus Christ. **Acts 2:38, 41.** Then Peter said unto them, Repent, and be baptized every one of you in the name of Jesus Christ for the remission of sins, and ye shall receive the gift of the Holy Ghost.... Then they that gladly received his word were baptized: and the same day there were added unto them about three thousand souls.

s. **Rom. 6:3–11.** Know ye not, that so many of us as were baptized into Jesus Christ were baptized into his death? Therefore we are buried with him by baptism into death: that like as Christ was raised up from the dead by the glory of the Father, even so we also should walk in newness of life. For if we have been planted together in the likeness of his death, we shall be also in the likeness of his resurrection: knowing this, that our old man is crucified with him, that the body of sin might be destroyed, that henceforth we should not serve sin. For he that is dead is freed from sin. Now if we

Chapter 29
Of the Lord's Supper

1. Our Lord Jesus, in the night wherein he was betrayed, instituted the sacrament of his body and blood, called the Lord's Supper, to be observed in his church, unto the end of the world, for the perpetual remembrance of the sacrifice of himself in his death; the sealing all benefits thereof unto true believers, their spiritual nourishment and growth in him, their further engagement in and to all duties which they owe unto him; and, to be a bond and pledge of their communion with him, and with each other, as members of his mystical body.[a]

2. In this sacrament, Christ is not offered up to his Father; nor any real sacrifice made at all, for remission of sins of the quick or dead;[b] but only a commemoration of that one offering up of himself,

be dead with Christ, we believe that we shall also live with him: knowing that Christ being raised from the dead dieth no more; death hath no more dominion over him. For in that he died, he died unto sin once: but in that he liveth, he liveth unto God. Likewise reckon ye also yourselves to be dead indeed unto sin, but alive unto God through Jesus Christ our Lord.

a. **1 Cor. 11:23–26.** For I have received of the Lord that which also I delivered unto you, That the Lord Jesus the same night in which he was betrayed took bread: and when he had given thanks, he brake it, and said, Take, eat: this is my body, which is broken for you: this do in remembrance of me. After the same manner also he took the cup, when he had supped, saying, This cup is the new testament in my blood: this do ye, as oft as ye drink it, in remembrance of me. For as often as ye eat this bread, and drink this cup, ye do shew the Lord's death till he come. **1 Cor. 10:16–17, 21.** The cup of blessing which we bless, is it not the communion of the blood of Christ? The bread which we break, is it not the communion of the body of Christ? For we being many are one bread, and one body: for we are all partakers of that one bread.… Ye cannot drink the cup of the Lord, and the cup of devils: ye cannot be partakers of the Lord's table, and of the table of devils. **1 Cor. 12:13.** For by one Spirit are we all baptized into one body, whether we be Jews or Gentiles, whether we be bond or free; and have been all made to drink into one Spirit.

b. **Heb. 9:22, 25–26, 28.** And almost all things are by the law purged with blood; and without shedding of blood is no remission.… Nor yet that he should offer himself often, as the high priest entereth into the holy place every year with blood of others; for then must he often have suffered since the foundation of the world: but now once in the end of the world hath he appeared to put away sin by the sacrifice of himself.… So Christ was once offered to bear the sins of many; and unto them that look for him shall he appear the second time without sin unto salvation. **Heb. 10:10–14.** By the which will we are sanctified through the offering of the body of Jesus

by himself, upon the cross, once for all: and a spiritual oblation of all possible praise unto God, for the same:[c] so that the popish sacrifice of the Mass (as they call it) is most abominably injurious to Christ's one, only sacrifice, the alone propitiation for all the sins of his elect.[d]

3. The Lord Jesus hath, in this ordinance, appointed his ministers to declare his word of institution to the people; to pray, and bless the elements of bread and wine, and thereby to set them apart from a common to an holy use; and to take and break the bread, to take the cup, and (they communicating also themselves) to give both to the communicants;[e] but to none who are not then present in the

Christ once for all. And every priest standeth daily ministering and offering oftentimes the same sacrifices, which can never take away sins: but this man, after he had offered one sacrifice for sins for ever, sat down on the right hand of God; from henceforth expecting till his enemies be made his footstool. For by one offering he hath perfected for ever them that are sanctified.

c. **1 Cor. 11:24–26.** And when he had given thanks, he brake it, and said, Take, eat: this is my body, which is broken for you: this do in remembrance of me. After the same manner also he took the cup, when he had supped, saying, This cup is the new testament in my blood: this do ye, as oft as ye drink it, in remembrance of me. For as often as ye eat this bread, and drink this cup, ye do shew the Lord's death till he come. **Matt. 26:26–27.** And as they were eating, Jesus took bread, and blessed it, and brake it, and gave it to the disciples, and said, Take, eat; this is my body. And he took the cup, and gave thanks, and gave it to them, saying, Drink ye all of it. **Luke 22:19–20.** And he took bread, and gave thanks, and brake it, and gave unto them, saying, This is my body which is given for you: this do in remembrance of me. Likewise also the cup after supper, saying, This cup is the new testament in my blood, which is shed for you.

d. **Heb. 7:23–24, 27.** And they truly were many priests, because they were not suffered to continue by reason of death: but this man, because he continueth ever, hath an unchangeable priesthood…. who needeth not daily, as those high priests, to offer up sacrifice, first for his own sins, and then for the people's: for this he did once, when he offered up himself. **Heb. 10:11–12, 14, 18.** And every priest standeth daily ministering and offering oftentimes the same sacrifices, which can never take away sins: but this man, after he had offered one sacrifice for sins for ever, sat down on the right hand of God…. For by one offering he hath perfected for ever them that are sanctified…. Now where remission of these is, there is no more offering for sin.

e. **Matt. 26:26–28.** And as they were eating, Jesus took bread, and blessed it, and brake it, and gave it to the disciples, and said, Take, eat; this is my body. And he took the cup, and gave thanks, and gave it to them, saying, Drink ye all of it; for this is my blood of the new testament, which is shed for many for the remission of sins. **Mark 14:22–24.** And as they did eat, Jesus took bread, and blessed, and brake it, and gave to them, and said, Take, eat: this is my body. And he took the cup, and when he had given thanks, he gave it to them: and they all drank of it. And he said unto them, This is my blood of the new testament, which is shed for many. **Luke 22:19–20.** And he took bread, and gave thanks, and brake it, and gave unto them, saying, This is my body which is given for you: this do in remembrance of me. Likewise also the cup after

congregation.[f]

4. Private Masses, or receiving this sacrament by a priest, or any other, alone;[g] as likewise, the denial of the cup to the people,[h] worshiping the elements, the lifting them up, or carrying them about, for adoration, and the reserving them for any pretended religious use; are all contrary to the nature of this sacrament, and to the institution of Christ.[i]

5. The outward elements in this sacrament, duly set apart to the uses ordained by Christ, have such relation to him crucified, as that, truly, yet sacramentally only, they are sometimes called by the name of the things they represent, to wit, the body and blood of Christ;[k]

supper, saying, This cup is the new testament in my blood, which is shed for you. **1 Cor. 10:16–17.** The cup of blessing which we bless, is it not the communion of the blood of Christ? The bread which we break, is it not the communion of the body of Christ? For we being many are one bread, and one body: for we are all partakers of that one bread. **1 Cor. 11:23–27.** For I have received of the Lord that which also I delivered unto you, That the Lord Jesus the same night in which he was betrayed took bread: and when he had given thanks, he brake it, and said, Take, eat: this is my body, which is broken for you: this do in remembrance of me. After the same manner also he took the cup, when he had supped, saying, This cup is the new testament in my blood: this do ye, as oft as ye drink it, in remembrance of me. For as often as ye eat this bread, and drink this cup, ye do shew the Lord's death till he come. Wherefore whosoever shall eat this bread, and drink this cup of the Lord, unworthily, shall be guilty of the body and blood of the Lord.

f. **Acts 20:7.** And upon the first day of the week, when the disciples came together to break bread, Paul preached unto them, ready to depart on the morrow; and continued his speech until midnight. **1 Cor. 11:20.** When ye come together therefore into one place, this is not to eat the Lord's supper.

g. **1 Cor. 10:16.** The cup of blessing which we bless, is it not the communion of the blood of Christ? The bread which we break, is it not the communion of the body of Christ?

h. **Matt. 26:27–28.** And he took the cup, and gave thanks, and gave it to them, saying, Drink ye all of it; for this is my blood of the new testament, which is shed for many for the remission of sins. **Mark 14:23.** And he took the cup, and when he had given thanks, he gave it to them: and they all drank of it. **1 Cor. 11:25–29.** After the same manner also he took the cup, when he had supped, saying, This cup is the new testament in my blood: this do ye, as oft as ye drink it, in remembrance of me. For as often as ye eat this bread, and drink this cup, ye do shew the Lord's death till he come. Wherefore whosoever shall eat this bread, and drink this cup of the Lord, unworthily, shall be guilty of the body and blood of the Lord. But let a man examine himself, and so let him eat of that bread, and drink of that cup. For he that eateth and drinketh unworthily, eateth and drinketh damnation to himself, not discerning the Lord's body.

i. **Matt. 15:9.** But in vain they do worship me, teaching for doctrines the commandments of men.

k. **Matt. 26:26–28.** And as they were eating, Jesus took bread, and blessed it,

albeit, in substance and nature, they still remain truly and only bread and wine, as they were before.[l]

6. That doctrine which maintains a change of the substance of bread and wine, into the substance of Christ's body and blood (commonly called transubstantiation) by consecration of a priest, or by any other way, is repugnant, not to Scripture alone, but even to common sense, and reason; overthroweth the nature of the sacrament, and hath been, and is, the cause of manifold superstitions; yea, of gross idolatries.[m]

7. Worthy receivers, outwardly partaking of the visible elements, in this sacrament,[n] do then also, inwardly by faith, really and indeed, yet not carnally and corporally, but spiritually, receive, and feed upon, Christ crucified, and all benefits of his death: the body and blood of Christ being then, not corporally or carnally, in, with, or under the bread and wine; yet, as really, but spiritually, present to the faith of believers in that ordinance, as the elements themselves are to their outward senses.[o]

8. Although ignorant and wicked men receive the outward elements in this sacrament; yet, they receive not the thing signified

and brake it, and gave it to the disciples, and said, Take, eat; this is my body. And he took the cup, and gave thanks, and gave it to them, saying, Drink ye all of it; for this is my blood of the new testament, which is shed for many for the remission of sins.

l. **1 Cor. 11:26–28.** For as often as ye eat this bread, and drink this cup, ye do shew the Lord's death till he come. Wherefore whosoever shall eat this bread, and drink this cup of the Lord, unworthily, shall be guilty of the body and blood of the Lord. But let a man examine himself, and so let him eat of that bread, and drink of that cup. **Matt. 26:29.** But I say unto you, I will not drink henceforth of this fruit of the vine, until that day when I drink it new with you in my Father's kingdom.

m. **Acts 3:21.** … whom the heaven must receive until the times of restitution of all things, which God hath spoken by the mouth of all his holy prophets since the world began. **1 Cor. 11:24–26.** And when he had given thanks, he brake it, and said, Take, eat: this is my body, which is broken for you: this do in remembrance of me. After the same manner also he took the cup, when he had supped, saying, This cup is the new testament in my blood: this do ye, as oft as ye drink it, in remembrance of me. For as often as ye eat this bread, and drink this cup, ye do shew the Lord's death till he come. **Luke 24:6, 39.** He is not here, but is risen: remember how he spake unto you when he was yet in Galilee.… Behold my hands and my feet, that it is I myself: handle me, and see; for a spirit hath not flesh and bones, as ye see me have.

n. **1 Cor. 11:28.** But let a man examine himself, and so let him eat of that bread, and drink of that cup.

o. **1 Cor. 10:16.** The cup of blessing which we bless, is it not the communion of the blood of Christ? The bread which we break, is it not the communion of the body of Christ? **See 1 Cor. 10:3–4.**

thereby; but, by their unworthy coming thereunto, are guilty of the body and blood of the Lord, to their own damnation. Wherefore, all ignorant and ungodly persons, as they are unfit to enjoy communion with him, so are they unworthy of the Lord's table; and cannot, without great sin against Christ, while they remain such, partake of these holy mysteries,[p] or be admitted thereunto.[q]

Chapter 30
Of Church Censures

1. The Lord Jesus, as King and Head of his church, hath therein appointed a government, in the hand of church officers, distinct from the civil magistrate.[a]

p. **1 Cor. 11:27–29.** Wherefore whosoever shall eat this bread, and drink this cup of the Lord, unworthily, shall be guilty of the body and blood of the Lord. But let a man examine himself, and so let him eat of that bread, and drink of that cup. For he that eateth and drinketh unworthily, eateth and drinketh damnation to himself, not discerning the Lord's body. **2 Cor. 6:14–16.** Be ye not unequally yoked together with unbelievers: for what fellowship hath righteousness with unrighteousness? and what communion hath light with darkness? And what concord hath Christ with Belial? or what part hath he that believeth with an infidel? And what agreement hath the temple of God with idols? for ye are the temple of the living God; as God hath said, I will dwell in them, and walk in them; and I will be their God, and they shall be my people. **1 Cor. 10:21.** Ye cannot drink the cup of the Lord, and the cup of devils: ye cannot be partakers of the Lord's table, and of the table of devils.

q. **1 Cor. 5:6–7, 13.** Your glorying is not good. Know ye not that a little leaven leaveneth the whole lump? Purge out therefore the old leaven, that ye may be a new lump, as ye are unleavened. For even Christ our passover is sacrificed for us.… But them that are without God judgeth. Therefore put away from among yourselves that wicked person. **2 Thess. 3:6, 14–15.** Now we command you, brethren, in the name of our Lord Jesus Christ, that ye withdraw yourselves from every brother that walketh disorderly, and not after the tradition which he received of us.… And if any man obey not our word by this epistle, note that man, and have no company with him, that he may be ashamed. Yet count him not as an enemy, but admonish him as a brother. **Matt. 7:6.** Give not that which is holy unto the dogs, neither cast ye your pearls before swine, lest they trample them under their feet, and turn again and rend you.

a. **Isa. 9:6–7.** For unto us a child is born, unto us a son is given: and the government shall be upon his shoulder: and his name shall be called Wonderful, Counseller, The mighty God, The everlasting Father, The Prince of Peace. Of the increase of his government and peace there shall be no end, upon the throne of David, and upon his kingdom, to order it, and to establish it with judgment and with justice from henceforth even for ever. The zeal of the LORD of hosts will perform this. **Col. 1:18.** And

2. To these officers the keys of the kingdom of heaven are committed; by virtue whereof, they have power, respectively, to retain, and remit sins; to shut that kingdom against the impenitent, both by the Word, and censures; and to open it unto penitent sinners, by the ministry of the gospel; and by absolution from censures, as occasion shall require.[b]

3. Church censures are necessary, for the reclaiming and gaining of offending brethren, for deterring of others from the like offenses, for purging out of that leaven which might infect the whole lump, for vindicating the honor of Christ, and the holy profession of the gos-

he is the head of the body, the church: who is the beginning, the firstborn from the dead; that in all things he might have the preeminence. **1 Tim. 5:17.** Let the elders that rule well be counted worthy of double honour, especially they who labour in the word and doctrine. **1 Thess. 5:12.** And we beseech you, brethren, to know them which labour among you, and are over you in the Lord, and admonish you. **Acts 20:17, 28.** And from Miletus he sent to Ephesus, and called the elders of the church.… Take heed therefore unto yourselves, and to all the flock, over the which the Holy Ghost hath made you overseers, to feed the church of God, which he hath purchased with his own blood. **Heb. 13:7, 17, 24.** Remember them which have the rule over you, who have spoken unto you the word of God: whose faith follow, considering the end of their conversation.… Obey them that have the rule over you, and submit yourselves: for they watch for your souls, as they that must give account, that they may do it with joy, and not with grief: for that is unprofitable for you.… Salute all them that have the rule over you, and all the saints. They of Italy salute you. **Eph. 4:11–12.** And he gave some, apostles; and some, prophets; and some, evangelists; and some, pastors and teachers; for the perfecting of the saints, for the work of the ministry, for the edifying of the body of Christ. **1 Cor. 12:28.** And God hath set some in the church, first apostles, secondarily prophets, thirdly teachers, after that miracles, then gifts of healings, helps, governments, diversities of tongues. **Matt. 28:18–20.** And Jesus came and spake unto them, saying, All power is given unto me in heaven and in earth. Go ye therefore, and teach all nations, baptizing them in the name of the Father, and of the Son, and of the Holy Ghost: teaching them to observe all things whatsoever I have commanded you: and, lo, I am with you alway, even unto the end of the world. Amen. **John 18:36.** Jesus answered, My kingdom is not of this world: if my kingdom were of this world, then would my servants fight, that I should not be delivered to the Jews: but now is my kingdom not from hence.

b. **Matt. 16:19.** And I will give unto thee the keys of the kingdom of heaven: and whatsoever thou shalt bind on earth shall be bound in heaven: and whatsoever thou shalt loose on earth shall be loosed in heaven. **Matt. 18:17–18.** And if he shall neglect to hear them, tell it unto the church: but if he neglect to hear the church, let him be unto thee as an heathen man and a publican. Verily I say unto you, Whatsoever ye shall bind on earth shall be bound in heaven: and whatsoever ye shall loose on earth shall be loosed in heaven. **John 20:21–23.** Then said Jesus to them again, Peace be unto you: as my Father hath sent me, even so send I you. And when he had said this, he breathed on them, and saith unto them, Receive ye the Holy Ghost:

pel, and for preventing the wrath of God, which might justly fall upon the church, if they should suffer his covenant, and the seals thereof, to be profaned by notorious and obstinate offenders.[c]

4. For the better attaining of these ends, the officers of the church are to proceed by admonition; suspension from the sacrament of the Lord's Supper for a season; and by excommunication from the church; according to the nature of the crime, and demerit of the person.[d]

whose soever sins ye remit, they are remitted unto them; and whose soever sins ye retain, they are retained. **2 Cor. 2:6–8.** Sufficient to such a man is this punishment, which was inflicted of many. So that contrariwise ye ought rather to forgive him, and comfort him, lest perhaps such a one should be swallowed up with overmuch sorrow. Wherefore I beseech you that ye would confirm your love toward him.

c. **1 Cor. 5:1–13.** It is reported commonly that there is fornication among you, and such fornication as is not so much as named among the Gentiles, that one should have his father's wife.… For I verily, as absent in body, but present in spirit, have judged already, as though I were present, concerning him that hath so done this deed, in the name of our Lord Jesus Christ, when ye are gathered together, and my spirit, with the power of our Lord Jesus Christ, to deliver such an one unto Satan for the destruction of the flesh, that the spirit may be saved in the day of the Lord Jesus. Your glorying is not good. Know ye not that a little leaven leaveneth the whole lump?… But now I have written unto you not to keep company, if any man that is called a brother be a fornicator, or covetous, or an idolater, or a railer, or a drunkard, or an extortioner; with such an one no not to eat. For what have I to do to judge them also that are without? do not ye judge them that are within? But them that are without God judgeth. Therefore put away from among yourselves that wicked person. **1 Tim. 5:20.** Them that sin rebuke before all, that others also may fear. **Matt. 7:6.** Give not that which is holy unto the dogs, neither cast ye your pearls before swine, lest they trample them under their feet, and turn again and rend you. **1 Tim. 1:20.** Of whom is Hymenaeus and Alexander; whom I have delivered unto Satan, that they may learn not to blaspheme. **1 Cor. 11:27–34.** Wherefore whosoever shall eat this bread, and drink this cup of the Lord, unworthily, shall be guilty of the body and blood of the Lord. But let a man examine himself, and so let him eat of that bread, and drink of that cup. For he that eateth and drinketh unworthily, eateth and drinketh damnation to himself, not discerning the Lord's body. For this cause many are weak and sickly among you, and many sleep. For if we would judge ourselves, we should not be judged.… **Jude 23.** And others save with fear, pulling them out of the fire; hating even the garment spotted by the flesh.

d. **1 Thess. 5:12.** And we beseech you, brethren, to know them which labour among you, and are over you in the Lord, and admonish you. **2 Thess. 3:6, 14–15.** Now we command you, brethren, in the name of our Lord Jesus Christ, that ye withdraw yourselves from every brother that walketh disorderly, and not after the tradition which he received of us.… And if any man obey not our word by this epistle, note that man, and have no company with him, that he may be ashamed. Yet count him not as an enemy, but admonish him as a brother. **1 Cor. 5:4–5, 13.** … in the name of our Lord Jesus Christ, when ye are gathered together, and my spirit, with the power of our

Chapter 31
Of Synods and Councils

1. For the better government, and further edification of the church, there ought to be such assemblies as are commonly called synods or councils:[a] and it belongeth to the overseers and other rulers of the particular churches, by virtue of their office, and the power which Christ hath given them for edification and not for destruction, to appoint such assemblies;[b] and to convene together in them, as often as they shall judge it expedient for the good of the church.[c]

2. It belongeth to synods and councils, ministerially to determine

Lord Jesus Christ, to deliver such an one unto Satan for the destruction of the flesh, that the spirit may be saved in the day of the Lord Jesus.… But them that are without God judgeth. Therefore put away from among yourselves that wicked person. **Matt. 18:17.** And if he shall neglect to hear them, tell it unto the church: but if he neglect to hear the church, let him be unto thee as an heathen man and a publican. **Titus 3:10.** A man that is an heretick after the first and second admonition reject.

a. **Acts 15:2, 4, 6.** When therefore Paul and Barnabas had no small dissension and disputation with them, they determined that Paul and Barnabas, and certain other of them, should go up to Jerusalem unto the apostles and elders about this question.… And when they were come to Jerusalem, they were received of the church, and of the apostles and elders, and they declared all things that God had done with them.… And the apostles and elders came together for to consider of this matter.

b. **Acts 15:1–35.** And certain men which came down from Judaea taught the brethren, and said, Except ye be circumcised after the manner of Moses, ye cannot be saved. When therefore Paul and Barnabas had no small dissension and disputation with them, they determined that Paul and Barnabas, and certain other of them, should go up to Jerusalem unto the apostles and elders about this question.… But there rose up certain of the sect of the Pharisees which believed, saying, That it was needful to circumcise them, and to command them to keep the law of Moses. And the apostles and elders came together for to consider of this matter.… Then pleased it the apostles and elders, with the whole church, to send chosen men of their own company to Antioch with Paul and Barnabas; namely, Judas surnamed Barsabas, and Silas, chief men among the brethren: and they wrote letters by them after this manner; The apostles and elders and brethren send greeting unto the brethren which are of the Gentiles in Antioch and Syria and Cilicia.… It seemed good unto us, being assembled with one accord, to send chosen men unto you with our beloved Barnabas and Paul.… For it seemed good to the Holy Ghost, and to us, to lay upon you no greater burden than these necessary things.… So when they were dismissed, they came to Antioch: and when they had gathered the multitude together, they delivered the epistle: which when they had read, they rejoiced for the consolation.…

c. **Acts 15:1–35. See footnote *b* above. Acts 20:17.** And from Miletus he sent to Ephesus, and called the elders of the church.

controversies of faith, and cases of conscience; to set down rules and directions for the better ordering of the public worship of God, and government of his church; to receive complaints in cases of maladministration, and authoritatively to determine the same: which decrees and determinations, if consonant to the Word of God, are to be received with reverence and submission; not only for their agreement with the Word, but also for the power whereby they are made, as being an ordinance of God appointed thereunto in his Word.[d]

3. All synods or councils, since the apostles' times, whether general or particular, may err; and many have erred. Therefore they are not to be made the rule of faith, or practice; but to be used as a help in both.[e]

4. Synods and councils are to handle, or conclude nothing, but that which is ecclesiastical: and are not to intermeddle with civil affairs which concern the commonwealth, unless by way of humble

d. **Acts 15:15, 19, 24, 27–31.** And to this agree the words of the prophets; as it is written … Wherefore my sentence is, that we trouble not them, which from among the Gentiles are turned to God.… Forasmuch as we have heard, that certain which went out from us have troubled you with words, subverting your souls, saying, Ye must be circumcised, and keep the law: to whom we gave no such commandment.… We have sent therefore Judas and Silas, who shall also tell you the same things by mouth. For it seemed good to the Holy Ghost, and to us, to lay upon you no greater burden than these necessary things; that ye abstain from meats offered to idols, and from blood, and from things strangled, and from fornication: from which if ye keep yourselves, ye shall do well. Fare ye well. So when they were dismissed, they came to Antioch: and when they had gathered the multitude together, they delivered the epistle: which when they had read, they rejoiced for the consolation. **Acts 16:4.** And as they went through the cities, they delivered them the decrees for to keep, that were ordained of the apostles and elders which were at Jerusalem. **Matt. 18:17–20.** And if he shall neglect to hear them, tell it unto the church: but if he neglect to hear the church, let him be unto thee as an heathen man and a publican. Verily I say unto you, Whatsoever ye shall bind on earth shall be bound in heaven: and whatsoever ye shall loose on earth shall be loosed in heaven. Again I say unto you, That if two of you shall agree on earth as touching any thing that they shall ask, it shall be done for them of my Father which is in heaven. For where two or three are gathered together in my name, there am I in the midst of them.

e. **Eph. 2:20.** … and are built upon the foundation of the apostles and prophets, Jesus Christ himself being the chief corner stone. **Acts 17:11.** These were more noble than those in Thessalonica, in that they received the word with all readiness of mind, and searched the scriptures daily, whether those things were so. **1 Cor. 2:5.** … that your faith should not stand in the wisdom of men, but in the power of God. **2 Cor. 1:24.** Not for that we have dominion over your faith, but are helpers of your joy: for by faith ye stand. **Cf. Isa. 8:19–20; Matt. 15:9.**

petition in cases extraordinary; or, by way of advice, for satisfaction of conscience, if they be thereunto required by the civil magistrate.[f]

Chapter 32
Of the State of Men after Death,
and of the Resurrection of the Dead

1. The bodies of men, after death, return to dust, and see corruption:[a] but their souls, which neither die nor sleep, having an immortal subsistence, immediately return to God who gave them:[b] the souls of the righteous, being then made perfect in holiness, are received into the highest heavens, where they behold the face of God, in light and glory, waiting for the full redemption of their bodies.[c]

f. **Luke 12:13–14.** And one of the company said unto him, Master, speak to my brother, that he divide the inheritance with me. And he said unto him, Man, who made me a judge or a divider over you? **John 18:36.** Jesus answered, My kingdom is not of this world: if my kingdom were of this world, then would my servants fight, that I should not be delivered to the Jews: but now is my kingdom not from hence. **Matt. 22:21.** They say unto him, Caesar's. Then saith he unto them, Render therefore unto Caesar the things which are Caesar's; and unto God the things that are God's.

a. **Gen. 3:19.** In the sweat of thy face shalt thou eat bread, till thou return unto the ground; for out of it wast thou taken: for dust thou art, and unto dust shalt thou return. **Acts 13:36.** For David, after he had served his own generation by the will of God, fell on sleep, and was laid unto his fathers, and saw corruption.

b. **Luke 23:43.** And Jesus said unto him, Verily I say unto thee, To day shalt thou be with me in paradise. **Eccl. 12:7.** Then shall the dust return to the earth as it was: and the spirit shall return unto God who gave it.

c. **Heb. 12:23.** … to the general assembly and church of the firstborn, which are written in heaven, and to God the Judge of all, and to the spirits of just men made perfect. **2 Cor. 5:1, 6, 8.** For we know that if our earthly house of this tabernacle were dissolved, we have a building of God, an house not made with hands, eternal in the heavens.… Therefore we are always confident, knowing that, whilst we are at home in the body, we are absent from the Lord.… We are confident, I say, and willing rather to be absent from the body, and to be present with the Lord. **Phil. 1:23.** For I am in a strait betwixt two, having a desire to depart, and to be with Christ; which is far better. **Acts 3:21.** … whom the heaven must receive until the times of restitution of all things, which God hath spoken by the mouth of all his holy prophets since the world began. **Eph. 4:10.** He that descended is the same also that ascended up far above all heavens, that he might fill all things. **Rom. 8:23.** And not only they, but ourselves also, which have the firstfruits of the Spirit, even we ourselves groan within ourselves, waiting for the adoption, to wit, the redemption of our body.

And the souls of the wicked are cast into hell, where they remain in torments and utter darkness, reserved to the judgment of the great day.[d] Beside these two places, for souls separated from their bodies, the Scripture acknowledgeth none.

2. At the last day, such as are found alive shall not die, but be changed:[e] and all the dead shall be raised up, with the selfsame bodies, and none other (although with different qualities), which shall be united again to their souls forever.[f]

3. The bodies of the unjust shall, by the power of Christ, be raised to dishonor: the bodies of the just, by his Spirit, unto honor;

d. **Luke 16:23–24.** And in hell he lift up his eyes, being in torments, and seeth Abraham afar off, and Lazarus in his bosom. And he cried and said, Father Abraham, have mercy on me, and send Lazarus, that he may dip the tip of his finger in water, and cool my tongue; for I am tormented in this flame. **Acts 1:25.** … that he may take part of this ministry and apostleship, from which Judas by transgression fell, that he might go to his own place. **Jude 6–7.** And the angels which kept not their first estate, but left their own habitation, he hath reserved in everlasting chains under darkness unto the judgment of the great day. Even as Sodom and Gomorrha, and the cities about them in like manner, giving themselves over to fornication, and going after strange flesh, are set forth for an example, suffering the vengeance of eternal fire. **1 Pet. 3:19.** … by which also he went and preached unto the spirits in prison.

e. **1 Thess. 4:17.** Then we which are alive and remain shall be caught up together with them in the clouds, to meet the Lord in the air: and so shall we ever be with the Lord. **1 Cor. 15:51–52.** Behold, I shew you a mystery; We shall not all sleep, but we shall all be changed, in a moment, in the twinkling of an eye, at the last trump: for the trumpet shall sound, and the dead shall be raised incorruptible, and we shall be changed.

f. **John 5:25–29.** Verily, verily, I say unto you, The hour is coming, and now is, when the dead shall hear the voice of the Son of God: and they that hear shall live. For as the Father hath life in himself; so hath he given to the Son to have life in himself; and hath given him authority to execute judgment also, because he is the Son of man. Marvel not at this: for the hour is coming, in the which all that are in the graves shall hear his voice, and shall come forth; they that have done good, unto the resurrection of life; and they that have done evil, unto the resurrection of damnation. **Acts 24:15.** And [I] have hope toward God, which they themselves also allow, that there shall be a resurrection of the dead, both of the just and unjust. **Job 19:26–27.** And though after my skin worms destroy this body, yet in my flesh shall I see God: whom I shall see for myself, and mine eyes shall behold, and not another; though my reins be consumed within me. **Dan. 12:2.** And many of them that sleep in the dust of the earth shall awake, some to everlasting life, and some to shame and everlasting contempt. **1 Cor. 15:42–44.** So also is the resurrection of the dead. It is sown in corruption; it is raised in incorruption: it is sown in dishonour; it is raised in glory: it is sown in weakness; it is raised in power: it is sown a natural body; it is raised a spiritual body. There is a natural body, and there is a spiritual body.

and be made conformable to his own glorious body.[g]

Chapter 33
Of the Last Judgment

1. God hath appointed a day, wherein he will judge the world, in righteousness, by Jesus Christ,[a] to whom all power and judgment is given of the Father.[b] In which day, not only the apostate angels shall be judged,[c] but likewise all persons that have lived upon earth shall appear before the tribunal of Christ, to give an account of their thoughts, words, and deeds; and to receive according to what they have done in the body, whether good or evil.[d]

g. **Acts 24:15.** And [I] have hope toward God, which they themselves also allow, that there shall be a resurrection of the dead, both of the just and unjust. **John 5:25–29.** Verily, verily, I say unto you, The hour is coming, and now is, when the dead shall hear the voice of the Son of God: and they that hear shall live. For as the Father hath life in himself; so hath he given to the Son to have life in himself; and hath given him authority to execute judgment also, because he is the Son of man. Marvel not at this: for the hour is coming, in the which all that are in the graves shall hear his voice, and shall come forth; they that have done good, unto the resurrection of life; and they that have done evil, unto the resurrection of damnation. **1 Cor. 15:43.** It is sown in dishonour; it is raised in glory: it is sown in weakness; it is raised in power. **Phil. 3:21.** … who shall change our vile body, that it may be fashioned like unto his glorious body, according to the working whereby he is able even to subdue all things unto himself.

a. **Acts 17:31.** … because he hath appointed a day, in the which he will judge the world in righteousness by that man whom he hath ordained; whereof he hath given assurance unto all men, in that he hath raised him from the dead.

b. **John 5:22, 27.** For the Father judgeth no man, but hath committed all judgment unto the Son.… And hath given him authority to execute judgment also, because he is the Son of man.

c. **Jude 6.** And the angels which kept not their first estate, but left their own habitation, he hath reserved in everlasting chains under darkness unto the judgment of the great day. **2 Pet. 2:4.** For if God spared not the angels that sinned, but cast them down to hell, and delivered them into chains of darkness, to be reserved unto judgment …

d. **2 Cor. 5:10.** For we must all appear before the judgment seat of Christ; that every one may receive the things done in his body, according to that he hath done, whether it be good or bad. **Eccl. 12:14.** For God shall bring every work into judgment, with every secret thing, whether it be good, or whether it be evil. **Rom. 2:16.** In the day when God shall judge the secrets of men by Jesus Christ according to my gospel. **Rom. 14:10, 12.** But why dost thou judge thy brother? or why dost thou set at nought thy brother? for we shall all stand before the judgment seat of Christ.… So

2. The end of God's appointing this day is for the manifestation of the glory of his mercy, in the eternal salvation of the elect; and of his justice, in the damnation of the reprobate, who are wicked and disobedient. For then shall the righteous go into everlasting life, and receive that fullness of joy and refreshing, which shall come from the presence of the Lord: but the wicked, who know not God, and obey not the gospel of Jesus Christ, shall be cast into eternal torments, and be punished with everlasting destruction from the presence of the Lord, and from the glory of his power.[e]

then every one of us shall give account of himself to God. **Matt. 12:36–37.** But I say unto you, That every idle word that men shall speak, they shall give account thereof in the day of judgment. For by thy words thou shalt be justified, and by thy words thou shalt be condemned.

e. **Matt. 25:31–46.** When the Son of man shall come in his glory, and all the holy angels with him, then shall he sit upon the throne of his glory: and before him shall be gathered all nations: and he shall separate them one from another, as a shepherd divideth his sheep from the goats: and he shall set the sheep on his right hand, but the goats on the left. Then shall the King say unto them on his right hand, Come, ye blessed of my Father, inherit the kingdom prepared for you from the foundation of the world: for I was an hungred, and ye gave me meat: I was thirsty, and ye gave me drink: I was a stranger, and ye took me in: naked, and ye clothed me: I was sick, and ye visited me: I was in prison, and ye came unto me.… Then shall he say also unto them on the left hand, Depart from me, ye cursed, into everlasting fire, prepared for the devil and his angels: for I was an hungred, and ye gave me no meat: I was thirsty, and ye gave me no drink: I was a stranger, and ye took me not in: naked, and ye clothed me not: sick, and in prison, and ye visited me not.… And these shall go away into everlasting punishment: but the righteous into life eternal. **Rom. 2:5–6.** But after thy hardness and impenitent heart treasurest up unto thyself wrath against the day of wrath and revelation of the righteous judgment of God; who will render to every man according to his deeds. **Rom. 9:22–23.** What if God, willing to shew his wrath, and to make his power known, endured with much longsuffering the vessels of wrath fitted to destruction: and that he might make known the riches of his glory on the vessels of mercy, which he had afore prepared unto glory. **Matt. 25:21.** His lord said unto him, Well done, thou good and faithful servant: thou hast been faithful over a few things, I will make thee ruler over many things: enter thou into the joy of thy lord. **Acts 3:19.** Repent ye therefore, and be converted, that your sins may be blotted out, when the times of refreshing shall come from the presence of the Lord. **2 Thess. 1:7–10.** … and to you who are troubled rest with us, when the Lord Jesus shall be revealed from heaven with his mighty angels, in flaming fire taking vengeance on them that know not God, and that obey not the gospel of our Lord Jesus Christ: who shall be punished with everlasting destruction from the presence of the Lord, and from the glory of his power; when he shall come to be glorified in his saints, and to be admired in all them that believe (because our testimony among you was believed) in that day. **Mark 9:48.** Where their worm dieth not, and the fire is not quenched.

3. As Christ would have us to be certainly persuaded that there shall be a day of judgment, both to deter all men from sin; and for the greater consolation of the godly in their adversity:[f] so will he have that day unknown to men, that they may shake off all carnal security, and be always watchful, because they know not at what hour the Lord will come; and may be ever prepared to say, Come Lord Jesus, come quickly, Amen.[g]

f. **2 Pet. 3:11, 14.** Seeing then that all these things shall be dissolved, what manner of persons ought ye to be in all holy conversation and godliness.... Wherefore, beloved, seeing that ye look for such things, be diligent that ye may be found of him in peace, without spot, and blameless. **2 Cor. 5:10–11.** For we must all appear before the judgment seat of Christ; that every one may receive the things done in his body, according to that he hath done, whether it be good or bad. Knowing therefore the terror of the Lord, we persuade men; but we are made manifest unto God; and I trust also are made manifest in your consciences. **2 Thess. 1:5–7.** Which is a manifest token of the righteous judgment of God, that ye may be counted worthy of the kingdom of God, for which ye also suffer: seeing it is a righteous thing with God to recompense tribulation to them that trouble you; and to you who are troubled rest with us, when the Lord Jesus shall be revealed from heaven with his mighty angels. **Luke 21:27–28.** And then shall they see the Son of man coming in a cloud with power and great glory. And when these things begin to come to pass, then look up, and lift up your heads; for your redemption draweth nigh. **Rom. 8:23–25.** And not only they, but ourselves also, which have the firstfruits of the Spirit, even we ourselves groan within ourselves, waiting for the adoption, to wit, the redemption of our body. For we are saved by hope: but hope that is seen is not hope: for what a man seeth, why doth he yet hope for? But if we hope for that we see not, then do we with patience wait for it.

g. **Matt. 24:36, 42–44.** But of that day and hour knoweth no man, no, not the angels of heaven, but my Father only.... Watch therefore: for ye know not what hour your Lord doth come. But know this, that if the goodman of the house had known in what watch the thief would come, he would have watched, and would not have suffered his house to be broken up. Therefore be ye also ready: for in such an hour as ye think not the Son of man cometh. **Mark 13:35–37.** Watch ye therefore: for ye know not when the master of the house cometh, at even, or at midnight, or at the cockcrowing, or in the morning: lest coming suddenly he find you sleeping. And what I say unto you I say unto all, Watch. **Luke 12:35–36.** Let your loins be girded about, and your lights burning; and ye yourselves like unto men that wait for their lord, when he will return from the wedding; that when he cometh and knocketh, they may open unto him immediately. **Rev. 22:20.** He which testifieth these things saith, Surely I come quickly. Amen. Even so, come, Lord Jesus.

THE

LARGER CATECHISM

Q. 1. *What is the chief and highest end of man?*

A. Man's chief and highest end is to glorify God,[a] and fully to enjoy him forever.[b]

a. **Rom. 11:36.** For of him, and through him, and to him, are all things: to whom be glory for ever. Amen. **1 Cor. 6:20.** For ye are bought with a price: therefore glorify God in your body, and in your spirit, which are God's. **1 Cor. 10:31.** Whether therefore ye eat, or drink, or whatsoever ye do, do all to the glory of God. **Ps. 86:9, 12.** All nations whom thou hast made shall come and worship before thee, O Lord; and shall glorify thy name.… I will praise thee, O Lord my God, with all my heart: and I will glorify thy name for evermore.

b. **Ps. 73:24–28.** Thou shalt guide me with thy counsel, and afterward receive me to glory. Whom have I in heaven but thee? and there is none upon earth that I desire beside thee. My flesh and my heart faileth: but God is the strength of my heart, and my portion for ever. For, lo, they that are far from thee shall perish: thou hast destroyed all them that go a whoring from thee. But it is good for me to draw near to God: I have put my trust in the Lord GOD, that I may declare all thy works. **John 17:21–23.** … that they all may be one; as thou, Father, art in me, and I in thee, that they also may be one in us: that the world may believe that thou hast sent me. And the glory which thou gavest me I have given them; that they may be one, even as we are one: I in them, and thou in me, that they may be made perfect in one; and that the world may know that thou hast sent me, and hast loved them, as thou hast loved me. **Ps. 16:5–11.** The LORD is the portion of mine inheritance and of my cup: thou maintainest my lot. The lines are fallen unto me in pleasant places; yea, I have a goodly heritage. I will bless the LORD, who hath given me counsel: my reins also instruct me in the night seasons. I have set the LORD always before me: because he is at my right hand, I shall not be moved. Therefore my heart is glad, and my glory rejoiceth: my flesh also shall rest in hope. For thou wilt not leave my soul in hell; neither wilt thou suffer thine Holy One to see corruption. Thou wilt shew me the path of life: in thy presence is fulness of joy; at thy right hand there are pleasures for evermore. **Rev. 21:3–4.** And I heard a great voice out of heaven saying, Behold, the tabernacle of God is with men, and he will dwell with them, and they shall be his people, and God

Q. 2. *How doth it appear that there is a God?*

A. The very light of nature in man, and the works of God, de-clare plainly that there is a God;[c] but his Word and Spirit only do sufficiently and effectually reveal him unto men for their salvation.[d]

Q. 3. *What is the Word of God?*

A. The Holy Scriptures of the Old and New Testament are the Word of God,[e] the only rule of faith and obedience.[f]

himself shall be with them, and be their God. And God shall wipe away all tears from their eyes; and there shall be no more death, neither sorrow, nor crying, neither shall there be any more pain: for the former things are passed away.

c. **Rom. 1:19–20.** Because that which may be known of God is manifest in them; for God hath shewed it unto them. For the invisible things of him from the creation of the world are clearly seen, being understood by the things that are made, even his eternal power and Godhead; so that they are without excuse. **Acts 17:28.** For in him we live, and move, and have our being; as certain also of your own poets have said, For we are also his offspring. **See Ps. 19:1–3.**

d. **1 Cor. 2:9–10.** But as it is written, Eye hath not seen, nor ear heard, neither have entered into the heart of man, the things which God hath prepared for them that love him. But God hath revealed them unto us by his Spirit: for the Spirit searcheth all things, yea, the deep things of God. **1 Cor. 1:20–21.** Where is the wise? where is the scribe? where is the disputer of this world? hath not God made foolish the wisdom of this world? For after that in the wisdom of God the world by wisdom knew not God, it pleased God by the foolishness of preaching to save them that believe. **2 Tim. 3:15–17.** … and that from a child thou hast known the holy scriptures, which are able to make thee wise unto salvation through faith which is in Christ Jesus. All scripture is given by inspiration of God, and is profitable for doctrine, for reproof, for correction, for instruction in righteousness: that the man of God may be perfect, thoroughly fur-nished unto all good works. **See Isa. 59:21.**

e. **2 Tim. 3:16.** All scripture is given by inspiration of God, and is profitable for doctrine, for reproof, for correction, for instruction in righteousness. **2 Pet. 1:19–21.** We have also a more sure word of prophecy; whereunto ye do well that ye take heed, as unto a light that shineth in a dark place, until the day dawn, and the day star arise in your hearts: knowing this first, that no prophecy of the scripture is of any private interpretation. For the prophecy came not in old time by the will of man: but holy men of God spake as they were moved by the Holy Ghost. **2 Pet. 3:2, 15–16.** … that ye may be mindful of the words which were spoken before by the holy prophets, and of the commandment of us the apostles of the Lord and Saviour.… And account that the longsuffering of our Lord is salvation; even as our beloved brother Paul also ac-cording to the wisdom given unto him hath written unto you; as also in all his epistles, speaking in them of these things; in which are some things hard to be understood, which they that are unlearned and unstable wrest, as they do also the other scriptures, unto their own destruction. **Matt. 19:4–5.** And he answered and said unto them, Have ye not read, that he which made them at the beginning made them male and female, and said, For this cause shall a man leave father and mother, and shall cleave to his wife: and they twain shall be one flesh? **With Gen. 2:24.** Therefore shall a man

Q. 4. *How doth it appear that the Scriptures are the Word of God?*

A. The Scriptures manifest themselves to be the Word of God, by their majesty[g] and purity;[h] by the consent of all the parts,[i] and the scope of the whole, which is to give all glory to God;[k] by their light

leave his father and his mother, and shall cleave unto his wife: and they shall be one flesh.

f. **Deut. 4:2.** Ye shall not add unto the word which I command you, neither shall ye diminish ought from it, that ye may keep the commandments of the Lord your God which I command you. **Eph. 2:20.** … and are built upon the foundation of the apostles and prophets, Jesus Christ himself being the chief corner stone. **Rev. 22:18– 19.** For I testify unto every man that heareth the words of the prophecy of this book, If any man shall add unto these things, God shall add unto him the plagues that are written in this book: and if any man shall take away from the words of the book of this prophecy, God shall take away his part out of the book of life, and out of the holy city, and from the things which are written in this book. **Isa. 8:20.** To the law and to the testimony: if they speak not according to this word, it is because there is no light in them. **Luke 16:29, 31.** Abraham saith unto him, They have Moses and the prophets; let them hear them.… And he said unto him, If they hear not Moses and the prophets, neither will they be persuaded, though one rose from the dead. **Gal. 1:8–9.** But though we, or an angel from heaven, preach any other gospel unto you than that which we have preached unto you, let him be accursed. As we said before, so say I now again, If any man preach any other gospel unto you than that ye have received, let him be accursed. **2 Tim. 3:15–16.** … and that from a child thou hast known the holy scriptures, which are able to make thee wise unto salvation through faith which is in Christ Jesus. All scripture is given by inspiration of God, and is profitable for doctrine, for reproof, for correction, for instruction in righteousness.

g. **Hos. 8:12.** I have written to him the great things of my law, but they were counted as a strange thing. **1 Cor. 2:6–7, 13.** Howbeit we speak wisdom among them that are perfect: yet not the wisdom of this world, nor of the princes of this world, that come to nought: but we speak the wisdom of God in a mystery, even the hidden wisdom, which God ordained before the world unto our glory.… Which things also we speak, not in the words which man's wisdom teacheth, but which the Holy Ghost teacheth; comparing spiritual things with spiritual. **Ps. 119:18, 129.** Open thou mine eyes, that I may behold wondrous things out of thy law.… Thy testimonies are wonderful: therefore doth my soul keep them.

h. **Ps. 12:6.** The words of the Lord are pure words: as silver tried in a furnace of earth, purified seven times. **Ps. 119:140.** Thy word is very pure: therefore thy servant loveth it.

i. **Luke 24:27.** And beginning at Moses and all the prophets, he expounded unto them in all the scriptures the things concerning himself. **Acts 10:43.** To him give all the prophets witness, that through his name whosoever believeth in him shall receive remission of sins. **Acts 26:22.** Having therefore obtained help of God, I continue unto this day, witnessing both to small and great, saying none other things than those which the prophets and Moses did say should come.

k. **Rom. 3:19, 27.** Now we know that what things soever the law saith, it saith to them who are under the law: that every mouth may be stopped, and all the world may

and power to convince and convert sinners, to comfort and build up believers unto salvation:[l] but the Spirit of God bearing witness by and with the Scriptures in the heart of man, is alone able fully to persuade it that they are the very Word of God.[m]

Q. 5. *What do the Scriptures principally teach?*

A. The Scriptures principally teach, what man is to believe concerning God,[n] and what duty God requires of man.[o]

become guilty before God.… Where is boasting then? It is excluded. By what law? of works? Nay: but by the law of faith. **Rom. 16:25–27.** Now to him that is of power to stablish you according to my gospel, and the preaching of Jesus Christ, according to the revelation of the mystery, which was kept secret since the world began, but now is made manifest, and by the scriptures of the prophets, according to the commandment of the everlasting God, made known to all nations for the obedience of faith: to God only wise, be glory through Jesus Christ for ever. Amen. **See 2 Cor. 3:6–11.**

l. **Acts 18:28.** For he mightily convinced the Jews, and that publickly, shewing by the scriptures that Jesus was Christ. **Heb. 4:12.** For the word of God is quick, and powerful, and sharper than any twoedged sword, piercing even to the dividing asunder of soul and spirit, and of the joints and marrow, and is a discerner of the thoughts and intents of the heart. **James 1:18.** Of his own will begat he us with the word of truth, that we should be a kind of firstfruits of his creatures. **Ps. 19:7–9.** The law of the LORD is perfect, converting the soul: the testimony of the LORD is sure, making wise the simple. The statutes of the LORD are right, rejoicing the heart: the commandment of the LORD is pure, enlightening the eyes. The fear of the LORD is clean, enduring for ever: the judgments of the LORD are true and righteous altogether. **Rom. 15:4.** For whatsoever things were written aforetime were written for our learning, that we through patience and comfort of the scriptures might have hope. **Acts 20:32.** And now, brethren, I commend you to God, and to the word of his grace, which is able to build you up, and to give you an inheritance among all them which are sanctified.

m. **John 16:13–14.** Howbeit when he, the Spirit of truth, is come, he will guide you into all truth: for he shall not speak of himself; but whatsoever he shall hear, that shall he speak: and he will shew you things to come. He shall glorify me: for he shall receive of mine, and shall shew it unto you. **See 1 John 2:20, 27. John 20:31.** But these are written, that ye might believe that Jesus is the Christ, the Son of God; and that believing ye might have life through his name.

n. **Gen. 1:1.** In the beginning God created the heaven and the earth. **Ex. 34:5–7.** And the LORD descended in the cloud, and stood with him there, and proclaimed the name of the LORD. And the LORD passed by before him, and proclaimed, The LORD, The LORD God, merciful and gracious, longsuffering, and abundant in goodness and truth, keeping mercy for thousands, forgiving iniquity and transgression and sin, and that will by no means clear the guilty; visiting the iniquity of the fathers upon the children, and upon the children's children, unto the third and to the fourth generation. **Ps. 48:1.** Great is the LORD, and greatly to be praised in the city of our God, in the mountain of his holiness. **John 20:31.** But these are written, that ye might believe that Jesus is the Christ, the Son of God; and that believing ye might have life through his name. **See 2 Tim. 3:15.**

WHAT MAN OUGHT TO BELIEVE CONCERNING GOD

Q. 6. *What do the Scriptures make known of God?*

A. The Scriptures make known what God is,[p] the persons in the Godhead,[q] his decrees,[r] and the execution of his decrees.[s]

o. **Deut. 10:12–13.** And now, Israel, what doth the LORD thy God require of thee, but to fear the LORD thy God, to walk in all his ways, and to love him, and to serve the LORD thy God with all thy heart and with all thy soul, To keep the commandments of the LORD, and his statutes, which I command thee this day for thy good? **2 Tim. 3:15–17.** … and that from a child thou hast known the holy scriptures, which are able to make thee wise unto salvation through faith which is in Christ Jesus. All scripture is given by inspiration of God, and is profitable for doctrine, for reproof, for correction, for instruction in righteousness: That the man of God may be perfect, throughly furnished unto all good works. **Acts 16:30–31.** And [the keeper of the prison] brought them out, and said, Sirs, what must I do to be saved? And they said, Believe on the Lord Jesus Christ, and thou shalt be saved, and thy house.

p. **John 4:24.** God is a Spirit: and they that worship him must worship him in spirit and in truth. **Ex. 34:6–7.** And the LORD passed by before him, and proclaimed, The LORD, The LORD God, merciful and gracious, longsuffering, and abundant in goodness and truth, keeping mercy for thousands, forgiving iniquity and transgression and sin, and that will by no means clear the guilty; visiting the iniquity of the fathers upon the children, and upon the children's children, unto the third and to the fourth generation. **Isa. 40:18, 21–23, 25, 28.** To whom then will ye liken God? or what likeness will ye compare unto him?… Have ye not known? have ye not heard? hath it not been told you from the beginning? have ye not understood from the foundations of the earth? It is he that sitteth upon the circle of the earth, and the inhabitants thereof are as grasshoppers; that stretcheth out the heavens as a curtain, and spreadeth them out as a tent to dwell in: that bringeth the princes to nothing; he maketh the judges of the earth as vanity.… To whom then will ye liken me, or shall I be equal? saith the Holy One.… Hast thou not known? hast thou not heard, that the everlasting God, the LORD, the Creator of the ends of the earth, fainteth not, neither is weary? there is no searching of his understanding. **Heb. 11:6.** But without faith it is impossible to please him: for he that cometh to God must believe that he is, and that he is a rewarder of them that diligently seek him.

q. **Matt. 3:16–17.** And Jesus, when he was baptized, went up straightway out of the water: and, lo, the heavens were opened unto him, and he saw the Spirit of God descending like a dove, and lighting upon him: and lo a voice from heaven, saying, This is my beloved Son, in whom I am well pleased. **Deut. 6:4–6.** Hear, O Israel: The LORD our God is one LORD: and thou shalt love the LORD thy God with all thine heart, and with all thy soul, and with all thy might. And these words, which I command thee this day, shall be in thine heart. **Compared with 1 Cor. 8:4, 6.** As concerning therefore the eating of those things that are offered in sacrifice unto idols, we know that an idol is nothing in the world, and that there is none other God but one.… But to us there is but one God, the Father, of whom are all things, and we in him; and one Lord Jesus Christ, by whom are all things, and we by him. **See Matt. 28:19–20; 2 Cor. 13:14.**

Q. 7. *What is God?*

A. God is a Spirit,[t] in and of himself infinite in being,[u] glory,[w] blessedness,[x] and perfection;[y] all-sufficient,[z] eternal,[a] unchangeable,[b] incomprehensible,[c] every where present,[d] almighty,[e] knowing all

r. **Acts 15:14–15, 18.** Simeon hath declared how God at the first did visit the Gentiles, to take out of them a people for his name. And to this agree the words of the prophets; as it is written, … Known unto God are all his works from the beginning of the world. **Isa. 46:9–10.** Remember the former things of old: for I am God, and there is none else; I am God, and there is none like me, declaring the end from the beginning, and from ancient times the things that are not yet done, saying, My counsel shall stand, and I will do all my pleasure.

s. **Acts 4:27–28.** For of a truth against thy holy child Jesus, whom thou hast anointed, both Herod, and Pontius Pilate, with the Gentiles, and the people of Israel, were gathered together, for to do whatsoever thy hand and thy counsel determined before to be done.

t. **John 4:24.** God is a Spirit: and they that worship him must worship him in spirit and in truth.

u. **Ex. 3:14.** And God said unto Moses, I AM THAT I AM: and he said, Thus shalt thou say unto the children of Israel, I AM hath sent me unto you. **Job 11:7–9.** Canst thou by searching find out God? canst thou find out the Almighty unto perfection? It is as high as heaven; what canst thou do? deeper than hell; what canst thou know? The measure thereof is longer than the earth, and broader than the sea. **Ps. 145:3.** Great is the LORD, and greatly to be praised; and his greatness is unsearchable. **Ps. 147:5.** Great is our Lord, and of great power: his understanding is infinite.

w. **Acts 7:2.** And he said, Men, brethren, and fathers, hearken; The God of glory appeared unto our father Abraham, when he was in Mesopotamia, before he dwelt in Charran.

x. **1 Tim. 6:15.** … which in his times he shall shew, who is the blessed and only Potentate, the King of kings, and Lord of lords.

y. **Matt. 5:48.** Be ye therefore perfect, even as your Father which is in heaven is perfect.

z. **Ex. 3:14.** And God said unto Moses, I AM THAT I AM: and he said, Thus shalt thou say unto the children of Israel, I AM hath sent me unto you. **Gen. 17:1.** And when Abram was ninety years old and nine, the LORD appeared to Abram, and said unto him, I am the Almighty God; walk before me, and be thou perfect. **Rom. 11:35–36.** Or who hath first given to him, and it shall be recompensed unto him again? For of him, and through him, and to him, are all things: to whom be glory for ever. Amen.

a. **Ps. 90:2.** Before the mountains were brought forth, or ever thou hadst formed the earth and the world, even from everlasting to everlasting, thou art God. **Deut. 33:27.** The eternal God is thy refuge, and underneath are the everlasting arms: and he shall thrust out the enemy from before thee; and shall say, Destroy them.

b. **Mal. 3:6.** For I am the LORD, I change not; therefore ye sons of Jacob are not consumed.

c. **1 Kings 8:27.** But will God indeed dwell on the earth? behold, the heaven and heaven of heavens cannot contain thee; how much less this house that I have

things,^{f} most wise,^{g} most holy,^{h} most just,^{i} most merciful and gracious, long-suffering, and abundant in goodness and truth.^{k}

builded? **Ps. 145:3.** Great is the LORD, and greatly to be praised; and his greatness is unsearchable. **See Rom. 11:34.**

d. **Ps. 139:1–13.** O LORD, thou hast searched me, and known me. Thou knowest my downsitting and mine uprising, thou understandest my thought afar off. Thou compassest my path and my lying down, and art acquainted with all my ways. For there is not a word in my tongue, but, lo, O LORD, thou knowest it altogether. Thou hast beset me behind and before, and laid thine hand upon me. Such knowledge is too wonderful for me; it is high, I cannot attain unto it. Whither shall I go from thy spirit? or whither shall I flee from thy presence? If I ascend up into heaven, thou art there: if I make my bed in hell, behold, thou art there. If I take the wings of the morning, and dwell in the uttermost parts of the sea; even there shall thy hand lead me, and thy right hand shall hold me. If I say, Surely the darkness shall cover me; even the night shall be light about me. Yea, the darkness hideth not from thee; but the night shineth as the day: the darkness and the light are both alike to thee. For thou hast possessed my reins: thou hast covered me in my mother's womb.

e. **Rev. 4:8.** And the four beasts had each of them six wings about him; and they were full of eyes within: and they rest not day and night, saying, Holy, holy, holy, Lord God Almighty, which was, and is, and is to come. **Gen. 17:1.** And when Abram was ninety years old and nine, the LORD appeared to Abram, and said unto him, I am the Almighty God; walk before me, and be thou perfect. **Matt. 19:26.** But Jesus beheld them, and said unto them, With men this is impossible; but with God all things are possible.

f. **Heb. 4:13.** Neither is there any creature that is not manifest in his sight: but all things are naked and opened unto the eyes of him with whom we have to do. **See Ps. 147:5.**

g. **Rom. 11:33–34.** O the depth of the riches both of the wisdom and knowledge of God! how unsearchable are his judgments, and his ways past finding out! For who hath known the mind of the Lord? or who hath been his counsellor? **Rom. 16:27.** To God only wise, be glory through Jesus Christ for ever. Amen.

h. **1 Pet. 1:15–16.** But as he which hath called you is holy, so be ye holy in all manner of conversation; because it is written, Be ye holy; for I am holy. **Rev. 15:4.** Who shall not fear thee, O Lord, and glorify thy name? for thou only art holy: for all nations shall come and worship before thee; for thy judgments are made manifest. **Isa. 6:3.** And one cried unto another, and said, Holy, holy, holy, is the LORD of hosts: the whole earth is full of his glory.

i. **Deut. 32:4.** He is the Rock, his work is perfect: for all his ways are judgment: a God of truth and without iniquity, just and right is he. **Rom. 3:5, 26.** But if our unrighteousness commend the righteousness of God, what shall we say? Is God unrighteous who taketh vengeance? (I speak as a man) … to declare, I say, at this time his righteousness: that he might be just, and the justifier of him which believeth in Jesus.

k. **Ex. 34:6.** And the LORD passed by before him, and proclaimed, The LORD, The LORD God, merciful and gracious, longsuffering, and abundant in goodness and truth. **Ps. 117:2.** For his merciful kindness is great toward us: and the truth of the LORD endureth for ever. Praise ye the LORD. **Deut. 32:4.** He is the Rock, his work is

Q. 8. *Are there more Gods than one?*

A. There is but one only,[l] the living and true God.[m]

Q. 9. *How many persons are there in the Godhead?*

A. There be three persons in the Godhead, the Father, the Son, and the Holy Ghost;[n] and these three are one true, eternal God, the same in substance, equal in power and glory; although distinguished by their personal properties.[o]

perfect: for all his ways are judgment: a God of truth and without iniquity, just and right is he.

l. **Deut. 6:4.** Hear, O Israel: The LORD our God is one LORD. **1 Cor. 8:4, 6.** As concerning therefore the eating of those things that are offered in sacrifice unto idols, we know that an idol is nothing in the world, and that there is none other God but one.… But to us there is but one God, the Father, of whom are all things, and we in him; and one Lord Jesus Christ, by whom are all things, and we by him. **Isa. 45:21–22.** Tell ye, and bring them near; yea, let them take counsel together: who hath declared this from ancient time? who hath told it from that time? have not I the LORD? and there is no God else beside me; a just God and a Saviour; there is none beside me. Look unto me, and be ye saved, all the ends of the earth: for I am God, and there is none else. **Isa. 44:6.** Thus saith the LORD the King of Israel, and his redeemer the LORD of hosts; I am the first, and I am the last; and beside me there is no God.

m. **Jer. 10:10.** But the LORD is the true God, he is the living God, and an everlasting king: at his wrath the earth shall tremble, and the nations shall not be able to abide his indignation. **John 17:3.** And this is life eternal, that they might know thee the only true God, and Jesus Christ, whom thou hast sent. **1 Thess. 1:9.** For they themselves shew of us what manner of entering in we had unto you, and how ye turned to God from idols to serve the living and true God. **1 John 5:20.** And we know that the Son of God is come, and hath given us an understanding, that we may know him that is true, and we are in him that is true, even in his Son Jesus Christ. This is the true God, and eternal life.

n. **Matt. 3:16–17.** And Jesus, when he was baptized, went up straightway out of the water: and, lo, the heavens were opened unto him, and he saw the Spirit of God descending like a dove, and lighting upon him: and lo a voice from heaven, saying, This is my beloved Son, in whom I am well pleased. **Matt. 28:19.** Go ye therefore, and teach all nations, baptizing them in the name of the Father, and of the Son, and of the Holy Ghost. **2 Cor. 13:14.** The grace of the Lord Jesus Christ, and the love of God, and the communion of the Holy Ghost, be with you all. Amen.

o. **John 1:1.** In the beginning was the Word, and the Word was with God, and the Word was God. **See also Gen. 1:1–3. John 17:5.** And now, O Father, glorify thou me with thine own self with the glory which I had with thee before the world was. **John 10:30.** I and my Father are one. **Ps. 45:6.** Thy throne, O God, is for ever and ever: the sceptre of thy kingdom is a right sceptre. **See also Heb. 1:8–9. Acts 5:3–4.** But Peter said, Ananias, why hath Satan filled thine heart to lie to the Holy Ghost, and to keep back part of the price of the land? Whiles it remained, was it not thine own? and after it was sold, was it not in thine own power? why hast thou conceived this thing in thine heart? thou hast not lied unto men, but unto God.

Q. 10. *What are the personal properties of the three persons in the Godhead?*

A. It is proper to the Father to beget the Son,[p] and to the Son to be begotten of the Father,[q] and to the Holy Ghost to proceed from the Father and the Son from all eternity.[r]

Q. 11. *How doth it appear that the Son and the Holy Ghost are God equal with the Father?*

A. The Scriptures manifest that the Son and the Holy Ghost are God equal with the Father, ascribing unto them such names,[s] attributes,[t] works,[u] and worship,[w] as are proper to God only.

Rom. 9:5. … whose are the fathers, and of whom as concerning the flesh Christ came, who is over all, God blessed for ever. Amen. **Col. 2:9.** For in him dwelleth all the fulness of the Godhead bodily.

p. **Heb. 1:5–6, 8.** For unto which of the angels said he at any time, Thou art my Son, this day have I begotten thee? And again, I will be to him a Father, and he shall be to me a Son? And again, when he bringeth in the firstbegotten into the world, he saith, And let all the angels of God worship him.… But unto the Son he saith, Thy throne, O God, is for ever and ever: a sceptre of righteousness is the sceptre of thy kingdom.

q. **John 1:14, 18.** And the Word was made flesh, and dwelt among us, (and we beheld his glory, the glory as of the only begotten of the Father,) full of grace and truth.… No man hath seen God at any time; the only begotten Son, which is in the bosom of the Father, he hath declared him.

r. **John 15:26.** But when the Comforter is come, whom I will send unto you from the Father, even the Spirit of truth, which proceedeth from the Father, he shall testify of me. **Gal. 4:6.** And because ye are sons, God hath sent forth the Spirit of his Son into your hearts, crying, Abba, Father.

s. **Isa. 6:3, 5, 8.** And one cried unto another, and said, Holy, holy, holy, is the LORD of hosts: the whole earth is full of his glory.… Then said I, Woe is me! for I am undone; because I am a man of unclean lips, and I dwell in the midst of a people of unclean lips: for mine eyes have seen the King, the LORD of hosts.… Also I heard the voice of the Lord, saying, Whom shall I send, and who will go for us? Then said I, Here am I; send me. **John 12:41.** These things said Esaias, when he saw his glory, and spake of him. **Acts 28:25.** And when they agreed not among themselves, they departed, after that Paul had spoken one word, Well spake the Holy Ghost by Esaias the prophet unto our fathers … **1 John 5:20.** And we know that the Son of God is come, and hath given us an understanding, that we may know him that is true, and we are in him that is true, even in his Son Jesus Christ. This is the true God, and eternal life. **Acts 5:3–4.** But Peter said, Ananias, why hath Satan filled thine heart to lie to the Holy Ghost, and to keep back part of the price of the land? Whiles it remained, was it not thine own? and after it was sold, was it not in thine own power? why hast thou conceived this thing in thine heart? thou hast not lied unto men, but unto God.

t. **John 1:1.** In the beginning was the Word, and the Word was with God, and the Word was God. **Isa. 9:6.** For unto us a child is born, unto us a son is given: and the government shall be upon his shoulder: and his name shall be called Wonderful, Counsellor, The mighty God, The everlasting Father, The Prince of Peace. **John 2:24–25.**

Q. 12. *What are the decrees of God?*

A. God's decrees are the wise, free, and holy acts of the counsel of his will,[x] whereby, from all eternity, he hath, for his own glory, unchangeably foreordained whatsoever comes to pass in time,[y] especially concerning angels and men.

But Jesus did not commit himself unto them, because he knew all men, and needed not that any should testify of man: for he knew what was in man. **1 Cor. 2:10–11.** But God hath revealed them unto us by his Spirit: for the Spirit searcheth all things, yea, the deep things of God. For what man knoweth the things of a man, save the spirit of man which is in him? even so the things of God knoweth no man, but the Spirit of God.

u. **Col. 1:16.** For by him were all things created, that are in heaven, and that are in earth, visible and invisible, whether they be thrones, or dominions, or principalities, or powers: all things were created by him, and for him. **Gen. 1:2.** And the earth was without form, and void; and darkness was upon the face of the deep. And the Spirit of God moved upon the face of the waters.

w. **Matt. 28:19.** Go ye therefore, and teach all nations, baptizing them in the name of the Father, and of the Son, and of the Holy Ghost. **2 Cor. 13:14.** The grace of the Lord Jesus Christ, and the love of God, and the communion of the Holy Ghost, be with you all. Amen.

x. **Isa. 45:6–7.** That they may know from the rising of the sun, and from the west, that there is none beside me. I am the LORD, and there is none else. I form the light, and create darkness: I make peace, and create evil: I the LORD do all these things. **Eph. 1:11.** … in whom also we have obtained an inheritance, being predestinated according to the purpose of him who worketh all things after the counsel of his own will. **Rom. 11:33.** O the depth of the riches both of the wisdom and knowledge of God! how unsearchable are his judgments, and his ways past finding out! **Rom. 9:14–15, 18.** What shall we say then? Is there unrighteousness with God? God forbid. For he saith to Moses, I will have mercy on whom I will have mercy, and I will have compassion on whom I will have compassion.… Therefore hath he mercy on whom he will have mercy, and whom he will he hardeneth.

y. **Ps. 33:11.** The counsel of the LORD standeth for ever, the thoughts of his heart to all generations. **Isa. 14:24.** The LORD of hosts hath sworn, saying, Surely as I have thought, so shall it come to pass; and as I have purposed, so shall it stand. **Acts 2:23.** Him, being delivered by the determinate counsel and foreknowledge of God, ye have taken, and by wicked hands have crucified and slain. **Acts 4:27–28.** For of a truth against thy holy child Jesus, whom thou hast anointed, both Herod, and Pontius Pilate, with the Gentiles, and the people of Israel, were gathered together, for to do whatsoever thy hand and thy counsel determined before to be done. **Rom. 9:22–23.** What if God, willing to shew his wrath, and to make his power known, endured with much longsuffering the vessels of wrath fitted to destruction: and that he might make known the riches of his glory on the vessels of mercy, which he had afore prepared unto glory. **Eph. 1:4, 11.** … according as he hath chosen us in him before the foundation of the world, that we should be holy and without blame before him in love.… in whom also we have obtained an inheritance, being predestinated according to the purpose of him who worketh all things after the counsel of his own will.

Q. 13. W*hat hath God especially decreed concerning angels and men?*

A. God, by an eternal and immutable decree, out of his mere love, for the praise of his glorious grace, to be manifested in due time, hath elected some angels to glory;[z] and in Christ hath chosen some men to eternal life, and the means thereof:[a] and also, according to his sovereign power, and the unsearchable counsel of his own will, (whereby he extendeth or withholdeth favor as he pleaseth,) hath passed by and foreordained the rest to dishonor and wrath, to be for their sin inflicted, to the praise of the glory of his justice.[b]

Q. 14. *How doth God execute his decrees?*

A. God executeth his decrees in the works of creation and

z. **1 Tim. 5:21.** I charge thee before God, and the Lord Jesus Christ, and the elect angels, that thou observe these things without preferring one before another, doing nothing by partiality.

a. **Eph. 1:4–6** … according as he hath chosen us in him before the foundation of the world, that we should be holy and without blame before him in love: having predestinated us unto the adoption of children by Jesus Christ to himself, according to the good pleasure of his will, to the praise of the glory of his grace, wherein he hath made us accepted in the beloved. **Eph. 2:10.** For we are his workmanship, created in Christ Jesus unto good works, which God hath before ordained that we should walk in them. **2 Thess. 2:13–14.** But we are bound to give thanks alway to God for you, brethren beloved of the Lord, because God hath from the beginning chosen you to salvation through sanctification of the Spirit and belief of the truth: whereunto he called you by our gospel, to the obtaining of the glory of our Lord Jesus Christ. **1 Pet. 1:2.** … elect according to the foreknowledge of God the Father, through sanctification of the Spirit, unto obedience and sprinkling of the blood of Jesus Christ: Grace unto you, and peace, be multiplied.

b. **Rom. 9:17–18, 21–22.** For the scripture saith unto Pharaoh, Even for this same purpose have I raised thee up, that I might shew my power in thee, and that my name might be declared throughout all the earth. Therefore hath he mercy on whom he will have mercy, and whom he will he hardeneth.… Hath not the potter power over the clay, of the same lump to make one vessel unto honour, and another unto dishonour? What if God, willing to shew his wrath, and to make his power known, endured with much longsuffering the vessels of wrath fitted to destruction. **Matt. 11:25–26.** At that time Jesus answered and said, I thank thee, O Father, Lord of heaven and earth, because thou hast hid these things from the wise and prudent, and hast revealed them unto babes. Even so, Father: for so it seemed good in thy sight. **2 Tim. 2:20.** But in a great house there are not only vessels of gold and of silver, but also of wood and of earth; and some to honour, and some to dishonour. **Jude 4.** For there are certain men crept in unawares, who were before of old ordained to this condemnation, ungodly men, turning the grace of our God into lasciviousness, and denying the only Lord God, and our Lord Jesus Christ. **1 Pet. 2:8.** … and a stone of stumbling, and a rock of offence, even to them which stumble at the word, being disobedient: whereunto also they were appointed.

providence,[c] according to his infallible foreknowledge, and the free and immutable counsel of his own will.[d]

Q. 15. *What is the work of creation?*

A. The work of creation is that wherein God did in the beginning, by the word of his power, make of nothing the world, and all things therein, for himself, within the space of six days, and all very good.[e]

Q. 16. *How did God create angels?*

A. God created all the angels[f] spirits,[g] immortal,[h] holy,[i] excelling

c. **Rev. 4:11.** Thou art worthy, O Lord, to receive glory and honour and power: for thou hast created all things, and for thy pleasure they are and were created. **See Isa. 40:12–31.**

d. **Eph. 1:11.** … in whom also we have obtained an inheritance, being predestinated according to the purpose of him who worketh all things after the counsel of his own will. **Ps. 148:8.** … fire, and hail; snow, and vapours; stormy wind fulfilling his word. **Dan. 4:35.** And all the inhabitants of the earth are reputed as nothing: and he doeth according to his will in the army of heaven, and among the inhabitants of the earth: and none can stay his hand, or say unto him, What doest thou? **Acts 4:24–28.** And when they heard that, they lifted up their voice to God with one accord, and said, Lord, thou art God, which hast made heaven, and earth, and the sea, and all that in them is: Who by the mouth of thy servant David hast said, Why did the heathen rage, and the people imagine vain things? The kings of the earth stood up, and the rulers were gathered together against the Lord, and against his Christ. For of a truth against thy holy child Jesus, whom thou hast anointed, both Herod, and Pontius Pilate, with the Gentiles, and the people of Israel, were gathered together, for to do whatsoever thy hand and thy counsel determined before to be done.

e. **Gen. 1:1.** In the beginning God created the heaven and the earth **(see entire chapter). Ps. 33:6, 9.** By the word of the LORD were the heavens made; and all the host of them by the breath of his mouth.… For he spake, and it was done; he commanded, and it stood fast. **Heb. 11:3.** Through faith we understand that the worlds were framed by the word of God, so that things which are seen were not made of things which do appear. **Rev. 4:11.** Thou art worthy, O Lord, to receive glory and honour and power: for thou hast created all things, and for thy pleasure they are and were created. **See Rom. 11:36.**

f. **Col. 1:16.** For by him were all things created, that are in heaven, and that are in earth, visible and invisible, whether they be thrones, or dominions, or principalities, or powers: all things were created by him, and for him.

g. **Ps. 104:4.** … who maketh his angels spirits; his ministers a flaming fire.

h. **Matt. 22:30.** For in the resurrection they neither marry, nor are given in marriage, but are as the angels of God in heaven. **Luke 20:36.** Neither can they die any more: for they are equal unto the angels; and are the children of God, being the children of the resurrection.

i. **Matt. 25:31.** When the Son of man shall come in his glory, and all the holy angels with him, then shall he sit upon the throne of his glory.

in knowledge,[k] mighty in power,[l] to execute his commandments, and to praise his name,[m] yet subject to change.[n]

Q. 17. *How did God create man?*

A. After God had made all other creatures, he created man male and female;[o] formed the body of the man of the dust of the ground,[p] and the woman of the rib of the man,[q] endued them with living, reasonable, and immortal souls;[r] made them after his own image,[s] in knowledge,[t] righteousness, and holiness;[u] having the law of God writ-

k. **2 Sam. 14:17.** Then thine handmaid said, The word of my lord the king shall now be comfortable: for as an angel of God, so is my lord the king to discern good and bad: therefore the LORD thy God will be with thee. **Matt. 24:36.** But of that day and hour knoweth no man, no, not the angels of heaven, but my Father only.

l. **2 Thess. 1:7.** … and to you who are troubled rest with us, when the Lord Jesus shall be revealed from heaven with his mighty angels.

m. **Ps. 91:11–12.** For he shall give his angels charge over thee, to keep thee in all thy ways. They shall bear thee up in their hands, lest thou dash thy foot against a stone. **Ps. 103:20–21.** Bless the LORD, ye his angels, that excel in strength, that do his commandments, hearkening unto the voice of his word. Bless ye the LORD, all ye his hosts; ye ministers of his, that do his pleasure.

n. **2 Pet. 2:4.** For if God spared not the angels that sinned, but cast them down to hell, and delivered them into chains of darkness, to be reserved unto judgment …

o. **Gen. 1:27.** So God created man in his own image, in the image of God created he him; male and female created he them. **Matt. 19:4.** And he answered and said unto them, Have ye not read, that he which made them at the beginning made them male and female.

p. **Gen. 2:7.** And the LORD God formed man of the dust of the ground, and breathed into his nostrils the breath of life; and man became a living soul.

q. **Gen. 2:22.** And the rib, which the LORD God had taken from man, made he a woman, and brought her unto the man.

r. **Gen. 2:7.** And the LORD God formed man of the dust of the ground, and breathed into his nostrils the breath of life; and man became a living soul. **Job 35:11.** Who teacheth us more than the beasts of the earth, and maketh us wiser than the fowls of heaven? **Eccl. 12:7.** Then shall the dust return to the earth as it was: and the spirit shall return unto God who gave it. **Matt. 10:28.** And fear not them which kill the body, but are not able to kill the soul: but rather fear him which is able to destroy both soul and body in hell. **Luke 23:43.** And Jesus said unto him, Verily I say unto thee, To day shalt thou be with me in paradise.

s. **Gen. 1:26–27.** And God said, Let us make man in our image, after our likeness: and let them have dominion over the fish of the sea, and over the fowl of the air, and over the cattle, and over all the earth, and over every creeping thing that creepeth upon the earth. So God created man in his own image, in the image of God created he him; male and female created he them.

t. **Col. 3:10.** And [ye] have put on the new man, which is renewed in knowledge after the image of him that created him.

ten in their hearts,[w] and power to fulfill it,[x] and dominion over the creatures;[y] yet subject to fall.[z]

Q. 18. *What are God's works of providence?*

A. God's works of providence are his most holy,[a] wise,[b] and powerful preserving[c] and governing[d] all his creatures; ordering them, and

u. **Eph. 4:24.** … and that ye put on the new man, which after God is created in righteousness and true holiness.

w. **Rom. 2:14–15.** For when the Gentiles, which have not the law, do by nature the things contained in the law, these, having not the law, are a law unto themselves: which shew the work of the law written in their hearts, their conscience also bearing witness, and their thoughts the mean while accusing or else excusing one another.

x. **Eccl. 7:29.** Lo, this only have I found, that God hath made man upright; but they have sought out many inventions.

y. **Gen. 1:28.** And God blessed them, and God said unto them, Be fruitful, and multiply, and replenish the earth, and subdue it: and have dominion over the fish of the sea, and over the fowl of the air, and over every living thing that moveth upon the earth. **Ps. 8:6–8.** Thou madest him to have dominion over the works of thy hands; thou hast put all things under his feet: all sheep and oxen, yea, and the beasts of the field; the fowl of the air, and the fish of the sea, and whatsoever passeth through the paths of the seas.

z. **Gen. 2:16–17.** And the Lord God commanded the man, saying, Of every tree of the garden thou mayest freely eat: but of the tree of the knowledge of good and evil, thou shalt not eat of it: for in the day that thou eatest thereof thou shalt surely die. **Gen. 3:6.** And when the woman saw that the tree was good for food, and that it was pleasant to the eyes, and a tree to be desired to make one wise, she took of the fruit thereof, and did eat, and gave also unto her husband with her; and he did eat. **Eccl. 7:29.** Lo, this only have I found, that God hath made man upright; but they have sought out many inventions.

a. **Ps. 145:17.** The Lord is righteous in all his ways, and holy in all his works. **Lev. 21:8.** Thou shalt sanctify him therefore; for he offereth the bread of thy God: he shall be holy unto thee: for I the Lord, which sanctify you, am holy.

b. **Ps. 104:24.** O Lord, how manifold are thy works! in wisdom hast thou made them all: the earth is full of thy riches. **Isa. 28:29.** This also cometh forth from the Lord of hosts, which is wonderful in counsel, and excellent in working.

c. **Heb. 1:3.** … who being the brightness of his glory, and the express image of his person, and upholding all things by the word of his power, when he had by himself purged our sins, sat down on the right hand of the Majesty on high. **Ps. 36:6.** Thy righteousness is like the great mountains; thy judgments are a great deep: O Lord, thou preservest man and beast. **Neh. 9:6.** Thou, even thou, art Lord alone; thou hast made heaven, the heaven of heavens, with all their host, the earth, and all things that are therein, the seas, and all that is therein, and thou preservest them all; and the host of heaven worshippeth thee.

d. **Ps. 103:19.** The Lord hath prepared his throne in the heavens; and his kingdom ruleth over all. **See Job 38–41; Ps. 145:14–16.**

all their actions,[e] to his own glory.[f]

Q. 19. *What is God's providence towards the angels?*

A. God by his providence permitted some of the angels, willfully and irrecoverably, to fall into sin and damnation,[g] limiting and ordering that, and all their sins, to his own glory;[h] and established the rest in holiness and happiness;[i] employing them all,[k] at his pleasure, in the administrations of his power, mercy, and justice.[l]

Q. 20. *What was the providence of God toward man in the estate in which he was created?*

A. The providence of God toward man in the estate in which he was created, was the placing him in paradise, appointing him to dress

e. **Matt. 10:29–31.** Are not two sparrows sold for a farthing? and one of them shall not fall on the ground without your Father. But the very hairs of your head are all numbered. Fear ye not therefore, ye are of more value than many sparrows. **Gen. 45:7.** And God sent me before you to preserve you a posterity in the earth, and to save your lives by a great deliverance. **Ps. 135:6.** Whatsoever the LORD pleased, that did he in heaven, and in earth, in the seas, and all deep places.

f. **Rom. 11:36.** For of him, and through him, and to him, are all things: to whom be glory for ever. Amen. **Isa. 63:14.** As a beast goeth down into the valley, the Spirit of the LORD caused him to rest: so didst thou lead thy people, to make thyself a glorious name.

g. **Jude 6.** And the angels which kept not their first estate, but left their own habitation, he hath reserved in everlasting chains under darkness unto the judgment of the great day. **See 2 Pet. 2:4; Heb. 2:16; John 8:44.**

h. **Job 1:12.** And the LORD said unto Satan, Behold, all that he hath is in thy power; only upon himself put not forth thine hand. So Satan went forth from the presence of the LORD. **Matt. 8:31.** So the devils besought him, saying, If thou cast us out, suffer us to go away into the herd of swine. **Luke 10:17.** And the seventy returned again with joy, saying, Lord, even the devils are subject unto us through thy name.

i. **1 Tim. 5:21.** I charge thee before God, and the Lord Jesus Christ, and the elect angels, that thou observe these things without preferring one before another, doing nothing by partiality. **Mark 8:38.** Whosoever therefore shall be ashamed of me and of my words in this adulterous and sinful generation; of him also shall the Son of man be ashamed, when he cometh in the glory of his Father with the holy angels. **Heb. 12:22.** But ye are come unto mount Sion, and unto the city of the living God, the heavenly Jerusalem, and to an innumerable company of angels.

k. **Ps. 103:20.** Bless the LORD, ye his angels, that excel in strength, that do his commandments, hearkening unto the voice of his word. **Ps. 104:4.** … who maketh his angels spirits; his ministers a flaming fire.

l. **Heb. 1:14.** Are they not all ministering spirits, sent forth to minister for them who shall be heirs of salvation? **See 2 Kings 19:35.**

it, giving him liberty to eat of the fruit of the earth;[m] putting the creatures under his dominion,[n] and ordaining marriage for his help;[o] affording him communion with himself;[p] instituting the Sabbath;[q] entering into a covenant of life with him, upon condition of personal, perfect, and perpetual obedience,[r] of which the tree of life was a pledge;[s] and forbidding to eat of the tree of the knowledge of good

m. **Gen. 2:8, 15–16.** And the LORD God planted a garden eastward in Eden; and there he put the man whom he had formed.… And the LORD God took the man, and put him into the garden of Eden to dress it and to keep it. And the LORD God commanded the man, saying, Of every tree of the garden thou mayest freely eat.

n. **Gen. 1:28.** And God blessed them, and God said unto them, Be fruitful, and multiply, and replenish the earth, and subdue it: and have dominion over the fish of the sea, and over the fowl of the air, and over every living thing that moveth upon the earth.

o. **Gen. 2:18.** And the LORD God said, It is not good that the man should be alone; I will make him an help meet for him. **See Matt. 19:3–9; Eph. 5:31.**

p. **Gen. 1:26–29.** And God said, Let us make man in our image, after our likeness: and let them have dominion over the fish of the sea, and over the fowl of the air, and over the cattle, and over all the earth, and over every creeping thing that creepeth upon the earth. So God created man in his own image, in the image of God created he him; male and female created he them. And God blessed them, and God said unto them, Be fruitful, and multiply, and replenish the earth, and subdue it: and have dominion over the fish of the sea, and over the fowl of the air, and over every living thing that moveth upon the earth. And God said, Behold, I have given you every herb bearing seed, which is upon the face of all the earth, and every tree, in the which is the fruit of a tree yielding seed; to you it shall be for meat. **Gen. 3:8.** And they heard the voice of the LORD God walking in the garden in the cool of the day: and Adam and his wife hid themselves from the presence of the LORD God amongst the trees of the garden.

q. **Gen. 2:3.** And God blessed the seventh day, and sanctified it: because that in it he had rested from all his work which God created and made. **Compared with Ex. 20:11.** For in six days the LORD made heaven and earth, the sea, and all that in them is, and rested the seventh day: wherefore the LORD blessed the sabbath day, and hallowed it.

r. **Gen. 2:16–17.** And the LORD God commanded the man, saying, Of every tree of the garden thou mayest freely eat: but of the tree of the knowledge of good and evil, thou shalt not eat of it: for in the day that thou eatest thereof thou shalt surely die. **Gal. 3:12.** And the law is not of faith: but, The man that doeth them shall live in them. **Rom. 10:5.** For Moses describeth the righteousness which is of the law, That the man which doeth those things shall live by them.

s. **Gen. 2:9.** And out of the ground made the LORD God to grow every tree that is pleasant to the sight, and good for food; the tree of life also in the midst of the garden, and the tree of knowledge of good and evil. **Gen. 3:22–24.** And the LORD God said, Behold, the man is become as one of us, to know good and evil: and now, lest he put forth his hand, and take also of the tree of life, and eat, and live for ever: therefore the LORD God sent him forth from the garden of Eden, to till the ground

and evil, upon the pain of death.[t]

Q. 21. *Did man continue in that estate wherein God at first created him?*

A. Our first parents being left to the freedom of their own will, through the temptation of Satan, transgressed the commandment of God in eating the forbidden fruit; and thereby fell from the estate of innocency wherein they were created.[u]

Q. 22. *Did all mankind fall in that first transgression?*

A. The covenant being made with Adam as a public person, not for himself only, but for his posterity, all mankind descending from him by ordinary generation,[w] sinned in him, and fell with him in that first transgression.[x]

from whence he was taken. So he drove out the man; and he placed at the east of the garden of Eden Cherubims, and a flaming sword which turned every way, to keep the way of the tree of life.

t. **Gen. 2:17.** But of the tree of the knowledge of good and evil, thou shalt not eat of it: for in the day that thou eatest thereof thou shalt surely die. **Compared with James 2:10.** For whosoever shall keep the whole law, and yet offend in one point, he is guilty of all.

u. **Gen. 3:6–8, 13.** And when the woman saw that the tree was good for food, and that it was pleasant to the eyes, and a tree to be desired to make one wise, she took of the fruit thereof, and did eat, and gave also unto her husband with her; and he did eat. And the eyes of them both were opened, and they knew that they were naked; and they sewed fig leaves together, and made themselves aprons. And they heard the voice of the LORD God walking in the garden in the cool of the day: and Adam and his wife hid themselves from the presence of the LORD God amongst the trees of the garden.… And the LORD God said unto the woman, What is this that thou hast done? And the woman said, The serpent beguiled me, and I did eat. **Eccl. 7:29.** Lo, this only have I found, that God hath made man upright; but they have sought out many inventions. **2 Cor. 11:3.** But I fear, lest by any means, as the serpent beguiled Eve through his subtilty, so your minds should be corrupted from the simplicity that is in Christ.

w. **Acts 17:26.** And [God] hath made of one blood all nations of men for to dwell on all the face of the earth, and hath determined the times before appointed, and the bounds of their habitation. **Rom. 3:23.** For all have sinned, and come short of the glory of God.

x. **Gen. 2:16–17.** And the LORD God commanded the man, saying, Of every tree of the garden thou mayest freely eat: but of the tree of the knowledge of good and evil, thou shalt not eat of it: for in the day that thou eatest thereof thou shalt surely die. **James 2:10.** For whosoever shall keep the whole law, and yet offend in one point, he is guilty of all. **Compared with Rom. 5:12–20.** Wherefore, as by one man sin entered into the world, and death by sin; and so death passed upon all men, for that all have sinned: (For until the law sin was in the world: but sin is not imputed

Q. 23. *Into what estate did the fall bring mankind?*
A. The fall brought mankind into an estate of sin and misery.ʸ

Q. 24. *What is sin?*
A. Sin is any want of conformity unto, or transgression of, any law of God, given as a rule to the reasonable creature.ᶻ

Q. 25. *Wherein consisteth the sinfulness of that estate whereinto man fell?*
A. The sinfulness of that estate whereinto man fell, consisteth in the guilt of Adam's first sin,ᵃ the want of that righteousness wherein

when there is no law. Nevertheless death reigned from Adam to Moses, even over them that had not sinned after the similitude of Adam's transgression, who is the figure of him that was to come. But not as the offence, so also is the free gift. For if through the offence of one many be dead, much more the grace of God, and the gift by grace, which is by one man, Jesus Christ, hath abounded unto many. And not as it was by one that sinned, so is the gift: for the judgment was by one to condemnation, but the free gift is of many offences unto justification. For if by one man's offence death reigned by one; much more they which receive abundance of grace and of the gift of righteousness shall reign in life by one, Jesus Christ.) therefore as by the offence of one judgment came upon all men to condemnation; even so by the righteousness of one the free gift came upon all men unto justification of life. For as by one man's disobedience many were made sinners, so by the obedience of one shall many be made righteous. Moreover the law entered, that the offence might abound. But where sin abounded, grace did much more abound. **1 Cor. 15:21–22.** For since by man came death, by man came also the resurrection of the dead. For as in Adam all die, even so in Christ shall all be made alive.

y. **Gen. 3:16–19.** Unto the woman he said, I will greatly multiply thy sorrow and thy conception; in sorrow thou shalt bring forth children; and thy desire shall be to thy husband, and he shall rule over thee. And unto Adam he said, Because thou hast hearkened unto the voice of thy wife, and hast eaten of the tree, of which I commanded thee, saying, Thou shalt not eat of it: cursed is the ground for thy sake; in sorrow shalt thou eat of it all the days of thy life; thorns also and thistles shall it bring forth to thee; and thou shalt eat the herb of the field; in the sweat of thy face shalt thou eat bread, till thou return unto the ground; for out of it wast thou taken: for dust thou art, and unto dust shalt thou return. **Rom. 5:12.** Wherefore, as by one man sin entered into the world, and death by sin; and so death passed upon all men, for that all have sinned … **Eph. 2:1.** And you hath he quickened, who were dead in trespasses and sins. **Rom. 3:16, 23.** Destruction and misery are in their ways.… For all have sinned, and come short of the glory of God.

z. **Lev. 5:17.** And if a soul sin, and commit any of these things which are forbidden to be done by the commandments of the Lᴏʀᴅ; though he wist it not, yet is he guilty, and shall bear his iniquity. **James 4:17.** Therefore to him that knoweth to do good, and doeth it not, to him it is sin. **1 John 3:4.** Whosoever committeth sin transgresseth also the law: for sin is the transgression of law. **See Gal. 3:10, 12.**

a. **Rom. 5:12, 19.** Wherefore, as by one man sin entered into the world, and

he was created, and the corruption of his nature, whereby he is utterly indisposed, disabled, and made opposite unto all that is spiritually good, and wholly inclined to all evil, and that continually;[b] which is commonly called original sin, and from which do proceed all actual transgressions.[c]

Q. 26. *How is original sin conveyed from our first parents unto their posterity?*

A. Original sin is conveyed from our first parents unto their posterity by natural generation, so as all that proceed from them in that way are conceived and born in sin.[d]

Q. 27. *What misery did the fall bring upon mankind?*

A. The fall brought upon mankind the loss of communion with

death by sin; and so death passed upon all men, for that all have sinned … For as by one man's disobedience many were made sinners, so by the obedience of one shall many be made righteous. **See 1 Cor. 15:22.**

b. **Rom. 3:10–12.** As it is written, There is none righteous, no, not one: there is none that understandeth, there is none that seeketh after God. They are all gone out of the way, they are together become unprofitable; there is none that doeth good, no, not one (**see verses 13–19**). **Eph. 2:1–3.** And you hath he quickened, who were dead in trespasses and sins: wherein in time past ye walked according to the course of this world, according to the prince of the power of the air, the spirit that now worketh in the children of disobedience: among whom also we all had our conversation in times past in the lusts of our flesh, fulfilling the desires of the flesh and of the mind; and were by nature the children of wrath, even as others. **Rom. 5:6.** For when we were yet without strength, in due time Christ died for the ungodly. **Rom. 8:7–8.** Because the carnal mind is enmity against God: for it is not subject to the law of God, neither indeed can be. So then they that are in the flesh cannot please God. **Gen. 6:5.** And God saw that the wickedness of man was great in the earth, and that every imagination of the thoughts of his heart was only evil continually. **See Col. 3:10; Eph. 4:24.**

c. **James 1:14–15.** But every man is tempted, when he is drawn away of his own lust, and enticed. Then when lust hath conceived, it bringeth forth sin: and sin, when it is finished, bringeth forth death. **Ps. 53:1–3.** The fool hath said in his heart, There is no God. Corrupt are they, and have done abominable iniquity: there is none that doeth good. God looked down from heaven upon the children of men, to see if there were any that did understand, that did seek God. Every one of them is gone back: they are altogether become filthy; there is none that doeth good, no, not one. **Matt. 15:19.** For out of the heart proceed evil thoughts, murders, adulteries, fornications, thefts, false witness, blasphemies. **See Rom. 3:10–18, 23; Gal. 5:19–21.**

d. **Ps. 51:5.** Behold, I was shapen in iniquity; and in sin did my mother conceive me. **Job 14:4.** Who can bring a clean thing out of an unclean? not one. **John 3:6.** That which is born of the flesh is flesh; and that which is born of the Spirit is spirit.

God,[e] his displeasure and curse;[f] so as we are by nature children of wrath,[g] bond slaves to Satan,[h] and justly liable to all punishments in

e. **Gen. 3:8, 10, 24.** And they heard the voice of the LORD God walking in the garden in the cool of the day: and Adam and his wife hid themselves from the presence of the LORD God amongst the trees of the garden.… And he said, I heard thy voice in the garden, and I was afraid, because I was naked; and I hid myself.… So he drove out the man; and he placed at the east of the garden of Eden Cherubims, and a flaming sword which turned every way, to keep the way of the tree of life. **John 8:34, 42, 44.** Jesus answered them, Verily, verily, I say unto you, Whosoever committeth sin is the servant of sin.… Jesus said unto them, If God were your Father, ye would love me: for I proceeded forth and came from God; neither came I of myself, but he sent me.… Ye are of your father the devil, and the lusts of your father ye will do. He was a murderer from the beginning, and abode not in the truth, because there is no truth in him. When he speaketh a lie, he speaketh of his own: for he is a liar, and the father of it. **Eph. 2:12.** … that at that time ye were without Christ, being aliens from the commonwealth of Israel, and strangers from the covenants of promise, having no hope, and without God in the world.

f. **Gen. 3:16–19.** Unto the woman he said, I will greatly multiply thy sorrow and thy conception; in sorrow thou shalt bring forth children; and thy desire shall be to thy husband, and he shall rule over thee. And unto Adam he said, Because thou hast hearkened unto the voice of thy wife, and hast eaten of the tree, of which I commanded thee, saying, Thou shalt not eat of it: cursed is the ground for thy sake; in sorrow shalt thou eat of it all the days of thy life; thorns also and thistles shall it bring forth to thee; and thou shalt eat the herb of the field; in the sweat of thy face shalt thou eat bread, till thou return unto the ground; for out of it wast thou taken: for dust thou art, and unto dust shalt thou return. **Job 5:7.** Yet man is born unto trouble, as the sparks fly upward. **Eccl. 2:22–23.** For what hath man of all his labour, and of the vexation of his heart, wherein he hath laboured under the sun? For all his days are sorrows, and his travail grief; yea, his heart taketh not rest in the night. This is also vanity. **Rom. 8:18–23.** For I reckon that the sufferings of this present time are not worthy to be compared with the glory which shall be revealed in us. For the earnest expectation of the creature waiteth for the manifestation of the sons of God. For the creature was made subject to vanity, not willingly, but by reason of him who hath subjected the same in hope, because the creature itself also shall be delivered from the bondage of corruption into the glorious liberty of the children of God. For we know that the whole creation groaneth and travaileth in pain together until now. And not only they, but ourselves also, which have the firstfruits of the Spirit, even we ourselves groan within ourselves, waiting for the adoption, to wit, the redemption of our body.

g. **Eph. 2:2–3.** … wherein in time past ye walked according to the course of this world, according to the prince of the power of the air, the spirit that now worketh in the children of disobedience: among whom also we all had our conversation in times past in the lusts of our flesh, fulfilling the desires of the flesh and of the mind; and were by nature the children of wrath, even as others. **John 3:36.** He that believeth on the Son hath everlasting life: and he that believeth not the Son shall not see life; but the wrath of God abideth on him. **Rom. 1:18.** For the wrath of God is revealed from heaven against all ungodliness and unrighteousness of men, who hold the truth in

this world, and that which is to come.[i]

Q. 28. *What are the punishments of sin in this world?*

A. The punishments of sin in this world are either inward, as blindness of mind,[k] a reprobate sense,[l] strong delusions,[m] hardness of heart,[n] horror of conscience,[o] and vile affections;[p] or outward, as the curse of God upon the creatures for our sakes,[q] and all other evils that befall us in our bodies, names, estates, relations, and employments;[r] together with death itself.[s]

unrighteousness. **Eph. 5:6.** Let no man deceive you with vain words: for because of these things cometh the wrath of God upon the children of disobedience.

h. **2 Tim. 2:26.** And that they may recover themselves out of the snare of the devil, who are taken captive by him at his will.

i. **Gen. 2:17.** But of the tree of the knowledge of good and evil, thou shalt not eat of it: for in the day that thou eatest thereof thou shalt surely die. **Lam. 3:39.** Wherefore doth a living man complain, a man for the punishment of his sins? **Rom. 6:23.** For the wages of sin is death; but the gift of God is eternal life through Jesus Christ our Lord. **Matt. 25:41, 46.** Then shall he say also unto them on the left hand, Depart from me, ye cursed, into everlasting fire, prepared for the devil and his angels.... And these shall go away into everlasting punishment: but the righteous into life eternal. **Jude 7.** Even as Sodom and Gomorrha, and the cities about them in like manner, giving themselves over to fornication, and going after strange flesh, are set forth for an example, suffering the vengeance of eternal fire.

k. **Eph. 4:18.** ... having the understanding darkened, being alienated from the life of God through the ignorance that is in them, because of the blindness of their heart.

l. **Rom. 1:28.** And even as they did not like to retain God in their knowledge, God gave them over to a reprobate mind, to do those things which are not convenient.

m. **2 Thess. 2:11.** And for this cause God shall send them strong delusion, that they should believe a lie.

n. **Rom. 2:5.** But after thy hardness and impenitent heart treasurest up unto thyself wrath against the day of wrath and revelation of the righteous judgment of God.

o. **Isa. 33:14.** The sinners in Zion are afraid; fearfulness hath surprised the hypocrites. Who among us shall dwell with the devouring fire? who among us shall dwell with everlasting burnings? **Gen. 4:13.** And Cain said unto the LORD, My punishment is greater than I can bear. **Matt. 27:4.** ... saying, I have sinned in that I have betrayed the innocent blood. And they said, What is that to us? see thou to that.

p. **Rom. 1:26.** For this cause God gave them up unto vile affections: for even their women did change the natural use into that which is against nature.

q. **Gen. 3:17.** And unto Adam he said, Because thou hast hearkened unto the voice of thy wife, and hast eaten of the tree, of which I commanded thee, saying, Thou shalt not eat of it: cursed is the ground for thy sake; in sorrow shalt thou eat of it all the days of thy life.

r. **Deut. 28:15.** But it shall come to pass, if thou wilt not hearken unto the voice of the LORD thy God, to observe to do all his commandments and his statutes which I

Q. 29. *What are the punishments of sin in the world to come?*

A. The punishments of sin in the world to come, are everlasting separation from the comfortable presence of God, and most grievous torments in soul and body, without intermission, in hellfire forever.[t]

Q. 30. *Doth God leave all mankind to perish in the estate of sin and misery?*

A. God doth not leave all men to perish in the estate of sin and misery,[u] into which they fell by the breach of the first covenant, commonly called the covenant of works;[w] but of his mere love and mercy delivereth his elect out of it, and bringeth them into an estate of salvation by the second covenant, commonly called the covenant of grace.[x]

command thee this day; that all these curses shall come upon thee, and overtake thee **(see verses 16–68).**

s. **Rom. 6:21, 23.** What fruit had ye then in those things whereof ye are now ashamed? for the end of those things is death.… For the wages of sin is death; but the gift of God is eternal life through Jesus Christ our Lord.

t. **2 Thess. 1:9.** … who shall be punished with everlasting destruction from the presence of the Lord, and from the glory of his power. **Mark 9:43–44, 46, 48.** And if thy hand offend thee, cut it off: it is better for thee to enter into life maimed, than having two hands to go into hell, into the fire that never shall be quenched: where their worm dieth not, and the fire is not quenched.… **Luke 16:24, 26.** And he cried and said, Father Abraham, have mercy on me, and send Lazarus, that he may dip the tip of his finger in water, and cool my tongue; for I am tormented in this flame.… And beside all this, between us and you there is a great gulf fixed: so that they which would pass from hence to you cannot; neither can they pass to us, that would come from thence. **See Matt. 25:41, 46; Rev. 14:11; John 3:36.**

u. **1 Thess. 5:9.** For God hath not appointed us to wrath, but to obtain salvation by our Lord Jesus Christ.

w. **Gen. 3:17.** And unto Adam he said, Because thou hast hearkened unto the voice of thy wife, and hast eaten of the tree, of which I commanded thee, saying, Thou shalt not eat of it: cursed is the ground for thy sake; in sorrow shalt thou eat of it all the days of thy life. **Rom. 5:12, 15.** Wherefore, as by one man sin entered into the world, and death by sin; and so death passed upon all men, for that all have sinned … But not as the offence, so also is the free gift. For if through the offence of one many be dead, much more the grace of God, and the gift by grace, which is by one man, Jesus Christ, hath abounded unto many. **Gal. 3:10, 12.** For as many as are of the works of the law are under the curse: for it is written, Cursed is every one that continueth not in all things which are written in the book of the law to do them.… And the law is not of faith: but, The man that doeth them shall live in them.

x. **Titus 3:4–7.** But after that the kindness and love of God our Saviour toward man appeared, not by works of righteousness which we have done, but according to his mercy he saved us, by the washing of regeneration, and renewing of the Holy Ghost; which he shed on us abundantly through Jesus Christ our Saviour; that being

Q. 31. *With whom was the covenant of grace made?*

A. The covenant of grace was made with Christ as the second Adam, and in him with all the elect as his seed.[y]

Q. 32. *How is the grace of God manifested in the second covenant?*

A. The grace of God is manifested in the second covenant, in that he freely provideth and offereth to sinners a Mediator,[z] and life and salvation by him;[a] and requiring faith as the condition to interest

justified by his grace, we should be made heirs according to the hope of eternal life. **Gal. 3:21.** Is the law then against the promises of God? God forbid: for if there had been a law given which could have given life, verily righteousness should have been by the law. **Rom. 3:20–22.** Therefore by the deeds of the law there shall no flesh be justified in his sight: for by the law is the knowledge of sin. But now the righteousness of God without the law is manifested, being witnessed by the law and the prophets; even the righteousness of God which is by faith of Jesus Christ unto all and upon all them that believe: for there is no difference. **2 Thess. 2:13–14.** But we are bound to give thanks alway to God for you, brethren beloved of the Lord, because God hath from the beginning chosen you to salvation through sanctification of the Spirit and belief of the truth: whereunto he called you by our gospel, to the obtaining of the glory of our Lord Jesus Christ. **See Acts 13:48; Eph. 1:4–5.**

y. **Gal. 3:16.** Now to Abraham and his seed were the promises made. He saith not, And to seeds, as of many; but as of one, And to thy seed, which is Christ. **Rom. 5:15.** But not as the offence, so also is the free gift. For if through the offence of one many be dead, much more the grace of God, and the gift by grace, which is by one man, Jesus Christ, hath abounded unto many. **See verses 16–21. Isa. 53:10–11.** Yet it pleased the Lord to bruise him; he hath put him to grief: when thou shalt make his soul an offering for sin, he shall see his seed, he shall prolong his days, and the pleasure of the Lord shall prosper in his hand. He shall see of the travail of his soul, and shall be satisfied: by his knowledge shall my righteous servant justify many; for he shall bear their iniquities. **Isa. 59:20–21.** And the Redeemer shall come to Zion, and unto them that turn from transgression in Jacob, saith the Lord. As for me, this is my covenant with them, saith the Lord; My spirit that is upon thee, and my words which I have put in thy mouth, shall not depart out of thy mouth, nor out of the mouth of thy seed, nor out of the mouth of thy seed's seed, saith the Lord, from henceforth and for ever.

z. **Gen. 3:15.** And I will put enmity between thee and the woman, and between thy seed and her seed; it shall bruise thy head, and thou shalt bruise his heel. **Isa. 42:6.** I the Lord have called thee in righteousness, and will hold thine hand, and will keep thee, and give thee for a covenant of the people, for a light of the Gentiles. **John 3:16.** For God so loved the world, that he gave his only begotten Son, that whosoever believeth in him should not perish, but have everlasting life. **John 6:27.** Labour not for the meat which perisheth, but for that meat which endureth unto everlasting life, which the Son of man shall give unto you: for him hath God the Father sealed. **1 Tim. 2:5.** For there is one God, and one mediator between God and men, the man Christ Jesus.

a. **1 John 5:11–12.** And this is the record, that God hath given to us eternal life,

them in him,[b] promiseth and giveth his Holy Spirit[c] to all his elect, to work in them that faith,[d] with all other saving graces;[e] and to enable them unto all holy obedience,[f] as the evidence of the truth of their

and this life is in his Son. He that hath the Son hath life; and he that hath not the Son of God hath not life.

b. **John 3:16, 36.** For God so loved the world, that he gave his only begotten Son, that whosoever believeth in him should not perish, but have everlasting life.... He that believeth on the Son hath everlasting life: and he that believeth not the Son shall not see life; but the wrath of God abideth on him. **John 1:12.** But as many as received him, to them gave he power to become the sons of God, even to them that believe on his name.

c. **Isa. 59:21.** As for me, this is my covenant with them, saith the LORD; My spirit that is upon thee, and my words which I have put in thy mouth, shall not depart out of thy mouth, nor out of the mouth of thy seed, nor out of the mouth of thy seed's seed, saith the LORD, from henceforth and for ever. **Luke 11:13.** If ye then, being evil, know how to give good gifts unto your children: how much more shall your heavenly Father give the Holy Spirit to them that ask him? **John 14:16–20.** And I will pray the Father, and he shall give you another Comforter, that he may abide with you for ever; even the Spirit of truth; whom the world cannot receive, because it seeth him not, neither knoweth him: but ye know him; for he dwelleth with you, and shall be in you. I will not leave you comfortless: I will come to you. Yet a little while, and the world seeth me no more; but ye see me: because I live, ye shall live also. At that day ye shall know that I am in my Father, and ye in me, and I in you. **1 Cor. 12:13.** For by one Spirit are we all baptized into one body, whether we be Jews or Gentiles, whether we be bond or free; and have been all made to drink into one Spirit. **Rom. 8:9.** But ye are not in the flesh, but in the Spirit, if so be that the Spirit of God dwell in you. Now if any man have not the Spirit of Christ, he is none of his (**see verses 4, 11, 14–16**).

d. **2 Cor. 4:13.** We having the same spirit of faith, according as it is written, I believed, and therefore have I spoken; we also believe, and therefore speak. **1 Cor. 12:3, 9.** Wherefore I give you to understand, that no man speaking by the Spirit of God calleth Jesus accursed: and that no man can say that Jesus is the Lord, but by the Holy Ghost.... to another faith [is given] by the same Spirit; to another the gifts of healing by the same Spirit. **Eph. 2:8–10.** For by grace are ye saved through faith; and that not of yourselves: it is the gift of God: not of works, lest any man should boast. For we are his workmanship, created in Christ Jesus unto good works, which God hath before ordained that we should walk in them. **Acts 16:14.** And a certain woman named Lydia, a seller of purple, of the city of Thyatira, which worshipped God, heard us: whose heart the Lord opened, that she attended unto the things which were spoken of Paul. **2 Pet. 1:1.** Simon Peter, a servant and an apostle of Jesus Christ, to them that have obtained like precious faith with us through the righteousness of God and our Saviour Jesus Christ.

e. **Gal. 5:22–23.** But the fruit of the Spirit is love, joy, peace, longsuffering, gentleness, goodness, faith, meekness, temperance: against such there is no law.

f. **Ezek. 36:27.** And I will put my spirit within you, and cause you to walk in my statutes, and ye shall keep my judgments, and do them. **Eph. 2:10.** For we are his workmanship, created in Christ Jesus unto good works, which God hath before

faith[g] and thankfulness to God,[h] and as the way which he hath appointed them to salvation.[i]

Q. 33. *Was the covenant of grace always administered after one and the same manner?*

A. The covenant of grace was not always administered after the same manner, but the administrations of it under the old testament were different from those under the new.[k]

Q. 34. *How was the covenant of grace administered under the old testament?*

A. The covenant of grace was administered under the old testament, by promises,[l] prophecies,[m] sacrifices,[n] circumcision,[o] the

ordained that we should walk in them.

g. **James 2:18, 22.** Yea, a man may say, Thou hast faith, and I have works: shew me thy faith without thy works, and I will shew thee my faith by my works.... Seest thou how faith wrought with his works, and by works was faith made perfect?

h. **2 Cor. 5:14–15.** For the love of Christ constraineth us; because we thus judge, that if one died for all, then were all dead: and that he died for all, that they which live should not henceforth live unto themselves, but unto him which died for them, and rose again.

i. **Eph. 2:10.** For we are his workmanship, created in Christ Jesus unto good works, which God hath before ordained that we should walk in them. **Titus 2:14.** ... who gave himself for us, that he might redeem us from all iniquity, and purify unto himself a peculiar people, zealous of good works.

k. **2 Cor. 3:6–9.** ... [God] hath made us able ministers of the new testament; not of the letter, but of the spirit: for the letter killeth, but the spirit giveth life. But if the ministration of death, written and engraven in stones, was glorious, so that the children of Israel could not stedfastly behold the face of Moses for the glory of his countenance; which glory was to be done away: how shall not the ministration of the spirit be rather glorious? For if the ministration of condemnation be glory, much more doth the ministration of righteousness exceed in glory. **See Heb. 8:7–13.**

l. **Rom. 15:8.** Now I say that Jesus Christ was a minister of the circumcision for the truth of God, to confirm the promises made unto the fathers. **See for example Gen. 3:15; 12:1–3; 15:5.**

m. **Acts 3:20, 24.** And he shall send Jesus Christ, which before was preached unto you.... Yea, and all the prophets from Samuel and those that follow after, as many as have spoken, have likewise foretold of these days. **See for example Isa. 52:13–53:12.**

n. **Heb. 10:1.** For the law having a shadow of good things to come, and not the very image of the things, can never with those sacrifices which they offered year by year continually make the comers thereunto perfect. **See Lev. 1–7.**

o. **Rom. 4:11.** And he received the sign of circumcision, a seal of the righteousness of the faith which he had yet being uncircumcised: that he might be the father of all them that believe, though they be not circumcised; that righteousness might be

Passover,[p] and other types and ordinances, which did all foresignify Christ then to come, and were for that time sufficient to build up the elect in faith in the promised Messiah,[q] by whom they then had full remission of sin, and eternal salvation.[r]

Q. 35. *How is the covenant of grace administered under the new testament?*

A. Under the new testament, when Christ the substance was exhibited, the same covenant of grace was and still is to be administered in the preaching of the Word,[s] and the administration of the sacraments of baptism[t] and the Lord's Supper;[u] in which grace and

imputed unto them also. **See Gen. 17:1–14.**

p. **1 Cor. 5:7.** Purge out therefore the old leaven, that ye may be a new lump, as ye are unleavened. For even Christ our passover is sacrificed for us. **Ex. 12:14, 17, 24.** And this day shall be unto you for a memorial; and ye shall keep it a feast to the Lord throughout your generations; ye shall keep it a feast by an ordinance for ever.… And ye shall observe the feast of unleavened bread; for in this selfsame day have I brought your armies out of the land of Egypt: therefore shall ye observe this day in your generations by an ordinance for ever.… And ye shall observe this thing for an ordinance to thee and to thy sons for ever **(see entire chapter).**

q. **Heb. 8:1–2.** Now of the things which we have spoken this is the sum: We have such an high priest, who is set on the right hand of the throne of the Majesty in the heavens; a minister of the sanctuary, and of the true tabernacle, which the Lord pitched, and not man. **See chapters 8–10. Heb. 11:13.** These all died in faith, not having received the promises, but having seen them afar off, and were persuaded of them, and embraced them, and confessed that they were strangers and pilgrims on the earth.

r. **Gal. 3:7–9, 14.** Know ye therefore that they which are of faith, the same are the children of Abraham. And the scripture, foreseeing that God would justify the heathen through faith, preached before the gospel unto Abraham, saying, In thee shall all nations be blessed. So then they which be of faith are blessed with faithful Abraham.… that the blessing of Abraham might come on the Gentiles through Jesus Christ; that we might receive the promise of the Spirit through faith.

s. **Luke 24:47–48.** … and that repentance and remission of sins should be preached in his name among all nations, beginning at Jerusalem. And ye are witnesses of these things. **See Matt. 28:19–20.**

t. **Matt. 28:19–20.** Go ye therefore, and teach all nations, baptizing them in the name of the Father, and of the Son, and of the Holy Ghost: teaching them to observe all things whatsoever I have commanded you: and, lo, I am with you alway, even unto the end of the world. Amen.

u. **Matt. 26:28.** For this is my blood of the new testament, which is shed for many for the remission of sins. **1 Cor. 11:23–25.** For I have received of the Lord that which also I delivered unto you, That the Lord Jesus the same night in which he was betrayed took bread: and when he had given thanks, he brake it, and said, Take, eat: this is my body, which is broken for you: this do in remembrance of me. After the same manner also he took the cup, when he had supped, saying, This cup is the new testament in my blood: this do ye, as oft as ye drink it, in remembrance of me.

salvation are held forth in more fullness, evidence, and efficacy, to all nations.ʷ

Q. 36. *Who is the Mediator of the covenant of grace?*

A. The only Mediator of the covenant of grace is the Lord Jesus Christ,ˣ who, being the eternal Son of God, of one substance and equal with the Father,ʸ in the fullness of time became man,ᶻ and so was and continues to be God and man, in two entire distinct natures,

w. **Rom. 1:16.** For I am not ashamed of the gospel of Christ: for it is the power of God unto salvation to every one that believeth; to the Jew first, and also to the Greek. **2 Cor. 3:6–9.** … [God] hath made us able ministers of the new testament; not of the letter, but of the spirit: for the letter killeth, but the spirit giveth life. But if the ministration of death, written and engraven in stones, was glorious, so that the children of Israel could not stedfastly behold the face of Moses for the glory of his countenance; which glory was to be done away: how shall not the ministration of the spirit be rather glorious? For if the ministration of condemnation be glory, much more doth the ministration of righteousness exceed in glory. **Heb. 8:6, 10–11.** But now hath he obtained a more excellent ministry, by how much also he is the mediator of a better covenant, which was established upon better promises.… For this is the covenant that I will make with the house of Israel after those days, saith the Lord; I will put my laws into their mind, and write them in their hearts: and I will be to them a God, and they shall be to me a people: and they shall not teach every man his neighbour, and every man his brother, saying, Know the Lord: for all shall know me, from the least to the greatest. **Matt. 28:19.** Go ye therefore, and teach all nations, baptizing them in the name of the Father, and of the Son, and of the Holy Ghost. **See Eph. 3:1–12.**

x. **1 Tim. 2:5.** For there is one God, and one mediator between God and men, the man Christ Jesus. **John 14:6.** Jesus saith unto him, I am the way, the truth, and the life: no man cometh unto the Father, but by me. **Acts 4:12.** Neither is there salvation in any other: for there is none other name under heaven given among men, whereby we must be saved.

y. **John 1:1, 14, 18.** In the beginning was the Word, and the Word was with God, and the Word was God.… And the Word was made flesh, and dwelt among us, (and we beheld his glory, the glory as of the only begotten of the Father,) full of grace and truth.… No man hath seen God at any time; the only begotten Son, which is in the bosom of the Father, he hath declared him. **John 10:30.** I and my Father are one. **Phil. 2:6.** … who, being in the form of God, thought it not robbery to be equal with God. **Ps. 2:7.** I will declare the decree: the Lᴏʀᴅ hath said unto me, Thou art my Son; this day have I begotten thee. **Matt. 3:17.** And lo a voice from heaven, saying, This is my beloved Son, in whom I am well pleased. **Matt. 17:5.** While he yet spake, behold, a bright cloud overshadowed them: and behold a voice out of the cloud, which said, This is my beloved Son, in whom I am well pleased; hear ye him.

z. **Gal. 4:4.** But when the fulness of the time was come, God sent forth his Son, made of a woman, made under the law. **Matt. 1:23.** Behold, a virgin shall be with child, and shall bring forth a son, and they shall call his name Emmanuel, which being interpreted is, God with us. **See John 1:14.**

and one person, forever.[a]

Q. 37. *How did Christ, being the Son of God, become man?*

A. Christ the Son of God became man, by taking to himself a true body, and a reasonable soul,[b] being conceived by the power of the Holy Ghost in the womb of the virgin Mary, of her substance, and born of her,[c] yet without sin.[d]

a. **Luke 1:35.** And the angel answered and said unto her, The Holy Ghost shall come upon thee, and the power of the Highest shall overshadow thee: therefore also that holy thing which shall be born of thee shall be called the Son of God. **Acts 1:11.** … which also said, Ye men of Galilee, why stand ye gazing up into heaven? this same Jesus, which is taken up from you into heaven, shall so come in like manner as ye have seen him go into heaven. **Rom. 9:5.** … whose are the fathers, and of whom as concerning the flesh Christ came, who is over all, God blessed for ever. Amen. **Col. 2:9.** For in him dwelleth all the fulness of the Godhead bodily. **Heb. 7:24–25.** But this man, because he continueth ever, hath an unchangeable priesthood. Wherefore he is able also to save them to the uttermost that come unto God by him, seeing he ever liveth to make intercession for them. **Heb. 13:8.** Jesus Christ the same yesterday, and to day, and for ever. **See Phil. 2:5–11.**

b. **John 1:14.** And the Word was made flesh, and dwelt among us, (and we beheld his glory, the glory as of the only begotten of the Father,) full of grace and truth. **Matt. 26:38.** Then saith he unto them, My soul is exceeding sorrowful, even unto death: tarry ye here, and watch with me. **Phil. 2:7.** … but made himself of no reputation, and took upon him the form of a servant, and was made in the likeness of men. **Heb. 2:14–17.** Forasmuch then as the children are partakers of flesh and blood, he also himself likewise took part of the same; that through death he might destroy him that had the power of death, that is, the devil; and deliver them who through fear of death were all their lifetime subject to bondage. For verily he took not on him the nature of angels; but he took on him the seed of Abraham. Wherefore in all things it behoved him to be made like unto his brethren, that he might be a merciful and faithful high priest in things pertaining to God, to make reconciliation for the sins of the people. **See Luke 2:40, 52; John 11:33.**

c. **Luke 1:27, 31, 35.** … to a virgin espoused to a man whose name was Joseph, of the house of David; and the virgin's name was Mary.… And, behold, thou shalt conceive in thy womb, and bring forth a son, and shalt call his name JESUS.… And the angel answered and said unto her, The Holy Ghost shall come upon thee, and the power of the Highest shall overshadow thee: therefore also that holy thing which shall be born of thee shall be called the Son of God. **Gal. 4:4.** But when the fulness of the time was come, God sent forth his Son, made of a woman, made under the law.

d. **Heb. 4:15.** For we have not an high priest which cannot be touched with the feeling of our infirmities; but was in all points tempted like as we are, yet without sin. **Heb. 7:26.** For such an high priest became us, who is holy, harmless, undefiled, separate from sinners, and made higher than the heavens. **2 Cor. 5:21.** For he hath made him to be sin for us, who knew no sin; that we might be made the righteousness of God in him. **1 John 3:5.** And ye know that he was manifested to take away our sins; and in him is no sin.

Q. 38. Why was it requisite that the Mediator should be God?

A. It was requisite that the Mediator should be God, that he might sustain and keep the human nature from sinking under the infinite wrath of God, and the power of death;ᵉ give worth and efficacy to his sufferings, obedience, and intercession;ᶠ and to satisfy God's justice,ᵍ procure his favor,ʰ purchase a peculiar people,ⁱ give his Spirit to them,ᵏ conquer all their enemies,ˡ and bring them to

e. **Acts 2:24–25.** … whom God hath raised up, having loosed the pains of death: because it was not possible that he should be holden of it. For David speaketh concerning him, I foresaw the Lord always before my face, for he is on my right hand, that I should not be moved. **Rom. 1:4.** … and declared to be the Son of God with power, according to the spirit of holiness, by the resurrection from the dead. **Rom. 4:25.** … who was delivered for our offences, and was raised again for our justification. **Heb. 9:14.** How much more shall the blood of Christ, who through the eternal Spirit offered himself without spot to God, purge your conscience from dead works to serve the living God?

f. **Acts 20:28.** Take heed therefore unto yourselves, and to all the flock, over the which the Holy Ghost hath made you overseers, to feed the church of God, which he hath purchased with his own blood. **Heb. 9:14.** How much more shall the blood of Christ, who through the eternal Spirit offered himself without spot to God, purge your conscience from dead works to serve the living God? **Heb. 7:25–28.** Wherefore he is able also to save them to the uttermost that come unto God by him, seeing he ever liveth to make intercession for them. For such an high priest became us, who is holy, harmless, undefiled, separate from sinners, and made higher than the heavens; who needeth not daily, as those high priests, to offer up sacrifice, first for his own sins, and then for the people's: for this he did once, when he offered up himself. For the law maketh men high priests which have infirmity; but the word of the oath, which was since the law, maketh the Son, who is consecrated for evermore. **See John 17.**

g. **Rom. 3:24–26.** … being justified freely by his grace through the redemption that is in Christ Jesus: whom God hath set forth to be a propitiation through faith in his blood, to declare his righteousness for the remission of sins that are past, through the forbearance of God; to declare, I say, at this time his righteousness: that he might be just, and the justifier of him which believeth in Jesus.

h. **Eph. 1:6.** … to the praise of the glory of his grace, wherein he hath made us accepted in the beloved. **Matt. 3:17.** And lo a voice from heaven, saying, This is my beloved Son, in whom I am well pleased.

i. **Titus 2:13–14.** … looking for that blessed hope, and the glorious appearing of the great God and our Saviour Jesus Christ; who gave himself for us, that he might redeem us from all iniquity, and purify unto himself a peculiar people, zealous of good works.

k. **Gal. 4:6.** And because ye are sons, God hath sent forth the Spirit of his Son into your hearts, crying, Abba, Father. **John 15:26.** But when the Comforter is come, whom I will send unto you from the Father, even the Spirit of truth, which proceedeth from the Father, he shall testify of me. **See John 16:7; 14:26.**

l. **Luke 1:68–69, 71, 74.** Blessed be the Lord God of Israel; for he hath visited

everlasting salvation.^m

Q. 39. *Why was it requisite that the Mediator should be man?*

A. It was requisite that the Mediator should be man, that he might advance our nature,ⁿ perform obedience to the law,^o suffer and make intercession for us in our nature,^p have a fellow feeling of our infirmities;^q that we might receive the adoption of sons,^r and have comfort and access with boldness unto the throne of grace.^s

and redeemed his people, and hath raised up an horn of salvation for us in the house of his servant David;… that we should be saved from our enemies, and from the hand of all that hate us;… that he would grant unto us, that we being delivered out of the hand of our enemies might serve him without fear.

m. **Heb. 5:8–9.** Though he were a Son, yet learned he obedience by the things which he suffered; and being made perfect, he became the author of eternal salvation unto all them that obey him. **Heb. 9:11–15.** But Christ being come an high priest of good things to come, by a greater and more perfect tabernacle, not made with hands, that is to say, not of this building; neither by the blood of goats and calves, but by his own blood he entered in once into the holy place, having obtained eternal redemption for us. For if the blood of bulls and of goats, and the ashes of an heifer sprinkling the unclean, sanctifieth to the purifying of the flesh: how much more shall the blood of Christ, who through the eternal Spirit offered himself without spot to God, purge your conscience from dead works to serve the living God? And for this cause he is the mediator of the new testament, that by means of death, for the redemption of the transgressions that were under the first testament, they which are called might receive the promise of eternal inheritance.

n. **Heb. 2:16.** For verily he took not on him the nature of angels; but he took on him the seed of Abraham. **2 Pet. 1:4.** … whereby are given unto us exceeding great and precious promises: that by these ye might be partakers of the divine nature, having escaped the corruption that is in the world through lust.

o. **Gal. 4:4.** But when the fulness of the time was come, God sent forth his Son, made of a woman, made under the law. **Matt. 5:17.** Think not that I am come to destroy the law, or the prophets: I am not come to destroy, but to fulfil. **Rom. 5:19.** For as by one man's disobedience many were made sinners, so by the obedience of one shall many be made righteous. **Phil. 2:8.** And being found in fashion as a man, he humbled himself, and became obedient unto death, even the death of the cross.

p. **Heb. 2:14.** Forasmuch then as the children are partakers of flesh and blood, he also himself likewise took part of the same; that through death he might destroy him that had the power of death, that is, the devil. **Heb. 7:24–25.** But this man, because he continueth ever, hath an unchangeable priesthood. Wherefore he is able also to save them to the uttermost that come unto God by him, seeing he ever liveth to make intercession for them.

q. **Heb. 4:15.** For we have not an high priest which cannot be touched with the feeling of our infirmities; but was in all points tempted like as we are, yet without sin.

r. **Gal. 4:5.** … to redeem them that were under the law, that we might receive the adoption of sons.

s. **Heb. 4:16.** Let us therefore come boldly unto the throne of grace, that we may

Q. 40. *Why was it requisite that the Mediator should be God and man in one person?*

A. It was requisite that the Mediator, who was to reconcile God and man, should himself be both God and man, and this in one person, that the proper works of each nature might be accepted of God for us,[t] and relied on by us, as the works of the whole person.[u]

Q. 41. *Why was our Mediator called Jesus?*

A. Our Mediator was called Jesus, because he saveth his people from their sins.[w]

Q. 42. *Why was our Mediator called Christ?*

A. Our Mediator was called Christ, because he was anointed with the Holy Ghost above measure;[x] and so set apart, and fully furnished with all authority and ability,[y] to execute the offices of prophet,[z] priest,[a]

obtain mercy, and find grace to help in time of need.

t. **Matt. 1:21, 23.** And she shall bring forth a son, and thou shalt call his name JESUS: for he shall save his people from their sins.… Behold, a virgin shall be with child, and shall bring forth a son, and they shall call his name Emmanuel, which being interpreted is, God with us. **Matt. 3:17.** And lo a voice from heaven, saying, This is my beloved Son, in whom I am well pleased. **Heb. 9:14.** How much more shall the blood of Christ, who through the eternal Spirit offered himself without spot to God, purge your conscience from dead works to serve the living God?

u. **1 Pet. 2:6.** Wherefore also it is contained in the scripture, Behold, I lay in Sion a chief corner stone, elect, precious: and he that believeth on him shall not be confounded.

w. **Matt. 1:21.** And she shall bring forth a son, and thou shalt call his name JESUS: for he shall save his people from their sins.

x. **Matt. 3:16.** And Jesus, when he was baptized, went up straightway out of the water: and, lo, the heavens were opened unto him, and he saw the Spirit of God descending like a dove, and lighting upon him. **Compared with Acts 10:37–38.** That word, I say, ye know, which was published throughout all Judaea, and began from Galilee, after the baptism which John preached; how God anointed Jesus of Nazareth with the Holy Ghost and with power: who went about doing good, and healing all that were oppressed of the devil; for God was with him. **John 3:34.** For he whom God hath sent speaketh the words of God: for God giveth not the Spirit by measure unto him. **Ps. 45:7.** Thou lovest righteousness, and hatest wickedness: therefore God, thy God, hath anointed thee with the oil of gladness above thy fellows.

y. **John 6:27.** Labour not for the meat which perisheth, but for that meat which endureth unto everlasting life, which the Son of man shall give unto you: for him hath God the Father sealed. **Matt. 28:18–20.** And Jesus came and spake unto them, saying, All power is given unto me in heaven and in earth. Go ye therefore, and teach all nations, baptizing them in the name of the Father, and of the Son, and of the Holy Ghost: teaching them to observe all things whatsoever I have commanded you: and, lo, I am with you alway, even unto the end of the world. Amen. **Rom. 1:3–4.**

and king of his church,[b] in the estate both of his humiliation and exaltation.

Q. 43. *How doth Christ execute the office of a prophet?*

A. Christ executeth the office of a prophet, in his revealing to the

… concerning his Son Jesus Christ our Lord, which was made of the seed of David according to the flesh; and declared to be the Son of God with power, according to the spirit of holiness, by the resurrection from the dead.

z. **Acts 3:21–22.** … whom the heaven must receive until the times of restitution of all things, which God hath spoken by the mouth of all his holy prophets since the world began. For Moses truly said unto the fathers, A prophet shall the Lord your God raise up unto you of your brethren, like unto me; him shall ye hear in all things whatsoever he shall say unto you. **Luke 4:18, 21.** The Spirit of the Lord is upon me, because he hath anointed me to preach the gospel to the poor; he hath sent me to heal the brokenhearted, to preach deliverance to the captives, and recovering of sight to the blind, to set at liberty them that are bruised.… And he began to say unto them, This day is this scripture fulfilled in your ears. **Heb. 1:1–2.** God, who at sundry times and in divers manners spake in time past unto the fathers by the prophets, hath in these last days spoken unto us by his Son, whom he hath appointed heir of all things, by whom also he made the worlds. **Deut. 18:18.** I will raise them up a Prophet from among their brethren, like unto thee, and will put my words in his mouth; and he shall speak unto them all that I shall command him.

a. **Heb. 5:5–7.** So also Christ glorified not himself to be made an high priest; but he that said unto him, Thou art my Son, to day have I begotten thee. As he saith also in another place, Thou art a priest for ever after the order of Melchisedec. Who in the days of his flesh, when he had offered up prayers and supplications with strong crying and tears unto him that was able to save him from death, and was heard in that he feared. **Heb. 4:14–15.** Seeing then that we have a great high priest, that is passed into the heavens, Jesus the Son of God, let us hold fast our profession. For we have not an high priest which cannot be touched with the feeling of our infirmities; but was in all points tempted like as we are, yet without sin.

b. **Ps. 2:6.** Yet have I set my king upon my holy hill of Zion. **Luke 1:32–34.** He shall be great, and shall be called the Son of the Highest: and the Lord God shall give unto him the throne of his father David: and he shall reign over the house of Jacob for ever; and of his kingdom there shall be no end. Then said Mary unto the angel, How shall this be, seeing I know not a man? **John 18:37.** Pilate therefore said unto him, Art thou a king then? Jesus answered, Thou sayest that I am a king. To this end was I born, and for this cause came I into the world, that I should bear witness unto the truth. Every one that is of the truth heareth my voice. **Matt. 21:5.** Tell ye the daughter of Sion, Behold, thy King cometh unto thee, meek, and sitting upon an ass, and a colt the foal of an ass. **Isa. 9:6–7.** For unto us a child is born, unto us a son is given: and the government shall be upon his shoulder: and his name shall be called Wonderful, Counsellor, The mighty God, The everlasting Father, The Prince of Peace. Of the increase of his government and peace there shall be no end, upon the throne of David, and upon his kingdom, to order it, and to establish it with judgment and with justice from henceforth even for ever. The zeal of the LORD of hosts will perform this. **Phil. 2:8–11.** And being found in fashion as a man, he humbled himself, and became obe-

church,^{c} in all ages, by his Spirit and Word,^{d} in divers ways of administration,^{e} the whole will of God,^{f} in all things concerning their edification and salvation.^{g}

Q. 44. *How doth Christ execute the office of a priest?*

A. Christ executeth the office of a priest, in his once offering himself a sacrifice without spot to God,^{h} to be a reconciliation for the sins of his people;^{i} and in making continual intercession for them.^{k}

dient unto death, even the death of the cross. Wherefore God also hath highly exalted him, and given him a name which is above every name: that at the name of Jesus every knee should bow, of things in heaven, and things in earth, and things under the earth; and that every tongue should confess that Jesus Christ is Lord, to the glory of God the Father.

c. **John 1:18.** No man hath seen God at any time; the only begotten Son, which is in the bosom of the Father, he hath declared him.

d. **1 Pet. 1:10–12.** Of which salvation the prophets have inquired and searched diligently, who prophesied of the grace that should come unto you: searching what, or what manner of time the Spirit of Christ which was in them did signify, when it testified beforehand the sufferings of Christ, and the glory that should follow. Unto whom it was revealed, that not unto themselves, but unto us they did minister the things, which are now reported unto you by them that have preached the gospel unto you with the Holy Ghost sent down from heaven; which things the angels desire to look into.

e. **Heb. 1:1–2.** God, who at sundry times and in divers manners spake in time past unto the fathers by the prophets, hath in these last days spoken unto us by his Son, whom he hath appointed heir of all things, by whom also he made the worlds.

f. **John 15:15.** Henceforth I call you not servants; for the servant knoweth not what his lord doeth: but I have called you friends; for all things that I have heard of my Father I have made known unto you.

g. **Acts 20:32.** And now, brethren, I commend you to God, and to the word of his grace, which is able to build you up, and to give you an inheritance among all them which are sanctified. **Eph. 4:11–13.** And he gave some, apostles; and some, prophets; and some, evangelists; and some, pastors and teachers; for the perfecting of the saints, for the work of the ministry, for the edifying of the body of Christ: till we all come in the unity of the faith, and of the knowledge of the Son of God, unto a perfect man, unto the measure of the stature of the fulness of Christ. **John 20:31.** But these are written, that ye might believe that Jesus is the Christ, the Son of God; and that believing ye might have life through his name.

h. **Heb. 9:14, 28.** How much more shall the blood of Christ, who through the eternal Spirit offered himself without spot to God, purge your conscience from dead works to serve the living God?... So Christ was once offered to bear the sins of many; and unto them that look for him shall he appear the second time without sin unto salvation. **Heb. 10:12.** But this man, after he had offered one sacrifice for sins for ever, sat down on the right hand of God. **See Isa. 53.**

i. **Heb. 2:17.** Wherefore in all things it behoved him to be made like unto his brethren, that he might be a merciful and faithful high priest in things pertaining to

Q. 45. *How doth Christ execute the office of a king?*

A. Christ executeth the office of a king, in calling out of the world a people to himself,[l] and giving them officers,[m] laws,[n] and censures, by which he visibly governs them;[o] in bestowing saving grace upon his elect,[p] rewarding their obedience,[q] and correcting them for their

God, to make reconciliation for the sins of the people. **2 Cor. 5:18.** And all things are of God, who hath reconciled us to himself by Jesus Christ, and hath given to us the ministry of reconciliation. **Col. 1:21–22.** And you, that were sometime alienated and enemies in your mind by wicked works, yet now hath he reconciled in the body of his flesh through death, to present you holy and unblameable and unreproveable in his sight.

k. **Heb. 7:25.** Wherefore he is able also to save them to the uttermost that come unto God by him, seeing he ever liveth to make intercession for them. **Heb. 9:24.** For Christ is not entered into the holy places made with hands, which are the figures of the true; but into heaven itself, now to appear in the presence of God for us.

l. **Acts 15:14–16.** Simeon hath declared how God at the first did visit the Gentiles, to take out of them a people for his name. And to this agree the words of the prophets; as it is written, After this I will return, and will build again the tabernacle of David, which is fallen down; and I will build again the ruins thereof, and I will set it up. **Gen. 49:10.** The sceptre shall not depart from Judah, nor a lawgiver from between his feet, until Shiloh come; and unto him shall the gathering of the people be. **Ps. 110:3.** Thy people shall be willing in the day of thy power, in the beauties of holiness from the womb of the morning: thou hast the dew of thy youth. **John 17:2.** … as thou hast given him power over all flesh, that he should give eternal life to as many as thou hast given him.

m. **Eph. 4:11–12.** And he gave some, apostles; and some, prophets; and some, evangelists; and some, pastors and teachers; for the perfecting of the saints, for the work of the ministry, for the edifying of the body of Christ. **1 Cor. 12:28.** And God hath set some in the church, first apostles, secondarily prophets, thirdly teachers, after that miracles, then gifts of healings, helps, governments, diversities of tongues.

n. **Isa. 33:22.** For the LORD is our judge, the LORD is our lawgiver, the LORD is our king; he will save us.

o. **Matt. 18:17–18.** And if he shall neglect to hear them, tell it unto the church: but if he neglect to hear the church, let him be unto thee as an heathen man and a publican. Verily I say unto you, Whatsoever ye shall bind on earth shall be bound in heaven: and whatsoever ye shall loose on earth shall be loosed in heaven. **1 Cor. 5: 4–5.** … in the name of our Lord Jesus Christ, when ye are gathered together, and my spirit, with the power of our Lord Jesus Christ, to deliver such an one unto Satan for the destruction of the flesh, that the spirit may be saved in the day of the Lord Jesus.

p. **Acts 5:31.** Him hath God exalted with his right hand to be a Prince and a Saviour, for to give repentance to Israel, and forgiveness of sins.

q. **Rev. 22:12.** And, behold, I come quickly; and my reward is with me, to give every man according as his work shall be. **Rev. 2:10.** Fear none of those things which thou shalt suffer: behold, the devil shall cast some of you into prison, that ye may be tried; and ye shall have tribulation ten days: be thou faithful unto death, and I will give thee a crown of life.

sins,[r] preserving and supporting them under all their temptations and sufferings,[s] restraining and overcoming all their enemies,[t] and powerfully ordering all things for his own glory,[u] and their good;[w] and also in taking vengeance on the rest, who know not God, and obey not the gospel.[x]

Q. 46. *What was the estate of Christ's humiliation?*

A. The estate of Christ's humiliation was that low condition, wherein he for our sakes, emptying himself of his glory, took upon him the form of a servant,[y] in his conception[z] and birth,[a] life,[b] death,[c]

r. **Rev. 3:19.** As many as I love, I rebuke and chasten: be zealous therefore, and repent.

s. **Isa. 63:9.** In all their affliction he was afflicted, and the angel of his presence saved them: in his love and in his pity he redeemed them; and he bare them, and carried them all the days of old.

t. **1 Cor. 15:25.** For he must reign, till he hath put all enemies under his feet. **Ps. 110:1–2.** The LORD said unto my Lord, Sit thou at my right hand, until I make thine enemies thy footstool. The LORD shall send the rod of thy strength out of Zion: rule thou in the midst of thine enemies.

u. **Rom. 14:10–11.** But why dost thou judge thy brother? or why dost thou set at nought thy brother? for we shall all stand before the judgment seat of Christ. For it is written, As I live, saith the Lord, every knee shall bow to me, and every tongue shall confess to God.

w. **Rom. 8:28.** And we know that all things work together for good to them that love God, to them who are the called according to his purpose.

x. **2 Thess. 1:8–9.** … in flaming fire taking vengeance on them that know not God, and that obey not the gospel of our Lord Jesus Christ: who shall be punished with everlasting destruction from the presence of the Lord, and from the glory of his power. **Ps. 2:8–9.** Ask of me, and I shall give thee the heathen for thine inheritance, and the uttermost parts of the earth for thy possession. Thou shalt break them with a rod of iron; thou shalt dash them in pieces like a potter's vessel.

y. **Phil. 2:6–8.** … who, being in the form of God, thought it not robbery to be equal with God: but made himself of no reputation, and took upon him the form of a servant, and was made in the likeness of men: and being found in fashion as a man, he humbled himself, and became obedient unto death, even the death of the cross.

z. **Luke 1:31.** And, behold, thou shalt conceive in thy womb, and bring forth a son, and shalt call his name JESUS.

a. **Luke 2:7.** And she brought forth her firstborn son, and wrapped him in swaddling clothes, and laid him in a manger; because there was no room for them in the inn.

b. **Gal. 4:4.** But when the fulness of the time was come, God sent forth his Son, made of a woman, made under the law. **2 Cor. 8:9.** For ye know the grace of our Lord Jesus Christ, that, though he was rich, yet for your sakes he became poor, that ye through his poverty might be rich. **Luke 9:58.** And Jesus said unto him, Foxes have holes, and birds of the air have nests; but the Son of man hath not where to lay his

and after his death,[d] until his resurrection.[e]

Q. 47. *How did Christ humble himself in his conception and birth?*

A. Christ humbled himself in his conception and birth, in that, being from all eternity the Son of God, in the bosom of the Father, he was pleased in the fullness of time to become the son of man, made of a woman of low estate, and to be born of her; with divers circumstances of more than ordinary abasement.[f]

Q. 48. *How did Christ humble himself in his life?*

A. Christ humbled himself in his life, by subjecting himself to the

head. **Heb. 2:18.** For in that he himself hath suffered being tempted, he is able to succour them that are tempted. **Isa. 53:3.** He is despised and rejected of men; a man of sorrows, and acquainted with grief: and we hid as it were our faces from him; he was despised, and we esteemed him not.

c. **Ps. 22:1.** My God, my God, why hast thou forsaken me? why art thou so far from helping me, and from the words of my roaring? **Compared with Matt. 27:46.** And about the ninth hour Jesus cried with a loud voice, saying, Eli, Eli, lama sabachthani? that is to say, My God, my God, why hast thou forsaken me? **Isa. 53:10.** Yet it pleased the LORD to bruise him; he hath put him to grief: when thou shalt make his soul an offering for sin, he shall see his seed, he shall prolong his days, and the pleasure of the LORD shall prosper in his hand. **1 John 2:2.** And he is the propitiation for our sins: and not for our's only, but also for the sins of the whole world. **Phil. 2:8.** And being found in fashion as a man, he humbled himself, and became obedient unto death, even the death of the cross.

d. **Matt. 12:40.** For as Jonas was three days and three nights in the whale's belly; so shall the Son of man be three days and three nights in the heart of the earth. **1 Cor. 15:3–4.** For I delivered unto you first of all that which I also received, how that Christ died for our sins according to the scriptures; and that he was buried, and that he rose again the third day according to the scriptures.

e. **Acts 2:24–27, 31.** … whom God hath raised up, having loosed the pains of death: because it was not possible that he should be holden of it. For David speaketh concerning him, I foresaw the Lord always before my face, for he is on my right hand, that I should not be moved: therefore did my heart rejoice, and my tongue was glad; moreover also my flesh shall rest in hope: because thou wilt not leave my soul in hell, neither wilt thou suffer thine Holy One to see corruption.… He seeing this before spake of the resurrection of Christ, that his soul was not left in hell, neither his flesh did see corruption.

f. **John 1:14, 18.** And the Word was made flesh, and dwelt among us, (and we beheld his glory, the glory as of the only begotten of the Father,) full of grace and truth.… No man hath seen God at any time; the only begotten Son, which is in the bosom of the Father, he hath declared him. **Gal. 4:4.** But when the fulness of the time was come, God sent forth his Son, made of a woman, made under the law. **Luke 2:7.** And she brought forth her firstborn son, and wrapped him in swaddling clothes, and laid him in a manger; because there was no room for them in the inn.

law,[g] which he perfectly fulfilled;[h] and by conflicting with the indignities of the world,[i] temptations of Satan,[k] and infirmities in his flesh, whether common to the nature of man, or particularly accompanying that his low condition.[l]

Q. 49. *How did Christ humble himself in his death?*

A. Christ humbled himself in his death, in that having been betrayed by Judas,[m] forsaken by his disciples,[n] scorned and rejected by the world,[o] condemned by Pilate, and tormented by his persecutors;[p]

g. **Gal. 4:4.** But when the fulness of the time was come, God sent forth his Son, made of a woman, made under the law.

h. **Matt. 5:17.** Think not that I am come to destroy the law, or the prophets: I am not come to destroy, but to fulfil. **Rom. 5:19.** For as by one man's disobedience many were made sinners, so by the obedience of one shall many be made righteous.

i. **Ps. 22:6.** But I am a worm, and no man; a reproach of men, and despised of the people. **Isa. 53:2–3.** For he shall grow up before him as a tender plant, and as a root out of a dry ground: he hath no form nor comeliness; and when we shall see him, there is no beauty that we should desire him. He is despised and rejected of men; a man of sorrows, and acquainted with grief: and we hid as it were our faces from him; he was despised, and we esteemed him not. **Heb. 12:2–3.** … looking unto Jesus the author and finisher of our faith; who for the joy that was set before him endured the cross, despising the shame, and is set down at the right hand of the throne of God. For consider him that endured such contradiction of sinners against himself, lest ye be wearied and faint in your minds.

k. **Matt. 4:1–11.** Then was Jesus led up of the Spirit into the wilderness to be tempted of the devil.… **Luke 4:13.** And when the devil had ended all the temptation, he departed from him for a season.

l. **Heb. 2:17–18.** Wherefore in all things it behoved him to be made like unto his brethren, that he might be a merciful and faithful high priest in things pertaining to God, to make reconciliation for the sins of the people. For in that he himself hath suffered being tempted, he is able to succour them that are tempted. **Heb. 4:15.** For we have not an high priest which cannot be touched with the feeling of our infirmities; but was in all points tempted like as we are, yet without sin. **Isa. 52:13–14.** Behold, my servant shall deal prudently, he shall be exalted and extolled, and be very high. As many were astonied at thee; his visage was so marred more than any man, and his form more than the sons of men.

m. **Matt. 27:4.** … saying, I have sinned in that I have betrayed the innocent blood. And they said, What is that to us? see thou to that.

n. **Matt. 26:56.** But all this was done, that the scriptures of the prophets might be fulfilled. Then all the disciples forsook him, and fled.

o. **Isa. 53:2–3.** For he shall grow up before him as a tender plant, and as a root out of a dry ground: he hath no form nor comeliness; and when we shall see him, there is no beauty that we should desire him. He is despised and rejected of men; a man of sorrows, and acquainted with grief: and we hid as it were our faces from him; he was despised, and we esteemed him not.

having also conflicted with the terrors of death, and the powers of darkness, felt and borne the weight of God's wrath,[q] he laid down his life an offering for sin,[r] enduring the painful, shameful, and cursed death of the cross.[s]

Q. 50. *Wherein consisted Christ's humiliation after his death?*

A. Christ's humiliation after his death consisted in his being buried,[t] and continuing in the state of the dead, and under the power of death till the third day;[u] which hath been otherwise expressed in these words, *He descended into hell.*

p. **Matt. 27:26–50.** Then released he Barabbas unto them: and when he had scourged Jesus, he delivered him to be crucified.... **John 19:34.** But one of the soldiers with a spear pierced his side, and forthwith came there out blood and water. **See Luke 22:63–64.**

q. **Luke 22:44.** And being in an agony he prayed more earnestly: and his sweat was as it were great drops of blood falling down to the ground. **Matt. 27:46.** And about the ninth hour Jesus cried with a loud voice, saying, Eli, Eli, lama sabachthani? that is to say, My God, my God, why hast thou forsaken me?

r. **Isa. 53:10.** Yet it pleased the LORD to bruise him; he hath put him to grief: when thou shalt make his soul an offering for sin, he shall see his seed, he shall prolong his days, and the pleasure of the LORD shall prosper in his hand. **Matt. 20:28.** ... even as the Son of man came not to be ministered unto, but to minister, and to give his life a ransom for many. **See Mark 10:45.**

s. **Phil. 2:8.** And being found in fashion as a man, he humbled himself, and became obedient unto death, even the death of the cross. **Heb. 12:2.** ... looking unto Jesus the author and finisher of our faith; who for the joy that was set before him endured the cross, despising the shame, and is set down at the right hand of the throne of God. **Gal. 3:13.** Christ hath redeemed us from the curse of the law, being made a curse for us: for it is written, Cursed is every one that hangeth on a tree.

t. **1 Cor. 15:3–4.** For I delivered unto you first of all that which I also received, how that Christ died for our sins according to the scriptures; and that he was buried, and that he rose again the third day according to the scriptures.

u. **Ps. 16:10.** For thou wilt not leave my soul in hell; neither wilt thou suffer thine Holy One to see corruption. **Acts 2:24–27, 31.** ... whom God hath raised up, having loosed the pains of death: because it was not possible that he should be holden of it. For David speaketh concerning him, I foresaw the Lord always before my face, for he is on my right hand, that I should not be moved: therefore did my heart rejoice, and my tongue was glad; moreover also my flesh shall rest in hope: because thou wilt not leave my soul in hell, neither wilt thou suffer thine Holy One to see corruption.... He seeing this before spake of the resurrection of Christ, that his soul was not left in hell, neither his flesh did see corruption. **Rom. 6:9.** ... knowing that Christ being raised from the dead dieth no more; death hath no more dominion over him. **Matt. 12:40.** For as Jonas was three days and three nights in the whale's belly; so shall the Son of man be three days and three nights in the heart of the earth.

Q. 51. *What was the estate of Christ's exaltation?*

A. The estate of Christ's exaltation comprehendeth his resurrection,[w] ascension,[x] sitting at the right hand of the Father,[y] and his coming again to judge the world.[z]

Q. 52. *How was Christ exalted in his resurrection?*

A. Christ was exalted in his resurrection, in that, not having seen corruption in death, (of which it was not possible for him to be held,[a]) and having the very same body in which he suffered, with the essential properties thereof,[b] (but without mortality, and other common infirmities belonging to this life,) really united to his soul,[c] he rose

w. **1 Cor. 15:4.** … and that he was buried, and that he rose again the third day according to the scriptures.

x. **Ps. 68:18.** Thou hast ascended on high, thou hast led captivity captive: thou hast received gifts for men; yea, for the rebellious also, that the LORD God might dwell among them. **Acts 1:11.** … which also said, Ye men of Galilee, why stand ye gazing up into heaven? this same Jesus, which is taken up from you into heaven, shall so come in like manner as ye have seen him go into heaven. **Eph. 4:8.** Wherefore he saith, When he ascended up on high, he led captivity captive, and gave gifts unto men.

y. **Eph. 1:20.** … which he wrought in Christ, when he raised him from the dead, and set him at his own right hand in the heavenly places. **Ps. 110:1.** The LORD said unto my Lord, Sit thou at my right hand, until I make thine enemies thy footstool. **Acts 2:33–34.** Therefore being by the right hand of God exalted, and having received of the Father the promise of the Holy Ghost, he hath shed forth this, which ye now see and hear. For David is not ascended into the heavens: but he saith himself, The LORD said unto my Lord, Sit thou on my right hand. **Heb. 1:3.** … who being the brightness of his glory, and the express image of his person, and upholding all things by the word of his power, when he had by himself purged our sins, sat down on the right hand of the Majesty on high.

z. **Acts 1:11.** … which also said, Ye men of Galilee, why stand ye gazing up into heaven? this same Jesus, which is taken up from you into heaven, shall so come in like manner as ye have seen him go into heaven. **Acts 17:31.** … because he hath appointed a day, in the which he will judge the world in righteousness by that man whom he hath ordained; whereof he hath given assurance unto all men, in that he hath raised him from the dead. **See Matt. 16:27.**

a. **Acts 2:24, 27.** … whom God hath raised up, having loosed the pains of death: because it was not possible that he should be holden of it.… because thou wilt not leave my soul in hell, neither wilt thou suffer thine Holy One to see corruption.

b. **Luke 24:39.** Behold my hands and my feet, that it is I myself: handle me, and see; for a spirit hath not flesh and bones, as ye see me have.

c. **Rom. 6:9.** … knowing that Christ being raised from the dead dieth no more; death hath no more dominion over him. **Rev. 1:18.** I am he that liveth, and was dead; and, behold, I am alive for evermore, Amen; and have the keys of hell and of death.

again from the dead the third day by his own power;[d] whereby he declared himself to be the Son of God,[e] to have satisfied divine justice,[f] to have vanquished death, and him that had the power of it,[g] and to be Lord of quick and dead:[h] all which he did as a public person,[i] the head of his church,[k] for their justification,[l] quickening in grace,[m]

d. **John 10:18.** No man taketh it from me, but I lay it down of myself. I have power to lay it down, and I have power to take it again. This commandment have I received of my Father.

e. **Rom. 1:4.** … and declared to be the Son of God with power, according to the spirit of holiness, by the resurrection from the dead.

f. **Rom. 8:34.** Who is he that condemneth? It is Christ that died, yea rather, that is risen again, who is even at the right hand of God, who also maketh intercession for us. **Rom. 3:25–26.** … whom God hath set forth to be a propitiation through faith in his blood, to declare his righteousness for the remission of sins that are past, through the forbearance of God; to declare, I say, at this time his righteousness: that he might be just, and the justifier of him which believeth in Jesus. **Heb. 9:13–14.** For if the blood of bulls and of goats, and the ashes of an heifer sprinkling the unclean, sanctifieth to the purifying of the flesh: how much more shall the blood of Christ, who through the eternal Spirit offered himself without spot to God, purge your conscience from dead works to serve the living God?

g. **Heb. 2:14.** Forasmuch then as the children are partakers of flesh and blood, he also himself likewise took part of the same; that through death he might destroy him that had the power of death, that is, the devil.

h. **Rom. 14:9.** For to this end Christ both died, and rose, and revived, that he might be Lord both of the dead and living.

i. **1 Cor. 15:21–22.** For since by man came death, by man came also the resurrection of the dead. For as in Adam all die, even so in Christ shall all be made alive. **Isa. 53:10–11.** Yet it pleased the LORD to bruise him; he hath put him to grief: when thou shalt make his soul an offering for sin, he shall see his seed, he shall prolong his days, and the pleasure of the LORD shall prosper in his hand. He shall see of the travail of his soul, and shall be satisfied: by his knowledge shall my righteous servant justify many; for he shall bear their iniquities.

k. **Eph. 1:20–23.** … which he wrought in Christ, when he raised him from the dead, and set him at his own right hand in the heavenly places, far above all principality, and power, and might, and dominion, and every name that is named, not only in this world, but also in that which is to come: and hath put all things under his feet, and gave him to be the head over all things to the church, which is his body, the fulness of him that filleth all in all. **Col. 1:18.** And he is the head of the body, the church: who is the beginning, the firstborn from the dead; that in all things he might have the preeminence.

l. **Rom. 4:25.** … who was delivered for our offences, and was raised again for our justification.

m. **Eph. 2:1, 5–6.** And you hath he quickened, who were dead in trespasses and sins.… Even when we were dead in sins, [God] hath quickened us together with Christ, (by grace ye are saved;) and hath raised us up together, and made us sit together in heavenly places in Christ Jesus. **Col. 2:12.** … buried with him in baptism, wherein

support against enemies,[n] and to assure them of their resurrection from the dead at the last day.[o]

Q. 53. *How was Christ exalted in his ascension?*

A. Christ was exalted in his ascension, in that having after his resurrection often appeared unto and conversed with his apostles, speaking to them of the things pertaining to the kingdom of God,[p] and giving them commission to preach the gospel to all nations,[q] forty days after his resurrection, he, in our nature, and as our head,[r] triumphing over enemies,[s] visibly went up into the highest heavens, there to receive gifts for men,[t] to raise up our affections thither,[u] and

also ye are risen with him through the faith of the operation of God, who hath raised him from the dead.

n. **1 Cor. 15:25–27.** For he must reign, till he hath put all enemies under his feet. The last enemy that shall be destroyed is death. For he hath put all things under his feet. But when he saith all things are put under him, it is manifest that he is excepted, which did put all things under him. **Ps. 2:7–9.** I will declare the decree: the LORD hath said unto me, Thou art my Son; this day have I begotten thee. Ask of me, and I shall give thee the heathen for thine inheritance, and the uttermost parts of the earth for thy possession. Thou shalt break them with a rod of iron; thou shalt dash them in pieces like a potter's vessel.

o. **1 Cor. 15:20.** But now is Christ risen from the dead, and become the firstfruits of them that slept. **1 Thess. 4:14.** For if we believe that Jesus died and rose again, even so them also which sleep in Jesus will God bring with him.

p. **Acts 1:2–3.** Until the day in which he was taken up, after that he through the Holy Ghost had given commandments unto the apostles whom he had chosen: to whom also he shewed himself alive after his passion by many infallible proofs, being seen of them forty days, and speaking of the things pertaining to the kingdom of God.

q. **Matt. 28:19–20.** Go ye therefore, and teach all nations, baptizing them in the name of the Father, and of the Son, and of the Holy Ghost: teaching them to observe all things whatsoever I have commanded you: and, lo, I am with you alway, even unto the end of the world. Amen.

r. **John 20:17.** Jesus saith unto her, Touch me not; for I am not yet ascended to my Father: but go to my brethren, and say unto them, I ascend unto my Father, and your Father; and to my God, and your God. **Heb. 6:20.** … whither the forerunner is for us entered, even Jesus, made an high priest for ever after the order of Melchisedec.

s. **Eph. 4:8.** Wherefore he saith, When he ascended up on high, he led captivity captive, and gave gifts unto men.

t. **Acts 1:9–11.** And when he had spoken these things, while they beheld, he was taken up; and a cloud received him out of their sight. And while they looked stedfastly toward heaven as he went up, behold, two men stood by them in white apparel; which also said, Ye men of Galilee, why stand ye gazing up into heaven? this same Jesus, which is taken up from you into heaven, shall so come in like manner as ye have seen him go into heaven. **Eph. 4:7–8.** But unto every one of us is given grace according to the measure of the gift of Christ. Wherefore he saith, When he ascended up on high,

to prepare a place for us,^w where himself is, and shall continue till his second coming at the end of the world.^x

Q. 54. *How is Christ exalted in his sitting at the right hand of God?*

A. Christ is exalted in his sitting at the right hand of God, in that as God-man he is advanced to the highest favor with God the Father,^y with all fullness of joy,^z glory,^a and power over all things in heaven and earth;^b and doth gather and defend his church, and subdue their enemies; furnisheth his ministers and people with gifts and graces,^c

he led captivity captive, and gave gifts unto men. **Ps. 68:18.** Thou hast ascended on high, thou hast led captivity captive: thou hast received gifts for men; yea, for the rebellious also, that the LORD God might dwell among them. **Eph. 4:10.** He that descended is the same also that ascended up far above all heavens, that he might fill all things. **Acts 2:33.** Therefore being by the right hand of God exalted, and having received of the Father the promise of the Holy Ghost, he hath shed forth this, which ye now see and hear.

u. **Col. 3:1–2.** If ye then be risen with Christ, seek those things which are above, where Christ sitteth on the right hand of God. Set your affection on things above, not on things on the earth.

w. **John 14:3.** And if I go and prepare a place for you, I will come again, and receive you unto myself; that where I am, there ye may be also.

x. **Acts 3:21.** … whom the heaven must receive until the times of restitution of all things, which God hath spoken by the mouth of all his holy prophets since the world began.

y. **Phil. 2:9.** Wherefore God also hath highly exalted him, and given him a name which is above every name.

z. **Acts 2:28.** Thou hast made known to me the ways of life; thou shalt make me full of joy with thy countenance. **Ps. 16:11.** Thou wilt shew me the path of life: in thy presence is fulness of joy; at thy right hand there are pleasures for evermore.

a. **John 17:5.** And now, O Father, glorify thou me with thine own self with the glory which I had with thee before the world was.

b. **Dan. 7:13–14.** I saw in the night visions, and, behold, one like the Son of man came with the clouds of heaven, and came to the Ancient of days, and they brought him near before him. And there was given him dominion, and glory, and a kingdom, that all people, nations, and languages, should serve him: his dominion is an everlasting dominion, which shall not pass away, and his kingdom that which shall not be destroyed. **Eph. 1:22.** … and hath put all things under his feet, and gave him to be the head over all things to the church. **1 Pet. 3:22.** … who is gone into heaven, and is on the right hand of God; angels and authorities and powers being made subject unto him.

c. **Eph. 4:10–12.** (… He that descended is the same also that ascended up far above all heavens, that he might fill all things.) And he gave some, apostles; and some, prophets; and some, evangelists; and some, pastors and teachers; for the perfecting of the saints, for the work of the ministry, for the edifying of the body of Christ. **Ps. 110:1.** The LORD said unto my Lord, Sit thou at my right hand, until I make thine

and maketh intercession for them.[d]

Q. 55. *How doth Christ make intercession?*

A. Christ maketh intercession, by his appearing in our nature continually before the Father in heaven,[e] in the merit of his obedience and sacrifice on earth,[f] declaring his will to have it applied to all believers;[g] answering all accusations against them,[h] and procuring for them quiet of conscience, notwithstanding daily failings,[i] access

enemies thy footstool. **Heb. 10:12–14.** But this man, after he had offered one sacrifice for sins for ever, sat down on the right hand of God; from henceforth expecting till his enemies be made his footstool. For by one offering he hath perfected for ever them that are sanctified. **Ezek. 37:24.** And David my servant shall be king over them; and they all shall have one shepherd: they shall also walk in my judgments, and observe my statutes, and do them.

d. **Rom. 8:34.** Who is he that condemneth? It is Christ that died, yea rather, that is risen again, who is even at the right hand of God, who also maketh intercession for us. **1 John 2:1.** My little children, these things write I unto you, that ye sin not. And if any man sin, we have an advocate with the Father, Jesus Christ the righteous. **Heb. 7:25.** Wherefore he is able also to save them to the uttermost that come unto God by him, seeing he ever liveth to make intercession for them.

e. **Heb. 9:12, 24.** Neither by the blood of goats and calves, but by his own blood he entered in once into the holy place, having obtained eternal redemption for us.… For Christ is not entered into the holy places made with hands, which are the figures of the true; but into heaven itself, now to appear in the presence of God for us.

f. **Isa. 53:12.** Therefore will I divide him a portion with the great, and he shall divide the spoil with the strong; because he hath poured out his soul unto death: and he was numbered with the transgressors; and he bare the sin of many, and made intercession for the transgressors. **Heb. 1:3.** … who being the brightness of his glory, and the express image of his person, and upholding all things by the word of his power, when he had by himself purged our sins, sat down on the right hand of the Majesty on high.

g. **John 3:16.** For God so loved the world, that he gave his only begotten Son, that whosoever believeth in him should not perish, but have everlasting life. **John 17:9, 20, 24.** I pray for them: I pray not for the world, but for them which thou hast given me; for they are thine.… Neither pray I for these alone, but for them also which shall believe on me through their word.… Father, I will that they also, whom thou hast given me, be with me where I am; that they may behold my glory, which thou hast given me: for thou lovedst me before the foundation of the world.

h. **Rom. 8:33–34.** Who shall lay any thing to the charge of God's elect? It is God that justifieth. Who is he that condemneth? It is Christ that died, yea rather, that is risen again, who is even at the right hand of God, who also maketh intercession for us.

i. **Rom. 5:1–2.** Therefore being justified by faith, we have peace with God through our Lord Jesus Christ: by whom also we have access by faith into this grace wherein we stand, and rejoice in hope of the glory of God. **1 John 2:1–2.** My little children,

with boldness to the throne of grace,[k] and acceptance of their persons[l] and services.[m]

Q. 56. *How is Christ to be exalted in his coming again to judge the world?*

A. Christ is to be exalted in his coming again to judge the world, in that he, who was unjustly judged and condemned by wicked men,[n] shall come again at the last day in great power,[o] and in the full manifestation of his own glory, and of his Father's, with all his holy angels,[p] with a shout, with the voice of the archangel, and with the trumpet of God,[q] to judge the world in righteousness.[r]

these things write I unto you, that ye sin not. And if any man sin, we have an advocate with the Father, Jesus Christ the righteous: and he is the propitiation for our sins: and not for ours only, but also for the sins of the whole world.

k. **Heb. 4:16.** Let us therefore come boldly unto the throne of grace, that we may obtain mercy, and find grace to help in time of need.

l. **Eph. 1:6.** ... to the praise of the glory of his grace, wherein he hath made us accepted in the beloved.

m. **1 Pet. 2:5.** Ye also, as lively stones, are built up a spiritual house, an holy priesthood, to offer up spiritual sacrifices, acceptable to God by Jesus Christ.

n. **Acts 3:14–15.** But ye denied the Holy One and the Just, and desired a murderer to be granted unto you; and killed the Prince of life, whom God hath raised from the dead; whereof we are witnesses.

o. **Matt. 24:30.** And then shall appear the sign of the Son of man in heaven: and then shall all the tribes of the earth mourn, and they shall see the Son of man coming in the clouds of heaven with power and great glory. **2 Thess. 1:9–10.** ... who shall be punished with everlasting destruction from the presence of the Lord, and from the glory of his power; when he shall come to be glorified in his saints, and to be admired in all them that believe (because our testimony among you was believed) in that day.

p. **Luke 9:26.** For whosoever shall be ashamed of me and of my words, of him shall the Son of man be ashamed, when he shall come in his own glory, and in his Father's, and of the holy angels. **Matt. 25:31.** When the Son of man shall come in his glory, and all the holy angels with him, then shall he sit upon the throne of his glory.

q. **1 Thess. 4:16.** For the Lord himself shall descend from heaven with a shout, with the voice of the archangel, and with the trump of God: and the dead in Christ shall rise first.

r. **Acts 17:31.** ... because he hath appointed a day, in the which he will judge the world in righteousness by that man whom he hath ordained; whereof he hath given assurance unto all men, in that he hath raised him from the dead. **2 Thess. 1:6–8.** ... seeing it is a righteous thing with God to recompense tribulation to them that trouble you; and to you who are troubled rest with us, when the Lord Jesus shall be revealed from heaven with his mighty angels, in flaming fire taking vengeance on them that know not God, and that obey not the gospel of our Lord Jesus Christ.

Q. 57. *What benefits hath Christ procured by his mediation?*

A. Christ, by his mediation, hath procured redemption,[s] with all other benefits of the covenant of grace.[t]

Q. 58. *How do we come to be made partakers of the benefits which Christ hath procured?*

A. We are made partakers of the benefits which Christ hath procured, by the application of them unto us,[u] which is the work especially of God the Holy Ghost.[w]

Q. 59. *Who are made partakers of redemption through Christ?*

A. Redemption is certainly applied, and effectually communicated, to all those for whom Christ hath purchased it;[x] who are in

s. **1 Tim. 2:5–6.** For there is one God, and one mediator between God and men, the man Christ Jesus; who gave himself a ransom for all, to be testified in due time. **Heb. 9:12.** Neither by the blood of goats and calves, but by his own blood he entered in once into the holy place, having obtained eternal redemption for us. **Eph. 1:7.** … in whom we have redemption through his blood, the forgiveness of sins, according to the riches of his grace.

t. **2 Cor. 1:20.** For all the promises of God in him are yea, and in him Amen, unto the glory of God by us. **Eph. 1:3–6.** Blessed be the God and Father of our Lord Jesus Christ, who hath blessed us with all spiritual blessings in heavenly places in Christ: according as he hath chosen us in him before the foundation of the world, that we should be holy and without blame before him in love: having predestinated us unto the adoption of children by Jesus Christ to himself, according to the good pleasure of his will, to the praise of the glory of his grace, wherein he hath made us accepted in the beloved. **2 Pet. 1:3–4.** … according as his divine power hath given unto us all things that pertain unto life and godliness, through the knowledge of him that hath called us to glory and virtue: whereby are given unto us exceeding great and precious promises: that by these ye might be partakers of the divine nature, having escaped the corruption that is in the world through lust.

u. **John 1:11–12.** He came unto his own, and his own received him not. But as many as received him, to them gave he power to become the sons of God, even to them that believe on his name.

w. **Titus 3:4–7.** But after that the kindness and love of God our Saviour toward man appeared, not by works of righteousness which we have done, but according to his mercy he saved us, by the washing of regeneration, and renewing of the Holy Ghost; which he shed on us abundantly through Jesus Christ our Saviour; that being justified by his grace, we should be made heirs according to the hope of eternal life. **John 16:14–15.** He shall glorify me: for he shall receive of mine, and shall shew it unto you. All things that the Father hath are mine: therefore said I, that he shall take of mine, and shall shew it unto you. **See John 3:3–8.**

x. **Eph. 1:13–14.** …in whom ye also trusted, after that ye heard the word of truth, the gospel of your salvation: in whom also after that ye believed, ye were sealed with that holy Spirit of promise, which is the earnest of our inheritance until the

time by the Holy Ghost enabled to believe in Christ according to the gospel.ʸ

Q. 60. *Can they who have never heard the gospel, and so know not Jesus Christ, nor believe in him, be saved by their living according to the light of nature?*

A. They who, having never heard the gospel,ᶻ know not Jesus Christ,ᵃ and believe not in him, cannot be saved,ᵇ be they never so diligent to frame their lives according to the light of nature,ᶜ or the

redemption of the purchased possession, unto the praise of his glory. **John 6:37, 39.** All that the Father giveth me shall come to me; and him that cometh to me I will in no wise cast out.... And this is the Father's will which hath sent me, that of all which he hath given me I should lose nothing, but should raise it up again at the last day. **John 10:15–16.** As the Father knoweth me, even so know I the Father: and I lay down my life for the sheep. And other sheep I have, which are not of this fold: them also I must bring, and they shall hear my voice; and there shall be one fold, and one shepherd.

y. **Rom. 10:17.** So then faith cometh by hearing, and hearing by the word of God. **1 Cor. 2:12–16.** Now we have received, not the spirit of the world, but the spirit which is of God; that we might know the things that are freely given to us of God. Which things also we speak, not in the words which man's wisdom teacheth, but which the Holy Ghost teacheth; comparing spiritual things with spiritual. But the natural man receiveth not the things of the Spirit of God: for they are foolishness unto him: neither can he know them, because they are spiritually discerned. But he that is spiritual judgeth all things, yet he himself is judged of no man. For who hath known the mind of the Lord, that he may instruct him? But we have the mind of Christ. **Eph. 2:8.** For by grace are ye saved through faith; and that not of yourselves: it is the gift of God. **Rom. 8:9, 14.** But ye are not in the flesh, but in the Spirit, if so be that the Spirit of God dwell in you. Now if any man have not the Spirit of Christ, he is none of his.... For as many as are led by the Spirit of God, they are the sons of God.

z. **Rom. 10:14.** How then shall they call on him in whom they have not believed? and how shall they believe in him of whom they have not heard? and how shall they hear without a preacher?

a. **2 Thess. 1:8–9.** ... in flaming fire taking vengeance on them that know not God, and that obey not the gospel of our Lord Jesus Christ: who shall be punished with everlasting destruction from the presence of the Lord, and from the glory of his power. **Eph. 2:12.** ... that at that time ye were without Christ, being aliens from the commonwealth of Israel, and strangers from the covenants of promise, having no hope, and without God in the world. **John 1:10–12.** He was in the world, and the world was made by him, and the world knew him not. He came unto his own, and his own received him not. But as many as received him, to them gave he power to become the sons of God, even to them that believe on his name.

b. **John 8:24.** I said therefore unto you, that ye shall die in your sins: for if ye believe not that I am he, ye shall die in your sins. **John 3:18.** He that believeth on him is not condemned: but he that believeth not is condemned already, because he hath not believed in the name of the only begotten Son of God.

c. **1 Cor. 1:20–24.** Where is the wise? where is the scribe? where is the disputer of this world? hath not God made foolish the wisdom of this world? For after that in

laws of that religion which they profess;[d] neither is there salvation in any other, but in Christ alone,[e] who is the Savior only of his body the church.[f]

Q. 61. *Are all they saved who hear the gospel, and live in the church?*

A. All that hear the gospel, and live in the visible church, are not saved; but they only who are true members of the church invisible.[g]

the wisdom of God the world by wisdom knew not God, it pleased God by the foolishness of preaching to save them that believe. For the Jews require a sign, and the Greeks seek after wisdom: but we preach Christ crucified, unto the Jews a stumblingblock, and unto the Greeks foolishness; but unto them which are called, both Jews and Greeks, Christ the power of God, and the wisdom of God.

d. **John 4:22.** Ye worship ye know not what: we know what we worship: for salvation is of the Jews. **Rom. 9:31–32.** But Israel, which followed after the law of righteousness, hath not attained to the law of righteousness. Wherefore? Because they sought it not by faith, but as it were by the works of the law. For they stumbled at that stumblingstone. **Phil. 3:4–9.** Though I might also have confidence in the flesh. If any other man thinketh that he hath whereof he might trust in the flesh, I more: circumcised the eighth day, of the stock of Israel, of the tribe of Benjamin, an Hebrew of the Hebrews; as touching the law, a Pharisee; concerning zeal, persecuting the church; touching the righteousness which is in the law, blameless. But what things were gain to me, those I counted loss for Christ. Yea doubtless, and I count all things but loss for the excellency of the knowledge of Christ Jesus my Lord: for whom I have suffered the loss of all things, and do count them but dung, that I may win Christ, and be found in him, not having mine own righteousness, which is of the law, but that which is through the faith of Christ, the righteousness which is of God by faith.

e. **Acts 4:12.** Neither is there salvation in any other: for there is none other name under heaven given among men, whereby we must be saved.

f. **Eph. 5:23.** For the husband is the head of the wife, even as Christ is the head of the church: and he is the saviour of the body.

g. **John 12:38–40.** … that the saying of Esaias the prophet might be fulfilled, which he spake, Lord, who hath believed our report? and to whom hath the arm of the Lord been revealed? Therefore they could not believe, because that Esaias said again, He hath blinded their eyes, and hardened their heart; that they should not see with their eyes, nor understand with their heart, and be converted, and I should heal them. **Rom. 9:6.** Not as though the word of God hath taken none effect. For they are not all Israel, which are of Israel. **Matt. 22:14.** For many are called, but few are chosen. **Matt. 7:21.** Not every one that saith unto me, Lord, Lord, shall enter into the kingdom of heaven; but he that doeth the will of my Father which is in heaven. **Rom. 11:7.** What then? Israel hath not obtained that which he seeketh for; but the election hath obtained it, and the rest were blinded. **1 Cor. 10:2–5.** And [our fathers] were all baptized unto Moses in the cloud and in the sea; and did all eat the same spiritual meat; and did all drink the same spiritual drink: for they drank of that spiritual Rock that followed them: and that Rock was Christ. But with many of them God was not well pleased: for they were overthrown in the wilderness.

Q. 62. *What is the visible church?*

A. The visible church is a society made up of all such as in all ages and places of the world do profess the true religion,[h] and of their children.[i]

Q. 63. *What are the special privileges of the visible church?*

A. The visible church hath the privilege of being under God's

---

h. **1 Cor. 1:2.** … unto the church of God which is at Corinth, to them that are sanctified in Christ Jesus, called to be saints, with all that in every place call upon the name of Jesus Christ our Lord, both theirs and ours. **1 Cor. 12:13.** For by one Spirit are we all baptized into one body, whether we be Jews or Gentiles, whether we be bond or free; and have been all made to drink into one Spirit. **Rom. 15:9–12.** … and that the Gentiles might glorify God for his mercy; as it is written, For this cause I will confess to thee among the Gentiles, and sing unto thy name. And again he saith, Rejoice, ye Gentiles, with his people. And again, Praise the Lord, all ye Gentiles; and laud him, all ye people. And again, Esaias saith, There shall be a root of Jesse, and he that shall rise to reign over the Gentiles; in him shall the Gentiles trust. **Rev. 7:9.** After this I beheld, and, lo, a great multitude, which no man could number, of all nations, and kindreds, and people, and tongues, stood before the throne, and before the Lamb, clothed with white robes, and palms in their hands. **Ps. 2:8.** Ask of me, and I shall give thee the heathen for thine inheritance, and the uttermost parts of the earth for thy possession. **Ps. 22:27–31.** All the ends of the world shall remember and turn unto the LORD: and all the kindreds of the nations shall worship before thee. For the kingdom is the LORD'S: and he is the governor among the nations. All they that be fat upon earth shall eat and worship: all they that go down to the dust shall bow before him: and none can keep alive his own soul. A seed shall serve him; it shall be accounted to the Lord for a generation. They shall come, and shall declare his righteousness unto a people that shall be born, that he hath done this. **Ps. 45:17.** I will make thy name to be remembered in all generations: therefore shall the people praise thee for ever and ever. **Matt. 28:19–20.** Go ye therefore, and teach all nations, baptizing them in the name of the Father, and of the Son, and of the Holy Ghost: Teaching them to observe all things whatsoever I have commanded you: and, lo, I am with you alway, even unto the end of the world. Amen. **Isa. 59:21.** As for me, this is my covenant with them, saith the LORD; My spirit that is upon thee, and my words which I have put in thy mouth, shall not depart out of thy mouth, nor out of the mouth of thy seed, nor out of the mouth of thy seed's seed, saith the LORD, from henceforth and for ever.

i. **1 Cor. 7:14.** For the unbelieving husband is sanctified by the wife, and the unbelieving wife is sanctified by the husband: else were your children unclean; but now are they holy. **Acts 2:39.** For the promise is unto you, and to your children, and to all that are afar off, even as many as the Lord our God shall call. **Rom. 11:16.** For if the firstfruit be holy, the lump is also holy: and if the root be holy, so are the branches. **Gen. 17:7.** And I will establish my covenant between me and thee and thy seed after thee in their generations for an everlasting covenant, to be a God unto thee, and to thy seed after thee.

special care and government;^k of being protected and preserved in all ages, notwithstanding the opposition of all enemies;^l and of enjoying the communion of saints, the ordinary means of salvation,^m

k. **Isa. 4:5–6.** And the LORD will create upon every dwelling place of mount Zion, and upon her assemblies, a cloud and smoke by day, and the shining of a flaming fire by night: for upon all the glory shall be a defence. And there shall be a tabernacle for a shadow in the daytime from the heat, and for a place of refuge, and for a covert from storm and from rain. **1 Tim. 4:10.** For therefore we both labour and suffer reproach, because we trust in the living God, who is the Saviour of all men, specially of those that believe. **Eph. 4:11–13.** And he gave some, apostles; and some, prophets; and some, evangelists; and some, pastors and teachers; for the perfecting of the saints, for the work of the ministry, for the edifying of the body of Christ: till we all come in the unity of the faith, and of the knowledge of the Son of God, unto a perfect man, unto the measure of the stature of the fulness of Christ.

l. **Ps. 115:1–2, 9.** Not unto us, O LORD, not unto us, but unto thy name give glory, for thy mercy, and for thy truth's sake. Wherefore should the heathen say, Where is now their God?… O Israel, trust thou in the LORD: he is their help and their shield. **Isa. 31:4–5.** For thus hath the LORD spoken unto me, Like as the lion and the young lion roaring on his prey, when a multitude of shepherds is called forth against him, he will not be afraid of their voice, nor abase himself for the noise of them: so shall the LORD of hosts come down to fight for mount Zion, and for the hill thereof. As birds flying, so will the LORD of hosts defend Jerusalem; defending also he will deliver it; and passing over he will preserve it. **Zech. 12:2–4, 8–9.** Behold, I will make Jerusalem a cup of trembling unto all the people round about, when they shall be in the siege both against Judah and against Jerusalem. And in that day will I make Jerusalem a burdensome stone for all people: all that burden themselves with it shall be cut in pieces, though all the people of the earth be gathered together against it. In that day, saith the LORD, I will smite every horse with astonishment, and his rider with madness: and I will open mine eyes upon the house of Judah, and will smite every horse of the people with blindness.… In that day shall the LORD defend the inhabitants of Jerusalem; and he that is feeble among them at that day shall be as David; and the house of David shall be as God, as the angel of the LORD before them. And it shall come to pass in that day, that I will seek to destroy all the nations that come against Jerusalem. **Matt. 16:18.** And I say also unto thee, That thou art Peter, and upon this rock I will build my church; and the gates of hell shall not prevail against it.

m. **Acts 2:39, 42.** For the promise is unto you, and to your children, and to all that are afar off, even as many as the Lord our God shall call.… And they continued stedfastly in the apostles' doctrine and fellowship, and in breaking of bread, and in prayers. **Matt. 28:19–20.** Go ye therefore, and teach all nations, baptizing them in the name of the Father, and of the Son, and of the Holy Ghost: teaching them to observe all things whatsoever I have commanded you: and, lo, I am with you alway, even unto the end of the world. Amen. **1 Cor. 12:12–13.** For as the body is one, and hath many members, and all the members of that one body, being many, are one body: so also is Christ. For by one Spirit are we all baptized into one body, whether we be Jews or Gentiles, whether we be bond or free; and have been all made to drink into one Spirit.

and offers of grace by Christ to all the members of it in the ministry of the gospel, testifying, that whosoever believes in him shall be saved,[n] and excluding none that will come unto him.[o]

Q. 64. *What is the invisible church?*

A. The invisible church is the whole number of the elect, that have been, are, or shall be gathered into one under Christ the head.[p]

Q. 65. *What special benefits do the members of the invisible church enjoy by Christ?*

A. The members of the invisible church by Christ enjoy union and communion with him in grace and glory.[q]

n. **Ps. 147:19–20.** He sheweth his word unto Jacob, his statutes and his judgments unto Israel. He hath not dealt so with any nation: and as for his judgments, they have not known them. Praise ye the LORD. **Rom. 9:4.** ... who are Israelites; to whom pertaineth the adoption, and the glory, and the covenants, and the giving of the law, and the service of God, and the promises. **Eph. 4:11–12.** And he gave some, apostles; and some, prophets; and some, evangelists; and some, pastors and teachers; for the perfecting of the saints, for the work of the ministry, for the edifying of the body of Christ. **Acts 22:16.** And now why tarriest thou? arise, and be baptized, and wash away thy sins, calling on the name of the Lord. **Acts 2:21.** And it shall come to pass, that whosoever shall call on the name of the Lord shall be saved. **See Joel 2:32. Rom. 10:10–13, 17.** For with the heart man believeth unto righteousness; and with the mouth confession is made unto salvation. For the scripture saith, Whosoever believeth on him shall not be ashamed. For there is no difference between the Jew and the Greek: for the same Lord over all is rich unto all that call upon him. For whosoever shall call upon the name of the Lord shall be saved.... So then faith cometh by hearing, and hearing by the word of God.

o. **Matt. 11:28–29.** Come unto me, all ye that labour and are heavy laden, and I will give you rest. Take my yoke upon you, and learn of me; for I am meek and lowly in heart: and ye shall find rest unto your souls. **John 6:37.** All that the Father giveth me shall come to me; and him that cometh to me I will in no wise cast out.

p. **Eph. 1:10.** ... that in the dispensation of the fulness of times he might gather together in one all things in Christ, both which are in heaven, and which are on earth; even in him. **Eph. 1:22–23.** ... and hath put all things under his feet, and gave him to be the head over all things to the church, which is his body, the fulness of him that filleth all in all. **John 10:16.** And other sheep I have, which are not of this fold: them also I must bring, and they shall hear my voice; and there shall be one fold, and one shepherd. **John 11:52.** ... and not for that nation only, but that also he should gather together in one the children of God that were scattered abroad. **Eph. 5:23, 27, 32.** For the husband is the head of the wife, even as Christ is the head of the church: and he is the saviour of the body.... that he might present it to himself a glorious church, not having spot, or wrinkle, or any such thing; but that it should be holy and without blemish.... This is a great mystery: but I speak concerning Christ and the church.

q. **John 17:21.** ... that they all may be one; as thou, Father, art in me, and I in

Q. 66. *What is that union which the elect have with Christ?*
A. The union which the elect have with Christ is the work of God's grace,[r] whereby they are spiritually and mystically, yet really and inseparably, joined to Christ as their head and husband;[s] which is done in their effectual calling.[t]

Q. 67. *What is effectual calling?*
A. Effectual calling is the work of God's almighty power and grace,[u] whereby (out of his free and special love to his elect, and from

thee, that they also may be one in us: that the world may believe that thou hast sent me. **Eph. 2:5–6.** Even when we were dead in sins, [God] hath quickened us together with Christ, (by grace ye are saved;) and hath raised us up together, and made us sit together in heavenly places in Christ Jesus. **John 17:24.** Father, I will that they also, whom thou hast given me, be with me where I am; that they may behold my glory, which thou hast given me: for thou lovedst me before the foundation of the world. **1 John 1:3.** That which we have seen and heard declare we unto you, that ye also may have fellowship with us: and truly our fellowship is with the Father, and with his Son Jesus Christ. **John 1:16.** And of his fulness have all we received, and grace for grace. **Eph. 3:16–19.** … that he would grant you, according to the riches of his glory, to be strengthened with might by his Spirit in the inner man; that Christ may dwell in your hearts by faith; that ye, being rooted and grounded in love, may be able to comprehend with all saints what is the breadth, and length, and depth, and height; and to know the love of Christ, which passeth knowledge, that ye might be filled with all the fulness of God. **Phil. 3:10.** … that I may know him, and the power of his resurrection, and the fellowship of his sufferings, being made conformable unto his death. **Rom. 6:5–6.** For if we have been planted together in the likeness of his death, we shall be also in the likeness of his resurrection: knowing this, that our old man is crucified with him, that the body of sin might be destroyed, that henceforth we should not serve sin.

r. **Eph. 2:6–7.** And hath raised us up together, and made us sit together in heavenly places in Christ Jesus: that in the ages to come he might shew the exceeding riches of his grace in his kindness toward us through Christ Jesus.

s. **Eph. 1:22.** … and hath put all things under his feet, and gave him to be the head over all things to the church. **1 Cor. 6:17.** But he that is joined unto the Lord is one spirit. **John 10:28.** And I give unto them eternal life; and they shall never perish, neither shall any man pluck them out of my hand. **Eph. 5:23, 30.** For the husband is the head of the wife, even as Christ is the head of the church: and he is the saviour of the body.… For we are members of his body, of his flesh, and of his bones. **John 15:5.** I am the vine, ye are the branches: He that abideth in me, and I in him, the same bringeth forth much fruit: for without me ye can do nothing. **Eph. 3:17.** … that Christ may dwell in your hearts by faith; that ye, being rooted and grounded in love …

t. **1 Pet. 5:10.** But the God of all grace, who hath called us unto his eternal glory by Christ Jesus, after that ye have suffered a while, make you perfect, stablish, strengthen, settle you. **1 Cor. 1:9.** God is faithful, by whom ye were called unto the fellowship of his Son Jesus Christ our Lord.

u. **Ezek. 37:9, 14.** Then said he unto me, Prophesy unto the wind, prophesy,

nothing in them moving him thereunto[w]) he doth, in his accepted time, invite and draw them to Jesus Christ, by his Word and Spirit;[x]

son of man, and say to the wind, Thus saith the Lord GOD; Come from the four winds, O breath, and breathe upon these slain, that they may live.… and [I] shall put my spirit in you, and ye shall live, and I shall place you in your own land: then shall ye know that I the LORD have spoken it, and performed it, saith the LORD. **John 5:25.** Verily, verily, I say unto you, The hour is coming, and now is, when the dead shall hear the voice of the Son of God: and they that hear shall live. **Eph. 1:18–20.** … the eyes of your understanding being enlightened; that ye may know what is the hope of his calling, and what the riches of the glory of his inheritance in the saints, and what is the exceeding greatness of his power to us-ward who believe, according to the working of his mighty power, which he wrought in Christ, when he raised him from the dead, and set him at his own right hand in the heavenly places. **2 Tim. 1:8–9.** Be not thou therefore ashamed of the testimony of our Lord, nor of me his prisoner: but be thou partaker of the afflictions of the gospel according to the power of God; who hath saved us, and called us with an holy calling, not according to our works, but according to his own purpose and grace, which was given us in Christ Jesus before the world began.

w. **Titus 3:4–5.** But after that the kindness and love of God our Saviour toward man appeared, not by works of righteousness which we have done, but according to his mercy he saved us, by the washing of regeneration, and renewing of the Holy Ghost. **Eph. 2:4–5, 7–9.** But God, who is rich in mercy, for his great love wherewith he loved us, even when we were dead in sins, hath quickened us together with Christ, (by grace ye are saved;) … that in the ages to come he might shew the exceeding riches of his grace in his kindness toward us through Christ Jesus. For by grace are ye saved through faith; and that not of yourselves: it is the gift of God: not of works, lest any man should boast. **Rom. 9:11.** … (for the children being not yet born, neither having done any good or evil, that the purpose of God according to election might stand, not of works, but of him that calleth;) … **Deut. 9:5.** Not for thy righteousness, or for the uprightness of thine heart, dost thou go to possess their land: but for the wickedness of these nations the LORD thy God doth drive them out from before thee, and that he may perform the word which the LORD sware unto thy fathers, Abraham, Isaac, and Jacob.

x. **John 3:5.** Jesus answered, Verily, verily, I say unto thee, Except a man be born of water and of the Spirit, he cannot enter into the kingdom of God. **Titus 3:5.** Not by works of righteousness which we have done, but according to his mercy he saved us, by the washing of regeneration, and renewing of the Holy Ghost. **2 Cor. 5:20.** Now then we are ambassadors for Christ, as though God did beseech you by us: we pray you in Christ's stead, be ye reconciled to God. **2 Cor. 6:1–2.** We then, as workers together with him, beseech you also that ye receive not the grace of God in vain. (For he saith, I have heard thee in a time accepted, and in the day of salvation have I succoured thee: behold, now is the accepted time; behold, now is the day of salvation.) **John 6:44–45.** No man can come to me, except the Father which hath sent me draw him: and I will raise him up at the last day. It is written in the prophets, And they shall be all taught of God. Every man therefore that hath heard, and hath learned of the Father, cometh unto me. **Acts 16:14.** And a certain woman named Lydia, a seller of purple, of the city of Thyatira, which worshipped God, heard us: whose heart the

savingly enlightening their minds,[y] renewing and powerfully determining their wills,[z] so as they (although in themselves dead in sin) are hereby made willing and able freely to answer his call, and to accept and embrace the grace offered and conveyed therein.[a]

Q. 68. *Are the elect only effectually called?*
A. All the elect, and they only, are effectually called;[b] although

Lord opened, that she attended unto the things which were spoken of Paul. **2 Thess. 2:13–14.** But we are bound to give thanks alway to God for you, brethren beloved of the Lord, because God hath from the beginning chosen you to salvation through sanctification of the Spirit and belief of the truth: whereunto he called you by our gospel, to the obtaining of the glory of our Lord Jesus Christ.

y. **Acts 26:18.** [I send thee] to open their eyes, and to turn them from darkness to light, and from the power of Satan unto God, that they may receive forgiveness of sins, and inheritance among them which are sanctified by faith that is in me. **1 Cor. 2:10, 12.** But God hath revealed them unto us by his Spirit: for the Spirit searcheth all things, yea, the deep things of God.… Now we have received, not the spirit of the world, but the spirit which is of God; that we might know the things that are freely given to us of God. **2 Cor. 4:6.** For God, who commanded the light to shine out of darkness, hath shined in our hearts, to give the light of the knowledge of the glory of God in the face of Jesus Christ. **Eph. 1:17–18.** … that the God of our Lord Jesus Christ, the Father of glory, may give unto you the spirit of wisdom and revelation in the knowledge of him: the eyes of your understanding being enlightened; that ye may know what is the hope of his calling, and what the riches of the glory of his inheritance in the saints.

z. **Ezek. 11:19.** And I will give them one heart, and I will put a new spirit within you; and I will take the stony heart out of their flesh, and will give them an heart of flesh. **Ezek. 36:26–27.** A new heart also will I give you, and a new spirit will I put within you: and I will take away the stony heart out of your flesh, and I will give you an heart of flesh. And I will put my spirit within you, and cause you to walk in my statutes, and ye shall keep my judgments, and do them. **John 6:45.** It is written in the prophets, And they shall be all taught of God. Every man therefore that hath heard, and hath learned of the Father, cometh unto me.

a. **Eph. 2:5.** Even when we were dead in sins, [God] hath quickened us together with Christ, (by grace ye are saved;) … **Phil. 2:13.** For it is God which worketh in you both to will and to do of his good pleasure. **Deut. 30:6.** And the Lord thy God will circumcise thine heart, and the heart of thy seed, to love the Lord thy God with all thine heart, and with all thy soul, that thou mayest live. **Isa. 45:22.** Look unto me, and be ye saved, all the ends of the earth: for I am God, and there is none else. **Matt. 11:28–30.** Come unto me, all ye that labour and are heavy laden, and I will give you rest. Take my yoke upon you, and learn of me; for I am meek and lowly in heart: and ye shall find rest unto your souls. For my yoke is easy, and my burden is light. **Rev. 22:17.** And the Spirit and the bride say, Come. And let him that heareth say, Come. And let him that is athirst come. And whosoever will, let him take the water of life freely.

b. **Acts 13:48.** And when the Gentiles heard this, they were glad, and glorified the word of the Lord: and as many as were ordained to eternal life believed.

others may be, and often are, outwardly called by the ministry of the Word,[c] and have some common operations of the Spirit;[d] who, for their willful neglect and contempt of the grace offered to them, being justly left in their unbelief, do never truly come to Jesus Christ.[e]

Q. 69. *What is the communion in grace which the members of the invisible church have with Christ?*

A. The communion in grace which the members of the invisible church have with Christ, is their partaking of the virtue of his media-

c. **Matt. 22:14.** For many are called, but few are chosen. **Acts 8:13, 20–21.** Then Simon himself believed also: and when he was baptized, he continued with Philip, and wondered, beholding the miracles and signs which were done.… But Peter said unto him, Thy money perish with thee, because thou hast thought that the gift of God may be purchased with money. Thou hast neither part nor lot in this matter: for thy heart is not right in the sight of God.

d. **Matt. 7:22.** Many will say to me in that day, Lord, Lord, have we not prophesied in thy name? and in thy name have cast out devils? and in thy name done many wonderful works? **Matt. 13:20–21.** But he that received the seed into stony places, the same is he that heareth the word, and anon with joy receiveth it; yet hath he not root in himself, but dureth for a while: for when tribulation or persecution ariseth because of the word, by and by he is offended. **Heb. 6:4–6.** For it is impossible for those who were once enlightened, and have tasted of the heavenly gift, and were made partakers of the Holy Ghost, and have tasted the good word of God, and the powers of the world to come, if they shall fall away, to renew them again unto repentance; seeing they crucify to themselves the Son of God afresh, and put him to an open shame.

e. **John 12:38–40.** … that the saying of Esaias the prophet might be fulfilled, which he spake, Lord, who hath believed our report? and to whom hath the arm of the Lord been revealed? Therefore they could not believe, because that Esaias said again, He hath blinded their eyes, and hardened their heart; that they should not see with their eyes, nor understand with their heart, and be converted, and I should heal them. **Acts 28:25–27.** And when they agreed not among themselves, they departed, after that Paul had spoken one word, Well spake the Holy Ghost by Esaias the prophet unto our fathers, saying, Go unto this people, and say, Hearing ye shall hear, and shall not understand; and seeing ye shall see, and not perceive: for the heart of this people is waxed gross, and their ears are dull of hearing, and their eyes have they closed; lest they should see with their eyes, and hear with their ears, and understand with their heart, and should be converted, and I should heal them. **John 6:64–65.** But there are some of you that believe not. For Jesus knew from the beginning who they were that believed not, and who should betray him. And he said, Therefore said I unto you, that no man can come unto me, except it were given unto him of my Father. **Ps. 81:11–12.** But my people would not hearken to my voice; and Israel would none of me. So I gave them up unto their own hearts' lust: and they walked in their own counsels. **Heb. 10:29.** Of how much sorer punishment, suppose ye, shall he be thought worthy, who hath trodden under foot the Son of God, and hath counted the blood of the

tion, in their justification,^f adoption,^g sanctification, and whatever else, in this life, manifests their union with him.^h

Q. 70. *What is justification?*

A. Justification is an act of God's free grace unto sinners,ⁱ in which he pardoneth all their sins, accepteth and accounteth their persons righteous in his sight;^k not for anything wrought in them, or done by them,^l but only for the perfect obedience and full satisfaction of Christ,

covenant, wherewith he was sanctified, an unholy thing, and hath done despite unto the Spirit of grace? **1 John 2:19.** They went out from us, but they were not of us; for if they had been of us, they would no doubt have continued with us: but they went out, that they might be made manifest that they were not all of us.

f. **Rom. 8:30.** Moreover whom he did predestinate, them he also called: and whom he called, them he also justified: and whom he justified, them he also glorified.

g. **Eph. 1:5.** ... having predestinated us unto the adoption of children by Jesus Christ to himself, according to the good pleasure of his will.

h. **1 Cor. 1:30.** But of him are ye in Christ Jesus, who of God is made unto us wisdom, and righteousness, and sanctification, and redemption. **1 Cor. 6:11.** And such were some of you: but ye are washed, but ye are sanctified, but ye are justified in the name of the Lord Jesus, and by the Spirit of our God.

i. **Rom. 3:22, 24–25.** ... even the righteousness of God which is by faith of Jesus Christ unto all and upon all them that believe: for there is no difference.... being justified freely by his grace through the redemption that is in Christ Jesus: whom God hath set forth to be a propitiation through faith in his blood, to declare his righteousness for the remission of sins that are past, through the forbearance of God. **Rom. 4:5.** But to him that worketh not, but believeth on him that justifieth the ungodly, his faith is counted for righteousness.

k. **Jer. 23:6.** In his days Judah shall be saved, and Israel shall dwell safely: and this is his name whereby he shall be called, THE LORD OUR RIGHTEOUSNESS. **Rom. 4:6–8.** Even as David also describeth the blessedness of the man, unto whom God imputeth righteousness without works, saying, Blessed are they whose iniquities are forgiven, and whose sins are covered. Blessed is the man to whom the Lord will not impute sin. **2 Cor. 5:19, 21.** ... to wit, that God was in Christ, reconciling the world unto himself, not imputing their trespasses unto them; and hath committed unto us the word of reconciliation.... For he hath made him to be sin for us, who knew no sin; that we might be made the righteousness of God in him. **Rom. 3:22, 24–25, 27–28.** ... even the righteousness of God which is by faith of Jesus Christ unto all and upon all them that believe: for there is no difference.... being justified freely by his grace through the redemption that is in Christ Jesus: whom God hath set forth to be a propitiation through faith in his blood, to declare his righteousness for the remission of sins that are past, through the forbearance of God.... Where is boasting then? It is excluded. By what law? of works? Nay: but by the law of faith. Therefore we conclude that a man is justified by faith without the deeds of the law.

l. **Titus 3:5, 7.** Not by works of righteousness which we have done, but according to his mercy he saved us, by the washing of regeneration, and renewing of the Holy Ghost.... that being justified by his grace, we should be made heirs according to

by God imputed to them,[m] and received by faith alone.[n]

Q. 71. *How is justification an act of God's free grace?*

A. Although Christ, by his obedience and death, did make a proper, real, and full satisfaction to God's justice in the behalf of them that are justified;[o] yet inasmuch as God accepteth the satisfaction from a surety, which he might have demanded of them, and did provide this surety, his own only Son,[p] imputing his righteousness to

the hope of eternal life. **Eph. 1:7.** … in whom we have redemption through his blood, the forgiveness of sins, according to the riches of his grace.

m. **Rom. 4:6–8, 11.** Even as David also describeth the blessedness of the man, unto whom God imputeth righteousness without works, saying, Blessed are they whose iniquities are forgiven, and whose sins are covered. Blessed is the man to whom the Lord will not impute sin.… And he received the sign of circumcision, a seal of the righteousness of the faith which he had yet being uncircumcised: that he might be the father of all them that believe, though they be not circumcised; that righteousness might be imputed unto them also. **Rom. 5:17–19.** … (For if by one man's offence death reigned by one; much more they which receive abundance of grace and of the gift of righteousness shall reign in life by one, Jesus Christ.) therefore as by the offence of one judgment came upon all men to condemnation; even so by the righteousness of one the free gift came upon all men unto justification of life. For as by one man's disobedience many were made sinners, so by the obedience of one shall many be made righteous.

n. **Acts 10:43.** To him give all the prophets witness, that through his name whosoever believeth in him shall receive remission of sins. **Gal. 2:16.** … knowing that a man is not justified by the works of the law, but by the faith of Jesus Christ, even we have believed in Jesus Christ, that we might be justified by the faith of Christ, and not by the works of the law: for by the works of the law shall no flesh be justified. **Phil. 3:9.** … and be found in him, not having mine own righteousness, which is of the law, but that which is through the faith of Christ, the righteousness which is of God by faith.

o. **Rom. 5:8–10, 19.** But God commendeth his love toward us, in that, while we were yet sinners, Christ died for us. Much more then, being now justified by his blood, we shall be saved from wrath through him. For if, when we were enemies, we were reconciled to God by the death of his Son, much more, being reconciled, we shall be saved by his life.… For as by one man's disobedience many were made sinners, so by the obedience of one shall many be made righteous.

p. **1 Tim. 2:5–6.** For there is one God, and one mediator between God and men, the man Christ Jesus; who gave himself a ransom for all, to be testified in due time. **Heb. 10:10.** By the which will we are sanctified through the offering of the body of Jesus Christ once for all. **Matt. 20:28.** … even as the Son of man came not to be ministered unto, but to minister, and to give his life a ransom for many. **Dan. 9:24, 26.** Seventy weeks are determined upon thy people and upon thy holy city, to finish the transgression, and to make an end of sins, and to make reconciliation for iniquity, and to bring in everlasting righteousness, and to seal up the vision and prophecy, and to anoint the most Holy.… And after threescore and two weeks shall Messiah

them,^{q} and requiring nothing of them for their justification but faith,^{r} which also is his gift,^{s} their justification is to them of free grace.^{t}

Q. 72. *What is justifying faith?*

A. Justifying faith is a saving grace,^{u} wrought in the heart of a

be cut off, but not for himself: and the people of the prince that shall come shall destroy the city and the sanctuary; and the end thereof shall be with a flood, and unto the end of the war desolations are determined. **Isa. 53:4–6, 10–12.** Surely he hath borne our griefs, and carried our sorrows: yet we did esteem him stricken, smitten of God, and afflicted. But he was wounded for our transgressions, he was bruised for our iniquities: the chastisement of our peace was upon him; and with his stripes we are healed. All we like sheep have gone astray; we have turned every one to his own way; and the LORD hath laid on him the iniquity of us all.... Yet it pleased the LORD to bruise him; he hath put him to grief: when thou shalt make his soul an offering for sin, he shall see his seed, he shall prolong his days, and the pleasure of the LORD shall prosper in his hand. He shall see of the travail of his soul, and shall be satisfied: by his knowledge shall my righteous servant justify many; for he shall bear their iniquities. Therefore will I divide him a portion with the great, and he shall divide the spoil with the strong; because he hath poured out his soul unto death: and he was numbered with the transgressors; and he bare the sin of many, and made intercession for the transgressors. **Heb. 7:22.** ... by so much was Jesus made a surety of a better testament. **Rom. 8:32.** He that spared not his own Son, but delivered him up for us all, how shall he not with him also freely give us all things? **1 Pet. 1:18–19.** ... forasmuch as ye know that ye were not redeemed with corruptible things, as silver and gold, from your vain conversation received by tradition from your fathers; but with the precious blood of Christ, as of a lamb without blemish and without spot.

q. **2 Cor. 5:21.** For he hath made him to be sin for us, who knew no sin; that we might be made the righteousness of God in him. **Rom. 4:6, 11.** Even as David also describeth the blessedness of the man, unto whom God imputeth righteousness without works.... And he received the sign of circumcision, a seal of the righteousness of the faith which he had yet being uncircumcised: that he might be the father of all them that believe, though they be not circumcised; that righteousness might be imputed unto them also.

r. **Rom. 3:24–25.** ... being justified freely by his grace through the redemption that is in Christ Jesus: whom God hath set forth to be a propitiation through faith in his blood, to declare his righteousness for the remission of sins that are past, through the forbearance of God.

s. **Eph. 2:8.** For by grace are ye saved through faith; and that not of yourselves: it is the gift of God.

t. **Eph. 1:7.** ... in whom we have redemption through his blood, the forgiveness of sins, according to the riches of his grace. **Rom. 3:24–25.** ... being justified freely by his grace through the redemption that is in Christ Jesus: whom God hath set forth to be a propitiation through faith in his blood, to declare his righteousness for the remission of sins that are past, through the forbearance of God.

u. **Heb. 10:39.** But we are not of them who draw back unto perdition; but of them that believe to the saving of the soul.

sinner by the Spirit^w and Word of God,^x whereby he, being convinced of his sin and misery, and of the disability in himself and all other creatures to recover him out of his lost condition,^y not only assenteth to the truth of the promise of the gospel,^z but receiveth and resteth upon Christ and his righteousness, therein held forth, for pardon of sin,^a and for the accepting and accounting of his person

w. **2 Cor. 4:13.** We having the same spirit of faith, according as it is written, I believed, and therefore have I spoken; we also believe, and therefore speak. **Eph. 1:17–19.** … that the God of our Lord Jesus Christ, the Father of glory, may give unto you the spirit of wisdom and revelation in the knowledge of him: the eyes of your understanding being enlightened; that ye may know what is the hope of his calling, and what the riches of the glory of his inheritance in the saints, and what is the exceeding greatness of his power to us-ward who believe, according to the working of his mighty power. **1 Cor. 12:3.** Wherefore I give you to understand, that no man speaking by the Spirit of God calleth Jesus accursed: and that no man can say that Jesus is the Lord, but by the Holy Ghost. **1 Pet. 1:2.** … elect according to the foreknowledge of God the Father, through sanctification of the Spirit, unto obedience and sprinkling of the blood of Jesus Christ: Grace unto you, and peace, be multiplied.

x. **Rom. 10:14–17.** How then shall they call on him in whom they have not believed? and how shall they believe in him of whom they have not heard? and how shall they hear without a preacher? And how shall they preach, except they be sent? as it is written, How beautiful are the feet of them that preach the gospel of peace, and bring glad tidings of good things! But they have not all obeyed the gospel. For Esaias saith, Lord, who hath believed our report? So then faith cometh by hearing, and hearing by the word of God. **1 Cor. 1:21.** For after that in the wisdom of God the world by wisdom knew not God, it pleased God by the foolishness of preaching to save them that believe.

y. **Acts 2:37.** Now when they heard this, they were pricked in their heart, and said unto Peter and to the rest of the apostles, Men and brethren, what shall we do? **Acts 16:30.** And [the keeper of the prison] brought them out, and said, Sirs, what must I do to be saved? **John 16:8–9.** And when he is come, he will reprove the world of sin, and of righteousness, and of judgment: of sin, because they believe not on me. **Rom. 6:6.** … knowing this, that our old man is crucified with him, that the body of sin might be destroyed, that henceforth we should not serve sin. **Eph. 2:1.** And you hath he quickened, who were dead in trespasses and sins. **Acts 4:12.** Neither is there salvation in any other: for there is none other name under heaven given among men, whereby we must be saved.

z. **Eph. 1:13.** … in whom ye also trusted, after that ye heard the word of truth, the gospel of your salvation: in whom also after that ye believed, ye were sealed with that holy Spirit of promise. **Heb. 11:13.** These all died in faith, not having received the promises, but having seen them afar off, and were persuaded of them, and embraced them, and confessed that they were strangers and pilgrims on the earth.

a. **John 1:12.** But as many as received him, to them gave he power to become the sons of God, even to them that believe on his name. **Acts 16:31.** And they said, Believe on the Lord Jesus Christ, and thou shalt be saved, and thy house. **Acts 10:43.** To him give all the prophets witness, that through his name whosoever believeth in

righteous in the sight of God for salvation.[b]

Q. 73. *How doth faith justify a sinner in the sight of God?*

A. Faith justifies a sinner in the sight of God, not because of those other graces which do always accompany it, or of good works that are the fruits of it,[c] nor as if the grace of faith, or any act thereof, were imputed to him for his justification;[d] but only as it is an instrument by which he receiveth and applieth Christ and his righteousness.[e]

Q. 74. *What is adoption?*

A. Adoption is an act of the free grace of God,[f] in and for his only Son Jesus Christ,[g] whereby all those that are justified are received into the number of his children,[h] have his name put upon

him shall receive remission of sins. **Zech. 3:8–9.** Hear now, O Joshua the high priest, thou, and thy fellows that sit before thee: for they are men wondered at: for, behold, I will bring forth my servant the BRANCH. For behold the stone that I have laid before Joshua; upon one stone shall be seven eyes: behold, I will engrave the graving thereof, saith the LORD of hosts, and I will remove the iniquity of that land in one day.

b. **Phil. 3:9.** … and be found in him, not having mine own righteousness, which is of the law, but that which is through the faith of Christ, the righteousness which is of God by faith. **Acts 15:11.** But we believe that through the grace of the Lord Jesus Christ we shall be saved, even as they.

c. **Gal. 3:11.** But that no man is justified by the law in the sight of God, it is evident: for, The just shall live by faith. **Rom. 3:28.** Therefore we conclude that a man is justified by faith without the deeds of the law.

d. **Rom. 4:5.** But to him that worketh not, but believeth on him that justifieth the ungodly, his faith is counted for righteousness. **Rom. 10:10.** For with the heart man believeth unto righteousness; and with the mouth confession is made unto salvation.

e. **John 1:12.** But as many as received him, to them gave he power to become the sons of God, even to them that believe on his name. **Phil. 3:9.** … and be found in him, not having mine own righteousness, which is of the law, but that which is through the faith of Christ, the righteousness which is of God by faith. **Gal. 2:16.** … knowing that a man is not justified by the works of the law, but by the faith of Jesus Christ, even we have believed in Jesus Christ, that we might be justified by the faith of Christ, and not by the works of the law: for by the works of the law shall no flesh be justified.

f. **1 John 3:1.** Behold, what manner of love the Father hath bestowed upon us, that we should be called the sons of God: therefore the world knoweth us not, because it knew him not.

g. **Eph. 1:5.** … having predestinated us unto the adoption of children by Jesus Christ to himself, according to the good pleasure of his will. **Gal. 4:4–5.** But when the fulness of the time was come, God sent forth his Son, made of a woman, made under the law, to redeem them that were under the law, that we might receive the adoption of sons.

h. **John 1:12.** But as many as received him, to them gave he power to become the sons of God, even to them that believe on his name. **Rom. 8:15–16.** For ye have

them,[i] the Spirit of his Son given to them,[k] are under his fatherly care and dispensations,[l] admitted to all the liberties and privileges of the sons of God, made heirs of all the promises, and fellow heirs with Christ in glory.[m]

Q. 75. *What is sanctification?*

A. Sanctification is a work of God's grace, whereby they whom God hath, before the foundation of the world, chosen to be holy, are in time, through the powerful operation of his Spirit[n] applying the

not received the spirit of bondage again to fear; but ye have received the Spirit of adoption, whereby we cry, Abba, Father. The Spirit itself beareth witness with our spirit, that we are the children of God.

i. **Num. 6:24–27.** The LORD bless thee, and keep thee: the LORD make his face shine upon thee, and be gracious unto thee: the LORD lift up his countenance upon thee, and give thee peace. And they shall put my name upon the children of Israel; and I will bless them. **Amos 9:12.** … that they may possess the remnant of Edom, and of all the heathen, which are called by my name, saith the LORD that doeth this. **2 Cor. 6:18.** … and will be a Father unto you, and ye shall be my sons and daughters, saith the Lord Almighty. **Rev. 3:12.** Him that overcometh will I make a pillar in the temple of my God, and he shall go no more out: and I will write upon him the name of my God, and the name of the city of my God, which is new Jerusalem, which cometh down out of heaven from my God: and I will write upon him my new name.

k. **Gal. 4:6.** And because ye are sons, God hath sent forth the Spirit of his Son into your hearts, crying, Abba, Father.

l. **Ps. 103:13.** Like as a father pitieth his children, so the LORD pitieth them that fear him. **Prov. 14:26.** In the fear of the LORD is strong confidence: and his children shall have a place of refuge. **Matt. 6:32.** … (for after all these things do the Gentiles seek:) for your heavenly Father knoweth that ye have need of all these things. **Heb. 12:5–7, 11.** And ye have forgotten the exhortation which speaketh unto you as unto children, My son, despise not thou the chastening of the Lord, nor faint when thou art rebuked of him: for whom the Lord loveth he chasteneth, and scourgeth every son whom he receiveth. If ye endure chastening, God dealeth with you as with sons; for what son is he whom the father chasteneth not?… Now no chastening for the present seemeth to be joyous, but grievous: nevertheless afterward it yieldeth the peaceable fruit of righteousness unto them which are exercised thereby.

m. **Heb. 6:12.** … that ye be not slothful, but followers of them who through faith and patience inherit the promises. **Rom. 8:17.** … and if children, then heirs; heirs of God, and joint-heirs with Christ; if so be that we suffer with him, that we may be also glorified together. **1 Pet. 1:3–4.** Blessed be the God and Father of our Lord Jesus Christ, which according to his abundant mercy hath begotten us again unto a lively hope by the resurrection of Jesus Christ from the dead, to an inheritance incorruptible, and undefiled, and that fadeth not away, reserved in heaven for you.

n. **Ezek. 36:27.** And I will put my spirit within you, and cause you to walk in my statutes, and ye shall keep my judgments, and do them. **Phil. 2:13.** For it is God which worketh in you both to will and to do of his good pleasure. **2 Thess. 2:13.** But

death and resurrection of Christ unto them,[o] renewed in their whole
man after the image of God;[p] having the seeds of repentance unto
life, and all other saving graces, put into their hearts,[q] and those graces
so stirred up, increased, and strengthened,[r] as that they more and
more die unto sin, and rise unto newness of life.[s]

we are bound to give thanks alway to God for you, brethren beloved of the Lord,
because God hath from the beginning chosen you to salvation through sanctification
of the Spirit and belief of the truth. **Eph. 1:4.** ... according as he hath chosen us in
him before the foundation of the world, that we should be holy and without blame
before him in love. **1 Cor. 6:11.** And such were some of you: but ye are washed, but
ye are sanctified, but ye are justified in the name of the Lord Jesus, and by the Spirit of
our God.

o. **Rom. 6:4–6.** Therefore we are buried with him by baptism into death: that
like as Christ was raised up from the dead by the glory of the Father, even so we also
should walk in newness of life. For if we have been planted together in the likeness of
his death, we shall be also in the likeness of his resurrection: knowing this, that our old
man is crucified with him, that the body of sin might be destroyed, that henceforth we
should not serve sin. **Col. 3:1–3.** If ye then be risen with Christ, seek those things
which are above, where Christ sitteth on the right hand of God. Set your affection on
things above, not on things on the earth. For ye are dead, and your life is hid with
Christ in God. **Phil. 3:10.** ... that I may know him, and the power of his resurrection, and the fellowship of his sufferings, being made conformable unto his death.

p. **2 Cor. 5:17.** Therefore if any man be in Christ, he is a new creature: old
things are passed away; behold, all things are become new. **Eph. 4:23–24.** ... and be
renewed in the spirit of your mind; and that ye put on the new man, which after God
is created in righteousness and true holiness. **1 Thess. 5:23.** And the very God of
peace sanctify you wholly; and I pray God your whole spirit and soul and body be
preserved blameless unto the coming of our Lord Jesus Christ.

q. **Acts 11:18.** When they heard these things, they held their peace, and glorified
God, saying, Then hath God also to the Gentiles granted repentance unto life.
1 John 3:9. Whosoever is born of God doth not commit sin; for his seed remaineth in
him: and he cannot sin, because he is born of God.

r. **Jude 20.** But ye, beloved, building up yourselves on your most holy faith,
praying in the Holy Ghost. **Heb. 6:11–12.** And we desire that every one of you do
shew the same diligence to the full assurance of hope unto the end: that ye be not
slothful, but followers of them who through faith and patience inherit the promises.
Eph. 3:16–19. ... that he would grant you, according to the riches of his glory, to be
strengthened with might by his Spirit in the inner man; that Christ may dwell in your
hearts by faith; that ye, being rooted and grounded in love, may be able to comprehend with all saints what is the breadth, and length, and depth, and height; and to
know the love of Christ, which passeth knowledge, that ye might be filled with all the
fulness of God. **Col. 1:10–11.** ... that ye might walk worthy of the Lord unto all
pleasing, being fruitful in every good work, and increasing in the knowledge of God;
strengthened with all might, according to his glorious power, unto all patience and
longsuffering with joyfulness.

s. **Ezek. 36:25–27.** Then will I sprinkle clean water upon you, and ye shall be

Q. 76. *What is repentance unto life?*

A. Repentance unto life is a saving grace,[t] wrought in the heart of a sinner by the Spirit[u] and Word of God,[w] whereby, out of the sight and sense, not only of the danger,[x] but also of the filthiness and

clean: from all your filthiness, and from all your idols, will I cleanse you. A new heart also will I give you, and a new spirit will I put within you: and I will take away the stony heart out of your flesh, and I will give you an heart of flesh. And I will put my spirit within you, and cause you to walk in my statutes, and ye shall keep my judgments, and do them. **Rom. 6:4, 6, 12–14.** Therefore we are buried with him by baptism into death: that like as Christ was raised up from the dead by the glory of the Father, even so we also should walk in newness of life.… knowing this, that our old man is crucified with him, that the body of sin might be destroyed, that henceforth we should not serve sin.… Let not sin therefore reign in your mortal body, that ye should obey it in the lusts thereof. Neither yield ye your members as instruments of unrighteousness unto sin: but yield yourselves unto God, as those that are alive from the dead, and your members as instruments of righteousness unto God. For sin shall not have dominion over you: for ye are not under the law, but under grace. **2 Cor. 7:1.** Having therefore these promises, dearly beloved, let us cleanse ourselves from all filthiness of the flesh and spirit, perfecting holiness in the fear of God. **1 Pet. 2:24.** … who his own self bare our sins in his own body on the tree, that we, being dead to sins, should live unto righteousness: by whose stripes ye were healed. **Gal. 5:24.** And they that are Christ's have crucified the flesh with the affections and lusts.

t. **2 Tim. 2:25.** … in meekness instructing those that oppose themselves; if God peradventure will give them repentance to the acknowledging of the truth. **Acts 11:18.** When they heard these things, they held their peace, and glorified God, saying, Then hath God also to the Gentiles granted repentance unto life.

u. **Zech. 12:10.** And I will pour upon the house of David, and upon the inhabitants of Jerusalem, the spirit of grace and of supplications: and they shall look upon me whom they have pierced, and they shall mourn for him, as one mourneth for his only son, and shall be in bitterness for him, as one that is in bitterness for his firstborn.

w. **Acts 11:18, 20–21.** When they heard these things, they held their peace, and glorified God, saying, Then hath God also to the Gentiles granted repentance unto life.… And some of them were men of Cyprus and Cyrene, which, when they were come to Antioch, spake unto the Grecians, preaching the Lord Jesus. And the hand of the Lord was with them: and a great number believed, and turned unto the Lord.

x. **Ezek. 18:28, 30, 32.** Because he considereth, and turneth away from all his transgressions that he hath committed, he shall surely live, he shall not die.… Therefore I will judge you, O house of Israel, every one according to his ways, saith the Lord GOD. Repent, and turn yourselves from all your transgressions; so iniquity shall not be your ruin.… For I have no pleasure in the death of him that dieth, saith the Lord GOD: wherefore turn yourselves, and live ye. **Luke 15:17–18.** And when he came to himself, he said, How many hired servants of my father's have bread enough and to spare, and I perish with hunger! I will arise and go to my father, and will say unto him, Father, I have sinned against heaven, and before thee. **Hos. 2:6–7.** Therefore, behold, I will hedge up thy way with thorns, and make a wall, that she shall not find her paths. And she shall follow after her lovers, but she shall not overtake them; and she

odiousness of his sins,[y] and upon the apprehension of God's mercy in Christ to such as are penitent,[z] he so grieves for[a] and hates his sins,[b] as that he turns from them all to God,[c] purposing and endeavoring

shall seek them, but shall not find them: then shall she say, I will go and return to my first husband; for then was it better with me than now.

y. **Ezek. 36:31.** Then shall ye remember your own evil ways, and your doings that were not good, and shall loathe yourselves in your own sight for your iniquities and for your abominations. **Isa. 30:22.** Ye shall defile also the covering of thy graven images of silver, and the ornament of thy molten images of gold: thou shalt cast them away as a menstruous cloth; thou shalt say unto it, Get thee hence. **Phil. 3:7–8.** But what things were gain to me, those I counted loss for Christ. Yea doubtless, and I count all things but loss for the excellency of the knowledge of Christ Jesus my Lord: for whom I have suffered the loss of all things, and do count them but dung, that I may win Christ.

z. **Joel 2:12–13.** Therefore also now, saith the LORD, turn ye even to me with all your heart, and with fasting, and with weeping, and with mourning: and rend your heart, and not your garments, and turn unto the LORD your God: for he is gracious and merciful, slow to anger, and of great kindness, and repenteth him of the evil. **Ps. 51:1–4.** Have mercy upon me, O God, according to thy lovingkindness: according unto the multitude of thy tender mercies blot out my transgressions. Wash me thoroughly from mine iniquity, and cleanse me from my sin. For I acknowledge my transgressions: and my sin is ever before me. Against thee, thee only, have I sinned, and done this evil in thy sight: that thou mightest be justified when thou speakest, and be clear when thou judgest. **Luke 15:7, 10.** I say unto you, that likewise joy shall be in heaven over one sinner that repenteth, more than over ninety and nine just persons, which need no repentance.… Likewise, I say unto you, there is joy in the presence of the angels of God over one sinner that repenteth. **Acts 2:37.** Now when they heard this, they were pricked in their heart, and said unto Peter and to the rest of the apostles, Men and brethren, what shall we do?

a. **Jer. 31:18–19.** I have surely heard Ephraim bemoaning himself thus; Thou hast chastised me, and I was chastised, as a bullock unaccustomed to the yoke: turn thou me, and I shall be turned; for thou art the LORD my God. Surely after that I was turned, I repented; and after that I was instructed, I smote upon my thigh: I was ashamed, yea, even confounded, because I did bear the reproach of my youth. **Ps. 32:5.** I acknowledged my sin unto thee, and mine iniquity have I not hid. I said, I will confess my transgressions unto the LORD; and thou forgavest the iniquity of my sin. Selah.

b. **2 Cor. 7:11.** For behold this selfsame thing, that ye sorrowed after a godly sort, what carefulness it wrought in you, yea, what clearing of yourselves, yea, what indignation, yea, what fear, yea, what vehement desire, yea, what zeal, yea, what revenge! In all things ye have approved yourselves to be clear in this matter.

c. **Luke 1:16–17.** And many of the children of Israel shall he turn to the Lord their God. And he shall go before him in the spirit and power of Elias, to turn the hearts of the fathers to the children, and the disobedient to the wisdom of the just; to make ready a people prepared for the Lord. **1 Thess. 1:9.** For they themselves shew of us what manner of entering in we had unto you, and how ye turned to God from

constantly to walk with him in all the ways of new obedience.[d]

Q. 77. *Wherein do justification and sanctification differ?*

A. Although sanctification be inseparably joined with justification,[e] yet they differ, in that God in justification imputeth the righteousness of Christ;[f] in sanctification his Spirit infuseth grace, and enableth to the exercise thereof;[g] in the former, sin is pardoned;[h] in

idols to serve the living and true God. **Acts 26:18.** [I send thee] to open their eyes, and to turn them from darkness to light, and from the power of Satan unto God, that they may receive forgiveness of sins, and inheritance among them which are sanctified by faith that is in me. **Ezek. 14:6.** Therefore say unto the house of Israel, Thus saith the Lord GOD; Repent, and turn yourselves from your idols; and turn away your faces from all your abominations. **1 Kings 8:47–48.** Yet if they shall bethink themselves in the land whither they were carried captives, and repent, and make supplication unto thee in the land of them that carried them captives, saying, We have sinned, and have done perversely, we have committed wickedness; and so return unto thee with all their heart, and with all their soul, in the land of their enemies, which led them away captive, and pray unto thee toward their land, which thou gavest unto their fathers, the city which thou hast chosen, and the house which I have built for thy name.

d. **2 Chron. 7:14.** If my people, which are called by my name, shall humble themselves, and pray, and seek my face, and turn from their wicked ways; then will I hear from heaven, and will forgive their sin, and will heal their land. **Ps. 119:57–64.** Thou art my portion, O LORD: I have said that I would keep thy words. I entreated thy favour with my whole heart: be merciful unto me according to thy word. I thought on my ways, and turned my feet unto thy testimonies. I made haste, and delayed not to keep thy commandments. The bands of the wicked have robbed me: but I have not forgotten thy law. At midnight I will rise to give thanks unto thee because of thy righteous judgments. I am a companion of all them that fear thee, and of them that keep thy precepts. The earth, O LORD, is full of thy mercy: teach me thy statutes. **Matt. 3:8.** Bring forth therefore fruits meet for repentance. **2 Cor. 7:10.** For godly sorrow worketh repentance to salvation not to be repented of: but the sorrow of the world worketh death. **Luke 1:6.** And they were both righteous before God, walking in all the commandments and ordinances of the Lord blameless.

e. **1 Cor. 6:11.** And such were some of you: but ye are washed, but ye are sanctified, but ye are justified in the name of the Lord Jesus, and by the Spirit of our God. **1 Cor. 1:30.** But of him are ye in Christ Jesus, who of God is made unto us wisdom, and righteousness, and sanctification, and redemption.

f. **Rom. 4:6, 8.** Even as David also describeth the blessedness of the man, unto whom God imputeth righteousness without works, … Blessed is the man to whom the Lord will not impute sin.

g. **Ezek. 36:27.** And I will put my spirit within you, and cause you to walk in my statutes, and ye shall keep my judgments, and do them. **Heb. 9:13–14.** For if the blood of bulls and of goats, and the ashes of an heifer sprinkling the unclean, sanctifieth to the purifying of the flesh: how much more shall the blood of Christ, who through the eternal Spirit offered himself without spot to God, purge your conscience from dead works to serve the living God?

the other, it is subdued:[i] the one doth equally free all believers from the revenging wrath of God, and that perfectly in this life, that they never fall into condemnation;[k] the other is neither equal in all,[l] nor in this life perfect in any,[m] but growing up to perfection.[n]

Q. 78. *Whence ariseth the imperfection of sanctification in believers?*

A. The imperfection of sanctification in believers ariseth from the remnants of sin abiding in every part of them, and the perpetual lustings of the flesh against the spirit; whereby they are often foiled with temptations, and fall into many sins,[o] are hindered in all their

h. **Rom. 3:24–25.** … being justified freely by his grace through the redemption that is in Christ Jesus: whom God hath set forth to be a propitiation through faith in his blood, to declare his righteousness for the remission of sins that are past, through the forbearance of God.

i. **Rom. 6:6, 14.** … knowing this, that our old man is crucified with him, that the body of sin might be destroyed, that henceforth we should not serve sin.… For sin shall not have dominion over you: for ye are not under the law, but under grace.

k. **Rom. 8:33–34.** Who shall lay any thing to the charge of God's elect? It is God that justifieth. Who is he that condemneth? It is Christ that died, yea rather, that is risen again, who is even at the right hand of God, who also maketh intercession for us.

l. **1 John 2:12–14.** I write unto you, little children, because your sins are forgiven you for his name's sake. I write unto you, fathers, because ye have known him that is from the beginning. I write unto you, young men, because ye have overcome the wicked one. I write unto you, little children, because ye have known the Father. I have written unto you, fathers, because ye have known him that is from the beginning. I have written unto you, young men, because ye are strong, and the word of God abideth in you, and ye have overcome the wicked one. **Heb. 5:12–14.** For when for the time ye ought to be teachers, ye have need that one teach you again which be the first principles of the oracles of God; and are become such as have need of milk, and not of strong meat. For every one that useth milk is unskilful in the word of righteousness: for he is a babe. But strong meat belongeth to them that are of full age, even those who by reason of use have their senses exercised to discern both good and evil.

m. **1 John 1:8, 10.** If we say that we have no sin, we deceive ourselves, and the truth is not in us.… If we say that we have not sinned, we make him a liar, and his word is not in us.

n. **2 Cor. 7:1.** Having therefore these promises, dearly beloved, let us cleanse ourselves from all filthiness of the flesh and spirit, perfecting holiness in the fear of God. **Phil. 3:12–14.** Not as though I had already attained, either were already perfect: but I follow after, if that I may apprehend that for which also I am apprehended of Christ Jesus. Brethren, I count not myself to have apprehended: but this one thing I do, forgetting those things which are behind, and reaching forth unto those things which are before, I press toward the mark for the prize of the high calling of God in Christ Jesus.

o. **Rom. 7:18, 23.** For I know that in me (that is, in my flesh,) dwelleth no good thing: for to will is present with me; but how to perform that which is good I find

spiritual services,ᵖ and their best works are imperfect and defiled in the sight of God.ۊ

Q. 79. *May not true believers, by reason of their imperfections, and the many temptations and sins they are overtaken with, fall away from the state of grace?*

A. True believers, by reason of the unchangeable love of God,ʳ and his decree and covenant to give them perseverance,ˢ their inseparable union with Christ,ᵗ his continual intercession for them,ᵘ

---

not.... But I see another law in my members, warring against the law of my mind, and bringing me into captivity to the law of sin which is in my members. **See Mark 14:66–72. Gal. 2:11–12.** But when Peter was come to Antioch, I withstood him to the face, because he was to be blamed. For before that certain came from James, he did eat with the Gentiles: but when they were come, he withdrew and separated himself, fearing them which were of the circumcision.

p. **Heb. 12:1.** Wherefore seeing we also are compassed about with so great a cloud of witnesses, let us lay aside every weight, and the sin which doth so easily beset us, and let us run with patience the race that is set before us.

q. **Isa. 64:6.** But we are all as an unclean thing, and all our righteousnesses are as filthy rags; and we all do fade as a leaf; and our iniquities, like the wind, have taken us away. **Ex. 28:38.** And it shall be upon Aaron's forehead, that Aaron may bear the iniquity of the holy things, which the children of Israel shall hallow in all their holy gifts; and it shall be always upon his forehead, that they may be accepted before the LORD. **Gal. 5:16–18.** This I say then, Walk in the Spirit, and ye shall not fulfil the lust of the flesh. For the flesh lusteth against the Spirit, and the Spirit against the flesh: and these are contrary the one to the other: so that ye cannot do the things that ye would. But if ye be led of the Spirit, ye are not under the law.

r. **Jer. 31:3.** The LORD hath appeared of old unto me, saying, Yea, I have loved thee with an everlasting love: therefore with lovingkindness have I drawn thee.

s. **2 Tim. 2:19.** Nevertheless the foundation of God standeth sure, having this seal, The Lord knoweth them that are his. And, Let every one that nameth the name of Christ depart from iniquity. **Heb. 13:20–21.** Now the God of peace, that brought again from the dead our Lord Jesus, that great shepherd of the sheep, through the blood of the everlasting covenant, make you perfect in every good work to do his will, working in you that which is wellpleasing in his sight, through Jesus Christ; to whom be glory for ever and ever. Amen. **2 Sam. 23:5.** Although my house be not so with God; yet he hath made with me an everlasting covenant, ordered in all things, and sure: for this is all my salvation, and all my desire, although he make it not to grow.

t. **1 Cor. 1:8–9.** Who shall also confirm you unto the end, that ye may be blameless in the day of our Lord Jesus Christ. God is faithful, by whom ye were called unto the fellowship of his Son Jesus Christ our Lord.

u. **Heb. 7:25.** Wherefore he is able also to save them to the uttermost that come unto God by him, seeing he ever liveth to make intercession for them. **Luke 22:32.** But I have prayed for thee, that thy faith fail not: and when thou art converted, strengthen thy brethren.

and the Spirit and seed of God abiding in them,[w] can neither totally nor finally fall away from the state of grace,[x] but are kept by the power of God through faith unto salvation.[y]

Q. 80. *Can true believers be infallibly assured that they are in the estate of grace, and that they shall persevere therein unto salvation?*

A. Such as truly believe in Christ, and endeavor to walk in all good conscience before him,[z] may, without extraordinary revelation, by faith grounded upon the truth of God's promises, and by the Spirit enabling them to discern in themselves those graces to which the promises of life are made,[a] and bearing witness with their spirits that

w. **1 John 3:9.** Whosoever is born of God doth not commit sin; for his seed remaineth in him: and he cannot sin, because he is born of God. **1 John 2:27.** But the anointing which ye have received of him abideth in you, and ye need not that any man teach you: but as the same anointing teacheth you of all things, and is truth, and is no lie, and even as it hath taught you, ye shall abide in him.

x. **Jer. 32:40.** And I will make an everlasting covenant with them, that I will not turn away from them, to do them good; but I will put my fear in their hearts, that they shall not depart from me. **John 10:28.** And I give unto them eternal life; and they shall never perish, neither shall any man pluck them out of my hand.

y. **1 Pet. 1:5.** … who are kept by the power of God through faith unto salvation ready to be revealed in the last time.

z. **1 John 2:3.** And hereby we do know that we know him, if we keep his commandments. **Heb. 10:19–23.** Having therefore, brethren, boldness to enter into the holiest by the blood of Jesus, by a new and living way, which he hath consecrated for us, through the veil, that is to say, his flesh; and having an high priest over the house of God; let us draw near with a true heart in full assurance of faith, having our hearts sprinkled from an evil conscience, and our bodies washed with pure water. Let us hold fast the profession of our faith without wavering; (for he is faithful that promised.)

a. **1 Cor. 2:12.** Now we have received, not the spirit of the world, but the spirit which is of God; that we might know the things that are freely given to us of God. **1 John 3:14, 18–19, 21, 24.** We know that we have passed from death unto life, because we love the brethren. He that loveth not his brother abideth in death.… My little children, let us not love in word, neither in tongue; but in deed and in truth. And hereby we know that we are of the truth, and shall assure our hearts before him.… Beloved, if our heart condemn us not, then have we confidence toward God.… And he that keepeth his commandments dwelleth in him, and he in him. And hereby we know that he abideth in us, by the Spirit which he hath given us. **1 John 4:13, 16.** Hereby know we that we dwell in him, and he in us, because he hath given us of his Spirit.… And we have known and believed the love that God hath to us. God is love; and he that dwelleth in love dwelleth in God, and God in him. **Heb. 6:11–12.** And we desire that every one of you do shew the same diligence to the full assurance of hope unto the end: that ye be not slothful, but followers of them who through faith and patience inherit the promises.

they are the children of God,[b] be infallibly assured that they are in the estate of grace, and shall persevere therein unto salvation.[c]

Q. 81. *Are all true believers at all times assured of their present being in the estate of grace, and that they shall be saved?*

A. Assurance of grace and salvation not being of the essence of faith,[d] true believers may wait long before they obtain it;[e] and, after the enjoyment thereof, may have it weakened and intermitted, through manifold distempers, sins, temptations, and desertions;[f] yet are they

b. **Rom. 8:15–16.** For ye have not received the spirit of bondage again to fear; but ye have received the Spirit of adoption, whereby we cry, Abba, Father. The Spirit itself beareth witness with our spirit, that we are the children of God.

c. **1 John 5:13.** These things have I written unto you that believe on the name of the Son of God; that ye may know that ye have eternal life, and that ye may believe on the name of the Son of God. **Heb. 6:19–20.** … which hope we have as an anchor of the soul, both sure and stedfast, and which entereth into that within the veil; whither the forerunner is for us entered, even Jesus, made an high priest for ever after the order of Melchisedec. **See 2 Pet. 1:5–11.**

d. **Eph. 1:13.** … in whom ye also trusted, after that ye heard the word of truth, the gospel of your salvation: in whom also after that ye believed, ye were sealed with that holy Spirit of promise.

e. **Isa. 50:10.** Who is among you that feareth the LORD, that obeyeth the voice of his servant, that walketh in darkness, and hath no light? let him trust in the name of the LORD, and stay upon his God. **Ps. 88:1–3, 6–7, 9–10, 13–15.** O LORD God of my salvation, I have cried day and night before thee: let my prayer come before thee: incline thine ear unto my cry; for my soul is full of troubles: and my life draweth nigh unto the grave.… Thou hast laid me in the lowest pit, in darkness, in the deeps. Thy wrath lieth hard upon me, and thou hast afflicted me with all thy waves. Selah.… Mine eye mourneth by reason of affliction: LORD, I have called daily upon thee, I have stretched out my hands unto thee. Wilt thou shew wonders to the dead? shall the dead arise and praise thee? Selah.… But unto thee have I cried, O LORD; and in the morning shall my prayer prevent thee. LORD, why castest thou off my soul? why hidest thou thy face from me? I am afflicted and ready to die from my youth up: while I suffer thy terrors I am distracted.

f. **Ps. 77:1–12.** I cried unto God with my voice, even unto God with my voice; and he gave ear unto me. In the day of my trouble I sought the Lord.… Will the Lord cast off for ever? and will he be favourable no more? Is his mercy clean gone for ever? doth his promise fail for evermore? Hath God forgotten to be gracious? hath he in anger shut up his tender mercies? Selah. And I said, This is my infirmity: but I will remember the years of the right hand of the most High. I will remember the works of the LORD: surely I will remember thy wonders of old. I will meditate also of all thy work, and talk of thy doings. **Ps. 51:8, 12.** Make me to hear joy and gladness; that the bones which thou hast broken may rejoice.… Restore unto me the joy of thy salvation; and uphold me with thy free spirit. **Ps. 31:22.** For I said in my haste, I am cut off from before thine eyes: nevertheless thou heardest the voice of my supplica-

never left without such a presence and support of the Spirit of God as keeps them from sinking into utter despair.[g]

Q. 82. *What is the communion in glory which the members of the invisible church have with Christ?*

A. The communion in glory which the members of the invisible church have with Christ, is in this life,[h] immediately after death,[i] and at last perfected at the resurrection and day of judgment.[k]

Q. 83. *What is the communion in glory with Christ which the members of the invisible church enjoy in this life?*

A. The members of the invisible church have communicated to

---

tions when I cried unto thee. **Ps. 22:1.** My God, my God, why hast thou forsaken me? why art thou so far from helping me, and from the words of my roaring? **Eph. 4:30.** And grieve not the holy Spirit of God, whereby ye are sealed unto the day of redemption. **Luke 22:31–34.** And the Lord said, Simon, Simon, behold, Satan hath desired to have you, that he may sift you as wheat: but I have prayed for thee, that thy faith fail not: and when thou art converted, strengthen thy brethren. And he said unto him, Lord, I am ready to go with thee, both into prison, and to death. And he said, I tell thee, Peter, the cock shall not crow this day, before that thou shalt thrice deny that thou knowest me.

g. **1 John 3:9.** Whosoever is born of God doth not commit sin; for his seed remaineth in him: and he cannot sin, because he is born of God. **Ps. 73:15, 23.** If I say, I will speak thus; behold, I should offend against the generation of thy children.... Nevertheless I am continually with thee: thou hast holden me by my right hand. **Isa. 54:7–10.** For a small moment have I forsaken thee; but with great mercies will I gather thee. In a little wrath I hid my face from thee for a moment; but with everlasting kindness will I have mercy on thee, saith the LORD thy Redeemer. For this is as the waters of Noah unto me: for as I have sworn that the waters of Noah should no more go over the earth; so have I sworn that I would not be wroth with thee, nor rebuke thee. For the mountains shall depart, and the hills be removed; but my kindness shall not depart from thee, neither shall the covenant of my peace be removed, saith the LORD that hath mercy on thee. **1 Pet. 4:12–14.** Beloved, think it not strange concerning the fiery trial which is to try you, as though some strange thing happened unto you: but rejoice, inasmuch as ye are partakers of Christ's sufferings; that, when his glory shall be revealed, ye may be glad also with exceeding joy. If ye be reproached for the name of Christ, happy are ye; for the spirit of glory and of God resteth upon you.

h. **2 Cor. 3:18.** But we all, with open face beholding as in a glass the glory of the Lord, are changed into the same image from glory to glory, even as by the Spirit of the Lord.

i. **Luke 23:43.** And Jesus said unto him, Verily I say unto thee, Today shalt thou be with me in paradise.

k. **1 Thess. 4:17.** Then we which are alive and remain shall be caught up together with them in the clouds, to meet the Lord in the air: and so shall we ever be with the Lord.

them in this life the firstfruits of glory with Christ, as they are members of him their head, and so in him are interested in that glory which he is fully possessed of;[l] and, as an earnest thereof, enjoy the sense of God's love,[m] peace of conscience, joy in the Holy Ghost, and hope of glory;[n] as, on the contrary, sense of God's revenging wrath, horror of conscience, and a fearful expectation of judgment, are to the wicked the beginning of their torments which they shall endure after death.[o]

Q. 84. *Shall all men die?*

A. Death being threatened as the wages of sin,[p] it is appointed unto all men once to die;[q] for that all have sinned.[r]

Q. 85. *Death being the wages of sin, why are not the righteous delivered from death, seeing all their sins are forgiven in Christ?*

A. The righteous shall be delivered from death itself at the last day, and even in death are delivered from the sting and curse of it;[s] so

l. **Eph. 2:5–6.** Even when we were dead in sins, [God] hath quickened us together with Christ, (by grace ye are saved;) and hath raised us up together, and made us sit together in heavenly places in Christ Jesus.

m. **Rom. 5:5.** And hope maketh not ashamed; because the love of God is shed abroad in our hearts by the Holy Ghost which is given unto us. **2 Cor. 1:22.** ... who hath also sealed us, and given the earnest of the Spirit in our hearts.

n. **Rom. 5:1–2.** Therefore being justified by faith, we have peace with God through our Lord Jesus Christ: by whom also we have access by faith into this grace wherein we stand, and rejoice in hope of the glory of God. **Rom. 14:17.** For the kingdom of God is not meat and drink; but righteousness, and peace, and joy in the Holy Ghost. **2 Pet. 3:18.** But grow in grace, and in the knowledge of our Lord and Saviour Jesus Christ. To him be glory both now and for ever. Amen.

o. **Gen. 4:13.** And Cain said unto the LORD, My punishment is greater than I can bear. **Matt. 27:4.** ... saying, I have sinned in that I have betrayed the innocent blood. And they said, What is that to us? see thou to that. **Heb. 10:27.** ... but a certain fearful looking for of judgment and fiery indignation, which shall devour the adversaries. **Rom. 2:9.** ... tribulation and anguish, upon every soul of man that doeth evil, of the Jew first, and also of the Gentile. **Mark 9:44.** ... where their worm dieth not, and the fire is not quenched.

p. **Rom. 6:23.** For the wages of sin is death; but the gift of God is eternal life through Jesus Christ our Lord.

q. **Heb. 9:27.** And as it is appointed unto men once to die, but after this the judgment ...

r. **Rom. 5:12.** Wherefore, as by one man sin entered into the world, and death by sin; and so death passed upon all men, for that all have sinned ...

s. **1 Cor. 15:26, 55–57.** The last enemy that shall be destroyed is death.... O death, where is thy sting? O grave, where is thy victory? The sting of death is sin; and

that, although they die, yet it is out of God's love,ᵗ to free them perfectly from sin and misery,ᵘ and to make them capable of further communion with Christ in glory, which they then enter upon.ʷ

Q. 86. *What is the communion in glory with Christ, which the members of the invisible church enjoy immediately after death?*

A. The communion in glory with Christ, which the members of the invisible church enjoy immediately after death, is, in that their souls are then made perfect in holiness,ˣ and received into the highest heavens,ʸ where they behold the face of God in light and

the strength of sin is the law. But thanks be to God, which giveth us the victory through our Lord Jesus Christ. **Heb. 2:15.** And deliver them who through fear of death were all their lifetime subject to bondage. **John 11:25–26.** Jesus said unto her, I am the resurrection, and the life: he that believeth in me, though he were dead, yet shall he live: and whosoever liveth and believeth in me shall never die. Believest thou this?

t. **Isa. 57:1–2.** The righteous perisheth, and no man layeth it to heart: and merciful men are taken away, none considering that the righteous is taken away from the evil to come. He shall enter into peace: they shall rest in their beds, each one walking in his uprightness. **2 Kings 22:20.** Behold therefore, I will gather thee unto thy fathers, and thou shalt be gathered into thy grave in peace; and thine eyes shall not see all the evil which I will bring upon this place. And they brought the king word again.

u. **Rev. 14:13.** And I heard a voice from heaven saying unto me, Write, Blessed are the dead which die in the Lord from henceforth: Yea, saith the Spirit, that they may rest from their labours; and their works do follow them. **Eph. 5:27.** … that he might present it to himself a glorious church, not having spot, or wrinkle, or any such thing; but that it should be holy and without blemish.

w. **Luke 23:43.** And Jesus said unto him, Verily I say unto thee, To day shalt thou be with me in paradise. **Phil. 1:23.** For I am in a strait betwixt two, having a desire to depart, and to be with Christ; which is far better.

x. **Heb. 12:23.** … to the general assembly and church of the firstborn, which are written in heaven, and to God the Judge of all, and to the spirits of just men made perfect. **Acts 7:55, 59.** But he, being full of the Holy Ghost, looked up stedfastly into heaven, and saw the glory of God, and Jesus standing on the right hand of God.… And they stoned Stephen, calling upon God, and saying, Lord Jesus, receive my spirit.

y. **2 Cor. 5:1, 6, 8.** For we know that if our earthly house of this tabernacle were dissolved, we have a building of God, an house not made with hands, eternal in the heavens.… Therefore we are always confident, knowing that, whilst we are at home in the body, we are absent from the Lord.… We are confident, I say, and willing rather to be absent from the body, and to be present with the Lord. **Phil. 1:23.** For I am in a strait betwixt two, having a desire to depart, and to be with Christ; which is far better. **Acts 3:21.** … whom the heaven must receive until the times of restitution of all things, which God hath spoken by the mouth of all his holy prophets since the world began. **Eph. 4:10.** He that descended is the same also that ascended up far above all heavens, that he might fill all things. **Luke 23:43.** And Jesus said unto him, Verily I

glory,[z] waiting for the full redemption of their bodies,[a] which even in death continue united to Christ,[b] and rest in their graves as in their beds,[c] till at the last day they be again united to their souls.[d] Whereas the souls of the wicked are at their death cast into hell, where they remain in torments and utter darkness, and their bodies kept in their graves, as in their prisons, till the resurrection and judgment of the great day.[e]

Q. 87. *What are we to believe concerning the resurrection?*

A. We are to believe, that at the last day there shall be a general resurrection of the dead, both of the just and unjust:[f] when they that are then found alive shall in a moment be changed; and the selfsame bodies of the dead which were laid in the grave, being then again

say unto thee, To day shalt thou be with me in paradise.

z. **1 John 3:2.** Beloved, now are we the sons of God, and it doth not yet appear what we shall be: but we know that, when he shall appear, we shall be like him; for we shall see him as he is. **1 Cor. 13:12.** For now we see through a glass, darkly; but then face to face: now I know in part; but then shall I know even as also I am known.

a. **Rom. 8:23.** And not only they, but ourselves also, which have the firstfruits of the Spirit, even we ourselves groan within ourselves, waiting for the adoption, to wit, the redemption of our body. **Ps. 16:9.** Therefore my heart is glad, and my glory rejoiceth: my flesh also shall rest in hope.

b. **1 Thess. 4:14, 16.** For if we believe that Jesus died and rose again, even so them also which sleep in Jesus will God bring with him.… For the Lord himself shall descend from heaven with a shout, with the voice of the archangel, and with the trump of God: and the dead in Christ shall rise first.

c. **Isa. 57:2.** He shall enter into peace: they shall rest in their beds, each one walking in his uprightness.

d. **Job 19:26–27.** And though after my skin worms destroy this body, yet in my flesh shall I see God: whom I shall see for myself, and mine eyes shall behold, and not another; though my reins be consumed within me.

e. **Luke 16:23–24.** And in hell he lift up his eyes, being in torments, and seeth Abraham afar off, and Lazarus in his bosom. And he cried and said, Father Abraham, have mercy on me, and send Lazarus, that he may dip the tip of his finger in water, and cool my tongue; for I am tormented in this flame. **Acts 1:25.** … that he may take part of this ministry and apostleship, from which Judas by transgression fell, that he might go to his own place. **Jude 6–7.** And the angels which kept not their first estate, but left their own habitation, he hath reserved in everlasting chains under darkness unto the judgment of the great day. Even as Sodom and Gomorrha, and the cities about them in like manner, giving themselves over to fornication, and going after strange flesh, are set forth for an example, suffering the vengeance of eternal fire.

f. **Dan. 12:2.** And many of them that sleep in the dust of the earth shall awake, some to everlasting life, and some to shame and everlasting contempt. **Acts 24:15.** And [I] have hope toward God, which they themselves also allow, that there shall be a resurrection of the dead, both of the just and unjust.

united to their souls forever, shall be raised up by the power of Christ.[g] The bodies of the just, by the Spirit of Christ, and by virtue of his resurrection as their head, shall be raised in power, spiritual, incorruptible, and made like to his glorious body;[h] and the bodies of the wicked shall be raised up in dishonor by him, as an offended judge.[i]

Q. 88. *What shall immediately follow after the resurrection?*

A. Immediately after the resurrection shall follow the general and final judgment of angels and men;[k] the day and hour whereof no

g. **Job 19:26.** And though after my skin worms destroy this body, yet in my flesh shall I see God. **1 Cor. 15:51–53.** Behold, I shew you a mystery; We shall not all sleep, but we shall all be changed, in a moment, in the twinkling of an eye, at the last trump: for the trumpet shall sound, and the dead shall be raised incorruptible, and we shall be changed. For this corruptible must put on incorruption, and this mortal must put on immortality. **1 Thess. 4:15–17.** For this we say unto you by the word of the Lord, that we which are alive and remain unto the coming of the Lord shall not prevent them which are asleep. For the Lord himself shall descend from heaven with a shout, with the voice of the archangel, and with the trump of God: and the dead in Christ shall rise first: then we which are alive and remain shall be caught up together with them in the clouds, to meet the Lord in the air: and so shall we ever be with the Lord. **John 5:28–29.** Marvel not at this: for the hour is coming, in the which all that are in the graves shall hear his voice, and shall come forth; they that have done good, unto the resurrection of life; and they that have done evil, unto the resurrection of damnation. **Rom. 8:11.** But if the Spirit of him that raised up Jesus from the dead dwell in you, he that raised up Christ from the dead shall also quicken your mortal bodies by his Spirit that dwelleth in you.

h. **1 Cor. 15:21–23, 42–44.** For since by man came death, by man came also the resurrection of the dead. For as in Adam all die, even so in Christ shall all be made alive. But every man in his own order: Christ the firstfruits; afterward they that are Christ's at his coming.… So also is the resurrection of the dead. It is sown in corruption; it is raised in incorruption: it is sown in dishonour; it is raised in glory: it is sown in weakness; it is raised in power: it is sown a natural body; it is raised a spiritual body. There is a natural body, and there is a spiritual body. **Phil. 3:21.** … who shall change our vile body, that it may be fashioned like unto his glorious body, according to the working whereby he is able even to subdue all things unto himself.

i. **John 5:27–29.** And hath given him authority to execute judgment also, because he is the Son of man. Marvel not at this: for the hour is coming, in the which all that are in the graves shall hear his voice, and shall come forth; they that have done good, unto the resurrection of life; and they that have done evil, unto the resurrection of damnation. **Matt. 25:33.** And he shall set the sheep on his right hand, but the goats on the left.

k. **Eccl. 12:14.** For God shall bring every work into judgment, with every secret thing, whether it be good, or whether it be evil. **2 Pet. 2:4, 6–7, 14–15.** For if God spared not the angels that sinned, but cast them down to hell, and delivered them into chains of darkness, to be reserved unto judgment … and turning the cities of Sodom

man knoweth, that all may watch and pray, and be ever ready for the coming of the Lord.[1]

Q. 89. *What shall be done to the wicked at the day of judgment?*

A. At the day of judgment, the wicked shall be set on Christ's left hand,[m] and, upon clear evidence, and full conviction of their own consciences,[n] shall have the fearful but just sentence of condemnation pronounced against them;[o] and thereupon shall be cast out from the favorable presence of God, and the glorious fellowship with Christ, his saints, and all his holy angels, into hell, to be punished with unspeakable torments, both of body and soul, with the devil and his angels forever.[p]

and Gomorrha into ashes condemned them with an overthrow, making them an ensample unto those that after should live ungodly; and delivered just Lot, vexed with the filthy conversation of the wicked … having eyes full of adultery, and that cannot cease from sin; beguiling unstable souls: an heart they have exercised with covetous practices; cursed children: which have forsaken the right way, and are gone astray, following the way of Balaam the son of Bosor, who loved the wages of unrighteousness. **Matt. 25:46.** And these shall go away into everlasting punishment: but the righteous into life eternal. **2 Cor. 5:10.** For we must all appear before the judgment seat of Christ; that every one may receive the things done in his body, according to that he hath done, whether it be good or bad. **Rom. 14:10, 12.** But why dost thou judge thy brother? or why dost thou set at nought thy brother? for we shall all stand before the judgment seat of Christ.… So then every one of us shall give account of himself to God.

l. **Matt. 24:36, 42, 44.** But of that day and hour knoweth no man, no, not the angels of heaven, but my Father only.… Watch therefore: for ye know not what hour your Lord doth come.… Therefore be ye also ready: for in such an hour as ye think not the Son of man cometh. **Mark 13:35–37.** Watch ye therefore: for ye know not when the master of the house cometh, at even, or at midnight, or at the cockcrowing, or in the morning: lest coming suddenly he find you sleeping. And what I say unto you I say unto all, Watch.

m. **Matt. 25:33.** And he shall set the sheep on his right hand, but the goats on the left.

n. **Rom. 2:15–16.** (… which shew the work of the law written in their hearts, their conscience also bearing witness, and their thoughts the mean while accusing or else excusing one another;) in the day when God shall judge the secrets of men by Jesus Christ according to my gospel.

o. **Matt. 25:41–43.** Then shall he say also unto them on the left hand, Depart from me, ye cursed, into everlasting fire, prepared for the devil and his angels: for I was an hungred, and ye gave me no meat: I was thirsty, and ye gave me no drink: I was a stranger, and ye took me not in: naked, and ye clothed me not: sick, and in prison, and ye visited me not.

p. **Luke 16:26.** And beside all this, between us and you there is a great gulf fixed: so that they which would pass from hence to you cannot; neither can they pass to us,

Q. 90. *What shall be done to the righteous at the day of judgment?*

A. At the day of judgment, the righteous, being caught up to Christ in the clouds,q shall be set on his right hand, and there openly acknowledged and acquitted,r shall join with him in the judging of reprobate angels and men,s and shall be received into heaven,t where they shall be fully and forever freed from all sin and misery;u filled with inconceivable joys,w made perfectly holy and happy both in body and soul, in the company of innumerable saints and holy angels,x but especially in the immediate vision and fruition of God the Father, of our Lord Jesus Christ, and of the Holy Spirit, to all eternity.y And

that would come from thence. **2 Thess. 1:8–9.** … in flaming fire taking vengeance on them that know not God, and that obey not the gospel of our Lord Jesus Christ: who shall be punished with everlasting destruction from the presence of the Lord, and from the glory of his power.

q. **1 Thess. 4:17.** Then we which are alive and remain shall be caught up together with them in the clouds, to meet the Lord in the air: and so shall we ever be with the Lord. **1 Cor. 15:42–43.** So also is the resurrection of the dead. It is sown in corruption; it is raised in incorruption: it is sown in dishonour; it is raised in glory: it is sown in weakness; it is raised in power.

r. **Matt. 25:33.** And he shall set the sheep on his right hand, but the goats on the left. **Matt. 10:32.** Whosoever therefore shall confess me before men, him will I confess also before my Father which is in heaven.

s. **1 Cor. 6:2–3.** Do ye not know that the saints shall judge the world? and if the world shall be judged by you, are ye unworthy to judge the smallest matters? Know ye not that we shall judge angels? how much more things that pertain to this life?

t. **Matt. 25:34, 46.** Then shall the King say unto them on his right hand, Come, ye blessed of my Father, inherit the kingdom prepared for you from the foundation of the world.… And these shall go away into everlasting punishment: but the righteous into life eternal.

u. **Eph. 5:27.** … that he might present it to himself a glorious church, not having spot, or wrinkle, or any such thing; but that it should be holy and without blemish. **Rev. 14:13.** And I heard a voice from heaven saying unto me, Write, Blessed are the dead which die in the Lord from henceforth: Yea, saith the Spirit, that they may rest from their labours; and their works do follow them.

w. **Ps. 16:11.** Thou wilt shew me the path of life: in thy presence is fulness of joy; at thy right hand there are pleasures for evermore.

x. **Heb. 12:22–23.** But ye are come unto mount Sion, and unto the city of the living God, the heavenly Jerusalem, and to an innumerable company of angels, to the general assembly and church of the firstborn, which are written in heaven, and to God the Judge of all, and to the spirits of just men made perfect.

y. **1 John 3:2.** Beloved, now are we the sons of God, and it doth not yet appear what we shall be: but we know that, when he shall appear, we shall be like him; for we shall see him as he is. **Rom. 8:29.** For whom he did foreknow, he also did predestinate to be conformed to the image of his Son, that he might be the firstborn among

this is the perfect and full communion, which the members of the invisible church shall enjoy with Christ in glory, at the resurrection and day of judgment.

HAVING SEEN WHAT THE SCRIPTURES PRINCIPALLY TEACH US TO BELIEVE CONCERNING GOD, IT FOLLOWS TO CONSIDER WHAT THEY REQUIRE AS THE DUTY OF MAN

Q. 91. *What is the duty which God requireth of man?*

A. The duty which God requireth of man, is obedience to his revealed will.[z]

Q. 92. *What did God at first reveal unto man as the rule of his obedience?*

A. The rule of obedience revealed to Adam in the estate of innocence, and to all mankind in him, besides a special command not to eat of the fruit of the tree of the knowledge of good and evil, was the moral law.[a]

many brethren. **1 Cor. 13:12.** For now we see through a glass, darkly; but then face to face: now I know in part; but then shall I know even as also I am known. **1 Thess. 4:17–18.** Then we which are alive and remain shall be caught up together with them in the clouds, to meet the Lord in the air: and so shall we ever be with the Lord. Wherefore comfort one another with these words.

z. **Deut. 29:29.** The secret things belong unto the LORD our God: but those things which are revealed belong unto us and to our children for ever, that we may do all the words of this law. **Mic. 6:8.** He hath shewed thee, O man, what is good; and what doth the LORD require of thee, but to do justly, and to love mercy, and to walk humbly with thy God? **1 John 5:2–3.** By this we know that we love the children of God, when we love God, and keep his commandments. For this is the love of God, that we keep his commandments: and his commandments are not grievous. **Rom. 12:1–2.** I beseech you therefore, brethren, by the mercies of God, that ye present your bodies a living sacrifice, holy, acceptable unto God, which is your reasonable service. And be not conformed to this world: but be ye transformed by the renewing of your mind, that ye may prove what is that good, and acceptable, and perfect, will of God. **1 Sam. 15:22.** And Samuel said, Hath the LORD as great delight in burnt offerings and sacrifices, as in obeying the voice of the LORD? Behold, to obey is better than sacrifice, and to hearken than the fat of rams.

a. **Gen. 1:26–27.** And God said, Let us make man in our image, after our likeness: and let them have dominion over the fish of the sea, and over the fowl of the air, and over the cattle, and over all the earth, and over every creeping thing that creepeth upon the earth. So God created man in his own image, in the image of God created he him; male and female created he them. **Rom. 2:14–15.** For when the Gentiles, which have not the law, do by nature the things contained in the law, these, having not the law, are a law unto themselves: which shew the work of the law written in their hearts, their conscience also bearing witness, and their thoughts the mean

Q. 93. *What is the moral law?*

A. The moral law is the declaration of the will of God to mankind, directing and binding everyone to personal, perfect, and perpetual conformity and obedience thereunto, in the frame and disposition of the whole man, soul and body,[b] and in performance of all those duties of holiness and righteousness which he oweth to God and man:[c] promising life upon the fulfilling, and threatening death upon the breach of it.[d]

Q. 94. *Is there any use of the moral law to man since the fall?*

A. Although no man, since the fall, can attain to righteousness and life by the moral law;[e] yet there is great use thereof, as well

while accusing or else excusing one another. **Rom. 10:5.** For Moses describeth the righteousness which is of the law, That the man which doeth those things shall live by them. **Gen. 2:17.** But of the tree of the knowledge of good and evil, thou shalt not eat of it: for in the day that thou eatest thereof thou shalt surely die.

b. **Deut. 5:1–3, 31, 33.** And Moses called all Israel, and said unto them, Hear, O Israel, the statutes and judgments which I speak in your ears this day, that ye may learn them, and keep, and do them. The LORD our God made a covenant with us in Horeb. The LORD made not this covenant with our fathers, but with us, even us, who are all of us here alive this day.… But as for thee, stand thou here by me, and I will speak unto thee all the commandments, and the statutes, and the judgments, which thou shalt teach them, that they may do them in the land which I give them to possess it.… Ye shall walk in all the ways which the LORD your God hath commanded you, that ye may live, and that it may be well with you, and that ye may prolong your days in the land which ye shall possess. **Luke 10:26–27.** He said unto him, What is written in the law? how readest thou? And he answering said, Thou shalt love the Lord thy God with all thy heart, and with all thy soul, and with all thy strength, and with all thy mind; and thy neighbour as thyself. **1 Thess. 5:23.** And the very God of peace sanctify you wholly; and I pray God your whole spirit and soul and body be preserved blameless unto the coming of our Lord Jesus Christ. **Eph. 4:24.** … and that ye put on the new man, which after God is created in righteousness and true holiness.

c. **Luke 1:75.** … in holiness and righteousness before him, all the days of our life. **Acts 24:16.** And herein do I exercise myself, to have always a conscience void of offence toward God, and toward men. **1 Pet. 1:15–16.** But as he which hath called you is holy, so be ye holy in all manner of conversation; because it is written, Be ye holy; for I am holy.

d. **Rom. 10:5.** For Moses describeth the righteousness which is of the law, That the man which doeth those things shall live by them. **Gal. 3:10, 12.** For as many as are of the works of the law are under the curse: for it is written, Cursed is every one that continueth not in all things which are written in the book of the law to do them.… And the law is not of faith: but, The man that doeth them shall live in them. **Rom. 5:12.** Wherefore, as by one man sin entered into the world, and death by sin; and so death passed upon all men, for that all have sinned …

e. **Rom. 8:3.** For what the law could not do, in that it was weak through the flesh,

common to all men, as peculiar either to the unregenerate, or the regenerate.[f]

Q. 95. *Of what use is the moral law to all men?*

A. The moral law is of use to all men, to inform them of the holy nature and will of God,[g] and of their duty, binding them to walk accordingly;[h] to convince them of their disability to keep it, and of the sinful pollution of their nature, hearts, and lives;[i] to humble them in the sense of their sin and misery,[k] and thereby help them to a clearer sight of the need they have of Christ,[l] and of the perfection

God sending his own Son in the likeness of sinful flesh, and for sin, condemned sin in the flesh. **Gal. 2:16.** … knowing that a man is not justified by the works of the law, but by the faith of Jesus Christ, even we have believed in Jesus Christ, that we might be justified by the faith of Christ, and not by the works of the law: for by the works of the law shall no flesh be justified.

f. **1 Tim. 1:8.** But we know that the law is good, if a man use it lawfully.

g. **Rom. 1:20.** For the invisible things of him from the creation of the world are clearly seen, being understood by the things that are made, even his eternal power and Godhead; so that they are without excuse. **Lev. 11:44–45.** For I am the LORD your God: ye shall therefore sanctify yourselves, and ye shall be holy; for I am holy: neither shall ye defile yourselves with any manner of creeping thing that creepeth upon the earth. For I am the LORD that bringeth you up out of the land of Egypt, to be your God: ye shall therefore be holy, for I am holy. **Lev. 20:7–8.** Sanctify yourselves therefore, and be ye holy: for I am the LORD your God. And ye shall keep my statutes, and do them: I am the LORD which sanctify you. **Rom. 7:12.** Wherefore the law is holy, and the commandment holy, and just, and good.

h. **Mic. 6:8.** He hath shewed thee, O man, what is good; and what doth the LORD require of thee, but to do justly, and to love mercy, and to walk humbly with thy God? **James 2:10–11.** For whosoever shall keep the whole law, and yet offend in one point, he is guilty of all. For he that said, Do not commit adultery, said also, Do not kill. Now if thou commit no adultery, yet if thou kill, thou art become a transgressor of the law. **Rom. 1:32.** … who knowing the judgment of God, that they which commit such things are worthy of death, not only do the same, but have pleasure in them that do them.

i. **Ps. 19:11–12.** Moreover by them is thy servant warned: and in keeping of them there is great reward. Who can understand his errors? cleanse thou me from secret faults. **Rom. 3:20.** Therefore by the deeds of the law there shall no flesh be justified in his sight: for by the law is the knowledge of sin. **Rom. 7:7.** What shall we say then? Is the law sin? God forbid. Nay, I had not known sin, but by the law: for I had not known lust, except the law had said, Thou shalt not covet.

k. **Rom. 3:9, 23.** What then? are we better than they? No, in no wise: for we have before proved both Jews and Gentiles, that they are all under sin.… For all have sinned, and come short of the glory of God.

l. **Gal. 3:21–22, 24.** Is the law then against the promises of God? God forbid: for if there had been a law given which could have given life, verily righteousness

of his obedience.[m]

Q. 96. *What particular use is there of the moral law to unregenerate men?*

A. The moral law is of use to unregenerate men, to awaken their consciences to flee from wrath to come,[n] and to drive them to Christ;[o] or, upon their continuance in the estate and way of sin, to leave them inexcusable,[p] and under the curse thereof.[q]

Q. 97. *What special use is there of the moral law to the regenerate?*

A. Although they that are regenerate, and believe in Christ, be delivered from the moral law as a covenant of works,[r] so as thereby

should have been by the law. But the scripture hath concluded all under sin, that the promise by faith of Jesus Christ might be given to them that believe.… Wherefore the law was our schoolmaster to bring us unto Christ, that we might be justified by faith.

m. **Rom. 10:4.** For Christ is the end of the law for righteousness to every one that believeth.

n. **Ps. 51:13.** Then will I teach transgressors thy ways; and sinners shall be converted unto thee. **1 Tim. 1:9–11.** … knowing this, that the law is not made for a righteous man, but for the lawless and disobedient, for the ungodly and for sinners, for unholy and profane, for murderers of fathers and murderers of mothers, for manslayers, for whoremongers, for them that defile themselves with mankind, for menstealers, for liars, for perjured persons, and if there be any other thing that is contrary to sound doctrine; according to the glorious gospel of the blessed God, which was committed to my trust.

o. **Gal. 3:24.** Wherefore the law was our schoolmaster to bring us unto Christ, that we might be justified by faith.

p. **Rom. 1:20.** For the invisible things of him from the creation of the world are clearly seen, being understood by the things that are made, even his eternal power and Godhead; so that they are without excuse. **Rom. 2:15.** … which shew the work of the law written in their hearts, their conscience also bearing witness, and their thoughts the mean while accusing or else excusing one another.

q. **Gal. 3:10.** For as many as are of the works of the law are under the curse: for it is written, Cursed is every one that continueth not in all things which are written in the book of the law to do them.

r. **Rom. 6:14.** For sin shall not have dominion over you: for ye are not under the law, but under grace. **Rom. 7:4, 6.** Wherefore, my brethren, ye also are become dead to the law by the body of Christ; that ye should be married to another, even to him who is raised from the dead, that we should bring forth fruit unto God.… But now we are delivered from the law, that being dead wherein we were held; that we should serve in newness of spirit, and not in the oldness of the letter. **Gal. 4:4–5.** But when the fulness of the time was come, God sent forth his Son, made of a woman, made under the law, to redeem them that were under the law, that we might receive the adoption of sons. **Col. 2:13–14.** And you, being dead in your sins and the uncircumcision of your flesh, hath he quickened together with him, having forgiven you all trespasses; blotting out the handwriting of ordinances that was against us, which was contrary to us, and took it out of the way, nailing it to his cross.

they are neither justified[s] nor condemned;[t] yet, besides the general uses thereof common to them with all men, it is of special use, to show them how much they are bound to Christ for his fulfilling it, and enduring the curse thereof in their stead, and for their good;[u] and thereby to provoke them to more thankfulness,[w] and to express the same in their greater care to conform themselves thereunto as the rule of their obedience.[x]

s. **Rom. 3:20.** Therefore by the deeds of the law there shall no flesh be justified in his sight: for by the law is the knowledge of sin.

t. **Gal. 5:23.** … meekness, temperance: against such there is no law. **Rom. 8:1.** There is therefore now no condemnation to them which are in Christ Jesus, who walk not after the flesh, but after the Spirit.

u. **Rom. 7:24–25.** O wretched man that I am! who shall deliver me from the body of this death? I thank God through Jesus Christ our Lord. So then with the mind I myself serve the law of God; but with the flesh the law of sin. **Gal. 3:13–14.** Christ hath redeemed us from the curse of the law, being made a curse for us: for it is written, Cursed is every one that hangeth on a tree: that the blessing of Abraham might come on the Gentiles through Jesus Christ; that we might receive the promise of the Spirit through faith. **Rom. 8:3–4.** For what the law could not do, in that it was weak through the flesh, God sending his own Son in the likeness of sinful flesh, and for sin, condemned sin in the flesh: that the righteousness of the law might be fulfilled in us, who walk not after the flesh, but after the Spirit. **Acts 13:38–39.** Be it known unto you therefore, men and brethren, that through this man is preached unto you the forgiveness of sins: and by him all that believe are justified from all things, from which ye could not be justified by the law of Moses.

w. **Luke 1:68–69, 74–75.** Blessed be the Lord God of Israel; for he hath visited and redeemed his people, and hath raised up an horn of salvation for us in the house of his servant David.… that he would grant unto us, that we being delivered out of the hand of our enemies might serve him without fear, in holiness and righteousness before him, all the days of our life. **Col. 1:12–14.** … giving thanks unto the Father, which hath made us meet to be partakers of the inheritance of the saints in light: who hath delivered us from the power of darkness, and hath translated us into the kingdom of his dear Son: in whom we have redemption through his blood, even the forgiveness of sins. **Rom. 6:14.** For sin shall not have dominion over you: for ye are not under the law, but under grace.

x. **Deut. 30:19–20.** I call heaven and earth to record this day against you, that I have set before you life and death, blessing and cursing: therefore choose life, that both thou and thy seed may live: that thou mayest love the LORD thy God, and that thou mayest obey his voice, and that thou mayest cleave unto him: for he is thy life, and the length of thy days: that thou mayest dwell in the land which the LORD sware unto thy fathers, to Abraham, to Isaac, and to Jacob, to give them. **Rom. 7:22.** For I delight in the law of God after the inward man. **Rom. 12:2.** And be not conformed to this world: but be ye transformed by the renewing of your mind, that ye may prove what is that good, and acceptable, and perfect, will of God. **Titus 2:11–14.** For the grace of God that bringeth salvation hath appeared to all men, teaching us that, denying un-

Q. 98. *Where is the moral law summarily comprehended?*

A. The moral law is summarily comprehended in the Ten Commandments, which were delivered by the voice of God upon Mount Sinai, and written by him in two tables of stone;[y] and are recorded in the twentieth chapter of Exodus: the four first commandments containing our duty to God, and the other six our duty to man.[z]

godliness and worldly lusts, we should live soberly, righteously, and godly, in this present world; looking for that blessed hope, and the glorious appearing of the great God and our Saviour Jesus Christ; who gave himself for us, that he might redeem us from all iniquity, and purify unto himself a peculiar people, zealous of good works. **James 1:25.** But whoso looketh into the perfect law of liberty, and continueth therein, he being not a forgetful hearer, but a doer of the work, this man shall be blessed in his deed.

y. **Deut. 4:13.** And he declared unto you his covenant, which he commanded you to perform, even ten commandments; and he wrote them upon two tables of stone. **Deut. 10:4.** And he wrote on the tables, according to the first writing, the ten commandments, which the LORD spake unto you in the mount out of the midst of the fire in the day of the assembly: and the LORD gave them unto me. **Ex. 34:1–4.** And the LORD said unto Moses, Hew thee two tables of stone like unto the first: and I will write upon these tables the words that were in the first tables, which thou brakest. And be ready in the morning, and come up in the morning unto mount Sinai, and present thyself there to me in the top of the mount. And no man shall come up with thee, neither let any man be seen throughout all the mount; neither let the flocks nor herds feed before that mount. And he hewed two tables of stone like unto the first; and Moses rose up early in the morning, and went up unto mount Sinai, as the LORD had commanded him, and took in his hand the two tables of stone. **Rom. 13:8–10.** Owe no man any thing, but to love one another: for he that loveth another hath fulfilled the law. For this, Thou shalt not commit adultery, Thou shalt not kill, Thou shalt not steal, Thou shalt not bear false witness, Thou shalt not covet; and if there be any other commandment, it is briefly comprehended in this saying, namely, Thou shalt love thy neighbour as thyself. Love worketh no ill to his neighbour: therefore love is the fulfilling of the law. **James 2:8, 10–12.** If ye fulfil the royal law according to the scripture, Thou shalt love thy neighbour as thyself, ye do well.… For whosoever shall keep the whole law, and yet offend in one point, he is guilty of all. For he that said, Do not commit adultery, said also, Do not kill. Now if thou commit no adultery, yet if thou kill, thou art become a transgressor of the law. So speak ye, and so do, as they that shall be judged by the law of liberty.

z. **Matt. 22:37–40.** Jesus said unto him, Thou shalt love the Lord thy God with all thy heart, and with all thy soul, and with all thy mind. This is the first and great commandment. And the second is like unto it, Thou shalt love thy neighbour as thyself. On these two commandments hang all the law and the prophets. **Matt. 19:17–19.** And he said unto him, Why callest thou me good? there is none good but one, that is, God: but if thou wilt enter into life, keep the commandments. He saith unto him, Which? Jesus said, Thou shalt do no murder, Thou shalt not commit adultery, Thou shalt not steal, Thou shalt not bear false witness, Honour thy father and thy mother: and, Thou shalt love thy neighbour as thyself.

Q. 99. *What rules are to be observed for the right understanding of the Ten Commandments?*

A. For the right understanding of the Ten Commandments, these rules are to be observed:

1. That the law is perfect, and bindeth everyone to full conformity in the whole man unto the righteousness thereof, and unto entire obedience forever; so as to require the utmost perfection of every duty, and to forbid the least degree of every sin.[a]

2. That it is spiritual, and so reacheth the understanding, will, affections, and all other powers of the soul; as well as words, works, and gestures.[b]

3. That one and the same thing, in divers respects, is required or

a. **Ps. 19:7.** The law of the LORD is perfect, converting the soul: the testimony of the LORD is sure, making wise the simple. **James 2:10.** For whosoever shall keep the whole law, and yet offend in one point, he is guilty of all. **Matt. 5:21–22.** Ye have heard that it was said by them of old time, Thou shalt not kill; and whosoever shall kill shall be in danger of the judgment: but I say unto you, That whosoever is angry with his brother without a cause shall be in danger of the judgment: and whosoever shall say to his brother, Raca, shall be in danger of the council: but whosoever shall say, Thou fool, shall be in danger of hell fire.

b. **Rom. 7:14.** For we know that the law is spiritual: but I am carnal, sold under sin. **Deut. 6:5.** And thou shalt love the LORD thy God with all thine heart, and with all thy soul, and with all thy might. **Matt. 22:37–39.** Jesus said unto him, Thou shalt love the Lord thy God with all thy heart, and with all thy soul, and with all thy mind. This is the first and great commandment. And the second is like unto it, Thou shalt love thy neighbour as thyself. **Matt. 5:21–22, 27–28, 33–34, 37–39, 43–44.** Ye have heard that it was said by them of old time, Thou shalt not kill; and whosoever shall kill shall be in danger of the judgment: but I say unto you, That whosoever is angry with his brother without a cause shall be in danger of the judgment: and whosoever shall say to his brother, Raca, shall be in danger of the council: but whosoever shall say, Thou fool, shall be in danger of hell fire.… Ye have heard that it was said by them of old time, Thou shalt not commit adultery: but I say unto you, That whosoever looketh on a woman to lust after her hath committed adultery with her already in his heart.… Again, ye have heard that it hath been said by them of old time, Thou shalt not forswear thyself, but shalt perform unto the Lord thine oaths: but I say unto you, Swear not at all; neither by heaven; for it is God's throne.… But let your communication be, Yea, yea; Nay, nay: for whatsoever is more than these cometh of evil. Ye have heard that it hath been said, An eye for an eye, and a tooth for a tooth: but I say unto you, That ye resist not evil: but whosoever shall smite thee on thy right cheek, turn to him the other also.… Ye have heard that it hath been said, Thou shalt love thy neighbour, and hate thine enemy. But I say unto you, Love your enemies, bless them that curse you, do good to them that hate you, and pray for them which despitefully use you, and persecute you.

forbidden in several commandments.[c]

4. That as, where a duty is commanded, the contrary sin is forbidden;[d] and, where a sin is forbidden, the contrary duty is commanded:[e] so, where a promise is annexed, the contrary threatening is included;[f] and, where a threatening is annexed, the contrary promise is included.[g]

c. **Col. 3:5.** Mortify therefore your members which are upon the earth; fornication, uncleanness, inordinate affection, evil concupiscence, and covetousness, which is idolatry. **Amos 8:5.** … saying, When will the new moon be gone, that we may sell corn? and the sabbath, that we may set forth wheat, making the ephah small, and the shekel great, and falsifying the balances by deceit? **Prov. 1:19.** So are the ways of every one that is greedy of gain; which taketh away the life of the owners thereof. **1 Tim. 6:10.** For the love of money is the root of all evil: which while some coveted after, they have erred from the faith, and pierced themselves through with many sorrows.

d. **Isa. 58:13.** If thou turn away thy foot from the sabbath, from doing thy pleasure on my holy day; and call the sabbath a delight, the holy of the LORD, honourable; and shalt honour him, not doing thine own ways, nor finding thine own pleasure, nor speaking thine own words. **Deut. 6:13.** Thou shalt fear the LORD thy God, and serve him, and shalt swear by his name. **Matt. 4:9–10.** And [the devil] saith unto him, All these things will I give thee, if thou wilt fall down and worship me. Then saith Jesus unto him, Get thee hence, Satan: for it is written, Thou shalt worship the Lord thy God, and him only shalt thou serve. **Matt. 15:4–6.** For God commanded, saying, Honour thy father and mother: and, He that curseth father or mother, let him die the death. But ye say, Whosoever shall say to his father or his mother, It is a gift, by whatsoever thou mightest be profited by me; and honour not his father or his mother, he shall be free. Thus have ye made the commandment of God of none effect by your tradition.

e. **Matt. 5:21–25.** Ye have heard that it was said by them of old time, Thou shalt not kill; and whosoever shall kill shall be in danger of the judgment: but I say unto you, That whosoever is angry with his brother without a cause shall be in danger of the judgment: and whosoever shall say to his brother, Raca, shall be in danger of the council: but whosoever shall say, Thou fool, shall be in danger of hell fire. Therefore if thou bring thy gift to the altar, and there rememberest that thy brother hath ought against thee; leave there thy gift before the altar, and go thy way; first be reconciled to thy brother, and then come and offer thy gift. Agree with thine adversary quickly, whiles thou art in the way with him; lest at any time the adversary deliver thee to the judge, and the judge deliver thee to the officer, and thou be cast into prison. **Eph. 4:28.** Let him that stole steal no more: but rather let him labour, working with his hands the thing which is good, that he may have to give to him that needeth.

f. **Ex. 20:12.** Honour thy father and thy mother: that thy days may be long upon the land which the LORD thy God giveth thee. **Prov. 30:17.** The eye that mocketh at his father, and despiseth to obey his mother, the ravens of the valley shall pick it out, and the young eagles shall eat it.

g. **Jer. 18:7–8.** At what instant I shall speak concerning a nation, and concerning a kingdom, to pluck up, and to pull down, and to destroy it; if that nation, against

5. That what God forbids, is at no time to be done;[h] what he commands, is always our duty;[i] and yet every particular duty is not to be done at all times.[k]

6. That under one sin or duty, all of the same kind are forbidden or commanded; together with all the causes, means, occasions, and appearances thereof, and provocations thereunto.[l]

whom I have pronounced, turn from their evil, I will repent of the evil that I thought to do unto them. **Ex. 20:7.** Thou shalt not take the name of the LORD thy God in vain; for the LORD will not hold him guiltless that taketh his name in vain. **Ps. 15:1, 4–5.** LORD, who shall abide in thy tabernacle? who shall dwell in thy holy hill?… In whose eyes a vile person is contemned; but he honoureth them that fear the LORD. He that sweareth to his own hurt, and changeth not. He that putteth not out his money to usury, nor taketh reward against the innocent. He that doeth these things shall never be moved. **Ps. 24:4–5.** He that hath clean hands, and a pure heart; who hath not lifted up his soul unto vanity, nor sworn deceitfully. He shall receive the blessing from the LORD, and righteousness from the God of his salvation.

h. **Job 13:7–8.** Will ye speak wickedly for God? and talk deceitfully for him? Will ye accept his person? will ye contend for God? **Rom. 3:8.** … and not rather, (as we be slanderously reported, and as some affirm that we say,) Let us do evil, that good may come? whose damnation is just. **Job 36:21.** Take heed, regard not iniquity: for this hast thou chosen rather than affliction. **Heb. 11:25.** … choosing rather to suffer affliction with the people of God, than to enjoy the pleasures of sin for a season.

i. **Deut. 4:8–9.** And what nation is there so great, that hath statutes and judgments so righteous as all this law, which I set before you this day? Only take heed to thyself, and keep thy soul diligently, lest thou forget the things which thine eyes have seen, and lest they depart from thy heart all the days of thy life: but teach them thy sons, and thy sons' sons. **Luke 17:10.** So likewise ye, when ye shall have done all those things which are commanded you, say, We are unprofitable servants: we have done that which was our duty to do.

k. **Matt. 12:7.** But if ye had known what this meaneth, I will have mercy, and not sacrifice, ye would not have condemned the guiltless.

l. **Matt. 5:21–22, 27–28.** Ye have heard that it was said by them of old time, Thou shalt not kill; and whosoever shall kill shall be in danger of the judgment: but I say unto you, That whosoever is angry with his brother without a cause shall be in danger of the judgment: and whosoever shall say to his brother, Raca, shall be in danger of the council: but whosoever shall say, Thou fool, shall be in danger of hell fire.… Ye have heard that it was said by them of old time, Thou shalt not commit adultery: but I say unto you, That whosoever looketh on a woman to lust after her hath committed adultery with her already in his heart. **Matt. 15:4–6.** For God commanded, saying, Honour thy father and mother: and, He that curseth father or mother, let him die the death. But ye say, Whosoever shall say to his father or his mother, It is a gift, by whatsoever thou mightest be profited by me; and honour not his father or his mother, he shall be free. Thus have ye made the commandment of God of none effect by your tradition. **1 Thess. 5:22.** Abstain from all appearance of evil. **Jude 23.** And others save with fear, pulling them out of the fire; hating even the garment spotted by the flesh. **Gal. 5:26.** Let us not be desirous of vain glory, provoking one

7. That what is forbidden or commanded to ourselves, we are bound, according to our places, to endeavor that it may be avoided or performed by others, according to the duty of their places.[m]

8. That in what is commanded to others, we are bound, according to our places and callings, to be helpful to them;[n] and to take heed of partaking with others in what is forbidden them.[o]

Q. 100. *What special things are we to consider in the Ten Commandments?*

A. We are to consider, in the Ten Commandments, the preface, the substance of the commandments themselves, and several reasons annexed to some of them, the more to enforce them.[p]

Q. 101. *What is the preface to the Ten Commandments?*

A. The preface to the Ten Commandments is contained in these words, *I am the LORD thy God, which have brought thee out of the land of*

another, envying one another. **Col. 3:21.** Fathers, provoke not your children to anger, lest they be discouraged.

m. **Ex. 20:10.** But the seventh day is the sabbath of the LORD thy God: in it thou shalt not do any work, thou, nor thy son, nor thy daughter, thy manservant, nor thy maidservant, nor thy cattle, nor thy stranger that is within thy gates. **Lev. 19:17.** Thou shalt not hate thy brother in thine heart: thou shalt in any wise rebuke thy neighbour, and not suffer sin upon him. **Gen. 18:19.** For I know him, that he will command his children and his household after him, and they shall keep the way of the LORD, to do justice and judgment; that the LORD may bring upon Abraham that which he hath spoken of him. **Josh. 24:15.** And if it seem evil unto you to serve the LORD, choose you this day whom ye will serve; whether the gods which your fathers served that were on the other side of the flood, or the gods of the Amorites, in whose land ye dwell: but as for me and my house, we will serve the LORD. **Deut. 6:6–7.** And these words, which I command thee this day, shall be in thine heart: and thou shalt teach them diligently unto thy children, and shalt talk of them when thou sittest in thine house, and when thou walkest by the way, and when thou liest down, and when thou risest up. **Heb. 10:24–25.** And let us consider one another to provoke unto love and to good works: not forsaking the assembling of ourselves together, as the manner of some is; but exhorting one another: and so much the more, as ye see the day approaching.

n. **2 Cor. 1:24.** Not for that we have dominion over your faith, but are helpers of your joy: for by faith ye stand.

o. **1 Tim. 5:22.** Lay hands suddenly on no man, neither be partaker of other men's sins: keep thyself pure. **Eph. 5:11.** And have no fellowship with the unfruitful works of darkness, but rather reprove them.

p. **As an example, Eph. 6:1–3.** Children, obey your parents in the Lord: for this is right. Honour thy father and mother; (which is the first commandment with promise;) that it may be well with thee, and thou mayest live long on the earth.

Egypt, out of the house of bondage.[q] Wherein God manifesteth his sovereignty, as being JEHOVAH, the eternal, immutable, and almighty God;[r] having his being in and of himself,[s] and giving being to all his words[t] and works:[u] and that he is a God in covenant, as with Israel of old, so with all his people;[w] who, as he brought them out of their bondage in Egypt, so he delivereth us from our spiritual thraldom;[x] and that therefore we are bound to take him for our God alone, and to keep all his commandments.[y]

Q. 102. *What is the sum of the four commandments which contain our duty to God?*

A. The sum of the four commandments containing our duty to God is, to love the Lord our God with all our heart, and with all our

q. **Ex. 20:2. Cf. Deut. 5:6.** I am the LORD thy God, which brought thee out of the land of Egypt, from the house of bondage.

r. **Isa. 44:6.** Thus saith the LORD the King of Israel, and his redeemer the LORD of hosts; I am the first, and I am the last; and beside me there is no God.

s. **Ex. 3:14.** And God said unto Moses, I AM THAT I AM: and he said, Thus shalt thou say unto the children of Israel, I AM hath sent me unto you.

t. **Ex. 6:3.** And I appeared unto Abraham, unto Isaac, and unto Jacob, by the name of God Almighty, but by my name JEHOVAH was I not known to them.

u. **Acts 17:24, 28.** God that made the world and all things therein, seeing that he is Lord of heaven and earth, dwelleth not in temples made with hands.... For in him we live, and move, and have our being; as certain also of your own poets have said, For we are also his offspring.

w. **Gen. 17:7.** And I will establish my covenant between me and thee and thy seed after thee in their generations for an everlasting covenant, to be a God unto thee, and to thy seed after thee. **Rom. 3:29.** Is he the God of the Jews only? is he not also of the Gentiles? Yes, of the Gentiles also.

x. **Luke 1:74–75.** ... that he would grant unto us, that we being delivered out of the hand of our enemies might serve him without fear, in holiness and righteousness before him, all the days of our life. **Gal. 5:1.** Stand fast therefore in the liberty wherewith Christ hath made us free, and be not entangled again with the yoke of bondage.

y. **1 Pet. 1:15–19.** But as he which hath called you is holy, so be ye holy in all manner of conversation; because it is written, Be ye holy; for I am holy. And if ye call on the Father, who without respect of persons judgeth according to every man's work, pass the time of your sojourning here in fear: forasmuch as ye know that ye were not redeemed with corruptible things, as silver and gold, from your vain conversation received by tradition from your fathers; but with the precious blood of Christ, as of a lamb without blemish and without spot. **Lev. 18:30.** Therefore shall ye keep mine ordinance, that ye commit not any one of these abominable customs, which were committed before you, and that ye defile not yourselves therein: I am the LORD your God. **Lev. 19:37.** Therefore shall ye observe all my statutes, and all my judgments, and do them: I am the LORD.

soul, and with all our strength, and with all our mind.ᶻ

Q. 103. *Which is the first commandment?*

A. The first commandment is, *Thou shall have no other gods before me.*ᵃ

Q. 104. *What are the duties required in the first commandment?*

A. The duties required in the first commandment are, the knowing and acknowledging of God to be the only true God, and our God;ᵇ and to worship and glorify him accordingly,ᶜ by thinking,ᵈ meditating,ᵉ remembering,ᶠ highly esteeming,ᵍ honoring,ʰ

z. **Luke 10:27.** And he answering said, Thou shalt love the Lord thy God with all thy heart, and with all thy soul, and with all thy strength, and with all thy mind; and thy neighbour as thyself. **Matt. 22:37–40.** Jesus said unto him, Thou shalt love the Lord thy God with all thy heart, and with all thy soul, and with all thy mind. This is the first and great commandment. And the second is like unto it, Thou shalt love thy neighbour as thyself. On these two commandments hang all the law and the prophets.

a. **Ex. 20:3. Cf. Deut. 5:7.** Thou shalt have none other gods before me.

b. **1 Chron. 28:9.** And thou, Solomon my son, know thou the God of thy father, and serve him with a perfect heart and with a willing mind: for the LORD searcheth all hearts, and understandeth all the imaginations of the thoughts: if thou seek him, he will be found of thee; but if thou forsake him, he will cast thee off for ever. **Deut. 26:7.** And when we cried unto the LORD God of our fathers, the LORD heard our voice, and looked on our affliction, and our labour, and our oppression. **Isa. 43:10.** Ye are my witnesses, saith the LORD, and my servant whom I have chosen: that ye may know and believe me, and understand that I am he: before me there was no God formed, neither shall there be after me. **See Jer. 14:22.**

c. **Ps. 95:6–7.** O come, let us worship and bow down: let us kneel before the LORD our maker. For he is our God; and we are the people of his pasture, and the sheep of his hand.… **Matt. 4:10.** Then saith Jesus unto him, Get thee hence, Satan: for it is written, Thou shalt worship the Lord thy God, and him only shalt thou serve. **Ps. 29:2.** Give unto the LORD the glory due unto his name; worship the LORD in the beauty of holiness.

d. **Mal. 3:16.** Then they that feared the LORD spake often one to another: and the LORD hearkened, and heard it, and a book of remembrance was written before him for them that feared the LORD, and that thought upon his name.

e. **Ps. 63:6.** … when I remember thee upon my bed, and meditate on thee in the night watches.

f. **Eccl. 12:1.** Remember now thy Creator in the days of thy youth, while the evil days come not, nor the years draw nigh, when thou shalt say, I have no pleasure in them.

g. **Ps. 71:19.** Thy righteousness also, O God, is very high, who hast done great things: O God, who is like unto thee!

h. **Mal. 1:6.** A son honoureth his father, and a servant his master: if then I be a father, where is mine honour? and if I be a master, where is my fear? saith the LORD of hosts unto you, O priests, that despise my name. And ye say, Wherein have we despised thy name?

adoring,[i] choosing,[k] loving,[l] desiring,[m] fearing of him;[n] believing him;[o] trusting,[p] hoping,[q] delighting,[r] rejoicing in him;[s] being zealous for him;[t] calling upon him, giving all praise and thanks,[u] and yielding all obedience and submission to him with the whole man;[w] being careful in all things to please him,[x] and sorrowful when in anything he is offended;[y] and walking humbly with him.[z]

i. **Isa. 45:23.** I have sworn by myself, the word is gone out of my mouth in righteousness, and shall not return, That unto me every knee shall bow, every tongue shall swear. **See Ps. 96.**

k. **Josh. 24:15, 22.** And if it seem evil unto you to serve the LORD, choose you this day whom ye will serve; whether the gods which your fathers served that were on the other side of the flood, or the gods of the Amorites, in whose land ye dwell: but as for me and my house, we will serve the LORD…. And Joshua said unto the people, Ye are witnesses against yourselves that ye have chosen you the LORD, to serve him. And they said, We are witnesses.

l. **Deut. 6:5.** And thou shalt love the LORD thy God with all thine heart, and with all thy soul, and with all thy might.

m. **Ps. 73:25.** Whom have I in heaven but thee? and there is none upon earth that I desire beside thee.

n. **Isa. 8:13.** Sanctify the LORD of hosts himself; and let him be your fear, and let him be your dread.

o. **Ex. 14:31.** And Israel saw that great work which the LORD did upon the Egyptians: and the people feared the LORD, and believed the LORD, and his servant Moses.

p. **Isa. 26:4.** Trust ye in the LORD for ever: for in the LORD JEHOVAH is everlasting strength.

q. **Ps. 130:7.** Let Israel hope in the LORD: for with the LORD there is mercy, and with him is plenteous redemption.

r. **Ps. 37:4.** Delight thyself also in the LORD; and he shall give thee the desires of thine heart.

s. **Ps. 32:11.** Be glad in the LORD, and rejoice, ye righteous: and shout for joy, all ye that are upright in heart.

t. **Rom. 12:11.** [Be] not slothful in business; fervent in spirit; serving the Lord. **See Num. 25:11.**

u. **Phil. 4:6.** Be careful for nothing; but in every thing by prayer and supplication with thanksgiving let your requests be made known unto God.

w. **Jer. 7:23.** But this thing commanded I them, saying, Obey my voice, and I will be your God, and ye shall be my people: and walk ye in all the ways that I have commanded you, that it may be well unto you. **James 4:7.** Submit yourselves therefore to God. Resist the devil, and he will flee from you.

x. **1 John 3:22.** And whatsoever we ask, we receive of him, because we keep his commandments, and do those things that are pleasing in his sight.

y. **Ps. 119:136.** Rivers of waters run down mine eyes, because they keep not thy law. **Jer. 31:18.** I have surely heard Ephraim bemoaning himself thus; Thou hast chastised me, and I was chastised, as a bullock unaccustomed to the yoke: turn thou me, and I shall be turned; for thou art the LORD my God.

Q. 105. *What are the sins forbidden in the first commandment?*

A. The sins forbidden in the first commandment are, atheism, in denying or not having a God;[a] idolatry, in having or worshiping more gods than one, or any with or instead of the true God;[b] the not having and avouching him for God, and our God;[c] the omission or neglect of anything due to him, required in this commandment;[d] ignorance,[e] forgetfulness,[f] misapprehensions,[g] false opinions,[h] unworthy

z. **Mic. 6:8.** He hath shewed thee, O man, what is good; and what doth the LORD require of thee, but to do justly, and to love mercy, and to walk humbly with thy God?

a. **Ps. 14:1.** The fool hath said in his heart, There is no God. They are corrupt, they have done abominable works, there is none that doeth good. **Eph. 2:12.** … that at that time ye were without Christ, being aliens from the commonwealth of Israel, and strangers from the covenants of promise, having no hope, and without God in the world.

b. **Jer. 2:27–28.** Saying to a stock, Thou art my father; and to a stone, Thou hast brought me forth: for they have turned their back unto me, and not their face: but in the time of their trouble they will say, Arise, and save us. But where are thy gods that thou hast made thee? let them arise, if they can save thee in the time of thy trouble: for according to the number of thy cities are thy gods, O Judah. **1 Thess. 1:9.** For they themselves shew of us what manner of entering in we had unto you, and how ye turned to God from idols to serve the living and true God.

c. **Ps. 81:10–11.** I am the LORD thy God, which brought thee out of the land of Egypt: open thy mouth wide, and I will fill it. But my people would not hearken to my voice; and Israel would none of me. **See Rom. 1:21.**

d. **Isa. 43:22–24.** But thou hast not called upon me, O Jacob; but thou hast been weary of me, O Israel. Thou hast not brought me the small cattle of thy burnt offerings; neither hast thou honoured me with thy sacrifices. I have not caused thee to serve with an offering, nor wearied thee with incense. Thou hast bought me no sweet cane with money, neither hast thou filled me with the fat of thy sacrifices: but thou hast made me to serve with thy sins, thou hast wearied me with thine iniquities.

e. **Jer. 4:22.** For my people is foolish, they have not known me; they are sottish children, and they have none understanding: they are wise to do evil, but to do good they have no knowledge. **Hos. 4:1, 6.** Hear the word of the LORD, ye children of Israel: for the LORD hath a controversy with the inhabitants of the land, because there is no truth, nor mercy, nor knowledge of God in the land.… My people are destroyed for lack of knowledge: because thou hast rejected knowledge, I will also reject thee, that thou shalt be no priest to me: seeing thou hast forgotten the law of thy God, I will also forget thy children.

f. **Jer. 2:32.** Can a maid forget her ornaments, or a bride her attire? yet my people have forgotten me days without number.

g. **Acts 17:23, 29.** For as I passed by, and beheld your devotions, I found an altar with this inscription, TO THE UNKNOWN GOD. Whom therefore ye ignorantly worship, him declare I unto you.… Forasmuch then as we are the offspring of God, we ought not to think that the Godhead is like unto gold, or silver, or stone, graven by

and wicked thoughts of him;[i] bold and curious searching into his secrets;[k] all profaneness,[l] hatred of God;[m] self-love,[n] self-seeking,[o] and all other inordinate and immoderate setting of our mind, will, or affections upon other things, and taking them off from him in whole or in part;[p] vain credulity,[q] unbelief,[r] heresy,[s] misbelief,[t] distrust,[u] despair,[w] incorrigibleness,[x] and insensibleness under judgments,[y]

art and man's device.

h. **Isa. 40:18.** To whom then will ye liken God? or what likeness will ye compare unto him?

i. **Ps. 50:21.** These things hast thou done, and I kept silence; thou thoughtest that I was altogether such an one as thyself: but I will reprove thee, and set them in order before thine eyes.

k. **Deut. 29:29.** The secret things belong unto the LORD our God: but those things which are revealed belong unto us and to our children for ever, that we may do all the words of this law.

l. **Titus 1:16.** They profess that they know God; but in works they deny him, being abominable, and disobedient, and unto every good work reprobate. **Heb. 12:16.** Lest there be any fornicator, or profane person, as Esau, who for one morsel of meat sold his birthright.

m. **Rom. 1:30.** … backbiters, haters of God, despiteful, proud, boasters, inventors of evil things, disobedient to parents.

n. **2 Tim. 3:2.** For men shall be lovers of their own selves, covetous, boasters, proud, blasphemers, disobedient to parents, unthankful, unholy.

o. **Phil. 2:21.** For all seek their own, not the things which are Jesus Christ's.

p. **1 John 2:15–16.** Love not the world, neither the things that are in the world. If any man love the world, the love of the Father is not in him. For all that is in the world, the lust of the flesh, and the lust of the eyes, and the pride of life, is not of the Father, but is of the world. **Col. 3:2, 5.** Set your affection on things above, not on things on the earth.… Mortify therefore your members which are upon the earth; fornication, uncleanness, inordinate affection, evil concupiscence, and covetousness, which is idolatry. **See 1 Sam. 2:29.**

q. **1 John 4:1.** Beloved, believe not every spirit, but try the spirits whether they are of God: because many false prophets are gone out into the world.

r. **Heb. 3:12.** Take heed, brethren, lest there be in any of you an evil heart of unbelief, in departing from the living God.

s. **Gal. 5:20.** … idolatry, witchcraft, hatred, variance, emulations, wrath, strife, seditions, heresies. **Titus 3:10.** A man that is an heretick after the first and second admonition reject.

t. **Acts 26:9.** I verily thought with myself, that I ought to do many things contrary to the name of Jesus of Nazareth.

u. **Ps. 78:22.** … because they believed not in God, and trusted not in his salvation.

w. **Gen. 4:13.** And Cain said unto the LORD, My punishment is greater than I can bear.

x. **Jer. 5:3.** O LORD, are not thine eyes upon the truth? thou hast stricken them,

hardness of heart,ᶻ pride,ᵃ´ presumption,ᵇ´ carnal security,ᶜ´ tempt-
ing of God;ᵈ´ using unlawful means,ᵉ´ and trusting in lawful means;ᶠ´
carnal delights and joys;ᵍ´ corrupt, blind, and indiscreet zeal;ʰ´ luke-
warmness,ⁱ´ and deadness in the things of God;ᵏ´ estranging ourselves,
and apostatizing from God;ˡ´ praying, or giving any religious worship, to saints, angels, or any other creatures;ᵐ´ all compacts and

but they have not grieved; thou hast consumed them, but they have refused to receive correction: they have made their faces harder than a rock; they have refused to return.

y. **Isa. 42:25.** Therefore he hath poured upon him the fury of his anger, and the strength of battle: and it hath set him on fire round about, yet he knew not; and it burned him, yet he laid it not to heart.

z. **Rom. 2:5.** But after thy hardness and impenitent heart treasurest up unto thyself wrath against the day of wrath and revelation of the righteous judgment of God.

a´. **Jer. 13:15.** Hear ye, and give ear; be not proud: for the LORD hath spoken.

b´. **Ps. 19:13.** Keep back thy servant also from presumptuous sins; let them not have dominion over me: then shall I be upright, and I shall be innocent from the great transgression.

c´. **Zeph. 1:12.** And it shall come to pass at that time, that I will search Jerusalem with candles, and punish the men that are settled on their lees: that say in their heart, The LORD will not do good, neither will he do evil.

d´. **Matt. 4:7.** Jesus said unto him, It is written again, Thou shalt not tempt the Lord thy God.

e´. **Rom. 3:8.** … and not rather, (as we be slanderously reported, and as some affirm that we say,) Let us do evil, that good may come? whose damnation is just.

f´. **Jer. 17:5.** Thus saith the LORD; Cursed be the man that trusteth in man, and maketh flesh his arm, and whose heart departeth from the LORD.

g´. **2 Tim. 3:4.** … traitors, heady, highminded, lovers of pleasures more than lovers of God.

h´. **Gal. 4:17.** They zealously affect you, but not well; yea, they would exclude you, that ye might affect them. **Rom. 10:2.** For I bear them record that they have a zeal of God, but not according to knowledge. **See John 16:2; Luke 9:54–55.**

i´. **Rev. 3:16.** So then because thou art lukewarm, and neither cold nor hot, I will spue thee out of my mouth.

k´. **Rev. 3:1.** And unto the angel of the church in Sardis write; These things saith he that hath the seven Spirits of God, and the seven stars; I know thy works, that thou hast a name that thou livest, and art dead.

l´. **Ezek. 14:5.** That I may take the house of Israel in their own heart, because they are all estranged from me through their idols. **Isa. 1:4–5.** Ah sinful nation, a people laden with iniquity, a seed of evildoers, children that are corrupters: they have forsaken the LORD, they have provoked the Holy One of Israel unto anger, they are gone away backward. Why should ye be stricken any more? ye will revolt more and more: the whole head is sick, and the whole heart faint.

m´. **Hos. 4:12.** My people ask counsel at their stocks, and their staff declareth unto them: for the spirit of whoredoms hath caused them to err, and they have gone a

consulting with the devil,$^{n'}$ and hearkening to his suggestions;$^{o'}$ making men the lords of our faith and conscience;$^{p'}$ slighting and despising God and his commands;$^{q'}$ resisting and grieving of his Spirit,$^{r'}$ discontent and impatience at his dispensations, charging him foolishly for the evils he inflicts on us;$^{s'}$ and ascribing the praise of any good we either are, have, or can do, to fortune,$^{t'}$ idols,$^{u'}$ ourselves,$^{w'}$

whoring from under their God. **Acts 10:25–26.** And as Peter was coming in, Cornelius met him, and fell down at his feet, and worshipped him. But Peter took him up, saying, Stand up; I myself also am a man. **Rev. 19:10.** And I fell at his feet to worship him. And he said unto me, See thou do it not: I am thy fellowservant, and of thy brethren that have the testimony of Jesus: worship God: for the testimony of Jesus is the spirit of prophecy. **Matt. 4:10.** Then saith Jesus unto him, Get thee hence, Satan: for it is written, Thou shalt worship the Lord thy God, and him only shalt thou serve. **Col. 2:18.** Let no man beguile you of your reward in a voluntary humility and worshipping of angels, intruding into those things which he hath not seen, vainly puffed up by his fleshly mind. **Rom. 1:25.** ... who changed the truth of God into a lie, and worshipped and served the creature more than the Creator, who is blessed for ever. Amen.

n´. **Lev. 20:6.** And the soul that turneth after such as have familiar spirits, and after wizards, to go a whoring after them, I will even set my face against that soul, and will cut him off from among his people. **See 1 Sam. 28:7, 11; 1 Chron. 10:13–14.**

o´. **Acts 5:3.** But Peter said, Ananias, why hath Satan filled thine heart to lie to the Holy Ghost, and to keep back part of the price of the land?

p´. **2 Cor. 1:24.** Not for that we have dominion over your faith, but are helpers of your joy: for by faith ye stand. **See Matt. 23:9.**

q´. **Deut. 32:15.** But Jeshurun waxed fat, and kicked: thou art waxen fat, thou art grown thick, thou art covered with fatness; then he forsook God which made him, and lightly esteemed the Rock of his salvation. **Prov. 13:13.** Whoso despiseth the word shall be destroyed: but he that feareth the commandment shall be rewarded. **See 2 Sam. 12:9.**

r´. **Acts 7:51.** Ye stiffnecked and uncircumcised in heart and ears, ye do always resist the Holy Ghost: as your fathers did, so do ye. **Eph. 4:30.** And grieve not the holy Spirit of God, whereby ye are sealed unto the day of redemption.

s´. **Job 1:22.** In all this Job sinned not, nor charged God foolishly. **Ps. 73:2–3.** But as for me, my feet were almost gone; my steps had well nigh slipped. For I was envious at the foolish, when I saw the prosperity of the wicked. **See verses 13–15, 22.**

t´. **1 Sam. 6:7–9.** Now therefore make a new cart, and take two milch kine, on which there hath come no yoke, and tie the kine to the cart, and bring their calves home from them: and take the ark of the LORD, and lay it upon the cart; and put the jewels of gold, which ye return him for a trespass offering, in a coffer by the side thereof; and send it away, that it may go. And see, if it goeth up by the way of his own coast to Bethshemesh, then he hath done us this great evil: but if not, then we shall know that it is not his hand that smote us; it was a chance that happened to us.

or any other creature.^{x´}

Q. 106. *What are we specially taught by these words* before me *in the first commandment?*

A. These words *before me* or before my face, in the first commandment, teach us, that God, who seeth all things, taketh special notice of, and is much displeased with, the sin of having any other God: that so it may be an argument to dissuade from it, and to aggravate it as a most impudent provocation:^y as also to persuade us to do as in his sight, whatever we do in his service.^z

Q. 107. *Which is the second commandment?*

A. The second commandment is, *Thou shalt not make unto thee any graven image, or any likeness of any thing that is in heaven above, or that is in the earth beneath, or that is in the water under the earth: thou shalt not bow down thyself to them, nor serve them: for I the LORD thy God am a jealous God, visiting the iniquity of the fathers upon the children unto the third and fourth generation of them that hate me; and shewing mercy unto thousands of them that love me, and keep my commandments.*^a

Luke 12:19. And I will say to my soul, Soul, thou hast much goods laid up for many years; take thine ease, eat, drink, and be merry.

u´. **Dan. 5:23.** But [thou, O Belshazzar] hast lifted up thyself against the Lord of heaven; and they have brought the vessels of his house before thee, and thou, and thy lords, thy wives, and thy concubines, have drunk wine in them; and thou hast praised the gods of silver, and gold, of brass, iron, wood, and stone, which see not, nor hear, nor know: and the God in whose hand thy breath is, and whose are all thy ways, hast thou not glorified.

w´. **Deut. 8:17.** … and thou say in thine heart, My power and the might of mine hand hath gotten me this wealth. **See Dan. 4:30.**

x´. **Hab. 1:16.** Therefore they sacrifice unto their net, and burn incense unto their drag; because by them their portion is fat, and their meat plenteous.

y. **Ps. 44:20–21.** If we have forgotten the name of our God, or stretched out our hands to a strange god; shall not God search this out? for he knoweth the secrets of the heart. **See Deut. 30:17–18; Ezek. 8:5–6, 12.**

z. **1 Chron. 28:9.** And thou, Solomon my son, know thou the God of thy father, and serve him with a perfect heart and with a willing mind: for the LORD searcheth all hearts, and understandeth all the imaginations of the thoughts: if thou seek him, he will be found of thee; but if thou forsake him, he will cast thee off for ever.

a. **Ex. 20:4–6. Cf. Deut. 5:8–10.** Thou shalt not make thee any graven image, or any likeness of any thing that is in heaven above, or that is in the earth beneath, or that is in the waters beneath the earth: thou shalt not bow down thyself unto them, nor serve them: for I the LORD thy God am a jealous God, visiting the iniquity of the fathers upon the children unto the third and fourth generation of them that hate me, and shewing mercy unto thousands of them that love me and keep my commandments.

Q. 108. *What are the duties required in the second commandment?*

A. The duties required in the second commandment are, the receiving, observing, and keeping pure and entire, all such religious worship and ordinances as God hath instituted in his Word;[b] particularly prayer and thanksgiving in the name of Christ;[c] the reading, preaching, and hearing of the Word;[d] the administration and receiving of the sacraments;[e] church government and discipline;[f] the

b. **Deut. 12:32.** What thing soever I command you, observe to do it: thou shalt not add thereto, nor diminish from it. **Deut. 32:46–47.** And he said unto them, Set your hearts unto all the words which I testify among you this day, which ye shall command your children to observe to do, all the words of this law. For it is not a vain thing for you; because it is your life: and through this thing ye shall prolong your days in the land, whither ye go over Jordan to possess it. **Matt. 28:20.** … teaching them to observe all things whatsoever I have commanded you: and, lo, I am with you alway, even unto the end of the world. Amen. **1 Tim. 6:13–14.** I give thee charge in the sight of God, who quickeneth all things, and before Christ Jesus, who before Pontius Pilate witnessed a good confession; that thou keep this commandment without spot, unrebukeable, until the appearing of our Lord Jesus Christ. **See Acts 2:42.**

c. **Phil. 4:6.** Be careful for nothing; but in every thing by prayer and supplication with thanksgiving let your requests be made known unto God. **Eph. 5:20.** Giving thanks always for all things unto God and the Father in the name of our Lord Jesus Christ.

d. **Deut. 17:18–19.** And it shall be, when he sitteth upon the throne of his kingdom, that he shall write him a copy of this law in a book out of that which is before the priests the Levites: and it shall be with him, and he shall read therein all the days of his life: that he may learn to fear the LORD his God, to keep all the words of this law and these statutes, to do them. **Acts 15:21.** For Moses of old time hath in every city them that preach him, being read in the synagogues every sabbath day. **2 Tim. 4:2.** Preach the word; be instant in season, out of season; reprove, rebuke, exhort with all longsuffering and doctrine. **James 1:21–22.** Wherefore lay apart all filthiness and superfluity of naughtiness, and receive with meekness the engrafted word, which is able to save your souls. But be ye doers of the word, and not hearers only, deceiving your own selves. **Acts 10:33.** Immediately therefore I sent to thee; and thou hast well done that thou art come. Now therefore are we all here present before God, to hear all things that are commanded thee of God.

e. **Matt. 28:19.** Go ye therefore, and teach all nations, baptizing them in the name of the Father, and of the Son, and of the Holy Ghost. **See 1 Cor. 11:23–30.**

f. **Matt. 18:15–17.** Moreover if thy brother shall trespass against thee, go and tell him his fault between thee and him alone: if he shall hear thee, thou hast gained thy brother. But if he will not hear thee, then take with thee one or two more, that in the mouth of two or three witnesses every word may be established. And if he shall neglect to hear them, tell it unto the church: but if he neglect to hear the church, let him be unto thee as a heathen man and a publican. **Matt. 16:19.** And I will give unto thee the keys of the kingdom of heaven: and whatsoever thou shalt bind on earth shall be bound in heaven: and whatsoever thou shalt loose on earth shall be loosed in

ministry and maintainance thereof;[g] religious fasting;[h] swearing by the name of God,[i] and vowing unto him:[k] as also the disapproving, detesting, opposing all false worship;[l] and, according to each one's place and calling, removing it, and all monuments of idolatry.[m]

Q. 109. *What are the sins forbidden in the second commandment?*

A. The sins forbidden in the second commandment are, all devising,[n] counseling,[o] commanding,[p] using,[q] and anywise approving,

heaven. **1 Cor. 12:28.** And God hath set some in the church, first apostles, secondarily prophets, thirdly teachers, after that miracles, then gifts of healings, helps, governments, diversities of tongues. **See 1 Cor. 5.**

g. **Eph. 4:11–12.** And he gave some, apostles; and some, prophets; and some, evangelists; and some, pastors and teachers; for the perfecting of the saints, for the work of the ministry, for the edifying of the body of Christ. **1 Tim. 5:17–18.** Let the elders that rule well be counted worthy of double honour, especially they who labour in the word and doctrine. For the scripture saith, Thou shalt not muzzle the ox that treadeth out the corn. And, The labourer is worthy of his reward. **See 1 Cor. 9:7–15.**

h. **Joel 2:12–13.** Therefore also now, saith the LORD, turn ye even to me with all your heart, and with fasting, and with weeping, and with mourning: and rend your heart, and not your garments, and turn unto the LORD your God: for he is gracious and merciful, slow to anger, and of great kindness, and repenteth him of the evil. **1 Cor. 7:5.** Defraud ye not one the other, except it be with consent for a time, that ye may give yourselves to fasting and prayer; and come together again, that Satan tempt you not for your incontinency.

i. **Deut. 6:13.** Thou shalt fear the LORD thy God, and serve him, and shalt swear by his name.

k. **Ps. 76:11.** Vow, and pay unto the LORD your God: let all that be round about him bring presents unto him that ought to be feared. **Isa. 19:21.** And the LORD shall be known to Egypt, and the Egyptians shall know the LORD in that day, and shall do sacrifice and oblation; yea, they shall vow a vow unto the LORD, and perform it. **See Ps. 116:14, 18.**

l. **Acts 17:16–17.** Now while Paul waited for them at Athens, his spirit was stirred in him, when he saw the city wholly given to idolatry. Therefore disputed he in the synagogue with the Jews, and with the devout persons, and in the market daily with them that met with him. **Ps. 16:4.** Their sorrows shall be multiplied that hasten after another god: their drink offerings of blood will I not offer, nor take up their names into my lips.

m. **Deut. 7:5.** But thus shall ye deal with them; ye shall destroy their altars, and break down their images, and cut down their groves, and burn their graven images with fire. **Isa. 30:22.** Ye shall defile also the covering of thy graven images of silver, and the ornament of thy molten images of gold: thou shalt cast them away as a menstruous cloth; thou shalt say unto it, Get thee hence.

n. **Num. 15:39.** And it shall be unto you for a fringe, that ye may look upon it, and remember all the commandments of the LORD, and do them; and that ye seek not after your own heart and your own eyes, after which ye use to go a whoring.

any religious worship not instituted by God himself;[r] the making any
representation of God, of all or of any of the three persons, either
inwardly in our mind, or outwardly in any kind of image or likeness
of any creature whatsoever;[s] all worshiping of it,[t] or God in it or by

o. **Deut. 13:6–8.** If thy brother, the son of thy mother, or thy son, or thy daughter, or the wife of thy bosom, or thy friend, which is as thine own soul, entice thee
secretly, saying, Let us go and serve other gods, which thou hast not known, thou, nor
thy fathers; namely, of the gods of the people which are round about you, nigh unto
thee, or far off from thee, from the one end of the earth even unto the other end of the
earth; thou shalt not consent unto him, nor hearken unto him; neither shall thine eye
pity him, neither shalt thou spare, neither shalt thou conceal him.

p. **Hos. 5:11.** Ephraim is oppressed and broken in judgment, because he willingly walked after the commandment. **Mic. 6:16.** For the statutes of Omri are kept,
and all the works of the house of Ahab, and ye walk in their counsels; that I should
make thee a desolation, and the inhabitants thereof an hissing: therefore ye shall bear
the reproach of my people.

q. **1 Kings 11:33.** Because that they have forsaken me, and have worshipped
Ashtoreth the goddess of the Zidonians, Chemosh the god of the Moabites, and Milcom
the god of the children of Ammon, and have not walked in my ways, to do that which
is right in mine eyes, and to keep my statutes and my judgments, as did David his
father. **1 Kings 12:33.** So he offered upon the altar which he had made in Bethel the
fifteenth day of the eighth month, even in the month which he had devised of his own
heart; and ordained a feast unto the children of Israel: and he offered upon the altar,
and burnt incense.

r. **Deut. 12:30–32.** Take heed to thyself that thou be not snared by following
them, after that they be destroyed from before thee; and that thou inquire not after
their gods, saying, How did these nations serve their gods? even so will I do likewise.
Thou shalt not do so unto the LORD thy God: for every abomination to the LORD,
which he hateth, have they done unto their gods; for even their sons and their daughters they have burnt in the fire to their gods. What thing soever I command you,
observe to do it: thou shalt not add thereto, nor diminish from it. **Lev. 10:1–2.** And
Nadab and Abihu, the sons of Aaron, took either of them his censer, and put fire
therein, and put incense thereon, and offered strange fire before the LORD, which he
commanded them not. And there went out fire from the LORD, and devoured them,
and they died before the LORD. **Jer. 19:5.** They have built also the high places of
Baal, to burn their sons with fire for burnt offerings unto Baal, which I commanded
not, nor spake it, neither came it into my mind.

s. **Deut. 4:15–16.** Take ye therefore good heed unto yourselves; for ye saw no
manner of similitude on the day that the LORD spake unto you in Horeb out of the
midst of the fire: lest ye corrupt yourselves, and make you a graven image, the similitude of any figure, the likeness of male or female. **See verses 17–19. Acts 17:29.**
Forasmuch then as we are the offspring of God, we ought not to think that the Godhead
is like unto gold, or silver, or stone, graven by art and man's device. **Rom. 1:21–23,
25.** … because that, when they knew God, they glorified him not as God, neither were
thankful; but became vain in their imaginations, and their foolish heart was darkened.
Professing themselves to be wise, they became fools, and changed the glory of the

it;[u] the making of any representation of feigned deities,[w] and all worship of them, or service belonging to them;[x] all superstitious devices,[y] corrupting the worship of God,[z] adding to it, or taking from it,[a] whether invented and taken up of ourselves,[b] or received by tradition from others,[c] though under the title of antiquity,[d] custom,[e]

uncorruptible God into an image made like to corruptible man, and to birds, and fourfooted beasts, and creeping things.… who changed the truth of God into a lie, and worshipped and served the creature more than the Creator, who is blessed for ever. Amen.

t. **Gal. 4:8.** Howbeit then, when ye knew not God, ye did service unto them which by nature are no gods. **See Dan. 3:18.**

u. **Ex. 32:5.** And when Aaron saw it, he built an altar before it; and Aaron made proclamation, and said, To morrow is a feast to the LORD.

w. **Ex. 32:8.** They have turned aside quickly out of the way which I commanded them: they have made them a molten calf, and have worshipped it, and have sacrificed thereunto, and said, These be thy gods, O Israel, which have brought thee up out of the land of Egypt.

x. **1 Kings 18:26, 28.** And they took the bullock which was given them, and they dressed it, and called on the name of Baal from morning even until noon, saying, O Baal, hear us. But there was no voice, nor any that answered. And they leaped upon the altar which was made.… And they cried aloud, and cut themselves after their manner with knives and lancets, till the blood gushed out upon them. **See Isa. 65:11.**

y. **Acts 17:22.** Then Paul stood in the midst of Mars' hill, and said, Ye men of Athens, I perceive that in all things ye are too superstitious. **Col. 2:21–23** … (touch not; taste not; handle not; which all are to perish with the using;) after the commandments and doctrines of men? Which things have indeed a shew of wisdom in will worship, and humility, and neglecting of the body; not in any honour to the satisfying of the flesh.

z. **Mal. 1:7–8, 14.** Ye offer polluted bread upon mine altar; and ye say, Wherein have we polluted thee? In that ye say, The table of the LORD is contemptible. And if ye offer the blind for sacrifice, is it not evil? and if ye offer the lame and sick, is it not evil? offer it now unto thy governor; will he be pleased with thee, or accept thy person? saith the LORD of hosts.… But cursed be the deceiver, which hath in his flock a male, and voweth, and sacrificeth unto the Lord a corrupt thing: for I am a great King, saith LORD of hosts, and my name is dreadful among the heathen.

a. **Deut. 4:2.** Ye shall not add unto the word which I command you, neither shall ye diminish ought from it, that ye may keep the commandments of the LORD your God which I command you.

b. **Ps. 106:39.** Thus were they defiled with their own works, and went a whoring with their own inventions.

c. **Matt. 15:9.** But in vain they do worship me, teaching for doctrines the commandments of men.

d. **1 Pet. 1:18.** … forasmuch as ye know that ye were not redeemed with corruptible things, as silver and gold, from your vain conversation received by tradition from your fathers.

e. **Jer. 44:17.** But we will certainly do whatsoever thing goeth forth out of our

devotion,[f] good intent, or any other pretense whatsoever;[g] simony;[h] sacrilege;[i] all neglect,[k] contempt,[l] hindering,[m] and opposing the worship and ordinances which God hath appointed.[n´]

own mouth, to burn incense unto the queen of heaven, and to pour out drink offerings unto her, as we have done, we, and our fathers, our kings, and our princes, in the cities of Judah, and in the streets of Jerusalem: for then had we plenty of victuals, and were well, and saw no evil.

f. **Isa. 65:3–5.** … a people that provoketh me to anger continually to my face; that sacrificeth in gardens, and burneth incense upon altars of brick; which remain among the graves, and lodge in the monuments, which eat swine's flesh, and broth of abominable things is in their vessels; which say, Stand by thyself, come not near to me; for I am holier than thou. These are a smoke in my nose, a fire that burneth all the day. **Gal. 1:13–14.** For ye have heard of my conversation in time past in the Jews' religion, how that beyond measure I persecuted the church of God, and wasted it: And profited in the Jews' religion above many my equals in mine own nation, being more exceedingly zealous of the traditions of my fathers.

g. **1 Sam. 13:11–12.** And Samuel said, What hast thou done? And Saul said, Because I saw that the people were scattered from me, and that thou camest not within the days appointed, and that the Philistines gathered themselves together at Michmash; therefore said I, The Philistines will come down now upon me to Gilgal, and I have not made supplication unto the LORD: I forced myself therefore, and offered a burnt offering. **1 Sam. 15:21.** But the people took of the spoil, sheep and oxen, the chief of the things which should have been utterly destroyed, to sacrifice unto the LORD thy God in Gilgal.

h. **Acts 8:18–19.** And when Simon saw that through laying on of the apostles' hands the Holy Ghost was given, he offered them money, saying, Give me also this power, that on whomsoever I lay hands, he may receive the Holy Ghost.

i. **Rom. 2:22.** Thou that sayest a man should not commit adultery, dost thou commit adultery? thou that abhorrest idols, dost thou commit sacrilege? **Mal. 3:8.** Will a man rob God? Yet ye have robbed me. But ye say, Wherein have we robbed thee? In tithes and offerings.

k. **Ex. 4:24–26.** And it came to pass by the way in the inn, that the LORD met him, and sought to kill him. Then Zipporah took a sharp stone, and cut off the foreskin of her son, and cast it at his feet, and said, Surely a bloody husband art thou to me. So he let him go: then she said, A bloody husband thou art, because of the circumcision.

l. **Matt. 22:5.** But they made light of it, and went their ways, one to his farm, another to his merchandise. **Mal. 1:7, 13.** Ye offer polluted bread upon mine altar; and ye say, Wherein have we polluted thee? In that ye say, The table of the LORD is contemptible.… Ye said also, Behold, what a weariness is it! and ye have snuffed at it, saith the LORD of hosts; and ye brought that which was torn, and the lame, and the sick; thus ye brought an offering: should I accept this of your hand? saith the LORD.

m. **Matt. 23:13.** But woe unto you, scribes and Pharisees, hypocrites! for ye shut up the kingdom of heaven against men: for ye neither go in yourselves, neither suffer ye them that are entering to go in.

n´. **Acts 13:44–45.** And the next sabbath day came almost the whole city

Q. 110. *What are the reasons annexed to the second commandment, the more to enforce it?*

A. The reasons annexed to the second commandment, the more to enforce it, contained in these words, *For I the* LORD *thy God am a jealous God, visiting the iniquity of the fathers upon the children unto the third and fourth generation of them that hate me; and shewing mercy unto thousands of them that love me, and keep my commandments;*[o] are, besides God's sovereignty over us, and propriety in us,[p] his fervent zeal for his own worship,[q] and his revengeful indignation against all false worship, as being a spiritual whoredom;[r] accounting the breakers of this commandment such as hate him, and threatening to punish them unto divers generations;[s] and esteeming the observers of it such as love him and keep his commandments, and promising mercy to them unto

---

together to hear the word of God. But when the Jews saw the multitudes, they were filled with envy, and spake against those things which were spoken by Paul, contradicting and blaspheming. **See 1 Thess. 2:15–16.**

o. **Ex. 20:5–6.**

p. **Ps. 45:11.** So shall the king greatly desire thy beauty: for he is thy Lord; and worship thou him. **Rev. 15:3–4.** And they sing the song of Moses the servant of God, and the song of the Lamb, saying, Great and marvellous are thy works, Lord God Almighty; just and true are thy ways, thou King of saints. Who shall not fear thee, O Lord, and glorify thy name? for thou only art holy: for all nations shall come and worship before thee; for thy judgments are made manifest. **See Ps. 95:2–3, 6–7; Ex. 19:5; Isa. 54:5.**

q. **Ex. 34:13–14.** But ye shall destroy their altars, break their images, and cut down their groves: for thou shalt worship no other god: for the LORD, whose name is Jealous, is a jealous God.

r. **1 Cor. 10:20–22.** But I say, that the things which the Gentiles sacrifice, they sacrifice to devils, and not to God: and I would not that ye should have fellowship with devils. Ye cannot drink the cup of the Lord, and the cup of devils: ye cannot be partakers of the Lord's table, and of the table of devils. Do we provoke the Lord to jealousy? are we stronger than he? **Ezek. 16:26–27.** Thou hast also committed fornication with the Egyptians thy neighbours, great of flesh; and hast increased thy whoredoms, to provoke me to anger. Behold, therefore I have stretched out my hand over thee, and have diminished thine ordinary food, and delivered thee unto the will of them that hate thee, the daughters of the Philistines, which are ashamed of thy lewd way. **See Jer. 7:18–20; Deut. 32:16–20.**

s. **Hos. 2:2–4.** Plead with your mother, plead: for she is not my wife, neither am I her husband: let her therefore put away her whoredoms out of her sight, and her adulteries from between her breasts; lest I strip her naked, and set her as in the day that she was born, and make her as a wilderness, and set her like a dry land, and slay her with thirst. And I will not have mercy upon her children; for they be the children of whoredoms.

many generations.[t]

Q. 111. *Which is the third commandment?*

A. The third commandment is, *Thou shalt not take the name of the* LORD *thy God in vain; for the* LORD *will not hold him guiltless that taketh his name in vain.*[u]

Q. 112. *What is required in the third commandment?*

A. The third commandment requires, that the name of God, his titles, attributes,[w] ordinances,[x] the Word,[y] sacraments,[z] prayer,[a] oaths,[b] vows,[c] lots,[d] his works,[e] and whatsoever else there is whereby he makes

t. **Deut. 5:29.** O that there were such an heart in them, that they would fear me, and keep all my commandments always, that it might be well with them, and with their children for ever!

u. **Ex. 20:7. Cf. Deut. 5:11.** Thou shalt not take the name of the LORD thy God in vain: for the LORD will not hold him guiltless that taketh his name in vain.

w. **Matt. 6:9.** After this manner therefore pray ye: Our Father which art in heaven, Hallowed be thy name. **Deut. 28:58.** If thou wilt not observe to do all the words of this law that are written in this book, that thou mayest fear this glorious and fearful name, THE LORD THY GOD … **Ps. 68:4.** Sing unto God, sing praises to his name: extol him that rideth upon the heavens by his name JAH, and rejoice before him. **See Ps. 29:2; 1 Chron. 29:10–13; Rev. 15:3–4.**

x. **Eccl. 5:1.** Keep thy foot when thou goest to the house of God, and be more ready to hear, than to give the sacrifice of fools: for they consider not that they do evil. **Luke 1:6.** And they were both righteous before God, walking in all the commandments and ordinances of the Lord blameless. **See Mal. 1:11, 14.**

y. **Ps. 138:2.** I will worship toward thy holy temple, and praise thy name for thy lovingkindness and for thy truth: for thou hast magnified thy word above all thy name.

z. **1 Cor. 11:24–25, 28–29.** And when he had given thanks, he brake it, and said, Take, eat: this is my body, which is broken for you: this do in remembrance of me. After the same manner also he took the cup, when he had supped, saying, This cup is the new testament in my blood: this do ye, as oft as ye drink it, in remembrance of me.… But let a man examine himself, and so let him eat of that bread, and drink of that cup. For he that eateth and drinketh unworthily, eateth and drinketh damnation to himself, not discerning the Lord's body.

a. **1 Tim. 2:8.** I will therefore that men pray every where, lifting up holy hands, without wrath and doubting.

b. **Jer. 4:2.** And thou shalt swear, The LORD liveth, in truth, in judgment, and in righteousness; and the nations shall bless themselves in him, and in him shall they glory.

c. **Eccl. 5:2, 4–6.** Be not rash with thy mouth, and let not thine heart be hasty to utter any thing before God: for God is in heaven, and thou upon earth: therefore let thy words be few.… When thou vowest a vow unto God, defer not to pay it; for he hath no pleasure in fools: pay that which thou hast vowed. Better is it that thou shouldest not vow, than that thou shouldest vow and not pay. Suffer not thy mouth to cause thy

himself known, be holily and reverently used in thought,[f] meditation,[g] word,[h] and writing;[i] by an holy profession,[k] and answerable conversation,[l] to the glory of God,[m] and the good of ourselves,[n] and others.[o]

Q. 113. *What are the sins forbidden in the third commandment?*

A. The sins forbidden in the third commandment are, the not using of God's name as is required;[p] and the abuse of it in an ignorant,[q] vain,[r] irreverent, profane,[s] superstitious,[t] or wicked men-

flesh to sin; neither say thou before the angel, that it was an error: wherefore should God be angry at thy voice, and destroy the work of thine hands?

d. **Acts 1:24, 26.** And they prayed, and said, Thou, Lord, which knowest the hearts of all men, shew whether of these two thou hast chosen.... And they gave forth their lots; and the lot fell upon Matthias; and he was numbered with the eleven apostles.

e. **Job 36:24.** Remember that thou magnify his work, which men behold.

f. **Mal. 3:16.** Then they that feared the LORD spake often one to another: and the LORD hearkened, and heard it, and a book of remembrance was written before him for them that feared the LORD, and that thought upon his name.

g. **Ps. 8:1, 3–4.** O LORD our Lord, how excellent is thy name in all the earth! who hast set thy glory above the heavens.... When I consider thy heavens, the work of thy fingers, the moon and the stars, which thou hast ordained; What is man, that thou art mindful of him? and the son of man, that thou visitest him?

h. **Ps. 105:2, 5.** Sing unto him, sing psalms unto him: talk ye of all his wondrous works.... Remember his marvellous works that he hath done; his wonders, and the judgments of his mouth. **See Col. 3:17.**

i. **Ps. 102:18.** This shall be written for the generation to come: and the people which shall be created shall praise the LORD.

k. **1 Pet. 3:15.** But sanctify the Lord God in your hearts: and be ready always to give an answer to every man that asketh you a reason of the hope that is in you with meekness and fear. **Mic. 4:5.** For all people will walk every one in the name of his god, and we will walk in the name of the LORD our God for ever and ever.

l. **Phil. 1:27.** Only let your conversation be as it becometh the gospel of Christ: that whether I come and see you, or else be absent, I may hear of your affairs, that ye stand fast in one spirit, with one mind striving together for the faith of the gospel.

m. **1 Cor. 10:31.** Whether therefore ye eat, or drink, or whatsoever ye do, do all to the glory of God.

n. **Jer. 32:39.** And I will give them one heart, and one way, that they may fear me for ever, for the good of them, and of their children after them.

o. **1 Pet. 2:12.** ... having your conversation honest among the Gentiles: that, whereas they speak against you as evildoers, they may by your good works, which they shall behold, glorify God in the day of visitation.

p. **Mal. 2:2.** If ye will not hear, and if ye will not lay it to heart, to give glory unto my name, saith the LORD of hosts, I will even send a curse upon you, and I will curse your blessings: yea, I have cursed them already, because ye do not lay it to heart.

q. **Acts 17:23.** For as I passed by, and beheld your devotions, I found an altar with this inscription, TO THE UNKNOWN GOD. Whom therefore ye ignorantly

tioning or otherwise using his titles, attributes,ᵘ ordinances,ʷ or works,ˣ

worship, him declare I unto you.

r. **Prov. 30:9.** … lest I be full, and deny thee, and say, Who is the LORD? or lest I be poor, and steal, and take the name of my God in vain.

s. **Mal. 1:6–7, 12.** A son honoureth his father, and a servant his master: if then I be a father, where is mine honour? and if I be a master, where is my fear? saith the LORD of hosts unto you, O priests, that despise my name. And ye say, Wherein have we despised thy name? Ye offer polluted bread upon mine altar; and ye say, Wherein have we polluted thee? In that ye say, The table of the LORD is contemptible…. But ye have profaned it, in that ye say, The table of the LORD is polluted; and the fruit thereof, even his meat, is contemptible. **Mal. 3:14.** Ye have said, It is vain to serve God: and what profit is it that we have kept his ordinance, and that we have walked mournfully before the LORD of hosts?

t. **1 Sam. 4:3–5.** And when the people were come into the camp, the elders of Israel said, Wherefore hath the LORD smitten us to day before the Philistines? Let us fetch the ark of the covenant of the LORD out of Shiloh unto us, that, when it cometh among us, it may save us out of the hand of our enemies. So the people sent to Shiloh, that they might bring from thence the ark of the covenant of the LORD of hosts, which dwelleth between the cherubims: and the two sons of Eli, Hophni and Phinehas, were there with the ark of the covenant of God. And when the ark of the covenant of the LORD came into the camp, all Israel shouted with a great shout, so that the earth rang again. **Jer. 7:4, 9–10, 14, 31.** Trust ye not in lying words, saying, The temple of the LORD, The temple of the LORD, The temple of the LORD, are these…. Will ye steal, murder, and commit adultery, and swear falsely, and burn incense unto Baal, and walk after other gods whom ye know not; and come and stand before me in this house, which is called by my name, and say, We are delivered to do all these abominations?… Therefore will I do unto this house, which is called by my name, wherein ye trust, and unto the place which I gave to you and to your fathers, as I have done to Shiloh…. And they have built the high places of Tophet, which is in the valley of the son of Hinnom, to burn their sons and their daughters in the fire; which I commanded them not, neither came it into my heart. **Col. 2:20–22.** Wherefore if ye be dead with Christ from the rudiments of the world, why, as though living in the world, are ye subject to ordinances, (touch not; taste not; handle not; which all are to perish with the using;) after the commandments and doctrines of men?

u. **2 Kings 18:30, 35.** Neither let Hezekiah make you trust in the LORD, saying, The LORD will surely deliver us, and this city shall not be delivered into the hand of the king of Assyria…. Who are they among all the gods of the countries, that have delivered their country out of mine hand, that the LORD should deliver Jerusalem out of mine hand? **Ex. 5:2.** And Pharaoh said, Who is the LORD, that I should obey his voice to let Israel go? I know not the LORD, neither will I let Israel go. **Ps. 139:20.** For they speak against thee wickedly, and thine enemies take thy name in vain.

w. **Ps. 50:16–17.** But unto the wicked God saith, What hast thou to do to declare my statutes, or that thou shouldest take my covenant in thy mouth? Seeing thou hatest instruction, and castest my words behind thee.

x. **Isa. 5:12.** And the harp, and the viol, the tabret, and pipe, and wine, are in their feasts: but they regard not the work of the LORD, neither consider the operation of his hands.

by blasphemy,[y] perjury;[z] all sinful cursings,[a] oaths,[b] vows,[c] and lots;[d] violating of our oaths and vows, if lawful,[e] and fulfilling them, if of

y. **2 Kings 19:22.** Whom hast thou reproached and blasphemed? and against whom hast thou exalted thy voice, and lifted up thine eyes on high? even against the Holy One of Israel. **Lev. 24:11.** And the Israelitish woman's son blasphemed the name of the LORD, and cursed. And they brought him unto Moses: (and his mother's name was Shelomith, the daughter of Dibri, of the tribe of Dan:) …

z. **Zech. 5:4.** I will bring it forth, saith the LORD of hosts, and it shall enter into the house of the thief, and into the house of him that sweareth falsely by my name: and it shall remain in the midst of his house, and shall consume it with the timber thereof and the stones thereof. **Zech. 8:17.** And let none of you imagine evil in your hearts against his neighbour; and love no false oath: for all these are things that I hate, saith the LORD.

a. **1 Sam. 17:43.** And the Philistine said unto David, Am I a dog, that thou comest to me with staves? And the Philistine cursed David by his gods. **2 Sam. 16:5.** And when king David came to Bahurim, behold, thence came out a man of the family of the house of Saul, whose name was Shimei, the son of Gera: he came forth, and cursed still as he came.

b. **Jer. 5:7.** How shall I pardon thee for this? thy children have forsaken me, and sworn by them that are no gods: when I had fed them to the full, they then committed adultery, and assembled themselves by troops in the harlots' houses. **Jer. 23:10.** For the land is full of adulterers; for because of swearing the land mourneth; the pleasant places of the wilderness are dried up, and their course is evil, and their force is not right.

c. **Deut. 23:18.** Thou shalt not bring the hire of a whore, or the price of a dog, into the house of the LORD thy God for any vow: for even both these are abomination unto the LORD thy God. **Acts 23:12, 14.** And when it was day, certain of the Jews banded together, and bound themselves under a curse, saying that they would neither eat nor drink till they had killed Paul.… And they came to the chief priests and elders, and said, We have bound ourselves under a great curse, that we will eat nothing until we have slain Paul.

d. **Est. 3:7.** In the first month, that is, the month Nisan, in the twelfth year of king Ahasuerus, they cast Pur, that is, the lot, before Haman from day to day, and from month to month, to the twelfth month, that is, the month Adar. **Est. 9:24.** Because Haman the son of Hammedatha, the Agagite, the enemy of all the Jews, had devised against the Jews to destroy them, and had cast Pur, that is, the lot, to consume them, and to destroy them. **Ps. 22:18.** They part my garments among them, and cast lots upon my vesture.

e. **Ps. 24:4.** He that hath clean hands, and a pure heart; who hath not lifted up his soul unto vanity, nor sworn deceitfully. **Ezek. 17:16, 18–19.** As I live, saith the Lord GOD, surely in the place where the king dwelleth that made him king, whose oath he despised, and whose covenant he brake, even with him in the midst of Babylon he shall die.… Seeing he despised the oath by breaking the covenant, when, lo, he had given his hand, and hath done all these things, he shall not escape. Therefore thus saith the Lord GOD; As I live, surely mine oath that he hath despised, and my covenant that he hath broken, even it will I recompense upon his own head.

things unlawful;[f] murmuring and quarreling at,[g] curious prying into,[h] and misapplying of God's decrees[i] and providences;[k] misinterpreting,[l]

f. **Mark 6:26.** And the king was exceeding sorry; yet for his oath's sake, and for their sakes which sat with him, he would not reject her. **1 Sam. 25:22, 32–34.** So and more also do God unto the enemies of David, if I leave of all that pertain to him by the morning light any that pisseth against the wall.... And David said to Abigail, Blessed be the LORD God of Israel, which sent thee this day to meet me: and blessed be thy advice, and blessed be thou, which hast kept me this day from coming to shed blood, and from avenging myself with mine own hand. For in very deed, as the LORD God of Israel liveth, which hath kept me back from hurting thee, except thou hadst hasted and come to meet me, surely there had not been left unto Nabal by the morning light any that pisseth against the wall.

g. **Rom. 9:14, 19–20.** What shall we say then? Is there unrighteousness with God? God forbid.... Thou wilt say then unto me, Why doth he yet find fault? For who hath resisted his will? Nay but, O man, who art thou that repliest against God? Shall the thing formed say to him that formed it, Why hast thou made me thus?

h. **Deut. 29:29.** The secret things belong unto the LORD our God: but those things which are revealed belong unto us and to our children for ever, that we may do all the words of this law.

i. **Rom. 3:5, 7.** But if our unrighteousness commend the righteousness of God, what shall we say? Is God unrighteous who taketh vengeance? (I speak as a man) ... For if the truth of God hath more abounded through my lie unto his glory; why yet am I also judged as a sinner? **Rom. 6:1–2.** What shall we say then? Shall we continue in sin, that grace may abound? God forbid. How shall we, that are dead to sin, live any longer therein?

k. **Eccl. 8:11.** Because sentence against an evil work is not executed speedily, therefore the heart of the sons of men is fully set in them to do evil. **Eccl. 9:3.** This is an evil among all things that are done under the sun, that there is one event unto all: yea, also the heart of the sons of men is full of evil, and madness is in their heart while they live, and after that they go to the dead. **See Ps. 39.**

l. **Matt. 5:21–22, 27–28, 31–35, 38–39, 43–44.** Ye have heard that it was said by them of old time, Thou shalt not kill; and whosoever shall kill shall be in danger of the judgment: but I say unto you, That whosoever is angry with his brother without a cause shall be in danger of the judgment: and whosoever shall say to his brother, Raca, shall be in danger of the council: but whosoever shall say, Thou fool, shall be in danger of hell fire.... Ye have heard that it was said by them of old time, Thou shalt not commit adultery: but I say unto you, That whosoever looketh on a woman to lust after her hath committed adultery with her already in his heart.... It hath been said, Whosoever shall put away his wife, let him give her a writing of divorcement: but I say unto you, That whosoever shall put away his wife, saving for the cause of fornication, causeth her to commit adultery: and whosoever shall marry her that is divorced committeth adultery. Again, ye have heard that it hath been said by them of old time, Thou shalt not forswear thyself, but shalt perform unto the Lord thine oaths: but I say unto you, Swear not at all; neither by heaven; for it is God's throne: nor by the earth; for it is his footstool: neither by Jerusalem; for it is the city of the great King.... Ye have heard that it hath been said, An eye for an eye, and a tooth for a tooth: but I say unto you, That ye resist not evil: but whosoever shall smite thee on thy right cheek, turn to

misapplying,[m] or anyway perverting the Word, or any part of it,[n] to profane jests,[o] curious or unprofitable questions, vain janglings, or the maintaining of false doctrines;[p'] abusing it, the creatures, or anything contained under the name of God, to charms,[q'] or sinful lusts

him the other also.… Ye have heard that it hath been said, Thou shalt love thy neighbour, and hate thine enemy. But I say unto you, Love your enemies, bless them that curse you, do good to them that hate you, and pray for them which despitefully use you, and persecute you.

m. **Ezek. 13:22.** Because with lies ye have made the heart of the righteous sad, whom I have not made sad; and strengthened the hands of the wicked, that he should not return from his wicked way, by promising him life …

n. **2 Pet. 3:16.** … as also in all his epistles, speaking in them of these things; in which are some things hard to be understood, which they that are unlearned and unstable wrest, as they do also the other scriptures, unto their own destruction. **See Matt. 22:24–31.**

o. **Isa. 22:13.** And behold joy and gladness, slaying oxen, and killing sheep, eating flesh, and drinking wine: let us eat and drink; for to morrow we shall die. **Jer. 23:34, 36, 38.** And as for the prophet, and the priest, and the people, that shall say, The burden of the LORD, I will even punish that man and his house.… And the burden of the LORD shall ye mention no more: for every man's word shall be his burden; for ye have perverted the words of the living God, of the LORD of hosts our God.… But since ye say, The burden of the LORD; therefore thus saith the LORD; Because ye say this word, The burden of the LORD, and I have sent unto you, saying, Ye shall not say, The burden of the LORD …

p'. **1 Tim. 1:4, 6–7.** Neither give heed to fables and endless genealogies, which minister questions, rather than godly edifying which is in faith: so do.… From which some having swerved have turned aside unto vain jangling; desiring to be teachers of the law; understanding neither what they say, nor whereof they affirm. **1 Tim. 6:4–5, 20.** He is proud, knowing nothing, but doting about questions and strifes of words, whereof cometh envy, strife, railings, evil surmisings, perverse disputings of men of corrupt minds, and destitute of the truth, supposing that gain is godliness: from such withdraw thyself.… O Timothy, keep that which is committed to thy trust, avoiding profane and vain babblings, and oppositions of science falsely so called. **2 Tim. 2:14.** Of these things put them in remembrance, charging them before the Lord that they strive not about words to no profit, but to the subverting of the hearers. **Titus 3:9.** But avoid foolish questions, and genealogies, and contentions, and strivings about the law; for they are unprofitable and vain.

q'. **Deut. 18:10–14.** There shall not be found among you any one that maketh his son or his daughter to pass through the fire, or that useth divination, or an observer of times, or an enchanter, or a witch, or a charmer, or a consulter with familiar spirits, or a wizard, or a necromancer. For all that do these things are an abomination unto the LORD: and because of these abominations the LORD thy God doth drive them out from before thee. Thou shalt be perfect with the LORD thy God. For these nations, which thou shalt possess, hearkened unto observers of times, and unto diviners: but as for thee, the LORD thy God hath not suffered thee so to do. **Acts 19:13.** Then certain of the vagabond Jews, exorcists, took upon them to call over them which had evil

and practices;^{r´} the maligning,^{s´} scorning,^{t´} reviling,^{u´} or anywise opposing of God's truth, grace, and ways;^{w´} making profession of reli-
gion in hypocrisy, or for sinister ends;^{x´} being ashamed of it,^{y´} or a

spirits the name of the Lord Jesus, saying, We adjure you by Jesus whom Paul preacheth.
   r´. **2 Tim. 4:3–4.** For the time will come when they will not endure sound
doctrine; but after their own lusts shall they heap to themselves teachers, having itch-
ing ears; and they shall turn away their ears from the truth, and shall be turned unto
fables. **1 Kings 21:9–10.** And she wrote in the letters, saying, Proclaim a fast, and set
Naboth on high among the people: and set two men, sons of Belial, before him, to
bear witness against him, saying, Thou didst blaspheme God and the king. And then
carry him out, and stone him, that he may die. **Jude 4.** For there are certain men
crept in unawares, who were before of old ordained to this condemnation, ungodly
men, turning the grace of our God into lasciviousness, and denying the only Lord
God, and our Lord Jesus Christ. **See Rom. 13:13–14.**
   s´. **Acts 13:45.** But when the Jews saw the multitudes, they were filled with envy,
and spake against those things which were spoken by Paul, contradicting and blaspheming. **1 John 3:12.** Not as Cain, who was of that wicked one, and slew his brother.
And wherefore slew he him? Because his own works were evil, and his brother's righteous.
   t´. **Ps. 1:1.** Blessed is the man that walketh not in the counsel of the ungodly, nor
standeth in the way of sinners, nor sitteth in the seat of the scornful. **2 Pet. 3:3.** …
knowing this first, that there shall come in the last days scoffers, walking after their
own lusts.
   u´. **1 Pet. 4:4.** … wherein they think it strange that ye run not with them to the
same excess of riot, speaking evil of you.
   w´. **Acts 13:45–46, 50.** But when the Jews saw the multitudes, they were filled
with envy, and spake against those things which were spoken by Paul, contradicting
and blaspheming. Then Paul and Barnabas waxed bold, and said, It was necessary
that the word of God should first have been spoken to you: but seeing ye put it from
you, and judge yourselves unworthy of everlasting life, lo, we turn to the Gentiles.…
But the Jews stirred up the devout and honourable women, and the chief men of the
city, and raised persecution against Paul and Barnabas, and expelled them out of their
coasts. **Acts 4:18.** And they called them, and commanded them not to speak at all
nor teach in the name of Jesus. **1 Thess. 2:16.** … forbidding us to speak to the
Gentiles that they might be saved, to fill up their sins alway: for the wrath is come upon
them to the uttermost. **Heb. 10:29.** Of how much sorer punishment, suppose ye,
shall he be thought worthy, who hath trodden under foot the Son of God, and hath
counted the blood of the covenant, wherewith he was sanctified, an unholy thing, and
hath done despite unto the Spirit of grace? **See Acts 19:9.**
   x´. **2 Tim. 3:5.** … having a form of godliness, but denying the power thereof:
from such turn away. **Matt. 23:14.** Woe unto you, scribes and Pharisees, hypocrites!
for ye devour widows' houses, and for a pretence make long prayer: therefore ye shall
receive the greater damnation. **See Matt. 6:1–2, 5, 16.**
   y´. **Mark 8:38.** Whosoever therefore shall be ashamed of me and of my words
in this adulterous and sinful generation; of him also shall the Son of man be ashamed,
when he cometh in the glory of his Father with the holy angels.

shame to it, by unconformable,[z'] unwise,[a'] unfruitful,[b'] and offensive walking,[c'] or backsliding from it.[d']

Q. 114. *What reasons are annexed to the third commandment?*

A. The reasons annexed to the third commandment, in these words, *The LORD thy God,* and, *For the LORD will not hold him guiltless that taketh his name in vain,*[e] are, because he is the Lord and our God, therefore his name is not to be profaned, or anyway abused by us;[f] especially because he will be so far from acquitting and sparing the transgressors of this commandment, as that he will not suffer them to escape his righteous judgment,[g] albeit many such escape the censures and punishments of men.[h]

Q. 115. *Which is the fourth commandment?*

A. The fourth commandment is, *Remember the sabbath day, to keep it*

z'. **Ps. 73:14–15.** For all the day long have I been plagued, and chastened every morning. If I say, I will speak thus; behold, I should offend against the generation of thy children.

a'. **Eph. 5:15–17.** See then that ye walk circumspectly, not as fools, but as wise, redeeming the time, because the days are evil. Wherefore be ye not unwise, but understanding what the will of the Lord is. **See 1 Cor. 6:5–6.**

b'. **Isa. 5:4.** What could have been done more to my vineyard, that I have not done in it? wherefore, when I looked that it should bring forth grapes, brought it forth wild grapes? **See 2 Pet. 1:8–9.**

c'. **Rom. 2:23–24.** Thou that makest thy boast of the law, through breaking the law dishonourest thou God? For the name of God is blasphemed among the Gentiles through you, as it is written.

d'. **Gal. 3:1, 3.** O foolish Galatians, who hath bewitched you, that ye should not obey the truth, before whose eyes Jesus Christ hath been evidently set forth, crucified among you?… Are ye so foolish? having begun in the Spirit, are ye now made perfect by the flesh? **See Heb. 6:6.**

e. **Ex. 20:7.**

f. **Lev. 19:12.** And ye shall not swear by my name falsely, neither shalt thou profane the name of thy God: I am the LORD.

g. **Deut. 28:58–59.** If thou wilt not observe to do all the words of this law that are written in this book, that thou mayest fear this glorious and fearful name, THE LORD THY GOD; then the LORD will make thy plagues wonderful, and the plagues of thy seed, even great plagues, and of long continuance, and sore sicknesses, and of long continuance. **See Ezek. 36:21–23.**

h. **1 Sam. 2:29.** Wherefore kick ye at my sacrifice and at mine offering, which I have commanded in my habitation; and honourest thy sons above me, to make yourselves fat with the chiefest of all the offerings of Israel my people? **1 Sam. 3:13.** For I have told him that I will judge his house for ever for the iniquity which he knoweth; because his sons made themselves vile, and he restrained them not. **See 1 Sam.**

holy. Six days shalt thou labour, and do all thy work: but the seventh day is the
sabbath of the LORD thy God: in it thou shalt not do any work, thou, nor thy son,
nor thy daughter, thy manservant, nor thy maidservant, nor thy cattle, nor thy
stranger that is within thy gates: for in six days the LORD made heaven and earth,
the sea, and all that in them is, and rested the seventh day: wherefore the LORD
blessed the sabbath day and hallowed it.[i]

Q. 116. *What is required in the fourth commandment?*

A. The fourth commandment requireth of all men the sanctifying or keeping holy to God such set times as he hath appointed in his
Word, expressly one whole day in seven; which was the seventh from
the beginning of the world to the resurrection of Christ, and the first
day of the week ever since, and so to continue to the end of the
world; which is the Christian sabbath,[k] and in the New Testament

2:12–17, 22–25.

i. **Ex. 20:8–11. Cf. Deut. 5:12–15.** Keep the sabbath day to sanctify it, as the
LORD thy God hath commanded thee. Six days thou shalt labour, and do all thy work:
but the seventh day is the sabbath of the LORD thy God: in it thou shalt not do any
work, thou, nor thy son, nor thy daughter, nor thy manservant, nor thy maidservant,
nor thine ox, nor thine ass, nor any of thy cattle, nor thy stranger that is within thy
gates; that thy manservant and thy maidservant may rest as well as thou. And remember that thou wast a servant in the land of Egypt, and that the LORD thy God brought
thee out thence through a mighty hand and by a stretched out arm: therefore the
LORD thy God commanded thee to keep the sabbath day.

k. **Deut. 5:12–14.** Keep the sabbath day to sanctify it, as the LORD thy God hath
commanded thee. Six days thou shalt labour, and do all thy work: but the seventh day
is the sabbath of the LORD thy God: in it thou shalt not do any work, thou, nor thy son,
nor thy daughter, nor thy manservant, nor thy maidservant, nor thine ox, nor thine
ass, nor any of thy cattle, nor thy stranger that is within thy gates; that thy manservant
and thy maidservant may rest as well as thou. **Gen. 2:2–3.** And on the seventh day
God ended his work which he had made; and he rested on the seventh day from all his
work which he had made. And God blessed the seventh day, and sanctified it: because
that in it he had rested from all his work which God created and made. **1 Cor.
16:1–2.** Now concerning the collection for the saints, as I have given order to the
churches of Galatia, even so do ye. Upon the first day of the week let every one of you
lay by him in store, as God hath prospered him, that there be no gatherings when I
come. **Acts 20:7.** And upon the first day of the week, when the disciples came together to break bread, Paul preached unto them, ready to depart on the morrow; and
continued his speech until midnight. **John 20:19, 26.** Then the same day at evening,
being the first day of the week, when the doors were shut where the disciples were
assembled for fear of the Jews, came Jesus and stood in the midst, and saith unto them,
Peace be unto you.… And after eight days again his disciples were within, and Thomas with them: then came Jesus, the doors being shut, and stood in the midst, and
said, Peace be unto you. **See Matt. 5:17–18; Isa. 56:2, 4, 6–7.**

called the Lord's Day.[l]

Q. 117. *How is the Sabbath or the Lord's Day to be sanctified?*

A. The Sabbath or Lord's Day is to be sanctified by an holy resting all the day,[m] not only from such works as are at all times sinful, but even from such worldly employments and recreations as are on other days lawful;[n] and making it our delight to spend the whole time (except so much of it as is to be taken up in works of necessity and mercy[o]) in the public and private exercises of God's worship:[p] and, to

l. **Rev. 1:10.** I was in the Spirit on the Lord's day, and heard behind me a great voice, as of a trumpet.

m. **Ex. 20:8, 10.** Remember the sabbath day, to keep it holy.... But the seventh day is the sabbath of the LORD thy God: in it thou shalt not do any work, thou, nor thy son, nor thy daughter, thy manservant, nor thy maidservant, nor thy cattle, nor thy stranger that is within thy gates.

n. **Ex. 16:25–28.** And Moses said, Eat that to day; for to day is a sabbath unto the LORD: to day ye shall not find it in the field. Six days ye shall gather it; but on the seventh day, which is the sabbath, in it there shall be none. And it came to pass, that there went out some of the people on the seventh day for to gather, and they found none. And the LORD said unto Moses, How long refuse ye to keep my commandments and my laws? **Jer. 17:21–22.** Thus saith the LORD; Take heed to yourselves, and bear no burden on the sabbath day, nor bring it in by the gates of Jerusalem; neither carry forth a burden out of your houses on the sabbath day, neither do ye any work, but hallow ye the sabbath day, as I commanded your fathers. **See Neh. 13:15–22.**

o. **Matt. 12:1–5.** At that time Jesus went on the sabbath day through the corn; and his disciples were an hungred, and began to pluck the ears of corn, and to eat. But when the Pharisees saw it, they said unto him, Behold, thy disciples do that which is not lawful to do upon the sabbath day. But he said unto them, Have ye not read what David did, when he was an hungred, and they that were with him; how he entered into the house of God, and did eat the shewbread, which was not lawful for him to eat, neither for them which were with him, but only for the priests? Or have ye not read in the law, how that on the sabbath days the priests in the temple profane the sabbath, and are blameless? **See verses 6–13.**

p. **Isa. 58:13–14.** If thou turn away thy foot from the sabbath, from doing thy pleasure on my holy day; and call the sabbath a delight, the holy of the LORD, honourable; and shalt honour him, not doing thine own ways, nor finding thine own pleasure, nor speaking thine own words: then shalt thou delight thyself in the LORD; and I will cause thee to ride upon the high places of the earth, and feed thee with the heritage of Jacob thy father: for the mouth of the LORD hath spoken it. **Luke 4:16.** And he came to Nazareth, where he had been brought up: and, as his custom was, he went into the synagogue on the sabbath day, and stood up for to read. **Acts 20:7.** And upon the first day of the week, when the disciples came together to break bread, Paul preached unto them, ready to depart on the morrow; and continued his speech until midnight. **1 Cor. 16:1–2.** Now concerning the collection for the saints, as I have given order to the churches of Galatia, even so do ye. Upon the first day of the

that end, we are to prepare our hearts, and with such foresight, diligence, and moderation, to dispose and seasonably dispatch our worldly business, that we may be the more free and fit for the duties of that day.[q]

Q. 118. *Why is the charge of keeping the Sabbath more specially directed to governors of families, and other superiors?*

A. The charge of keeping the Sabbath is more specially directed to governors of families, and other superiors, because they are bound not only to keep it themselves, but to see that it be observed by all those that are under their charge; and because they are prone ofttimes to hinder them by employments of their own.[r]

Q. 119. *What are the sins forbidden in the fourth commandment?*

A. The sins forbidden in the fourth commandment are, all omissions of the duties required,[s] all careless, negligent, and unprofitable

week let every one of you lay by him in store, as God hath prospered him, that there be no gatherings when I come. **Lev. 23:3.** Six days shall work be done: but the seventh day is the sabbath of rest, an holy convocation; ye shall do no work therein: it is the sabbath of the LORD in all your dwellings. **See Ps. 92 title; Isa. 66:23.**

q. **Ex. 20:8.** Remember the sabbath day, to keep it holy. **Luke 23:54, 56.** And that day was the preparation, and the sabbath drew on.... And they returned, and prepared spices and ointments; and rested the sabbath day according to the commandment. **Ex. 16:22, 25–26, 29.** And it came to pass, that on the sixth day they gathered twice as much bread, two omers for one man: and all the rulers of the congregation came and told Moses.... And Moses said, Eat that to day; for to day is a sabbath unto the LORD: to day ye shall not find it in the field. Six days ye shall gather it; but on the seventh day, which is the sabbath, in it there shall be none.... See, for that the LORD hath given you the sabbath, therefore he giveth you on the sixth day the bread of two days; abide ye every man in his place, let no man go out of his place on the seventh day. **Neh. 13:19.** And it came to pass, that when the gates of Jerusalem began to be dark before the sabbath, I commanded that the gates should be shut, and charged that they should not be opened till after the sabbath: and some of my servants set I at the gates, that there should no burden be brought in on the sabbath day.

r. **Ex. 20:10.** But the seventh day is the sabbath of the LORD thy God: in it thou shalt not do any work, thou, nor thy son, nor thy daughter, thy manservant, nor thy maidservant, nor thy cattle, nor thy stranger that is within thy gates. **Ex. 23:12.** Six days thou shalt do thy work, and on the seventh day thou shalt rest: that thine ox and thine ass may rest, and the son of thy handmaid, and the stranger, may be refreshed. **See Josh. 24:15; Neh. 13:15–17; Jer. 17:20–22.**

s. **Ezek. 22:26.** Her priests have violated my law, and have profaned mine holy things: they have put no difference between the holy and profane, neither have they shewed difference between the unclean and the clean, and have hid their eyes from my sabbaths, and I am profaned among them.

performing of them, and being weary of them;[t] all profaning the day by idleness, and doing that which is in itself sinful;[u] and by all needless works, words, and thoughts, about our worldly employments and recreations.[w]

Q. 120. *What are the reasons annexed to the fourth commandment, the more to enforce it?*

A. The reasons annexed to the fourth commandment, the more to enforce it, are taken from the equity of it, God allowing us six days of seven for our own affairs, and reserving but one for himself, in these words, *Six days shalt thou labour, and do all thy work:*[x] from God's challenging a special propriety in that day, *The seventh day is the sabbath of the LORD thy God:*[y] from the example of God, who *in six days ... made heaven and earth, the sea, and all that in them is, and rested the seventh day:* and from that blessing which God put upon that day, not only in sanctifying it to be a day for his service, but in ordaining it to be a means of blessing to us in our sanctifying it; *Wherefore the LORD blessed the sabbath day, and hallowed it.*[z]

Q. 121. *Why is the word* Remember *set in the beginning of the fourth commandment?*

A. The word *Remember* is set in the beginning of the fourth commandment,[a] partly, because of the great benefit of remembering it, we being thereby helped in our preparation to keep it,[b] and, in

t. **Amos 8:5.** ... saying, When will the new moon be gone, that we may sell corn? and the sabbath, that we may set forth wheat, making the ephah small, and the shekel great, and falsifying the balances by deceit? **See Acts 20:7, 9; Ezek. 33:30–32; Mal. 1:13.**

u. **Ezek. 23:38.** Moreover this they have done unto me: they have defiled my sanctuary in the same day, and have profaned my sabbaths.

w. **Jer. 17:24, 27.** And it shall come to pass, if ye diligently hearken unto me, saith the LORD, to bring in no burden through the gates of this city on the sabbath day, but hallow the sabbath day, to do no work therein ... But if ye will not hearken unto me to hallow the sabbath day, and not to bear a burden, even entering in at the gates of Jerusalem on the sabbath day; then will I kindle a fire in the gates thereof, and it shall devour the palaces of Jerusalem, and it shall not be quenched. **See Isa. 58:13–14.**

x. **Ex. 20:9.**

y. **Ex. 20:10.**

z. **Ex. 20:11.**

a. **Ex. 20:8.** Remember the sabbath day, to keep it holy.

b. **Ex. 16:23.** And he said unto them, This is that which the LORD hath said, To

keeping it, better to keep all the rest of the commandments,[c] and to continue a thankful remembrance of the two great benefits of creation and redemption, which contain a short abridgment of religion;[d] and partly, because we are very ready to forget it,[e] for that there is less light of nature for it,[f] and yet it restraineth our natural liberty in things at other times lawful;[g] that it cometh but once in seven days, and many worldly businesses come between, and too often take off our minds from thinking of it, either to prepare for it, or to sanctify it;[h] and that Satan with his instruments much labor to blot out the

morrow is the rest of the holy sabbath unto the LORD: bake that which ye will bake to day, and seethe that ye will seethe; and that which remaineth over lay up for you to be kept until the morning. **Luke 23:54, 56.** And that day was the preparation, and the sabbath drew on.… And they returned, and prepared spices and ointments; and rested the sabbath day according to the commandment. **See Mark 15:42; Neh. 13:19.**

c. **Ezek. 20:12, 19–20.** Moreover also I gave them my sabbaths, to be a sign between me and them, that they might know that I am the LORD that sanctify them.… I am the LORD your God; walk in my statutes, and keep my judgments, and do them; and hallow my sabbaths; and they shall be a sign between me and you, that ye may know that I am the LORD your God. **Ps. 92:13–14.** Those that be planted in the house of the LORD shall flourish in the courts of our God. They shall still bring forth fruit in old age; they shall be fat and flourishing. **See Ps. 92 title.**

d. **Gen. 2:2–3.** And on the seventh day God ended his work which he had made; and he rested on the seventh day from all his work which he had made. And God blessed the seventh day, and sanctified it: because that in it he had rested from all his work which God created and made. **Ps. 118:22, 24.** The stone which the builders refused is become the head stone of the corner.… This is the day which the LORD hath made; we will rejoice and be glad in it. **Rev. 1:10.** I was in the Spirit on the Lord's day, and heard behind me a great voice, as of a trumpet.

e. **Ezek. 22:26.** Her priests have violated my law, and have profaned mine holy things: they have put no difference between the holy and profane, neither have they shewed difference between the unclean and the clean, and have hid their eyes from my sabbaths, and I am profaned among them.

f. **Neh. 9:14.** … and madest known unto them thy holy sabbath, and commandedst them precepts, statutes, and laws, by the hand of Moses thy servant.

g. **Ex. 34:21.** Six days thou shalt work, but on the seventh day thou shalt rest: in earing time and in harvest thou shalt rest.

h. **Deut. 5:14–15.** But the seventh day is the sabbath of the LORD thy God: in it thou shalt not do any work, thou, nor thy son, nor thy daughter, nor thy manservant, nor thy maidservant, nor thine ox, nor thine ass, nor any of thy cattle, nor thy stranger that is within thy gates; that thy manservant and thy maidservant may rest as well as thou. And remember that thou wast a servant in the land of Egypt, and that the LORD thy God brought thee out thence through a mighty hand and by a stretched out arm: therefore the LORD thy God commanded thee to keep the sabbath day. **Amos 8:5.** … saying, When will the new moon be gone, that we may sell corn? and the sabbath, that we may set forth wheat, making the ephah small, and the shekel great, and falsifying

glory, and even the memory of it, to bring in all irreligion and impiety.[i]

Q. 122. *What is the sum of the six commandments which contain our duty to man?*

A. The sum of the six commandments which contain our duty to man is, to love our neighbor as ourselves,[k] and to do to others what we would have them to do to us.[l]

Q. 123. *Which is the fifth commandment?*

A. The fifth commandment is, *Honour thy father and thy mother: that thy days may be long upon the land which the LORD thy God giveth thee.*[m]

Q. 124. *Who are meant by* father *and* mother *in the fifth commandment?*

A. By *father* and *mother*, in the fifth commandment, are meant, not only natural parents,[n] but all superiors in age[o] and gifts;[p] and especially such as, by God's ordinance, are over us in place of authority,

the balances by deceit?

i. **Lam. 1:7.** Jerusalem remembered in the days of her affliction and of her miseries all her pleasant things that she had in the days of old, when her people fell into the hand of the enemy, and none did help her: the adversaries saw her, and did mock at her sabbaths. **Jer. 17:21–23.** Thus saith the LORD; Take heed to yourselves, and bear no burden on the sabbath day, nor bring it in by the gates of Jerusalem; neither carry forth a burden out of your houses on the sabbath day, neither do ye any work, but hallow ye the sabbath day, as I commanded your fathers. But they obeyed not, neither inclined their ear, but made their neck stiff, that they might not hear, nor receive instruction. **See Neh. 13:15–22.**

k. **Matt. 22:39.** And the second is like unto it, Thou shalt love thy neighbour as thyself.

l. **Matt. 7:12.** Therefore all things whatsoever ye would that men should do to you, do ye even so to them: for this is the law and the prophets.

m. **Ex. 20:12. Cf. Deut. 5:16.** Honour thy father and thy mother, as the LORD thy God hath commanded thee; that thy days may be prolonged, and that it may go well with thee, in the land which the LORD thy God giveth thee.

n. **Prov. 23:22, 25.** Hearken unto thy father that begat thee, and despise not thy mother when she is old.… Thy father and thy mother shall be glad, and she that bare thee shall rejoice. **See Eph. 6:1–2.**

o. **1 Tim. 5:1–2.** Rebuke not an elder, but intreat him as a father; and the younger men as brethren; the elder women as mothers; the younger as sisters, with all purity.

p. **Gen. 4:20–21.** And Adah bare Jabal: he was the father of such as dwell in tents, and of such as have cattle. And his brother's name was Jubal: he was the father of all such as handle the harp and organ. **Gen. 45:8.** So now it was not you that sent me hither, but God: and he hath made me a father to Pharaoh, and lord of all his house, and a ruler throughout all the land of Egypt.

whether in family,[q] church,[r] or commonwealth.[s]

Q. 125. *Why are superiors styled* father *and* mother?
A. Superiors are styled *father* and *mother*, both to teach them in all duties toward their inferiors, like natural parents, to express love and tenderness to them, according to their several relations;[t] and to work inferiors to a greater willingness and cheerfulness in performing their duties to their superiors, as to their parents.[u]

Q. 126. *What is the general scope of the fifth commandment?*
A. The general scope of the fifth commandment is, the performance of those duties which we mutually owe in our several relations, as inferiors, superiors, or equals.[w]

Q. 127. *What is the honor that inferiors owe to their superiors?*
A. The honor which inferiors owe to their superiors is, all due

q. **2 Kings 5:13.** And his servants came near, and spake unto him, and said, My father, if the prophet had bid thee do some great thing, wouldest thou not have done it? how much rather then, when he saith to thee, Wash, and be clean?

r. **2 Kings 2:12.** And Elisha saw it, and he cried, My father, my father, the chariot of Israel, and the horsemen thereof. And he saw him no more: and he took hold of his own clothes, and rent them in two pieces. **Gal. 4:19.** My little children, of whom I travail in birth again until Christ be formed in you … **See 2 Kings 13:14.**

s. **Isa. 49:23.** And kings shall be thy nursing fathers, and their queens thy nursing mothers: they shall bow down to thee with their face toward the earth, and lick up the dust of thy feet; and thou shalt know that I am the LORD: for they shall not be ashamed that wait for me.

t. **Eph. 6:4.** And, ye fathers, provoke not your children to wrath: but bring them up in the nurture and admonition of the Lord. **2 Cor. 12:14.** Behold, the third time I am ready to come to you; and I will not be burdensome to you: for I seek not yours, but you: for the children ought not to lay up for the parents, but the parents for the children. **1 Thess. 2:7–8, 11.** But we were gentle among you, even as a nurse cherisheth her children: so being affectionately desirous of you, we were willing to have imparted unto you, not the gospel of God only, but also our own souls, because ye were dear unto us.… As ye know how we exhorted and comforted and charged every one of you, as a father doth his children. **See Num. 11:11–12.**

u. **1 Cor. 4:14–16.** I write not these things to shame you, but as my beloved sons I warn you. For though ye have ten thousand instructors in Christ, yet have ye not many fathers: for in Christ Jesus I have begotten you through the gospel. Wherefore I beseech you, be ye followers of me. **See 2 Kings 5:13.**

w. **Eph. 5:21.** … submitting yourselves one to another in the fear of God. **1 Pet. 2:17.** Honour all men. Love the brotherhood. Fear God. Honour the king. **Rom. 12:10.** Be kindly affectioned one to another with brotherly love; in honour preferring one another. **See Rom. 13:1, 7; Eph. 5:22, 24; 6:1, 4–5, 9.**

reverence in heart,[x] word,[y] and behavior;[z] prayer and thanksgiving for them;[a] imitation of their virtues and graces;[b] willing obedience to their lawful commands and counsels;[c] due submission to their corrections;[d] fidelity to,[e] defense,[f] and maintenance of their persons

x. **Mal. 1:6.** A son honoureth his father, and a servant his master: if then I be a father, where is mine honour? and if I be a master, where is my fear? saith the LORD of hosts unto you, O priests, that despise my name. And ye say, Wherein have we despised thy name? **Lev. 19:3.** Ye shall fear every man his mother, and his father, and keep my sabbaths: I am the LORD your God.

y. **Prov. 31:28.** Her children arise up, and call her blessed; her husband also, and he praiseth her. **1 Pet. 3:6.** … even as Sara obeyed Abraham, calling him lord: whose daughters ye are, as long as ye do well, and are not afraid with any amazement.

z. **Lev. 19:32.** Thou shalt rise up before the hoary head, and honour the face of the old man, and fear thy God: I am the LORD. **1 Kings 2:19.** Bathsheba therefore went unto king Solomon, to speak unto him for Adonijah. And the king rose up to meet her, and bowed himself unto her, and sat down on his throne, and caused a seat to be set for the king's mother; and she sat on his right hand.

a. **1 Tim. 2:1–2.** I exhort therefore, that, first of all, supplications, prayers, intercessions, and giving of thanks, be made for all men; for kings, and for all that are in authority; that we may lead a quiet and peaceable life in all godliness and honesty.

b. **Heb. 13:7.** Remember them which have the rule over you, who have spoken unto you the word of God: whose faith follow, considering the end of their conversation. **Phil. 3:17.** Brethren, be followers together of me, and mark them which walk so as ye have us for an ensample.

c. **Eph. 6:1–2, 5–7.** Children, obey your parents in the Lord: for this is right. Honour thy father and mother; (which is the first commandment with promise;) … Servants, be obedient to them that are your masters according to the flesh, with fear and trembling, in singleness of your heart, as unto Christ; not with eyeservice, as menpleasers; but as the servants of Christ, doing the will of God from the heart; with good will doing service, as to the Lord, and not to men. **1 Pet. 2:13–14.** Submit yourselves to every ordinance of man for the Lord's sake: whether it be to the king, as supreme; or unto governors, as unto them that are sent by him for the punishment of evildoers, and for the praise of them that do well. **Heb. 13:17.** Obey them that have the rule over you, and submit yourselves: for they watch for your souls, as they that must give account, that they may do it with joy, and not with grief: for that is unprofitable for you. **See Rom. 13:1–5; Prov. 4:3–4; 23:22; Ex. 18:19, 24.**

d. **Heb. 12:9.** Furthermore we have had fathers of our flesh which corrected us, and we gave them reverence: shall we not much rather be in subjection unto the Father of spirits, and live? **1 Pet. 2:18–20.** Servants, be subject to your masters with all fear; not only to the good and gentle, but also to the froward. For this is thankworthy, if a man for conscience toward God endure grief, suffering wrongfully. For what glory is it, if, when ye be buffeted for your faults, ye shall take it patiently? but if, when ye do well, and suffer for it, ye take it patiently, this is acceptable with God.

e. **Titus 2:9–10.** Exhort servants to be obedient unto their own masters, and to please them well in all things; not answering again; not purloining, but shewing all good fidelity; that they may adorn the doctrine of God our Saviour in all things.

and authority, according to their several ranks, and the nature of their places;[g] bearing with their infirmities, and covering them in love,[h] that so they may be an honor to them and to their government.[i]

Q. 128. *What are the sins of inferiors against their superiors?*

A. The sins of inferiors against their superiors are, all neglect of the duties required toward them;[k] envying at,[l] contempt of,[m] and

f. **1 Sam. 26:15–16**. And David said to Abner, Art not thou a valiant man? and who is like to thee in Israel? wherefore then hast thou not kept thy lord the king? for there came one of the people in to destroy the king thy lord. This thing is not good that thou hast done. As the LORD liveth, ye are worthy to die, because ye have not kept your master, the LORD's anointed. And now see where the king's spear is, and the cruse of water that was at his bolster. **See 2 Sam. 18:3; Est. 6:2.**

g. **Matt. 22:21.** They say unto him, Caesar's. Then saith he unto them, Render therefore unto Caesar the things which are Caesar's; and unto God the things that are God's. **Rom. 13:6–7.** For for this cause pay ye tribute also: for they are God's ministers, attending continually upon this very thing. Render therefore to all their dues: tribute to whom tribute is due; custom to whom custom; fear to whom fear; honour to whom honour. **1 Tim. 5:17–18.** Let the elders that rule well be counted worthy of double honour, especially they who labour in the word and doctrine. For the scripture saith, Thou shalt not muzzle the ox that treadeth out the corn. And, The labourer is worthy of his reward. **See Gal. 6:6; Gen. 45:11; 47:12.**

h. **Gen. 9:23.** And Shem and Japheth took a garment, and laid it upon both their shoulders, and went backward, and covered the nakedness of their father; and their faces were backward, and they saw not their father's nakedness. **See 1 Pet. 2:18; Prov. 23:22.**

i. **Ps. 127:3–5.** Lo, children are an heritage of the LORD: and the fruit of the womb is his reward. As arrows are in the hand of a mighty man; so are children of the youth. Happy is the man that hath his quiver full of them: they shall not be ashamed, but they shall speak with the enemies in the gate. **Prov. 31:23.** Her husband is known in the gates, when he sitteth among the elders of the land.

k. **Matt. 15:4–6.** For God commanded, saying, Honour thy father and mother: and, He that curseth father or mother, let him die the death. But ye say, Whosoever shall say to his father or his mother, It is a gift, by whatsoever thou mightest be profited by me; and honour not his father or his mother, he shall be free. Thus have ye made the commandment of God of none effect by your tradition. **Rom. 13:8.** Owe no man any thing, but to love one another: for he that loveth another hath fulfilled the law.

l. **Num. 11:28–29.** And Joshua the son of Nun, the servant of Moses, one of his young men, answered and said, My lord Moses, forbid them. And Moses said unto him, Enviest thou for my sake? would God that all the LORD's people were prophets, and that the LORD would put his spirit upon them!

m. **1 Sam. 8:7.** And the LORD said unto Samuel, Hearken unto the voice of the people in all that they say unto thee: for they have not rejected thee, but they have rejected me, that I should not reign over them. **Isa. 3:5.** And the people shall be oppressed, every one by another, and every one by his neighbour: the child shall

rebellion[n] against, their persons[o] and places,[p] in their lawful counsels,[q] commands, and corrections;[r] cursing, mocking,[s] and all such refractory and scandalous carriage, as proves a shame and dishonor to them and their government.[t]

Q. 129. *What is required of superiors towards their inferiors?*

A. It is required of superiors, according to that power they receive from God, and that relation wherein they stand, to love,[u] pray for,[w] and bless their inferiors;[x] to instruct,[y] counsel, and admonish

behave himself proudly against the ancient, and the base against the honourable.

n. **2 Sam. 15:10.** But Absalom sent spies throughout all the tribes of Israel, saying, As soon as ye hear the sound of the trumpet, then ye shall say, Absalom reigneth in Hebron. **See verses 1–12.**

o. **Ex. 21:15.** And he that smiteth his father, or his mother, shall be surely put to death.

p. **1 Sam. 10:27.** But the children of Belial said, How shall this man save us? And they despised him, and brought him no presents. But he held his peace.

q. **1 Sam. 2:25.** If one man sin against another, the judge shall judge him: but if a man sin against the LORD, who shall intreat for him? Notwithstanding they hearkened not unto the voice of their father, because the LORD would slay them.

r. **Deut. 21:18–21.** If a man have a stubborn and rebellious son, which will not obey the voice of his father, or the voice of his mother, and that, when they have chastened him, will not hearken unto them: then shall his father and his mother lay hold on him, and bring him out unto the elders of his city, and unto the gate of his place; and they shall say unto the elders of his city, This our son is stubborn and rebellious, he will not obey our voice; he is a glutton, and a drunkard. And all the men of his city shall stone him with stones, that he die: so shalt thou put evil away from among you; and all Israel shall hear, and fear.

s. **Prov. 30:11, 17.** There is a generation that curseth their father, and doth not bless their mother. The eye that mocketh at his father, and despiseth to obey his mother, the ravens of the valley shall pick it out, and the young eagles shall eat it.

t. **Prov. 19:26.** He that wasteth his father, and chaseth away his mother, is a son that causeth shame, and bringeth reproach.

u. **Col. 3:19.** Husbands, love your wives, and be not bitter against them. **Titus 2:4.** … that they may teach the young women to be sober, to love their husbands, to love their children.

w. **1 Sam. 12:23.** Moreover as for me, God forbid that I should sin against the LORD in ceasing to pray for you: but I will teach you the good and the right way. **Job 1:5.** And it was so, when the days of their feasting were gone about, that Job sent and sanctified them, and rose up early in the morning, and offered burnt offerings according to the number of them all: for Job said, It may be that my sons have sinned, and cursed God in their hearts. Thus did Job continually.

x. **1 Kings 8:55–56.** And he stood, and blessed all the congregation of Israel with a loud voice, saying, Blessed be the LORD, that hath given rest unto his people Israel, according to all that he promised: there hath not failed one word of all his good promise, which he promised by the hand of Moses his servant. **Heb. 7:7.** And

them;[z] countenancing,[a] commending,[b] and rewarding such as do well;[c] and discountenancing,[d] reproving, and chastising such as do ill;[e] protecting,[f] and providing for them all things necessary for soul[g] and body:[h] and by grave, wise, holy, and exemplary carriage, to procure glory to God,[i] honor to themselves,[k] and so to preserve that authority which God hath put upon them.[l]

without all contradiction the less is blessed of the better. **See Gen. 49:28.**

y. **Deut. 6:6–7.** And these words, which I command thee this day, shall be in thine heart: and thou shalt teach them diligently unto thy children, and shalt talk of them when thou sittest in thine house, and when thou walkest by the way, and when thou liest down, and when thou risest up.

z. **Eph. 6:4.** And, ye fathers, provoke not your children to wrath: but bring them up in the nurture and admonition of the Lord.

a. **1 Pet. 3:7.** Likewise, ye husbands, dwell with them according to knowledge, giving honour unto the wife, as unto the weaker vessel, and as being heirs together of the grace of life; that your prayers be not hindered.

b. **1 Pet. 2:14.** … or unto governors, as unto them that are sent by him for the punishment of evildoers, and for the praise of them that do well. **Rom. 13:3.** For rulers are not a terror to good works, but to the evil. Wilt thou then not be afraid of the power? do that which is good, and thou shalt have praise of the same.

c. **Est. 6:3.** And the king said, What honour and dignity hath been done to Mordecai for this? Then said the king's servants that ministered unto him, There is nothing done for him.

d. **Rom. 13:3–4.** For rulers are not a terror to good works, but to the evil. Wilt thou then not be afraid of the power? do that which is good, and thou shalt have praise of the same: for he is the minister of God to thee for good. But if thou do that which is evil, be afraid; for he beareth not the sword in vain: for he is the minister of God, a revenger to execute wrath upon him that doeth evil.

e. **Prov. 29:15.** The rod and reproof give wisdom: but a child left to himself bringeth his mother to shame. **1 Pet. 2:14.** … or unto governors, as unto them that are sent by him for the punishment of evildoers, and for the praise of them that do well.

f. **Isa. 1:10, 17.** Hear the word of the LORD, ye rulers of Sodom; give ear unto the law of our God, ye people of Gomorrah.… Learn to do well; seek judgment, relieve the oppressed, judge the fatherless, plead for the widow. **See Job 29:12–17.**

g. **Eph. 6:4.** And, ye fathers, provoke not your children to wrath: but bring them up in the nurture and admonition of the Lord.

h. **1 Tim. 5:8.** But if any provide not for his own, and specially for those of his own house, he hath denied the faith, and is worse than an infidel.

j. **1 Tim. 4:12.** Let no man despise thy youth; but be thou an example of the believers, in word, in conversation, in charity, in spirit, in faith, in purity. **See Titus 2:3–5.**

k. **1 Kings 3:28.** And all Israel heard of the judgment which the king had judged; and they feared the king: for they saw that the wisdom of God was in him, to do judgment.

l. **Titus 2:15.** These things speak, and exhort, and rebuke with all authority. Let

Q. 130. *What are the sins of superiors?*

A. The sins of superiors are, besides the neglect of the duties required of them,^m and inordinate seeking of themselves,ⁿ their own glory,^o ease, profit, or pleasure;^p commanding things unlawful,^q or not in the power of inferiors to perform;^r counseling,^s encouraging,^t or favoring them in that which is evil;^u dissuading, discouraging, or

no man despise thee.

m. **Ezek. 34:2–4.** Son of man, prophesy against the shepherds of Israel, prophesy, and say unto them, Thus saith the Lord God unto the shepherds; Woe be to the shepherds of Israel that do feed themselves! should not the shepherds feed the flocks? Ye eat the fat, and ye clothe you with the wool, ye kill them that are fed: but ye feed not the flock. The diseased have ye not strengthened, neither have ye healed that which was sick, neither have ye bound up that which was broken, neither have ye brought again that which was driven away, neither have ye sought that which was lost; but with force and with cruelty have ye ruled them.

n. **Phil. 2:21.** For all seek their own, not the things which are Jesus Christ's.

o. **John 5:44.** How can ye believe, which receive honour one of another, and seek not the honour that cometh from God only? **See John 7:18.**

p. **Isa. 56:10–11.** His watchmen are blind: they are all ignorant, they are all dumb dogs, they cannot bark; sleeping, lying down, loving to slumber. Yea, they are greedy dogs which can never have enough, and they are shepherds that cannot understand: they all look to their own way, every one for his gain, from his quarter. **See Deut. 17:17.**

q. **Acts 4:17–18.** But that it spread no further among the people, let us straitly threaten them, that they speak henceforth to no man in this name. And they called them, and commanded them not to speak at all nor teach in the name of Jesus. **See Dan. 3:4–6.**

r. **Ex. 5:18.** Go therefore now, and work; for there shall no straw be given you, yet shall ye deliver the tale of bricks. **See verses 10–19. Matt. 23:2, 4.** … saying, The scribes and the Pharisees sit in Moses' seat.… For they bind heavy burdens and grievous to be borne, and lay them on men's shoulders; but they themselves will not move them with one of their fingers.

s. **Matt. 14:8.** And she, being before instructed of her mother, said, Give me here John Baptist's head in a charger. **See Mark 6:24.**

t. **2 Sam. 13:28.** Now Absalom had commanded his servants, saying, Mark ye now when Amnon's heart is merry with wine, and when I say unto you, Smite Amnon; then kill him, fear not: have not I commanded you? be courageous, and be valiant.

u. **Jer. 6:13–14.** For from the least of them even unto the greatest of them every one is given to covetousness; and from the prophet even unto the priest every one dealeth falsely. They have healed also the hurt of the daughter of my people slightly, saying, Peace, peace; when there is no peace. **Judg. 20:13–14.** Now therefore deliver us the men, the children of Belial, which are in Gibeah, that we may put them to death, and put away evil from Israel. But the children of Benjamin would not hearken to the voice of their brethren the children of Israel: but the children of Benjamin gathered themselves together out of the cities unto Gibeah, to go out to battle against the children of Israel. **See entire chapter.**

discountenancing them in that which is good;[w] correcting them unduly;[x] careless exposing, or leaving them to wrong, temptation, and danger;[y] provoking them to wrath;[z] or anyway dishonoring themselves, or lessening their authority, by an unjust, indiscreet, rigorous, or remiss behavior.[a]

Q. 131. *What are the duties of equals?*

A. The duties of equals are, to regard the dignity and worth of each other,[b] in giving honor to go one before another;[c] and to rejoice

w. **John 7:46–49.** The officers answered, Never man spake like this man. Then answered them the Pharisees, Are ye also deceived? Have any of the rulers or of the Pharisees believed on him? But this people who knoweth not the law are cursed. **See Col. 3:21; Ex. 5:17; John 9:28.**

x. **1 Pet. 2:18–20.** Servants, be subject to your masters with all fear; not only to the good and gentle, but also to the froward. For this is thankworthy, if a man for conscience toward God endure grief, suffering wrongfully. For what glory is it, if, when ye be buffeted for your faults, ye shall take it patiently? but if, when ye do well, and suffer for it, ye take it patiently, this is acceptable with God. **Deut. 25:3.** Forty stripes he may give him, and not exceed: lest, if he should exceed, and beat him above these with many stripes, then thy brother should seem vile unto thee.

y. **Gen. 38:11, 26.** Then said Judah to Tamar his daughter in law, Remain a widow at thy father's house, till Shelah my son be grown: for he said, Lest peradventure he die also, as his brethren did. And Tamar went and dwelt in her father's house.… And Judah acknowledged them, and said, She hath been more righteous than I; because that I gave her not to Shelah my son. And he knew her again no more. **Acts 18:17.** Then all the Greeks took Sosthenes, the chief ruler of the synagogue, and beat him before the judgment seat. And Gallio cared for none of those things. **See 1 Sam. 23:15–17; Lev. 19:29; Isa. 58:7.**

z. **Eph. 6:4.** And, ye fathers, provoke not your children to wrath: but bring them up in the nurture and admonition of the Lord.

a. **Gen. 9:21.** And he drank of the wine, and was drunken; and he was uncovered within his tent. **1 Kings 12:13–16.** And the king answered the people roughly, and forsook the old men's counsel that they gave him; and spake to them after the counsel of the young men, saying, My father made your yoke heavy, and I will add to your yoke: my father also chastised you with whips, but I will chastise you with scorpions. Wherefore the king hearkened not unto the people; for the cause was from the LORD, that he might perform his saying, which the LORD spake by Ahijah the Shilonite unto Jeroboam the son of Nebat. So when all Israel saw that the king hearkened not unto them, the people answered the king, saying, What portion have we in David? neither have we inheritance in the son of Jesse: to your tents, O Israel: now see to thine own house, David. So Israel departed unto their tents. **1 Kings 1:6.** And his father had not displeased him at any time in saying, Why hast thou done so? and he also was a very goodly man; and his mother bare him after Absalom. **See 1 Sam. 2:29–31; 3:13.**

b. **1 Pet. 2:17.** Honour all men. Love the brotherhood. Fear God. Honour the king.

in each other's gifts and advancement, as their own.[d]

Q. 132. *What are the sins of equals?*

A. The sins of equals are, besides the neglect of the duties required,[e] the undervaluing of the worth,[f] envying the gifts,[g] grieving at the advancement of prosperity one of another;[h] and usurping preeminence one over another.[i]

Q. 133. *What is the reason annexed to the fifth commandment, the more to enforce it?*

A. The reason annexed to the fifth commandment, in these words, *That thy days may be long upon the land which the LORD thy God giveth thee,*[k] is an express promise of long life and prosperity, as far as it shall serve for God's glory and their own good, to all such as keep this commandment.[l]

Q. 134. *Which is the sixth commandment?*

A. The sixth commandment is, *Thou shalt not kill.*[m]

c. **Rom. 12:10.** Be kindly affectioned one to another with brotherly love; in honour preferring one another. **Phil. 2:3.** Let nothing be done through strife or vainglory; but in lowliness of mind let each esteem other better than themselves.

d. **Rom. 12:15–16.** Rejoice with them that do rejoice, and weep with them that weep. Be of the same mind one toward another. Mind not high things, but condescend to men of low estate. Be not wise in your own conceits. **Phil. 2:3.** Let nothing be done through strife or vainglory; but in lowliness of mind let each esteem other better than themselves.

e. **Rom. 13:8.** Owe no man any thing, but to love one another: for he that loveth another hath fulfilled the law.

f. **2 Tim. 3:3.** … without natural affection, trucebreakers, false accusers, incontinent, fierce, despisers of those that are good. **See Prov. 14:21; Isa. 65:5.**

g. **Acts 7:9.** And the patriarchs, moved with envy, sold Joseph into Egypt: but God was with him. **Gal. 5:26.** Let us not be desirous of vain glory, provoking one another, envying one another.

h. **Num. 12:2.** And they said, Hath the LORD indeed spoken only by Moses? hath he not spoken also by us? And the LORD heard it.

i. **3 John 9.** I wrote unto the church: but Diotrephes, who loveth to have the preeminence among them, receiveth us not. **Luke 22:24.** And there was also a strife among them, which of them should be accounted the greatest.

k. **Ex. 20:12.**

l. **Eph. 6:2–3.** Honour thy father and mother; (which is the first commandment with promise;) that it may be well with thee, and thou mayest live long on the earth. **See Deut. 5:16; 1 Kings 8:25.**

m. **Ex. 20:13. Cf. Deut. 5:17.** Thou shalt not kill.

Q. 135. *What are the duties required in the sixth commandment?*

A. The duties required in the sixth commandment are, all careful studies, and lawful endeavors, to preserve the life of ourselves[n] and others[o] by resisting all thoughts and purposes,[p] subduing all passions,[q] and avoiding all occasions,[r] temptations,[s] and practices, which tend to the unjust taking away the life of any;[t] by just defense thereof against violence,[u] patient bearing of the hand of God,[w] quiet-

n. **Eph. 5:28–29.** So ought men to love their wives as their own bodies. He that loveth his wife loveth himself. For no man ever yet hated his own flesh; but nourisheth and cherisheth it, even as the Lord the church.

o. **1 Kings 18:4.** For it was so, when Jezebel cut off the prophets of the LORD, that Obadiah took an hundred prophets, and hid them by fifty in a cave, and fed them with bread and water.

p. **Jer. 26:15–16.** But know ye for certain, that if ye put me to death, ye shall surely bring innocent blood upon yourselves, and upon this city, and upon the inhabitants thereof: for of a truth the LORD hath sent me unto you to speak all these words in your ears. Then said the princes and all the people unto the priests and to the prophets; This man is not worthy to die: for he hath spoken to us in the name of the LORD our God. **See Acts 23:12, 16–17, 21, 27.**

q. **Eph. 4:26–27.** Be ye angry, and sin not: let not the sun go down upon your wrath: neither give place to the devil.

r. **2 Sam. 2:22–23.** And Abner said again to Asahel, Turn thee aside from following me: wherefore should I smite thee to the ground? how then should I hold up my face to Joab thy brother? Howbeit he refused to turn aside: wherefore Abner with the hinder end of the spear smote him under the fifth rib, that the spear came out behind him; and he fell down there, and died in the same place: and it came to pass, that as many as came to the place where Asahel fell down and died stood still. **Deut. 22:8.** When thou buildest a new house, then thou shalt make a battlement for thy roof, that thou bring not blood upon thine house, if any man fall from thence.

s. **Matt. 4:6–7.** And [the devil] saith unto him, If thou be the Son of God, cast thyself down: for it is written, He shall give his angels charge concerning thee: and in their hands they shall bear thee up, lest at any time thou dash thy foot against a stone. Jesus said unto him, It is written again, Thou shalt not tempt the Lord thy God. **Prov. 1:10–11, 15–16.** My son, if sinners entice thee, consent thou not. If they say, Come with us, let us lay wait for blood, let us lurk privily for the innocent without cause.… My son, walk not thou in the way with them; refrain thy foot from their path: for their feet run to evil, and make haste to shed blood.

t. **Gen. 37:21–22.** And Reuben heard it, and he delivered him out of their hands; and said, Let us not kill him. And Reuben said unto them, Shed no blood, but cast him into this pit that is in the wilderness, and lay no hand upon him; that he might rid him out of their hands, to deliver him to his father again. **See 1 Sam. 24:12; 26:9–11.**

u. **Ps. 82:4.** Deliver the poor and needy: rid them out of the hand of the wicked. **Prov. 24:11–12.** If thou forbear to deliver them that are drawn unto death, and those that are ready to be slain; if thou sayest, Behold, we knew it not; doth not he that

ness of mind,[x] cheerfulness of spirit;[y] a sober use of meat,[z] drink,[a] physic,[b] sleep,[c] labor,[d] and recreations;[e] by charitable thoughts,[f]

pondereth the heart consider it? and he that keepeth thy soul, doth not he know it? and shall not he render to every man according to his works? **See 1 Sam. 14:45; Jer. 38:7–13.**

w. **James 5:10–11.** Take, my brethren, the prophets, who have spoken in the name of the Lord, for an example of suffering affliction, and of patience. Behold, we count them happy which endure. Ye have heard of the patience of Job, and have seen the end of the Lord; that the Lord is very pitiful, and of tender mercy. **Heb. 12:9.** Furthermore we have had fathers of our flesh which corrected us, and we gave them reverence: shall we not much rather be in subjection unto the Father of spirits, and live? **See 2 Sam. 16:10–12.**

x. **1 Thess. 4:11.** … and that ye study to be quiet, and to do your own business, and to work with your own hands, as we commanded you. **1 Pet. 3:3–4.** Whose adorning let it not be that outward adorning of plaiting the hair, and of wearing of gold, or of putting on of apparel; but let it be the hidden man of the heart, in that which is not corruptible, even the ornament of a meek and quiet spirit, which is in the sight of God of great price. **Ps. 37:8, 11**. Cease from anger, and forsake wrath: fret not thyself in any wise to do evil.… But the meek shall inherit the earth; and shall delight themselves in the abundance of peace.

y. **Prov. 17:22.** A merry heart doeth good like a medicine: but a broken spirit drieth the bones.

z. **Prov. 23:20.** Be not among winebibbers; among riotous eaters of flesh. **Prov. 25:16, 27.** Hast thou found honey? eat so much as is sufficient for thee, lest thou be filled therewith, and vomit it.… It is not good to eat much honey: so for men to search their own glory is not glory.

a. **1 Tim. 5:23.** Drink no longer water, but use a little wine for thy stomach's sake and thine often infirmities.

b. **Isa. 38:21.** For Isaiah had said, Let them take a lump of figs, and lay it for a plaister upon the boil, and he shall recover.

c. **Ps. 127:2.** It is vain for you to rise up early, to sit up late, to eat the bread of sorrows: for so he giveth his beloved sleep.

d. **2 Thess. 3:12.** Now them that are such we command and exhort by our Lord Jesus Christ, that with quietness they work, and eat their own bread. **See Eccl. 5:12.**

e. **Eccl. 3:4, 11.** … a time to weep, and a time to laugh; a time to mourn, and a time to dance … He hath made every thing beautiful in his time: also he hath set the world in their heart, so that no man can find out the work that God maketh from the beginning to the end. **Mark 6:31.** And he said unto them, Come ye yourselves apart into a desert place, and rest a while: for there were many coming and going, and they had no leisure so much as to eat.

f. **1 Sam. 19:4–5.** And Jonathan spake good of David unto Saul his father, and said unto him, Let not the king sin against his servant, against David; because he hath not sinned against thee, and because his works have been to thee-ward very good: for he did put his life in his hand, and slew the Philistine, and the LORD wrought a great salvation for all Israel: thou sawest it, and didst rejoice: wherefore then wilt thou sin against innocent blood, to slay David without a cause? **See 1 Sam. 22:13–14.**

love,[g] compassion,[h] meekness, gentleness, kindness;[i] peaceable,[k] mild, and courteous speeches and behavior;[l] forbearance, readiness to be reconciled, patient bearing and forgiving of injuries, and requiting good for evil;[m] comforting and succoring the distressed, and protecting and defending the innocent.[n´]

Q. 136. *What are the sins forbidden in the sixth commandment?*

A. The sins forbidden in the sixth commandment are, all taking

g. **Rom. 13:10.** Love worketh no ill to his neighbour: therefore love is the fulfilling of the law.

h. **Luke 10:33–34.** But a certain Samaritan, as he journeyed, came where he was: and when he saw him, he had compassion on him, and went to him, and bound up his wounds, pouring in oil and wine, and set him on his own beast, and brought him to an inn, and took care of him.

i. **Col. 3:12–13.** Put on therefore, as the elect of God, holy and beloved, bowels of mercies, kindness, humbleness of mind, meekness, longsuffering; forbearing one another, and forgiving one another, if any man have a quarrel against any: even as Christ forgave you, so also do ye.

k. **James 3:17.** But the wisdom that is from above is first pure, then peaceable, gentle, and easy to be intreated, full of mercy and good fruits, without partiality, and without hypocrisy.

l. **1 Pet. 3:8–11.** Finally, be ye all of one mind, having compassion one of another, love as brethren, be pitiful, be courteous: not rendering evil for evil, or railing for railing: but contrariwise blessing; knowing that ye are thereunto called, that ye should inherit a blessing. For he that will love life, and see good days, let him refrain his tongue from evil, and his lips that they speak no guile: let him eschew evil, and do good; let him seek peace, and ensue it. **1 Cor. 4:12–13.** And [we] labour, working with our own hands: being reviled, we bless; being persecuted, we suffer it: being defamed, we intreat: we are made as the filth of the world, and are the offscouring of all things unto this day. **See Prov. 15:1; Judg. 8:1–3.**

m. **Matt. 5:24.** Leave there thy gift before the altar, and go thy way; first be reconciled to thy brother, and then come and offer thy gift. **Eph. 4:2, 32.** … with all lowliness and meekness, with longsuffering, forbearing one another in love … And be ye kind one to another, tenderhearted, forgiving one another, even as God for Christ's sake hath forgiven you. **Rom. 12:17, 20–21.** Recompense to no man evil for evil.… Therefore if thine enemy hunger, feed him; if he thirst, give him drink: for in so doing thou shalt heap coals of fire on his head. Be not overcome of evil, but overcome evil with good.

n´. **1 Thess. 5:14.** Now we exhort you, brethren, warn them that are unruly, comfort the feebleminded, support the weak, be patient toward all men. **Matt. 25:35–36.** For I was an hungred, and ye gave me meat: I was thirsty, and ye gave me drink: I was a stranger, and ye took me in: naked, and ye clothed me: I was sick, and ye visited me: I was in prison, and ye came unto me. **Prov. 31:8–9.** Open thy mouth for the dumb in the cause of all such as are appointed to destruction. Open thy mouth, judge righteously, and plead the cause of the poor and needy. **See Job 31:19–20; Isa. 58:7.**

away the life of ourselves,^o or of others,^p except in case of public justice,^q lawful war,^r or necessary defense;^s the neglecting or withdrawing the lawful and necessary means of preservation of life;^t sinful anger,^u hatred,^w envy,^x desire of revenge;^y all excessive passions,^z distracting cares;^a immoderate use of meat, drink,^b labor,^c and

o. **Acts 16:28.** But Paul cried with a loud voice, saying, Do thyself no harm: for we are all here.

p. **Gen. 9:6.** Whoso sheddeth man's blood, by man shall his blood be shed: for in the image of God made he man.

q. **Num. 35:31, 33.** Moreover ye shall take no satisfaction for the life of a murderer, which is guilty of death: but he shall be surely put to death.... So ye shall not pollute the land wherein ye are: for blood it defileth the land: and the land cannot be cleansed of the blood that is shed therein, but by the blood of him that shed it. **Rom. 13:4.** For he is the minister of God to thee for good. But if thou do that which is evil, be afraid; for he beareth not the sword in vain: for he is the minister of God, a revenger to execute wrath upon him that doeth evil.

r. **See Deut. 20 compared with Heb. 11:32–34.** And what shall I more say? for the time would fail me to tell of Gedeon, and of Barak, and of Samson, and of Jephthah; of David also, and Samuel, and of the prophets: who through faith subdued kingdoms, wrought righteousness, obtained promises, stopped the mouths of lions, quenched the violence of fire, escaped the edge of the sword, out of weakness were made strong, waxed valiant in fight, turned to flight the armies of the aliens.

s. **Ex. 22:2.** If a thief be found breaking up, and be smitten that he die, there shall no blood be shed for him.

t. **Matt. 25:42–43.** For I was an hungred, and ye gave me no meat: I was thirsty, and ye gave me no drink: I was a stranger, and ye took me not in: naked, and ye clothed me not: sick, and in prison, and ye visited me not. **James 2:15–16.** If a brother or sister be naked, and destitute of daily food, and one of you say unto them, Depart in peace, be ye warmed and filled; notwithstanding ye give them not those things which are needful to the body; what doth it profit?

u. **Matt. 5:22.** But I say unto you, That whosoever is angry with his brother without a cause shall be in danger of the judgment: and whosoever shall say to his brother, Raca, shall be in danger of the council: but whosoever shall say, Thou fool, shall be in danger of hell fire.

w. **1 John 3:15.** Whosoever hateth his brother is a murderer: and ye know that no murderer hath eternal life abiding in him. **Lev. 19:17.** Thou shalt not hate thy brother in thine heart: thou shalt in any wise rebuke thy neighbour, and not suffer sin upon him.

x. **Prov. 14:30.** A sound heart is the life of the flesh: but envy the rottenness of the bones.

y. **Rom. 12:19.** Dearly beloved, avenge not yourselves, but rather give place unto wrath: for it is written, Vengeance is mine; I will repay, saith the Lord.

z. **Eph. 4:31.** Let all bitterness, and wrath, and anger, and clamour, and evil speaking, be put away from you, with all malice.

a. **Matt. 6:31, 34.** Therefore take no thought, saying, What shall we eat? or, What shall we drink? or, Wherewithal shall we be clothed?... Take therefore no thought

recreations;^d provoking words,^e oppression,^f quarreling,^g striking, wounding,^h and whatsoever else tends to the destruction of the life of any.ⁱ

Q. 137. *Which is the seventh commandment?*

A. The seventh commandment is, *Thou shalt not commit adultery.*^k

Q. 138. *What are the duties required in the seventh commandment?*

A. The duties required in the seventh commandment are, chastity in body, mind, affections,^l words,^m and behavior;ⁿ and the preser-

for the morrow: for the morrow shall take thought for the things of itself. Sufficient unto the day is the evil thereof.

b. **Luke 21:34.** And take heed to yourselves, lest at any time your hearts be overcharged with surfeiting, and drunkenness, and cares of this life, and so that day come upon you unawares. **Rom. 13:13.** Let us walk honestly, as in the day; not in rioting and drunkenness, not in chambering and wantonness, not in strife and envying.

c. **Eccl. 12:12.** And further, by these, my son, be admonished: of making many books there is no end; and much study is a weariness of the flesh. **Eccl. 2:22–23.** For what hath man of all his labour, and of the vexation of his heart, wherein he hath laboured under the sun? For all his days are sorrows, and his travail grief; yea, his heart taketh not rest in the night. This is also vanity.

d. **Isa. 5:12.** And the harp, and the viol, the tabret, and pipe, and wine, are in their feasts: but they regard not the work of the LORD, neither consider the operation of his hands.

e. **Prov. 15:1.** A soft answer turneth away wrath: but grievous words stir up anger. **Prov. 12:18.** There is that speaketh like the piercings of a sword: but the tongue of the wise is health.

f. **Ex. 1:14.** And they made their lives bitter with hard bondage, in mortar, and in brick, and in all manner of service in the field: all their service, wherein they made them serve, was with rigour. **See Isa. 3:15.**

g. **Gal. 5:15.** But if ye bite and devour one another, take heed that ye be not consumed one of another. **Prov. 23:29.** Who hath woe? who hath sorrow? who hath contentions? who hath babbling? who hath wounds without cause? who hath redness of eyes?

h. **Num. 35:16–17.** And if he smite him with an instrument of iron, so that he die, he is a murderer: the murderer shall surely be put to death. And if he smite him with throwing a stone, wherewith he may die, and he die, he is a murderer: the murderer shall surely be put to death. **See verses 18–21.**

i. **Ex. 21:29.** But if the ox were wont to push with his horn in time past, and it hath been testified to his owner, and he hath not kept him in, but that he hath killed a man or a woman; the ox shall be stoned, and his owner also shall be put to death. **See verses 18–36.**

k. **Ex. 20:14. Cf. Deut. 5:18.** Neither shalt thou commit adultery.

l. **1 Thess. 4:4–5.** That every one of you should know how to possess his vessel in sanctification and honour, not in the lust of concupiscence, even as the Gentiles

vation of it in ourselves and others;[o] watchfulness over the eyes and all the senses;[p] temperance,[q] keeping of chaste company,[r] modesty in apparel;[s] marriage by those that have not the gift of continency,[t]

which know not God. **Job 31:1.** I made a covenant with mine eyes; why then should I think upon a maid? **1 Cor. 7:34.** There is difference also between a wife and a virgin. The unmarried woman careth for the things of the Lord, that she may be holy both in body and in spirit: but she that is married careth for the things of the world, how she may please her husband.

m. **Eph. 4:29.** Let no corrupt communication proceed out of your mouth, but that which is good to the use of edifying, that it may minister grace unto the hearers. **Col. 4:6.** Let your speech be alway with grace, seasoned with salt, that ye may know how ye ought to answer every man.

n. **1 Pet. 3:2.** While they behold your chaste conversation coupled with fear.

o. **1 Cor. 7:2–5, 34–36.** Nevertheless, to avoid fornication, let every man have his own wife, and let every woman have her own husband. Let the husband render unto the wife due benevolence: and likewise also the wife unto the husband. The wife hath not power of her own body, but the husband: and likewise also the husband hath not power of his own body, but the wife. Defraud ye not one the other, except it be with consent for a time, that ye may give yourselves to fasting and prayer; and come together again, that Satan tempt you not for your incontinency.... There is difference also between a wife and a virgin. The unmarried woman careth for the things of the Lord, that she may be holy both in body and in spirit: but she that is married careth for the things of the world, how she may please her husband. And this I speak for your own profit; not that I may cast a snare upon you, but for that which is comely, and that ye may attend upon the Lord without distraction. But if any man think that he behaveth himself uncomely toward his virgin, if she pass the flower of her age, and need so require, let him do what he will, he sinneth not: let them marry.

p. **Matt. 5:28.** But I say unto you, That whosoever looketh on a woman to lust after her hath committed adultery with her already in his heart. **Job 31:1.** I made a covenant with mine eyes; why then should I think upon a maid?

q. **Acts 24:24–25.** And after certain days, when Felix came with his wife Drusilla, which was a Jewess, he sent for Paul, and heard him concerning the faith in Christ. And as he reasoned of righteousness, temperance, and judgment to come, Felix trembled, and answered, Go thy way for this time; when I have a convenient season, I will call for thee.

r. **Prov. 2:16–20.** ... to deliver thee from the strange woman, even from the stranger which flattereth with her words; which forsaketh the guide of her youth, and forgetteth the covenant of her God. For her house inclineth unto death, and her paths unto the dead. None that go unto her return again, neither take they hold of the paths of life. That thou mayest walk in the way of good men, and keep the paths of the righteous.

s. **1 Tim. 2:9.** In like manner also, that women adorn themselves in modest apparel, with shamefacedness and sobriety; not with broided hair, or gold, or pearls, or costly array.

t. **1 Cor. 7:2, 9.** Nevertheless, to avoid fornication, let every man have his own wife, and let every woman have her own husband.... But if they cannot contain, let them marry: for it is better to marry than to burn.

conjugal love,[u] and cohabitation;[w] diligent labor in our callings;[x] shunning all occasions of uncleanness, and resisting temptations thereunto.[y]

Q. 139. *What are the sins forbidden in the seventh commandment?*

A. The sins forbidden in the seventh commandment, besides the neglect of the duties required,[z] are, adultery, fornication,[a] rape, incest,[b] sodomy, and all unnatural lusts;[c] all unclean imaginations, thoughts, purposes, and affections;[d] all corrupt or filthy communications, or

u. **Prov. 5:19–20.** Let her be as the loving hind and pleasant roe; let her breasts satisfy thee at all times; and be thou ravished always with her love. And why wilt thou, my son, be ravished with a strange woman, and embrace the bosom of a stranger?

w. **1 Pet. 3:7.** Likewise, ye husbands, dwell with them according to knowledge, giving honour unto the wife, as unto the weaker vessel, and as being heirs together of the grace of life; that your prayers be not hindered. **1 Cor. 7:5.** Defraud ye not one the other, except it be with consent for a time, that ye may give yourselves to fasting and prayer; and come together again, that Satan tempt you not for your incontinency.

x. **Prov. 31:11, 27–28.** The heart of her husband doth safely trust in her, so that he shall have no need of spoil…. She looketh well to the ways of her household, and eateth not the bread of idleness. Her children arise up, and call her blessed; her husband also, and he praiseth her.

y. **Prov. 5:8.** Remove thy way far from her, and come not nigh the door of her house. **See Gen. 39:8–10.**

z. **Prov. 5:7.** Hear me now therefore, O ye children, and depart not from the words of my mouth. **See Prov. 4:23, 27.**

a. **Heb. 13:4.** Marriage is honourable in all, and the bed undefiled: but whoremongers and adulterers God will judge. **Eph. 5:5.** For this ye know, that no whoremonger, nor unclean person, nor covetous man, who is an idolater, hath any inheritance in the kingdom of God. **See Gal. 5:19.**

b. **2 Sam. 13:14.** Howbeit he would not hearken unto her voice: but, being stronger than she, forced her, and lay with her. **1 Cor. 5:1.** It is reported commonly that there is fornication among you, and such fornication as is not so much as named among the Gentiles, that one should have his father's wife. **Mark 6:18.** For John had said unto Herod, It is not lawful for thee to have thy brother's wife.

c. **Rom. 1:24, 26–27.** Wherefore God also gave them up to uncleanness through the lusts of their own hearts, to dishonour their own bodies between themselves…. For this cause God gave them up unto vile affections: for even their women did change the natural use into that which is against nature: and likewise also the men, leaving the natural use of the woman, burned in their lust one toward another; men with men working that which is unseemly, and receiving in themselves that recompence of their error which was meet. **Lev. 20:15–16.** And if a man lie with a beast, he shall surely be put to death: and ye shall slay the beast. And if a woman approach unto any beast, and lie down thereto, thou shalt kill the woman, and the beast: they shall surely be put to death; their blood shall be upon them.

d. **Matt. 5:28.** But I say unto you, That whosoever looketh on a woman to lust after her hath committed adultery with her already in his heart. **Matt. 15:19.** For

listening thereunto;ᵉ wanton looks,ᶠ impudent or light behavior, immodest apparel;ᵍ prohibiting of lawful,ʰ and dispensing with unlawful marriages;ⁱ allowing, tolerating, keeping of stews, and resorting to them;ᵏ entangling vows of single life,ˡ undue delay of marriage,ᵐ

out of the heart proceed evil thoughts, murders, adulteries, fornications, thefts, false witness, blasphemies. **Col. 3:5.** Mortify therefore your members which are upon the earth; fornication, uncleanness, inordinate affection, evil concupiscence, and covetousness, which is idolatry.

e. **Eph. 5:3–4.** But fornication, and all uncleanness, or covetousness, let it not be once named among you, as becometh saints; neither filthiness, nor foolish talking, nor jesting, which are not convenient: but rather giving of thanks. **See Prov. 7:5, 21–22.**

f. **Isa. 3:16.** Moreover the LORD saith, Because the daughters of Zion are haughty, and walk with stretched forth necks and wanton eyes, walking and mincing as they go, and making a tinkling with their feet … **2 Pet. 2:14.** … having eyes full of adultery, and that cannot cease from sin; beguiling unstable souls: an heart they have exercised with covetous practices; cursed children.

g. **Prov. 7:10, 13.** And, behold, there met him a woman with the attire of an harlot, and subtil of heart.… So she caught him, and kissed him, and with an impudent face said unto him …

h. **1 Tim. 4:3.** … forbidding to marry, and commanding to abstain from meats, which God hath created to be received with thanksgiving of them which believe and know the truth.

i. **Mark 6:18.** For John had said unto Herod, It is not lawful for thee to have thy brother's wife. **Mal. 2:11–12.** Judah hath dealt treacherously, and an abomination is committed in Israel and in Jerusalem; for Judah hath profaned the holiness of the LORD which he loved, and hath married the daughter of a strange god. The LORD will cut off the man that doeth this, the master and the scholar, out of the tabernacles of Jacob, and him that offereth an offering unto the LORD of hosts. **See Lev. 18:1–21.**

k. **1 Kings 15:12.** And he took away the sodomites out of the land, and removed all the idols that his fathers had made. **2 Kings 23:7.** And he brake down the houses of the sodomites, that were by the house of the LORD, where the women wove hangings for the grove. **Lev. 19:29.** Do not prostitute thy daughter, to cause her to be a whore; lest the land fall to whoredom, and the land become full of wickedness. **Jer. 5:7.** How shall I pardon thee for this? thy children have forsaken me, and sworn by them that are no gods: when I had fed them to the full, they then committed adultery, and assembled themselves by troops in the harlots' houses. **See Deut. 23:17–18; Prov. 7:24–27.**

l. **Matt. 19:10–11.** His disciples say unto him, If the case of the man be so with his wife, it is not good to marry. But he said unto them, All men cannot receive this saying, save they to whom it is given.

m. **1 Cor. 7:7–9.** For I would that all men were even as I myself. But every man hath his proper gift of God, one after this manner, and another after that. I say therefore to the unmarried and widows, It is good for them if they abide even as I. But if they cannot contain, let them marry: for it is better to marry than to burn. **Gen. 38:26.** And Judah acknowledged them, and said, She hath been more righteous than I; because that I gave her not to Shelah my son. And he knew her again no more.

having more wives or husbands than one at the same time;[n] unjust divorce,[o] or desertion;[p] idleness, gluttony, drunkenness,[q] unchaste company;[r] lascivious songs, books, pictures, dancings, stage plays;[s] and all other provocations to, or acts of uncleanness, either in ourselves or others.[t]

n. **Mal. 2:14–15.** Yet ye say, Wherefore? Because the LORD hath been witness between thee and the wife of thy youth, against whom thou hast dealt treacherously: yet is she thy companion, and the wife of thy covenant. And did not he make one? Yet had he the residue of the spirit. And wherefore one? That he might seek a godly seed. Therefore take heed to your spirit, and let none deal treacherously against the wife of his youth. **Matt. 19:5.** … and said, For this cause shall a man leave father and mother, and shall cleave to his wife: and they twain shall be one flesh?

o. **Mal. 2:16.** For the LORD, the God of Israel, saith that he hateth putting away: for one covereth violence with his garment, saith the LORD of hosts: therefore take heed to your spirit, that ye deal not treacherously. **Matt. 5:32.** But I say unto you, That whosoever shall put away his wife, saving for the cause of fornication, causeth her to commit adultery: and whosoever shall marry her that is divorced committeth adultery. **Matt. 19:8–9.** He saith unto them, Moses because of the hardness of your hearts suffered you to put away your wives: but from the beginning it was not so. And I say unto you, Whosoever shall put away his wife, except it be for fornication, and shall marry another, committeth adultery: and whoso marrieth her which is put away doth commit adultery.

p. **1 Cor. 7:12–13.** But to the rest speak I, not the Lord: If any brother hath a wife that believeth not, and she be pleased to dwell with him, let him not put her away. And the woman which hath an husband that believeth not, and if he be pleased to dwell with her, let her not leave him.

q. **Ezek. 16:49.** Behold, this was the iniquity of thy sister Sodom, pride, fulness of bread, and abundance of idleness was in her and in her daughters, neither did she strengthen the hand of the poor and needy. **See Prov. 23:30–33.**

r. **Gen. 39:19.** And it came to pass, when his master heard the words of his wife, which she spake unto him, saying, After this manner did thy servant to me; that his wrath was kindled. **See Prov. 5:8.**

s. **Eph. 5:4.** … neither filthiness, nor foolish talking, nor jesting, which are not convenient: but rather giving of thanks. **Rom. 13:13.** Let us walk honestly, as in the day; not in rioting and drunkenness, not in chambering and wantonness, not in strife and envying. **1 Pet. 4:3.** For the time past of our life may suffice us to have wrought the will of the Gentiles, when we walked in lasciviousness, lusts, excess of wine, revellings, banquetings, and abominable idolatries. **See Ezek. 23:14–16; Isa. 3:16; 23:15–17; Mark 6:22.**

t. **2 Kings 9:30.** And when Jehu was come to Jezreel, Jezebel heard of it; and she painted her face, and tired her head, and looked out at a window. **Jer. 4:30.** And when thou art spoiled, what wilt thou do? Though thou clothest thyself with crimson, though thou deckest thee with ornaments of gold, though thou rentest thy face with painting, in vain shalt thou make thyself fair; thy lovers will despise thee, they will seek thy life. **Ezek. 23:40.** And furthermore, that ye have sent for men to come from far, unto whom a messenger was sent; and, lo, they came: for whom thou didst wash

Q. 140. *Which is the eighth commandment?*

A. The eighth commandment is, *Thou shalt not steal.*[u]

Q. 141. *What are the duties required in the eighth commandment?*

A. The duties required in the eighth commandment are, truth, faithfulness, and justice in contracts and commerce between man and man;[w] rendering to everyone his due;[x] restitution of goods unlawfully detained from the right owners thereof;[y] giving and lending freely, according to our abilities, and the necessities of others;[z] moderation of our judgments, wills, and affections concerning worldly goods;[a] a

---

thyself, paintedst thy eyes, and deckedst thyself with ornaments.

u. **Ex. 20:15. Cf. Deut. 5:19.** Neither shalt thou steal.

w. **Ps. 15:2, 4.** He that walketh uprightly, and worketh righteousness, and speaketh the truth in his heart.… In whose eyes a vile person is contemned; but he honoureth them that fear the LORD. He that sweareth to his own hurt, and changeth not. **Mic. 6:8.** He hath shewed thee, O man, what is good; and what doth the LORD require of thee, but to do justly, and to love mercy, and to walk humbly with thy God? **Zech. 8:16–17.** These are the things that ye shall do; Speak ye every man the truth to his neighbour; execute the judgment of truth and peace in your gates: and let none of you imagine evil in your hearts against his neighbour; and love no false oath: for all these are things that I hate, saith the LORD. **See Zech. 7:4, 10.**

x. **Rom. 13:7.** Render therefore to all their dues: tribute to whom tribute is due; custom to whom custom; fear to whom fear; honour to whom honour.

y. **Lev. 6:2–5.** If a soul sin, and commit a trespass against the LORD, and lie unto his neighbour in that which was delivered him to keep, or in fellowship, or in a thing taken away by violence, or hath deceived his neighbour; or have found that which was lost, and lieth concerning it, and sweareth falsely; in any of all these that a man doeth, sinning therein: then it shall be, because he hath sinned, and is guilty, that he shall restore that which he took violently away, or the thing which he hath deceitfully gotten, or that which was delivered him to keep, or the lost thing which he found, or all that about which he hath sworn falsely; he shall even restore it in the principal, and shall add the fifth part more thereto, and give it unto him to whom it appertaineth, in the day of his trespass offering. **See Luke 19:8.**

z. **Luke 6:30, 38.** Give to every man that asketh of thee; and of him that taketh away thy goods ask them not again.… Give, and it shall be given unto you; good measure, pressed down, and shaken together, and running over, shall men give into your bosom. For with the same measure that ye mete withal it shall be measured to you again. **1 John 3:17.** But whoso hath this world's good, and seeth his brother have need, and shutteth up his bowels of compassion from him, how dwelleth the love of God in him? **Eph. 4:28.** Let him that stole steal no more: but rather let him labour, working with his hands the thing which is good, that he may have to give to him that needeth. **Gal. 6:10.** As we have therefore opportunity, let us do good unto all men, especially unto them who are of the household of faith.

a. **1 Tim. 6:6–9.** But godliness with contentment is great gain. For we brought nothing into this world, and it is certain we can carry nothing out. And having food

provident care and study to get,[b] keep, use, and dispose these things which are necessary and convenient for the sustentation of our nature, and suitable to our condition;[c] a lawful calling,[d] and diligence in it;[e] frugality;[f] avoiding unnecessary lawsuits,[g] and suretyship, or other like engagements;[h] and an endeavor, by all just and lawful means, to procure, preserve, and further the wealth and outward estate of others, as well as our own.[i]

Q. 142. *What are the sins forbidden in the eighth commandment?*
A. The sins forbidden in the eighth commandment, besides the

and raiment let us be therewith content. But they that will be rich fall into temptation and a snare, and into many foolish and hurtful lusts, which drown men in destruction and perdition. **See Gal. 6:14.**

b. **1 Tim. 5:8.** But if any provide not for his own, and specially for those of his own house, he hath denied the faith, and is worse than an infidel.

c. **Prov. 27:23.** Be thou diligent to know the state of thy flocks, and look well to thy herds. **See verses 24–27. Eccl. 2:24.** There is nothing better for a man, than that he should eat and drink, and that he should make his soul enjoy good in his labour. This also I saw, that it was from the hand of God. **Eccl. 3:12–13.** I know that there is no good in them, but for a man to rejoice, and to do good in his life. And also that every man should eat and drink, and enjoy the good of all his labour, it is the gift of God. **1 Tim. 6:17–18.** Charge them that are rich in this world, that they be not highminded, nor trust in uncertain riches, but in the living God, who giveth us richly all things to enjoy; that they do good, that they be rich in good works, ready to distribute, willing to communicate. **See Isa. 38:1; Matt. 11:8.**

d. **1 Cor. 7:20.** Let every man abide in the same calling wherein he was called. **See Gen. 2:15; 3:19.**

e. **Eph. 4:28.** Let him that stole steal no more: but rather let him labour, working with his hands the thing which is good, that he may have to give to him that needeth. **Prov. 10:4.** He becometh poor that dealeth with a slack hand: but the hand of the diligent maketh rich. **Rom. 12:11.** [Be] not slothful in business; fervent in spirit; serving the Lord.

f. **John 6:12.** When they were filled, he said unto his disciples, Gather up the fragments that remain, that nothing be lost. **Prov. 21:20.** There is treasure to be desired and oil in the dwelling of the wise; but a foolish man spendeth it up.

g. **1 Cor. 6:1.** Dare any of you, having a matter against another, go to law before the unjust, and not before the saints? **See verses 2–9.**

h. **Prov. 11:15.** He that is surety for a stranger shall smart for it: and he that hateth suretiship is sure. **See Prov. 6:1–6.**

i. **Lev. 25:35.** And if thy brother be waxen poor, and fallen in decay with thee; then thou shalt relieve him: yea, though he be a stranger, or a sojourner; that he may live with thee. **Phil. 2:4.** Look not every man on his own things, but every man also on the things of others. **See Deut. 22:1–4; Ex. 23:4–5; Gen. 47:14, 20; Matt. 22:39.**

neglect of the duties required,[k] are, theft,[l] robbery,[m] manstealing,[n] and receiving anything that is stolen;[o] fraudulent dealing,[p] false weights and measures,[q] removing landmarks,[r] injustice and unfaithfulness in contracts between man and man,[s] or in matters of trust;[t] oppression,[u] extortion,[w] usury,[x] bribery,[y] vexatious lawsuits,[z] unjust enclosures

k. **James 2:15–16.** If a brother or sister be naked, and destitute of daily food, and one of you say unto them, Depart in peace, be ye warmed and filled; notwithstanding ye give them not those things which are needful to the body; what doth it profit? **1 John 3:17.** But whoso hath this world's good, and seeth his brother have need, and shutteth up his bowels of compassion from him, how dwelleth the love of God in him?

l. **Eph. 4:28.** Let him that stole steal no more: but rather let him labour, working with his hands the thing which is good, that he may have to give to him that needeth.

m. **Ps. 62:10.** Trust not in oppression, and become not vain in robbery: if riches increase, set not your heart upon them.

n. **1 Tim. 1:10.** … for whoremongers, for them that defile themselves with mankind, for menstealers, for liars, for perjured persons, and if there be any other thing that is contrary to sound doctrine.

o. **Prov. 29:24.** Whoso is partner with a thief hateth his own soul: he heareth cursing, and bewrayeth it not. **Ps. 50:18.** When thou sawest a thief, then thou consentedst with him, and hast been partaker with adulterers.

p. **1 Thess. 4:6.** … that no man go beyond and defraud his brother in any matter: because that the Lord is the avenger of all such, as we also have forewarned you and testified. **Lev. 19:13.** Thou shalt not defraud thy neighbour, neither rob him: the wages of him that is hired shall not abide with thee all night until the morning.

q. **Prov. 11:1.** A false balance is abomination to the LORD: but a just weight is his delight. **Prov. 20:10.** Divers weights, and divers measures, both of them are alike abomination to the LORD.

r. **Deut. 19:14.** Thou shalt not remove thy neighbour's landmark, which they of old time have set in thine inheritance, which thou shalt inherit in the land that LORD thy God giveth thee to possess it. **See Prov. 23:10.**

s. **Amos 8:5.** … saying, When will the new moon be gone, that we may sell corn? and the sabbath, that we may set forth wheat, making the ephah small, and the shekel great, and falsifying the balances by deceit? **Ps. 37:21.** The wicked borroweth, and payeth not again: but the righteous sheweth mercy, and giveth.

t. **Luke 16:10–12.** He that is faithful in that which is least is faithful also in much: and he that is unjust in the least is unjust also in much. If therefore ye have not been faithful in the unrighteous mammon, who will commit to your trust the true riches? And if ye have not been faithful in that which is another man's, who shall give you that which is your own?

u. **Ezek. 22:29.** The people of the land have used oppression, and exercised robbery, and have vexed the poor and needy: yea, they have oppressed the stranger wrongfully. **Lev. 25:17.** Ye shall not therefore oppress one another; but thou shalt fear thy God: for I am the LORD your God.

w. **Matt. 23:25.** Woe unto you, scribes and Pharisees, hypocrites! for ye make clean the outside of the cup and of the platter, but within they are full of extortion and

and depredation;[a] engrossing commodities to enhance the price;[b] unlawful callings,[c] and all other unjust or sinful ways of taking or withholding from our neighbor what belongs to him, or of enriching ourselves;[d] covetousness;[e] inordinate prizing and affecting worldly goods;[f] distrustful and distracting cares and studies in getting, keeping, and using them;[g] envying at the prosperity of others;[h] as likewise

excess. **Ezek. 22:12.** In thee have they taken gifts to shed blood; thou hast taken usury and increase, and thou hast greedily gained of thy neighbours by extortion, and hast forgotten me, saith the Lord GOD.

x. **Ps. 15:5.** He that putteth not out his money to usury, nor taketh reward against the innocent. He that doeth these things shall never be moved.

y. **Job 15:34.** For the congregation of hypocrites shall be desolate, and fire shall consume the tabernacles of bribery.

z. **1 Cor. 6:6–8.** But brother goeth to law with brother, and that before the unbelievers. Now therefore there is utterly a fault among you, because ye go to law one with another. Why do ye not rather take wrong? why do ye not rather suffer yourselves to be defrauded? Nay, ye do wrong, and defraud, and that your brethren. **Prov. 3:29–30.** Devise not evil against thy neighbour, seeing he dwelleth securely by thee. Strive not with a man without cause, if he have done thee no harm.

a. **Isa. 5:8.** Woe unto them that join house to house, that lay field to field, till there be no place, that they may be placed alone in the midst of the earth! **Mic. 2:2.** And they covet fields, and take them by violence; and houses, and take them away: so they oppress a man and his house, even a man and his heritage.

b. **Prov. 11:26.** He that withholdeth corn, the people shall curse him: but blessing shall be upon the head of him that selleth it.

c. **Acts 19:19.** Many of them also which used curious arts brought their books together, and burned them before all men: and they counted the price of them, and found it fifty thousand pieces of silver. **See verses 24–25.**

d. **James 5:4.** Behold, the hire of the labourers who have reaped down your fields, which is of you kept back by fraud, crieth: and the cries of them which have reaped are entered into the ears of the Lord of sabaoth. **Prov. 21:6.** The getting of treasures by a lying tongue is a vanity tossed to and fro of them that seek death. **See Job 20:19.**

e. **Luke 12:15.** And he said unto them, Take heed, and beware of covetousness: for a man's life consisteth not in the abundance of the things which he possesseth.

f. **1 Tim. 6:5.** … perverse disputings of men of corrupt minds, and destitute of the truth, supposing that gain is godliness: from such withdraw thyself. **Col. 3:2.** Set your affection on things above, not on things on the earth. **1 John 2:15–16.** Love not the world, neither the things that are in the world. If any man love the world, the love of the Father is not in him. For all that is in the world, the lust of the flesh, and the lust of the eyes, and the pride of life, is not of the Father, but is of the world. **See Prov. 23:5; Ps. 62:10.**

g. **Matt. 6:25, 31, 34.** Therefore I say unto you, Take no thought for your life, what ye shall eat, or what ye shall drink; nor yet for your body, what ye shall put on. Is not the life more than meat, and the body than raiment?… Therefore take no thought,

idleness,[i] prodigality, wasteful gaming; and all other ways whereby we do unduly prejudice our own outward estate,[k'] and defrauding ourselves of the due use and comfort of that estate which God hath given us.[l']

Q. 143. *Which is the ninth commandment?*

A. The ninth commandment is, *Thou shalt not bear false witness against thy neighbour.*[m]

Q. 144. *What are the duties required in the ninth commandment?*

A. The duties required in the ninth commandment are, the preserving and promoting of truth between man and man,[n] and the

saying, What shall we eat? or, What shall we drink? or, Wherewithal shall we be clothed?... Take therefore no thought for the morrow: for the morrow shall take thought for the things of itself. Sufficient unto the day is the evil thereof. **Eccl. 5:12.** The sleep of a labouring man is sweet, whether he eat little or much: but the abundance of the rich will not suffer him to sleep.

h. **Ps. 73:3.** For I was envious at the foolish, when I saw the prosperity of the wicked. **See Ps. 37:1, 7.**

i. **2 Thess. 3:10–11.** For even when we were with you, this we commanded you, that if any would not work, neither should he eat. For we hear that there are some which walk among you disorderly, working not at all, but are busybodies. **See Prov. 18:9.**

k'. **Prov. 21:17.** He that loveth pleasure shall be a poor man: he that loveth wine and oil shall not be rich. **Prov. 23:20–21.** Be not among winebibbers; among riotous eaters of flesh: for the drunkard and the glutton shall come to poverty: and drowsiness shall clothe a man with rags. **See Prov. 28:19.**

l'. **Eccl. 4:8.** There is one alone, and there is not a second; yea, he hath neither child nor brother: yet is there no end of all his labour; neither is his eye satisfied with riches; neither saith he, For whom do I labour, and bereave my soul of good? This is also vanity, yea, it is a sore travail. **Eccl. 6:2.** ... a man to whom God hath given riches, wealth, and honour, so that he wanteth nothing for his soul of all that he desireth, yet God giveth him not power to eat thereof, but a stranger eateth it: this is vanity, and it is an evil disease. **1 Tim. 4:3–5.** ... forbidding to marry, and commanding to abstain from meats, which God hath created to be received with thanksgiving of them which believe and know the truth. For every creature of God is good, and nothing to be refused, if it be received with thanksgiving: for it is sanctified by the word of God and prayer. **1 Tim. 5:8.** But if any provide not for his own, and specially for those of his own house, he hath denied the faith, and is worse than an infidel.

m. **Ex. 20:16. Cf. Deut. 5:20.** Neither shalt thou bear false witness against thy neighbour.

n. **Zech. 8:16.** These are the things that ye shall do; Speak ye every man the truth to his neighbour; execute the judgment of truth and peace in your gates. **Eph. 4:25.** Wherefore putting away lying, speak every man truth with his neighbour: for we are members one of another.

good name of our neighbor, as well as our own;[o] appearing and standing for the truth;[p] and from the heart,[q] sincerely,[r] freely,[s] clearly,[t] and fully,[u] speaking the truth, and only the truth, in matters of judgment and justice,[w] and in all other things whatsoever;[x] a charitable esteem of our neighbors;[y] loving, desiring, and rejoicing in their good name;[z]

o. **3 John 12.** Demetrius hath good report of all men, and of the truth itself: yea, and we also bear record; and ye know that our record is true.

p. **Prov. 31:8–9.** Open thy mouth for the dumb in the cause of all such as are appointed to destruction. Open thy mouth, judge righteously, and plead the cause of the poor and needy.

q. **Ps. 15:2.** He that walketh uprightly, and worketh righteousness, and speaketh the truth in his heart.

r. **2 Chron. 19:9.** And he charged them, saying, Thus shall ye do in the fear of the LORD, faithfully, and with a perfect heart.

s. **1 Sam. 19:4–5.** And Jonathan spake good of David unto Saul his father, and said unto him, Let not the king sin against his servant, against David; because he hath not sinned against thee, and because his works have been to thee-ward very good: for he did put his life in his hand, and slew the Philistine, and the LORD wrought a great salvation for all Israel: thou sawest it, and didst rejoice: wherefore then wilt thou sin against innocent blood, to slay David without a cause?

t. **Josh. 7:19.** And Joshua said unto Achan, My son, give, I pray thee, glory to the LORD God of Israel, and make confession unto him; and tell me now what thou hast done; hide it not from me. **See verses 15–20.**

u. **2 Sam. 14:18.** Then the king answered and said unto the woman, Hide not from me, I pray thee, the thing that I shall ask thee. And the woman said, Let my lord the king now speak. **See verses 19–20. Acts 20:27.** For I have not shunned to declare unto you all the counsel of God.

w. **Lev. 19:15.** Ye shall do no unrighteousness in judgment: thou shalt not respect the person of the poor, nor honour the person of the mighty: but in righteousness shalt thou judge thy neighbour. **Prov. 14:5, 25.** A faithful witness will not lie: but a false witness will utter lies.... A true witness delivereth souls: but a deceitful witness speaketh lies.

x. **2 Cor. 1:17–18.** When I therefore was thus minded, did I use lightness? or the things that I purpose, do I purpose according to the flesh, that with me there should be yea yea, and nay nay? But as God is true, our word toward you was not yea and nay. **Eph. 4:25.** Wherefore putting away lying, speak every man truth with his neighbour: for we are members one of another. **See Col. 3:9.**

y. **Heb. 6:9.** But, beloved, we are persuaded better things of you, and things that accompany salvation, though we thus speak. **1 Cor. 13:7.** [Charity] beareth all things, believeth all things, hopeth all things, endureth all things.

z. **Rom. 1:8.** First, I thank my God through Jesus Christ for you all, that your faith is spoken of throughout the whole world. **2 John 4.** I rejoiced greatly that I found of thy children walking in truth, as we have received a commandment from the Father. **3 John 3–4.** For I rejoiced greatly, when the brethren came and testified of the truth that is in thee, even as thou walkest in the truth. I have no greater joy than to hear that my children walk in truth.

sorrowing for,[a] and covering of their infirmities;[b] freely acknowledging of their gifts and graces,[c] defending their innocency;[d] a ready receiving of a good report,[e] and unwillingness to admit of an evil report,[f] concerning them; discouraging talebearers,[g] flatterers,[h] and slanderers;[i] love and care of our own good name, and defending it when need requireth;[k] keeping of lawful promises;[l] studying and practicing of whatsoever things are true, honest, lovely, and of good report.[m]

Q. 145. *What are the sins forbidden in the ninth commandment?*

A. The sins forbidden in the ninth commandment are, all prejudicing the truth, and the good name of our neighbors, as well as our

a. **2 Cor. 2:4.** For out of much affliction and anguish of heart I wrote unto you with many tears; not that ye should be grieved, but that ye might know the love which I have more abundantly unto you. **2 Cor. 12:21.** And [I fear] lest, when I come again, my God will humble me among you, and that I shall bewail many which have sinned already, and have not repented of the uncleanness and fornication and lasciviousness which they have committed. **See Ps. 119:158.**

b. **Prov. 17:9.** He that covereth a transgression seeketh love; but he that repeateth a matter separateth very friends. **1 Pet. 4:8.** And above all things have fervent charity among yourselves: for charity shall cover the multitude of sins.

c. **1 Cor. 1:4–5, 7.** I thank my God always on your behalf, for the grace of God which is given you by Jesus Christ; that in every thing ye are enriched by him, in all utterance, and in all knowledge.… So that ye come behind in no gift; waiting for the coming of our Lord Jesus Christ. **See 2 Tim. 1:4–5.**

d. **1 Sam. 22:14.** Then Ahimelech answered the king, and said, And who is so faithful among all thy servants as David, which is the king's son in law, and goeth at thy bidding, and is honourable in thine house?

e. **1 Cor. 13:6–7.** [Charity] rejoiceth not in iniquity, but rejoiceth in the truth; beareth all things, believeth all things, hopeth all things, endureth all things.

f. **Ps. 15:3.** He that backbiteth not with his tongue, nor doeth evil to his neighbour, nor taketh up a reproach against his neighbour.

g. **Prov. 25:23.** The north wind driveth away rain: so doth an angry countenance a backbiting tongue.

h. **Prov. 26:24–25.** He that hateth dissembleth with his lips, and layeth up deceit within him; when he speaketh fair, believe him not: for there are seven abominations in his heart.

i. **Ps. 101:5.** Whoso privily slandereth his neighbour, him will I cut off: him that hath an high look and a proud heart will not I suffer.

k. **Prov. 22:1.** A good name is rather to be chosen than great riches, and loving favour rather than silver and gold. **John 8:49.** Jesus answered, I have not a devil; but I honour my Father, and ye do dishonour me. **See 2 Cor. 11:1–12:13.**

l. **Ps. 15:4.** … He that sweareth to his own hurt, and changeth not.

m. **Phil. 4:8.** Finally, brethren, whatsoever things are true, whatsoever things are honest, whatsoever things are just, whatsoever things are pure, whatsoever things are

own,[n] especially in public judicature;[o] giving false evidence,[p] suborning false witnesses,[q] wittingly appearing and pleading for an evil cause, outfacing and overbearing the truth;[r] passing unjust sentence,[s] calling evil good, and good evil; rewarding the wicked according to the work of the righteous, and the righteous according to the work of the wicked;[t] forgery,[u] concealing the truth, undue silence in a just cause,[w] and holding our peace when iniquity calleth for either a reproof from ourselves,[x] or complaint to others;[y] speaking the truth unseasonably,[z]

lovely, whatsoever things are of good report; if there be any virtue, and if there be any praise, think on these things.

n. **Luke 3:14.** And the soldiers likewise demanded of him, saying, And what shall we do? And he said unto them, Do violence to no man, neither accuse any falsely; and be content with your wages. **See 1 Sam. 17:28; 2 Sam. 16:3; 1:9–10, 15–16.**

o. **Lev. 19:15.** Ye shall do no unrighteousness in judgment: thou shalt not respect the person of the poor, nor honour the person of the mighty: but in righteousness shalt thou judge thy neighbour. **See Hab. 1:4.**

p. **Prov. 19:5.** A false witness shall not be unpunished, and he that speaketh lies shall not escape. **See Prov. 6:16, 19.**

q. **Acts 6:13.** And set up false witnesses, which said, This man ceaseth not to speak blasphemous words against this holy place, and the law.

r. **Jer. 9:3, 5.** And they bend their tongues like their bow for lies: but they are not valiant for the truth upon the earth; for they proceed from evil to evil, and they know not me, saith the LORD.… And they will deceive every one his neighbour, and will not speak the truth: they have taught their tongue to speak lies, and weary themselves to commit iniquity. **Ps. 12:3–4.** The LORD shall cut off all flattering lips, and the tongue that speaketh proud things: who have said, With our tongue will we prevail; our lips are our own: who is lord over us? **See Acts 24:2, 5; Ps. 52:1–4.**

s. **Prov. 17:15.** He that justifieth the wicked, and he that condemneth the just, even they both are abomination to the LORD. **See 1 Kings 21:9–14.**

t. **Isa. 5:23.** Which justify the wicked for reward, and take away the righteousness of the righteous from him!

u. **1 Kings 21:8.** So she wrote letters in Ahab's name, and sealed them with his seal, and sent the letters unto the elders and to the nobles that were in his city, dwelling with Naboth.

w. **Lev. 5:1.** And if a soul sin, and hear the voice of swearing, and is a witness, whether he hath seen or known of it; if he do not utter it, then he shall bear his iniquity. **Acts 5:3.** But Peter said, Ananias, why hath Satan filled thine heart to lie to the Holy Ghost, and to keep back part of the price of the land? **See verses 8–9; Deut. 13:8; 2 Tim. 4:16.**

x. **1 Kings 1:6.** And his father had not displeased him at any time in saying, Why hast thou done so? and he also was a very goodly man; and his mother bare him after Absalom. **Lev. 19:17.** Thou shalt not hate thy brother in thine heart: thou shalt in any wise rebuke thy neighbour, and not suffer sin upon him.

y. **Isa. 59:4.** None calleth for justice, nor any pleadeth for truth: they trust in vanity, and speak lies; they conceive mischief, and bring forth iniquity.

or maliciously to a wrong end,[a] or perverting it to a wrong meaning,[b] or in doubtful and equivocal expressions, to the prejudice of truth or justice;[c] speaking untruth,[d] lying,[e] slandering,[f] backbiting,[g] detracting,[h] talebearing,[i] whispering,[k] scoffing,[l] reviling,[m] rash,[n´]

z. **Prov. 29:11.** A fool uttereth all his mind: but a wise man keepeth it in till afterwards.

a. **1 Sam. 22:9–10.** Then answered Doeg the Edomite, which was set over the servants of Saul, and said, I saw the son of Jesse coming to Nob, to Ahimelech the son of Ahitub. And he inquired of the LORD for him, and gave him victuals, and gave him the sword of Goliath the Philistine. **Ps. 52:1–5.** Why boastest thou thyself in mischief, O mighty man? the goodness of God endureth continually. Thy tongue deviseth mischiefs; like a sharp razor, working deceitfully. Thou lovest evil more than good; and lying rather than to speak righteousness. Selah. Thou lovest all devouring words, O thou deceitful tongue. God shall likewise destroy thee for ever, he shall take thee away, and pluck thee out of thy dwelling place, and root thee out of the land of the living. Selah.

b. **Ps. 56:5.** Every day they wrest my words: all their thoughts are against me for evil. **Matt. 26:60–61.** … but found none: yea, though many false witnesses came, yet found they none. At the last came two false witnesses, and said, This fellow said, I am able to destroy the temple of God, and to build it in three days. **See John 2:19.**

c. **Gen. 3:5.** For God doth know that in the day ye eat thereof, then your eyes shall be opened, and ye shall be as gods, knowing good and evil. **See Gen. 26:7, 9.**

d. **Isa. 59:13.** … in transgressing and lying against the LORD, and departing away from our God, speaking oppression and revolt, conceiving and uttering from the heart words of falsehood.

e. **Col. 3:9.** Lie not one to another, seeing that ye have put off the old man with his deeds. **See Lev. 19:11.**

f. **Ps. 50:20.** Thou sittest and speakest against thy brother; thou slanderest thine own mother's son.

g. **Ps. 15:3.** He that backbiteth not with his tongue, nor doeth evil to his neighbour, nor taketh up a reproach against his neighbour.

h. **James 4:11.** Speak not evil one of another, brethren. He that speaketh evil of his brother, and judgeth his brother, speaketh evil of the law, and judgeth the law: but if thou judge the law, thou art not a doer of the law, but a judge. **See Jer. 38:4.**

i. **Lev. 19:16.** Thou shalt not go up and down as a talebearer among thy people: neither shalt thou stand against the blood of thy neighbour: I am the LORD.

k. **Rom. 1:29–30.** … being filled with all unrighteousness, fornication, wickedness, covetousness, maliciousness; full of envy, murder, debate, deceit, malignity; whisperers, backbiters, haters of God, despiteful, proud, boasters, inventors of evil things, disobedient to parents.

l. **Gen. 21:9.** And Sarah saw the son of Hagar the Egyptian, which she had born unto Abraham, mocking. **Gal. 4:29.** But as then he that was born after the flesh persecuted him that was born after the Spirit, even so it is now.

m. **1 Cor. 6:10.** Nor thieves, nor covetous, nor drunkards, nor revilers, nor extortioners, shall inherit the kingdom of God.

n´. **Matt. 7:1.** Judge not, that ye be not judged.

harsh,[o′] and partial censuring;[p′] misconstructing intentions, words, and actions;[q′] flattering,[r′] vainglorious boasting;[s′] thinking or speaking too highly or too meanly of ourselves or others;[t′] denying the gifts and graces of God;[u′] aggravating smaller faults;[w′] hiding, excusing,

o′. **Acts 28:4.** And when the barbarians saw the venomous beast hang on his hand, they said among themselves, No doubt this man is a murderer, whom, though he hath escaped the sea, yet vengeance suffereth not to live. **See James 2:13.**

p′. **Gen. 38:24.** And it came to pass about three months after, that it was told Judah, saying, Tamar thy daughter in law hath played the harlot; and also, behold, she is with child by whoredom. And Judah said, Bring her forth, and let her be burnt. **Rom. 2:1.** Therefore thou art inexcusable, O man, whosoever thou art that judgest: for wherein thou judgest another, thou condemnest thyself; for thou that judgest doest the same things.

q′. **Rom. 3:8.** … and not rather, (as we be slanderously reported, and as some affirm that we say,) Let us do evil, that good may come? whose damnation is just. **Ps. 69:10.** When I wept, and chastened my soul with fasting, that was to my reproach. **See Neh. 6:6–8; 1 Sam. 1:13–15; 2 Sam. 10:3.**

r′. **Ps. 12:2–3.** They speak vanity every one with his neighbour: with flattering lips and with a double heart do they speak. The LORD shall cut off all flattering lips, and the tongue that speaketh proud things.

s′. **2 Tim. 3:2.** For men shall be lovers of their own selves, covetous, boasters, proud, blasphemers, disobedient to parents, unthankful, unholy.

t′. **Luke 18:9, 11.** And he spake this parable unto certain which trusted in themselves that they were righteous, and despised others.… The Pharisee stood and prayed thus with himself, God, I thank thee, that I am not as other men are, extortioners, unjust, adulterers, or even as this publican. **Acts 12:22.** And the people gave a shout, saying, It is the voice of a god, and not of a man. **Ex. 4:10–14.** And Moses said unto the LORD, O my Lord, I am not eloquent, neither heretofore, nor since thou hast spoken unto thy servant: but I am slow of speech, and of a slow tongue. And the LORD said unto him, Who hath made man's mouth? or who maketh the dumb, or deaf, or the seeing, or the blind? have not I the LORD? Now therefore go, and I will be with thy mouth, and teach thee what thou shalt say. And he said, O my Lord, send, I pray thee, by the hand of him whom thou wilt send. And the anger of the LORD was kindled against Moses, and he said, Is not Aaron the Levite thy brother? I know that he can speak well. And also, behold, he cometh forth to meet thee: and when he seeth thee, he will be glad in his heart. **See Rom. 12:16; Gal. 5:26; 1 Cor. 4:6.**

u′. **Luke 9:49–50.** And John answered and said, Master, we saw one casting out devils in thy name; and we forbad him, because he followeth not with us. And Jesus said unto him, Forbid him not: for he that is not against us is for us. **2 Cor. 10:10.** For his letters, say they, are weighty and powerful; but his bodily presence is weak, and his speech contemptible. **Acts 2:13.** Others mocking said, These men are full of new wine. **See Job 27:5–6; 4:6.**

w′. **Matt. 7:3–5.** And why beholdest thou the mote that is in thy brother's eye, but considerest not the beam that is in thine own eye? Or how wilt thou say to thy brother, Let me pull out the mote out of thine eye; and, behold, a beam is in thine own eye? Thou hypocrite, first cast out the beam out of thine own eye; and then shalt thou

or extenuating of sins, when called to a free confession;^{x´} unnecessary discovering of infirmities;^{y´} raising false rumors,^{z´} receiving and countenancing evil reports,^{a´} and stopping our ears against just defense;^{b´} evil suspicion;^{c´} envying or grieving at the deserved credit of any,^{d´} endeavoring or desiring to impair it,^{e´} rejoicing in their disgrace and infamy;^{f´} scornful contempt,^{g´} fond admiration;^{h´} breach

see clearly to cast out the mote out of thy brother's eye.

x´. **Prov. 28:13.** He that covereth his sins shall not prosper: but whoso confesseth and forsaketh them shall have mercy. **Gen. 3:12–13.** And the man said, The woman whom thou gavest to be with me, she gave me of the tree, and I did eat. And the LORD God said unto the woman, What is this that thou hast done? And the woman said, The serpent beguiled me, and I did eat. **See Prov. 30:20; Jer. 2:35; 2 Kings 5:25; Gen. 4:9.**

y´. **Prov. 25:9–10.** Debate thy cause with thy neighbour himself; and discover not a secret to another: lest he that heareth it put thee to shame, and thine infamy turn not away. **See Gen. 9:22.**

z´. **Ex. 23:1.** Thou shalt not raise a false report: put not thine hand with the wicked to be an unrighteous witness.

a´. **Prov. 29:12.** If a ruler hearken to lies, all his servants are wicked. **See Ps. 41:7–8.**

b´. **Acts 7:56–57.** And [Stephen] said, Behold, I see the heavens opened, and the Son of man standing on the right hand of God. Then they cried out with a loud voice, and stopped their ears, and ran upon him with one accord. **Job 31:13–14.** If I did despise the cause of my manservant or of my maidservant, when they contended with me; what then shall I do when God riseth up? and when he visiteth, what shall I answer him?

c´. **1 Cor. 13:5.** [Charity] doth not behave itself unseemly, seeketh not her own, is not easily provoked, thinketh no evil. **See 1 Tim. 6:4.**

d´. **Matt. 21:15.** And when the chief priests and scribes saw the wonderful things that he did, and the children crying in the temple, and saying, Hosanna to the son of David; they were sore displeased. **See Num. 11:29.**

e´. **Ezra 4:12–13.** Be it known unto the king, that the Jews which came up from thee to us are come unto Jerusalem, building the rebellious and the bad city, and have set up the walls thereof, and joined the foundations. Be it known now unto the king, that, if this city be builded, and the walls set up again, then will they not pay toll, tribute, and custom, and so thou shalt endamage the revenue of the kings. **See Dan. 6:3–4.**

f´. **Jer. 48:27.** For was not Israel a derision unto thee? was he found among thieves? for since thou spakest of him, thou skippedst for joy.

g´. **Matt. 27:28–29.** And they stripped him, and put on him a scarlet robe. And when they had platted a crown of thorns, they put it upon his head, and a reed in his right hand: and they bowed the knee before him, and mocked him, saying, Hail, King of the Jews! **See Ps. 35:15–16, 21.**

h´. **Jude 16.** These are murmurers, complainers, walking after their own lusts; and their mouth speaketh great swelling words, having men's persons in admiration because of advantage. **Acts 12:22.** And the people gave a shout, saying, It is the

of lawful promises;[i'] neglecting such things as are of good report,[k'] and practicing, or not avoiding ourselves, or not hindering what we can in others, such things as procure an ill name.[l']

Q. 146. *Which is the tenth commandment?*

A. The tenth commandment is, *Thou shalt not covet thy neighbour's house, thou shall not covet they neighbour's wife, nor his manservant, nor his maidservant, nor his ox, nor his ass, nor any thing that is thy neighbour's.*[m]

Q. 147. *What are the duties required in the tenth commandment?*

A. The duties required in the tenth commandment are, such a full contentment with our own condition,[n] and such a charitable frame of the whole soul toward our neighbor, as that all our inward motions and affections touching him, tend unto, and further all that good which is his.[o]

Q. 148. *What are the sins forbidden in the tenth commandment?*

A. The sins forbidden in the tenth commandment are, discontentment with our own estate;[p] envying[q] and grieving at the good of

voice of a god, and not of a man.

i'. **Rom. 1:31.** ... without understanding, covenantbreakers, without natural affection, implacable, unmerciful. **2 Tim. 3:3.** ... without natural affection, trucebreakers, false accusers, incontinent, fierce, despisers of those that are good.

k'. **1 Sam. 2:24.** Nay, my sons; for it is no good report that I hear: ye make the LORD's people to transgress.

l'. **2 Sam. 13:12–13.** And she answered him, Nay, my brother, do not force me; for no such thing ought to be done in Israel: do not thou this folly. And I, whither shall I cause my shame to go? and as for thee, thou shalt be as one of the fools in Israel. Now therefore, I pray thee, speak unto the king; for he will not withhold me from thee. **Prov. 5:8–9.** Remove thy way far from her, and come not nigh the door of her house: lest thou give thine honour unto others, and thy years unto the cruel. **Prov. 6:33.** A wound and dishonour shall he get; and his reproach shall not be wiped away.

m. **Ex. 20:17. Cf. Deut. 5:21.** Neither shalt thou desire thy neighbour's wife, neither shalt thou covet thy neighbour's house, his field, or his manservant, or his maidservant, his ox, or his ass, or any thing that is thy neighbour's.

n. **Heb. 13:5.** Let your conversation be without covetousness; and be content with such things as ye have: for he hath said, I will never leave thee, nor forsake thee. **1 Tim. 6:6.** But godliness with contentment is great gain. **See Phil. 4:11.**

o. **Job 31:29.** If I rejoiced at the destruction of him that hated me, or lifted up myself when evil found him ... **Rom. 12:15.** Rejoice with them that do rejoice, and weep with them that weep. **See Ps. 122:7–9; 1 Tim. 1:5; Est. 10:3; 1 Cor. 13:4–7.**

p. **1 Cor. 10:10.** Neither murmur ye, as some of them also murmured, and were destroyed of the destroyer. **See 1 Kings 21:4; Est. 5:13.**

our neighbor,[r] together with all inordinate motions and affections to anything that is his.[s]

Q. 149. *Is any man able perfectly to keep the commandments of God?*

A. No man is able, either of himself,[t] or by any grace received in this life, perfectly to keep the commandments of God;[u] but doth daily break them in thought,[w] word, and deed.[x]

q. **Gal. 5:26.** Let us not be desirous of vain glory, provoking one another, envying one another. **James 3:14, 16.** But if ye have bitter envying and strife in your hearts, glory not, and lie not against the truth.… For where envying and strife is, there is confusion and every evil work.

r. **Ps. 112:9–10.** He hath dispersed, he hath given to the poor; his righteousness endureth for ever; his horn shall be exalted with honour. The wicked shall see it, and be grieved; he shall gnash with his teeth, and melt away: the desire of the wicked shall perish. **See Neh. 2:10.**

s. **Rom. 7:7–8.** What shall we say then? Is the law sin? God forbid. Nay, I had not known sin, but by the law: for I had not known lust, except the law had said, Thou shalt not covet. But sin, taking occasion by the commandment, wrought in me all manner of concupiscence. For without the law sin was dead. **Rom. 13:9.** For this, Thou shalt not commit adultery, Thou shalt not kill, Thou shalt not steal, Thou shalt not bear false witness, Thou shalt not covet; and if there be any other commandment, it is briefly comprehended in this saying, namely, Thou shalt love thy neighbour as thyself. **Col. 3:5.** Mortify therefore your members which are upon the earth; fornication, uncleanness, inordinate affection, evil concupiscence, and covetousness, which is idolatry. **Deut. 5:21.** Neither shalt thou desire thy neighbour's wife, neither shalt thou covet thy neighbour's house, his field, or his manservant, or his maidservant, his ox, or his ass, or any thing that is thy neighbour's.

t. **James 3:2.** For in many things we offend all. If any man offend not in word, the same is a perfect man, and able also to bridle the whole body. **John 15:5.** I am the vine, ye are the branches: He that abideth in me, and I in him, the same bringeth forth much fruit: for without me ye can do nothing. **Rom. 8:3.** For what the law could not do, in that it was weak through the flesh, God sending his own Son in the likeness of sinful flesh, and for sin, condemned sin in the flesh.

u. **Eccl. 7:20.** For there is not a just man upon earth, that doeth good, and sinneth not. **1 John 1:8, 10.** If we say that we have no sin, we deceive ourselves, and the truth is not in us.… If we say that we have not sinned, we make him a liar, and his word is not in us. **Gal. 5:17.** For the flesh lusteth against the Spirit, and the Spirit against the flesh: and these are contrary the one to the other: so that ye cannot do the things that ye would. **Rom. 7:18–19.** For I know that in me (that is, in my flesh,) dwelleth no good thing: for to will is present with me; but how to perform that which is good I find not. For the good that I would I do not: but the evil which I would not, that I do.

w. **Gen. 6:5.** And God saw that the wickedness of man was great in the earth, and that every imagination of the thoughts of his heart was only evil continually. **Gen. 8:21.** And the LORD smelled a sweet savour; and the LORD said in his heart, I will not again curse the ground any more for man's sake; for the imagination of man's

Q. 150. *Are all transgressions of the law of God equally heinous in themselves, and in the sight of God?*

A. All transgressions of the law of God are not equally heinous; but some sins in themselves, and by reason of several aggravations, are more heinous in the sight of God than others.[y]

Q. 151. *What are those aggravations that make some sins more heinous than others?*

A. Sins receive their aggravations,

1. From the persons offending:[z] if they be of riper age,[a] greater experience or grace,[b] eminent for profession,[c] gifts,[d] place,[e]

heart is evil from his youth; neither will I again smite any more every thing living, as I have done. **James 1:14.** But every man is tempted, when he is drawn away of his own lust, and enticed.

x. **Rom. 3:9.** What then? are we better than they? No, in no wise: for we have before proved both Jews and Gentiles, that they are all under sin. **See verses 10–19; James 3:2–13.**

y. **John 19:11.** Jesus answered, Thou couldest have no power at all against me, except it were given thee from above: therefore he that delivered me unto thee hath the greater sin. **1 John 5:16.** If any man see his brother sin a sin which is not unto death, he shall ask, and he shall give him life for them that sin not unto death. There is a sin unto death: I do not say that he shall pray for it. **Heb. 2:2–3.** For if the word spoken by angels was stedfast, and every transgression and disobedience received a just recompence of reward; how shall we escape, if we neglect so great salvation; which at the first began to be spoken by the Lord, and was confirmed unto us by them that heard him. **See Ps. 78:17, 32, 56; Ezek. 8:6, 13, 15.**

z. **Jer. 2:8.** The priests said not, Where is the LORD? and they that handle the law knew me not: the pastors also transgressed against me, and the prophets prophesied by Baal, and walked after things that do not profit.

a. **Job 32:7, 9.** I said, Days should speak, and multitude of years should teach wisdom…. Great men are not always wise: neither do the aged understand judgment. **Eccl. 4:13.** Better is a poor and a wise child than an old and foolish king, who will no more be admonished.

b. **1 Kings 11:4, 9.** For it came to pass, when Solomon was old, that his wives turned away his heart after other gods: and his heart was not perfect with the LORD his God, as was the heart of David his father…. And the LORD was angry with Solomon, because his heart was turned from the LORD God of Israel, which had appeared unto him twice.

c. **2 Sam. 12:14.** Howbeit, because by this deed thou hast given great occasion to the enemies of the LORD to blaspheme, the child also that is born unto thee shall surely die. **1 Cor. 5:1.** It is reported commonly that there is fornication among you, and such fornication as is not so much as named among the Gentiles, that one should have his father's wife.

d. **James 4:17.** Therefore to him that knoweth to do good, and doeth it not, to him it is sin. **Luke 12:47–48.** And that servant, which knew his lord's will, and

office,^{f} guides to others,^{g} and whose example is likely to be followed by others.^{h}

2. From the parties offended:^{i} if immediately against God,^{k} his

prepared not himself, neither did according to his will, shall be beaten with many stripes. But he that knew not, and did commit things worthy of stripes, shall be beaten with few stripes. For unto whomsoever much is given, of him shall be much required: and to whom men have committed much, of him they will ask the more.

e. **Jer. 5:4–5.** Therefore I said, Surely these are poor; they are foolish: for they know not the way of the LORD, nor the judgment of their God. I will get me unto the great men, and will speak unto them; for they have known the way of the LORD, and the judgment of their God: but these have altogether broken the yoke, and burst the bonds.

f. **2 Sam. 12:7–9.** And Nathan said to David, Thou art the man. Thus saith the LORD God of Israel, I anointed thee king over Israel, and I delivered thee out of the hand of Saul; and I gave thee thy master's house, and thy master's wives into thy bosom, and gave thee the house of Israel and of Judah; and if that had been too little, I would moreover have given unto thee such and such things. Wherefore hast thou despised the commandment of the LORD, to do evil in his sight? thou hast killed Uriah the Hittite with the sword, and hast taken his wife to be thy wife, and hast slain him with the sword of the children of Ammon. **Ezek. 8:11–12.** And there stood before them seventy men of the ancients of the house of Israel, and in the midst of them stood Jaazaniah the son of Shaphan, with every man his censer in his hand; and a thick cloud of incense went up. Then said he unto me, Son of man, hast thou seen what the ancients of the house of Israel do in the dark, every man in the chambers of his imagery? for they say, The LORD seeth us not; the LORD hath forsaken the earth.

g. **Rom. 2:17–24.** Behold, thou art called a Jew, and restest in the law, and makest thy boast of God, and knowest his will, and approvest the things that are more excellent, being instructed out of the law; and art confident that thou thyself art a guide of the blind, a light of them which are in darkness, an instructor of the foolish, a teacher of babes, which hast the form of knowledge and of the truth in the law. Thou therefore which teachest another, teachest thou not thyself? thou that preachest a man should not steal, dost thou steal? thou that sayest a man should not commit adultery, dost thou commit adultery? thou that abhorrest idols, dost thou commit sacrilege? thou that makest thy boast of the law, through breaking the law dishonourest thou God? For the name of God is blasphemed among the Gentiles through you, as it is written.

h. **Gal. 2:11–14.** But when Peter was come to Antioch, I withstood him to the face, because he was to be blamed. For before that certain came from James, he did eat with the Gentiles: but when they were come, he withdrew and separated himself, fearing them which were of the circumcision. And the other Jews dissembled likewise with him; insomuch that Barnabas also was carried away with their dissimulation. But when I saw that they walked not uprightly according to the truth of the gospel, I said unto Peter before them all, If thou, being a Jew, livest after the manner of Gentiles, and not as do the Jews, why compellest thou the Gentiles to live as do the Jews?

i. **Ps. 2:12.** Kiss the Son, lest he be angry, and ye perish from the way, when his wrath is kindled but a little. Blessed are all they that put their trust in him. **Matt. 21:38–39.** But when the husbandmen saw the son, they said among themselves, This

attributes,[l] and worship;[m] against Christ, and his grace;[n] the Holy Spirit,[o] his witness,[p] and workings;[q] against superiors, men of eminency,[r] and such as we stand especially related and

is the heir; come, let us kill him, and let us seize on his inheritance. And they caught him, and cast him out of the vineyard, and slew him.

k. **1 Sam. 2:25.** If one man sin against another, the judge shall judge him: but if a man sin against the Lord, who shall intreat for him? Notwithstanding they hearkened not unto the voice of their father, because the Lord would slay them. **Acts 5:4.** Whiles it remained, was it not thine own? and after it was sold, was it not in thine own power? why hast thou conceived this thing in thine heart? thou hast not lied unto men, but unto God. **Ps. 5:4.** For thou art not a God that hath pleasure in wickedness: neither shall evil dwell with thee.

l. **Rom. 2:4.** Or despisest thou the riches of his goodness and forbearance and longsuffering; not knowing that the goodness of God leadeth thee to repentance?

m. **Mal. 1:8, 14.** And if ye offer the blind for sacrifice, is it not evil? and if ye offer the lame and sick, is it not evil? offer it now unto thy governor; will he be pleased with thee, or accept thy person? saith the Lord of hosts.… But cursed be the deceiver, which hath in his flock a male, and voweth, and sacrificeth unto the Lord a corrupt thing: for I am a great King, saith the Lord of hosts, and my name is dreadful among the heathen.

n. **Heb. 2:2–3.** For if the word spoken by angels was stedfast, and every transgression and disobedience received a just recompence of reward; how shall we escape, if we neglect so great salvation; which at the first began to be spoken by the Lord, and was confirmed unto us by them that heard him. **Heb. 12:25.** See that ye refuse not him that speaketh. For if they escaped not who refused him that spake on earth, much more shall not we escape, if we turn away from him that speaketh from heaven.

o. **Heb. 10:28–29.** He that despised Moses' law died without mercy under two or three witnesses: of how much sorer punishment, suppose ye, shall he be thought worthy, who hath trodden under foot the Son of God, and hath counted the blood of the covenant, wherewith he was sanctified, an unholy thing, and hath done despite unto the Spirit of grace? **Matt. 12:31–32.** Wherefore I say unto you, All manner of sin and blasphemy shall be forgiven unto men: but the blasphemy against the Holy Ghost shall not be forgiven unto men. And whosoever speaketh a word against the Son of man, it shall be forgiven him: but whosoever speaketh against the Holy Ghost, it shall not be forgiven him, neither in this world, neither in the world to come.

p. **Eph. 4:30.** And grieve not the holy Spirit of God, whereby ye are sealed unto the day of redemption.

q. **Heb. 6:4–6.** For it is impossible for those who were once enlightened, and have tasted of the heavenly gift, and were made partakers of the Holy Ghost, and have tasted the good word of God, and the powers of the world to come, if they shall fall away, to renew them again unto repentance; seeing they crucify to themselves the Son of God afresh, and put him to an open shame.

r. **Jude 8.** Likewise also these filthy dreamers defile the flesh, despise dominion, and speak evil of dignities. **Num. 12:8–9.** With him will I speak mouth to mouth, even apparently, and not in dark speeches; and the similitude of the Lord shall he behold: wherefore then were ye not afraid to speak against my servant Moses? And the anger of the Lord was kindled against them; and he departed. **Isa. 3:5.** And the

engaged unto;[s] against any of the saints,[t] particularly weak
brethren,[u] the souls of them, or any other,[w] and the common

people shall be oppressed, every one by another, and every one by his neighbour: the
child shall behave himself proudly against the ancient, and the base against the
honourable.

s. **Prov. 30:17.** The eye that mocketh at his father, and despiseth to obey his
mother, the ravens of the valley shall pick it out, and the young eagles shall eat it.
2 Cor. 12:15. And I will very gladly spend and be spent for you; though the more
abundantly I love you, the less I be loved. **Ps. 55:12–15.** For it was not an enemy that
reproached me; then I could have borne it: neither was it he that hated me that did
magnify himself against me; then I would have hid myself from him: but it was thou,
a man mine equal, my guide, and mine acquaintance. We took sweet counsel together,
and walked unto the house of God in company. Let death seize upon them, and let
them go down quick into hell: for wickedness is in their dwellings, and among them.

t. **Zeph. 2:8, 10–11.** I have heard the reproach of Moab, and the revilings of
the children of Ammon, whereby they have reproached my people, and magnified
themselves against their border.… This shall they have for their pride, because they
have reproached and magnified themselves against the people of the LORD of hosts.
The LORD will be terrible unto them: for he will famish all the gods of the earth; and
men shall worship him, every one from his place, even all the isles of the heathen.
Matt. 18:6. But whoso shall offend one of these little ones which believe in me, it
were better for him that a millstone were hanged about his neck, and that he were
drowned in the depth of the sea. **1 Cor. 6:8.** Nay, ye do wrong, and defraud, and that
your brethren. **Rev. 17:6.** And I saw the woman drunken with the blood of the
saints, and with the blood of the martyrs of Jesus: and when I saw her, I wondered
with great admiration.

u. **1 Cor. 8:11–12.** And through thy knowledge shall the weak brother perish,
for whom Christ died? But when ye sin so against the brethren, and wound their weak
conscience, ye sin against Christ. **Rom. 14:13, 15, 21.** Let us not therefore judge
one another any more: but judge this rather, that no man put a stumblingblock or an
occasion to fall in his brother's way.… But if thy brother be grieved with thy meat,
now walkest thou not charitably. Destroy not him with thy meat, for whom Christ
died.… It is good neither to eat flesh, nor to drink wine, nor any thing whereby thy
brother stumbleth, or is offended, or is made weak.

w. **Ezek. 13:19.** And will ye pollute me among my people for handfuls of barley
and for pieces of bread, to slay the souls that should not die, and to save the souls alive
that should not live, by your lying to my people that hear your lies? **1 Cor. 8:12.** But
when ye sin so against the brethren, and wound their weak conscience, ye sin against
Christ. **Rev. 18:12–13.** The merchandise of gold, and silver, and precious stones,
and of pearls, and fine linen, and purple, and silk, and scarlet, and all thyine wood,
and all manner vessels of ivory, and all manner vessels of most precious wood, and of
brass, and iron, and marble, and cinnamon, and odours, and ointments, and frankin-
cense, and wine, and oil, and fine flour, and wheat, and beasts, and sheep, and horses,
and chariots, and slaves, and souls of men. **Matt. 23:15.** Woe unto you, scribes and
Pharisees, hypocrites! for ye compass sea and land to make one proselyte, and when he
is made, ye make him twofold more the child of hell than yourselves.

good of all or many.[x]

3. From the nature and quality of the offense:[y] if it be against the express letter of the law,[z] break many commandments, contain in it many sins:[a] if not only conceived in the heart, but breaks forth in words and actions,[b] scandalize others,[c] and

x. **1 Thess. 2:15–16.** … who both killed the Lord Jesus, and their own prophets, and have persecuted us; and they please not God, and are contrary to all men: forbidding us to speak to the Gentiles that they might be saved, to fill up their sins alway: for the wrath is come upon them to the uttermost. **Josh. 22:20.** Did not Achan the son of Zerah commit a trespass in the accursed thing, and wrath fell on all the congregation of Israel? and that man perished not alone in his iniquity.

y. **Prov. 6:30–33.** Men do not despise a thief, if he steal to satisfy his soul when he is hungry; but if he be found, he shall restore sevenfold; he shall give all the substance of his house. But whoso committeth adultery with a woman lacketh understanding: he that doeth it destroyeth his own soul. A wound and dishonour shall he get; and his reproach shall not be wiped away.

z. **Ezra 9:10–12.** And now, O our God, what shall we say after this? for we have forsaken thy commandments, which thou hast commanded by thy servants the prophets, saying, The land, unto which ye go to possess it, is an unclean land with the filthiness of the people of the lands, with their abominations, which have filled it from one end to another with their uncleanness. Now therefore give not your daughters unto their sons, neither take their daughters unto your sons, nor seek their peace or their wealth for ever: that ye may be strong, and eat the good of the land, and leave it for an inheritance to your children for ever. **1 Kings 11:9–10.** And the LORD was angry with Solomon, because his heart was turned from the LORD God of Israel, which had appeared unto him twice, and had commanded him concerning this thing, that he should not go after other gods: but he kept not that which the LORD commanded.

a. **Col. 3:5.** Mortify therefore your members which are upon the earth; fornication, uncleanness, inordinate affection, evil concupiscence, and covetousness, which is idolatry. **1 Tim. 6:10.** For the love of money is the root of all evil: which while some coveted after, they have erred from the faith, and pierced themselves through with many sorrows. **Prov. 5:8–12.** Remove thy way far from her, and come not nigh the door of her house: lest thou give thine honour unto others, and thy years unto the cruel: lest strangers be filled with thy wealth; and thy labours be in the house of a stranger; and thou mourn at the last, when thy flesh and thy body are consumed, and say, How have I hated instruction, and my heart despised reproof. **Prov. 6:32–33.** But whoso committeth adultery with a woman lacketh understanding: he that doeth it destroyeth his own soul. A wound and dishonour shall he get; and his reproach shall not be wiped away. **Josh. 7:21.** When I saw among the spoils a goodly Babylonish garment, and two hundred shekels of silver, and a wedge of gold of fifty shekels weight, then I coveted them, and took them; and, behold, they are hid in the earth in the midst of my tent, and the silver under it.

b. **James 1:14–15.** But every man is tempted, when he is drawn away of his own lust, and enticed. Then when lust hath conceived, it bringeth forth sin: and sin, when it is finished, bringeth forth death. **Matt. 5:22.** But I say unto you, That whosoever is angry with his brother without a cause shall be in danger of the judgment: and

admit of no reparation:^d if against means,^e mercies,^f judgments,^g light of nature,^h conviction of conscience,ⁱ public or

whosoever shall say to his brother, Raca, shall be in danger of the council: but whosoever shall say, Thou fool, shall be in danger of hell fire. **Mic. 2:1.** Woe to them that
devise iniquity, and work evil upon their beds! when the morning is light, they practise
it, because it is in the power of their hand.

c. **Matt. 18:7.** Woe unto the world because of offences! for it must needs be that
offences come; but woe to that man by whom the offence cometh! **Rom. 2:23–24.**
Thou that makest thy boast of the law, through breaking the law dishonourest thou
God? For the name of God is blasphemed among the Gentiles through you, as it is
written.

d. **Deut. 22:22, 28–29.** If a man be found lying with a woman married to an
husband, then they shall both of them die, both the man that lay with the woman, and
the woman: so shalt thou put away evil from Israel.… If a man find a damsel that is a
virgin, which is not betrothed, and lay hold on her, and lie with her, and they be found;
then the man that lay with her shall give unto the damsel's father fifty shekels of silver,
and she shall be his wife; because he hath humbled her, he may not put her away all his
days. **Prov. 6:32–35.** But whoso committeth adultery with a woman lacketh understanding: he that doeth it destroyeth his own soul. A wound and dishonour shall he
get; and his reproach shall not be wiped away. For jealousy is the rage of a man:
therefore he will not spare in the day of vengeance. He will not regard any ransom;
neither will he rest content, though thou givest many gifts.

e. **Matt. 11:21–24.** Woe unto thee, Chorazin! woe unto thee, Bethsaida! for if
the mighty works, which were done in you, had been done in Tyre and Sidon, they
would have repented long ago in sackcloth and ashes. But I say unto you, It shall be
more tolerable for Tyre and Sidon at the day of judgment, than for you. And thou,
Capernaum, which art exalted unto heaven, shalt be brought down to hell: for if the
mighty works, which have been done in thee, had been done in Sodom, it would have
remained until this day. But I say unto you, That it shall be more tolerable for the land
of Sodom in the day of judgment, than for thee. **John 15:22.** If I had not come and
spoken unto them, they had not had sin: but now they have no cloak for their sin.

f. **Isa. 1:3.** The ox knoweth his owner, and the ass his master's crib: but Israel
doth not know, my people doth not consider. **Deut. 32:6.** Do ye thus requite the
LORD, O foolish people and unwise? is not he thy father that hath bought thee? hath
he not made thee, and established thee?

g. **Amos 4:8–11.** So two or three cities wandered unto one city, to drink water;
but they were not satisfied: yet have ye not returned unto me, saith the LORD. I have
smitten you with blasting and mildew: when your gardens and your vineyards and
your fig trees and your olive trees increased, the palmerworm devoured them: yet have
ye not returned unto me, saith the LORD. I have sent among you the pestilence after
the manner of Egypt: your young men have I slain with the sword, and have taken
away your horses; and I have made the stink of your camps to come up unto your
nostrils: yet have ye not returned unto me, saith the LORD. I have overthrown some of
you, as God overthrew Sodom and Gomorrah, and ye were as a firebrand plucked out
of the burning: yet have ye not returned unto me, saith the LORD. **Jer. 5:3.** O LORD,
are not thine eyes upon the truth? thou hast stricken them, but they have not grieved;
thou hast consumed them, but they have refused to receive correction: they have made

private admonition,[k] censures of the church,[l] civil punishments;[m] and our prayers, purposes, promises,[n] vows,[o]
covenants,[p] and engagements to God or men:[q] if done

their faces harder than a rock; they have refused to return.

h. **Rom. 1:26–27.** For this cause God gave them up unto vile affections: for even their women did change the natural use into that which is against nature: and likewise also the men, leaving the natural use of the woman, burned in their lust one toward another; men with men working that which is unseemly, and receiving in themselves that recompence of their error which was meet.

i. **Rom. 1:32.** … who knowing the judgment of God, that they which commit such things are worthy of death, not only do the same, but have pleasure in them that do them. **Dan. 5:22.** And thou his son, O Belshazzar, hast not humbled thine heart, though thou knewest all this. **Titus 3:10–11.** A man that is an heretick after the first and second admonition reject; knowing that he that is such is subverted, and sinneth, being condemned of himself.

k. **Prov. 29:1.** He, that being often reproved hardeneth his neck, shall suddenly be destroyed, and that without remedy.

l. **Titus 3:10.** A man that is an heretick after the first and second admonition reject. **Matt. 18:17.** And if he shall neglect to hear them, tell it unto the church: but if he neglect to hear the church, let him be unto thee as a heathen man and a publican.

m. **Prov. 27:22.** Though thou shouldest bray a fool in a mortar among wheat with a pestle, yet will not his foolishness depart from him. **Prov. 23:35.** They have stricken me, shalt thou say, and I was not sick; they have beaten me, and I felt it not: when shall I awake? I will seek it yet again.

n. **Ps. 78:34–37.** When he slew them, then they sought him: and they returned and inquired early after God. And they remembered that God was their rock, and the high God their redeemer. Nevertheless they did flatter him with their mouth, and they lied unto him with their tongues. For their heart was not right with him, neither were they stedfast in his covenant. **Jer. 2:20.** For of old time I have broken thy yoke, and burst thy bands; and thou saidst, I will not transgress; when upon every high hill and under every green tree thou wanderest, playing the harlot. **Jer. 13:5–6, 20–21.** So I went, and hid it by Euphrates, as the LORD commanded me. And it came to pass after many days, that the LORD said unto me, Arise, go to Euphrates, and take the girdle from thence, which I commanded thee to hide there.… Lift up your eyes, and behold them that come from the north: where is the flock that was given thee, thy beautiful flock? What wilt thou say when he shall punish thee? for thou hast taught them to be captains, and as chief over thee: shall not sorrows take thee, as a woman in travail?

o. **Eccl. 5:4–6.** When thou vowest a vow unto God, defer not to pay it; for he hath no pleasure in fools: pay that which thou hast vowed. Better is it that thou shouldest not vow, than that thou shouldest vow and not pay. Suffer not thy mouth to cause thy flesh to sin; neither say thou before the angel, that it was an error: wherefore should God be angry at thy voice, and destroy the work of thine hands? **Prov. 20:25.** It is a snare to the man who devoureth that which is holy, and after vows to make inquiry.

p. **Lev. 26:25.** And I will bring a sword upon you, that shall avenge the quarrel of my covenant: and when ye are gathered together within your cities, I will send the pestilence among you; and ye shall be delivered into the hand of the enemy.

q. **Prov. 2:17.** … which forsaketh the guide of her youth, and forgetteth the

deliberately,[r] willfully,[s] presumptuously,[t] impudently,[u] boastingly,[w] maliciously,[x] frequently,[y′] obstinately,[z′] with delight,[a′] continuance,[b′] or relapsing after repentance.[c′]

covenant of her God. **Ezek. 7:18–19.** They shall also gird themselves with sackcloth, and horror shall cover them; and shame shall be upon all faces, and baldness upon all their heads. They shall cast their silver in the streets, and their gold shall be removed: their silver and their gold shall not be able to deliver them in the day of the wrath of the LORD: they shall not satisfy their souls, neither fill their bowels: because it is the stumblingblock of their iniquity.

r. **Ps. 36:4.** He deviseth mischief upon his bed; he setteth himself in a way that is not good; he abhorreth not evil.

s. **Jer. 6:16.** Thus saith the LORD, Stand ye in the ways, and see, and ask for the old paths, where is the good way, and walk therein, and ye shall find rest for your souls. But they said, We will not walk therein.

t. **Num. 15:30.** But the soul that doeth ought presumptuously, whether he be born in the land, or a stranger, the same reproacheth the LORD; and that soul shall be cut off from among his people. **Ex. 21:14.** But if a man come presumptuously upon his neighbour, to slay him with guile; thou shalt take him from mine altar, that he may die.

u. **Jer. 3:3.** Therefore the showers have been withholden, and there hath been no latter rain; and thou hadst a whore's forehead, thou refusedst to be ashamed. **Prov. 7:13.** So she caught him, and kissed him, and with an impudent face said unto him …

w. **Ps. 52:1.** Why boastest thou thyself in mischief, O mighty man? the goodness of God endureth continually.

x. **3 John 10.** Wherefore, if I come, I will remember his deeds which he doeth, prating against us with malicious words …

y′. **Num. 14:22.** Because all those men which have seen my glory, and my miracles, which I did in Egypt and in the wilderness, and have tempted me now these ten times, and have not hearkened to my voice …

z′. **Zech. 7:11–12.** But they refused to hearken, and pulled away the shoulder, and stopped their ears, that they should not hear. Yea, they made their hearts as an adamant stone, lest they should hear the law, and the words which the LORD of hosts hath sent in his spirit by the former prophets: therefore came a great wrath from the LORD of hosts.

a′. **Prov. 2:14.** … who rejoice to do evil, and delight in the frowardness of the wicked.

b′. **Isa. 57:17.** For the iniquity of his covetousness was I wroth, and smote him: I hid me, and was wroth, and he went on frowardly in the way of his heart.

c′. **Jer. 34:8–11.** This is the word that came unto Jeremiah from the LORD, after that the king Zedekiah had made a covenant with all the people which were at Jerusalem, to proclaim liberty unto them; that every man should let his manservant, and every man his maidservant, being an Hebrew or an Hebrewess, go free; that none should serve himself of them, to wit, of a Jew his brother. Now when all the princes, and all the people, which had entered into the covenant, heard that every one should let his manservant, and every one his maidservant, go free, that none should serve themselves of them any more, then they obeyed, and let them go. But afterward they turned, and caused the servants and the handmaids, whom they had let go free, to

4. From circumstances of time[d] and place:[e] if on the Lord's Day,[f] or other times of divine worship;[g] or immediately before[h] or after these,[i] or other helps to prevent or remedy such mis-

return, and brought them into subjection for servants and for handmaids. **2 Pet. 2:20–22.** For if after they have escaped the pollutions of the world through the knowledge of the Lord and Saviour Jesus Christ, they are again entangled therein, and overcome, the latter end is worse with them than the beginning. For it had been better for them not to have known the way of righteousness, than, after they have known it, to turn from the holy commandment delivered unto them. But it is happened unto them according to the true proverb, The dog is turned to his own vomit again; and the sow that was washed to her wallowing in the mire.

d. **2 Kings 5:26.** And he said unto him, Went not mine heart with thee, when the man turned again from his chariot to meet thee? Is it a time to receive money, and to receive garments, and oliveyards, and vineyards, and sheep, and oxen, and menservants, and maidservants?

e. **Jer. 7:10.** And [will ye] come and stand before me in this house, which is called by my name, and say, We are delivered to do all these abominations? **Isa. 26:10.** Let favour be shewed to the wicked, yet will he not learn righteousness: in the land of uprightness will he deal unjustly, and will not behold the majesty of the LORD.

f. **Ezek. 23:37–39.** [Declare] that they have committed adultery, and blood is in their hands, and with their idols have they committed adultery, and have also caused their sons, whom they bare unto me, to pass for them through the fire, to devour them. Moreover this they have done unto me: they have defiled my sanctuary in the same day, and have profaned my sabbaths. For when they had slain their children to their idols, then they came the same day into my sanctuary to profane it; and, lo, thus have they done in the midst of mine house.

g. **Isa. 58:3–5.** Wherefore have we fasted, say they, and thou seest not? wherefore have we afflicted our soul, and thou takest no knowledge? Behold, in the day of your fast ye find pleasure, and exact all your labours. Behold, ye fast for strife and debate, and to smite with the fist of wickedness: ye shall not fast as ye do this day, to make your voice to be heard on high. Is it such a fast that I have chosen? a day for a man to afflict his soul? is it to bow down his head as a bulrush, and to spread sackcloth and ashes under him? wilt thou call this a fast, and an acceptable day to the LORD? **Num. 25:6–7.** And, behold, one of the children of Israel came and brought unto his brethren a Midianitish woman in the sight of Moses, and in the sight of all the congregation of the children of Israel, who were weeping before the door of the tabernacle of the congregation. And when Phinehas, the son of Eleazar, the son of Aaron the priest, saw it, he rose up from among the congregation, and took a javelin in his hand.

h. **1 Cor. 11:20–21.** When ye come together therefore into one place, this is not to eat the Lord's supper. For in eating every one taketh before other his own supper: and one is hungry, and another is drunken. **Jer. 7:8–10.** Behold, ye trust in lying words, that cannot profit. Will ye steal, murder, and commit adultery, and swear falsely, and burn incense unto Baal, and walk after other gods whom ye know not; and come and stand before me in this house, which is called by my name, and say, We are delivered to do all these abominations?

i. **Prov. 7:14–15.** I have peace offerings with me; this day have I payed my vows.

carriages:[k] if in public, or in the presence of others, who are thereby likely to be provoked or defiled.[l]

Q. 152. *What doth every sin deserve at the hands of God?*

A. Every sin, even the least, being against the sovereignty,[m] goodness,[n] and holiness of God,[o] and against his righteous law,[p] deserveth his wrath and curse,[q] both in this life,[r] and that which is to

Therefore came I forth to meet thee, diligently to seek thy face, and I have found thee. **John 13:27, 30.** And after the sop Satan entered into him. Then said Jesus unto him, That thou doest, do quickly.... He then having received the sop went immediately out: and it was night.

k. **Ezra 9:13–14.** And after all that is come upon us for our evil deeds, and for our great trespass, seeing that thou our God hast punished us less than our iniquities deserve, and hast given us such deliverance as this; should we again break thy commandments, and join in affinity with the people of these abominations? wouldest not thou be angry with us till thou hadst consumed us, so that there should be no remnant nor escaping?

l. **2 Sam. 16:22.** So they spread Absalom a tent upon the top of the house; and Absalom went in unto his father's concubines in the sight of all Israel. **1 Sam. 2:22–24.** Now Eli was very old, and heard all that his sons did unto all Israel; and how they lay with the women that assembled at the door of the tabernacle of the congregation. And he said unto them, Why do ye such things? for I hear of your evil dealings by all this people. Nay, my sons; for it is no good report that I hear: ye make the LORD's people to transgress.

m. **James 2:10–11.** For whosoever shall keep the whole law, and yet offend in one point, he is guilty of all. For he that said, Do not commit adultery, said also, Do not kill. Now if thou commit no adultery, yet if thou kill, thou art become a transgressor of the law.

n. **Ex. 20:1–2.** And God spake all these words, saying, I am the LORD thy God, which have brought thee out of the land of Egypt, out of the house of bondage.

o. **Hab. 1:13.** Thou art of purer eyes than to behold evil, and canst not look on iniquity: wherefore lookest thou upon them that deal treacherously, and holdest thy tongue when the wicked devoureth the man that is more righteous than he? **Lev. 10:3.** Then Moses said unto Aaron, This is it that the LORD spake, saying, I will be sanctified in them that come nigh me, and before all the people I will be glorified.... **Lev. 11:44–45.** For I am the LORD your God: ye shall therefore sanctify yourselves, and ye shall be holy; for I am holy: neither shall ye defile yourselves with any manner of creeping thing that creepeth upon the earth. For I am the LORD that bringeth you up out of the land of Egypt, to be your God: ye shall therefore be holy, for I am holy.

p. **1 John 3:4.** Whosoever committeth sin transgresseth also the law: for sin is the transgression of the law. **Rom. 7:12.** Wherefore the law is holy, and the commandment holy, and just, and good.

q. **Eph. 5:6.** Let no man deceive you with vain words: for because of these things cometh the wrath of God upon the children of disobedience. **Gal. 3:10.** For as many as are of the works of the law are under the curse: for it is written, Cursed is every one

come;[s] and cannot be expiated but by the blood of Christ.[t]

Q. 153. *What doth God require of us, that we may escape his wrath and curse due to us by reason of the transgression of the law?*

A. That we may escape the wrath and curse of God due to us by reason of the transgression of the law, he requireth of us repentance toward God, and faith toward our Lord Jesus Christ,[u] and the diligent use of the outward means whereby Christ communicates to us the benefits of his mediation.[w]

that continueth not in all things which are written in the book of the law to do them.
r. **Lam. 3:39.** Wherefore doth a living man complain, a man for the punishment of his sins? **Deut. 28:15–68.** But it shall come to pass, if thou wilt not hearken unto the voice of the LORD thy God, to observe to do all his commandments and his statutes which I command thee this day; that all these curses shall come upon thee, and overtake thee: Cursed shalt thou be in the city, and cursed shalt thou be in the field. Cursed shall be thy basket and thy store....
s. **Matt. 25:41.** Then shall he say also unto them on the left hand, Depart from me, ye cursed, into everlasting fire, prepared for the devil and his angels.
t. **Heb. 9:22.** And almost all things are by the law purged with blood; and without shedding of blood is no remission. **1 Pet. 1:18–19.** ... forasmuch as ye know that ye were not redeemed with corruptible things, as silver and gold, from your vain conversation received by tradition from your fathers; but with the precious blood of Christ, as of a lamb without blemish and without spot.
u. **Acts 20:21.** ... testifying both to the Jews, and also to the Greeks, repentance toward God, and faith toward our Lord Jesus Christ. **Matt. 3:7–8.** But when he saw many of the Pharisees and Sadducees come to his baptism, he said unto them, O generation of vipers, who hath warned you to flee from the wrath to come? Bring forth therefore fruits meet for repentance. **Luke 13:3, 5.** I tell you, Nay: but, except ye repent, ye shall all likewise perish. **Acts 16:30–31.** And [the keeper of the prison] brought them out, and said, Sirs, what must I do to be saved? And they said, Believe on the Lord Jesus Christ, and thou shalt be saved, and thy house. **John 3:16, 18.** For God so loved the world, that he gave his only begotten Son, that whosoever believeth in him should not perish, but have everlasting life.... He that believeth on him is not condemned: but he that believeth not is condemned already, because he hath not believed in the name of the only begotten Son of God.
w. **Prov. 2:1–5.** My son, if thou wilt receive my words, and hide my commandments with thee; so that thou incline thine ear unto wisdom, and apply thine heart to understanding; yea, if thou criest after knowledge, and liftest up thy voice for understanding; if thou seekest her as silver, and searchest for her as for hid treasures; then shalt thou understand the fear of the LORD, and find the knowledge of God. **Prov. 8:33–36.** Hear instruction, and be wise, and refuse it not. Blessed is the man that heareth me, watching daily at my gates, waiting at the posts of my doors. For whoso findeth me findeth life, and shall obtain favour of the LORD. But he that sinneth against me wrongeth his own soul: all they that hate me love death.

Q. 154. *What are the outward means whereby Christ communicates to us the benefits of his mediation?*

A. The outward and ordinary means whereby Christ communicates to his church the benefits of his mediation, are all his ordinances; especially the Word, sacraments, and prayer; all which are made effectual to the elect for their salvation.[x]

Q. 155. *How is the Word made effectual to salvation?*

A. The Spirit of God maketh the reading, but especially the preaching of the Word, an effectual means of enlightening,[y] convincing, and humbling sinners;[z] of driving them out of themselves, and drawing them unto Christ;[a] of conforming them to his image,[b] and subduing them to his will;[c] of strengthening them against

x. **Matt. 28:19–20.** Go ye therefore, and teach all nations, baptizing them in the name of the Father, and of the Son, and of the Holy Ghost: teaching them to observe all things whatsoever I have commanded you: and, lo, I am with you alway, even unto the end of the world. Amen. **Acts 2:42, 46–47.** And they continued stedfastly in the apostles' doctrine and fellowship, and in breaking of bread, and in prayers.… And they, continuing daily with one accord in the temple, and breaking bread from house to house, did eat their meat with gladness and singleness of heart, praising God, and having favour with all the people. And the Lord added to the church daily such as should be saved.

y. **Neh. 8:8.** So they read in the book in the law of God distinctly, and gave the sense, and caused them to understand the reading. **Acts 26:18.** [I send thee] to open their eyes, and to turn them from darkness to light, and from the power of Satan unto God, that they may receive forgiveness of sins, and inheritance among them which are sanctified by faith that is in me. **Ps. 19:8.** The statutes of the LORD are right, rejoicing the heart: the commandment of the LORD is pure, enlightening the eyes.

z. **1 Cor. 14:24–25.** But if all prophesy, and there come in one that believeth not, or one unlearned, he is convinced of all, he is judged of all: and thus are the secrets of his heart made manifest; and so falling down on his face he will worship God, and report that God is in you of a truth. **See 2 Chron. 34:18–19, 26–28.**

a. **Acts 2:37, 41.** Now when they heard this, they were pricked in their heart, and said unto Peter and to the rest of the apostles, Men and brethren, what shall we do?… Then they that gladly received his word were baptized: and the same day were added unto them about three thousand souls. **See Acts 8:27–38.**

b. **2 Cor. 3:18.** But we all, with open face beholding as in a glass the glory of the Lord, are changed into the same image from glory to glory, even as by the Spirit of the Lord. **See Col. 1:27.**

c. **2 Cor. 10:4–6.** … (for the weapons of our warfare are not carnal, but mighty through God to the pulling down of strong holds;) casting down imaginations, and every high thing that exalteth itself against the knowledge of God, and bringing into captivity every thought to the obedience of Christ; and having in a readiness to revenge all disobedience, when your obedience is fulfilled. **See Rom. 6:17–18.**

temptations and corruptions;[d] of building them up in grace,[e] and establishing their hearts in holiness and comfort through faith unto salvation.[f]

Q. 156. *Is the Word of God to be read by all?*

A. Although all are not to be permitted to read the Word publicly to the congregation,[g] yet all sorts of people are bound to read it apart by themselves,[h] and with their families:[i] to which end, the Holy

d. **Eph. 6:16–17.** … above all, taking the shield of faith, wherewith ye shall be able to quench all the fiery darts of the wicked. And take the helmet of salvation, and the sword of the Spirit, which is the word of God. **Col. 1:28.** … whom we preach, warning every man, and teaching every man in all wisdom; that we may present every man perfect in Christ Jesus. **Ps. 19:11.** Moreover by them is thy servant warned: and in keeping of them there is great reward. **See Matt. 4:4, 7, 10; 1 Cor. 10:11.**

e. **Eph. 4:11–12.** And he gave some, apostles; and some, prophets; and some, evangelists; and some, pastors and teachers; for the perfecting of the saints, for the work of the ministry, for the edifying of the body of Christ. **Acts 20:32.** And now, brethren, I commend you to God, and to the word of his grace, which is able to build you up, and to give you an inheritance among all them which are sanctified. **See 2 Tim. 3:15–17.**

f. **Rom. 16:25.** Now to him that is of power to stablish you according to my gospel, and the preaching of Jesus Christ, according to the revelation of the mystery, which was kept secret since the world began … **1 Thess. 3:2, 10–11, 13.** And [we] sent Timotheus, our brother, and minister of God, and our fellowlabourer in the gospel of Christ, to establish you, and to comfort you concerning your faith.… night and day praying exceedingly that we might see your face, and might perfect that which is lacking in your faith? Now God himself and our Father, and our Lord Jesus Christ, direct our way unto you.… to the end he may stablish your hearts unblameable in holiness before God, even our Father, at the coming of our Lord Jesus Christ with all his saints. **See Rom. 15:4; 10:13–17; 1:16.**

g. **Deut. 31:9, 11–13.** And Moses wrote this law, and delivered it unto the priests the sons of Levi, which bare the ark of the covenant of the LORD, and unto all the elders of Israel.… When all Israel is come to appear before the LORD thy God in the place which he shall choose, thou shalt read this law before all Israel in their hearing. Gather the people together, men, and women, and children, and thy stranger that is within thy gates, that they may hear, and that they may learn, and fear the LORD your God, and observe to do all the words of this law: and that their children, which have not known any thing, may hear, and learn to fear the LORD your God, as long as ye live in the land whither ye go over Jordan to possess it. **See Neh. 8:2–3; 9:3–5.**

h. **Deut. 17:19.** And it shall be with him, and he shall read therein all the days of his life: that he may learn to fear the LORD his God, to keep all the words of this law and these statutes, to do them. **Rev. 1:3.** Blessed is he that readeth, and they that hear the words of this prophecy, and keep those things which are written therein: for the time is at hand. **John 5:39.** Search the scriptures; for in them ye think ye have eternal life: and they are they which testify of me. **Isa. 34:16.** Seek ye out of the book of the LORD, and read: no one of these shall fail.…

Scriptures are to be translated out of the original into vulgar languages.[k]

Q. 157. *How is the Word of God to be read?*

A. The Holy Scriptures are to be read with an high and reverent esteem of them;[l] with a firm persuasion that they are the very Word

i. **Deut. 6:6–9.** And these words, which I command thee this day, shall be in thine heart: and thou shalt teach them diligently unto thy children, and shalt talk of them when thou sittest in thine house, and when thou walkest by the way, and when thou liest down, and when thou risest up. And thou shalt bind them for a sign upon thine hand, and they shall be as frontlets between thine eyes. And thou shalt write them upon the posts of thy house, and on thy gates. **Gen. 18:17, 19.** And the LORD said, Shall I hide from Abraham that thing which I do …? For I know him, that he will command his children and his household after him, and they shall keep the way of the LORD, to do justice and judgment; that the LORD may bring upon Abraham that which he hath spoken of him. **Ps. 78:5–7.** For he established a testimony in Jacob, and appointed a law in Israel, which he commanded our fathers, that they should make them known to their children: that the generation to come might know them, even the children which should be born; who should arise and declare them to their children: that they might set their hope in God, and not forget the works of God, but keep his commandments.

k. **1 Cor. 14:6, 9, 11–12, 15–16, 24, 27–28.** Now, brethren, if I come unto you speaking with tongues, what shall I profit you, except I shall speak to you either by revelation, or by knowledge, or by prophesying, or by doctrine?… So likewise ye, except ye utter by the tongue words easy to be understood, how shall it be known what is spoken? for ye shall speak into the air.… Therefore if I know not the meaning of the voice, I shall be unto him that speaketh a barbarian, and he that speaketh shall be a barbarian unto me. Even so ye, forasmuch as ye are zealous of spiritual gifts, seek that ye may excel to the edifying of the church.… What is it then? I will pray with the spirit, and I will pray with the understanding also: I will sing with the spirit, and I will sing with the understanding also. Else when thou shalt bless with the spirit, how shall he that occupieth the room of the unlearned say Amen at thy giving of thanks, seeing he understandeth not what thou sayest?… But if all prophesy, and there come in one that believeth not, or one unlearned, he is convinced of all, he is judged of all.… If any man speak in an unknown tongue, let it be by two, or at the most by three, and that by course; and let one interpret. But if there be no interpreter, let him keep silence in the church; and let him speak to himself, and to God. **Neh. 8:8.** So they read in the book in the law of God distinctly, and gave the sense, and caused them to understand the reading.

l. **Ps. 119:97.** O how love I thy law! it is my meditation all the day. **Ps. 19:10.** More to be desired are they than gold, yea, than much fine gold: sweeter also than honey and the honeycomb. **Ex. 24:7.** And he took the book of the covenant, and read in the audience of the people: and they said, All that the LORD hath said will we do, and be obedient. **2 Chron. 34:27.** Because thine heart was tender, and thou didst humble thyself before God, when thou heardest his words against this place, and against the inhabitants thereof, and humbledst thyself before me, and didst rend thy

of God,[m] and that he only can enable us to understand them;[n] with desire to know, believe, and obey the will of God revealed in them;[o] with diligence,[p] and attention to the matter and scope of them;[q] with meditation,[r] application,[s] self-denial,[t] and prayer.[u]

clothes, and weep before me; I have even heard thee also, saith the LORD. **Isa. 66:2.** For all those things hath mine hand made, and all those things have been, saith the LORD: but to this man will I look, even to him that is poor and of a contrite spirit, and trembleth at my word. **See Neh. 8:3–10.**

m. **2 Pet. 1:19–21.** We have also a more sure word of prophecy; whereunto ye do well that ye take heed, as unto a light that shineth in a dark place, until the day dawn, and the day star arise in your hearts: knowing this first, that no prophecy of the scripture is of any private interpretation. For the prophecy came not in old time by the will of man: but holy men of God spake as they were moved by the Holy Ghost. **Matt. 4:4.** But he answered and said, It is written, Man shall not live by bread alone, but by every word that proceedeth out of the mouth of God. **1 Thess. 2:13.** For this cause also thank we God without ceasing, because, when ye received the word of God which ye heard of us, ye received it not as the word of men, but as it is in truth, the word of God, which effectually worketh also in you that believe. **See Mark 7:13.**

n. **Luke 24:45.** Then opened he their understanding, that they might understand the scriptures. **2 Cor. 3:13–16.** And not as Moses, which put a vail over his face, that the children of Israel could not stedfastly look to the end of that which is abolished: but their minds were blinded: for until this day remaineth the same vail untaken away in the reading of the old testament; which vail is done away in Christ. But even unto this day, when Moses is read, the vail is upon their heart. Nevertheless when it shall turn to the Lord, the vail shall be taken away.

o. **Deut. 17:10, 20.** And thou shalt do according to the sentence, which they of that place which the LORD shall choose shall shew thee; and thou shalt observe to do according to all that they inform thee.… that his heart be not lifted up above his brethren, and that he turn not aside from the commandment, to the right hand, or to the left: to the end that he may prolong his days in his kingdom, he, and his children, in the midst of Israel.

p. **Acts 17:11.** These were more noble than those in Thessalonica, in that they received the word with all readiness of mind, and searched the scriptures daily, whether those things were so.

q. **Acts 8:30, 34.** And Philip ran thither to him, and heard him read the prophet Esaias, and said, Understandest thou what thou readest?… And the eunuch answered Philip, and said, I pray thee, of whom speaketh the prophet this? of himself, or of some other man? **Luke 10:26–28.** He said unto him, What is written in the law? how readest thou? And he answering said, Thou shalt love the Lord thy God with all thy heart, and with all thy soul, and with all thy strength, and with all thy mind; and thy neighbour as thyself. And he said unto him, Thou hast answered right: this do, and thou shalt live.

r. **Ps. 1:2.** But his delight is in the law of the LORD; and in his law doth he meditate day and night. **Ps. 119:97.** O how love I thy law! it is my meditation all the day.

s. **2 Chron. 34:21.** Go, inquire of the LORD for me, and for them that are left in

Q. 158. *By whom is the Word of God to be preached?*
A. The Word of God is to be preached only by such as are sufficiently gifted,[w] and also duly approved and called to that office.[x]

Israel and in Judah, concerning the words of the book that is found: for great is the
wrath of the LORD that is poured out upon us, because our fathers have not kept the
word of the LORD, to do after all that is written in this book.

t. **Prov. 3:5.** Trust in the LORD with all thine heart; and lean not unto thine own
understanding. **Deut. 33:3.** Yea, he loved the people; all his saints are in thy hand:
and they sat down at thy feet; every one shall receive of thy words. **Matt. 16:24.**
Then said Jesus unto his disciples, If any man will come after me, let him deny himself,
and take up his cross, and follow me. **See Luke 9:23; Gal. 1:15–16.**

u. **Prov. 2:1–6.** My son, if thou wilt receive my words, and hide my commandments with thee; so that thou incline thine ear unto wisdom, and apply thine heart to
understanding; yea, if thou criest after knowledge, and liftest up thy voice for understanding; if thou seekest her as silver, and searchest for her as for hid treasures; then
shalt thou understand the fear of the LORD, and find the knowledge of God. For the
LORD giveth wisdom: out of his mouth cometh knowledge and understanding. **Ps.
119:18.** Open thou mine eyes, that I may behold wondrous things out of thy law.
Neh. 8:6, 8. And Ezra blessed the LORD, the great God. And all the people answered, Amen, Amen, with lifting up their hands: and they bowed their heads, and
worshipped the LORD with their faces to the ground.... So they read in the book in the
law of God distinctly, and gave the sense, and caused them to understand the reading.

w. **1 Tim. 3:2, 6.** A bishop then must be blameless, the husband of one wife,
vigilant, sober, of good behaviour, given to hospitality, apt to teach.... Not a novice,
lest being lifted up with pride he fall into the condemnation of the devil. **Eph. 4:8–
11.** Wherefore he saith, When he ascended up on high, he led captivity captive, and
gave gifts unto men. (Now that he ascended, what is it but that he also descended first
into the lower parts of the earth? He that descended is the same also that ascended up
far above all heavens, that he might fill all things.) And he gave some, apostles; and
some, prophets; and some, evangelists; and some, pastors and teachers. **Mal. 2:7.** For
the priest's lips should keep knowledge, and they should seek the law at his mouth: for
he is the messenger of the LORD of hosts. **2 Cor. 3:6.** ... [God] hath made us able
ministers of the new testament; not of the letter, but of the spirit: for the letter killeth,
but the spirit giveth life. **2 Tim. 2:2.** And the things that thou hast heard of me
among many witnesses, the same commit thou to faithful men, who shall be able to
teach others also.

x. **Jer. 14:15.** Therefore thus saith the LORD concerning the prophets that prophesy
in my name, and I sent them not, yet they say, Sword and famine shall not be in this
land; by sword and famine shall those prophets be consumed. **Rom. 10:15.** And
how shall they preach, except they be sent? as it is written, How beautiful are the feet
of them that preach the gospel of peace, and bring glad tidings of good things! **Heb.
5:4.** And no man taketh this honour unto himself, but he that is called of God, as was
Aaron. **1 Cor. 12:28–29.** And God hath set some in the church, first apostles, secondarily prophets, thirdly teachers, after that miracles, then gifts of healings, helps,
governments, diversities of tongues. Are all apostles? are all prophets? are all teachers?
are all workers of miracles? **1 Tim. 3:10.** And let these also first be proved; then let

Q. 159. *How is the Word of God to be preached by those that are called thereunto?*

A. They that are called to labor in the ministry of the Word, are to preach sound doctrine,[y] diligently,[z] in season and out of season;[a] plainly,[b] not in the enticing words of man's wisdom, but in demonstration of the Spirit, and of power;[c] faithfully,[d] making known the whole counsel of God;[e] wisely,[f] applying themselves to the necessities and capacities of the hearers;[g] zealously,[h] with fervent love to

them use the office of a deacon, being found blameless. **1 Tim. 4:14.** Neglect not the gift that is in thee, which was given thee by prophecy, with the laying on of the hands of the presbytery. **1 Tim. 5:22.** Lay hands suddenly on no man, neither be partaker of other men's sins: keep thyself pure.

y. **Titus 2:1, 8.** But speak thou the things which become sound doctrine.… sound speech, that cannot be condemned; that he that is of the contrary part may be ashamed, having no evil thing to say of you.

z. **Acts 18:25.** This man was instructed in the way of the Lord; and being fervent in the spirit, he spake and taught diligently the things of the Lord, knowing only the baptism of John.

a. **2 Tim. 4:2.** Preach the word; be instant in season, out of season; reprove, rebuke, exhort with all longsuffering and doctrine.

b. **1 Cor. 14:9.** So likewise ye, except ye utter by the tongue words easy to be understood, how shall it be known what is spoken? for ye shall speak into the air. **See verses 10–19.**

c. **1 Cor. 2:4.** And my speech and my preaching was not with enticing words of man's wisdom, but in demonstration of the Spirit and of power.

d. **Jer. 23:28.** The prophet that hath a dream, let him tell a dream; and he that hath my word, let him speak my word faithfully. What is the chaff to the wheat? saith the LORD. **1 Cor. 4:1–2.** Let a man so account of us, as of the ministers of Christ, and stewards of the mysteries of God. Moreover it is required in stewards, that a man be found faithful.

e. **Acts 20:27.** For I have not shunned to declare unto you all the counsel of God.

f. **Col. 1:28.** … whom we preach, warning every man, and teaching every man in all wisdom; that we may present every man perfect in Christ Jesus. **2 Tim. 2:15.** Study to shew thyself approved unto God, a workman that needeth not to be ashamed, rightly dividing the word of truth.

g. **1 Cor. 3:2.** I have fed you with milk, and not with meat: for hitherto ye were not able to bear it, neither yet now are ye able. **Heb. 5:12–14.** For when for the time ye ought to be teachers, ye have need that one teach you again which be the first principles of the oracles of God; and are become such as have need of milk, and not of strong meat. For every one that useth milk is unskilful in the word of righteousness: for he is a babe. But strong meat belongeth to them that are of full age, even those who by reason of use have their senses exercised to discern both good and evil. **Luke 12:42.** And the Lord said, Who then is that faithful and wise steward, whom his lord shall make ruler over his household, to give them their portion of meat in due season?

God[i] and the souls of his people;[k] sincerely,[l] aiming at his glory,[m] and their conversion,[n] edification,[o] and salvation.[p]

h. **Acts 18:25.** This man was instructed in the way of the Lord; and being fervent in the spirit, he spake and taught diligently the things of the Lord, knowing only the baptism of John. **Ps. 119:139.** My zeal hath consumed me, because mine enemies have forgotten thy words. **2 Tim. 4:5.** But watch thou in all things, endure afflictions, do the work of an evangelist, make full proof of thy ministry.

i. **2 Cor. 5:13–14.** For whether we be beside ourselves, it is to God: or whether we be sober, it is for your cause. For the love of Christ constraineth us; because we thus judge, that if one died for all, then were all dead. **Phil. 1:15–17.** Some indeed preach Christ even of envy and strife; and some also of good will: the one preach Christ of contention, not sincerely, supposing to add affliction to my bonds: but the other of love, knowing that I am set for the defence of the gospel.

k. **Col. 4:12.** Epaphras, who is one of you, a servant of Christ, saluteth you, always labouring fervently for you in prayers, that ye may stand perfect and complete in all the will of God. **2 Cor. 12:15.** And I will very gladly spend and be spent for you; though the more abundantly I love you, the less I be loved.

l. **2 Cor. 2:17.** For we are not as many, which corrupt the word of God: but as of sincerity, but as of God, in the sight of God speak we in Christ. **2 Cor. 4:2.** But [we] have renounced the hidden things of dishonesty, not walking in craftiness, nor handling the word of God deceitfully; but by manifestation of the truth commending ourselves to every man's conscience in the sight of God.

m. **1 Thess. 2:4–6.** But as we were allowed of God to be put in trust with the gospel, even so we speak; not as pleasing men, but God, which trieth our hearts. For neither at any time used we flattering words, as ye know, nor a cloak of covetousness; God is witness: nor of men sought we glory, neither of you, nor yet of others, when we might have been burdensome, as the apostles of Christ. **John 7:18.** He that speaketh of himself seeketh his own glory: but he that seeketh his glory that sent him, the same is true, and no unrighteousness is in him.

n. **1 Cor. 9:19–22.** For though I be free from all men, yet have I made myself servant unto all, that I might gain the more. And unto the Jews I became as a Jew, that I might gain the Jews; to them that are under the law, as under the law, that I might gain them that are under the law; to them that are without law, as without law, (being not without law to God, but under the law to Christ,) that I might gain them that are without law. To the weak became I as weak, that I might gain the weak: I am made all things to all men, that I might by all means save some.

o. **2 Cor. 12:19.** Again, think ye that we excuse ourselves unto you? we speak before God in Christ: but we do all things, dearly beloved, for your edifying. **Eph. 4:12.** … for the perfecting of the saints, for the work of the ministry, for the edifying of the body of Christ.

p. **1 Tim. 4:16.** Take heed unto thyself, and unto the doctrine; continue in them: for in doing this thou shalt both save thyself, and them that hear thee. **Acts 26:16–18.** But rise, and stand upon thy feet: for I have appeared unto thee for this purpose, to make thee a minister and a witness both of these things which thou hast seen, and of those things in the which I will appear unto thee; delivering thee from the people, and from the Gentiles, unto whom now I send thee, to open their eyes, and to turn them from darkness to light, and from the power of Satan unto God, that they may receive

Q. 160. *What is required of those that hear the Word preached?*

A. It is required of those that hear the Word preached, that they attend upon it with diligence,[q] preparation,[r] and prayer;[s] examine what they hear by the Scriptures;[t] receive the truth with faith,[u] love,[w]meekness,[x] and readiness of mind,[y] as the Word of God;[z] meditate,[a] and confer of it;[b] hide it in their hearts,[c] and bring forth

forgiveness of sins, and inheritance among them which are sanctified by faith that is in me.

q. **Prov. 8:34.** Blessed is the man that heareth me, watching daily at my gates, waiting at the posts of my doors.

r. **1 Pet. 2:1–2.** Wherefore laying aside all malice, and all guile, and hypocrisies, and envies, and all evil speakings, as newborn babes, desire the sincere milk of the word, that ye may grow thereby. **Luke 8:18.** Take heed therefore how ye hear: for whosoever hath, to him shall be given; and whosoever hath not, from him shall be taken even that which he seemeth to have.

s. **Ps. 119:18.** Open thou mine eyes, that I may behold wondrous things out of thy law. **Eph. 6:18–19.** … praying always with all prayer and supplication in the Spirit, and watching thereunto with all perseverance and supplication for all saints; and for me, that utterance may be given unto me, that I may open my mouth boldly, to make known the mystery of the gospel.

t. **Acts 17:11.** These were more noble than those in Thessalonica, in that they received the word with all readiness of mind, and searched the scriptures daily, whether those things were so.

u. **Heb. 4:2.** For unto us was the gospel preached, as well as unto them: but the word preached did not profit them, not being mixed with faith in them that heard it.

w. **2 Thess. 2:10.** … and with all deceivableness of unrighteousness in them that perish; because they received not the love of the truth, that they might be saved.

x. **James 1:21.** Wherefore lay apart all filthiness and superfluity of naughtiness, and receive with meekness the engrafted word, which is able to save your souls.

y. **Acts 17:11.** These were more noble than those in Thessalonica, in that they received the word with all readiness of mind, and searched the scriptures daily, whether those things were so.

z. **1 Thess. 2:13.** For this cause also thank we God without ceasing, because, when ye received the word of God which ye heard of us, ye received it not as the word of men, but as it is in truth, the word of God, which effectually worketh also in you that believe.

a. **Luke 9:44.** Let these sayings sink down into your ears: for the Son of man shall be delivered into the hands of men. **Heb. 2:1.** Therefore we ought to give the more earnest heed to the things which we have heard, lest at any time we should let them slip.

b. **Luke 24:14.** And they talked together of all these things which had happened. **Deut. 6:6–7.** And these words, which I command thee this day, shall be in thine heart: and thou shalt teach them diligently unto thy children, and shalt talk of them when thou sittest in thine house, and when thou walkest by the way, and when thou liest down, and when thou risest up.

the fruit of it in their lives.[d]

Q. 161. *How do the sacraments become effectual means of salvation?*

A. The sacraments become effectual means of salvation, not by any power in themselves, or any virtue derived from the piety or intention of him by whom they are administered, but only by the working of the Holy Ghost, and the blessing of Christ, by whom they are instituted.[e]

Q. 162. *What is a sacrament?*

A. A sacrament is an holy ordinance instituted by Christ in his church,[f] to signify, seal, and exhibit[g] unto those that are within the

c. **Prov. 2:1.** My son, if thou wilt receive my words, and hide my commandments with thee … **Ps. 119:11.** Thy word have I hid in mine heart, that I might not sin against thee.

d. **Luke 8:15.** But that on the good ground are they, which in an honest and good heart, having heard the word, keep it, and bring forth fruit with patience. **James 1:25.** But whoso looketh into the perfect law of liberty, and continueth therein, he being not a forgetful hearer, but a doer of the work, this man shall be blessed in his deed.

e. **1 Pet. 3:21.** The like figure whereunto even baptism doth also now save us (not the putting away of the filth of the flesh, but the answer of a good conscience toward God,) by the resurrection of Jesus Christ. **Acts 8:13, 23.** Then Simon himself believed also: and when he was baptized, he continued with Philip, and wondered, beholding the miracles and signs which were done.… For I perceive that thou art in the gall of bitterness, and in the bond of iniquity. **1 Cor. 3:5–7.** Who then is Paul, and who is Apollos, but ministers by whom ye believed, even as the Lord gave to every man? I have planted, Apollos watered; but God gave the increase. So then neither is he that planteth any thing, neither he that watereth; but God that giveth the increase. **Compared with 1 Cor. 1:12–17.** Now this I say, that every one of you saith, I am of Paul; and I of Apollos; and I of Cephas; and I of Christ. Is Christ divided? was Paul crucified for you? or were ye baptized in the name of Paul? I thank God that I baptized none of you, but Crispus and Gaius; lest any should say that I had baptized in mine own name. And I baptized also the household of Stephanas: besides, I know not whether I baptized any other. For Christ sent me not to baptize, but to preach the gospel: not with wisdom of words, lest the cross of Christ should be made of none effect. **1 Cor. 12:13.** For by one Spirit are we all baptized into one body, whether we be Jews or Gentiles, whether we be bond or free; and have been all made to drink into one Spirit. **1 Cor. 6:11.** And such were some of you: but ye are washed, but ye are sanctified, but ye are justified in the name of the Lord Jesus, and by the Spirit of our God.

f. **Gen. 17:7, 10.** And I will establish my covenant between me and thee and thy seed after thee in their generations for an everlasting covenant, to be a God unto thee, and to thy seed after thee.… This is my covenant, which ye shall keep, between me and you and thy seed after thee; Every man child among you shall be circumcised.

covenant of grace,[h] the benefits of his mediation;[i] to strengthen and increase their faith, and all other graces;[k] to oblige them to obedience;[l] to testify and cherish their love and communion one with another;[m]

Ex. 12 (containing the institution of the passover). Matt. 28:19. Go ye therefore, and teach all nations, baptizing them in the name of the Father, and of the Son, and of the Holy Ghost. **Matt. 26:26–28.** And as they were eating, Jesus took bread, and blessed it, and brake it, and gave it to the disciples, and said, Take, eat; this is my body. And he took the cup, and gave thanks, and gave it to them, saying, Drink ye all of it; for this is my blood of the new testament, which is shed for many for the remission of sins. **See Mark 14:22–25; Luke 22:19–20; 1 Cor. 11:22–26.**

g. **Rom. 4:11.** And he received the sign of circumcision, a seal of the righteousness of the faith which he had yet being uncircumcised: that he might be the father of all them that believe, though they be not circumcised; that righteousness might be imputed unto them also. **1 Cor. 11:24–25.** And when he had given thanks, he brake it, and said, Take, eat: this is my body, which is broken for you: this do in remembrance of me. After the same manner also he took the cup, when he had supped, saying, This cup is the new testament in my blood: this do ye, as oft as ye drink it, in remembrance of me.

h. **Rom. 15:8.** Now I say that Jesus Christ was a minister of the circumcision for the truth of God, to confirm the promises made unto the fathers. **Ex. 12:48.** And when a stranger shall sojourn with thee, and will keep the passover to the LORD, let all his males be circumcised, and then let him come near and keep it; and he shall be as one that is born in the land: for no uncircumcised person shall eat thereof. **Rom. 9:8.** That is, They which are the children of the flesh, these are not the children of God: but the children of the promise are counted for the seed. **Gal. 3:27, 29.** For as many of you as have been baptized into Christ have put on Christ.… And if ye be Christ's, then are ye Abraham's seed, and heirs according to the promise.

i. **Acts 2:38.** Then Peter said unto them, Repent, and be baptized every one of you in the name of Jesus Christ for the remission of sins, and ye shall receive the gift of the Holy Ghost. **1 Cor. 10:16.** The cup of blessing which we bless, is it not the communion of the blood of Christ? The bread which we break, is it not the communion of the body of Christ?

k. **Rom. 4:11.** And he received the sign of circumcision, a seal of the righteousness of the faith which he had yet being uncircumcised: that he might be the father of all them that believe, though they be not circumcised; that righteousness might be imputed unto them also. **Gal. 3:27.** For as many of you as have been baptized into Christ have put on Christ.

l. **Rom. 6:3–4.** Know ye not, that so many of us as were baptized into Jesus Christ were baptized into his death? Therefore we are buried with him by baptism into death: that like as Christ was raised up from the dead by the glory of the Father, even so we also should walk in newness of life. **1 Cor. 10:21.** Ye cannot drink the cup of the Lord, and the cup of devils: ye cannot be partakers of the Lord's table, and of the table of devils.

m. **Eph. 4:2–5.** … with all lowliness and meekness, with longsuffering, forbearing one another in love; endeavouring to keep the unity of the Spirit in the bond of peace. There is one body, and one Spirit, even as ye are called in one hope of your

and to distinguish them from those that are without.[n]

Q. 163. *What are the parts of a sacrament?*

A. The parts of a sacrament are two; the one an outward and sensible sign, used according to Christ's own appointment; the other an inward and spiritual grace thereby signified.[o]

Q. 164. *How many sacraments hath Christ instituted in his church under the new testament?*

A. Under the new testament Christ hath instituted in his church only two sacraments, baptism and the Lord's Supper.[p]

Q. 165. *What is baptism?*

A. Baptism is a sacrament of the new testament, wherein Christ

calling; one Lord, one faith, one baptism. **1 Cor. 12:13.** For by one Spirit are we all baptized into one body, whether we be Jews or Gentiles, whether we be bond or free; and have been all made to drink into one Spirit. **1 Cor. 10:16–17.** The cup of blessing which we bless, is it not the communion of the blood of Christ? The bread which we break, is it not the communion of the body of Christ? For we being many are one bread, and one body: for we are all partakers of that one bread.

n. **Eph. 2:11–12.** Wherefore remember, that ye being in time past Gentiles in the flesh, who are called Uncircumcision by that which is called the Circumcision in the flesh made by hands; that at that time ye were without Christ, being aliens from the commonwealth of Israel, and strangers from the covenants of promise, having no hope, and without God in the world. **Gen. 34:14.** And they said unto them, We cannot do this thing, to give our sister to one that is uncircumcised; for that were a reproach unto us.

o. **Matt. 3:11.** I indeed baptize you with water unto repentance: but he that cometh after me is mightier than I, whose shoes I am not worthy to bear: he shall baptize you with the Holy Ghost, and with fire. **1 Pet. 3:21.** The like figure whereunto even baptism doth also now save us (not the putting away of the filth of the flesh, but the answer of a good conscience toward God,) by the resurrection of Jesus Christ. **Titus 3:5.** Not by works of righteousness which we have done, but according to his mercy he saved us, by the washing of regeneration, and renewing of the Holy Ghost. **Cf. Confession of Faith 27.2 and the passages cited thereunder. Cf. also Deut. 10:16; 30:6; Jer. 4:4.**

p. **Matt. 28:19.** Go ye therefore, and teach all nations, baptizing them in the name of the Father, and of the Son, and of the Holy Ghost. **1 Cor. 11:20, 23.** When ye come together therefore into one place, this is not to eat the Lord's supper.... For I have received of the Lord that which also I delivered unto you, That the Lord Jesus the same night in which he was betrayed took bread. **Matt. 26:26–28.** And as they were eating, Jesus took bread, and blessed it, and brake it, and gave it to the disciples, and said, Take, eat; this is my body. And he took the cup, and gave thanks, and gave it to them, saying, Drink ye all of it; for this is my blood of the new testament, which is shed for many for the remission of sins.

hath ordained the washing with water in the name of the Father, and of the Son, and of the Holy Ghost,^{q} to be a sign and seal of ingrafting into himself,^{r} of remission of sins by his blood,^{s} and regeneration by his Spirit;^{t} of adoption,^{u} and resurrection unto everlasting life;^{w} and whereby the parties baptized are solemnly admitted into the visible church,^{x} and enter into an open and professed engagement to be wholly and only the Lord's.^{y}

Q. 166. *Unto whom is baptism to be administered?*

A. Baptism is not to be administered to any that are out of the visible church, and so strangers from the covenant of promise, till they profess their faith in Christ, and obedience to him,^{z} but infants

q. **Matt. 28:19.** Go ye therefore, and teach all nations, baptizing them in the name of the Father, and of the Son, and of the Holy Ghost.

r. **Gal. 3:27.** For as many of you as have been baptized into Christ have put on Christ. **Rom. 6:3.** Know ye not, that so many of us as were baptized into Jesus Christ were baptized into his death?

s. **Mark 1:4.** John did baptize in the wilderness, and preach the baptism of repentance for the remission of sins. **Rev. 1:5.** … Unto him that loved us, and washed us from our sins in his own blood. **Acts 2:38.** Then Peter said unto them, Repent, and be baptized every one of you in the name of Jesus Christ for the remission of sins, and ye shall receive the gift of the Holy Ghost. **Acts 22:16.** And now why tarriest thou? arise, and be baptized, and wash away thy sins, calling on the name of the Lord. **1 Pet. 3:21.** The like figure whereunto even baptism doth also now save us (not the putting away of the filth of the flesh, but the answer of a good conscience toward God,) by the resurrection of Jesus Christ.

t. **Titus 3:5.** Not by works of righteousness which we have done, but according to his mercy he saved us, by the washing of regeneration, and renewing of the Holy Ghost. **Eph. 5:26.** … that he might sanctify and cleanse it with the washing of water by the word. **See Acts 2:38.**

u. **Gal. 3:26–27.** For ye are all the children of God by faith in Christ Jesus. For as many of you as have been baptized into Christ have put on Christ.

w. **1 Cor. 15:29.** Else what shall they do which are baptized for the dead, if the dead rise not at all? why are they then baptized for the dead? **Rom. 6:5.** For if we have been planted together in the likeness of his death, we shall be also in the likeness of his resurrection.

x. **1 Cor. 12:13.** For by one Spirit are we all baptized into one body, whether we be Jews or Gentiles, whether we be bond or free; and have been all made to drink into one Spirit. **Acts 2:41.** Then they that gladly received his word were baptized: and the same day there were added unto them about three thousand souls.

y. **Rom. 6:4.** Therefore we are buried with him by baptism into death: that like as Christ was raised up from the dead by the glory of the Father, even so we also should walk in newness of life. **See Acts 2:38–42.**

z. **Acts 2:38–39, 41.** Then Peter said unto them, Repent, and be baptized every one of you in the name of Jesus Christ for the remission of sins, and ye shall receive

descending from parents, either both, or but one of them, professing faith in Christ, and obedience to him, are in that respect within the covenant, and to be baptized.[a]

Q. 167. *How is our baptism to be improved by us?*

A. The needful but much neglected duty of improving our baptism, is to be performed by us all our life long, especially in the time of temptation, and when we are present at the administration of it to others;[b] by serious and thankful consideration of the nature of it, and of the ends for which Christ instituted it, the privileges and benefits

the gift of the Holy Ghost. For the promise is unto you, and to your children, and to all that are afar off, even as many as the Lord our God shall call.… Then they that gladly received his word were baptized: and the same day there were added unto them about three thousand souls. **Acts 8:12, 36, 38.** But when they believed Philip preaching the things concerning the kingdom of God, and the name of Jesus Christ, they were baptized, both men and women.… And as they went on their way, they came unto a certain water: and the eunuch said, See, here is water; what doth hinder me to be baptized?… And he commanded the chariot to stand still: and they went down both into the water, both Philip and the eunuch; and he baptized him. **Acts 16:15.** And when she was baptized, and her household, she besought us, saying, If ye have judged me to be faithful to the Lord, come into my house, and abide there. And she constrained us.

a. **Col. 2:11–12.** … in whom also ye are circumcised with the circumcision made without hands, in putting off the body of the sins of the flesh by the circumcision of Christ: buried with him in baptism, wherein also ye are risen with him through the faith of the operation of God, who hath raised him from the dead. **Acts 2:38–39.** Then Peter said unto them, Repent, and be baptized every one of you in the name of Jesus Christ for the remission of sins, and ye shall receive the gift of the Holy Ghost. For the promise is unto you, and to your children, and to all that are afar off, even as many as the Lord our God shall call. **Rom. 4:11–12.** And he received the sign of circumcision, a seal of the righteousness of the faith which he had yet being uncircumcised: that he might be the father of all them that believe, though they be not circumcised; that righteousness might be imputed unto them also: and the father of circumcision to them who are not of the circumcision only, but who also walk in the steps of that faith of our father Abraham, which he had being yet uncircumcised. **1 Cor. 7:14.** For the unbelieving husband is sanctified by the wife, and the unbelieving wife is sanctified by the husband: else were your children unclean; but now are they holy. **Luke 18:15–16.** And they brought unto him also infants, that he would touch them: but when his disciples saw it, they rebuked them. But Jesus called them unto him, and said, Suffer little children to come unto me, and forbid them not: for of such is the kingdom of God. **See Gen. 17:7–9; Gal. 3:9–14; Rom. 11:16.**

b. **Col. 2:11–12.** … in whom also ye are circumcised with the circumcision made without hands, in putting off the body of the sins of the flesh by the circumcision of Christ: buried with him in baptism, wherein also ye are risen with him through the faith of the operation of God, who hath raised him from the dead. **Rom. 6:4, 6,**

conferred and sealed thereby, and our solemn vow made therein;[c] by being humbled for our sinful defilement, our falling short of, and walking contrary to, the grace of baptism, and our engagements;[d] by growing up to assurance of pardon of sin, and of all other blessings sealed to us in that sacrament;[e] by drawing strength from the death and resurrection of Christ, into whom we are baptized, for the mortifying of sin, and quickening of grace;[f] and by endeavoring to live

11. Therefore we are buried with him by baptism into death: that like as Christ was raised up from the dead by the glory of the Father, even so we also should walk in newness of life.… knowing this, that our old man is crucified with him, that the body of sin might be destroyed, that henceforth we should not serve sin.… Likewise reckon ye also yourselves to be dead indeed unto sin, but alive unto God through Jesus Christ our Lord.

c. **Rom. 6:3–5.** Know ye not, that so many of us as were baptized into Jesus Christ were baptized into his death? Therefore we are buried with him by baptism into death: that like as Christ was raised up from the dead by the glory of the Father, even so we also should walk in newness of life. For if we have been planted together in the likeness of his death, we shall be also in the likeness of his resurrection. **1 Pet. 3:21.** The like figure whereunto even baptism doth also now save us (not the putting away of the filth of the flesh, but the answer of a good conscience toward God,) by the resurrection of Jesus Christ.

d. **1 Cor. 1:11–13.** For it hath been declared unto me of you, my brethren, by them which are of the house of Chloe, that there are contentions among you. Now this I say, that every one of you saith, I am of Paul; and I of Apollos; and I of Cephas; and I of Christ. Is Christ divided? was Paul crucified for you? or were ye baptized in the name of Paul? **Rom. 6:2–3.** God forbid. How shall we, that are dead to sin, live any longer therein? Know ye not, that so many of us as were baptized into Jesus Christ were baptized into his death?

e. **Rom. 6:4–7, 22.** Therefore we are buried with him by baptism into death: that like as Christ was raised up from the dead by the glory of the Father, even so we also should walk in newness of life. For if we have been planted together in the likeness of his death, we shall be also in the likeness of his resurrection: knowing this, that our old man is crucified with him, that the body of sin might be destroyed, that henceforth we should not serve sin. For he that is dead is freed from sin.… But now being made free from sin, and become servants to God, ye have your fruit unto holiness, and the end everlasting life. **1 Pet. 3:21.** The like figure whereunto even baptism doth also now save us (not the putting away of the filth of the flesh, but the answer of a good conscience toward God,) by the resurrection of Jesus Christ. **Rom. 5:1–2.** Therefore being justified by faith, we have peace with God through our Lord Jesus Christ: by whom also we have access by faith into this grace wherein we stand, and rejoice in hope of the glory of God. **Jer. 33:8.** And I will cleanse them from all their iniquity, whereby they have sinned against me; and I will pardon all their iniquities, whereby they have sinned, and whereby they have transgressed against me.

f. **Rom. 6:3–5.** Know ye not, that so many of us as were baptized into Jesus Christ were baptized into his death? Therefore we are buried with him by baptism

by faith,[g] to have our conversation in holiness and righteousness,[h] as those that have therein given up their names to Christ;[i] and to walk in brotherly love, as being baptized by the same Spirit into one body.[k]

Q. 168. *What is the Lord's Supper?*

A. The Lord's Supper is a sacrament of the new testament,[l] wherein, by giving and receiving bread and wine according to the appointment of Jesus Christ, his death is showed forth; and they that worthily communicate feed upon his body and blood, to their spiritual nourishment and growth in grace;[m] have their union and communion with him confirmed;[n] testify and renew their thankfulness,[o]

into death: that like as Christ was raised up from the dead by the glory of the Father, even so we also should walk in newness of life. For if we have been planted together in the likeness of his death, we shall be also in the likeness of his resurrection.

g. **Gal. 3:26–27.** For ye are all the children of God by faith in Christ Jesus. For as many of you as have been baptized into Christ have put on Christ.

h. **Rom. 6:22.** But now being made free from sin, and become servants to God, ye have your fruit unto holiness, and the end everlasting life.

i. **Acts 2:38.** Then Peter said unto them, Repent, and be baptized every one of you in the name of Jesus Christ for the remission of sins, and ye shall receive the gift of the Holy Ghost. **Compared with Gal. 2:20.** I am crucified with Christ: nevertheless I live; yet not I, but Christ liveth in me: and the life which I now live in the flesh I live by the faith of the Son of God, who loved me, and gave himself for me. **See also Rev. 2:17.**

k. **1 Cor. 12:13, 25.** For by one Spirit are we all baptized into one body, whether we be Jews or Gentiles, whether we be bond or free; and have been all made to drink into one Spirit.… That there should be no schism in the body; but that the members should have the same care one for another.

l. **Luke 22:20.** Likewise also [he took] the cup after supper, saying, This cup is the new testament in my blood, which is shed for you.

m. **Matt. 26:26–28.** And as they were eating, Jesus took bread, and blessed it, and brake it, and gave it to the disciples, and said, Take, eat; this is my body. And he took the cup, and gave thanks, and gave it to them, saying, Drink ye all of it; for this is my blood of the new testament, which is shed for many for the remission of sins. **1 Cor. 11:23–26.** For I have received of the Lord that which also I delivered unto you, That the Lord Jesus the same night in which he was betrayed took bread: and when he had given thanks, he brake it, and said, Take, eat: this is my body, which is broken for you: this do in remembrance of me. After the same manner also he took the cup, when he had supped, saying, This cup is the new testament in my blood: this do ye, as oft as ye drink it, in remembrance of me. For as often as ye eat this bread, and drink this cup, ye do shew the Lord's death till he come.

n. **1 Cor. 10:16.** The cup of blessing which we bless, is it not the communion of the blood of Christ? The bread which we break, is it not the communion of the body of Christ?

o. **1 Cor. 11:24.** And when he had given thanks, he brake it, and said, Take, eat:

and engagement to God,[p] and their mutual love and fellowship each with other, as members of the same mystical body.[q]

Q. 169. *How hath Christ appointed bread and wine to be given and received in the sacrament of the Lord's Supper?*

A. Christ hath appointed the ministers of his Word, in the administration of this sacrament of the Lord's Supper, to set apart the bread and wine from common use, by the word of institution, thanksgiving, and prayer; to take and break the bread, and to give both the bread and the wine to the communicants: who are, by the same appointment, to take and eat the bread, and to drink the wine, in thankful remembrance that the body of Christ was broken and given, and his blood shed, for them.[r]

Q. 170. *How do they that worthily communicate in the Lord's supper feed upon the body and blood of Christ therein?*

A. As the body and blood of Christ are not corporally or carnally present in, with, or under the bread and wine in the Lord's Supper,[s] and yet are spiritually present to the faith of the receiver, no less truly and really than the elements themselves are to their outward senses;[t] so they that worthily communicate in the sacrament of

this is my body, which is broken for you: this do in remembrance of me.

p. **1 Cor. 10:14–16, 21.** Wherefore, my dearly beloved, flee from idolatry. I speak as to wise men; judge ye what I say. The cup of blessing which we bless, is it not the communion of the blood of Christ? The bread which we break, is it not the communion of the body of Christ?… Ye cannot drink the cup of the Lord, and the cup of devils: ye cannot be partakers of the Lord's table, and of the table of devils. **Compared with Rom. 7:4.** Wherefore, my brethren, ye also are become dead to the law by the body of Christ; that ye should be married to another, even to him who is raised from the dead, that we should bring forth fruit unto God.

q. **1 Cor. 10:17.** For we being many are one bread, and one body: for we are all partakers of that one bread.

r. **1 Cor. 11:23–24.** For I have received of the Lord that which also I delivered unto you, That the Lord Jesus the same night in which he was betrayed took bread: and when he had given thanks, he brake it, and said, Take, eat: this is my body, which is broken for you: this do in remembrance of me. **See Matt. 26:26–28; Mark 14:22–24; Luke 22:19–20.**

s. **Acts 3:21.** … whom the heaven must receive until the times of restitution of all things, which God hath spoken by the mouth of all his holy prophets since the world began.

t. **Matt. 26:26, 28.** And as they were eating, Jesus took bread, and blessed it, and brake it, and gave it to the disciples, and said, Take, eat; this is my body.… For this is my blood of the new testament, which is shed for many for the remission of sins.

the Lord's Supper, do therein feed upon the body and blood of Christ, not after a corporal and carnal, but in a spiritual manner; yet truly and really,[u] while by faith they receive and apply unto themselves Christ crucified, and all the benefits of his death.[w]

Q. 171. *How are they that receive the sacrament of the Lord's Supper to prepare themselves before they come unto it?*

A. They that receive the sacrament of the Lord's Supper are, before they come, to prepare themselves thereunto, by examining themselves[x] of their being in Christ,[y] of their sins and wants;[z] of the truth and measure of their knowledge,[a] faith,[b] repentance;[c] love to

u. **1 Cor. 11:24–29.** And when he had given thanks, he brake it, and said, Take, eat: this is my body, which is broken for you: this do in remembrance of me. After the same manner also he took the cup, when he had supped, saying, This cup is the new testament in my blood: this do ye, as oft as ye drink it, in remembrance of me. For as often as ye eat this bread, and drink this cup, ye do shew the Lord's death till he come. Wherefore whosoever shall eat this bread, and drink this cup of the Lord, unworthily, shall be guilty of the body and blood of the Lord. But let a man examine himself, and so let him eat of that bread, and drink of that cup. For he that eateth and drinketh unworthily, eateth and drinketh damnation to himself, not discerning the Lord's body. **Cf. Confession of Faith 27.2. Cf. also John 6:51, 53.**

w. **1 Cor. 10:16.** The cup of blessing which we bless, is it not the communion of the blood of Christ? The bread which we break, is it not the communion of the body of Christ?

x. **1 Cor. 11:28.** But let a man examine himself, and so let him eat of that bread, and drink of that cup.

y. **2 Cor. 13:5.** Examine yourselves, whether ye be in the faith; prove your own selves. Know ye not your own selves, how that Jesus Christ is in you, except ye be reprobates?

z. **1 Cor. 5:7.** Purge out therefore the old leaven, that ye may be a new lump, as ye are unleavened. For even Christ our passover is sacrificed for us. **Ex. 12:15**. Seven days shall ye eat unleavened bread; even the first day ye shall put away leaven out of your houses: for whosoever eateth leavened bread from the first day until the seventh day, that soul shall be cut off from Israel.

a. **1 Cor. 11:29.** For he that eateth and drinketh unworthily, eateth and drinketh damnation to himself, not discerning the Lord's body.

b. **2 Cor. 13:5.** Examine yourselves, whether ye be in the faith; prove your own selves. Know ye not your own selves, how that Jesus Christ is in you, except ye be reprobates? **Matt. 26:28.** For this is my blood of the new testament, which is shed for many for the remission of sins.

c. **Zech. 12:10.** And I will pour upon the house of David, and upon the inhabitants of Jerusalem, the spirit of grace and of supplications: and they shall look upon me whom they have pierced, and they shall mourn for him, as one mourneth for his only son, and shall be in bitterness for him, as one that is in bitterness for his firstborn. **1 Cor. 11:31.** For if we would judge ourselves, we should not be judged.

God and the brethren,[d] charity to all men,[e] forgiving those that have done them wrong;[f] of their desires after Christ,[g] and of their new obedience;[h] and by renewing the exercise of these graces,[i] by serious meditation,[k] and fervent prayer.[l]

d. **1 Cor. 10:16–17.** The cup of blessing which we bless, is it not the communion of the blood of Christ? The bread which we break, is it not the communion of the body of Christ? For we being many are one bread, and one body: for we are all partakers of that one bread. **Acts 2:46–47.** And they, continuing daily with one accord in the temple, and breaking bread from house to house, did eat their meat with gladness and singleness of heart, praising God, and having favour with all the people. And the Lord added to the church daily such as should be saved.

e. **1 Cor. 5:8.** Therefore let us keep the feast, not with old leaven, neither with the leaven of malice and wickedness; but with the unleavened bread of sincerity and truth. **1 Cor. 11:18, 20.** For first of all, when ye come together in the church, I hear that there be divisions among you; and I partly believe it.… When ye come together therefore into one place, this is not to eat the Lord's supper.

f. **Matt. 5:23–24.** Therefore if thou bring thy gift to the altar, and there rememberest that thy brother hath ought against thee; leave there thy gift before the altar, and go thy way; first be reconciled to thy brother, and then come and offer thy gift.

g. **Isa. 55:1.** Ho, every one that thirsteth, come ye to the waters, and he that hath no money; come ye, buy, and eat; yea, come, buy wine and milk without money and without price. **John 7:37.** In the last day, that great day of the feast, Jesus stood and cried, saying, If any man thirst, let him come unto me, and drink.

h. **1 Cor. 5:7–8.** Purge out therefore the old leaven, that ye may be a new lump, as ye are unleavened. For even Christ our passover is sacrificed for us: therefore let us keep the feast, not with old leaven, neither with the leaven of malice and wickedness; but with the unleavened bread of sincerity and truth.

i. **1 Cor. 11:25–26, 28.** After the same manner also he took the cup, when he had supped, saying, This cup is the new testament in my blood: this do ye, as oft as ye drink it, in remembrance of me. For as often as ye eat this bread, and drink this cup, ye do shew the Lord's death till he come.… But let a man examine himself, and so let him eat of that bread, and drink of that cup. **Heb. 10:21–22, 24.** … and having an high priest over the house of God; let us draw near with a true heart in full assurance of faith, having our hearts sprinkled from an evil conscience, and our bodies washed with pure water.… And let us consider one another to provoke unto love and to good works. **Ps. 26:6.** I will wash mine hands in innocency: so will I compass thine altar, O LORD.

k. **1 Cor. 11:24–25.** And when he had given thanks, he brake it, and said, Take, eat: this is my body, which is broken for you: this do in remembrance of me. After the same manner also he took the cup, when he had supped, saying, This cup is the new testament in my blood: this do ye, as oft as ye drink it, in remembrance of me.

l. **2 Chron. 30:18–19.** For a multitude of the people, even many of Ephraim, and Manasseh, Issachar, and Zebulun, had not cleansed themselves, yet did they eat the passover otherwise than it was written. But Hezekiah prayed for them, saying, The good LORD pardon every one that prepareth his heart to seek God, the LORD God of his fathers, though he be not cleansed according to the purification of the sanctuary. **Matt. 26:26.** And as they were eating, Jesus took bread, and blessed it, and brake it,

Q. 172. *May one who doubteth of his being in Christ, or of his due prepa-ration, come to the Lord's Supper?*

A. One who doubteth of his being in Christ, or of his due prepa-ration to the sacrament of the Lord's Supper, may have true interest in Christ, though he be not yet assured thereof;[m] and in God's ac-count hath it, if he be duly affected with the apprehension of the want of it,[n] and unfeignedly desires to be found in Christ,[o] and to

and gave it to the disciples, and said, Take, eat; this is my body.

m. **Isa. 50:10.** Who is among you that feareth the Lord, that obeyeth the voice of his servant, that walketh in darkness, and hath no light? let him trust in the name of the Lord, and stay upon his God. **1 John 5:13.** These things have I written unto you that believe on the name of the Son of God; that ye may know that ye have eternal life, and that ye may believe on the name of the Son of God. **Ps. 88.** O Lord God of my salvation, I have cried day and night before thee: let my prayer come before thee: incline thine ear unto my cry; for my soul is full of troubles: and my life draweth nigh unto the grave.... Thy wrath lieth hard upon me, and thou hast afflicted me with all thy waves. Selah.... Mine eye mourneth by reason of affliction: Lord, I have called daily upon thee, I have stretched out my hands unto thee. Wilt thou shew wonders to the dead? shall the dead arise and praise thee? Selah.... Lord, why castest thou off my soul? why hidest thou thy face from me?... Thy fierce wrath goeth over me; thy terrors have cut me off.... Lover and friend hast thou put far from me, and mine acquain-tance into darkness. **Ps. 77:1–4, 7–10.** I cried unto God with my voice, even unto God with my voice; and he gave ear unto me. In the day of my trouble I sought the Lord: my sore ran in the night, and ceased not: my soul refused to be comforted. I remembered God, and was troubled: I complained, and my spirit was overwhelmed. Selah. Thou holdest mine eyes waking: I am so troubled that I cannot speak.... Will the Lord cast off for ever? and will he be favourable no more? Is his mercy clean gone for ever? doth his promise fail for evermore? Hath God forgotten to be gracious? hath he in anger shut up his tender mercies? Selah. And I said, This is my infirmity: but I will remember the years of the right hand of the most High. **Jonah 2:4.** Then I said, I am cast out of thy sight; yet I will look again toward thy holy temple.

n. **Isa. 54:7–10.** For a small moment have I forsaken thee; but with great mer-cies will I gather thee. In a little wrath I hid my face from thee for a moment; but with everlasting kindness will I have mercy on thee, saith the Lord thy Redeemer. For this is as the waters of Noah unto me: for as I have sworn that the waters of Noah should no more go over the earth; so have I sworn that I would not be wroth with thee, nor rebuke thee. For the mountains shall depart, and the hills be removed; but my kindness shall not depart from thee, neither shall the covenant of my peace be removed, saith the Lord that hath mercy on thee. **Matt. 5:3–4.** Blessed are the poor in spirit: for theirs is the kingdom of heaven. Blessed are they that mourn: for they shall be com-forted. **Ps. 31:22.** For I said in my haste, I am cut off from before thine eyes: never-theless thou heardest the voice of my supplications when I cried unto thee. **Ps. 73:13, 22–23.** Verily I have cleansed my heart in vain, and washed my hands in innocency.... So foolish was I, and ignorant: I was as a beast before thee. Nevertheless I am continu-ally with thee: thou hast holden me by my right hand.

depart from iniquity:P in which case (because promises are made, and this sacrament is appointed, for the relief even of weak and doubting Christians^q) he is to bewail his unbelief,^r and labor to have his doubts resolved;^s and, so doing, he may and ought to come to the Lord's Supper, that he may be further strengthened.^t

o. **Phil. 3:8–9.** Yea doubtless, and I count all things but loss for the excellency of the knowledge of Christ Jesus my Lord: for whom I have suffered the loss of all things, and do count them but dung, that I may win Christ, and be found in him, not having mine own righteousness, which is of the law, but that which is through the faith of Christ, the righteousness which is of God by faith. **Ps. 10:17.** LORD, thou hast heard the desire of the humble: thou wilt prepare their heart, thou wilt cause thine ear to hear. **Ps. 42:1–2, 5, 11.** As the hart panteth after the water brooks, so panteth my soul after thee, O God. My soul thirsteth for God, for the living God: when shall I come and appear before God?… Why art thou cast down, O my soul? and why art thou disquieted in me? hope thou in God: for I shall yet praise him for the help of his countenance.… Why art thou cast down, O my soul? and why art thou disquieted within me? hope thou in God: for I shall yet praise him, who is the health of my countenance, and my God.

p. **2 Tim. 2:19.** Nevertheless the foundation of God standeth sure, having this seal, The Lord knoweth them that are his. And, Let every one that nameth the name of Christ depart from iniquity. **Isa. 50:10.** Who is among you that feareth the LORD, that obeyeth the voice of his servant, that walketh in darkness, and hath no light? let him trust in the name of the LORD, and stay upon his God. **Ps. 66:18–20.** If I regard iniquity in my heart, the Lord will not hear me: but verily God hath heard me; he hath attended to the voice of my prayer. Blessed be God, which hath not turned away my prayer, nor his mercy from me.

q. **Isa. 40:11, 29, 31.** He shall feed his flock like a shepherd: he shall gather the lambs with his arm, and carry them in his bosom, and shall gently lead those that are with young.… He giveth power to the faint; and to them that have no might he increaseth strength.… But they that wait upon the LORD shall renew their strength; they shall mount up with wings as eagles; they shall run, and not be weary; and they shall walk, and not faint. **Matt. 11:28.** Come unto me, all ye that labour and are heavy laden, and I will give you rest. **Matt. 12:20.** A bruised reed shall he not break, and smoking flax shall he not quench, till he send forth judgment unto victory. **Matt. 26:28.** For this is my blood of the new testament, which is shed for many for the remission of sins.

r. **Mark 9:24.** And straightway the father of the child cried out, and said with tears, Lord, I believe; help thou mine unbelief.

s. **Acts 2:37.** Now when they heard this, they were pricked in their heart, and said unto Peter and to the rest of the apostles, Men and brethren, what shall we do? **Acts 16:30.** And [the keeper of the prison] brought them out, and said, Sirs, what must I do to be saved?

t. **Rom. 4:11.** And he received the sign of circumcision, a seal of the righteousness of the faith which he had yet being uncircumcised: that he might be the father of all them that believe, though they be not circumcised; that righteousness might be imputed unto them also. **1 Cor. 11:28.** But let a man examine himself, and so let him eat of that bread, and drink of that cup.

Q. 173. *May any who profess the faith, and desire to come to the Lord's Supper, be kept from it?*

A. Such as are found to be ignorant or scandalous, notwithstanding their profession of the faith, and desire to come to the Lord's Supper, may and ought to be kept from that sacrament, by the power which Christ hath left in his church,ᵘ until they receive instruction, and manifest their reformation.ʷ

Q. 174. *What is required of them that receive the sacrament of the Lord's Supper in the time of the administration of it?*

A. It is required of them that receive the sacrament of the Lord's Supper, that, during the time of the administration of it, with all holy reverence and attention they wait upon God in that ordinance,ˣ

---

u. **1 Cor. 11:27–34.** Wherefore whosoever shall eat this bread, and drink this cup of the Lord, unworthily, shall be guilty of the body and blood of the Lord. But let a man examine himself, and so let him eat of that bread, and drink of that cup. For he that eateth and drinketh unworthily, eateth and drinketh damnation to himself, not discerning the Lord's body. For this cause many are weak and sickly among you, and many sleep. For if we would judge ourselves, we should not be judged. But when we are judged, we are chastened of the Lord, that we should not be condemned with the world. Wherefore, my brethren, when ye come together to eat, tarry one for another. And if any man hunger, let him eat at home; that ye come not together unto condemnation. And the rest will I set in order when I come. **Matt. 7:6.** Give not that which is holy unto the dogs, neither cast ye your pearls before swine, lest they trample them under their feet, and turn again and rend you. **1 Cor. 5.** It is reported commonly that there is fornication among you, and such fornication as is not so much as named among the Gentiles, that one should have his father's wife.... For I verily, as absent in body, but present in spirit, have judged already, as though I were present, concerning him that hath so done this deed, in the name of our Lord Jesus Christ, when ye are gathered together, and my spirit, with the power of our Lord Jesus Christ, to deliver such an one unto Satan for the destruction of the flesh, that the spirit may be saved in the the day of the Lord Jesus.... For even Christ our passover is sacrificed for us: therefore let us keep the feast, not with old leaven, neither with the leaven of malice and wickedness; but with the unleavened bread of sincerity and truth.... But now I have written unto you not to keep company, if any man that is called a brother be a fornicator, or covetous, or an idolater, or a railer, or a drunkard, or an extortioner; with such an one no not to eat.... Therefore put away from among yourselves that wicked person. **Jude 23.** And others save with fear, pulling them out of the fire; hating even the garment spotted by the flesh. **1 Tim. 5:22.** Lay hands suddenly on no man, neither be partaker of other men's sins: keep thyself pure.

w. **2 Cor. 2:7.** So that contrariwise ye ought rather to forgive him, and comfort him, lest perhaps such a one should be swallowed up with overmuch sorrow.

x. **Lev. 10:3.** Then Moses said unto Aaron, This is it that the LORD spake, saying, I will be sanctified in them that come nigh me, and before all the people I will be

diligently observe the sacramental elements and actions,[y] heedfully discern the Lord's body,[z] and affectionately meditate on his death and sufferings,[a] and thereby stir up themselves to a vigorous exercise of their graces;[b] in judging themselves,[c] and sorrowing for sin;[d] in earnest hungering and thirsting after Christ,[e] feeding on him by faith,[f] receiving of his fullness,[g] trusting in his merits,[h] rejoicing in his love,[i]

glorified.… **Heb. 12:28.** Wherefore we receiving a kingdom which cannot be moved, let us have grace, whereby we may serve God acceptably with reverence and godly fear. **Ps. 5:7.** But as for me, I will come into thy house in the multitude of thy mercy: and in thy fear will I worship toward thy holy temple. **1 Cor. 11:17, 26–27.** Now in this that I declare unto you I praise you not, that ye come together not for the better, but for the worse.… For as often as ye eat this bread, and drink this cup, ye do shew the Lord's death till he come. Wherefore whosoever shall eat this bread, and drink this cup of the Lord, unworthily, shall be guilty of the body and blood of the Lord.

y. **Ex. 24:8.** And Moses took the blood, and sprinkled it on the people, and said, Behold the blood of the covenant, which the LORD hath made with you concerning all these words. **Matt. 26:28.** For this is my blood of the new testament, which is shed for many for the remission of sins.

z. **1 Cor. 11:29.** For he that eateth and drinketh unworthily, eateth and drinketh damnation to himself, not discerning the Lord's body.

a. **Luke 22:19.** And he took bread, and gave thanks, and brake it, and gave unto them, saying, This is my body which is given for you: this do in remembrance of me.

b. **1 Cor. 11:26.** For as often as ye eat this bread, and drink this cup, ye do shew the Lord's death till he come. **1 Cor. 10:3–5, 11, 14.** And [our fathers] did all eat the same spiritual meat; and did all drink the same spiritual drink: for they drank of that spiritual Rock that followed them: and that Rock was Christ. But with many of them God was not well pleased: for they were overthrown in the wilderness.… Now all these things happened unto them for ensamples: and they are written for our admonition, upon whom the ends of the world are come.… Wherefore, my dearly beloved, flee from idolatry.

c. **1 Cor. 11:31.** For if we would judge ourselves, we should not be judged.

d. **Zech. 12:10.** And I will pour upon the house of David, and upon the inhabitants of Jerusalem, the spirit of grace and of supplications: and they shall look upon me whom they have pierced, and they shall mourn for him, as one mourneth for his only son, and shall be in bitterness for him, as one that is in bitterness for his firstborn.

e. **Rev. 22:17.** And the Spirit and the bride say, Come. And let him that heareth say, Come. And let him that is athirst come. And whosoever will, let him take the water of life freely. **See Matt. 5:6.**

f. **John 6:35.** And Jesus said unto them, I am the bread of life: he that cometh to me shall never hunger; and he that believeth on me shall never thirst. **See verses 47–58.**

g. **John 1:16.** And of his fulness have all we received, and grace for grace.

h. **Phil. 3:9.** … and be found in him, not having mine own righteousness, which is of the law, but that which is through the faith of Christ, the righteousness which is of God by faith.

giving thanks for his grace;^k in renewing of their covenant with God,^l and love to all the saints.^m

Q. 175. *What is the duty of Christians, after they have received the sacrament of the Lord's Supper?*

A. The duty of Christians, after they have received the sacrament of the Lord's Supper, is seriously to consider how they have behaved themselves therein, and with what success;ⁿ if they find quickening and comfort, to bless God for it,^o beg the continuance of it,^p

i. **Ps. 63:4–5.** Thus will I bless thee while I live: I will lift up my hands in thy name. My soul shall be satisfied as with marrow and fatness; and my mouth shall praise thee with joyful lips. **2 Chron. 30:21.** And the children of Israel that were present at Jerusalem kept the feast of unleavened bread seven days with great gladness: and the Levites and the priests praised the LORD day by day, singing with loud instruments unto the LORD.

k. **Ps. 22:26.** The meek shall eat and be satisfied: they shall praise the LORD that seek him: your heart shall live for ever. **See 1 Cor. 10:16.**

l. **Jer. 50:5.** They shall ask the way to Zion with their faces thitherward, saying, Come, and let us join ourselves to the LORD in a perpetual covenant that shall not be forgotten. **Ps. 50:5.** Gather my saints together unto me; those that have made a covenant with me by sacrifice.

m. **Acts 2:42.** And they continued stedfastly in the apostles' doctrine and fellowship, and in breaking of bread, and in prayers.

n. **Ps. 28:7.** The LORD is my strength and my shield; my heart trusted in him, and I am helped: therefore my heart greatly rejoiceth; and with my song will I praise him. **Ps. 85:8.** I will hear what God the LORD will speak: for he will speak peace unto his people, and to his saints: but let them not turn again to folly. **1 Cor. 11:17, 30–31.** Now in this that I declare unto you I praise you not, that ye come together not for the better, but for the worse.… For this cause many are weak and sickly among you, and many sleep. For if we would judge ourselves, we should not be judged.

o. **2 Chron. 30:21–23, 25–26.** And the children of Israel that were present at Jerusalem kept the feast of unleavened bread seven days with great gladness: and the Levites and the priests praised the LORD day by day, singing with loud instruments unto the LORD. And Hezekiah spake comfortably unto all the Levites that taught the good knowledge of the LORD: and they did eat throughout the feast seven days, offering peace offerings, and making confession to the LORD God of their fathers. And the whole assembly took counsel to keep other seven days: and they kept other seven days with gladness.… And all the congregation of Judah, with the priests and the Levites, and all the congregation that came out of Israel, and the strangers that came out of the land of Israel, and that dwelt in Judah, rejoiced. So there was great joy in Jerusalem: for since the time of Solomon the son of David king of Israel there was not the like in Jerusalem. **Acts 2:42, 46–47.** And they continued stedfastly in the apostles' doctrine and fellowship, and in breaking of bread, and in prayers.… And they, continuing daily with one accord in the temple, and breaking bread from house to house, did eat their meat with gladness and singleness of heart, praising God, and having

watch against relapses,[q] fulfill their vows,[r] and encourage themselves
to a frequent attendance on that ordinance:[s] but if they find no present
benefit, more exactly to review their preparation to, and carriage at,
the sacrament;[t] in both which, if they can approve themselves to God
and their own consciences, they are to wait for the fruit of it in due
time:[u] but, if they see they have failed in either, they are to be

favour with all the people. And the Lord added to the church daily such as should be
saved.

p. **Ps. 36:10.** O continue thy lovingkindness unto them that know thee; and thy
righteousness to the upright in heart. **Song 3:4.** It was but a little that I passed from
them, but I found him whom my soul loveth: I held him, and would not let him go,
until I had brought him into my mother's house, and into the chamber of her that
conceived me. **1 Chron. 29:18.** O LORD God of Abraham, Isaac, and of Israel, our
fathers, keep this for ever in the imagination of the thoughts of the heart of thy people,
and prepare their heart unto thee.

q. **1 Cor. 10:3–5, 12.** And [our fathers] did all eat the same spiritual meat; and
did all drink the same spiritual drink: for they drank of that spiritual Rock that followed them: and that Rock was Christ. But with many of them God was not well
pleased: for they were overthrown in the wilderness.... Wherefore let him that thinketh
he standeth take heed lest he fall.

r. **Ps. 50:14.** Offer unto God thanksgiving; and pay thy vows unto the most High.

s. **1 Cor. 11:25–26.** After the same manner also he took the cup, when he had
supped, saying, This cup is the new testament in my blood: this do ye, as oft as ye drink
it, in remembrance of me. For as often as ye eat this bread, and drink this cup, ye do
shew the Lord's death till he come. **Acts 2:42, 46.** And they continued stedfastly in
the apostles' doctrine and fellowship, and in breaking of bread, and in prayers.... And
they, continuing daily with one accord in the temple, and breaking bread from house
to house, did eat their meat with gladness and singleness of heart.

t. **Eccl. 5:1–6.** Keep thy foot when thou goest to the house of God, and be more
ready to hear, than to give the sacrifice of fools: for they consider not that they do evil.
Be not rash with thy mouth, and let not thine heart be hasty to utter any thing before
God: for God is in heaven, and thou upon earth: therefore let thy words be few. For a
dream cometh through the multitude of business; and a fool's voice is known by multitude of words. When thou vowest a vow unto God, defer not to pay it; for he hath no
pleasure in fools: pay that which thou hast vowed. Better is it that thou shouldest not
vow, than that thou shouldest vow and not pay. Suffer not thy mouth to cause thy flesh
to sin; neither say thou before the angel, that it was an error: wherefore should God be
angry at thy voice, and destroy the work of thine hands? **Ps. 139:23–24.** Search me,
O God, and know my heart: try me, and know my thoughts: and see if there be any
wicked way in me, and lead me in the way everlasting.

u. **Ps. 123:1–2.** Unto thee lift I up mine eyes, O thou that dwellest in the heavens. Behold, as the eyes of servants look unto the hand of their masters, and as the eyes
of a maiden unto the hand of her mistress; so our eyes wait upon the LORD our God,
until that he have mercy upon us. **Ps. 42:5, 8.** Why art thou cast down, O my soul?
and why art thou disquieted in me? hope thou in God: for I shall yet praise him for the
help of his countenance.... Yet the LORD will command his lovingkindness in the

humbled,ʷ and to attend upon it afterwards with more care and diligence.ˣ

Q. 176. *Wherein do the sacraments of baptism and the Lord's Supper agree?*
A. The sacraments of baptism and the Lord's Supper agree, in that the author of both is God;ʸ the spiritual part of both is Christ and his benefits;ᶻ both are seals of the same covenant,ᵃ are to be

daytime, and in the night his song shall be with me, and my prayer unto the God of my life. **Ps. 43:3–5.** O send out thy light and thy truth: let them lead me; let them bring me unto thy holy hill, and to thy tabernacles. Then will I go unto the altar of God, unto God my exceeding joy: yea, upon the harp will I praise thee, O God my God. Why art thou cast down, O my soul? and why art thou disquieted within me? hope in God: for I shall yet praise him, who is the health of my countenance, and my God.

w. **2 Chron. 30:18–19.** For a multitude of the people, even many of Ephraim, and Manasseh, Issachar, and Zebulun, had not cleansed themselves, yet did they eat the passover otherwise than it was written. But Hezekiah prayed for them, saying, The good Lᴏʀᴅ pardon every one that prepareth his heart to seek God, the Lᴏʀᴅ God of his fathers, though he be not cleansed according to the purification of the sanctuary.

x. **2 Cor. 7:11.** For behold this selfsame thing, that ye sorrowed after a godly sort, what carefulness it wrought in you, yea, what clearing of yourselves, yea, what indignation, yea, what fear, yea, what vehement desire, yea, what zeal, yea, what revenge! In all things ye have approved yourselves to be clear in this matter. **1 Chron. 15:12–14.** And [David] said unto them, Ye are the chief of the fathers of the Levites: sanctify yourselves, both ye and your brethren, that ye may bring up the ark of the Lᴏʀᴅ God of Israel unto the place that I have prepared for it. For because ye did it not at the first, the Lᴏʀᴅ our God made a breach upon us, for that we sought him not after the due order. So the priests and the Levites sanctified themselves to bring up the ark of the Lᴏʀᴅ God of Israel.

y. **Matt. 28:19.** Go ye therefore, and teach all nations, baptizing them in the name of the Father, and of the Son, and of the Holy Ghost. **1 Cor. 11:23.** For I have received of the Lord that which also I delivered unto you, That the Lord Jesus the same night in which he was betrayed took bread.

z. **Rom. 6:3–4.** Know ye not, that so many of us as were baptized into Jesus Christ were baptized into his death? Therefore we are buried with him by baptism into death: that like as Christ was raised up from the dead by the glory of the Father, even so we also should walk in newness of life. **1 Cor. 10:16.** The cup of blessing which we bless, is it not the communion of the blood of Christ? The bread which we break, is it not the communion of the body of Christ?

a. **Rom. 4:11.** And he received the sign of circumcision, a seal of the righteousness of the faith which he had yet being uncircumcised: that he might be the father of all them that believe, though they be not circumcised; that righteousness might be imputed unto them also. **Compared with Col. 2:12.** … buried with him in baptism, wherein also ye are risen with him through the faith of the operation of God, who hath raised him from the dead. **Matt. 26:27–28.** And he took the cup, and gave thanks, and gave it to them, saying, Drink ye all of it; for this is my blood of the new

dispensed by ministers of the gospel, and by none other;[b] and to be continued in the church of Christ until his second coming.[c]

Q. 177. *Wherein do the sacraments of baptism and the Lord's Supper differ?*

A. The sacraments of baptism and the Lord's Supper differ, in that baptism is to be administered but once, with water, to be a sign and seal of our regeneration and ingrafting into Christ,[d] and that even to infants;[e] whereas the Lord's Supper is to be administered often, in the elements of bread and wine, to represent and exhibit Christ as spiritual nourishment to the soul,[f] and to confirm our

testament, which is shed for many for the remission of sins.

b. **John 1:33.** And I knew him not: but he that sent me to baptize with water, the same said unto me, Upon whom thou shalt see the Spirit descending, and remaining on him, the same is he which baptizeth with the Holy Ghost. **Matt. 28:19.** Go ye therefore, and teach all nations, baptizing them in the name of the Father, and of the Son, and of the Holy Ghost. **1 Cor. 11:23.** For I have received of the Lord that which also I delivered unto you, That the Lord Jesus the same night in which he was betrayed took bread. **1 Cor. 4:1.** Let a man so account of us, as of the ministers of Christ, and stewards of the mysteries of God. **Heb. 5:4.** And no man taketh this honour unto himself, but he that is called of God, as was Aaron.

c. **Matt. 28:19–20.** Go ye therefore, and teach all nations, baptizing them in the name of the Father, and of the Son, and of the Holy Ghost: teaching them to observe all things whatsoever I have commanded you: and, lo, I am with you alway, even unto the end of the world. Amen. **1 Cor. 11:26.** For as often as ye eat this bread, and drink this cup, ye do shew the Lord's death till he come.

d. **Matt. 3:11.** I indeed baptize you with water unto repentance: but he that cometh after me is mightier than I, whose shoes I am not worthy to bear: he shall baptize you with the Holy Ghost, and with fire. **Titus 3:5.** Not by works of righteousness which we have done, but according to his mercy he saved us, by the washing of regeneration, and renewing of the Holy Ghost. **Gal. 3:27.** For as many of you as have been baptized into Christ have put on Christ.

e. **Gen. 17:7, 9.** And I will establish my covenant between me and thee and thy seed after thee in their generations for an everlasting covenant, to be a God unto thee, and to thy seed after thee.… And God said unto Abraham, Thou shalt keep my covenant therefore, thou, and thy seed after thee in their generations. **Acts 2:38–39.** Then Peter said unto them, Repent, and be baptized every one of you in the name of Jesus Christ for the remission of sins, and ye shall receive the gift of the Holy Ghost. For the promise is unto you, and to your children, and to all that are afar off, even as many as the Lord our God shall call. **1 Cor. 7:14.** For the unbelieving husband is sanctified by the wife, and the unbelieving wife is sanctified by the husband: else were your children unclean; but now are they holy.

f. **1 Cor. 11:23–26.** For I have received of the Lord that which also I delivered unto you, That the Lord Jesus the same night in which he was betrayed took bread: and when he had given thanks, he brake it, and said, Take, eat: this is my body, which

continuance and growth in him,[g] and that only to such as are of years and ability to examine themselves.[h]

Q. 178. *What is prayer?*
A. Prayer is an offering up of our desires unto God,[i] in the name of Christ,[k] by the help of his Spirit;[l] with confession of our sins,[m] and thankful acknowledgment of his mercies.[n]

Q. 179. *Are we to pray unto God only?*
A. God only being able to search the hearts,[o] hear the requests,[p]

is broken for you: this do in remembrance of me. After the same manner also he took the cup, when he had supped, saying, This cup is the new testament in my blood: this do ye, as oft as ye drink it, in remembrance of me. For as often as ye eat this bread, and drink this cup, ye do shew the Lord's death till he come.

g. **1 Cor. 10:16.** The cup of blessing which we bless, is it not the communion of the blood of Christ? The bread which we break, is it not the communion of the body of Christ?

h. **1 Cor. 11:28–29.** But let a man examine himself, and so let him eat of that bread, and drink of that cup. For he that eateth and drinketh unworthily, eateth and drinketh damnation to himself, not discerning the Lord's body.

i. **Ps. 10:17.** Lord, thou hast heard the desire of the humble: thou wilt prepare their heart, thou wilt cause thine ear to hear. **Ps. 62:8.** Trust in him at all times; ye people, pour out your heart before him: God is a refuge for us. Selah. **Matt. 7:7–8.** Ask, and it shall be given you; seek, and ye shall find; knock, and it shall be opened unto you: for every one that asketh receiveth; and he that seeketh findeth; and to him that knocketh it shall be opened.

k. **John 16:23.** And in that day ye shall ask me nothing. Verily, verily, I say unto you, Whatsoever ye shall ask the Father in my name, he will give it you.

l. **Rom. 8:26.** Likewise the Spirit also helpeth our infirmities: for we know not what we should pray for as we ought: but the Spirit itself maketh intercession for us with groanings which cannot be uttered.

m. **Ps. 32:5–6.** I acknowledged my sin unto thee, and mine iniquity have I not hid. I said, I will confess my transgressions unto the Lord; and thou forgavest the iniquity of my sin. Selah. For this shall every one that is godly pray unto thee in a time when thou mayest be found: surely in the floods of great waters they shall not come nigh unto him. **1 John 1:9.** If we confess our sins, he is faithful and just to forgive us our sins, and to cleanse us from all unrighteousness. **See Dan. 9:4–19.**

n. **Phil. 4:6.** Be careful for nothing; but in every thing by prayer and supplication with thanksgiving let your requests be made known unto God. **Ps. 103:1–5.** Bless the Lord, O my soul: and all that is within me, bless his holy name. Bless the Lord, O my soul, and forget not all his benefits: who forgiveth all thine iniquities; who healeth all thy diseases; who redeemeth thy life from destruction; who crowneth thee with loving-kindness and tender mercies; who satisfieth thy mouth with good things; so that thy youth is renewed like the eagle's. **See Ps. 136.**

o. **1 Kings 8:39.** Then hear thou in heaven thy dwelling place, and forgive, and do, and give to every man according to his ways, whose heart thou knowest; (for thou,

pardon the sins,^{q} and fulfill the desires of all;^{r} and only to be believed in,^{s} and worshiped with religious worship;^{t} prayer, which is a special part thereof,^{u} is to be made by all to him alone,^{w} and to none other.^{x}

Q. 180. *What is it to pray in the name of Christ?*

A. To pray in the name of Christ is, in obedience to his command, and in confidence on his promises, to ask mercy for his sake;^{y} not by bare mentioning of his name,^{z} but by drawing our encouragement to pray, and our boldness, strength, and hope of acceptance in prayer, from Christ and his mediation.^{a}

even thou only, knowest the hearts of all the children of men;) … **Acts 1:24.** And they prayed, and said, Thou, Lord, which knowest the hearts of all men, shew whether of these two thou hast chosen. **Rom. 8:27.** And he that searcheth the hearts knoweth what is the mind of the Spirit, because he maketh intercession for the saints according to the will of God.

p. **Ps. 65:2.** O thou that hearest prayer, unto thee shall all flesh come.

q. **Mic. 7:18.** Who is a God like unto thee, that pardoneth iniquity, and passeth by the transgression of the remnant of his heritage? he retaineth not his anger for ever, because he delighteth in mercy.

r. **Ps. 145:18.** The LORD is nigh unto all them that call upon him, to all that call upon him in truth.

s. **Rom. 10:14.** How then shall they call on him in whom they have not believed? and how shall they believe in him of whom they have not heard? and how shall they hear without a preacher?

t. **Matt. 4:10.** Then saith Jesus unto him, Get thee hence, Satan: for it is written, Thou shalt worship the Lord thy God, and him only shalt thou serve.

u. **1 Cor. 1:2.** … unto the church of God which is at Corinth, to them that are sanctified in Christ Jesus, called to be saints, with all that in every place call upon the name of Jesus Christ our Lord, both theirs and ours …

w. **Isa. 45:22.** Look unto me, and be ye saved, all the ends of the earth: for I am God, and there is none else. **Matt. 6:9.** After this manner therefore pray ye: Our Father which art in heaven, Hallowed be thy name. **Ps. 50:15.** And call upon me in the day of trouble: I will deliver thee, and thou shalt glorify me.

x. **Isa. 43:11.** I, even I, am the LORD; and beside me there is no saviour. **Isa. 46:9.** Remember the former things of old: for I am God, and there is none else; I am God, and there is none like me (**see entire chapter**).

y. **John 14:13–14.** And whatsoever ye shall ask in my name, that will I do, that the Father may be glorified in the Son. If ye shall ask any thing in my name, I will do it. **John 16:24.** Hitherto have ye asked nothing in my name: ask, and ye shall receive, that your joy may be full. **Dan. 9:17.** Now therefore, O our God, hear the prayer of thy servant, and his supplications, and cause thy face to shine upon thy sanctuary that is desolate, for the Lord's sake.

z. **Matt. 7:21.** Not every one that saith unto me, Lord, Lord, shall enter into the kingdom of heaven; but he that doeth the will of my Father which is in heaven.

a. **Heb. 4:14–16.** Seeing then that we have a great high priest, that is passed into

Q. 181. *Why are we to pray in the name of Christ?*

A. The sinfulness of man, and his distance from God by reason thereof, being so great, as that we can have no access into his presence without a mediator;[b] and there being none in heaven or earth appointed to, or fit for, that glorious work but Christ alone,[c] we are to pray in no other name but his only.[d]

Q. 182. *How doth the Spirit help us to pray?*

A. We not knowing what to pray for as we ought, the Spirit helpeth our infirmities, by enabling us to understand both for whom, and what, and how prayer is to be made; and by working and quickening in our hearts (although not in all persons, nor at all times, in the same measure) those apprehensions, affections, and graces which are requisite for the right performance of that duty.[e]

the heavens, Jesus the Son of God, let us hold fast our profession. For we have not an high priest which cannot be touched with the feeling of our infirmities; but was in all points tempted like as we are, yet without sin. Let us therefore come boldly unto the throne of grace, that we may obtain mercy, and find grace to help in time of need. **1 John 5:13–15.** These things have I written unto you that believe on the name of the Son of God; that ye may know that ye have eternal life, and that ye may believe on the name of the Son of God. And this is the confidence that we have in him, that, if we ask any thing according to his will, he heareth us: and if we know that he hear us, whatsoever we ask, we know that we have the petitions that we desired of him.

b. **John 14:6.** Jesus saith unto him, I am the way, the truth, and the life: no man cometh unto the Father, but by me. **Isa. 59:2.** But your iniquities have separated between you and your God, and your sins have hid his face from you, that he will not hear. **Eph. 3:12.** … in whom we have boldness and access with confidence by the faith of him.

c. **John 6:27.** Labour not for the meat which perisheth, but for that meat which endureth unto everlasting life, which the Son of man shall give unto you: for him hath God the Father sealed. **Heb. 7:25–27.** Wherefore he is able also to save them to the uttermost that come unto God by him, seeing he ever liveth to make intercession for them. For such an high priest became us, who is holy, harmless, undefiled, separate from sinners, and made higher than the heavens; who needeth not daily, as those high priests, to offer up sacrifice, first for his own sins, and then for the people's: for this he did once, when he offered up himself. **1 Tim. 2:5.** For there is one God, and one mediator between God and men, the man Christ Jesus.

d. **Col. 3:17.** And whatsoever ye do in word or deed, do all in the name of the Lord Jesus, giving thanks to God and the Father by him. **Heb. 13:15.** By him therefore let us offer the sacrifice of praise to God continually, that is, the fruit of our lips giving thanks to his name.

e. **Rom. 8:26–27.** Likewise the Spirit also helpeth our infirmities: for we know not what we should pray for as we ought: but the Spirit itself maketh intercession for us with groanings which cannot be uttered. And he that searcheth the hearts knoweth

Q. 183. *For whom are we to pray?*

A. We are to pray for the whole church of Christ upon earth;[f] for magistrates,[g] and ministers;[h] for ourselves,[i] our brethren,[k] yea, our enemies;[l] and for all sorts of men living,[m] or that shall live hereafter;[n] but not for the dead,[o] nor for those that are known to have sinned the sin unto death.[p]

what is the mind of the Spirit, because he maketh intercession for the saints according to the will of God. **Ps. 10:17.** LORD, thou hast heard the desire of the humble: thou wilt prepare their heart, thou wilt cause thine ear to hear. **Zech. 12:10.** And I will pour upon the house of David, and upon the inhabitants of Jerusalem, the spirit of grace and of supplications: and they shall look upon me whom they have pierced, and they shall mourn for him, as one mourneth for his only son, and shall be in bitterness for him, as one that is in bitterness for his firstborn.

f. **Eph. 6:18.** … praying always with all prayer and supplication in the Spirit, and watching thereunto with all perseverance and supplication for all saints. **Ps. 28:9.** Save thy people, and bless thine inheritance: feed them also, and lift them up for ever.

g. **1 Tim. 2:1–2.** I exhort therefore, that, first of all, supplications, prayers, intercessions, and giving of thanks, be made for all men; for kings, and for all that are in authority; that we may lead a quiet and peaceable life in all godliness and honesty.

h. **Col. 4:3.** … withal praying also for us, that God would open unto us a door of utterance, to speak the mystery of Christ, for which I am also in bonds.

i. **Gen. 32:11.** Deliver me, I pray thee, from the hand of my brother, from the hand of Esau: for I fear him, lest he will come and smite me, and the mother with the children.

k. **James 5:16.** Confess your faults one to another, and pray one for another, that ye may be healed. The effectual fervent prayer of a righteous man availeth much.

l. **Matt. 5:44.** But I say unto you, Love your enemies, bless them that curse you, do good to them that hate you, and pray for them which despitefully use you, and persecute you.

m. **1 Tim. 2:1–2.** I exhort therefore, that, first of all, supplications, prayers, intercessions, and giving of thanks, be made for all men; for kings, and for all that are in authority; that we may lead a quiet and peaceable life in all godliness and honesty.

n. **John 17:20.** Neither pray I for these alone, but for them also which shall believe on me through their word. **2 Sam. 7:29.** Therefore now let it please thee to bless the house of thy servant, that it may continue for ever before thee: for thou, O Lord GOD, hast spoken it: and with thy blessing let the house of thy servant be blessed for ever.

o. **2 Sam. 12:21–23.** Then said his servants unto him, What thing is this that thou hast done? thou didst fast and weep for the child, while it was alive; but when the child was dead, thou didst rise and eat bread. And he said, While the child was yet alive, I fasted and wept: for I said, Who can tell whether GOD will be gracious to me, that the child may live? But now he is dead, wherefore should I fast? can I bring him back again? I shall go to him, but he shall not return to me.

p. **1 John 5:16.** If any man see his brother sin a sin which is not unto death, he shall ask, and he shall give him life for them that sin not unto death. There is a sin unto

Q. 184. *For what things are we to pray?*

A. We are to pray for all things tending to the glory of God,[q] the welfare of the church,[r] our own[s] or others' good;[t] but not for anything that is unlawful.[u]

Q. 185. *How are we to pray?*

A. We are to pray with an awful apprehension of the majesty of God,[w] and deep sense of our own unworthiness,[x] necessities,[y] and sins;[z] with penitent,[a] thankful,[b] and enlarged hearts;[c] with under-

---

death: I do not say that he shall pray for it.

q. **Matt. 6:9.** After this manner therefore pray ye: Our Father which art in heaven, Hallowed be thy name.

r. **Ps. 51:18.** Do good in thy good pleasure unto Zion: build thou the walls of Jerusalem. **Ps. 122:6.** Pray for the peace of Jerusalem: they shall prosper that love thee.

s. **Matt. 7:11.** If ye then, being evil, know how to give good gifts unto your children, how much more shall your Father which is in heaven give good things to them that ask him?

t. **Ps. 125:4.** Do good, O LORD, unto those that be good, and to them that are upright in their hearts.

u. **1 John 5:14.** And this is the confidence that we have in him, that, if we ask any thing according to his will, he heareth us.

w. **Ps. 33:8.** Let all the earth fear the LORD: let all the inhabitants of the world stand in awe of him. **Ps. 95:6.** O come, let us worship and bow down: let us kneel before the LORD our maker. **Ps. 145:5.** I will speak of the glorious honour of thy majesty, and of thy wondrous works.

x. **Gen. 18:27.** And Abraham answered and said, Behold now, I have taken upon me to speak unto the Lord, which am but dust and ashes. **Gen. 32:10.** I am not worthy of the least of all the mercies, and of all the truth, which thou hast shewed unto thy servant; for with my staff I passed over this Jordan; and now I am become two bands.

y. **Luke 15:17–19.** And when he came to himself, he said, How many hired servants of my father's have bread enough and to spare, and I perish with hunger! I will arise and go to my father, and will say unto him, Father, I have sinned against heaven, and before thee, and am no more worthy to be called thy son: make me as one of thy hired servants.

z. **Luke 18:13–14.** And the publican, standing afar off, would not lift up so much as his eyes unto heaven, but smote upon his breast, saying, God be merciful to me a sinner. I tell you, this man went down to his house justified rather than the other: for every one that exalteth himself shall be abased; and he that humbleth himself shall be exalted.

a. **Ps. 51:17.** The sacrifices of God are a broken spirit: a broken and a contrite heart, O God, thou wilt not despise.

b. **Phil. 4:6.** Be careful for nothing; but in every thing by prayer and supplication with thanksgiving let your requests be made known unto God.

standing,[d] faith,[e] sincerity,[f] fervency,[g] love,[h] and perseverance,[i] waiting upon him,[k] with humble submission to his will.[l]

Q. 186. *What rule hath God given for our direction in the duty of prayer?*
A. The whole Word of God is of use to direct us in the duty of prayer;[m] but the special rule of direction is that form of prayer which our Savior Christ taught his disciples, commonly called the Lord's Prayer.[n]

c. **1 Sam. 1:15.** And Hannah answered and said, No, my lord, I am a woman of a sorrowful spirit: I have drunk neither wine nor strong drink, but have poured out my soul before the LORD. **1 Sam. 2:1.** And Hannah prayed, and said, My heart rejoiceth in the LORD, mine horn is exalted in the LORD: my mouth is enlarged over mine enemies; because I rejoice in thy salvation.

d. **1 Cor. 14:15.** What is it then? I will pray with the spirit, and I will pray with the understanding also: I will sing with the spirit, and I will sing with the understanding also.

e. **Mark 11:24.** Therefore I say unto you, What things soever ye desire, when ye pray, believe that ye receive them, and ye shall have them. **James 1:6.** But let him ask in faith, nothing wavering. For he that wavereth is like a wave of the sea driven with the wind and tossed.

f. **Ps. 145:18.** The LORD is nigh unto all them that call upon him, to all that call upon him in truth. **Ps. 17:1.** Hear the right, O LORD, attend unto my cry, give ear unto my prayer, that goeth not out of feigned lips.

g. **James 5:16.** Confess your faults one to another, and pray one for another, that ye may be healed. The effectual fervent prayer of a righteous man availeth much.

h. **Ps. 116:1–2.** I love the LORD, because he hath heard my voice and my supplications. Because he hath inclined his ear unto me, therefore will I call upon him as long as I live. **Rom. 15:30.** Now I beseech you, brethren, for the Lord Jesus Christ's sake, and for the love of the Spirit, that ye strive together with me in your prayers to God for me.

i. **Eph. 6:18.** … praying always with all prayer and supplication in the Spirit, and watching thereunto with all perseverance and supplication for all saints.

k. **Mic. 7:7.** Therefore I will look unto the LORD; I will wait for the God of my salvation: my God will hear me.

l. **Matt. 26:39.** And he went a little farther, and fell on his face, and prayed, saying, O my Father, if it be possible, let this cup pass from me: nevertheless not as I will, but as thou wilt.

m. **1 John 5:14.** And this is the confidence that we have in him, that, if we ask any thing according to his will, he heareth us.

n. **Matt. 6:9–13.** After this manner therefore pray ye: Our Father which art in heaven, Hallowed be thy name. Thy kingdom come. Thy will be done in earth, as it is in heaven. Give us this day our daily bread. And forgive us our debts, as we forgive our debtors. And lead us not into temptation, but deliver us from evil: For thine is the kingdom, and the power, and the glory, for ever. Amen. **Luke 11:2–4.** And he said unto them, When ye pray, say, Our Father which art in heaven, Hallowed be thy name. Thy kingdom come. Thy will be done, as in heaven, so in earth. Give us day by

Q. 187. *How is the Lord's Prayer to be used?*

A. The Lord's Prayer is not only for direction, as a pattern, according to which we are to make other prayers; but may also be used as a prayer, so that it be done with understanding, faith, reverence, and other graces necessary to the right performance of the duty of prayer.[o]

Q. 188. *Of how many parts doth the Lord's Prayer consist?*

A. The Lord's Prayer consists of three parts; a preface, petitions, and a conclusion.

Q. 189. *What doth the preface of the Lord's Prayer teach us?*

A. The preface of the Lord's Prayer (contained in these words, *Our Father which art in heaven*,[p]) teacheth us, when we pray, to draw near to God with confidence of his fatherly goodness, and our interest therein;[q] with reverence, and all other childlike dispositions,[r] heavenly affections,[s] and due apprehensions of his sovereign power, majesty, and gracious condescension:[t] as also, to pray with and for others.[u]

day our daily bread. And forgive us our sins; for we also forgive every one that is indebted to us. And lead us not into temptation; but deliver us from evil.

o. **Matt. 6:9.** After this manner therefore pray ye: Our Father which art in heaven, Hallowed be thy name. **Luke 11:2.** And he said unto them, When ye pray, say, Our Father which art in heaven, Hallowed be thy name....

p. **Matt. 6:9. Cf. Luke 11:2.** ... Our Father which art in heaven ...

q. **Ps. 103:13.** Like as a father pitieth his children, so the LORD pitieth them that fear him. **Luke 11:13.** If ye then, being evil, know how to give good gifts unto your children: how much more shall your heavenly Father give the Holy Spirit to them that ask him? **Rom. 8:15.** For ye have not received the spirit of bondage again to fear; but ye have received the Spirit of adoption, whereby we cry, Abba, Father.

r. **Isa. 64:9.** Be not wroth very sore, O LORD, neither remember iniquity for ever: behold, see, we beseech thee, we are all thy people.

s. **Col. 3:1–2.** If ye then be risen with Christ, seek those things which are above, where Christ sitteth on the right hand of God. Set your affection on things above, not on things on the earth. **Ps. 123:1.** Unto thee lift I up mine eyes, O thou that dwellest in the heavens. **Lam. 3:41.** Let us lift up our heart with our hands unto God in the heavens.

t. **Isa. 63:15–16.** Look down from heaven, and behold from the habitation of thy holiness and of thy glory: where is thy zeal and thy strength, the sounding of thy bowels and of thy mercies toward me? are they restrained? Doubtless thou art our father, though Abraham be ignorant of us, and Israel acknowledge us not: thou, O LORD, art our father, our redeemer; thy name is from everlasting. **Neh. 1:4–6.** And it came to pass, when I heard these words, that I sat down and wept, and mourned certain days, and fasted, and prayed before the God of heaven, and said, I beseech thee, O LORD God of heaven, the great and terrible God, that keepeth covenant and

Q. 190. *What do we pray for in the first petition?*

A. In the first petition, (which is, *Hallowed be thy name,*[w]) acknowledging the utter inability and indisposition that is in ourselves and all men to honor God aright,[x] we pray, that God would by his grace enable and incline us and others to know, to acknowledge, and highly to esteem him,[y] his titles,[z] attributes,[a] ordinances, Word,[b] works, and

mercy for them that love him and observe his commandments: let thine ear now be attentive, and thine eyes open, that thou mayest hear the prayer of thy servant, which I pray before thee now, day and night, for the children of Israel thy servants, and confess the sins of the children of Israel, which we have sinned against thee: both I and my father's house have sinned. **See Ps. 113:4–6.**

u. **Acts 12:5.** Peter therefore was kept in prison: but prayer was made without ceasing of the church unto God for him. **1 Tim. 2:1–2.** I exhort therefore, that, first of all, supplications, prayers, intercessions, and giving of thanks, be made for all men; for kings, and for all that are in authority; that we may lead a quiet and peaceable life in all godliness and honesty. **Eph. 6:18.** … praying always with all prayer and supplication in the Spirit, and watching thereunto with all perseverance and supplication for all saints.

w. **Matt. 6:9. Cf. Luke 11:2.** … Hallowed be thy name.…

x. **2 Cor. 3:5.** Not that we are sufficient of ourselves to think any thing as of ourselves; but our sufficiency is of God. **Ps. 51:15.** O Lord, open thou my lips; and my mouth shall shew forth thy praise.

y. **Ps. 67:2–3.** That thy way may be known upon earth, thy saving health among all nations. Let the people praise thee, O God; let all the people praise thee. **Ps. 99:1–3.** The LORD reigneth; let the people tremble: he sitteth between the cherubims; let the earth be moved. The LORD is great in Zion; and he is high above all the people. Let them praise thy great and terrible name; for it is holy.

z. **Ps. 83:18.** … that men may know that thou, whose name alone is JEHOVAH, art the most high over all the earth.

a. **Ps. 86:10–13, 15.** For thou art great, and doest wondrous things: thou art God alone. Teach me thy way, O LORD; I will walk in thy truth: unite my heart to fear thy name. I will praise thee, O Lord my God, with all my heart: and I will glorify thy name for evermore. For great is thy mercy toward me: and thou hast delivered my soul from the lowest hell.… But thou, O Lord, art a God full of compassion, and gracious, longsuffering, and plenteous in mercy and truth.

b. **2 Thess. 3:1.** Finally, brethren, pray for us, that the word of the Lord may have free course, and be glorified, even as it is with you. **Ps. 147:19–20.** He sheweth his word unto Jacob, his statutes and his judgments unto Israel. He hath not dealt so with any nation: and as for his judgments, they have not known them. Praise ye the LORD. **Ps. 138:1–3.** I will praise thee with my whole heart: before the gods will I sing praise unto thee. I will worship toward thy holy temple, and praise thy name for thy lovingkindness and for thy truth: for thou hast magnified thy word above all thy name. In the day when I cried thou answeredst me, and strengthenedst me with strength in my soul. **2 Cor. 2:14–15.** Now thanks be unto God, which always causeth us to triumph in Christ, and maketh manifest the savour of his knowledge by us in every place. For we are unto God a sweet savour of Christ, in them that are saved, and in

whatsoever he is pleased to make himself known by;^c and to glorify him in thought, word,^d and deed:^e that he would prevent and remove atheism,^f ignorance,^g idolatry,^h profaneness,ⁱ and whatsoever is dishonorable to him;^k and, by his overruling providence, direct and dispose of all things to his own glory.^l

them that perish.

c. **Ps. 145.** I will extol thee, my God, O king; and I will bless thy name for ever and ever.... **Ps. 8.** O LORD our Lord, how excellent is thy name in all the earth! who hast set thy glory above the heavens....

d. **Ps. 103:1.** Bless the LORD, O my soul: and all that is within me, bless his holy name. **Ps. 19:14.** Let the words of my mouth, and the meditation of my heart, be acceptable in thy sight, O LORD, my strength, and my redeemer.

e. **Phil. 1:9, 11.** And this I pray, that your love may abound yet more and more in knowledge and in all judgment.... being filled with the fruits of righteousness, which are by Jesus Christ, unto the glory and praise of God. **Ps. 100:3–4.** Know ye that the LORD he is God: it is he that hath made us, and not we ourselves; we are his people, and the sheep of his pasture. Enter into his gates with thanksgiving, and into his courts with praise: be thankful unto him, and bless his name.

f. **Ps. 67:1–4.** God be merciful unto us, and bless us; and cause his face to shine upon us; Selah. That thy way may be known upon earth, thy saving health among all nations. Let the people praise thee, O God; let all the people praise thee. O let the nations be glad and sing for joy: for thou shalt judge the people righteously, and govern the nations upon earth. Selah.

g. **Eph. 1:17–18.** ... that the God of our Lord Jesus Christ, the Father of glory, may give unto you the spirit of wisdom and revelation in the knowledge of him: the eyes of your understanding being enlightened; that ye may know what is the hope of his calling, and what the riches of the glory of his inheritance in the saints.

h. **Ps. 97:7.** Confounded be all they that serve graven images, that boast themselves of idols: worship him, all ye gods.

i. **Ps. 74:18, 22–23.** Remember this, that the enemy hath reproached, O LORD, and that the foolish people have blasphemed thy name.... Arise, O God, plead thine own cause: remember how the foolish man reproacheth thee daily. Forget not the voice of thine enemies: the tumult of those that rise up against thee increaseth continually.

k. **2 Kings 19:15–16.** And Hezekiah prayed before the LORD, and said, O LORD God of Israel, which dwellest between the cherubims, thou art the God, even thou alone, of all the kingdoms of the earth; thou hast made heaven and earth. LORD, bow down thine ear, and hear: open, LORD, thine eyes, and see: and hear the words of Sennacherib, which hath sent him to reproach the living God.

l. **2 Chron. 20:6.** And [Jehoshaphat] said, O LORD God of our fathers, art not thou God in heaven? and rulest not thou over all the kingdoms of the heathen? and in thine hand is there not power and might, so that none is able to withstand thee? **See verses 10–12. Rom. 11:33–36.** O the depth of the riches both of the wisdom and knowledge of God! how unsearchable are his judgments, and his ways past finding out! For who hath known the mind of the Lord? or who hath been his counsellor? Or who hath first given to him, and it shall be recompensed unto him again? For of him,

Q. 191. *What do we pray for in the second petition?*

A. In the second petition, (which is, *Thy kingdom come*,[m]) acknowledging ourselves and all mankind to be by nature under the dominion of sin and Satan,[n] we pray, that the kingdom of sin and Satan may be destroyed,[o] the gospel propagated throughout the world,[p] the Jews called,[q] the fullness of the Gentiles brought in;[r] the church furnished with all gospel officers and ordinances,[s] purged from corruption,[t] countenanced and maintained by the civil magistrate:[u]

and through him, and to him, are all things: to whom be glory for ever. Amen. **Rev. 4:11.** Thou art worthy, O Lord, to receive glory and honour and power: for thou hast created all things, and for thy pleasure they are and were created. **See Pss. 83; 140:4, 8.**

m. **Matt. 6:10. Cf. Luke 11:2.** … Thy kingdom come.…

n. **Eph. 2:2–3.** … wherein in time past ye walked according to the course of this world, according to the prince of the power of the air, the spirit that now worketh in the children of disobedience: among whom also we all had our conversation in times past in the lusts of our flesh, fulfilling the desires of the flesh and of the mind; and were by nature the children of wrath, even as others.

o. **Ps. 68:1, 18.** Let God arise, let his enemies be scattered: let them also that hate him flee before him.… Thou hast ascended on high, thou hast led captivity captive: thou hast received gifts for men; yea, for the rebellious also, that the LORD God might dwell among them. **Rev. 12:10–11.** And I heard a loud voice saying in heaven, Now is come salvation, and strength, and the kingdom of our God, and the power of his Christ: for the accuser of our brethren is cast down, which accused them before our God day and night. And they overcame him by the blood of the Lamb, and by the word of their testimony; and they loved not their lives unto the death.

p. **Ps. 67:1–2.** God be merciful unto us, and bless us; and cause his face to shine upon us; Selah. That thy way may be known upon earth, thy saving health among all nations. **2 Thess. 3:1.** Finally, brethren, pray for us, that the word of the Lord may have free course, and be glorified, even as it is with you.

q. **Rom. 10:1.** Brethren, my heart's desire and prayer to God for Israel is, that they might be saved.

r. **John 17:9, 20.** I pray for them: I pray not for the world, but for them which thou hast given me; for they are thine.… Neither pray I for these alone, but for them also which shall believe on me through their word. **Rom. 11:25–26.** For I would not, brethren, that ye should be ignorant of this mystery, lest ye should be wise in your own conceits; that blindness in part is happened to Israel, until the fulness of the Gentiles be come in. And so all Israel shall be saved: as it is written, There shall come out of Sion the Deliverer, and shall turn away ungodliness from Jacob. **See Ps. 67.**

s. **Matt. 9:38.** Pray ye therefore the Lord of the harvest, that he will send forth labourers into his harvest. **2 Thess. 3:1.** Finally, brethren, pray for us, that the word of the Lord may have free course, and be glorified, even as it is with you.

t. **Mal. 1:11.** For from the rising of the sun even unto the going down of the same my name shall be great among the Gentiles; and in every place incense shall be offered unto my name, and a pure offering: for my name shall be great among the hea-

that the ordinances of Christ may be purely dispensed, and made effectual to the converting of those that are yet in their sins, and the confirming, comforting, and building up of those that are already converted:ʷ that Christ would rule in our hearts here,ˣ and hasten the time of his second coming, and our reigning with him forever:ʸ

then, saith the Lord of hosts. **Zeph. 3:9.** For then will I turn to the people a pure language, that they may all call upon the name of the Lord, to serve him with one consent.
    u. **1 Tim. 2:1–2.** I exhort therefore, that, first of all, supplications, prayers, intercessions, and giving of thanks, be made for all men; for kings, and for all that are in authority; that we may lead a quiet and peaceable life in all godliness and honesty. **Isa. 49:23.** And kings shall be thy nursing fathers, and their queens thy nursing mothers: they shall bow down to thee with their face toward the earth, and lick up the dust of thy feet; and thou shalt know that I am the Lord: for they shall not be ashamed that wait for me.
    w. **Acts 4:29–30.** And now, Lord, behold their threatenings: and grant unto thy servants, that with all boldness they may speak thy word, by stretching forth thine hand to heal; and that signs and wonders may be done by the name of thy holy child Jesus. **Eph. 6:18–20.** … praying always with all prayer and supplication in the Spirit, and watching thereunto with all perseverance and supplication for all saints; and for me, that utterance may be given unto me, that I may open my mouth boldly, to make known the mystery of the gospel, for which I am an ambassador in bonds: that therein I may speak boldly, as I ought to speak. **Rom. 15:29–30, 32.** And I am sure that, when I come unto you, I shall come in the fulness of the blessing of the gospel of Christ. Now I beseech you, brethren, for the Lord Jesus Christ's sake, and for the love of the Spirit, that ye strive together with me in your prayers to God for me…. that I may come unto you with joy by the will of God, and may with you be refreshed. **2 Thess. 1:11.** Wherefore also we pray always for you, that our God would count you worthy of this calling, and fulfil all the good pleasure of his goodness, and the work of faith with power. **2 Thess. 2:16–17.** Now our Lord Jesus Christ himself, and God, even our Father, which hath loved us, and hath given us everlasting consolation and good hope through grace, comfort your hearts, and stablish you in every good word and work.
    x. **Eph. 3:14–20.** For this cause I bow my knees unto the Father of our Lord Jesus Christ, of whom the whole family in heaven and earth is named, that he would grant you, according to the riches of his glory, to be strengthened with might by his Spirit in the inner man; that Christ may dwell in your hearts by faith; that ye, being rooted and grounded in love, may be able to comprehend with all saints what is the breadth, and length, and depth, and height; and to know the love of Christ, which passeth knowledge, that ye might be filled with all the fulness of God. Now unto him that is able to do exceeding abundantly above all that we ask or think, according to the power that worketh in us … **Col. 3:15.** And let the peace of God rule in your hearts, to the which also ye are called in one body; and be ye thankful.
    y. **Rev. 22:20.** He which testifieth these things saith, Surely I come quickly. Amen. Even so, come, Lord Jesus. **2 Tim. 2:12.** If we suffer, we shall also reign with him: if we deny him, he also will deny us. **2 Pet. 3:12.** … looking for and hasting unto the coming of the day of God, wherein the heavens being on fire shall be dissolved, and

and that he would be pleased so to exercise the kingdom of his power in all the world, as may best conduce to these ends.ᶻ

Q. 192. *What do we pray for in the third petition?*
A. In the third petition, (which is, *Thy will be done in earth, as it is in heaven,*ᵃ) acknowledging, that by nature we and all men are not only utterly unable and unwilling to know and do the will of God,ᵇ but prone to rebel against his Word,ᶜ to repine and murmur against his providence,ᵈ and wholly inclined to do the will of the flesh, and of the devil:ᵉ we pray, that God would by his Spirit take away from ourselves and others all blindness,ᶠ weakness,ᵍ indisposedness,ʰ and

the elements shall melt with fervent heat?

z. **Isa. 64:1–2.** Oh that thou wouldest rend the heavens, that thou wouldest come down, that the mountains might flow down at thy presence, as when the melting fire burneth, the fire causeth the waters to boil, to make thy name known to thine adversaries, that the nations may tremble at thy presence! **Rev. 4:8–11.** And the four beasts had each of them six wings about him; and they were full of eyes within: and they rest not day and night, saying, Holy, holy, holy, Lord God Almighty, which was, and is, and is to come. And when those beasts give glory and honour and thanks to him that sat on the throne, who liveth for ever and ever, the four and twenty elders fall down before him that sat on the throne, and worship him that liveth for ever and ever, and cast their crowns before the throne, saying, Thou art worthy, O Lord, to receive glory and honour and power: for thou hast created all things, and for thy pleasure they are and were created.

a. **Matt. 6:10. Cf. Luke 11:2.** ... Thy will be done, as in heaven, so in earth.

b. **Rom. 7:18.** For I know that in me (that is, in my flesh,) dwelleth no good thing: for to will is present with me; but how to perform that which is good I find not. **Job 21:14.** Therefore they say unto God, Depart from us; for we desire not the knowledge of thy ways. **1 Cor. 2:14.** But the natural man receiveth not the things of the Spirit of God: for they are foolishness unto him: neither can he know them, because they are spiritually discerned.

c. **Rom. 8:7.** Because the carnal mind is enmity against God: for it is not subject to the law of God, neither indeed can be.

d. **Ex. 17:7.** And he called the name of the place Massah, and Meribah, because of the chiding of the children of Israel, and because they tempted the Lᴏʀᴅ, saying, Is the Lᴏʀᴅ among us, or not? **Num. 14:2.** And all the children of Israel murmured against Moses and against Aaron: and the whole congregation said unto them, Would God that we had died in the land of Egypt! or would God we had died in this wilderness!

e. **Eph. 2:2.** ... wherein in time past ye walked according to the course of this world, according to the prince of the power of the air, the spirit that now worketh in the children of disobedience.

f. **Eph. 1:17–18.** ... that the God of our Lord Jesus Christ, the Father of glory, may give unto you the spirit of wisdom and revelation in the knowledge of him: the eyes of your understanding being enlightened; that ye may know what is the hope of

perverseness of heart;[i] and by his grace make us able and willing to know, do, and submit to his will in all things,[k] with the like humility,[l] cheerfulness,[m] faithfulness,[n] diligence,[o] zeal,[p] sincerity,[q] and constancy,[r] as the angels do in heaven.[s]

his calling, and what the riches of the glory of his inheritance in the saints.

g. **Eph. 3:16.** … that he would grant you, according to the riches of his glory, to be strengthened with might by his Spirit in the inner man.

h. **Matt. 26:40–41.** And he cometh unto the disciples, and findeth them asleep, and saith unto Peter, What, could ye not watch with me one hour? Watch and pray, that ye enter not into temptation: the spirit indeed is willing, but the flesh is weak.

i. **Jer. 31:18–19.** I have surely heard Ephraim bemoaning himself thus; Thou hast chastised me, and I was chastised, as a bullock unaccustomed to the yoke: turn thou me, and I shall be turned; for thou art the LORD my God. Surely after that I was turned, I repented; and after that I was instructed, I smote upon my thigh: I was ashamed, yea, even confounded, because I did bear the reproach of my youth.

k. **Ps. 19:14.** Let the words of my mouth, and the meditation of my heart, be acceptable in thy sight, O LORD, my strength, and my redeemer. **Acts 21:14.** And when he would not be persuaded, we ceased, saying, The will of the Lord be done. **See Ps. 119; 1 Thess. 5:23; Heb. 13:20–21.**

l. **Mic. 6:8.** He hath shewed thee, O man, what is good; and what doth the LORD require of thee, but to do justly, and to love mercy, and to walk humbly with thy God?

m. **Ps. 100:2.** Serve the LORD with gladness: come before his presence with singing. **Job 1:21.** And said, Naked came I out of my mother's womb, and naked shall I return thither: the LORD gave, and the LORD hath taken away; blessed be the name of the LORD. **2 Sam. 15:25–26.** And the king said unto Zadok, Carry back the ark of God into the city: if I shall find favour in the eyes of the LORD, he will bring me again, and shew me both it, and his habitation: but if he thus say, I have no delight in thee; behold, here am I, let him do to me as seemeth good unto him.

n. **Isa. 38:3.** And said, Remember now, O LORD, I beseech thee, how I have walked before thee in truth and with a perfect heart, and have done that which is good in thy sight. And Hezekiah wept sore.

o. **Ps. 119:4–5.** Thou hast commanded us to keep thy precepts diligently. O that my ways were directed to keep thy statutes!

p. **Ps. 69:9.** For the zeal of thine house hath eaten me up; and the reproaches of them that reproached thee are fallen upon me. **John 2:17.** And his disciples remembered that it was written, The zeal of thine house hath eaten me up. **Rom. 12:11.** [Be] not slothful in business; fervent in spirit; serving the Lord.

q. **Josh. 24:14.** Now therefore fear the LORD, and serve him in sincerity and in truth: and put away the gods which your fathers served on the other side of the flood, and in Egypt; and serve ye the LORD. **Ps. 119:80.** Let my heart be sound in thy statutes; that I be not ashamed. **1 Cor. 5:8.** Therefore let us keep the feast, not with old leaven, neither with the leaven of malice and wickedness; but with the unleavened bread of sincerity and truth. **See 2 Cor. 1:12.**

r. **Ps. 119:112.** I have inclined mine heart to perform thy statutes alway, even unto the end.

s. **Isa. 6:2–3.** Above it stood the seraphims: each one had six wings; with twain

Q. 193. *What do we pray for in the fourth petition?*

A. In the fourth petition, (which is, *Give us this day our daily bread,*[t]) acknowledging, that in Adam, and by our own sin, we have forfeited our right to all the outward blessings of this life, and deserve to be wholly deprived of them by God, and to have them cursed to us in the use of them;[u] and that neither they of themselves are able to sustain us,[w] nor we to merit,[x] or by our own industry to procure them;[y] but prone to desire,[z] get,[a] and use them unlawfully:[b] we pray for

he covered his face, and with twain he covered his feet, and with twain he did fly. And one cried unto another, and said, Holy, holy, holy, is the LORD of hosts: the whole earth is full of his glory. **Ps. 103:20–21.** Bless the LORD, ye his angels, that excel in strength, that do his commandments, hearkening unto the voice of his word. Bless ye the LORD, all ye his hosts; ye ministers of his, that do his pleasure. **Matt. 18:10.** Take heed that ye despise not one of these little ones; for I say unto you, That in heaven their angels do always behold the face of my Father which is in heaven.

t. **Matt. 6:11. Cf. Luke 11:3.** Give us day by day our daily bread.

u. **Gen. 2:17.** But of the tree of the knowledge of good and evil, thou shalt not eat of it: for in the day that thou eatest thereof thou shalt surely die. **Gen. 3:17.** And unto Adam he said, Because thou hast hearkened unto the voice of thy wife, and hast eaten of the tree, of which I commanded thee, saying, Thou shalt not eat of it: cursed is the ground for thy sake; in sorrow shalt thou eat of it all the days of thy life. **Rom. 8:20–22.** For the creature was made subject to vanity, not willingly, but by reason of him who hath subjected the same in hope, because the creature itself also shall be delivered from the bondage of corruption into the glorious liberty of the children of God. For we know that the whole creation groaneth and travaileth in pain together until now. **Jer. 5:25.** Your iniquities have turned away these things, and your sins have withholden good things from you. **Deut. 28:15–68.** But it shall come to pass, if thou wilt not hearken unto the voice of the LORD thy God, to observe to do all his commandments and his statutes which I command thee this day; that all these curses shall come upon thee, and overtake thee: Cursed shalt thou be in the city, and cursed shalt thou be in the field. Cursed shall be thy basket and thy store....

w. **Deut. 8:3.** And he humbled thee, and suffered thee to hunger, and fed thee with manna, which thou knewest not, neither did thy fathers know; that he might make thee know that man doth not live by bread only, but by every word that proceedeth out of the mouth of the LORD doth man live.

x. **Gen. 32:10.** I am not worthy of the least of all the mercies, and of all the truth, which thou hast shewed unto thy servant; for with my staff I passed over this Jordan; and now I am become two bands.

y. **Deut. 8:17–18.** ... and thou say in thine heart, My power and the might of mine hand hath gotten me this wealth. But thou shalt remember the LORD thy God: for it is he that giveth thee power to get wealth, that he may establish his covenant which he sware unto thy fathers, as it is this day.

z. **Jer. 6:13.** For from the least of them even unto the greatest of them every one is given to covetousness; and from the prophet even unto the priest every one dealeth falsely. **Mark 7:21–22.** For from within, out of the heart of men, proceed evil thoughts,

ourselves and others, that both they and we, waiting upon the providence of God from day to day in the use of lawful means, may, of his free gift, and as to his fatherly wisdom shall seem best, enjoy a competent portion of them;^c and have the same continued and blessed unto us in our holy and comfortable use of them,^d and contentment in them;^e and be kept from all things that are contrary to our temporal support and comfort.^f

Q. 194. *What do we pray for in the fifth petition?*

A. In the fifth petition, (which is, *Forgive us our debts, as we forgive our debtors,*^g) acknowledging, that we and all others are guilty both of original and actual sin, and thereby become debtors to the justice of God;

adulteries, fornications, murders, thefts, covetousness, wickedness, deceit, lasciviousness, an evil eye, blasphemy, pride, foolishness.

a. **Hos. 12:7.** He is a merchant, the balances of deceit are in his hand: he loveth to oppress.

b. **James 4:3.** Ye ask, and receive not, because ye ask amiss, that ye may consume it upon your lusts.

c. **Gen. 43:12–14.** And take double money in your hand; and the money that was brought again in the mouth of your sacks, carry it again in your hand; peradventure it was an oversight: take also your brother, and arise, go again unto the man: and God Almighty give you mercy before the man, that he may send away your other brother, and Benjamin. If I be bereaved of my children, I am bereaved. **Gen. 28:20.** And Jacob vowed a vow, saying, If God will be with me, and will keep me in this way that I go, and will give me bread to eat, and raiment to put on … **Eph. 4:28.** Let him that stole steal no more: but rather let him labour, working with his hands the thing which is good, that he may have to give to him that needeth. **2 Thess. 3:11–12.** For we hear that there are some which walk among you disorderly, working not at all, but are busybodies. Now them that are such we command and exhort by our Lord Jesus Christ, that with quietness they work, and eat their own bread. **Phil. 4:6.** Be careful for nothing; but in every thing by prayer and supplication with thanksgiving let your requests be made known unto God.

d. **1 Tim. 4:3–5.** … forbidding to marry, and commanding to abstain from meats, which God hath created to be received with thanksgiving of them which believe and know the truth. For every creature of God is good, and nothing to be refused, if it be received with thanksgiving: for it is sanctified by the word of God and prayer.

e. **1 Tim. 6:6–8.** But godliness with contentment is great gain. For we brought nothing into this world, and it is certain we can carry nothing out. And having food and raiment let us be therewith content.

f. **Prov. 30:8–9.** Remove far from me vanity and lies: give me neither poverty nor riches; feed me with food convenient for me: lest I be full, and deny thee, and say, Who is the Lord? or lest I be poor, and steal, and take the name of my God in vain.

g. **Matt. 6:12. Cf. Luke 11:4.** And forgive us our sins; for we also forgive every one that is indebted to us.…

and that neither we, nor any other creature, can make the least satisfaction for that debt:[h] we pray for ourselves and others, that God of
his free grace would, through the obedience and satisfaction of Christ,
apprehended and applied by faith, acquit us both from the guilt and
punishment of sin,[i] accept us in his Beloved;[k] continue his favor and
grace to us,[l] pardon our daily failings,[m] and fill us with peace and joy,
in giving us daily more and more assurance of forgiveness;[n] which
we are the rather emboldened to ask, and encouraged to expect, when

h. **Rom. 3:9–22.** What then? are we better than they? No, in no wise: for we
have before proved both Jews and Gentiles, that they are all under sin; as it is written,
There is none righteous, no, not one: there is none that understandeth, there is none
that seeketh after God. They are all gone out of the way, they are together become
unprofitable; there is none that doeth good, no, not one.… Now we know that what
things soever the law saith, it saith to them who are under the law: that every mouth
may be stopped, and all the world may become guilty before God.… **Matt. 18:24–
25.** And when he had begun to reckon, one was brought unto him, which owed him
ten thousand talents. But forasmuch as he had not to pay, his lord commanded him to
be sold, and his wife, and children, and all that he had, and payment to be made. **Ps.
130:3–4.** If thou, LORD, shouldest mark iniquities, O Lord, who shall stand? But
there is forgiveness with thee, that thou mayest be feared.

i. **Rom. 3:24–26.** … being justified freely by his grace through the redemption
that is in Christ Jesus: whom God hath set forth to be a propitiation through faith in his
blood, to declare his righteousness for the remission of sins that are past, through the
forbearance of God; to declare, I say, at this time his righteousness: that he might be
just, and the justifier of him which believeth in Jesus. **Heb. 9:22.** And almost all
things are by the law purged with blood; and without shedding of blood is no remission.

k. **Eph. 1:6–7.** … to the praise of the glory of his grace, wherein he hath made
us accepted in the beloved. In whom we have redemption through his blood, the forgiveness of sins, according to the riches of his grace.

l. **2 Pet. 1:2.** Grace and peace be multiplied unto you through the knowledge of
God, and of Jesus our Lord.

m. **Hos. 14:2.** Take with you words, and turn to the LORD: say unto him, Take
away all iniquity, and receive us graciously: so will we render the calves of our lips.
Jer. 14:7. O LORD, though our iniquities testify against us, do thou it for thy name's
sake: for our backslidings are many; we have sinned against thee. **1 John 1:9.** If we
confess our sins, he is faithful and just to forgive us our sins, and to cleanse us from all
unrighteousness. **See Dan. 9:17–19.**

n. **Rom. 15:13.** Now the God of hope fill you with all joy and peace in believing,
that ye may abound in hope, through the power of the Holy Ghost. **Ps. 51:7–10, 12.**
Purge me with hyssop, and I shall be clean: wash me, and I shall be whiter than snow.
Make me to hear joy and gladness; that the bones which thou hast broken may rejoice.
Hide thy face from my sins, and blot out all mine iniquities. Create in me a clean heart,
O God; and renew a right spirit within me.… Restore unto me the joy of thy salvation;
and uphold me with thy free spirit.

we have this testimony in ourselves, that we from the heart forgive others their offenses.[o]

Q. 195. *What do we pray for in the sixth petition?*

A. In the sixth petition, (which is, *And lead us not into temptation, but deliver us from evil,*[p]) acknowledging, that the most wise, righteous, and gracious God, for divers holy and just ends, may so order things, that we may be assaulted, foiled, and for a time led captive by temptations;[q] that Satan,[r] the world,[s] and the flesh, are ready powerfully to draw us aside, and ensnare us;[t] and that we, even after the pardon of our sins, by reason of our corruption,[u] weakness, and want of watchfulness,[w] are not only subject to be tempted, and forward to expose ourselves unto temptations,[x] but also of ourselves unable and unwilling to

o. **Luke 11:4.** And forgive us our sins; for we also forgive every one that is indebted to us.... **Matt. 6:14–15.** For if ye forgive men their trespasses, your heavenly Father will also forgive you: but if ye forgive not men their trespasses, neither will your Father forgive your trespasses. **Eph. 4:32.** And be ye kind one to another, tenderhearted, forgiving one another, even as God for Christ's sake hath forgiven you. **Col. 3:13.** ... forbearing one another, and forgiving one another, if any man have a quarrel against any: even as Christ forgave you, so also do ye. **See Matt. 18:21–35.**

p. **Matt. 6:13. Cf. Luke 11:4.** ... And lead us not into temptation; but deliver us from evil.

q. **2 Chron. 32:31.** Howbeit in the business of the ambassadors of the princes of Babylon, who sent unto him to inquire of the wonder that was done in the land, God left him, to try him, that he might know all that was in his heart.

r. **1 Chron. 21:1.** And Satan stood up against Israel, and provoked David to number Israel.

s. **Luke 21:34.** And take heed to yourselves, lest at any time your hearts be overcharged with surfeiting, and drunkenness, and cares of this life, and so that day come upon you unawares. **Mark 4:19.** And the cares of this world, and the deceitfulness of riches, and the lusts of other things entering in, choke the word, and it becometh unfruitful.

t. **James 1:14.** But every man is tempted, when he is drawn away of his own lust, and enticed.

u. **Gal. 5:17.** For the flesh lusteth against the Spirit, and the Spirit against the flesh: and these are contrary the one to the other: so that ye cannot do the things that ye would.

w. **Matt. 26:41.** Watch and pray, that ye enter not into temptation: the spirit indeed is willing, but the flesh is weak.

x. **Matt. 26:69–72.** Now Peter sat without in the palace: and a damsel came unto him, saying, Thou also wast with Jesus of Galilee. But he denied before them all, saying, I know not what thou sayest. And when he was gone out into the porch, another maid saw him, and said unto them that were there, This fellow was also with Jesus of Nazareth. And again he denied with an oath, I do not know the man.

resist them, to recover out of them, and to improve them;[y] and worthy to be left under the power of them:[z] we pray, that God would so overrule the world and all in it,[a] subdue the flesh,[b] and restrain Satan,[c]

Gal. 2:11–14. But when Peter was come to Antioch, I withstood him to the face, because he was to be blamed. For before that certain came from James, he did eat with the Gentiles: but when they were come, he withdrew and separated himself, fearing them which were of the circumcision. And the other Jews dissembled likewise with him; insomuch that Barnabas also was carried away with their dissimulation. But when I saw that they walked not uprightly according to the truth of the gospel, I said unto Peter before them all, If thou, being a Jew, livest after the manner of Gentiles, and not as do the Jews, why compellest thou the Gentiles to live as do the Jews? **2 Chron. 18:3.** And Ahab king of Israel said unto Jehoshaphat king of Judah, Wilt thou go with me to Ramothgilead? And he answered him, I am as thou art, and my people as thy people; and we will be with thee in the war. **2 Chron. 19:2.** And Jehu the son of Hanani the seer went out to meet him, and said to king Jehoshaphat, Shouldest thou help the ungodly, and love them that hate the LORD? therefore is wrath upon thee from before the LORD.

y. **Rom. 7:23–24.** But I see another law in my members, warring against the law of my mind, and bringing me into captivity to the law of sin which is in my members. O wretched man that I am! who shall deliver me from the body of this death? **1 Chron. 21:1–4.** And Satan stood up against Israel, and provoked David to number Israel. And David said to Joab and to the rulers of the people, Go, number Israel from Beersheba even to Dan; and bring the number of them to me, that I may know it. And Joab answered, The LORD make his people an hundred times so many more as they be: but, my lord the king, are they not all my lord's servants? why then doth my lord require this thing? why will he be a cause of trespass to Israel? Nevertheless the king's word prevailed against Joab. Wherefore Joab departed, and went throughout all Israel, and came to Jerusalem. **2 Chron. 16:7–10.** And at that time Hanani the seer came to Asa king of Judah, and said unto him, Because thou hast relied on the king of Syria, and not relied on the LORD thy God, therefore is the host of the king of Syria escaped out of thine hand. Were not the Ethiopians and the Lubims a huge host, with very many chariots and horsemen? yet, because thou didst rely on the LORD, he delivered them into thine hand. For the eyes of the LORD run to and fro throughout the whole earth, to shew himself strong in the behalf of them whose heart is perfect toward him. Herein thou hast done foolishly: therefore from henceforth thou shalt have wars. Then Asa was wroth with the seer, and put him in a prison house; for he was in a rage with him because of this thing. And Asa oppressed some of the people the same time.

z. **Ps. 81:11–12.** But my people would not hearken to my voice; and Israel would none of me. So I gave them up unto their own hearts' lust: and they walked in their own counsels.

a. **John 17:15.** I pray not that thou shouldest take them out of the world, but that thou shouldest keep them from the evil.

b. **Ps. 51:10.** Create in me a clean heart, O God; and renew a right spirit within me. **Ps. 119:133.** Order my steps in thy word: and let not any iniquity have dominion over me.

order all things,[d] bestow and bless all means of grace,[e] and quicken us to watchfulness in the use of them, that we and all his people may by his providence be kept from being tempted to sin;[f] or, if tempted, that by his Spirit we may be powerfully supported and enabled to stand in the hour of temptation;[g] or when fallen, raised again and recovered out of it,[h] and have a sanctified use and improvement thereof:[i] that our sanctification and salvation may be perfected,[k]

c. **2 Cor. 12:7–8.** And lest I should be exalted above measure through the abundance of the revelations, there was given to me a thorn in the flesh, the messenger of Satan to buffet me, lest I should be exalted above measure. For this thing I besought the Lord thrice, that it might depart from me.

d. **1 Cor. 10:12–13.** Wherefore let him that thinketh he standeth take heed lest he fall. There hath no temptation taken you but such as is common to man: but God is faithful, who will not suffer you to be tempted above that ye are able; but will with the temptation also make a way to escape, that ye may be able to bear it.

e. **Heb. 13:20–21.** Now the God of peace, that brought again from the dead our Lord Jesus, that great shepherd of the sheep, through the blood of the everlasting covenant, make you perfect in every good work to do his will, working in you that which is wellpleasing in his sight, through Jesus Christ; to whom be glory for ever and ever. Amen.

f. **Matt. 26:41.** Watch and pray, that ye enter not into temptation: the spirit indeed is willing, but the flesh is weak. **Ps. 19:13.** Keep back thy servant also from presumptuous sins; let them not have dominion over me: then shall I be upright, and I shall be innocent from the great transgression.

g. **Eph. 3:14–17.** For this cause I bow my knees unto the Father of our Lord Jesus Christ, of whom the whole family in heaven and earth is named, that he would grant you, according to the riches of his glory, to be strengthened with might by his Spirit in the inner man; that Christ may dwell in your hearts by faith; that ye, being rooted and grounded in love … **1 Thess. 3:13.** … to the end he may stablish your hearts unblameable in holiness before God, even our Father, at the coming of our Lord Jesus Christ with all his saints. **Jude 24.** Now unto him that is able to keep you from falling, and to present you faultless before the presence of his glory with exceeding joy …

h. **Ps. 51:12.** Restore unto me the joy of thy salvation; and uphold me with thy free spirit.

i. **1 Pet. 5:8–10.** Be sober, be vigilant; because your adversary the devil, as a roaring lion, walketh about, seeking whom he may devour: whom resist stedfast in the faith, knowing that the same afflictions are accomplished in your brethren that are in the world. But the God of all grace, who hath called us unto his eternal glory by Christ Jesus, after that ye have suffered a while, make you perfect, stablish, strengthen, settle you.

k. **2 Cor. 13:7, 9.** Now I pray to God that ye do no evil; not that we should appear approved, but that ye should do that which is honest, though we be as reprobates.… For we are glad, when we are weak, and ye are strong: and this also we wish, even your perfection.

Satan trodden under our feet,[l] and we fully freed from sin, temptation, and all evil, forever.[m]

Q 196. *What doth the conclusion of the Lord's Prayer teach us?*

A. The conclusion of the Lord's Prayer, (which is, *For thine is the kingdom, and the power, and the glory, for ever. Amen.*[n]) teacheth us to enforce our petitions with arguments,[o] which are to be taken, not from any worthiness in ourselves, or in any other creature, but from God;[p] and with our prayers to join praises,[q] ascribing to God alone eternal sovereignty, omnipotency, and glorious excellency;[r] in regard whereof,

l. **Rom. 16:20.** And the God of peace shall bruise Satan under your feet shortly. The grace of our Lord Jesus Christ be with you. Amen. **Luke 22:31–32.** And the Lord said, Simon, Simon, behold, Satan hath desired to have you, that he may sift you as wheat: but I have prayed for thee, that thy faith fail not: and when thou art converted, strengthen thy brethren.

m. **John 17:15.** I pray not that thou shouldest take them out of the world, but that thou shouldest keep them from the evil. **1 Thess. 5:23.** And the very God of peace sanctify you wholly; and I pray God your whole spirit and soul and body be preserved blameless unto the coming of our Lord Jesus Christ.

n. **Matt. 6:13.** ... For thine is the kingdom, and the power, and the glory, for ever. Amen [*found in some, but not all, Greek manuscripts*].

o. **Rom. 15:30.** Now I beseech you, brethren, for the Lord Jesus Christ's sake, and for the love of the Spirit, that ye strive together with me in your prayers to God for me.

p. **Dan. 9:4, 7–9, 16–19.** And I prayed unto the LORD my God, and made my confession, and said, O Lord, the great and dreadful God, keeping the covenant and mercy to them that love him, and to them that keep his commandments.... O Lord, righteousness belongeth unto thee, but unto us confusion of faces, as at this day.... O Lord, to us belongeth confusion of face, to our kings, to our princes, and to our fathers, because we have sinned against thee. To the Lord our God belong mercies and forgivenesses, though we have rebelled against him.... O Lord, according to all thy righteousness, I beseech thee, let thine anger and thy fury be turned away from thy city Jerusalem.... Now therefore, O our God, hear the prayer of thy servant, and his supplications, and cause thy face to shine upon thy sanctuary that is desolate, for the Lord's sake. O my God, incline thine ear, and hear; open thine eyes, and behold our desolations, and the city which is called by thy name: for we do not present our supplications before thee for our righteousnesses, but for thy great mercies. O Lord, hear; O Lord, forgive; O Lord, hearken and do; defer not, for thine own sake, O my God: for thy city and thy people are called by thy name.

q. **Phil. 4:6.** Be careful for nothing; but in every thing by prayer and supplication with thanksgiving let your requests be made known unto God.

r. **1 Chron. 29:10–13.** Wherefore David blessed the LORD before all the congregation: and David said, Blessed be thou, LORD God of Israel our father, for ever and ever. Thine, O LORD, is the greatness, and the power, and the glory, and the victory, and the majesty: for all that is in the heaven and in the earth is thine; thine is the

as he is able and willing to help us,[s] so we by faith are emboldened to plead with him that he would,[t] and quietly to rely upon him, that he will fulfill our requests.[u] And, to testify this our desire and assurance, we say, *Amen*.[w]

kingdom, O LORD, and thou art exalted as head above all. Both riches and honour come of thee, and thou reignest over all; and in thine hand is power and might; and in thine hand it is to make great, and to give strength unto all. Now therefore, our God, we thank thee, and praise thy glorious name. **1 Tim. 1:17.** Now unto the King eternal, immortal, invisible, the only wise God, be honour and glory for ever and ever. Amen. **Rev. 5:11–13.** And I beheld, and I heard the voice of many angels round about the throne and the beasts and the elders: and the number of them was ten thousand times ten thousand, and thousands of thousands; saying with a loud voice, Worthy is the Lamb that was slain to receive power, and riches, and wisdom, and strength, and honour, and glory, and blessing. And every creature which is in heaven, and on the earth, and under the earth, and such as are in the sea, and all that are in them, heard I saying, Blessing, and honour, and glory, and power, be unto him that sitteth upon the throne, and unto the Lamb for ever and ever.

s. **Eph. 3:20–21.** Now unto him that is able to do exceeding abundantly above all that we ask or think, according to the power that worketh in us, unto him be glory in the church by Christ Jesus throughout all ages, world without end. Amen. **Luke 11:13.** If ye then, being evil, know how to give good gifts unto your children: how much more shall your heavenly Father give the Holy Spirit to them that ask him?

t. **2 Chron. 20:6, 11.** And [Jehoshaphat] said, O LORD God of our fathers, art not thou God in heaven? and rulest not thou over all the kingdoms of the heathen? and in thine hand is there not power and might, so that none is able to withstand thee?… Behold, I say, how they reward us, to come to cast us out of thy possession, which thou hast given us to inherit.

u. **2 Chron. 14:11.** And Asa cried unto the LORD his God, and said, LORD, it is nothing with thee to help, whether with many, or with them that have no power: help us, O LORD our God; for we rest on thee, and in thy name we go against this multitude. O LORD, thou art our God; let not man prevail against thee.

w. **1 Cor. 14:16.** Else when thou shalt bless with the spirit, how shall he that occupieth the room of the unlearned say Amen at thy giving of thanks, seeing he understandeth not what thou sayest? **Rev. 22:20–21.** He which testifieth these things saith, Surely I come quickly. Amen. Even so, come, Lord Jesus. The grace of our Lord Jesus Christ be with you all. Amen.

THE

SHORTER CATECHISM

Q. 1. *What is the chief end of man?*
A. Man's chief end is to glorify God,[a] and to enjoy him forever.[b]

   a. **Ps. 86:9.** All nations whom thou hast made shall come and worship before thee, O Lord; and shall glorify thy name. **Isa. 60:21.** Thy people also shall be all righteous: they shall inherit the land for ever, the branch of my planting, the work of my hands, that I may be glorified. **Rom. 11:36.** For of him, and through him, and to him, are all things: to whom be glory for ever. Amen. **1 Cor. 6:20.** For ye are bought with a price: therefore glorify God in your body, and in your spirit, which are God's. **1 Cor. 10:31.** Whether therefore ye eat, or drink, or whatsoever ye do, do all to the glory of God. **Rev. 4:11.** Thou art worthy, O Lord, to receive glory and honour and power: for thou hast created all things, and for thy pleasure they are and were created.

   b. **Ps. 16:5–11.** The LORD is the portion of mine inheritance and of my cup: thou maintainest my lot. The lines are fallen unto me in pleasant places; yea, I have a goodly heritage. I will bless the LORD, who hath given me counsel: my reins also instruct me in the night seasons. I have set the LORD always before me: because he is at my right hand, I shall not be moved. Therefore my heart is glad, and my glory rejoiceth: my flesh also shall rest in hope. For thou wilt not leave my soul in hell; neither wilt thou suffer thine Holy One to see corruption. Thou wilt shew me the path of life: in thy presence is fulness of joy; at thy right hand there are pleasures for evermore. **Ps. 144:15.** Happy is that people, that is in such a case: yea, happy is that people, whose God is the LORD. **Isa. 12:2.** Behold, God is my salvation; I will trust, and not be afraid: for the LORD JEHOVAH is my strength and my song; he also is become my salvation. **Luke 2:10.** And the angel said unto them, Fear not: for, behold, I bring you good tidings of great joy, which shall be to all people. **Phil. 4:4.** Rejoice in the Lord alway: and again I say, Rejoice. **Rev. 21:3–4.** And I heard a great voice out of heaven saying, Behold, the tabernacle of God is with men, and he will dwell with them, and they shall be his people, and God himself shall be with them, and be their God. And God shall wipe away all tears from their eyes; and there shall be no more death, neither sorrow, nor crying, neither shall there be any more pain: for the former things are passed away.

Q. 2. *What rule hath God given to direct us how we may glorify and enjoy him?*

A. The Word of God, which is contained in the Scriptures of the Old and New Testaments,^c is the only rule to direct us how we may glorify and enjoy him.^d

c. **Matt. 19:4–5.** And he answered and said unto them, Have ye not read, that he which made them at the beginning made them male and female, and said, For this cause shall a man leave father and mother, and shall cleave to his wife: and they twain shall be one flesh? **With Gen. 2:24.** Therefore shall a man leave his father and his mother, and shall cleave unto his wife: and they shall be one flesh. **Luke 24:27, 44.** And beginning at Moses and all the prophets, he expounded unto them in all the scriptures the things concerning himself.... And he said unto them, These are the words which I spake unto you, while I was yet with you, that all things must be fulfilled, which were written in the law of Moses, and in the prophets, and in the psalms, concerning me. **1 Cor. 2:13.** ... which things also we speak, not in the words which man's wisdom teacheth, but which the Holy Ghost teacheth; comparing spiritual things with spiritual. **1 Cor. 14:37.** If any man think himself to be a prophet, or spiritual, let him acknowledge that the things that I write unto you are the commandments of the Lord. **2 Pet. 1:20–21.** ... knowing this first, that no prophecy of the scripture is of any private interpretation. For the prophecy came not in old time by the will of man: but holy men of God spake as they were moved by the Holy Ghost. **2 Pet. 3:2, 15–16.** ... that ye may be mindful of the words which were spoken before by the holy prophets, and of the commandment of us the apostles of the Lord and Saviour.... And account that the longsuffering of our Lord is salvation; even as our beloved brother Paul also according to the wisdom given unto him hath written unto you; as also in all his epistles, speaking in them of these things; in which are some things hard to be understood, which they that are unlearned and unstable wrest, as they do also the other scriptures, unto their own destruction.

d. **Deut. 4:2.** Ye shall not add unto the word which I command you, neither shall ye diminish ought from it, that ye may keep the commandments of the LORD your God which I command you. **Ps. 19:7–11.** The law of the LORD is perfect, converting the soul: the testimony of the LORD is sure, making wise the simple. The statutes of the LORD are right, rejoicing the heart: the commandment of the LORD is pure, enlightening the eyes. The fear of the LORD is clean, enduring for ever: the judgments of the LORD are true and righteous altogether. More to be desired are they than gold, yea, than much fine gold: sweeter also than honey and the honeycomb. Moreover by them is thy servant warned: and in keeping of them there is great reward. **Isa. 8:20.** To the law and to the testimony: if they speak not according to this word, it is because there is no light in them. **John 15:11.** These things have I spoken unto you, that my joy might remain in you, and that your joy might be full. **John 20:30–31.** And many other signs truly did Jesus in the presence of his disciples, which are not written in this book: but these are written, that ye might believe that Jesus is the Christ, the Son of God; and that believing ye might have life through his name. **Acts 17:11.** These were more noble than those in Thessalonica, in that they received the word with all readiness of mind, and searched the scriptures daily, whether those things were so. **2 Tim. 3:15–17.** ... and that from a child thou hast known the holy

Q. 3. *What do the Scriptures principally teach?*

A. The Scriptures principally teach, what man is to believe concerning God,[e] and what duty God requires of man.[f]

Q. 4. *What is God?*

A. God is a Spirit,[g] infinite,[h] eternal,[i] and unchangeable,[k] in his

scriptures, which are able to make thee wise unto salvation through faith which is in Christ Jesus. All scripture is given by inspiration of God, and is profitable for doctrine, for reproof, for correction, for instruction in righteousness: that the man of God may be perfect, thoroughly furnished unto all good works. **1 John 1:4.** And these things write we unto you, that your joy may be full.

e. **Gen. 1:1.** In the beginning God created the heaven and the earth. **John 5:39.** Search the scriptures; for in them ye think ye have eternal life: and they are they which testify of me. **John 20:31.** But these are written, that ye might believe that Jesus is the Christ, the Son of God; and that believing ye might have life through his name. **Rom. 10:17.** So then faith cometh by hearing, and hearing by the word of God. **2 Tim. 3:15.** … and that from a child thou hast known the holy scriptures, which are able to make thee wise unto salvation through faith which is in Christ Jesus.

f. **Deut. 10:12–13.** And now, Israel, what doth the LORD thy God require of thee, but to fear the LORD thy God, to walk in all his ways, and to love him, and to serve the LORD thy God with all thy heart and with all thy soul, to keep the commandments of the LORD, and his statutes, which I command thee this day for thy good? **Josh. 1:8.** This book of the law shall not depart out of thy mouth; but thou shalt meditate therein day and night, that thou mayest observe to do according to all that is written therein: for then thou shalt make thy way prosperous, and then thou shalt have good success. **Ps. 119:105.** Thy word is a lamp unto my feet, and a light unto my path. **Mic. 6:8.** He hath shewed thee, O man, what is good; and what doth the LORD require of thee, but to do justly, and to love mercy, and to walk humbly with thy God? **2 Tim. 3:16–17.** All scripture is given by inspiration of God, and is profitable for doctrine, for reproof, for correction, for instruction in righteousness: that the man of God may be perfect, thoroughly furnished unto all good works.

g. **Deut. 4:15–19.** Take ye therefore good heed unto yourselves; for ye saw no manner of similitude on the day that the LORD spake unto you in Horeb out of the midst of the fire: lest ye corrupt yourselves, and make you a graven image, the similitude of any figure, the likeness of male or female, the likeness of any beast that is on the earth, the likeness of any winged fowl that flieth in the air, the likeness of any thing that creepeth on the ground, the likeness of any fish that is in the waters beneath the earth: and lest thou lift up thine eyes unto heaven, and when thou seest the sun, and the moon, and the stars, even all the host of heaven, shouldest be driven to worship them, and serve them, which the LORD thy God hath divided unto all nations under the whole heaven. **Luke 24:39.** Behold my hands and my feet, that it is I myself: handle me, and see; for a spirit hath not flesh and bones, as ye see me have. **John 1:18.** No man hath seen God at any time; the only begotten Son, which is in the bosom of the Father, he hath declared him. **John 4:24.** God is a Spirit: and they that worship him must worship him in spirit and in truth. **Acts 17:29.** Forasmuch then as we are the offspring of God, we ought not to think that the Godhead is like unto gold,

being,[l] wisdom,[m] power,[n] holiness,[o] justice,[p] goodness,[q] and truth.[r]

or silver, or stone, graven by art and man's device.

h. **1 Kings 8:27.** But will God indeed dwell on the earth? behold, the heaven and heaven of heavens cannot contain thee; how much less this house that I have builded? **Ps. 139:7–10.** Whither shall I go from thy spirit? or whither shall I flee from thy presence? If I ascend up into heaven, thou art there: if I make my bed in hell, behold, thou art there. If I take the wings of the morning, and dwell in the uttermost parts of the sea; even there shall thy hand lead me, and thy right hand shall hold me. **Ps. 145:3.** Great is the LORD, and greatly to be praised; and his greatness is unsearchable. **Ps. 147:5.** Great is our Lord, and of great power: his understanding is infinite. **Jer. 23:24.** Can any hide himself in secret places that I shall not see him? saith the LORD. Do not I fill heaven and earth? saith the LORD. **Rom. 11:33–36.** O the depth of the riches both of the wisdom and knowledge of God! how unsearchable are his judgments, and his ways past finding out! For who hath known the mind of the Lord? or who hath been his counsellor? Or who hath first given to him, and it shall be recompensed unto him again? For of him, and through him, and to him, are all things: to whom be glory for ever. Amen.

i. **Deut. 33:27.** The eternal God is thy refuge, and underneath are the everlasting arms: and he shall thrust out the enemy from before thee; and shall say, Destroy them. **Ps. 90:2.** Before the mountains were brought forth, or ever thou hadst formed the earth and the world, even from everlasting to everlasting, thou art God. **Ps. 102:12, 24–27.** But thou, O LORD, shalt endure for ever; and thy remembrance unto all generations.… I said, O my God, take me not away in the midst of my days: thy years are throughout all generations. Of old hast thou laid the foundation of the earth: and the heavens are the work of thy hands. They shall perish, but thou shalt endure: yea, all of them shall wax old like a garment; as a vesture shalt thou change them, and they shall be changed: but thou art the same, and thy years shall have no end. **Rev. 1:4, 8.** JOHN to the seven churches which are in Asia: Grace be unto you, and peace, from him which is, and which was, and which is to come; and from the seven Spirits which are before his throne.… I am Alpha and Omega, the beginning and the ending, saith the Lord, which is, and which was, and which is to come, the Almighty.

k. **Ps. 33:11.** The counsel of the LORD standeth for ever, the thoughts of his heart to all generations. **Mal. 3:6.** For I am the LORD, I change not; therefore ye sons of Jacob are not consumed. **Heb. 1:12.** And as a vesture shalt thou fold them up, and they shall be changed: but thou art the same, and thy years shall not fail. **Heb. 6:17–18.** Wherein God, willing more abundantly to shew unto the heirs of promise the immutability of his counsel, confirmed it by an oath: that by two immutable things, in which it was impossible for God to lie, we might have a strong consolation, who have fled for refuge to lay hold upon the hope set before us. **Heb. 13:8.** Jesus Christ the same yesterday, and to day, and for ever. **James 1:17.** Every good gift and every perfect gift is from above, and cometh down from the Father of lights, with whom is no variableness, neither shadow of turning.

l. **Ex. 3:14.** And God said unto Moses, I AM THAT I AM: and he said, Thus shalt thou say unto the children of Israel, I AM hath sent me unto you. **Ps. 115:2–3.** Wherefore should the heathen say, Where is now their God? But our God is in the heavens: he hath done whatsoever he hath pleased. **1 Tim. 1:17.** Now unto the King eternal, immortal, invisible, the only wise God, be honour and glory for ever and ever.

Amen. **1 Tim. 6:15–16.** ... which in his times he shall shew, who is the blessed and only Potentate, the King of kings, and Lord of lords; who only hath immortality, dwelling in the light which no man can approach unto; whom no man hath seen, nor can see: to whom be honour and power everlasting. Amen.

m. **Ps. 104:24.** O Lord, how manifold are thy works! in wisdom hast thou made them all: the earth is full of thy riches. **Rom. 11:33–34.** O the depth of the riches both of the wisdom and knowledge of God! how unsearchable are his judgments, and his ways past finding out! For who hath known the mind of the Lord? or who hath been his counsellor? **Heb. 4:13.** Neither is there any creature that is not manifest in his sight: but all things are naked and opened unto the eyes of him with whom we have to do. **1 John 3:20.** For if our heart condemn us, God is greater than our heart, and knoweth all things.

n. **Gen. 17:1.** And when Abram was ninety years old and nine, the Lord appeared to Abram, and said unto him, I am the Almighty God; walk before me, and be thou perfect. **Ps. 62:11.** God hath spoken once; twice have I heard this; that power belongeth unto God. **Jer. 32:17.** Ah Lord God! behold, thou hast made the heaven and the earth by thy great power and stretched out arm, and there is nothing too hard for thee. **Matt. 19:26.** But Jesus beheld them, and said unto them, With men this is impossible; but with God all things are possible. **Rev. 1:8.** I am Alpha and Omega, the beginning and the ending, saith the Lord, which is, and which was, and which is to come, the Almighty.

o. **Hab. 1:13.** Thou art of purer eyes than to behold evil, and canst not look on iniquity: wherefore lookest thou upon them that deal treacherously, and holdest thy tongue when the wicked devoureth the man that is more righteous than he? **1 Pet. 1:15–16.** But as he which hath called you is holy, so be ye holy in all manner of conversation; because it is written, Be ye holy; for I am holy. **1 John 3:3, 5.** And every man that hath this hope in him purifieth himself, even as he is pure.... And ye know that he was manifested to take away our sins; and in him is no sin. **Rev. 15:4.** Who shall not fear thee, O Lord, and glorify thy name? for thou only art holy: for all nations shall come and worship before thee; for thy judgments are made manifest.

p. **Gen. 18:25.** That be far from thee to do after this manner, to slay the righteous with the wicked: and that the righteous should be as the wicked, that be far from thee: Shall not the Judge of all the earth do right? **Ex. 34:6–7.** And the Lord passed by before him, and proclaimed, The Lord, The Lord God, merciful and gracious, longsuffering, and abundant in goodness and truth, keeping mercy for thousands, forgiving iniquity and transgression and sin, and that will by no means clear the guilty; visiting the iniquity of the fathers upon the children, and upon the children's children, unto the third and to the fourth generation. **Deut. 32:4.** He is the Rock, his work is perfect: for all his ways are judgment: a God of truth and without iniquity, just and right is he. **Ps. 96:13.** ... before the Lord: for he cometh, for he cometh to judge the earth: he shall judge the world with righteousness, and the people with his truth. **Rom. 3:5, 26.** But if our unrighteousness commend the righteousness of God, what shall we say? Is God unrighteous who taketh vengeance? (I speak as a man) ... to declare, I say, at this time his righteousness: that he might be just, and the justifier of him which believeth in Jesus.

q. **Ps. 103:5.** ... who satisfieth thy mouth with good things; so that thy youth is renewed like the eagle's. **Ps. 107:8.** Oh that men would praise the Lord for his goodness, and for his wonderful works to the children of men! **Matt. 19:17.** And he

Q. 5. *Are there more Gods than one?*

A. There is but one only,[s] the living and true God.[t]

Q. 6. *How many persons are there in the Godhead?*

A. There are three persons in the Godhead; the Father, the Son, and the Holy Ghost;[u] and these three are one God, the same in sub-

said unto him, Why callest thou me good? there is none good but one, that is, God: but if thou wilt enter into life, keep the commandments. **Rom. 2:4.** Or despisest thou the riches of his goodness and forbearance and longsuffering; not knowing that the goodness of God leadeth thee to repentance?

r. **Ex. 34:6.** And the LORD passed by before him, and proclaimed, The LORD, The LORD God, merciful and gracious, longsuffering, and abundant in goodness and truth. **Deut. 32:4.** He is the Rock, his work is perfect: for all his ways are judgment: a God of truth and without iniquity, just and right is he. **Ps. 86:15.** But thou, O Lord, art a God full of compassion, and gracious, longsuffering, and plenteous in mercy and truth. **Ps. 117:2.** For his merciful kindness is great toward us: and the truth of the LORD endureth for ever. Praise ye the LORD. **Heb. 6:18.** That by two immutable things, in which it was impossible for God to lie, we might have a strong consolation, who have fled for refuge to lay hold upon the hope set before us.

s. **Deut. 6:4.** Hear, O Israel: The LORD our God is one LORD. **Isa. 44:6.** Thus saith the LORD the King of Israel, and his redeemer the LORD of hosts; I am the first, and I am the last; and beside me there is no God. **Isa. 45:21–22.** Tell ye, and bring them near; yea, let them take counsel together: who hath declared this from ancient time? who hath told it from that time? have not I the LORD? and there is no God else beside me; a just God and a Saviour; there is none beside me. Look unto me, and be ye saved, all the ends of the earth: for I am God, and there is none else. **1 Cor. 8:4–6.** As concerning therefore the eating of those things that are offered in sacrifice unto idols, we know that an idol is nothing in the world, and that there is none other God but one. For though there be that are called gods, whether in heaven or in earth, (as there be gods many, and lords many,) but to us there is but one God, the Father, of whom are all things, and we in him; and one Lord Jesus Christ, by whom are all things, and we by him.

t. **Jer. 10:10.** But the LORD is the true God, he is the living God, and an everlasting king: at his wrath the earth shall tremble, and the nations shall not be able to abide his indignation. **John 17:3.** And this is life eternal, that they might know thee the only true God, and Jesus Christ, whom thou hast sent. **1 Thess. 1:9.** For they themselves shew of us what manner of entering in we had unto you, and how ye turned to God from idols to serve the living and true God. **1 John 5:20.** And we know that the Son of God is come, and hath given us an understanding, that we may know him that is true, and we are in him that is true, even in his Son Jesus Christ. This is the true God, and eternal life.

u. **Matt. 3:16–17.** And Jesus, when he was baptized, went up straightway out of the water: and, lo, the heavens were opened unto him, and he saw the Spirit of God descending like a dove, and lighting upon him: and lo a voice from heaven, saying, This is my beloved Son, in whom I am well pleased. **Matt. 28:19.** Go ye therefore, and teach all nations, baptizing them in the name of the Father, and of the Son, and

stance, equal in power and glory.ʷ

Q. 7. *What are the decrees of God?*
A. The decrees of God are, his eternal purpose, according to the counsel of his will, whereby, for his own glory, he hath foreordained whatsoever comes to pass.ˣ

Q. 8. *How doth God execute his decrees?*
A. God executeth his decrees in the works of creation and providence.ʸ

of the Holy Ghost. **2 Cor. 13:14.** The grace of the Lord Jesus Christ, and the love of God, and the communion of the Holy Ghost, be with you all. Amen. **1 Pet. 1:2.** … elect according to the foreknowledge of God the Father, through sanctification of the Spirit, unto obedience and sprinkling of the blood of Jesus Christ: Grace unto you, and peace, be multiplied.

w. **Ps. 45:6.** Thy throne, O God, is for ever and ever: the sceptre of thy kingdom is a right sceptre. **John 1:1.** In the beginning was the Word, and the Word was with God, and the Word was God. **John 17:5.** And now, O Father, glorify thou me with thine own self with the glory which I had with thee before the world was. **Acts 5:3–4.** But Peter said, Ananias, why hath Satan filled thine heart to lie to the Holy Ghost, and to keep back part of the price of the land? Whiles it remained, was it not thine own? and after it was sold, was it not in thine own power? why hast thou conceived this thing in thine heart? thou hast not lied unto men, but unto God. **Rom. 9:5.** … whose are the fathers, and of whom as concerning the flesh Christ came, who is over all, God blessed for ever. Amen. **Col. 2:9.** For in him dwelleth all the fulness of the Godhead bodily. **Jude 24–25.** Now unto him that is able to keep you from falling, and to present you faultless before the presence of his glory with exceeding joy, to the only wise God our Saviour, be glory and majesty, dominion and power, both now and ever. Amen.

x. **Ps. 33:11.** The counsel of the LORD standeth for ever, the thoughts of his heart to all generations. **Isa. 14:24.** The LORD of hosts hath sworn, saying, Surely as I have thought, so shall it come to pass; and as I have purposed, so shall it stand. **Acts 2:23.** Him, being delivered by the determinate counsel and foreknowledge of God, ye have taken, and by wicked hands have crucified and slain. **Eph. 1:11–12.** … in whom also we have obtained an inheritance, being predestinated according to the purpose of him who worketh all things after the counsel of his own will: that we should be to the praise of his glory, who first trusted in Christ.

y. **Ps. 148:8.** … fire, and hail; snow, and vapours; stormy wind fulfilling his word. **Isa. 40:26.** Lift up your eyes on high, and behold who hath created these things, that bringeth out their host by number: he calleth them all by names by the greatness of his might, for that he is strong in power; not one faileth. **Dan. 4:35.** And all the inhabitants of the earth are reputed as nothing: and he doeth according to his will in the army of heaven, and among the inhabitants of the earth: and none can stay his hand, or say unto him, What doest thou? **Acts 4:24–28.** And when they heard that, they lifted up their voice to God with one accord, and said, Lord, thou art God, which hast made heaven, and earth, and the sea, and all that in them is: who by the mouth of thy servant David hast said, Why did the heathen rage, and the people

Q. 9. *What is the work of creation?*

A. The work of creation is, God's making all things of nothing, by the word of his power,[z] in the space of six days, and all very good.[a]

Q. 10. *How did God create man?*

A. God created man male and female, after his own image,[b] in knowledge,[c] righteousness, and holiness,[d] with dominion over the creatures.[e]

Q. 11. *What are God's works of providence?*

A. God's works of providence are, his most holy,[f] wise,[g] and powerful[h] preserving[i] and governing[k] all his creatures, and all their

imagine vain things? The kings of the earth stood up, and the rulers were gathered together against the Lord, and against his Christ. For of a truth against thy holy child Jesus, whom thou hast anointed, both Herod, and Pontius Pilate, with the Gentiles, and the people of Israel, were gathered together, For to do whatsoever thy hand and thy counsel determined before to be done. **Rev. 4:11.** Thou art worthy, O Lord, to receive glory and honour and power: for thou hast created all things, and for thy pleasure they are and were created.

z. **Gen. 1:1.** In the beginning God created the heaven and the earth. **Ps. 33:6, 9.** By the word of the LORD were the heavens made; and all the host of them by the breath of his mouth.… For he spake, and it was done; he commanded, and it stood fast. **Heb. 11:3.** Through faith we understand that the worlds were framed by the word of God, so that things which are seen were not made of things which do appear.

a. **Gen. 1:31.** And God saw every thing that he had made, and, behold, it was very good. And the evening and the morning were the sixth day.

b. **Gen. 1:27.** So God created man in his own image, in the image of God created he him; male and female created he them.

c. **Col. 3:10.** And [ye] have put on the new man, which is renewed in knowledge after the image of him that created him.

d. **Eph. 4:24.** … and that ye put on the new man, which after God is created in righteousness and true holiness.

e. **Gen. 1:28.** And God blessed them, and God said unto them, Be fruitful, and multiply, and replenish the earth, and subdue it: and have dominion over the fish of the sea, and over the fowl of the air, and over every living thing that moveth upon the earth. **See Ps. 8.**

f. **Ps. 145:17.** The LORD is righteous in all his ways, and holy in all his works.

g. **Ps. 104:24.** O LORD, how manifold are thy works! in wisdom hast thou made them all: the earth is full of thy riches.

h. **Heb. 1:3.** … who being the brightness of his glory, and the express image of his person, and upholding all things by the word of his power, when he had by himself purged our sins, sat down on the right hand of the Majesty on high.

i. **Neh. 9:6.** Thou, even thou, art LORD alone; thou hast made heaven, the heaven of heavens, with all their host, the earth, and all things that are therein, the seas, and all that is therein, and thou preservest them all; and the host of heaven worshippeth thee.

actions.[1]

Q. 12. *What special act of providence did God exercise towards man in the estate wherein he was created?*

A. When God had created man, he entered into a covenant of life with him, upon condition of perfect obedience; forbidding him to eat of the tree of the knowledge of good and evil, upon pain of death.[m]

Q. 13. *Did our first parents continue in the estate wherein they were created?*

A. Our first parents, being left to the freedom of their own will, fell from the estate wherein they were created, by sinning against God.[n]

Q. 14. *What is sin?*

A. Sin is any want of conformity unto, or transgression of, the law of God.[o]

k. **Eph. 1:19–22.** … and what is the exceeding greatness of his power to us-ward who believe, according to the working of his mighty power, which he wrought in Christ, when he raised him from the dead, and set him at his own right hand in the heavenly places, far above all principality, and power, and might, and dominion, and every name that is named, not only in this world, but also in that which is to come: and hath put all things under his feet, and gave him to be the head over all things to the church.

l. **Ps. 36:6.** Thy righteousness is like the great mountains; thy judgments are a great deep: O LORD, thou preservest man and beast. **Prov. 16:33.** The lot is cast into the lap; but the whole disposing thereof is of the LORD. **Matt. 10:30.** But the very hairs of your head are all numbered.

m. **Gen. 2:16–17.** And the LORD God commanded the man, saying, Of every tree of the garden thou mayest freely eat: but of the tree of the knowledge of good and evil, thou shalt not eat of it: for in the day that thou eatest thereof thou shalt surely die. **James 2:10.** For whosoever shall keep the whole law, and yet offend in one point, he is guilty of all.

n. **Gen. 3:6–8, 13.** And when the woman saw that the tree was good for food, and that it was pleasant to the eyes, and a tree to be desired to make one wise, she took of the fruit thereof, and did eat, and gave also unto her husband with her; and he did eat. And the eyes of them both were opened, and they knew that they were naked; and they sewed fig leaves together, and made themselves aprons. And they heard the voice of the LORD God walking in the garden in the cool of the day: and Adam and his wife hid themselves from the presence of the LORD God amongst the trees of the garden.… And the LORD God said unto the woman, What is this that thou hast done? And the woman said, The serpent beguiled me, and I did eat. **2 Cor. 11:3.** But I fear, lest by any means, as the serpent beguiled Eve through his subtilty, so your minds should be corrupted from the simplicity that is in Christ.

o. **Lev. 5:17.** And if a soul sin, and commit any of these things which are

Q. 15. *What was the sin whereby our first parents fell from the estate wherein they were created?*

A. The sin whereby our first parents fell from the estate wherein they were created, was their eating the forbidden fruit.[p]

Q. 16. *Did all mankind fall in Adam's first transgression?*

A. The covenant being made with Adam,[q] not only for himself, but for his posterity; all mankind, descending from him by ordinary generation, sinned in him, and fell with him, in his first transgression.[r]

Q. 17. *Into what estate did the fall bring mankind?*

A. The fall brought mankind into an estate of sin and misery.[s]

forbidden to be done by the commandments of the LORD; though he wist it not, yet is he guilty, and shall bear his iniquity. **James 4:17.** Therefore to him that knoweth to do good, and doeth it not, to him it is sin. **1 John 3:4.** Whosoever committeth sin transgresseth also the law: for sin is the transgression of the law.

p. **Gen. 3:6.** And when the woman saw that the tree was good for food, and that it was pleasant to the eyes, and a tree to be desired to make one wise, she took of the fruit thereof, and did eat, and gave also unto her husband with her; and he did eat.

q. **Gen. 2:16–17.** And the LORD God commanded the man, saying, Of every tree of the garden thou mayest freely eat: but of the tree of the knowledge of good and evil, thou shalt not eat of it: for in the day that thou eatest thereof thou shalt surely die. **James 2:10.** For whosoever shall keep the whole law, and yet offend in one point, he is guilty of all.

r. **Rom. 5:12–21.** Wherefore, as by one man sin entered into the world, and death by sin; and so death passed upon all men, for that all have sinned: (For until the law sin was in the world: but sin is not imputed when there is no law. Nevertheless death reigned from Adam to Moses, even over them that had not sinned after the similitude of Adam's transgression, who is the figure of him that was to come. But not as the offence, so also is the free gift. For if through the offence of one many be dead, much more the grace of God, and the gift by grace, which is by one man, Jesus Christ, hath abounded unto many. And not as it was by one that sinned, so is the gift: for the judgment was by one to condemnation, but the free gift is of many offences unto justification. For if by one man's offence death reigned by one; much more they which receive abundance of grace and of the gift of righteousness shall reign in life by one, Jesus Christ.) Therefore as by the offence of one judgment came upon all men to condemnation; even so by the righteousness of one the free gift came upon all men unto justification of life. For as by one man's disobedience many were made sinners, so by the obedience of one shall many be made righteous. Moreover the law entered, that the offence might abound. But where sin abounded, grace did much more abound: that as sin hath reigned unto death, even so might grace reign through righteousness unto eternal life by Jesus Christ our Lord. **1 Cor. 15:22.** For as in Adam all die, even so in Christ shall all be made alive.

s. **Gen. 3:16–19, 23.** Unto the woman he said, I will greatly multiply thy sorrow and thy conception; in sorrow thou shalt bring forth children; and thy desire shall be to thy husband, and he shall rule over thee. And unto Adam he said, Because thou

Q. 18. *Wherein consists the sinfulness of that estate whereinto man fell?*

A. The sinfulness of that estate whereinto man fell, consists in the guilt of Adam's first sin,[t] the want of original righteousness,[u] and the corruption of his whole nature,[w] which is commonly called original sin; together with all actual transgressions which proceed from it.[x]

hast hearkened unto the voice of thy wife, and hast eaten of the tree, of which I commanded thee, saying, Thou shalt not eat of it: cursed is the ground for thy sake; in sorrow shalt thou eat of it all the days of thy life; thorns also and thistles shall it bring forth to thee; and thou shalt eat the herb of the field; in the sweat of thy face shalt thou eat bread, till thou return unto the ground; for out of it wast thou taken: for dust thou art, and unto dust shalt thou return.… Therefore the LORD God sent him forth from the garden of Eden, to till the ground from whence he was taken. **Rom. 3:16.** Destruction and misery are in their ways. **Rom. 5:12.** Wherefore, as by one man sin entered into the world, and death by sin; and so death passed upon all men, for that all have sinned … **Eph. 2:1.** And you hath he quickened, who were dead in trespasses and sins.

t. **Rom. 5:12, 19.** Wherefore, as by one man sin entered into the world, and death by sin; and so death passed upon all men, for that all have sinned … For as by one man's disobedience many were made sinners, so by the obedience of one shall many be made righteous.

u. **Rom. 3:10.** As it is written, There is none righteous, no, not one. **Col. 3:10.** And [ye] have put on the new man, which is renewed in knowledge after the image of him that created him. **Eph. 4:24.** … and that ye put on the new man, which after God is created in righteousness and true holiness.

w. **Ps. 51:5.** Behold, I was shapen in iniquity; and in sin did my mother conceive me. **John 3:6.** That which is born of the flesh is flesh; and that which is born of the Spirit is spirit. **Rom. 3:18.** There is no fear of God before their eyes. **Rom. 8:7–8.** Because the carnal mind is enmity against God: for it is not subject to the law of God, neither indeed can be. So then they that are in the flesh cannot please God. **Eph. 2:3.** … among whom also we all had our conversation in times past in the lusts of our flesh, fulfilling the desires of the flesh and of the mind; and were by nature the children of wrath, even as others.

x. **Gen. 6:5.** And God saw that the wickedness of man was great in the earth, and that every imagination of the thoughts of his heart was only evil continually. **Ps. 53:1–3.** The fool hath said in his heart, There is no God. Corrupt are they, and have done abominable iniquity: there is none that doeth good. God looked down from heaven upon the children of men, to see if there were any that did understand, that did seek God. Every one of them is gone back: they are altogether become filthy; there is none that doeth good, no, not one. **Matt. 15:19.** For out of the heart proceed evil thoughts, murders, adulteries, fornications, thefts, false witness, blasphemies. **Rom. 3:10–18, 23.** As it is written, There is none righteous, no, not one: there is none that understandeth, there is none that seeketh after God. They are all gone out of the way, they are together become unprofitable; there is none that doeth good, no, not one. Their throat is an open sepulchre; with their tongues they have used deceit; the poison of asps is under their lips: whose mouth is full of cursing and bitterness: their feet are

Q. 19. *What is the misery of that estate whereinto man fell?*

A. All mankind by their fall lost communion with God,[y] are under his wrath[z] and curse,[a] and so made liable to all the miseries of this life,[b] to death[c] itself, and to the pains of hell forever.[d]

swift to shed blood: destruction and misery are in their ways: and the way of peace have they not known: there is no fear of God before their eyes.... For all have sinned, and come short of the glory of God. **Gal. 5:19–21.** Now the works of the flesh are manifest, which are these; Adultery, fornication, uncleanness, lasciviousness, idolatry, witchcraft, hatred, variance, emulations, wrath, strife, seditions, heresies, envyings, murders, drunkenness, revellings, and such like: of the which I tell you before, as I have also told you in time past, that they which do such things shall not inherit the kingdom of God. **James 1:14–15.** But every man is tempted, when he is drawn away of his own lust, and enticed. Then when lust hath conceived, it bringeth forth sin: and sin, when it is finished, bringeth forth death.

y. **Gen. 3:8, 24.** And they heard the voice of the LORD God walking in the garden in the cool of the day: and Adam and his wife hid themselves from the presence of the LORD God amongst the trees of the garden.... So he drove out the man; and he placed at the east of the garden of Eden Cherubims, and a flaming sword which turned every way, to keep the way of the tree of life. **John 8:34, 42, 44.** Jesus answered them, Verily, verily, I say unto you, Whosoever committeth sin is the servant of sin.... Jesus said unto them, If God were your Father, ye would love me: for I proceeded forth and came from God; neither came I of myself, but he sent me.... Ye are of your father the devil, and the lusts of your father ye will do. He was a murderer from the beginning, and abode not in the truth, because there is no truth in him. When he speaketh a lie, he speaketh of his own: for he is a liar, and the father of it. **Eph. 2:12.** ... that at that time ye were without Christ, being aliens from the commonwealth of Israel, and strangers from the covenants of promise, having no hope, and without God in the world. **Eph. 4:18.** ... having the understanding darkened, being alienated from the life of God through the ignorance that is in them, because of the blindness of their heart.

z. **John 3:36.** He that believeth on the Son hath everlasting life: and he that believeth not the Son shall not see life; but the wrath of God abideth on him. **Rom. 1:18.** For the wrath of God is revealed from heaven against all ungodliness and unrighteousness of men, who hold the truth in unrighteousness. **Eph. 2:3.** ... among whom also we all had our conversation in times past in the lusts of our flesh, fulfilling the desires of the flesh and of the mind; and were by nature the children of wrath, even as others. **Eph. 5:6.** Let no man deceive you with vain words: for because of these things cometh the wrath of God upon the children of disobedience.

a. **Gal. 3:10.** For as many as are of the works of the law are under the curse: for it is written, Cursed is every one that continueth not in all things which are written in the book of the law to do them. **Rev. 22:3.** And there shall be no more curse: but the throne of God and of the Lamb shall be in it; and his servants shall serve him.

b. **Gen. 3:16–19.** Unto the woman he said, I will greatly multiply thy sorrow and thy conception; in sorrow thou shalt bring forth children; and thy desire shall be to thy husband, and he shall rule over thee. And unto Adam he said, Because thou hast hearkened unto the voice of thy wife, and hast eaten of the tree, of which I

Q. 20. *Did God leave all mankind to perish in the estate of sin and misery?*
A. God, having out of his mere good pleasure, from all eternity, elected some to everlasting life,[e] did enter into a covenant of grace to

commanded thee, saying, Thou shalt not eat of it: cursed is the ground for thy sake; in sorrow shalt thou eat of it all the days of thy life; thorns also and thistles shall it bring forth to thee; and thou shalt eat the herb of the field; in the sweat of thy face shalt thou eat bread, till thou return unto the ground; for out of it wast thou taken: for dust thou art, and unto dust shalt thou return. **Job 5:7.** Yet man is born unto trouble, as the sparks fly upward. **Eccl. 2:22–23.** For what hath man of all his labour, and of the vexation of his heart, wherein he hath laboured under the sun? For all his days are sorrows, and his travail grief; yea, his heart taketh not rest in the night. This is also vanity. **Rom. 8:18–23.** For I reckon that the sufferings of this present time are not worthy to be compared with the glory which shall be revealed in us. For the earnest expectation of the creature waiteth for the manifestation of the sons of God. For the creature was made subject to vanity, not willingly, but by reason of him who hath subjected the same in hope, because the creature itself also shall be delivered from the bondage of corruption into the glorious liberty of the children of God. For we know that the whole creation groaneth and travaileth in pain together until now. And not only they, but ourselves also, which have the firstfruits of the Spirit, even we ourselves groan within ourselves, waiting for the adoption, to wit, the redemption of our body.

c. **Ezek. 18:4.** Behold, all souls are mine; as the soul of the father, so also the soul of the son is mine: the soul that sinneth, it shall die. **Rom. 5:12.** Wherefore, as by one man sin entered into the world, and death by sin; and so death passed upon all men, for that all have sinned … **Rom. 6:23.** For the wages of sin is death; but the gift of God is eternal life through Jesus Christ our Lord.

d. **Matt. 25:41, 46.** Then shall he say also unto them on the left hand, Depart from me, ye cursed, into everlasting fire, prepared for the devil and his angels.… And these shall go away into everlasting punishment: but the righteous into life eternal. **2 Thess. 1:9.** … who shall be punished with everlasting destruction from the presence of the Lord, and from the glory of his power. **Rev. 14:9–11.** And the third angel followed them, saying with a loud voice, If any man worship the beast and his image, and receive his mark in his forehead, or in his hand, the same shall drink of the wine of the wrath of God, which is poured out without mixture into the cup of his indignation; and he shall be tormented with fire and brimstone in the presence of the holy angels, and in the presence of the Lamb: and the smoke of their torment ascendeth up for ever and ever: and they have no rest day nor night, who worship the beast and his image, and whosoever receiveth the mark of his name.

e. **Acts 13:48.** And when the Gentiles heard this, they were glad, and glorified the word of the Lord: and as many as were ordained to eternal life believed. **Eph. 1:4–5.** … according as he hath chosen us in him before the foundation of the world, that we should be holy and without blame before him in love: having predestinated us unto the adoption of children by Jesus Christ to himself, according to the good pleasure of his will. **2 Thess. 2:13–14.** But we are bound to give thanks alway to God for you, brethren beloved of the Lord, because God hath from the beginning chosen you to salvation through sanctification of the Spirit and belief of the truth: whereunto he called you by our gospel, to the obtaining of the glory of our Lord Jesus Christ.

deliver them out of the estate of sin and misery, and to bring them into an estate of salvation by a Redeemer.[f]

Q. 21. *Who is the Redeemer of God's elect?*

A. The only Redeemer of God's elect is the Lord Jesus Christ,[g] who, being the eternal Son of God,[h] became man,[i] and so was, and

f. **Gen. 3:15.** And I will put enmity between thee and the woman, and between thy seed and her seed; it shall bruise thy head, and thou shalt bruise his heel. **Gen. 17:7.** And I will establish my covenant between me and thee and thy seed after thee in their generations for an everlasting covenant, to be a God unto thee, and to thy seed after thee. **Ex. 19:5–6.** Now therefore, if ye will obey my voice indeed, and keep my covenant, then ye shall be a peculiar treasure unto me above all people: for all the earth is mine: and ye shall be unto me a kingdom of priests, and an holy nation. These are the words which thou shalt speak unto the children of Israel. **Jer. 31:31–34.** Behold, the days come, saith the LORD, that I will make a new covenant with the house of Israel and with the house of Judah: not according to the covenant that I made with their fathers in the day that I took them by the hand to bring them out of the land of Egypt; which my covenant they brake, although I was an husband unto them, saith the LORD: but this shall be the covenant that I will make with the house of Israel; After those days, saith the LORD, I will put my law in their inward parts, and write it in their hearts; and will be their God, and they shall be my people. And they shall teach no more every man his neighbour, and every man his brother, saying, Know the LORD: for they shall all know me, from the least of them unto the greatest of them, saith the LORD: for I will forgive their iniquity, and I will remember their sin no more. **Matt. 20:28.** … even as the Son of man came not to be ministered unto, but to minister, and to give his life a ransom for many. **1 Cor. 11:25.** After the same manner also he took the cup, when he had supped, saying, This cup is the new testament in my blood: this do ye, as oft as ye drink it, in remembrance of me. **Heb. 9:15.** And for this cause he is the mediator of the new testament, that by means of death, for the redemption of the transgressions that were under the first testament, they which are called might receive the promise of eternal inheritance.

g. **John 14:6.** Jesus saith unto him, I am the way, the truth, and the life: no man cometh unto the Father, but by me. **Acts 4:12.** Neither is there salvation in any other: for there is none other name under heaven given among men, whereby we must be saved. **1 Tim. 2:5–6.** For there is one God, and one mediator between God and men, the man Christ Jesus; who gave himself a ransom for all, to be testified in due time.

h. **Ps. 2:7.** I will declare the decree: the LORD hath said unto me, Thou art my Son; this day have I begotten thee. **Matt. 3:17.** And lo a voice from heaven, saying, This is my beloved Son, in whom I am well pleased. **Matt. 17:5.** While he yet spake, behold, a bright cloud overshadowed them: and behold a voice out of the cloud, which said, This is my beloved Son, in whom I am well pleased; hear ye him. **John 1:18.** No man hath seen God at any time; the only begotten Son, which is in the bosom of the Father, he hath declared him.

i. **Isa. 9:6.** For unto us a child is born, unto us a son is given: and the government shall be upon his shoulder: and his name shall be called Wonderful, Counsellor, The

continueth to be, God and man in two distinct natures, and one person, forever.[k]

Q. 22. *How did Christ, being the Son of God, become man?*

A. Christ, the Son of God, became man, by taking to himself a true body, and a reasonable soul,[l] being conceived by the power of the Holy Ghost, in the womb of the Virgin Mary, and born of her,[m] yet without sin.[n]

Q. 23. *What offices doth Christ execute as our Redeemer?*

A. Christ, as our Redeemer, executeth the offices of a prophet,[o]

mighty God, The everlasting Father, The Prince of Peace. **Matt. 1:23.** Behold, a virgin shall be with child, and shall bring forth a son, and they shall call his name Emmanuel, which being interpreted is, God with us. **John 1:14.** And the Word was made flesh, and dwelt among us, (and we beheld his glory, the glory as of the only begotten of the Father,) full of grace and truth. **Gal. 4:4.** But when the fulness of the time was come, God sent forth his Son, made of a woman, made under the law.

k. **Acts 1:11.** … which also said, Ye men of Galilee, why stand ye gazing up into heaven? this same Jesus, which is taken up from you into heaven, shall so come in like manner as ye have seen him go into heaven. **Heb. 7:24–25.** But this man, because he continueth ever, hath an unchangeable priesthood. Wherefore he is able also to save them to the uttermost that come unto God by him, seeing he ever liveth to make intercession for them.

l. **Phil. 2:7.** … but made himself of no reputation, and took upon him the form of a servant, and was made in the likeness of men. **Heb. 2:14, 17.** Forasmuch then as the children are partakers of flesh and blood, he also himself likewise took part of the same; that through death he might destroy him that had the power of death, that is, the devil.… Wherefore in all things it behoved him to be made like unto his brethren, that he might be a merciful and faithful high priest in things pertaining to God, to make reconciliation for the sins of the people.

m. **Luke 1:27, 31, 35.** … to a virgin espoused to a man whose name was Joseph, of the house of David; and the virgin's name was Mary.… And, behold, thou shalt conceive in thy womb, and bring forth a son, and shalt call his name JESUS.… And the angel answered and said unto her, The Holy Ghost shall come upon thee, and the power of the Highest shall overshadow thee: therefore also that holy thing which shall be born of thee shall be called the Son of God.

n. **2 Cor. 5:21.** For he hath made him to be sin for us, who knew no sin; that we might be made the righteousness of God in him. **Heb. 4:15.** For we have not an high priest which cannot be touched with the feeling of our infirmities; but was in all points tempted like as we are, yet without sin. **Heb. 7:26.** For such an high priest became us, who is holy, harmless, undefiled, separate from sinners, and made higher than the heavens. **1 John 3:5.** And ye know that he was manifested to take away our sins; and in him is no sin.

o. **Deut. 18:18.** I will raise them up a Prophet from among their brethren, like unto thee, and will put my words in his mouth; and he shall speak unto them all that I shall command him. **Acts 2:33.** Therefore being by the right hand of God exalted,

of a priest,[p] and of a king,[q] both in his estate of humiliation and exaltation.

Q. 24. *How doth Christ execute the office of a prophet?*

A. Christ executeth the office of a prophet, in revealing to us, by his Word[r] and Spirit,[s] the will of God for our salvation.[t]

and having received of the Father the promise of the Holy Ghost, he hath shed forth this, which ye now see and hear. **Acts 3:22–23.** For Moses truly said unto the fathers, A prophet shall the Lord your God raise up unto you of your brethren, like unto me; him shall ye hear in all things whatsoever he shall say unto you. And it shall come to pass, that every soul, which will not hear that prophet, shall be destroyed from among the people. **Heb. 1:1–2.** God, who at sundry times and in divers manners spake in time past unto the fathers by the prophets, hath in these last days spoken unto us by his Son, whom he hath appointed heir of all things, by whom also he made the worlds.

p. **Heb. 4:14–15.** Seeing then that we have a great high priest, that is passed into the heavens, Jesus the Son of God, let us hold fast our profession. For we have not an high priest which cannot be touched with the feeling of our infirmities; but was in all points tempted like as we are, yet without sin. **Heb. 5:5–6.** So also Christ glorified not himself to be made an high priest; but he that said unto him, Thou art my Son, to day have I begotten thee. As he saith also in another place, Thou art a priest for ever after the order of Melchisedec.

q. **Isa. 9:6–7.** For unto us a child is born, unto us a son is given: and the government shall be upon his shoulder: and his name shall be called Wonderful, Counsellor, The mighty God, The everlasting Father, The Prince of Peace. Of the increase of his government and peace there shall be no end, upon the throne of David, and upon his kingdom, to order it, and to establish it with judgment and with justice from henceforth even for ever. The zeal of the Lord of hosts will perform this. **Luke 1:32–33.** He shall be great, and shall be called the Son of the Highest: and the Lord God shall give unto him the throne of his father David: and he shall reign over the house of Jacob for ever; and of his kingdom there shall be no end. **John 18:37.** Pilate therefore said unto him, Art thou a king then? Jesus answered, Thou sayest that I am a king. To this end was I born, and for this cause came I into the world, that I should bear witness unto the truth. Every one that is of the truth heareth my voice. **1 Cor. 15:25.** For he must reign, till he hath put all enemies under his feet.

r. **Luke 4:18–19, 21.** The Spirit of the Lord is upon me, because he hath anointed me to preach the gospel to the poor; he hath sent me to heal the brokenhearted, to preach deliverance to the captives, and recovering of sight to the blind, to set at liberty them that are bruised, to preach the acceptable year of the Lord.… And he began to say unto them, This day is this scripture fulfilled in your ears. **Acts 1:1–2.** The former treatise have I made, O Theophilus, of all that Jesus began both to do and teach, until the day in which he was taken up, after that he through the Holy Ghost had given commandments unto the apostles whom he had chosen. **Heb. 2:3.** How shall we escape, if we neglect so great salvation; which at the first began to be spoken by the Lord, and was confirmed unto us by them that heard him.

s. **John 15:26–27.** But when the Comforter is come, whom I will send unto you from the Father, even the Spirit of truth, which proceedeth from the Father, he shall

Q. 25. *How doth Christ execute the office of a priest?*

A. Christ executeth the office of a priest, in his once offering up of himself a sacrifice to satisfy divine justice,[u] and reconcile us to God,[w] and in making continual intercession for us.[x]

testify of me: and ye also shall bear witness, because ye have been with me from the beginning. **Acts 1:8.** But ye shall receive power, after that the Holy Ghost is come upon you: and ye shall be witnesses unto me both in Jerusalem, and in all Judaea, and in Samaria, and unto the uttermost part of the earth. **1 Pet. 1:11.** ... searching what, or what manner of time the Spirit of Christ which was in them did signify, when it testified beforehand the sufferings of Christ, and the glory that should follow.

t. **John 4:41–42.** And many more believed because of his own word; and said unto the woman, Now we believe, not because of thy saying: for we have heard him ourselves, and know that this is indeed the Christ, the Saviour of the world. **John 20:30–31.** And many other signs truly did Jesus in the presence of his disciples, which are not written in this book: but these are written, that ye might believe that Jesus is the Christ, the Son of God; and that believing ye might have life through his name.

u. **Isa. 53.** ... All we like sheep have gone astray; we have turned every one to his own way; and the LORD hath laid on him the iniquity of us all. He was oppressed, and he was afflicted, yet he opened not his mouth: he is brought as a lamb to the slaughter, and as a sheep before her shearers is dumb, so he openeth not his mouth. He was taken from prison and from judgment: and who shall declare his generation? for he was cut off out of the land of the living: for the transgression of my people was he stricken.... Yet it pleased the LORD to bruise him; he hath put him to grief: when thou shalt make his soul an offering for sin, he shall see his seed, he shall prolong his days, and the pleasure of the LORD shall prosper in his hand. He shall see of the travail of his soul, and shall be satisfied: by his knowledge shall my righteous servant justify many; for he shall bear their iniquities.... **Acts 8:32–35.** The place of the scripture which he read was this, He was led as a sheep to the slaughter; and like a lamb dumb before his shearer, so opened he not his mouth: in his humiliation his judgment was taken away: and who shall declare his generation? for his life is taken from the earth. And the eunuch answered Philip, and said, I pray thee, of whom speaketh the prophet this? of himself, or of some other man? Then Philip opened his mouth, and began at the same scripture, and preached unto him Jesus. **Heb. 9:26–28.** For then must he often have suffered since the foundation of the world: but now once in the end of the world hath he appeared to put away sin by the sacrifice of himself. And as it is appointed unto men once to die, but after this the judgment: so Christ was once offered to bear the sins of many; and unto them that look for him shall he appear the second time without sin unto salvation. **Heb. 10:12.** But this man, after he had offered one sacrifice for sins for ever, sat down on the right hand of God.

w. **Rom. 5:10–11.** For if, when we were enemies, we were reconciled to God by the death of his Son, much more, being reconciled, we shall be saved by his life. And not only so, but we also joy in God through our Lord Jesus Christ, by whom we have now received the atonement. **2 Cor. 5:18.** And all things are of God, who hath reconciled us to himself by Jesus Christ, and hath given to us the ministry of reconciliation. **Col. 1:21–22.** And you, that were sometime alienated and enemies in your mind by wicked works, yet now hath he reconciled in the body of his flesh through

Q. 26. *How doth Christ execute the office of a king?*

A. Christ executeth the office of a king, in subduing us to himself, in ruling and defending us,[y] and in restraining and conquering all his and our enemies.[z]

Q. 27. *Wherein did Christ's humiliation consist?*

A. Christ's humiliation consisted in his being born, and that in a low condition,[a] made under the law,[b] undergoing the miseries of this

death, to present you holy and unblameable and unreproveable in his sight.

x. **Rom. 8:34.** Who is he that condemneth? It is Christ that died, yea rather, that is risen again, who is even at the right hand of God, who also maketh intercession for us. **Heb. 7:25.** Wherefore he is able also to save them to the uttermost that come unto God by him, seeing he ever liveth to make intercession for them. **Heb. 9:24.** For Christ is not entered into the holy places made with hands, which are the figures of the true; but into heaven itself, now to appear in the presence of God for us.

y. **Ps. 110:3.** Thy people shall be willing in the day of thy power, in the beauties of holiness from the womb of the morning: thou hast the dew of thy youth. **Matt. 28:18–20.** And Jesus came and spake unto them, saying, All power is given unto me in heaven and in earth. Go ye therefore, and teach all nations, baptizing them in the name of the Father, and of the Son, and of the Holy Ghost: teaching them to observe all things whatsoever I have commanded you: and, lo, I am with you alway, even unto the end of the world. Amen. **John 17:2.** … as thou hast given him power over all flesh, that he should give eternal life to as many as thou hast given him. **Col. 1:13.** … who hath delivered us from the power of darkness, and hath translated us into the kingdom of his dear Son.

z. **Ps. 2:6–9.** Yet have I set my king upon my holy hill of Zion. I will declare the decree: the LORD hath said unto me, Thou art my Son; this day have I begotten thee. Ask of me, and I shall give thee the heathen for thine inheritance, and the uttermost parts of the earth for thy possession. Thou shalt break them with a rod of iron; thou shalt dash them in pieces like a potter's vessel. **Ps. 110:1–2.** The LORD said unto my Lord, Sit thou at my right hand, until I make thine enemies thy footstool. The LORD shall send the rod of thy strength out of Zion: rule thou in the midst of thine enemies. **Matt. 12:28.** But if I cast out devils by the Spirit of God, then the kingdom of God is come unto you. **1 Cor. 15:24–26.** Then cometh the end, when he shall have delivered up the kingdom to God, even the Father; when he shall have put down all rule and all authority and power. For he must reign, till he hath put all enemies under his feet. The last enemy that shall be destroyed is death. **Col. 2:15.** And having spoiled principalities and powers, he made a shew of them openly, triumphing over them in it.

a. **Luke 2:7.** And she brought forth her firstborn son, and wrapped him in swaddling clothes, and laid him in a manger; because there was no room for them in the inn. **2 Cor. 8:9.** For ye know the grace of our Lord Jesus Christ, that, though he was rich, yet for your sakes he became poor, that ye through his poverty might be rich. **Gal. 4:4.** But when the fulness of the time was come, God sent forth his Son, made of a woman, made under the law.

life,^{c} the wrath of God,^{d} and the cursed death of the cross;^{e} in being buried, and continuing under the power of death for a time.^{f}

Q. 28. *Wherein consisteth Christ's exaltation?*

A. Christ's exaltation consisteth in his rising again from the dead on the third day,^{g} in ascending up into heaven,^{h} in sitting at the right hand of God the Father,^{i} and in coming to judge the world at

b. **Gal. 4:4.** But when the fulness of the time was come, God sent forth his Son, made of a woman, made under the law.

c. **Isa. 53:3.** He is despised and rejected of men; a man of sorrows, and acquainted with grief: and we hid as it were our faces from him; he was despised, and we esteemed him not. **Luke 9:58.** And Jesus said unto him, Foxes have holes, and birds of the air have nests; but the Son of man hath not where to lay his head. **John 4:6.** Now Jacob's well was there. Jesus therefore, being wearied with his journey, sat thus on the well: and it was about the sixth hour. **John 11:35.** Jesus wept. **Heb. 2:18.** For in that he himself hath suffered being tempted, he is able to succour them that are tempted.

d. **Ps. 22:1.** My God, my God, why hast thou forsaken me? why art thou so far from helping me, and from the words of my roaring? (**Matt. 27:46.** And about the ninth hour Jesus cried with a loud voice, saying, Eli, Eli, lama sabachthani? that is to say, My God, my God, why hast thou forsaken me?) **Isa. 53:10.** Yet it pleased the LORD to bruise him; he hath put him to grief: when thou shalt make his soul an offering for sin, he shall see his seed, he shall prolong his days, and the pleasure of the LORD shall prosper in his hand. **1 John 2:2.** And he is the propitiation for our sins: and not for ours only, but also for the sins of the whole world.

e. **Gal. 3:13.** Christ hath redeemed us from the curse of the law, being made a curse for us: for it is written, Cursed is every one that hangeth on a tree. **Phil. 2:8.** And being found in fashion as a man, he humbled himself, and became obedient unto death, even the death of the cross.

f. **Matt. 12:40.** For as Jonas was three days and three nights in the whale's belly; so shall the Son of man be three days and three nights in the heart of the earth. **1 Cor. 15:3–4.** For I delivered unto you first of all that which I also received, how that Christ died for our sins according to the scriptures; and that he was buried, and that he rose again the third day according to the scriptures.

g. **1 Cor. 15:4.** … and that he was buried, and that he rose again the third day according to the scriptures.

h. **Ps. 68:18.** Thou hast ascended on high, thou hast led captivity captive: thou hast received gifts for men; yea, for the rebellious also, that the LORD God might dwell among them. **Acts 1:11.** … which also said, Ye men of Galilee, why stand ye gazing up into heaven? this same Jesus, which is taken up from you into heaven, shall so come in like manner as ye have seen him go into heaven. **Eph. 4:8.** Wherefore he saith, When he ascended up on high, he led captivity captive, and gave gifts unto men.

i. **Ps. 110:1.** The LORD said unto my Lord, Sit thou at my right hand, until I make thine enemies thy footstool. **Acts 2:33–34.** Therefore being by the right hand of God exalted, and having received of the Father the promise of the Holy Ghost, he hath shed forth this, which ye now see and hear. For David is not ascended into the heavens: but he saith himself, The Lord said unto my Lord, Sit thou on my right hand.

the last day.[k]

Q. 29. *How are we made partakers of the redemption purchased by Christ?*

A. We are made partakers of the redemption purchased by Christ, by the effectual application of it to us by his Holy Spirit.[l]

Q. 30. *How doth the Spirit apply to us the redemption purchased by Christ?*

A. The Spirit applieth to us the redemption purchased by Christ, by working faith in us,[m] and thereby uniting us to Christ in our effectual calling.[n]

Q. 31. *What is effectual calling?*

A. Effectual calling is the work of God's Spirit, whereby, convincing us of our sin and misery, enlightening our minds in the knowl-

Heb. 1:3. … who being the brightness of his glory, and the express image of his person, and upholding all things by the word of his power, when he had by himself purged our sins, sat down on the right hand of the Majesty on high.

k. **Matt. 16:27.** For the Son of man shall come in the glory of his Father with his angels; and then he shall reward every man according to his works. **Acts 17:31.** … because he hath appointed a day, in the which he will judge the world in righteousness by that man whom he hath ordained; whereof he hath given assurance unto all men, in that he hath raised him from the dead.

l. **Titus 3:4–7.** But after that the kindness and love of God our Saviour toward man appeared, not by works of righteousness which we have done, but according to his mercy he saved us, by the washing of regeneration, and renewing of the Holy Ghost; which he shed on us abundantly through Jesus Christ our Saviour; that being justified by his grace, we should be made heirs according to the hope of eternal life.

m. **Rom. 10:17.** So then faith cometh by hearing, and hearing by the word of God. **1 Cor. 2:12–16.** Now we have received, not the spirit of the world, but the spirit which is of God; that we might know the things that are freely given to us of God. Which things also we speak, not in the words which man's wisdom teacheth, but which the Holy Ghost teacheth; comparing spiritual things with spiritual. But the natural man receiveth not the things of the Spirit of God: for they are foolishness unto him: neither can he know them, because they are spiritually discerned. But he that is spiritual judgeth all things, yet he himself is judged of no man. For who hath known the mind of the Lord, that he may instruct him? But we have the mind of Christ. **Eph. 2:8.** For by grace are ye saved through faith; and that not of yourselves: it is the gift of God. **Phil. 1:29.** For unto you it is given in the behalf of Christ, not only to believe on him, but also to suffer for his sake.

n. **John 15:5.** I am the vine, ye are the branches: He that abideth in me, and I in him, the same bringeth forth much fruit: for without me ye can do nothing. **1 Cor. 1:9.** God is faithful, by whom ye were called unto the fellowship of his Son Jesus Christ our Lord. **Eph. 3:17.** … that Christ may dwell in your hearts by faith; that ye, being rooted and grounded in love …

edge of Christ,[o] and renewing our wills,[p] he doth persuade and enable us to embrace Jesus Christ,[q] freely offered to us in the gospel.[r]

Q. 32. *What benefits do they that are effectually called partake of in this life?*

A. They that are effectually called do in this life partake of justification, adoption, and sanctification, and the several benefits which in this life do either accompany or flow from them.[s]

o. **Acts 26:18.** [I send thee] to open their eyes, and to turn them from darkness to light, and from the power of Satan unto God, that they may receive forgiveness of sins, and inheritance among them which are sanctified by faith that is in me. **1 Cor. 2:10, 12.** But God hath revealed them unto us by his Spirit: for the Spirit searcheth all things, yea, the deep things of God.... Now we have received, not the spirit of the world, but the spirit which is of God; that we might know the things that are freely given to us of God. **2 Cor. 4:6.** For God, who commanded the light to shine out of darkness, hath shined in our hearts, to give the light of the knowledge of the glory of God in the face of Jesus Christ. **Eph. 1:17–18.** ... that the God of our Lord Jesus Christ, the Father of glory, may give unto you the spirit of wisdom and revelation in the knowledge of him: the eyes of your understanding being enlightened; that ye may know what is the hope of his calling, and what the riches of the glory of his inheritance in the saints.

p. **Deut. 30:6.** And the LORD thy God will circumcise thine heart, and the heart of thy seed, to love the LORD thy God with all thine heart, and with all thy soul, that thou mayest live. **Ezek. 36:26–27.** A new heart also will I give you, and a new spirit will I put within you: and I will take away the stony heart out of your flesh, and I will give you an heart of flesh. And I will put my spirit within you, and cause you to walk in my statutes, and ye shall keep my judgments, and do them. **John 3:5.** Jesus answered, Verily, verily, I say unto thee, Except a man be born of water and of the Spirit, he cannot enter into the kingdom of God. **Titus 3:5.** Not by works of righteousness which we have done, but according to his mercy he saved us, by the washing of regeneration, and renewing of the Holy Ghost.

q. **John 6:44–45.** No man can come to me, except the Father which hath sent me draw him: and I will raise him up at the last day. It is written in the prophets, And they shall be all taught of God. Every man therefore that hath heard, and hath learned of the Father, cometh unto me. **Acts 16:14.** And a certain woman named Lydia, a seller of purple, of the city of Thyatira, which worshipped God, heard us: whose heart the Lord opened, that she attended unto the things which were spoken of Paul.

r. **Isa. 45:22.** Look unto me, and be ye saved, all the ends of the earth: for I am God, and there is none else. **Matt. 11:28–30.** Come unto me, all ye that labour and are heavy laden, and I will give you rest. Take my yoke upon you, and learn of me; for I am meek and lowly in heart: and ye shall find rest unto your souls. For my yoke is easy, and my burden is light. **Rev. 22:17.** And the Spirit and the bride say, Come. And let him that heareth say, Come. And let him that is athirst come. And whosoever will, let him take the water of life freely.

s. **Rom. 8:30.** Moreover whom he did predestinate, them he also called: and whom he called, them he also justified: and whom he justified, them he also glorified.

Q. 33. *What is justification?*

A. Justification is an act of God's free grace,[t] wherein he pardoneth all our sins,[u] and accepteth us as righteous in his sight,[w] only for the righteousness of Christ imputed to us,[x] and received by faith alone.[y]

Q. 34. *What is adoption?*

A. Adoption is an act of God's free grace,[z] whereby we are received into the number, and have a right to all the privileges, of the sons of God.[a]

1 Cor. 1:30. But of him are ye in Christ Jesus, who of God is made unto us wisdom, and righteousness, and sanctification, and redemption. **1 Cor. 6:11.** And such were some of you: but ye are washed, but ye are sanctified, but ye are justified in the name of the Lord Jesus, and by the Spirit of our God. **Eph. 1:5.** … having predestinated us unto the adoption of children by Jesus Christ to himself, according to the good pleasure of his will.

t. **Rom. 3:24.** … being justified freely by his grace through the redemption that is in Christ Jesus.

u. **Rom. 4:6–8.** Even as David also describeth the blessedness of the man, unto whom God imputeth righteousness without works, saying, Blessed are they whose iniquities are forgiven, and whose sins are covered. Blessed is the man to whom the Lord will not impute sin. **2 Cor. 5:19.** … to wit, that God was in Christ, reconciling the world unto himself, not imputing their trespasses unto them; and hath committed unto us the word of reconciliation.

w. **2 Cor. 5:21.** For he hath made him to be sin for us, who knew no sin; that we might be made the righteousness of God in him.

x. **Rom. 4:6, 11.** Even as David also describeth the blessedness of the man, unto whom God imputeth righteousness without works.… And he received the sign of circumcision, a seal of the righteousness of the faith which he had yet being uncircumcised: that he might be the father of all them that believe, though they be not circumcised; that righteousness might be imputed unto them also. **Rom. 5:19.** For as by one man's disobedience many were made sinners, so by the obedience of one shall many be made righteous.

y. **Gal. 2:16.** … knowing that a man is not justified by the works of the law, but by the faith of Jesus Christ, even we have believed in Jesus Christ, that we might be justified by the faith of Christ, and not by the works of the law: for by the works of the law shall no flesh be justified. **Phil. 3:9.** … and be found in him, not having mine own righteousness, which is of the law, but that which is through the faith of Christ, the righteousness which is of God by faith.

z. **1 John 3:1.** Behold, what manner of love the Father hath bestowed upon us, that we should be called the sons of God: therefore the world knoweth us not, because it knew him not.

a. **John 1:12.** But as many as received him, to them gave he power to become the sons of God, even to them that believe on his name. **Rom. 8:17.** … and if children, then heirs; heirs of God, and joint-heirs with Christ; if so be that we suffer with him, that we may be also glorified together.

Q. 35. *What is sanctification?*

A. Sanctification is the work of God's free grace,[b] whereby we are renewed in the whole man after the image of God,[c] and are enabled more and more to die unto sin, and live unto righteousness.[d]

Q. 36. *What are the benefits which in this life do accompany or flow from justification, adoption, and sanctification?*

A. The benefits which in this life do accompany or flow from justification, adoption, and sanctification, are, assurance of God's love,[e] peace of conscience,[f] joy in the Holy Ghost,[g] increase of grace,[h]

b. **Ezek. 36:27.** And I will put my spirit within you, and cause you to walk in my statutes, and ye shall keep my judgments, and do them. **Phil. 2:13.** For it is God which worketh in you both to will and to do of his good pleasure. **2 Thess. 2:13.** But we are bound to give thanks alway to God for you, brethren beloved of the Lord, because God hath from the beginning chosen you to salvation through sanctification of the Spirit and belief of the truth.

c. **2 Cor. 5:17.** Therefore if any man be in Christ, he is a new creature: old things are passed away; behold, all things are become new. **Eph. 4:23–24.** … and be renewed in the spirit of your mind; and that ye put on the new man, which after God is created in righteousness and true holiness. **1 Thess. 5:23.** And the very God of peace sanctify you wholly; and I pray God your whole spirit and soul and body be preserved blameless unto the coming of our Lord Jesus Christ.

d. **Ezek. 36:25–27.** Then will I sprinkle clean water upon you, and ye shall be clean: from all your filthiness, and from all your idols, will I cleanse you. A new heart also will I give you, and a new spirit will I put within you: and I will take away the stony heart out of your flesh, and I will give you an heart of flesh. And I will put my spirit within you, and cause you to walk in my statutes, and ye shall keep my judgments, and do them. **Rom. 6:4, 6, 12–14.** Therefore we are buried with him by baptism into death: that like as Christ was raised up from the dead by the glory of the Father, even so we also should walk in newness of life.… knowing this, that our old man is crucified with him, that the body of sin might be destroyed, that henceforth we should not serve sin.… Let not sin therefore reign in your mortal body, that ye should obey it in the lusts thereof. Neither yield ye your members as instruments of unrighteousness unto sin: but yield yourselves unto God, as those that are alive from the dead, and your members as instruments of righteousness unto God. For sin shall not have dominion over you: for ye are not under the law, but under grace. **2 Cor. 7:1.** Having therefore these promises, dearly beloved, let us cleanse ourselves from all filthiness of the flesh and spirit, perfecting holiness in the fear of God. **1 Pet. 2:24.** … who his own self bare our sins in his own body on the tree, that we, being dead to sins, should live unto righteousness: by whose stripes ye were healed.

e. **Rom. 5:5.** And hope maketh not ashamed; because the love of God is shed abroad in our hearts by the Holy Ghost which is given unto us.

f. **Rom. 5:1.** Therefore being justified by faith, we have peace with God through our Lord Jesus Christ.

g. **Rom. 14:17.** For the kingdom of God is not meat and drink; but righteous-

and perseverance therein to the end.[i]

Q. 37. *What benefits do believers receive from Christ at death?*

A. The souls of believers are at their death made perfect in holiness,[k] and do immediately pass into glory;[l] and their bodies, being still united to Christ,[m] do rest in their graves, till the resurrection.[n]

Q. 38. *What benefits do believers receive from Christ at the resurrection?*

A. At the resurrection, believers, being raised up in glory,[o] shall be openly acknowledged and acquitted in the day of judgment,[p] and made perfectly blessed in the full enjoying of God[q] to all eternity.[r]

ness, and peace, and joy in the Holy Ghost.

h. **2 Pet. 3:18.** But grow in grace, and in the knowledge of our Lord and Saviour Jesus Christ. To him be glory both now and for ever. Amen.

i. **Phil. 1:6.** … being confident of this very thing, that he which hath begun a good work in you will perform it until the day of Jesus Christ. **1 Pet. 1:5.** … who are kept by the power of God through faith unto salvation ready to be revealed in the last time.

k. **Heb. 12:23.** … to the general assembly and church of the firstborn, which are written in heaven, and to God the Judge of all, and to the spirits of just men made perfect.

l. **Luke 23:43.** And Jesus said unto him, Verily I say unto thee, To day shalt thou be with me in paradise. **2 Cor. 5:6, 8.** Therefore we are always confident, knowing that, whilst we are at home in the body, we are absent from the Lord.… We are confident, I say, and willing rather to be absent from the body, and to be present with the Lord. **Phil. 1:23.** For I am in a strait betwixt two, having a desire to depart, and to be with Christ; which is far better.

m. **1 Thess. 4:14.** For if we believe that Jesus died and rose again, even so them also which sleep in Jesus will God bring with him.

n. **Dan. 12:2.** And many of them that sleep in the dust of the earth shall awake, some to everlasting life, and some to shame and everlasting contempt. **John 5:28–29.** Marvel not at this: for the hour is coming, in the which all that are in the graves shall hear his voice, and shall come forth; they that have done good, unto the resurrection of life; and they that have done evil, unto the resurrection of damnation. **Acts 24:15.** And [I] have hope toward God, which they themselves also allow, that there shall be a resurrection of the dead, both of the just and unjust.

o. **1 Cor. 15:42–43.** So also is the resurrection of the dead. It is sown in corruption; it is raised in incorruption: it is sown in dishonour; it is raised in glory: it is sown in weakness; it is raised in power.

p. **Matt. 25:33–34, 46.** And he shall set the sheep on his right hand, but the goats on the left. Then shall the King say unto them on his right hand, Come, ye blessed of my Father, inherit the kingdom prepared for you from the foundation of the world.… And these shall go away into everlasting punishment: but the righteous into life eternal.

q. **Rom. 8:29.** For whom he did foreknow, he also did predestinate to be conformed to the image of his Son, that he might be the firstborn among many brethren.

Q. 39. *What is the duty which God requireth of man?*

A. The duty which God requireth of man, is obedience to his revealed will.[s]

Q. 40. *What did God at first reveal to man for the rule of his obedience?*

A. The rule which God at first revealed to man for his obedience, was the moral law.[t]

Q. 41. *Wherein is the moral law summarily comprehended?*

A. The moral law is summarily comprehended in the Ten Commandments.[u]

Q. 42. *What is the sum of the Ten Commandments?*

A. The sum of the Ten Commandments is, to love the Lord our God with all our heart, with all our soul, with all our strength, and with all our mind; and our neighbor as ourselves.[w]

1 John 3:2. Beloved, now are we the sons of God, and it doth not yet appear what we shall be: but we know that, when he shall appear, we shall be like him; for we shall see him as he is.

r. **Ps. 16:11.** Thou wilt shew me the path of life: in thy presence is fulness of joy; at thy right hand there are pleasures for evermore. **1 Thess. 4:17.** Then we which are alive and remain shall be caught up together with them in the clouds, to meet the Lord in the air: and so shall we ever be with the Lord.

s. **Deut. 29:29.** The secret things belong unto the LORD our God: but those things which are revealed belong unto us and to our children for ever, that we may do all the words of this law. **Mic. 6:8.** He hath shewed thee, O man, what is good; and what doth the LORD require of thee, but to do justly, and to love mercy, and to walk humbly with thy God? **1 John 5:2–3.** By this we know that we love the children of God, when we love God, and keep his commandments. For this is the love of God, that we keep his commandments: and his commandments are not grievous.

t. **Rom. 2:14–15.** For when the Gentiles, which have not the law, do by nature the things contained in the law, these, having not the law, are a law unto themselves: which shew the work of the law written in their hearts, their conscience also bearing witness, and their thoughts the mean while accusing or else excusing one another. **Rom. 10:5.** For Moses describeth the righteousness which is of the law, that the man which doeth those things shall live by them.

u. **Deut. 4:13.** And he declared unto you his covenant, which he commanded you to perform, even ten commandments; and he wrote them upon two tables of stone. **Matt. 19:17–19.** And he said unto him, Why callest thou me good? there is none good but one, that is, God: but if thou wilt enter into life, keep the commandments. He saith unto him, Which? Jesus said, Thou shalt do no murder, Thou shalt not commit adultery, Thou shalt not steal, Thou shalt not bear false witness, Honour thy father and thy mother: and, Thou shalt love thy neighbour as thyself.

w. **Matt. 22:37–40.** Jesus said unto him, Thou shalt love the Lord thy God with all thy heart, and with all thy soul, and with all thy mind. This is the first and great

Q. 43. *What is the preface to the Ten Commandments?*

A. The preface to the Ten Commandments is in these words, *I am the* LORD *thy God, which have brought thee out of the land of Egypt, out of the house of bondage.*[x]

Q. 44. *What doth the preface to the Ten Commandments teach us?*

A. The preface to the Ten Commandments teacheth us, that because God is the Lord, and our God, and Redeemer, therefore we are bound to keep all his commandments.[y]

Q. 45. *Which is the first commandment?*

A. The first commandment is, *Thou shalt have no other gods before me.*[z]

Q. 46. *What is required in the first commandment?*

A. The first commandment requireth us to know and acknowledge God to be the only true God, and our God; and to worship and glorify him accordingly.[a]

commandment. And the second is like unto it, Thou shalt love thy neighbour as thyself. On these two commandments hang all the law and the prophets.

x. **Ex. 20:2. Deut. 5:6.** I am the LORD thy God, which brought thee out of the land of Egypt, from the house of bondage.

y. **Luke 1:74–75.** … that he would grant unto us, that we being delivered out of the hand of our enemies might serve him without fear, in holiness and righteousness before him, all the days of our life. **1 Pet. 1:14–19.** … as obedient children, not fashioning yourselves according to the former lusts in your ignorance: but as he which hath called you is holy, so be ye holy in all manner of conversation; because it is written, Be ye holy; for I am holy. And if ye call on the Father, who without respect of persons judgeth according to every man's work, pass the time of your sojourning here in fear: forasmuch as ye know that ye were not redeemed with corruptible things, as silver and gold, from your vain conversation received by tradition from your fathers; but with the precious blood of Christ, as of a lamb without blemish and without spot.

z. **Ex. 20:3. Deut. 5:7.** Thou shalt have none other gods before me.

a. **1 Chron. 28:9.** And thou, Solomon my son, know thou the God of thy father, and serve him with a perfect heart and with a willing mind: for the LORD searcheth all hearts, and understandeth all the imaginations of the thoughts: if thou seek him, he will be found of thee; but if thou forsake him, he will cast thee off for ever. **Isa. 45:20–25.** Assemble yourselves and come; draw near together, ye that are escaped of the nations: they have no knowledge that set up the wood of their graven image, and pray unto a god that cannot save. Tell ye, and bring them near; yea, let them take counsel together: who hath declared this from ancient time? who hath told it from that time? have not I the LORD? and there is no God else beside me; a just God and a Saviour; there is none beside me. Look unto me, and be ye saved, all the ends of the earth: for I am God, and there is none else. I have sworn by myself, the word is gone out of my mouth in righteousness, and shall not return, That unto me every knee shall

Q. 47. *What is forbidden in the first commandment?*

A. The first commandment forbiddeth the denying,[b] or not worshiping and glorifying, the true God as God,[c] and our God;[d] and the giving of that worship and glory to any other, which is due to him alone.[e]

Q. 48. *What are we specially taught by these words,* before me, *in the first commandment?*

A. These words, *before me,* in the first commandment teach us, that God, who seeth all things, taketh notice of, and is much displeased with, the sin of having any other God.[f]

bow, every tongue shall swear. Surely, shall one say, in the LORD have I righteousness and strength: even to him shall men come; and all that are incensed against him shall be ashamed. In the LORD shall all the seed of Israel be justified, and shall glory. **Matt. 4:10.** Then saith Jesus unto him, Get thee hence, Satan: for it is written, Thou shalt worship the Lord thy God, and him only shalt thou serve.

b. **Ps. 14:1.** The fool hath said in his heart, There is no God. They are corrupt, they have done abominable works, there is none that doeth good.

c. **Rom. 1:20–21.** For the invisible things of him from the creation of the world are clearly seen, being understood by the things that are made, even his eternal power and Godhead; so that they are without excuse: because that, when they knew God, they glorified him not as God, neither were thankful; but became vain in their imaginations, and their foolish heart was darkened.

d. **Ps. 81:10–11.** I am the LORD thy God, which brought thee out of the land of Egypt: open thy mouth wide, and I will fill it. But my people would not hearken to my voice; and Israel would none of me.

e. **Ezek. 8:16–18.** And he brought me into the inner court of the LORD'S house, and, behold, at the door of the temple of the LORD, between the porch and the altar, were about five and twenty men, with their backs toward the temple of the LORD, and their faces toward the east; and they worshipped the sun toward the east. Then he said unto me, Hast thou seen this, O son of man? Is it a light thing to the house of Judah that they commit the abominations which they commit here? for they have filled the land with violence, and have returned to provoke me to anger: and, lo, they put the branch to their nose. Therefore will I also deal in fury: mine eye shall not spare, neither will I have pity: and though they cry in mine ears with a loud voice, yet will I not hear them. **Rom. 1:25.** … who changed the truth of God into a lie, and worshipped and served the creature more than the Creator, who is blessed for ever. Amen.

f. **Deut. 30:17–18.** But if thine heart turn away, so that thou wilt not hear, but shalt be drawn away, and worship other gods, and serve them; I denounce unto you this day, that ye shall surely perish, and that ye shall not prolong your days upon the land, whither thou passest over Jordan to go to possess it. **Ps. 44:20–21.** If we have forgotten the name of our God, or stretched out our hands to a strange god; shall not God search this out? for he knoweth the secrets of the heart. **Ezek. 8:12.** Then said he unto me, Son of man, hast thou seen what the ancients of the house of Israel do in the dark, every man in the chambers of his imagery? for they say, The LORD seeth us

Q. 49. *Which is the second commandment?*

A. The second commandment is, *Thou shalt not make unto thee any graven image, or any likeness of any thing that is in heaven above, or that is in the earth beneath, or that is in the water under the earth: thou shalt not bow down thyself to them, nor serve them: for I the LORD thy God am a jealous God, visiting the iniquity of the fathers upon the children unto the third and fourth generation of them that hate me; and shewing mercy unto thousands of them that love me, and keep my commandments.*[g]

Q. 50. *What is required in the second commandment?*

A. The second commandment requireth the receiving, observing, and keeping pure and entire, all such religious worship and ordinances as God hath appointed in his Word.[h]

Q. 51. *What is forbidden in the second commandment?*

A. The second commandment forbiddeth the worshiping of God by images,[i] or any other way not appointed in his Word.[k]

not; the LORD hath forsaken the earth.

g. **Ex. 20:4–6. Deut. 5:8–10.** Thou shalt not make thee any graven image, or any likeness of any thing that is in heaven above, or that is in the earth beneath, or that is in the waters beneath the earth: thou shalt not bow down thyself unto them, nor serve them: for I the LORD thy God am a jealous God, visiting the iniquity of the fathers upon the children unto the third and fourth generation of them that hate me, and shewing mercy unto thousands of them that love me and keep my commandments.

h. **Deut. 12:32.** What thing soever I command you, observe to do it: thou shalt not add thereto, nor diminish from it. **Matt. 28:20.** … teaching them to observe all things whatsoever I have commanded you: and, lo, I am with you alway, even unto the end of the world. Amen.

i. **Deut. 4:15–19.** Take ye therefore good heed unto yourselves; for ye saw no manner of similitude on the day that the LORD spake unto you in Horeb out of the midst of the fire: lest ye corrupt yourselves, and make you a graven image, the similitude of any figure, the likeness of male or female, the likeness of any beast that is on the earth, the likeness of any winged fowl that flieth in the air, the likeness of any thing that creepeth on the ground, the likeness of any fish that is in the waters beneath the earth: and lest thou lift up thine eyes unto heaven, and when thou seest the sun, and the moon, and the stars, even all the host of heaven, shouldest be driven to worship them, and serve them, which the LORD thy God hath divided unto all nations under the whole heaven. **Rom. 1:22–23.** Professing themselves to be wise, they became fools, and changed the glory of the uncorruptible God into an image made like to corruptible man, and to birds, and fourfooted beasts, and creeping things.

k. **Lev. 10:1–2.** And Nadab and Abihu, the sons of Aaron, took either of them his censer, and put fire therein, and put incense thereon, and offered strange fire before the LORD, which he commanded them not. And there went out fire from the

Q. 52. *What are the reasons annexed to the second commandment?*

A. The reasons annexed to the second commandment are, God's sovereignty over us,[l] his propriety in us,[m] and the zeal he hath to his own worship.[n]

Q. 53. *Which is the third commandment?*

A. The third commandment is, *Thou shalt not take the name of the* LORD *thy God in vain: for the* LORD *will not hold him guiltless that taketh his name in vain.*[o]

Q. 54. *What is required in the third commandment?*

A. The third commandment requireth the holy and reverent use

LORD, and devoured them, and they died before the LORD. **Jer. 19:4–5.** Because they have forsaken me, and have estranged this place, and have burned incense in it unto other gods, whom neither they nor their fathers have known, nor the kings of Judah, and have filled this place with the blood of innocents; they have built also the high places of Baal, to burn their sons with fire for burnt offerings unto Baal, which I commanded not, nor spake it, neither came it into my mind. **Col. 2:18–23.** Let no man beguile you of your reward in a voluntary humility and worshipping of angels, intruding into those things which he hath not seen, vainly puffed up by his fleshly mind, and not holding the Head, from which all the body by joints and bands having nourishment ministered, and knit together, increaseth with the increase of God. Wherefore if ye be dead with Christ from the rudiments of the world, why, as though living in the world, are ye subject to ordinances, (touch not; taste not; handle not; which all are to perish with the using;) after the commandments and doctrines of men? Which things have indeed a shew of wisdom in will worship, and humility, and neglecting of the body; not in any honour to the satisfying of the flesh.

l. **Ps. 95:2–3, 6–7.** Let us come before his presence with thanksgiving, and make a joyful noise unto him with psalms. For the LORD is a great God, and a great King above all gods.… O come, let us worship and bow down: let us kneel before the LORD our maker. For he is our God; and we are the people of his pasture, and the sheep of his hand.… **Ps. 96:9–10.** O worship the LORD in the beauty of holiness: fear before him, all the earth. Say among the heathen that the LORD reigneth: the world also shall be established that it shall not be moved: he shall judge the people righteously.

m. **Ex. 19:5.** Now therefore, if ye will obey my voice indeed, and keep my covenant, then ye shall be a peculiar treasure unto me above all people: for all the earth is mine. **Ps. 45:11.** So shall the king greatly desire thy beauty: for he is thy Lord; and worship thou him. **Isa. 54:5.** For thy Maker is thine husband; the LORD of hosts is his name; and thy Redeemer the Holy One of Israel; The God of the whole earth shall he be called.

n. **Ex. 34:14.** For thou shalt worship no other god: for the LORD, whose name is Jealous, is a jealous God. **1 Cor. 10:22.** Do we provoke the Lord to jealousy? are we stronger than he?

o. **Ex. 20:7. Deut. 5:11.** Thou shalt not take the name of the LORD thy God in vain: for the LORD will not hold him guiltless that taketh his name in vain.

of God's names, titles,[p] attributes,[q] ordinances,[r] Word,[s] and works.[t]

Q. 55. *What is forbidden in the third commandment?*

A. The third commandment forbiddeth all profaning or abusing of anything whereby God maketh himself known.[u]

p. **Deut. 10:20.** Thou shalt fear the Lord thy God; him shalt thou serve, and to him shalt thou cleave, and swear by his name. **Ps. 29:2.** Give unto the Lord the glory due unto his name; worship the Lord in the beauty of holiness. **Matt. 6:9.** After this manner therefore pray ye: Our Father which art in heaven, Hallowed be thy name.

q. **1 Chron. 29:10–13.** Wherefore David blessed the Lord before all the congregation: and David said, Blessed be thou, Lord God of Israel our father, for ever and ever. Thine, O Lord, is the greatness, and the power, and the glory, and the victory, and the majesty: for all that is in the heaven and in the earth is thine; thine is the kingdom, O Lord, and thou art exalted as head above all. Both riches and honour come of thee, and thou reignest over all; and in thine hand is power and might; and in thine hand it is to make great, and to give strength unto all. Now therefore, our God, we thank thee, and praise thy glorious name. **Rev. 15:3–4.** And they sing the song of Moses the servant of God, and the song of the Lamb, saying, Great and marvellous are thy works, Lord God Almighty; just and true are thy ways, thou King of saints. Who shall not fear thee, O Lord, and glorify thy name? for thou only art holy: for all nations shall come and worship before thee; for thy judgments are made manifest.

r. **Acts 2:42.** And they continued stedfastly in the apostles' doctrine and fellowship, and in breaking of bread, and in prayers. **1 Cor. 11:27–28.** Wherefore whosoever shall eat this bread, and drink this cup of the Lord, unworthily, shall be guilty of the body and blood of the Lord. But let a man examine himself, and so let him eat of that bread, and drink of that cup.

s. **Ps. 138:2.** I will worship toward thy holy temple, and praise thy name for thy lovingkindness and for thy truth: for thou hast magnified thy word above all thy name. **Rev. 22:18–19.** For I testify unto every man that heareth the words of the prophecy of this book, If any man shall add unto these things, God shall add unto him the plagues that are written in this book: and if any man shall take away from the words of the book of this prophecy, God shall take away his part out of the book of life, and out of the holy city, and from the things which are written in this book.

t. **Ps. 107:21–22.** Oh that men would praise the Lord for his goodness, and for his wonderful works to the children of men! And let them sacrifice the sacrifices of thanksgiving, and declare his works with rejoicing. **Rev. 4:11.** Thou art worthy, O Lord, to receive glory and honour and power: for thou hast created all things, and for thy pleasure they are and were created.

u. **Lev. 19:12.** And ye shall not swear by my name falsely, neither shalt thou profane the name of thy God: I am the Lord. **Matt. 5:33–37.** Again, ye have heard that it hath been said by them of old time, Thou shalt not forswear thyself, but shalt perform unto the Lord thine oaths: but I say unto you, Swear not at all; neither by heaven; for it is God's throne: nor by the earth; for it is his footstool: neither by Jerusalem; for it is the city of the great King. Neither shalt thou swear by thy head, because thou canst not make one hair white or black. But let your communication be, Yea, yea; Nay, nay: for whatsoever is more than these cometh of evil. **James 5:12.** But above

Q. 56. *What is the reason annexed to the third commandment?*

A. The reason annexed to the third commandment is, that however the breakers of this commandment may escape punishment from men, yet the Lord our God will not suffer them to escape his righteous judgment.[w]

Q. 57. *Which is the fourth commandment?*

A. The fourth commandment is, *Remember the sabbath day, to keep it holy. Six days shalt thou labour, and do all thy work: but the seventh day is the sabbath of the LORD thy God: in it thou shalt not do any work, thou, nor thy son, nor thy daughter, thy manservant, nor thy maidservant, nor thy cattle, nor thy stranger that is within thy gates: for in six days the LORD made heaven and earth, the sea, and all that in them is, and rested the seventh day: wherefore the LORD blessed the sabbath day, and hallowed it.*[x]

Q. 58. *What is required in the fourth commandment?*

A. The fourth commandment requireth the keeping holy to God such set times as he hath appointed in his Word; expressly one whole day in seven, to be a holy Sabbath to himself.[y]

all things, my brethren, swear not, neither by heaven, neither by the earth, neither by any other oath: but let your yea be yea; and your nay, nay; lest ye fall into condemnation.

w. **Deut. 28:58–59.** If thou wilt not observe to do all the words of this law that are written in this book, that thou mayest fear this glorious and fearful name, THE LORD THY GOD; then the LORD will make thy plagues wonderful, and the plagues of thy seed, even great plagues, and of long continuance, and sore sicknesses, and of long continuance. **1 Sam. 3:13.** For I have told him that I will judge his house for ever for the iniquity which he knoweth; because his sons made themselves vile, and he restrained them not. **1 Sam. 4:11.** And the ark of God was taken; and the two sons of Eli, Hophni and Phinehas, were slain.

x. **Ex. 20:8–11. Deut. 5:12–15.** Keep the sabbath day to sanctify it, as the LORD thy God hath commanded thee. Six days thou shalt labour, and do all thy work: but the seventh day is the sabbath of the LORD thy God: in it thou shalt not do any work, thou, nor thy son, nor thy daughter, nor thy manservant, nor thy maidservant, nor thine ox, nor thine ass, nor any of thy cattle, nor thy stranger that is within thy gates; that thy manservant and thy maidservant may rest as well as thou. And remember that thou wast a servant in the land of Egypt, and that the LORD thy God brought thee out thence through a mighty hand and by a stretched out arm: therefore the LORD thy God commanded thee to keep the sabbath day.

y. **Ex. 31:13, 16–17.** Speak thou also unto the children of Israel, saying, Verily my sabbaths ye shall keep: for it is a sign between me and you throughout your generations; that ye may know that I am the LORD that doth sanctify you.… Wherefore the children of Israel shall keep the sabbath, to observe the sabbath throughout their

Q. 59. *Which day of the seven hath God appointed to be the weekly Sabbath?*

A. From the beginning of the world to the resurrection of Christ, God appointed the seventh day of the week to be the weekly Sabbath;[z] and the first day of the week ever since, to continue to the end of the world, which is the Christian Sabbath.[a]

Q. 60. *How is the Sabbath to be sanctified?*

A. The Sabbath is to be sanctified by a holy resting all that day, even from such worldly employments and recreations as are lawful on other days;[b] and spending the whole time in the public and pri-

generations, for a perpetual covenant. It is a sign between me and the children of Israel for ever: for in six days the LORD made heaven and earth, and on the seventh day he rested, and was refreshed.

z. **Gen. 2:2–3.** And on the seventh day God ended his work which he had made; and he rested on the seventh day from all his work which he had made. And God blessed the seventh day, and sanctified it: because that in it he had rested from all his work which God created and made. **Ex. 20:11.** For in six days the LORD made heaven and earth, the sea, and all that in them is, and rested the seventh day: wherefore the LORD blessed the sabbath day, and hallowed it.

a. **Mark 2:27–28.** And he said unto them, The sabbath was made for man, and not man for the sabbath: therefore the Son of man is Lord also of the sabbath. **Acts 20:7.** And upon the first day of the week, when the disciples came together to break bread, Paul preached unto them, ready to depart on the morrow; and continued his speech until midnight. **1 Cor. 16:2.** Upon the first day of the week let every one of you lay by him in store, as God hath prospered him, that there be no gatherings when I come. **Rev. 1:10.** I was in the Spirit on the Lord's day, and heard behind me a great voice, as of a trumpet.

b. **Ex. 20:10.** But the seventh day is the sabbath of the LORD thy God: in it thou shalt not do any work, thou, nor thy son, nor thy daughter, thy manservant, nor thy maidservant, nor thy cattle, nor thy stranger that is within thy gates. **Neh. 13:15–22.** In those days saw I in Judah some treading wine presses on the sabbath, and bringing in sheaves, and lading asses; as also wine, grapes, and figs, and all manner of burdens, which they brought into Jerusalem on the sabbath day: and I testified against them in the day wherein they sold victuals.… Then I contended with the nobles of Judah, and said unto them, What evil thing is this that ye do, and profane the sabbath day? Did not your fathers thus, and did not our God bring all this evil upon us, and upon this city? yet ye bring more wrath upon Israel by profaning the sabbath. And it came to pass, that when the gates of Jerusalem began to be dark before the sabbath, I commanded that the gates should be shut, and charged that they should not be opened till after the sabbath: and some of my servants set I at the gates, that there should no burden be brought in on the sabbath day.… **Isa. 58:13–14.** If thou turn away thy foot from the sabbath, from doing thy pleasure on my holy day; and call the sabbath a delight, the holy of the LORD, honourable; and shalt honour him, not doing thine own ways, nor finding thine own pleasure, nor speaking thine own words: then shalt thou

vate exercises of God's worship,[c] except so much as is to be taken up in the works of necessity and mercy.[d]

Q. 61. *What is forbidden in the fourth commandment?*

A. The fourth commandment forbiddeth the omission, or careless performance, of the duties required, and the profaning the day by idleness, or doing that which is in itself sinful, or by unnecessary thoughts, words, or works, about our worldly employments or recreations.[e]

delight thyself in the LORD; and I will cause thee to ride upon the high places of the earth, and feed thee with the heritage of Jacob thy father: for the mouth of the LORD hath spoken it.

c. **Ex. 20:8.** Remember the sabbath day, to keep it holy. **Lev. 23:3.** Six days shall work be done: but the seventh day is the sabbath of rest, an holy convocation; ye shall do no work therein: it is the sabbath of the LORD in all your dwellings. **Luke 4:16.** And he came to Nazareth, where he had been brought up: and, as his custom was, he went into the synagogue on the sabbath day, and stood up for to read. **Acts 20:7.** And upon the first day of the week, when the disciples came together to break bread, Paul preached unto them, ready to depart on the morrow; and continued his speech until midnight.

d. **Matt. 12:1–13.** At that time Jesus went on the sabbath day through the corn; and his disciples were an hungred, and began to pluck the ears of corn, and to eat. But when the Pharisees saw it, they said unto him, Behold, thy disciples do that which is not lawful to do upon the sabbath day. But he said unto them, Have ye not read what David did, when he was an hungred, and they that were with him; how he entered into the house of God, and did eat the shewbread, which was not lawful for him to eat, neither for them which were with him, but only for the priests? Or have ye not read in the law, how that on the sabbath days the priests in the temple profane the sabbath, and are blameless? But I say unto you, That in this place is one greater than the temple. But if ye had known what this meaneth, I will have mercy, and not sacrifice, ye would not have condemned the guiltless. For the Son of man is Lord even of the sabbath day. And when he was departed thence, he went into their synagogue: and, behold, there was a man which had his hand withered. And they asked him, saying, Is it lawful to heal on the sabbath days? that they might accuse him. And he said unto them, What man shall there be among you, that shall have one sheep, and if it fall into a pit on the sabbath day, will he not lay hold on it, and lift it out? How much then is a man better than a sheep? Wherefore it is lawful to do well on the sabbath days. Then saith he to the man, Stretch forth thine hand. And he stretched it forth; and it was restored whole, like as the other.

e. **Neh. 13:15–22. See footnote** *b* **above. Isa. 58:13–14. See footnote** *b* **above. Amos 8:4–6.** Hear this, O ye that swallow up the needy, even to make the poor of the land to fail, saying, When will the new moon be gone, that we may sell corn? and the sabbath, that we may set forth wheat, making the ephah small, and the shekel great, and falsifying the balances by deceit? That we may buy the poor for silver, and the needy for a pair of shoes; yea, and sell the refuse of the wheat?

Q. 62. *What are the reasons annexed to the fourth commandment?*

A. The reasons annexed to the fourth commandment are, God's allowing us six days of the week for our own employments,[f] his challenging a special propriety in the seventh, his own example, and his blessing the Sabbath day.[g]

Q. 63. *Which is the fifth commandment?*

A. The fifth commandment is, *Honour thy father and thy mother: that thy days may be long upon the land which the LORD thy God giveth thee.*[h]

Q. 64. *What is required in the fifth commandment?*

A. The fifth commandment requireth the preserving the honor, and performing the duties, belonging to everyone in their several places and relations, as superiors, inferiors, or equals.[i]

---

f. **Ex. 20:9.** Six days shalt thou labour, and do all thy work. **Ex. 31:15.** Six days may work be done; but in the seventh is the sabbath of rest, holy to the LORD: whosoever doeth any work in the sabbath day, he shall surely be put to death. **Lev. 23:3.** Six days shall work be done: but the seventh day is the sabbath of rest, an holy convocation; ye shall do no work therein: it is the sabbath of the LORD in all your dwellings.

g. **Gen. 2:2–3.** And on the seventh day God ended his work which he had made; and he rested on the seventh day from all his work which he had made. And God blessed the seventh day, and sanctified it: because that in it he had rested from all his work which God created and made. **Ex. 20:11.** For in six days the LORD made heaven and earth, the sea, and all that in them is, and rested the seventh day: wherefore the LORD blessed the sabbath day, and hallowed it. **Ex. 31:17.** It is a sign between me and the children of Israel for ever: for in six days the LORD made heaven and earth, and on the seventh day he rested, and was refreshed.

h. **Ex. 20:12. Deut. 5:16.** Honour thy father and thy mother, as the LORD thy God hath commanded thee; that thy days may be prolonged, and that it may go well with thee, in the land which the LORD thy God giveth thee.

i. **Rom. 13:1, 7.** Let every soul be subject unto the higher powers. For there is no power but of God: the powers that be are ordained of God.… Render therefore to all their dues: tribute to whom tribute is due; custom to whom custom; fear to whom fear; honour to whom honour. **Eph. 5:21–22, 24.** … submitting yourselves one to another in the fear of God. Wives, submit yourselves unto your own husbands, as unto the Lord.… Therefore as the church is subject unto Christ, so let the wives be to their own husbands in every thing. **Eph. 6:1, 4–5, 9.** Children, obey your parents in the Lord: for this is right.… And, ye fathers, provoke not your children to wrath: but bring them up in the nurture and admonition of the Lord. Servants, be obedient to them that are your masters according to the flesh, with fear and trembling, in singleness of your heart, as unto Christ.… And, ye masters, do the same things unto them, forbearing threatening: knowing that your Master also is in heaven; neither is there respect of persons with him. **1 Pet. 2:17.** Honour all men. Love the brotherhood. Fear God. Honour the king.

Q. 65. *What is forbidden in the fifth commandment?*

A. The fifth commandment forbiddeth the neglecting of, or doing anything against, the honor and duty which belongeth to everyone in their several places and relations.[k]

Q. 66. *What is the reason annexed to the fifth commandment?*

A. The reason annexed to the fifth commandment is, a promise of long life and prosperity (as far as it shall serve for God's glory and their own good) to all such as keep this commandment.[l]

Q. 67. *Which is the sixth commandment?*

A. The sixth commandment is, *Thou shalt not kill.*[m]

Q. 68. *What is required in the sixth commandment?*

A. The sixth commandment requireth all lawful endeavors to preserve our own life, and the life of others.[n]

Q. 69. *What is forbidden in the sixth commandment?*

A. The sixth commandment forbiddeth the taking away of our own life, or the life of our neighbor unjustly, or whatsoever tendeth thereunto.[o]

k. **Matt. 15:4–6.** For God commanded, saying, Honour thy father and mother: and, He that curseth father or mother, let him die the death. But ye say, Whosoever shall say to his father or his mother, It is a gift, by whatsoever thou mightest be profited by me; and honour not his father or his mother, he shall be free. Thus have ye made the commandment of God of none effect by your tradition. **Rom. 13:8.** Owe no man any thing, but to love one another: for he that loveth another hath fulfilled the law.

l. **Ex. 20:12.** Honour thy father and thy mother: that thy days may be long upon the land which the LORD thy God giveth thee. **Deut. 5:16.** Honour thy father and thy mother, as the LORD thy God hath commanded thee; that thy days may be prolonged, and that it may go well with thee, in the land which the LORD thy God giveth thee. **Eph. 6:2–3.** Honour thy father and mother; (which is the first commandment with promise;) that it may be well with thee, and thou mayest live long on the earth.

m. **Ex. 20:13. Deut. 5:17.** Thou shalt not kill.

n. **Eph. 5:28–29.** So ought men to love their wives as their own bodies. He that loveth his wife loveth himself. For no man ever yet hated his own flesh; but nourisheth and cherisheth it, even as the Lord the church.

o. **Gen. 9:6.** Whoso sheddeth man's blood, by man shall his blood be shed: for in the image of God made he man. **Matt. 5:22.** But I say unto you, That whosoever is angry with his brother without a cause shall be in danger of the judgment: and whosoever shall say to his brother, Raca, shall be in danger of the council: but whosoever shall say, Thou fool, shall be in danger of hell fire. **1 John 3:15.** Whosoever hateth his brother is a murderer: and ye know that no murderer hath eternal life abiding in him.

Q. 70. *Which is the seventh commandment?*

A. The seventh commandment is, *Thou shalt not commit adultery.*[p]

Q. 71. *What is required in the seventh commandment?*

A. The seventh commandment requireth the preservation of our own and our neighbor's chastity, in heart, speech, and behavior.[q]

Q. 72. *What is forbidden in the seventh commandment?*

A. The seventh commandment forbiddeth all unchaste thoughts, words, and actions.[r]

Q. 73. *Which is the eighth commandment?*

A. The eighth commandment is, *Thou shalt not steal.*[s]

Q. 74. *What is required in the eighth commandment?*

A. The eighth commandment requireth the lawful procuring and furthering the wealth and outward estate of ourselves and others.[t]

Q. 75. *What is forbidden in the eighth commandment?*

A. The eighth commandment forbiddeth whatsoever doth, or may, unjustly hinder our own, or our neighbor's, wealth or outward estate.[u]

p. **Ex. 20:14. Deut. 5:18.** Neither shalt thou commit adultery.

q. **1 Cor. 7:2–3, 5.** Nevertheless, to avoid fornication, let every man have his own wife, and let every woman have her own husband. Let the husband render unto the wife due benevolence: and likewise also the wife unto the husband.… Defraud ye not one the other, except it be with consent for a time, that ye may give yourselves to fasting and prayer; and come together again, that Satan tempt you not for your incontinency. **1 Thess. 4:3–5.** For this is the will of God, even your sanctification, that ye should abstain from fornication: that every one of you should know how to possess his vessel in sanctification and honour; not in the lust of concupiscence, even as the Gentiles which know not God.

r. **Matt. 5:28.** But I say unto you, That whosoever looketh on a woman to lust after her hath committed adultery with her already in his heart. **Eph. 5:3–4.** But fornication, and all uncleanness, or covetousness, let it not be once named among you, as becometh saints; neither filthiness, nor foolish talking, nor jesting, which are not convenient: but rather giving of thanks.

s. **Ex. 20:15. Deut. 5:19.** Neither shalt thou steal.

t. **Lev. 25:35.** And if thy brother be waxen poor, and fallen in decay with thee; then thou shalt relieve him: yea, though he be a stranger, or a sojourner; that he may live with thee. **Eph. 4:28b.** … but rather let him labour, working with his hands the thing which is good, that he may have to give to him that needeth. **Phil. 2:4.** Look not every man on his own things, but every man also on the things of others.

u. **Prov. 28:19ff.** He that tilleth his land shall have plenty of bread: but he that followeth after vain persons shall have poverty enough. A faithful man shall abound

Q. 76. *Which is the ninth commandment?*

A. The ninth commandment is, *Thou shalt not bear false witness against thy neighbour.*[w]

Q. 77. *What is required in the ninth commandment?*

A. The ninth commandment requireth the maintaining and promoting of truth between man and man, and of our own and our neighbor's good name,[x] especially in witness bearing.[y]

Q. 78. *What is forbidden in the ninth commandment?*

A. The ninth commandment forbiddeth whatsoever is prejudicial to truth, or injurious to our own, or our neighbor's, good name.[z]

Q. 79. *Which is the tenth commandment?*

A. The tenth commandment is, *Thou shalt not covet thy neighbour's house, thou shalt not covet thy neighbour's wife, nor his manservant, nor his maid-*

---

with blessings: but he that maketh haste to be rich shall not be innocent.... He that hasteth to be rich hath an evil eye, and considereth not that poverty shall come upon him.... Whoso robbeth his father or his mother, and saith, It is no transgression; the same is the companion of a destroyer.... **Eph. 4:28a.** Let him that stole steal no more. **2 Thess. 3:10.** For even when we were with you, this we commanded you, that if any would not work, neither should he eat. **1 Tim. 5:8.** But if any provide not for his own, and specially for those of his own house, he hath denied the faith, and is worse than an infidel.

w. **Ex. 20:16. Deut. 5:20.** Neither shalt thou bear false witness against thy neighbour.

x. **Zech. 8:16.** These are the things that ye shall do; Speak ye every man the truth to his neighbour; execute the judgment of truth and peace in your gates. **Acts 25:10.** Then said Paul, I stand at Caesar's judgment seat, where I ought to be judged: to the Jews have I done no wrong, as thou very well knowest. **3 John 12.** Demetrius hath good report of all men, and of the truth itself: yea, and we also bear record; and ye know that our record is true.

y. **Prov. 14:5, 25.** A faithful witness will not lie: but a false witness will utter lies.... A true witness delivereth souls: but a deceitful witness speaketh lies.

z. **Lev. 19:16.** Thou shalt not go up and down as a talebearer among thy people: neither shalt thou stand against the blood of thy neighbour: I am the LORD. **Ps. 15:3.** He that backbiteth not with his tongue, nor doeth evil to his neighbour, nor taketh up a reproach against his neighbour. **Prov. 6:16–19.** These six things doth the LORD hate: yea, seven are an abomination unto him: a proud look, a lying tongue, and hands that shed innocent blood, an heart that deviseth wicked imaginations, feet that be swift in running to mischief, a false witness that speaketh lies, and he that soweth discord among brethren. **Luke 3:14.** And the soldiers likewise demanded of him, saying, And what shall we do? And he said unto them, Do violence to no man, neither accuse any falsely; and be content with your wages.

servant, nor his ox, nor his ass, nor any thing that is thy neighbour's.[a]

Q. 80. *What is required in the tenth commandment?*

A. The tenth commandment requireth full contentment with our own condition,[b] with a right and charitable frame of spirit toward our neighbor, and all that is his.[c]

Q. 81. *What is forbidden in the tenth commandment?*

A. The tenth commandment forbiddeth all discontentment with our own estate,[d] envying or grieving at the good of our neighbor, and all inordinate motions and affections to anything that is his.[e]

a. **Ex. 20:17. Deut. 5:21.** Neither shalt thou desire thy neighbour's wife, neither shalt thou covet thy neighbour's house, his field, or his manservant, or his maidservant, his ox, or his ass, or any thing that is thy neighbour's.

b. **Ps. 34:1.** I will bless the LORD at all times: his praise shall continually be in my mouth. **Phil. 4:11.** Not that I speak in respect of want: for I have learned, in whatsoever state I am, therewith to be content. **1 Tim. 6:6.** But godliness with contentment is great gain. **Heb. 13:5.** Let your conversation be without covetousness; and be content with such things as ye have: for he hath said, I will never leave thee, nor forsake thee.

c. **Luke 15:6, 9, 11–32.** And when he cometh home, he calleth together his friends and neighbours, saying unto them, Rejoice with me; for I have found my sheep which was lost.... And when she hath found it, she calleth her friends and her neighbours together, saying, Rejoice with me; for I have found the piece which I had lost.... And he said, A certain man had two sons: and the younger of them said to his father, Father, give me the portion of goods that falleth to me. And he divided unto them his living. And not many days after the younger son gathered all together, and took his journey into a far country, and there wasted his substance with riotous living.... And when he came to himself, he said, ... I will arise and go to my father, and will say unto him, Father, I have sinned against heaven, and before thee.... But when he was yet a great way off, his father saw him, and had compassion, and ran, and fell on his neck, and kissed him. And ... the father said to his servants, ... [B]ring hither the fatted calf, and kill it; and let us eat, and be merry.... Now his elder son ... was angry, and would not go in: therefore came his father out, and entreated him.... And he said unto him, Son, thou art ever with me, and all that I have is thine. It was meet that we should make merry, and be glad: for this thy brother was dead, and is alive again; and was lost, and is found. **Rom. 12:15.** Rejoice with them that do rejoice, and weep with them that weep. **Phil. 2:4.** Look not every man on his own things, but every man also on the things of others.

d. **1 Cor. 10:10.** Neither murmur ye, as some of them also murmured, and were destroyed of the destroyer. **James 3:14–16.** But if ye have bitter envying and strife in your hearts, glory not, and lie not against the truth. This wisdom descendeth not from above, but is earthly, sensual, devilish. For where envying and strife is, there is confusion and every evil work.

e. **Gal. 5:26.** Let us not be desirous of vain glory, provoking one another,

Q. 82. *Is any man able perfectly to keep the commandments of God?*

A. No mere man, since the fall, is able in this life perfectly to keep the commandments of God, but doth daily break them in thought, word, and deed.[f]

Q. 83. *Are all transgressions of the law equally heinous?*

A. Some sins in themselves, and by reason of several aggravations, are more heinous in the sight of God than others.[g]

Q. 84. *What doth every sin deserve?*

A. Every sin deserveth God's wrath and curse, both in this life, and that which is to come.[h]

envying one another. **Col. 3:5.** Mortify therefore your members which are upon the earth; fornication, uncleanness, inordinate affection, evil concupiscence, and covetousness, which is idolatry.

f. **Gen. 8:21.** And the LORD smelled a sweet savour; and the LORD said in his heart, I will not again curse the ground any more for man's sake; for the imagination of man's heart is evil from his youth; neither will I again smite any more every thing living, as I have done. **Rom. 3:9ff., 23.** What then? are we better than they? No, in no wise: for we have before proved both Jews and Gentiles, that they are all under sin; as it is written, There is none righteous, no, not one: there is none that understandeth, there is none that seeketh after God.... For all have sinned, and come short of the glory of God.

g. **Ezek. 8:6, 13, 15.** He said furthermore unto me, Son of man, seest thou what they do? even the great abominations that the house of Israel committeth here, that I should go far off from my sanctuary? but turn thee yet again, and thou shalt see greater abominations.... He said also unto me, Turn thee yet again, and thou shalt see greater abominations that they do.... Then said he unto me, Hast thou seen this, O son of man? turn thee yet again, and thou shalt see greater abominations than these. **Matt. 11:20–24.** Then began he to upbraid the cities wherein most of his mighty works were done, because they repented not: Woe unto thee, Chorazin! woe unto thee, Bethsaida! for if the mighty works, which were done in you, had been done in Tyre and Sidon, they would have repented long ago in sackcloth and ashes. But I say unto you, It shall be more tolerable for Tyre and Sidon at the day of judgment, than for you. And thou, Capernaum, which art exalted unto heaven, shalt be brought down to hell: for if the mighty works, which have been done in thee, had been done in Sodom, it would have remained until this day. But I say unto you, That it shall be more tolerable for the land of Sodom in the day of judgment, than for thee. **John 19:11.** Jesus answered, Thou couldest have no power at all against me, except it were given thee from above: therefore he that delivered me unto thee hath the greater sin.

h. **Matt. 25:41.** Then shall he say also unto them on the left hand, Depart from me, ye cursed, into everlasting fire, prepared for the devil and his angels. **Gal. 3:10.** For as many as are of the works of the law are under the curse: for it is written, Cursed is every one that continueth not in all things which are written in the book of the law to do them. **Eph. 5:6.** Let no man deceive you with vain words: for because of these

Q. 85. *What doth God require of us, that we may escape his wrath and curse, due to us for sin?*

A. To escape the wrath and curse of God, due to us for sin, God requireth of us faith in Jesus Christ, repentance unto life,[i] with the diligent use of all the outward means whereby Christ communicateth to us the benefits of redemption.[k]

Q. 86. *What is faith in Jesus Christ?*

A. Faith in Jesus Christ is a saving grace,[l] whereby we receive and rest upon him alone for salvation, as he is offered to us in the gospel.[m]

things cometh the wrath of God upon the children of disobedience. **James 2:10.** For whosoever shall keep the whole law, and yet offend in one point, he is guilty of all.

i. **Mark 1:15.** … and saying, The time is fulfilled, and the kingdom of God is at hand: repent ye, and believe the gospel. **Acts 20:21.** … testifying both to the Jews, and also to the Greeks, repentance toward God, and faith toward our Lord Jesus Christ.

k. **Acts 2:38.** Then Peter said unto them, Repent, and be baptized every one of you in the name of Jesus Christ for the remission of sins, and ye shall receive the gift of the Holy Ghost. **1 Cor. 11:24–25.** And when he had given thanks, he brake it, and said, Take, eat: this is my body, which is broken for you: this do in remembrance of me. After the same manner also he took the cup, when he had supped, saying, This cup is the new testament in my blood: this do ye, as oft as ye drink it, in remembrance of me. **Col. 3:16.** Let the word of Christ dwell in you richly in all wisdom; teaching and admonishing one another in psalms and hymns and spiritual songs, singing with grace in your hearts to the Lord.

l. **Eph. 2:8–9.** For by grace are ye saved through faith; and that not of yourselves: it is the gift of God: not of works, lest any man should boast. **Cf. Rom. 4:16.** Therefore it is of faith, that it might be by grace; to the end the promise might be sure to all the seed; not to that only which is of the law, but to that also which is of the faith of Abraham; who is the father of us all.

m. **John 20:30–31.** And many other signs truly did Jesus in the presence of his disciples, which are not written in this book: but these are written, that ye might believe that Jesus is the Christ, the Son of God; and that believing ye might have life through his name. **Gal. 2:15–16.** We who are Jews by nature, and not sinners of the Gentiles, knowing that a man is not justified by the works of the law, but by the faith of Jesus Christ, even we have believed in Jesus Christ, that we might be justified by the faith of Christ, and not by the works of the law: for by the works of the law shall no flesh be justified. **Phil. 3:3–11.** For we are the circumcision, which worship God in the spirit, and rejoice in Christ Jesus, and have no confidence in the flesh.… Yea doubtless, and I count all things but loss for the excellency of the knowledge of Christ Jesus my Lord: for whom I have suffered the loss of all things, and do count them but dung, that I may win Christ, and be found in him, not having mine own righteousness, which is of the law, but that which is through the faith of Christ, the righteousness which is of God by faith: that I may know him, and the power of his resurrection, and the fellowship of his sufferings, being made conformable unto his death; if by any

Q. 87. *What is repentance unto life?*

A. Repentance unto life is a saving grace,[n] whereby a sinner, out of a true sense of his sin, and apprehension of the mercy of God in Christ,[o] doth, with grief and hatred of his sin, turn from it unto God,[p] with full purpose of, and endeavor after, new obedience.[q]

means I might attain unto the resurrection of the dead.

n. **Acts 11:18.** When they heard these things, they held their peace, and glorified God, saying, Then hath God also to the Gentiles granted repentance unto life. **2 Tim. 2:25.** … in meekness instructing those that oppose themselves; if God peradventure will give them repentance to the acknowledging of the truth.

o. **Ps. 51:1–4.** Have mercy upon me, O God, according to thy lovingkindness: according unto the multitude of thy tender mercies blot out my transgressions. Wash me thoroughly from mine iniquity, and cleanse me from my sin. For I acknowledge my transgressions: and my sin is ever before me. Against thee, thee only, have I sinned, and done this evil in thy sight: that thou mightest be justified when thou speakest, and be clear when thou judgest. **Joel 2:13.** And rend your heart, and not your garments, and turn unto the LORD your God: for he is gracious and merciful, slow to anger, and of great kindness, and repenteth him of the evil. **Luke 15:7, 10.** I say unto you, that likewise joy shall be in heaven over one sinner that repenteth, more than over ninety and nine just persons, which need no repentance.… Likewise, I say unto you, there is joy in the presence of the angels of God over one sinner that repenteth. **Acts 2:37.** Now when they heard this, they were pricked in their heart, and said unto Peter and to the rest of the apostles, Men and brethren, what shall we do?

p. **Jer. 31:18–19.** I have surely heard Ephraim bemoaning himself thus; Thou hast chastised me, and I was chastised, as a bullock unaccustomed to the yoke: turn thou me, and I shall be turned; for thou art the LORD my God. Surely after that I was turned, I repented; and after that I was instructed, I smote upon my thigh: I was ashamed, yea, even confounded, because I did bear the reproach of my youth. **Luke 1:16–17.** And many of the children of Israel shall he turn to the Lord their God. And he shall go before him in the spirit and power of Elias, to turn the hearts of the fathers to the children, and the disobedient to the wisdom of the just; to make ready a people prepared for the Lord. **1 Thess. 1:9.** For they themselves shew of us what manner of entering in we had unto you, and how ye turned to God from idols to serve the living and true God.

q. **2 Chron. 7:14.** If my people, which are called by my name, shall humble themselves, and pray, and seek my face, and turn from their wicked ways; then will I hear from heaven, and will forgive their sin, and will heal their land. **Ps. 119:57–64.** Thou art my portion, O LORD: I have said that I would keep thy words. I intreated thy favour with my whole heart: be merciful unto me according to thy word. I thought on my ways, and turned my feet unto thy testimonies. I made haste, and delayed not to keep thy commandments. The bands of the wicked have robbed me: but I have not forgotten thy law. At midnight I will rise to give thanks unto thee because of thy righteous judgments. I am a companion of all them that fear thee, and of them that keep thy precepts. The earth, O LORD, is full of thy mercy: teach me thy statutes. **Matt. 3:8.** Bring forth therefore fruits meet for repentance. **2 Cor. 7:10.** For godly sorrow

Q. 88. *What are the outward and ordinary means whereby Christ communicateth to us the benefits of redemption?*

A. The outward and ordinary means whereby Christ communicateth to us the benefits of redemption are, his ordinances, especially the Word, sacraments, and prayer; all which are made effectual to the elect for salvation.ʳ

Q. 89. *How is the Word made effectual to salvation?*

A. The Spirit of God maketh the reading, but especially the preaching, of the Word, an effectual means of convincing and converting sinners, and of building them up in holiness and comfort, through faith, unto salvation.ˢ

Q. 90. *How is the Word to be read and heard, that it may become effectual to salvation?*

A. That the Word may become effectual to salvation, we must

worketh repentance to salvation not to be repented of: but the sorrow of the world worketh death.

r. **Matt. 28:18–20.** And Jesus came and spake unto them, saying, All power is given unto me in heaven and in earth. Go ye therefore, and teach all nations, baptizing them in the name of the Father, and of the Son, and of the Holy Ghost: teaching them to observe all things whatsoever I have commanded you: and, lo, I am with you alway, even unto the end of the world. Amen. **Acts 2:41–42.** Then they that gladly received his word were baptized: and the same day there were added unto them about three thousand souls. And they continued stedfastly in the apostles' doctrine and fellowship, and in breaking of bread, and in prayers.

s. **Neh. 8:8–9.** So they read in the book in the law of God distinctly, and gave the sense, and caused them to understand the reading. And Nehemiah, which is the Tirshatha, and Ezra the priest the scribe, and the Levites that taught the people, said unto all the people, This day is holy unto the LORD your God; mourn not, nor weep. For all the people wept, when they heard the words of the law. **Acts 20:32.** And now, brethren, I commend you to God, and to the word of his grace, which is able to build you up, and to give you an inheritance among all them which are sanctified. **Rom. 10:14–17.** How then shall they call on him in whom they have not believed? and how shall they believe in him of whom they have not heard? and how shall they hear without a preacher? And how shall they preach, except they be sent? as it is written, How beautiful are the feet of them that preach the gospel of peace, and bring glad tidings of good things! But they have not all obeyed the gospel. For Esaias saith, Lord, who hath believed our report? So then faith cometh by hearing, and hearing by the word of God. **2 Tim. 3:15–17.** … and that from a child thou hast known the holy scriptures, which are able to make thee wise unto salvation through faith which is in Christ Jesus. All scripture is given by inspiration of God, and is profitable for doctrine, for reproof, for correction, for instruction in righteousness: that the man of God may be perfect, thoroughly furnished unto all good works.

attend thereunto with diligence, preparation, and prayer;[t] receive it with faith and love, lay it up in our hearts, and practice it in our lives.[u]

Q. 91. *How do the sacraments become effectual means of salvation?*

A. The sacraments become effectual means of salvation, not from any virtue in them, or in him that doth administer them; but only by the blessing of Christ, and the working of his Spirit in them that by faith receive them.[w]

Q. 92. *What is a sacrament?*

A. A sacrament is a holy ordinance instituted by Christ;[x] wherein,

t. **Deut. 6:16ff.** Ye shall not tempt the LORD your God, as ye tempted him in Massah. Ye shall diligently keep the commandments of the LORD your God, and his testimonies, and his statutes, which he hath commanded thee. And thou shalt do that which is right and good in the sight of the LORD: that it may be well with thee, and that thou mayest go in and possess the good land which the LORD sware unto thy fathers.… **Ps. 119:18.** Open thou mine eyes, that I may behold wondrous things out of thy law. **1 Pet. 2:1–2.** Wherefore laying aside all malice, and all guile, and hypocrisies, and envies, and all evil speakings, as newborn babes, desire the sincere milk of the word, that ye may grow thereby.

u. **Ps. 119:11.** Thy word have I hid in mine heart, that I might not sin against thee. **2 Thess. 2:10.** … and with all deceivableness of unrighteousness in them that perish; because they received not the love of the truth, that they might be saved. **Heb. 4:2.** For unto us was the gospel preached, as well as unto them: but the word preached did not profit them, not being mixed with faith in them that heard it. **James 1:22–25.** But be ye doers of the word, and not hearers only, deceiving your own selves. For if any be a hearer of the word, and not a doer, he is like unto a man beholding his natural face in a glass: for he beholdeth himself, and goeth his way, and straightway forgetteth what manner of man he was. But whoso looketh into the perfect law of liberty, and continueth therein, he being not a forgetful hearer, but a doer of the work, this man shall be blessed in his deed.

w. **1 Cor. 3:7.** So then neither is he that planteth any thing, neither he that watereth; but God that giveth the increase. **Cf. 1 Cor. 1:12–17.** Now this I say, that every one of you saith, I am of Paul; and I of Apollos; and I of Cephas; and I of Christ. Is Christ divided? was Paul crucified for you? or were ye baptized in the name of Paul? I thank God that I baptized none of you, but Crispus and Gaius; lest any should say that I had baptized in mine own name. And I baptized also the household of Stephanas: besides, I know not whether I baptized any other. For Christ sent me not to baptize, but to preach the gospel: not with wisdom of words, lest the cross of Christ should be made of none effect.

x. **Matt. 28:19.** Go ye therefore, and teach all nations, baptizing them in the name of the Father, and of the Son, and of the Holy Ghost. **Matt. 26:26–28.** And as they were eating, Jesus took bread, and blessed it, and brake it, and gave it to the disciples, and said, Take, eat; this is my body. And he took the cup, and gave thanks, and gave it to them, saying, Drink ye all of it; For this is my blood of the new testament, which is shed for many for the remission of sins. **Mark 14:22–25.** And as they

by sensible signs, Christ, and the benefits of the new covenant, are represented, sealed, and applied to believers.[y]

Q. 93. *Which are the sacraments of the New Testament?*

A. The sacraments of the New Testament are, baptism,[z] and the Lord's Supper.[a]

Q. 94. *What is baptism?*

A. Baptism is a sacrament, wherein the washing with water in the name of the Father, and of the Son, and of the Holy Ghost,[b] doth signify and seal our ingrafting into Christ, and partaking of the benefits of the covenant of grace, and our engagement to be the Lord's.[c]

did eat, Jesus took bread, and blessed, and brake it, and gave to them, and said, Take, eat: this is my body. And he took the cup, and when he had given thanks, he gave it to them: and they all drank of it. And he said unto them, This is my blood of the new testament, which is shed for many. Verily I say unto you, I will drink no more of the fruit of the vine, until that day that I drink it new in the kingdom of God. **Luke 22:19–20.** And he took bread, and gave thanks, and brake it, and gave unto them, saying, This is my body which is given for you: this do in remembrance of me. Likewise also the cup after supper, saying, This cup is the new testament in my blood, which is shed for you. **1 Cor. 1:22–26.** For the Jews require a sign, and the Greeks seek after wisdom: but we preach Christ crucified, unto the Jews a stumblingblock, and unto the Greeks foolishness; but unto them which are called, both Jews and Greeks, Christ the power of God, and the wisdom of God. Because the foolishness of God is wiser than men; and the weakness of God is stronger than men. For ye see your calling, brethren, how that not many wise men after the flesh, not many mighty, not many noble, are called.

y. **Gal. 3:27.** For as many of you as have been baptized into Christ have put on Christ. **1 Cor. 10:16–17.** The cup of blessing which we bless, is it not the communion of the blood of Christ? The bread which we break, is it not the communion of the body of Christ? For we being many are one bread, and one body: for we are all partakers of that one bread.

z. **Matt. 28:19.** Go ye therefore, and teach all nations, baptizing them in the name of the Father, and of the Son, and of the Holy Ghost.

a. **1 Cor. 11:23–26.** For I have received of the Lord that which also I delivered unto you, That the Lord Jesus the same night in which he was betrayed took bread: and when he had given thanks, he brake it, and said, Take, eat: this is my body, which is broken for you: this do in remembrance of me. After the same manner also he took the cup, when he had supped, saying, This cup is the new testament in my blood: this do ye, as oft as ye drink it, in remembrance of me. For as often as ye eat this bread, and drink this cup, ye do shew the Lord's death till he come.

b. **Matt. 28:19.** Go ye therefore, and teach all nations, baptizing them in the name of the Father, and of the Son, and of the Holy Ghost.

c. **Acts 2:38–42.** Then Peter said unto them, Repent, and be baptized every one

Q. 95. *To whom is baptism to be administered?*

A. Baptism is not to be administered to any that are out of the visible church, till they profess their faith in Christ, and obedience to him;[d] but the infants of such as are members of the visible church are to be baptized.[e]

of you in the name of Jesus Christ for the remission of sins, and ye shall receive the gift of the Holy Ghost. For the promise is unto you, and to your children, and to all that are afar off, even as many as the Lord our God shall call. And with many other words did he testify and exhort, saying, Save yourselves from this untoward generation. Then they that gladly received his word were baptized: and the same day there were added unto them about three thousand souls. And they continued stedfastly in the apostles' doctrine and fellowship, and in breaking of bread, and in prayers. **Acts 22:16.** And now why tarriest thou? arise, and be baptized, and wash away thy sins, calling on the name of the Lord. **Rom. 6:3–4.** Know ye not, that so many of us as were baptized into Jesus Christ were baptized into his death? Therefore we are buried with him by baptism into death: that like as Christ was raised up from the dead by the glory of the Father, even so we also should walk in newness of life. **Gal. 3:26–27.** For ye are all the children of God by faith in Christ Jesus. For as many of you as have been baptized into Christ have put on Christ. **1 Pet. 3:21.** The like figure whereunto even baptism doth also now save us (not the putting away of the filth of the flesh, but the answer of a good conscience toward God,) by the resurrection of Jesus Christ.

d. **Acts 2:41.** Then they that gladly received his word were baptized: and the same day there were added unto them about three thousand souls. **Acts 8:12, 36, 38.** But when they believed Philip preaching the things concerning the kingdom of God, and the name of Jesus Christ, they were baptized, both men and women.… And as they went on their way, they came unto a certain water: and the eunuch said, See, here is water; what doth hinder me to be baptized?… And he commanded the chariot to stand still: and they went down both into the water, both Philip and the eunuch; and he baptized him. **Acts 18:8.** And Crispus, the chief ruler of the synagogue, believed on the Lord with all his house; and many of the Corinthians hearing believed, and were baptized.

e. **Gen. 17:7, 9–11.** And I will establish my covenant between me and thee and thy seed after thee in their generations for an everlasting covenant, to be a God unto thee, and to thy seed after thee.… And God said unto Abraham, Thou shalt keep my covenant therefore, thou, and thy seed after thee in their generations. This is my covenant, which ye shall keep, between me and you and thy seed after thee; Every man child among you shall be circumcised. And ye shall circumcise the flesh of your foreskin; and it shall be a token of the covenant betwixt me and you. **Acts 2:38–39.** Then Peter said unto them, Repent, and be baptized every one of you in the name of Jesus Christ for the remission of sins, and ye shall receive the gift of the Holy Ghost. For the promise is unto you, and to your children, and to all that are afar off, even as many as the Lord our God shall call. **Acts 16:32–33.** And they spake unto him the word of the Lord, and to all that were in his house. And he took them the same hour of the night, and washed their stripes; and was baptized, he and all his, straightway. **Col. 2:11–12.** … in whom also ye are circumcised with the circumcision made without hands, in putting off the body of the sins of the flesh by the circumcision of

Q. 96. *What is the Lord's Supper?*

A. The Lord's Supper is a sacrament, wherein, by giving and receiving bread and wine, according to Christ's appointment, his death is showed forth;[f] and the worthy receivers are, not after a corporal and carnal manner, but by faith, made partakers of his body and blood, with all his benefits, to their spiritual nourishment, and growth in grace.[g]

Q. 97. *What is required for the worthy receiving of the Lord's Supper?*

A. It is required of them that would worthily partake of the Lord's Supper, that they examine themselves of their knowledge to discern the Lord's body, of their faith to feed upon him, of their repentance, love, and new obedience; lest, coming unworthily, they eat and drink judgment to themselves.[h]

Q. 98. *What is prayer?*

A. Prayer is an offering up of our desires unto God,[i] for things

Christ: buried with him in baptism, wherein also ye are risen with him through the faith of the operation of God, who hath raised him from the dead.

f. **Luke 22:19–20.** And he took bread, and gave thanks, and brake it, and gave unto them, saying, This is my body which is given for you: this do in remembrance of me. Likewise also the cup after supper, saying, This cup is the new testament in my blood, which is shed for you. **1 Cor. 11:23–26.** For I have received of the Lord that which also I delivered unto you, That the Lord Jesus the same night in which he was betrayed took bread: and when he had given thanks, he brake it, and said, Take, eat: this is my body, which is broken for you: this do in remembrance of me. After the same manner also he took the cup, when he had supped, saying, This cup is the new testament in my blood: this do ye, as oft as ye drink it, in remembrance of me. For as often as ye eat this bread, and drink this cup, ye do shew the Lord's death till he come.

g. **1 Cor. 10:16–17.** The cup of blessing which we bless, is it not the communion of the blood of Christ? The bread which we break, is it not the communion of the body of Christ? For we being many are one bread, and one body: for we are all partakers of that one bread.

h. **1 Cor. 11:27–32.** Wherefore whosoever shall eat this bread, and drink this cup of the Lord, unworthily, shall be guilty of the body and blood of the Lord. But let a man examine himself, and so let him eat of that bread, and drink of that cup. For he that eateth and drinketh unworthily, eateth and drinketh damnation to himself, not discerning the Lord's body. For this cause many are weak and sickly among you, and many sleep. For if we would judge ourselves, we should not be judged. But when we are judged, we are chastened of the Lord, that we should not be condemned with the world.

i. **Ps. 10:17.** LORD, thou hast heard the desire of the humble: thou wilt prepare their heart, thou wilt cause thine ear to hear. **Ps. 62:8.** Trust in him at all times; ye people, pour out your heart before him: God is a refuge for us. Selah. **Matt. 7:7–8.**

agreeable to his will,^{k} in the name of Christ,^{l} with confession of our sins,^{m} and thankful acknowledgment of his mercies.^{n}

Q. 99. *What rule hath God given for our direction in prayer?*
A. The whole Word of God is of use to direct us in prayer;^{o} but

Ask, and it shall be given you; seek, and ye shall find; knock, and it shall be opened unto you: for every one that asketh receiveth; and he that seeketh findeth; and to him that knocketh it shall be opened.

k. **1 John 5:14.** And this is the confidence that we have in him, that, if we ask any thing according to his will, he heareth us.

l. **John 16:23–24.** And in that day ye shall ask me nothing. Verily, verily, I say unto you, Whatsoever ye shall ask the Father in my name, he will give it you. Hitherto have ye asked nothing in my name: ask, and ye shall receive, that your joy may be full.

m. **Ps. 32:5–6.** I acknowledged my sin unto thee, and mine iniquity have I not hid. I said, I will confess my transgressions unto the Lord; and thou forgavest the iniquity of my sin. Selah. For this shall every one that is godly pray unto thee in a time when thou mayest be found: surely in the floods of great waters they shall not come nigh unto him. **Dan. 9:4–19.** And I prayed unto the Lord my God, and made my confession, and said, O Lord, the great and dreadful God, keeping the covenant and mercy to them that love him, and to them that keep his commandments; we have sinned, and have committed iniquity, and have done wickedly, and have rebelled, even by departing from thy precepts and from thy judgments…. To the Lord our God belong mercies and forgivenesses, though we have rebelled against him; neither have we obeyed the voice of the Lord our God, to walk in his laws, which he set before us by his servants the prophets…. O my God, incline thine ear, and hear; open thine eyes, and behold our desolations, and the city which is called by thy name: for we do not present our supplications before thee for our righteousnesses, but for thy great mercies. O Lord, hear; O Lord, forgive; O Lord, hearken and do; defer not, for thine own sake, O my God: for thy city and thy people are called by thy name. **1 John 1:9.** If we confess our sins, he is faithful and just to forgive us our sins, and to cleanse us from all unrighteousness.

n. **Ps. 103:1–5.** Bless the Lord, O my soul: and all that is within me, bless his holy name. Bless the Lord, O my soul, and forget not all his benefits: who forgiveth all thine iniquities; who healeth all thy diseases; who redeemeth thy life from destruction; who crowneth thee with lovingkindness and tender mercies; who satisfieth thy mouth with good things; so that thy youth is renewed like the eagle's. **Ps. 136.** O give thanks unto the Lord; for he is good: for his mercy endureth for ever. O give thanks unto the God of gods: for his mercy endureth for ever. O give thanks to the Lord of lords: for his mercy endureth for ever. To him who alone doeth great wonders: for his mercy endureth for ever…. Who remembered us in our low estate: for his mercy endureth for ever: and hath redeemed us from our enemies: for his mercy endureth for ever. Who giveth food to all flesh: for his mercy endureth for ever. O give thanks unto the God of heaven: for his mercy endureth for ever. **Phil. 4:6.** Be careful for nothing; but in every thing by prayer and supplication with thanksgiving let your requests be made known unto God.

o. **1 John 5:14.** And this is the confidence that we have in him, that, if we ask any thing according to his will, he heareth us.

the special rule of direction is that form of prayer which Christ taught his disciples, commonly called the Lord's Prayer.[p]

Q. 100. *What doth the preface of the Lord's Prayer teach us?*

A. The preface of the Lord's Prayer, which is, *Our Father which art in heaven,* teacheth us to draw near to God with all holy reverence[q] and confidence,[r] as children to a father,[s] able and ready to help us;[t] and that we should pray with and for others.[u]

Q. 101. *What do we pray for in the first petition?*

A. In the first petition, which is, *Hallowed be thy name,* we pray that God would enable us, and others, to glorify him in all that whereby he maketh himself known;[w] and that he would dispose all things to

p. **Matt. 6:9–13.** After this manner therefore pray ye: Our Father which art in heaven, Hallowed be thy name. Thy kingdom come. Thy will be done in earth, as it is in heaven. Give us this day our daily bread. And forgive us our debts, as we forgive our debtors. And lead us not into temptation, but deliver us from evil: For thine is the kingdom, and the power, and the glory, for ever. Amen.

q. **Ps. 95:6.** O come, let us worship and bow down: let us kneel before the LORD our maker.

r. **Eph. 3:12.** … in whom we have boldness and access with confidence by the faith of him.

s. **Matt. 7:9–11.** Or what man is there of you, whom if his son ask bread, will he give him a stone? Or if he ask a fish, will he give him a serpent? If ye then, being evil, know how to give good gifts unto your children, how much more shall your Father which is in heaven give good things to them that ask him? **Cf. Luke 11:11–13.** If a son shall ask bread of any of you that is a father, will he give him a stone? or if he ask a fish, will he for a fish give him a serpent? Or if he shall ask an egg, will he offer him a scorpion? If ye then, being evil, know how to give good gifts unto your children: how much more shall your heavenly Father give the Holy Spirit to them that ask him? **Rom. 8:15.** For ye have not received the spirit of bondage again to fear; but ye have received the Spirit of adoption, whereby we cry, Abba, Father.

t. **Eph. 3:20.** Now unto him that is able to do exceeding abundantly above all that we ask or think, according to the power that worketh in us …

u. **Eph. 6:18.** … praying always with all prayer and supplication in the Spirit, and watching thereunto with all perseverance and supplication for all saints. **1 Tim. 2:1–2.** I exhort therefore, that, first of all, supplications, prayers, intercessions, and giving of thanks, be made for all men; for kings, and for all that are in authority; that we may lead a quiet and peaceable life in all godliness and honesty.

w. **Ps. 67:1–3.** God be merciful unto us, and bless us; and cause his face to shine upon us; Selah. That thy way may be known upon earth, thy saving health among all nations. Let the people praise thee, O God; let all the people praise thee. **Ps. 99:3.** Let them praise thy great and terrible name; for it is holy. **Ps. 100:3–4.** Know ye that the LORD he is God: it is he that hath made us, and not we ourselves; we are his people, and the sheep of his pasture. Enter into his gates with thanksgiving, and into his courts

his own glory.[x]

Q. 102. *What do we pray for in the second petition?*

A. In the second petition, which is, *Thy kingdom come*, we pray that Satan's kingdom may be destroyed;[y] and that the kingdom of grace may be advanced,[z] ourselves and others brought into it, and kept in it;[a] and that the kingdom of glory may be hastened.[b]

with praise: be thankful unto him, and bless his name.

    x. **Rom. 11:33–36.** O the depth of the riches both of the wisdom and knowledge of God! how unsearchable are his judgments, and his ways past finding out! For who hath known the mind of the Lord? or who hath been his counsellor? Or who hath first given to him, and it shall be recompensed unto him again? For of him, and through him, and to him, are all things: to whom be glory for ever. Amen. **Rev. 4:11.** Thou art worthy, O Lord, to receive glory and honour and power: for thou hast created all things, and for thy pleasure they are and were created.

    y. **Matt. 12:25–28.** And Jesus knew their thoughts, and said unto them, Every kingdom divided against itself is brought to desolation; and every city or house divided against itself shall not stand: and if Satan cast out Satan, he is divided against himself; how shall then his kingdom stand? And if I by Beelzebub cast out devils, by whom do your children cast them out? therefore they shall be your judges. But if I cast out devils by the Spirit of God, then the kingdom of God is come unto you. **Rom. 16:20.** And the God of peace shall bruise Satan under your feet shortly. The grace of our Lord Jesus Christ be with you. Amen. **1 John 3:8.** He that committeth sin is of the devil; for the devil sinneth from the beginning. For this purpose the Son of God was manifested, that he might destroy the works of the devil.

    z. **Ps. 72:8–11.** He shall have dominion also from sea to sea, and from the river unto the ends of the earth. They that dwell in the wilderness shall bow before him; and his enemies shall lick the dust. The kings of Tarshish and of the isles shall bring presents: the kings of Sheba and Seba shall offer gifts. Yea, all kings shall fall down before him: all nations shall serve him. **Matt. 24:14.** And this gospel of the kingdom shall be preached in all the world for a witness unto all nations; and then shall the end come. **1 Cor. 15:24–25.** Then cometh the end, when he shall have delivered up the kingdom to God, even the Father; when he shall have put down all rule and all authority and power. For he must reign, till he hath put all enemies under his feet.

    a. **Ps. 119:5.** O that my ways were directed to keep thy statutes! **Luke 22:32.** But I have prayed for thee, that thy faith fail not: and when thou art converted, strengthen thy brethren. **2 Thess. 3:1–5.** Finally, brethren, pray for us, that the word of the Lord may have free course, and be glorified, even as it is with you: and that we may be delivered from unreasonable and wicked men: for all men have not faith. But the Lord is faithful, who shall stablish you, and keep you from evil. And we have confidence in the Lord touching you, that ye both do and will do the things which we command you. And the Lord direct your hearts into the love of God, and into the patient waiting for Christ.

    b. **Rev. 22:20.** He which testifieth these things saith, Surely I come quickly. Amen. Even so, come, Lord Jesus.

Q. 103. *What do we pray for in the third petition?*

A. In the third petition, which is, *Thy will be done in earth, as it is in heaven,* we pray that God, by his grace, would make us able and willing to know, obey, and submit to his will in all things,[c] as the angels do in heaven.[d]

Q. 104. *What do we pray for in the fourth petition?*

A. In the fourth petition, which is, *Give us this day our daily bread,* we pray that of God's free gift we may receive a competent portion of the good things of this life, and enjoy his blessing with them.[e]

c. **Ps. 19:14.** Let the words of my mouth, and the meditation of my heart, be acceptable in thy sight, O LORD, my strength, and my redeemer. **Ps. 119.** Blessed are the undefiled in the way, who walk in the law of the LORD. Blessed are they that keep his testimonies, and that seek him with the whole heart. They also do no iniquity: they walk in his ways. Thou hast commanded us to keep thy precepts diligently. O that my ways were directed to keep thy statutes! Then shall I not be ashamed, when I have respect unto all thy commandments. I will praise thee with uprightness of heart, when I shall have learned thy righteous judgments. I will keep thy statutes: O forsake me not utterly.… **1 Thess. 5:23.** And the very God of peace sanctify you wholly; and I pray God your whole spirit and soul and body be preserved blameless unto the coming of our Lord Jesus Christ. **Heb. 13:20–21.** Now the God of peace, that brought again from the dead our Lord Jesus, that great shepherd of the sheep, through the blood of the everlasting covenant, make you perfect in every good work to do his will, working in you that which is wellpleasing in his sight, through Jesus Christ; to whom be glory for ever and ever. Amen.

d. **Ps. 103:20–21.** Bless the LORD, ye his angels, that excel in strength, that do his commandments, hearkening unto the voice of his word. Bless ye the LORD, all ye his hosts; ye ministers of his, that do his pleasure. **Heb. 1:14.** Are they not all ministering spirits, sent forth to minister for them who shall be heirs of salvation?

e. **Prov. 30:8–9.** Remove far from me vanity and lies: give me neither poverty nor riches; feed me with food convenient for me: lest I be full, and deny thee, and say, Who is the LORD? or lest I be poor, and steal, and take the name of my God in vain. **Matt. 6:31–34.** Therefore take no thought, saying, What shall we eat? or, What shall we drink? or, Wherewithal shall we be clothed? (For after all these things do the Gentiles seek:) for your heavenly Father knoweth that ye have need of all these things. But seek ye first the kingdom of God, and his righteousness; and all these things shall be added unto you. Take therefore no thought for the morrow: for the morrow shall take thought for the things of itself. Sufficient unto the day is the evil thereof. **Phil. 4:11, 19.** Not that I speak in respect of want: for I have learned, in whatsoever state I am, therewith to be content.… But my God shall supply all your need according to his riches in glory by Christ Jesus. **1 Tim. 6:6–8.** But godliness with contentment is great gain. For we brought nothing into this world, and it is certain we can carry nothing out. And having food and raiment let us be therewith content.

Q. 105. *What do we pray for in the fifth petition?*

A. In the fifth petition, which is, *And forgive us our debts, as we forgive our debtors,* we pray that God, for Christ's sake, would freely pardon all our sins;[f] which we are the rather encouraged to ask, because by his grace we are enabled from the heart to forgive others.[g]

Q. 106. *What do we pray for in the sixth petition?*

A. In the sixth petition, which is, *And lead us not into temptation, but deliver us from evil,* we pray that God would either keep us from being tempted to sin,[h] or support and deliver us when we are tempted.[i]

f. **Ps. 51:1–2, 7, 9.** Have mercy upon me, O God, according to thy lovingkindness: according unto the multitude of thy tender mercies blot out my transgressions. Wash me thoroughly from mine iniquity, and cleanse me from my sin.… Purge me with hyssop, and I shall be clean: wash me, and I shall be whiter than snow.… Hide thy face from my sins, and blot out all mine iniquities. **Dan. 9:17–19.** Now therefore, O our God, hear the prayer of thy servant, and his supplications, and cause thy face to shine upon thy sanctuary that is desolate, for the Lord's sake. O my God, incline thine ear, and hear; open thine eyes, and behold our desolations, and the city which is called by thy name: for we do not present our supplications before thee for our righteousnesses, but for thy great mercies. O Lord, hear; O Lord, forgive; O Lord, hearken and do; defer not, for thine own sake, O my God: for thy city and thy people are called by thy name. **1 John 1:7.** But if we walk in the light, as he is in the light, we have fellowship one with another, and the blood of Jesus Christ his Son cleanseth us from all sin.

g. **Matt. 18:21–35.** Then came Peter to him, and said, Lord, how oft shall my brother sin against me, and I forgive him? till seven times? Jesus saith unto him, I say not unto thee, Until seven times: but, Until seventy times seven. Therefore is the kingdom of heaven likened unto a certain king, which would take account of his servants. And when he had begun to reckon, one was brought unto him, which owed him ten thousand talents.… Then the lord of that servant was moved with compassion, and loosed him, and forgave him the debt. But the same servant went out, and found one of his fellowservants, which owed him an hundred pence: and he … cast him into prison, till he should pay the debt.… Then his lord, after that he had called him, said unto him, O thou wicked servant, … shouldest not thou also have had compassion on thy fellowservant, even as I had pity on thee? And his lord was wroth, and delivered him to the tormentors, till he should pay all that was due unto him. So likewise shall my heavenly Father do also unto you, if ye from your hearts forgive not every one his brother their trespasses. **Eph. 4:32.** And be ye kind one to another, tenderhearted, forgiving one another, even as God for Christ's sake hath forgiven you. **Col. 3:13.** … forbearing one another, and forgiving one another, if any man have a quarrel against any: even as Christ forgave you, so also do ye.

h. **Ps. 19:13.** Keep back thy servant also from presumptuous sins; let them not have dominion over me: then shall I be upright, and I shall be innocent from the great transgression. **Matt. 26:41.** Watch and pray, that ye enter not into temptation: the spirit indeed is willing, but the flesh is weak. **John 17:15.** I pray not that thou shouldest take them out of the world, but that thou shouldest keep them from the evil.

Q. 107. *What doth the conclusion of the Lord's Prayer teach us?*

A. The conclusion of the Lord's Prayer, which is, *For thine is the kingdom, and the power, and the glory, for ever. Amen,* teacheth us to take our encouragement in prayer from God only,[k] and in our prayers to praise him, ascribing kingdom, power, and glory to him;[l] and, in testimony

i. **Luke 22:31–32.** And the Lord said, Simon, Simon, behold, Satan hath desired to have you, that he may sift you as wheat: but I have prayed for thee, that thy faith fail not: and when thou art converted, strengthen thy brethren. **1 Cor. 10:13.** There hath no temptation taken you but such as is common to man: but God is faithful, who will not suffer you to be tempted above that ye are able; but will with the temptation also make a way to escape, that ye may be able to bear it. **2 Cor. 12:7–9.** And lest I should be exalted above measure through the abundance of the revelations, there was given to me a thorn in the flesh, the messenger of Satan to buffet me, lest I should be exalted above measure. For this thing I besought the Lord thrice, that it might depart from me. And he said unto me, My grace is sufficient for thee: for my strength is made perfect in weakness. Most gladly therefore will I rather glory in my infirmities, that the power of Christ may rest upon me. **Heb. 2:18.** For in that he himself hath suffered being tempted, he is able to succour them that are tempted.

k. **Dan. 9:4, 7–9, 16–19.** And I prayed unto the LORD my God, and made my confession, and said, O Lord, the great and dreadful God, keeping the covenant and mercy to them that love him, and to them that keep his commandments.… O Lord, righteousness belongeth unto thee, but unto us confusion of faces, as at this day; to the men of Judah, and to the inhabitants of Jerusalem, and unto all Israel, that are near, and that are far off, through all the countries whither thou hast driven them, because of their trespass that they have trespassed against thee. O Lord, to us belongeth confusion of face, to our kings, to our princes, and to our fathers, because we have sinned against thee. To the Lord our God belong mercies and forgivenesses, though we have rebelled against him.… O Lord, according to all thy righteousness, I beseech thee, let thine anger and thy fury be turned away from thy city Jerusalem, thy holy mountain: because for our sins, and for the iniquities of our fathers, Jerusalem and thy people are become a reproach to all that are about us. Now therefore, O our God, hear the prayer of thy servant, and his supplications, and cause thy face to shine upon thy sanctuary that is desolate, for the Lord's sake. O my God, incline thine ear, and hear; open thine eyes, and behold our desolations, and the city which is called by thy name: for we do not present our supplications before thee for our righteousnesses, but for thy great mercies. O Lord, hear; O Lord, forgive; O Lord, hearken and do; defer not, for thine own sake, O my God: for thy city and thy people are called by thy name. **Luke 18:1, 7–8.** And he spake a parable unto them to this end, that men ought always to pray, and not to faint.… And shall not God avenge his own elect, which cry day and night unto him, though he bear long with them? I tell you that he will avenge them speedily. Nevertheless when the Son of man cometh, shall he find faith on the earth?

l. **1 Chron. 29:10–13.** Wherefore David blessed the LORD before all the congregation: and David said, Blessed be thou, LORD God of Israel our father, for ever and ever. Thine, O LORD, is the greatness, and the power, and the glory, and the victory, and the majesty: for all that is in the heaven and in the earth is thine; thine is the

of our desire, and assurance to be heard, we say, *Amen*.[m]

kingdom, O LORD, and thou art exalted as head above all. Both riches and honour come of thee, and thou reignest over all; and in thine hand is power and might; and in thine hand it is to make great, and to give strength unto all. Now therefore, our God, we thank thee, and praise thy glorious name. **1 Tim. 1:17.** Now unto the King eternal, immortal, invisible, the only wise God, be honour and glory for ever and ever. Amen. **Rev. 5:11–13.** And I beheld, and I heard the voice of many angels round about the throne and the beasts and the elders: and the number of them was ten thousand times ten thousand, and thousands of thousands; saying with a loud voice, Worthy is the Lamb that was slain to receive power, and riches, and wisdom, and strength, and honour, and glory, and blessing. And every creature which is in heaven, and on the earth, and under the earth, and such as are in the sea, and all that are in them, heard I saying, Blessing, and honour, and glory, and power, be unto him that sitteth upon the throne, and unto the Lamb for ever and ever.

m. **1 Cor. 14:16.** Else when thou shalt bless with the spirit, how shall he that occupieth the room of the unlearned say Amen at thy giving of thanks, seeing he understandeth not what thou sayest? **Rev. 22:20.** He which testifieth these things saith, Surely I come quickly. Amen. Even so, come, Lord Jesus.

Scripture Index

410

414

Psalms (*cont.*)

418

420

424

426

428

434

435

438

440

442

1 Thessalonians

2 Thessalonians

444

446

447

448

450